THIS ITEM HAS BEEN
DISCARDED BY THE
UNIVERSITY
OF PUGET SOUND
COLLINS MEMORIAL LIBRARY

EDUCATIONAL ORGANIZATION AND ADMINISTRATION

Concepts, Practices,
and Issues

third edition

EDUCATIONAL AND

Concepts, Practices,

PRENTICE-HALL, INC., Englewood Cliffs, N.J.

ORGANIZATION ADMINISTRATION

and Issues

EDGAR L. MORPHET
Professor of Education Emeritus
University of California, Berkeley

ROE L. JOHNS
Professor of Educational Administration
University of Florida

THEODORE L. RELLER
Professor of Education
University of California, Berkeley

Library of Congress Cataloging in Publication Data

MORPHET, EDGAR LEROY
    Educational organization and administration.

    First published in 1959 under title: Educational administration.
    Includes bibliographies.
    1. School management and organization. I. Johns, Roe Lyell, joint author. II. Reller, Theodore Lee, joint author. III. Title.
LB2805.M68 1974   371.2   73-18138
ISBN 0-13-236711-4

To our wives

CAMILLA, GLADYS, and MARGERY

EDUCATIONAL ORGANIZATION AND ADMINISTRATION
Concepts, Practices, and Issues

by Edgar L. Morphet, Roe L. Johns, and Theodore L. Reller

© 1974, 1967, 1959 by PRENTICE-HALL, INC., Englewood Cliffs, New Jersey

*All rights reserved. No part of this book
may be reproduced in any form or by any means
without permission in writing from the publisher.*

10 9 8 7 6 5 4 3 2 1

Printed in the United States of America

PRENTICE-HALL INTERNATIONAL, INC., London
PRENTICE-HALL OF AUSTRALIA PTY. LTD., Sydney
PRENTICE-HALL OF CANADA LTD., Toronto
PRENTICE-HALL OF INDIA PRIVATE LIMITED, New Delhi
PRENTICE-HALL OF JAPAN, INC., Tokyo

Contents

Preface   ix

part I
BASIC PRINCIPLES, CONCEPTS, AND ISSUES

1 The Evolving Systems of Education   3

Some International Concerns 3, Significance of Change 8, Educational Administration and the Behavioral Sciences 13, Unique Features of Education in the United States 15, Provisions for Organization and Administration 20, Some Important Problems and Issues 23, Selected References 28

2 The Legal Basis for Education   30

Bases for Legal Provisions 31, Constitutional Provisions 36, Laws and Administrative Policies Relating to Education 39, Court Decisions 49, Some Important Problems and Issues 52, Selected References 57

3 Theory and Research Relating to Educational Administration   58

General Systems Theory 59, Some Theoretical Models 67, Some Important Problems and Issues 79, Selected References 82

4 Concepts and Principles of Organization and Administration   85

Some Characteristics of Organizations 87, Concepts of Organization and Administration 96, Traditional and Emerging Concepts of Organization and Administration 102, The Emerging Pluralistic, Collegial Concept 109, Some Contrasts Between the Monocratic, Bureaucratic and the Pluralistic, Collegial Concepts 114, Some Important Problems and Issues 120, Selected References 124

5 Role of Educational Leadership   126

Some Concepts of Leadership 127, Trends in Studies of Leadership 130, The Group 135, Some Generalizations on Leadership 139, Leadership and Educational Administration 143, Executive Behavior 149, Some Important Problems and Issues 155, Selected References 161

6 Planning and Effecting Improvements in Education   163

Rationale and Basic Considerations 165, Preparing to Plan Systematically 168, The Nature and Processes of Planning 173, Effecting Needed Changes 180, Some Important Problems and Issues 183, Selected References 188

7 The Environment and the Schools   189

Some Background Considerations 190, Changed Local Conditions 197, Changes in Federal and State Activity 201, Other Organizations and Agencies 203, Power in the Local School District Area 205, Building an Integrated School Community 207, Studies of the Community 209, Action Based on Community Study 213, The Community and Its Schools 216, Some Important Problems and Issues 217, Selected References 223

part II
THE ORGANIZATION FOR EDUCATION

8 The Federal Government and Education   227

Federal Constitutional Authority 228, Early Historical Relationships 233, Federal Educational Activities Since 1958 243, The Federal Education Agency 250, Some Important Problems and Issues 252, Selected References 254

Contents vii

9 State Organization and Responsibilities
for Education   255
Evolution of State Systems of Education 256, State Provisions for
Education 258, The State Education Agency 259, Emerging State
Responsibilities and Relations 265, Preparing for the Future 270,
Some Important Problems and Issues 274, Selected References 278

10 School Districts and Area Service Agencies   280
Local School Districts 281, Schools and Other Educational Centers 293,
Intermediate Units and Regional Service Agencies 294, Decentralization
of Large Districts 298, Some Important Problems and Issues 299,
Selected References 304

11 The Local Education Agency   305
The Significance of the Local Authority 305,
The State-Local Partnership 308, The Board of Education 310,
The Superintendent of Schools 313, The Policy and Procedure Guide 318,
Some Important Problems and Issues 319, Selected References 333

12 Organization and Administration of Education
in Metropolitan Areas   335
The Inner City and the Metropolitan Area 336, District Structure in the
Metropolitan Area 340, State and Federal Governments and the
Metropolitan Area 344, Decentralization in the Metropolitan Area 345,
Planning and Development in the Metropolitan Area 348,
Some Important Problems and Issues 350, Selected References 354

13 The Administration of the Community Education Center 356
The Decision-Making Roles of the Community School Center 359,
The Principal 361, Relationship of the Principal to the Central Staff 364,
Organizing the Staff 366, Working with the Staff 368,
The Principal as Instructional Leader 369, Working with Students 370,
Ways of Working with the Community 371,
Some Important Problems and Issues 374, Selected References 383

part III
DEVELOPMENT AND ADMINISTRATION
OF PROGRAMS AND SERVICES

14 Provisions for Learning   387
The Environment for Learning 388,
New Insights and Changing Concepts 390,
Planning Improvements 393, Purposes, Goals, and Objectives 395,
Determination of Needs 398, Identification and Analysis
of Alternatives 398, Implementing Plans 399,
Characteristics of Effective Programs and Procedures 400,
Special Provisions and Programs 406,
Some Important Problems and Issues 412, Selected References 414

viii CONTENTS

15 Personnel Development and Administration   416
Structuring the Personnel Function 418, Planning the Personnel Function 420, Staffing the System 422, Improving Personnel Performance 427, Maintaining and Improving Personnel Service 433, Personnel Security 434, Personnel Participation 437, Some Important Problems and Issues 439, Selected References 442

16 Facilities for Education   443
School Facilities in an Era of Change 443, Buildings and Instruction 447, Schoolhousing Needs 448, Administrative-Staff Time Involved 449, Determining Need and Ability 450, Selecting and Employing an Architect 453, Selecting Sites 454, Educational Specifications and Architectural Plans 455, Reviewing Sketches and Plans 456, Contracting for and Constructing the Plant 457, Supervising the Construction 457, Equipping and Utilizing the Plant 458, Some Important Problems and Issues 459, Selected References 468

17 Business Administration Operations and Services   469
Major Concepts and Procedures 470, School Budgeting 475, Financial Accounting and Administration 480, Business Administration Services 484, Safeguarding School Funds, Property, and Persons 493, Some Important Problems and Issues 498, Selected References 500

18 Provisions for Financing Education   502
Early History of School Financing 503, Present Status of School Financing 504, Criteria for Evaluation of Taxes 509, Evolution of School Finance Theories 511, Evaluation of State Provisions for Financing Public Schools 515, Alternative State School Finance Models 518, Measuring the Cost of the Program 519, The Measurement of Local Taxpaying Ability 522, Evaluation of Alternative State School Finance Models 523, Some Important Problems and Issues 525, Selected References 528

19 Evaluation and Accountability   530
Appraisal and Assessment 532, Evaluation 534, Accountability 541, Some Important Problems and Issues 552, Selected References 559

Index   561

Preface

In the preface to the first edition of this book (1959) the authors stated their conviction that:

> The kind and quality of leadership provided in educational administration is particularly important in the democratic society in which we live, because education is so basic to the satisfactory functioning of that society and superior leadership is essential for the development of an adequate program of education. The educational leader of the future ... must be a highly competent person who believes in democracy, in the potentialities inherent in people, and in the significance of the educational process; a person who has the knowledge, insights, ability, and skills needed to function successfully as a recognized educational leader in helping people identify, analyze, and solve satisfactorily the problems with which they and their society are confronted.

In the preface to the second edition (1967) the authors commented that because there had been so many significant changes during the eight years since the first edition was published, "the original materials have been almost completely rewritten and many new concepts introduced."

Although many of the developments and concepts discussed in the first two editions are still pertinent, it has become apparent to the authors that major revisions are again needed because during the past few years (1) on the basis of new information and insights, there have been many significant changes in the perspectives, value systems, attitudes, and expectations of most citizens in the nation and even further changes seem inevitable; (2) there has been a growing recognition of the fact that, even though improvements have been made in some aspects of education, these changes have been inadequate to meet the needs of a dynamic society; and (3) further systematically planned changes in education are essential to meet the emerging as well as presently recognized needs.

In this edition considerable attention has been devoted to the processes of planning and effecting improvements in all aspects of education; to the continuous monitoring of progress and the revision of plans as necessary; and to the responsibility for ensuring adequate, appropriate, and effective provisions for education. The modern educational administrator, therefore, is viewed primarily as a well-informed, perceptive, creative, and future-oriented leader in human relations as well as in the technical aspects of planning; in effecting needed changes; in developing and implementing effective management procedures; and in ensuring that education is continuously adapted to the needs of a changing pluralistic society. Moreover, if he is to function effectively, every administrator needs to understand social systems, their interrelations, and the ways in which they identify and seek to attain their goals.

Although educational administration has not yet become a science based on rational and defensible theory (and probably will continue to be considered an art as well as a science in certain respects), considerable progress has been made. For example, much research during recent years has been based on, or related to, some theory that seems to be appropriate. As a result of these and other similar developments, many defensible criteria and guidelines discussed in this edition are now available for use by school boards and administrators in planning and effecting improvements in education. This volume, therefore, should be helpful to school board members and administrators as well as to college and university students who are preparing to become administrators and to teachers and other staff members who are interested in or concerned about the organization and administration of education.

Part I of this volume is primarily concerned with basic theories, concepts, and principles; Part II, with the major provisions and implications for organization and administration; and Part III, with the development and implementation of relevant provisions and programs. One of the distinctive features of this volume, as in previous editions, is the discussion of pertinent problems and issues relating to the concepts and developments considered in each chapter.

EDGAR L. MORPHET
ROE L. JOHNS
THEODORE L. RELLER

part 1

BASIC PRINCIPLES, CONCEPTS, AND ISSUES

1

The Evolving Systems of Education

The leaders of most nations now recognize that appropriate education, or the lack of it, could mean the difference between orderly progress and chaos. However, the assumptions they have made in developing and implementing provisions for education vary greatly. Such assumptions have a direct bearing on the purposes and goals that will be accepted, on the plans for organization and administration that will be developed, and on the procedures that will be utilized to implement the program of education. These provisions may not only affect the progress of a nation, but also may help to promote understanding or serve to create international tensions.

SOME INTERNATIONAL CONCERNS

Every nation has developed or "inherited" some kind of *system* of education but these systems differ in many important ways. The purposes of education that are accepted and the procedures utilized by a nation's leaders in developing and implementing the provisions for education may promote enlightenment and progress for all citizens, or may perpetuate ignorance and misery or generate dangerous biases for many. Education has tremendous potential for good or for evil. Among the problems faced by nations that attempt to develop adequate plans and provisions for education are one or more of the following:[1]

1. The leaders or the group in power may not want the masses to be educated or may not even recognize the importance of an adequate program of education for all citizens—especially for minorities against whom there may be strong biases.
2. The members of the controlling group may be so interested in promoting some ideology or fostering some form of nationalism that they fail to recognize the dangers inherent in such a policy and ignore the importance of attempting to provide a sound basis for encouraging better understanding among the peoples of the world.
3. A nation's resources may be so limited that little progress can be made, even though the people and their leaders recognize the importance of a good program of education for all and want to develop such a program.
4. Although a nation may have the resources needed to provide an excellent program of education, the people or their leaders may insist on continuing outmoded policies and practices or may become complacent because their material needs have been satisfied and, may, therefore, fail to devote a sufficient proportion of their attention and resources to education to ensure good schools and institutions of higher learning.

Recent Developments and Needed Studies

During recent years, most nations have become increasingly interested in providing better and more defensible systems and programs of education. This interest has been stimulated by many developments, including the establishment and contributions of the United Nations Educational, Scientific, and Cultural Organization (UNESCO). The UNESCO constitution succinctly states some basic goals for all member nations and, hopefully, for all nations. However, these trends do not suggest that nations will or should adopt identical systems of education. Some differences, growing out of the diverse cultures, are to be expected and may, in fact, be stimulating and challenging to others. At this stage, most national plans have some weaknesses as well as some strengths. Continuing study is needed to provide background and information that will enable the people of each country to gain better insights into some of their own problems and possibilities.

[1] Adapted from Theodore L. Reller and Edgar L. Morphet, eds., *Comparative Educational Administration* (Englewood Cliffs, N.J.: Prentice-Hall, Inc., 1962), pp. 1–6.

Improved communication and transportation, provisions for exchange of educational personnel, programs of international cooperation, the establishment of international professional societies and organizations, and many other recent trends have contributed to a growing interest in educational policies, problems, and procedures in all countries. Such trends have also led to an awareness of major developments and problem areas that transcend national boundaries. Systematic analytical and comparative studies in many areas, in which present "solutions" or ways of dealing with problems often differ significantly, should be of interest and benefit to the people in many nations. A few of these studies are noted below.

- The major educational problems, needs, and ways of meeting them in a changing society—especially in the congested cities and rapidly growing metropolitan areas in many countries.
- Ways of making the curriculum and learning opportunities more functional and meaningful for students at all levels, and of placing in proper perspective the traditional "classical" emphasis, especially in underdeveloped countries.
- The extent to which theories, policies, and practices relating to instruction and learning and to the organization and administration of education are culturally oriented, and the possibility of developing culture-free theories.
- The extent of control of education by political, religious, and other groups and the implications for organization, administration, teaching, and learning.
- The procedures used and the ways in which people are involved in the development of national and other educational policies as related to the kinds of policies developed and to the appropriateness of the programs provided.
- The procedures utilized (and the implications) in developing and implementing long-range plans for organizing, administering, and financing education, and in revising plans to meet emerging needs.

The Purposes and Goals of Education

Every society and nation has been and will continue to be confronted with the same basic problem: How can its members, especially the children and youth, best learn what is necessary to survive and to contribute to the welfare and improvement of the human condition and of the society in which they live?

Each society or nation has not only established procedures for educating the young but has also come to accept purposes of education such as one or more of the following: to ensure conformity, to preserve stability, to promote nationalism, to perpetuate the existing political system, to facilitate international understanding, to develop the potentialities of each individual, or to provide for the continuous improvement of society. The purposes and goals of education grow out of the ideas, beliefs, and values of the people and tend to be modified somewhat over a period of years but, in the absence of unusual conditions, generally change slowly. There is usually considerable resistance to major changes regardless of the need.

Issues Relating to Educational Organization and Administration

In developing a system of education, the leaders—or the people—of each nation have been confronted at one time or another with the four basic issues discussed below, each of which has implications for the others. The manner in which each of these issues was resolved had direct implications for the educational structure as well as for programs and procedures.

RELATION TO RELIGION. In many countries in which the leaders and a majority of the people belong to one church or religious organization, that organization has either been given control of education or has had a decisive voice in determining how the schools should be organized and operated. For example, the Concordat at Rome signed by Spain in 1857 provided that "Public instruction in the universities, colleges, and seminaries, public and private schools of every description must be at all points in harmony with the teaching of the Catholic Church."[2] In the Concordat of 1953, the right of the Church to control education was again affirmed. Apparently at the other extreme is the Soviet Union, which has sought to prevent religious groups from having any active role in education. The United States has attempted to avoid both extremes, providing for the separation of Church and State but recognizing the right of religious groups to organize and operate their own schools.

RELATION TO THE POLITICAL STATE. Education may be either partly or entirely an instrument of the group in control of the national government or political state, or may have a more autonomous position. Communist Russia and other totalitarian countries have made education a definite arm of the group controlling the political state for the purpose of perpetuating and promoting communist or fascist ideologies. On the other hand, the people and leaders in the United States have gone to great lengths to ensure that education is not dominated by any partisan political organization or controlled by any agency of the federal government. However, this does not imply that education has been isolated from political considerations, or that it should be.

EDUCATION AND THE INDIVIDUAL. The relation of education to the individual citizen has also varied greatly from country to country. The medieval concept of preparing leaders for a society controlled by the elite

---

[2] Nicholas A. Hans, *Comparative Education* (London: Routledge and Kegan Paul, Ltd., 1950), p. 111.

constituted one basis for the class systems of education developed in many European nations. The emphasis in those countries was on the organization of a system of higher education for the elite, often the most wealthy, with only schools of lower grade for the others. In the United States, however, schools presumably have been organized to provide opportunities for all rather than primarily for selected leaders or the privileged, but only during the last few decades has significant progress been made toward reaching this goal.

THE STATE AND THE INDIVIDUAL. One of the key issues to be resolved in the various nations concerns the relationship of the central government to each individual citizen and his development.[3] In totalitarian countries, chief emphasis has been placed on preserving and perpetuating the state by molding and using individuals for state purposes. In most democratically organized nations, on the other hand, the emphasis presumably has been placed on the development of the individual citizen as a contributing member of the group. Most people believe that if each citizen is helped to develop in accordance with his potential, and is encouraged to learn to think and evaluate for himself, he will contribute more to the national welfare than a citizen who is molded in some predetermined pattern. As stated in the 1956 report of the White House Conference on Education: "This policy of encouraging each child to develop his individual talents will be of greatest use to the nation, for in the long run, if no talent is wasted in our land, no skill will be lacking."[4]

Organization and Administration
Related to Purposes and Goals

Not only the different purposes and goals of education as recognized and accepted by the nations existing today, but also the different policy decisions relating to the basic issues previously discussed have tended to determine the plan for organization, control, and administration of schools that each country has developed. The nations which have accepted the assumption that education should serve the interests of the controlling group—whether that group be political or religious or a political-religious partnership—have generally developed a highly centralized system of education. In such countries, the policies are developed primarily by the leaders and must be observed by all schools and by the groups involved in operating the schools. The entire educational program must be operated

---

[3] I. L. Kandel, *Comparative Education* (Boston: Houghton Mifflin Company, 1933), Chap. 3.

[4] *A Report to the President* (Washington, D.C.: Government Printing Office, 1956), p. 10.

within the pattern established for the purpose of developing citizens who will contribute directly to the goals and welfare of the group that controls the government. Any thinking that is encouraged must be within the framework of the ideologies accepted by the controlling group.

In the more democratically organized nations, however, especially in the United States and England, most people have been seriously concerned about avoiding centralized partisan control of education by any group, especially in matters relating to what is taught and how it is taught. In most of these nations the assumption is made that the national welfare is best promoted by educating citizens to think through problems and reach sound conclusions. The control of schools has generally been primarily in the hands of the citizens instead of being vested in religious or political leaders.

Thus, in any society the establishment of a system for education calls for some kind of plan and an organization for making it effective. In primitive groups the organization was usually relatively simple. As society became more complex and formal educational institutions were developed, the need for an appropriate organization to facilitate achievement of the accepted purposes and goals of education became apparent. As modern nations began to develop, they came to accept different purposes and goals for education, consistent with what seemed to be their national interests and concerns. Each attempted to create a system of education and an organization that seemed appropriate to carry out its purposes. As would be expected, these systems and organizations differ considerably in both structure and functions.

SIGNIFICANCE OF CHANGE

Changes that affect people in one way or another have occurred throughout the history of man. Some of these resulted from natural events; others were brought about by man himself. Thus, the fact of change is not new. What is new is the sharply increasing rate at which changes have occurred during recent years, the variety and kinds of changes that have been taking place, and the role of man in the process of effecting changes.

This challenging and, to many people, disturbing new situation has come about largely because (1) a far larger proportion of the people in many countries are much better educated and informed than ever before and, consequently, are more able to understand problems, recognize inconsistencies, and contribute to solutions; (2) the great increase in new knowledge and understanding tends to stimulate and facilitate the development of further knowledge, discoveries, and inventions; and (3) in many countries an increasing share of the resources is being devoted to research that often results in new knowledge, new theories, and, in some cases, in discrediting traditionally accepted assumptions.

All available information points to the conclusion that the rate of discovery, change, and the addition of new knowledge will continue to increase. In the immediate future, however, the rate of increase will be much greater in some parts of the world and perhaps in certain areas of knowledge and action than in others. The resulting imbalances are almost certain to create major tensions and problems that will need to be resolved.

This rapid expansion of knowledge and insights carries tremendous —probably even some unanticipated—implications for the future of mankind. It could and should lead to the further liberation of man from biases and to marked improvements in civilization, but it will also bring new dangers and problems. Many of the assumptions and myths to which substantial numbers of people presently subscribe will be so completely discredited they will have to be abandoned. Even some of the values and value systems held by individuals and groups in various parts of the world will have to be modified. There will probably be difficult periods of confusion and uncertainty for many, but new possibilities and hope for almost everyone should emerge if mankind can learn how to manage and utilize new knowledge and to plan cooperatively and wisely for the improvement of civilization.

Implications for Education

Not only new knowledge and insights but many innovations and changes in society have important implications for education. Perhaps the most obvious are the implications for learning and the curriculum of new theories, information, and discoveries that have already resulted in some major adjustments. Curriculum changes require not only new instructional materials but also modifications in teaching-learning procedures and probably even in learning centers and in organization and administration. But even more far-reaching changes involving many aspects of the entire educational system are already in prospect as a result of developments during the past few years.

In most organizations there are some people who might well be classified as perennial advocates of change. They seem to view change as something that is highly desirable, regardless of the evidence pertinent to a particular situation. At the other extreme are some—often many—who resist change. Their reaction to any proposal for change tends to be negative, perhaps because they view change as a threat to their established values, habits, and patterns of thought. Between these two extremes are those who view change as something that may be either beneficial or harmful, depending on the factors involved, and who support the kinds of change that should enhance their own potential or enrich and improve the society in which they live.

The above statements are apparently as applicable to those serving in educational agencies, institutions, and organizations as to people generally. There is considerable evidence that many school systems and institutions of higher learning have been quite slow in adopting important changes and innovations in education.[5] This evidence indicates that many educators, for some reason, have failed to adopt a number of changes found to be beneficial. In view of the rapidly increasing rate at which change is taking place in society and the wide variety of changes that are occurring, any serious lag in making needed adaptations or changes in education should become a major concern, and vigorous steps should be taken to remedy the situation. Some of these should be concerned with the goals, organization, and procedures; others with the perceptions and points of view of the personnel involved.

As Gardner has so appropriately pointed out, "It is necessary to discuss not only the vitality of societies but the vitality of institutions and individuals. They are the same subject. A society decays when its institutions and individuals lose their vitality."[6] The vitality of an organization, an institution, or a society (its ability to become self-renewing) is basically determined by the vitality and perceptions of its personnel. In education, this means that the vitality of administrators, of the facilitating staff, of the teachers and other employees, and of the students is directly related to the vitality of schools and institutions of higher learning.

The attitudes (of administrators, teachers, and others involved in education) toward change and innovation—as reflected in teaching and learning processes—are important in any society. If teachers encourage their students to court change indiscriminately, they may help to establish the climate for chaos. If, on the other hand, teachers assist their students to develop a sound basis for appraising the implications of change and to bring the results into line with the evolving purposes of society, they are contributing to orderly progress.

These observations, supplemented by evidence already available concerning the teaching and learning processes, point to the conclusion that all "teachers" must clearly recognize and accept their responsibility for helping to prepare every student to: (1) look forward to a future that will bring many changes and to accept the responsibility for helping to shape that future; (2) recognize his special aptitudes and abilities, and thus

---

[5]See D. H. Ross, ed., *Administration for Adaptability* (New York: Metropolitan School Study Council, Teachers College, Columbia University, 1958).

[6]John W. Gardner, *Self Renewal: The Individual and the Innovative Society* (New York: Harper & Row, Publishers, 1964), p. 2.

facilitate the development of his individuality; (3) develop a sound basis for accepting a defensible and evolving system of moral and ethical values for guidance in exercising his responsibilities as a citizen; (4) understand that happiness comes primarily from progress in achieving, and in helping others to achieve, worthwhile goals and objectives; (5) seek and utilize learning and knowledge as a basis for understanding meanings in relationship to his life and to society; and (6) learn to use appropriate and defensible procedures as a basis for studying and resolving the problems he encounters.

Implications for Organization and Administration

If teachers and other educators are to contribute significantly to the vitality and progress of students and of society, the organization (agency, school system, or institution) with which they are associated must make a serious effort to provide a favorable environment and climate for education. Among other things, this means that the citizens need to insist on high quality education (continuously seeking to achieve excellence) and that the purposes, policies, and regulations facilitate the employment and effective functioning of competent personnel who are interested in preparing students to contribute to planned, constructive, and orderly change. This kind of climate is least likely to be found in communities in which substantial numbers are fearful of any change and suspicious of those who believe in preparing for change. Moreover, it is unlikely to be favorable in situations in which board members, administrators, and staff are primarily concerned with stability based on traditional concepts, as contrasted with the "stability in motion" that should be associated with progress.

In every community and state, there are pressures for and against change that come from individuals and groups. These pressures create problems that, unless resolved, can result in confusion or chaos for students as well as for staff. One important step is for administrators, teachers, and all other members of the staff to find ways of helping people realize that many of the changes that are occurring in society require adjustments to be made in educational programs and processes if emerging needs are to be met. Another is for everyone, especially administrators, to develop a better understanding of social systems (discussed in Chapter 3) and the processes—the dynamics—of planning and effecting constructive change (discussed in Chapter 6). These are matters concerning which many people have been poorly informed, and about which greater understanding is urgently needed.

Before much progress can be made, the major barriers to change must be identified. Gardner listed several under the heading, "Obstacles to

Renewal,"[7] and noted that most of these are to be found in the *minds of people,* rather than in external arrangements. Thus, major barriers (or obstacles) often include the habits, attitudes, precedents, and belief systems of people. He also noted the tendency of people to become nostalgic about the "good old days" and to defend present practices by relating them to "high moral principles." Among the obstacles are vested interests, detailed and stultifying rules and regulations, an overconcern with how to do things the "approved" way, and a tendency to be suspicious of innovators and attempt to discredit them.

Carlson, after expressing concern "about the ability of the public schools to make rapid and adequate adaptation to our fast changing times,"[8] listed three barriers to change: (1) the absence of an institutional "change agent" position, such as the county agent for agriculture, who has as his major function the advocacy and introduction of innovations into practice; (2) a weak knowledge base about new educational practices, evidenced by the limited research, experiment, and development practices; and (3) the establishment of the public school system as a "domesticated" organization which cannot select its clients and whose clients must accept its services. He noted that when important elements of the environment are stable, the necessity (or at least, the pressure) for changes is reduced. He might have added that, as important changes occur in certain aspects of the environment of the schools, the situation becomes less stable and change may be facilitated.

In most school systems, the administrators are in a position to play a key role in facilitating or in retarding changes in education. Those who operate as "facilitators" can attempt to serve directly as "change agents" or advocates of particular changes, or as what has been called "process initiators." When the evidence regarding the need for a change is reasonably conclusive, an administrator might be justified in assuming the role of *advocate.* When the evidence is weak or controversial, the administrator might better assume the role of *process initiator*—that is, of appointing or arranging for the appointment of a committee or taking other steps to ensure that all aspects and implications of the proposal are carefully studied and discussed as a basis for recommendations. A third role, which would be appropriate under certain conditions, might be that of a *mediator* or catalyst whose purpose is to facilitate agreement so decisions can be made.

[7] *Ibid.,* Chap. 5.
[8] Richard O. Carlson, "Barriers to Change in Public Schools," in *Change Processes in the Public Schools* (Eugene, Ore.: Institute for the Advanced Study of Educational Administration, University of Oregon, 1965), pp. 3–8.

Miles has noted that "... successful efforts at planned change must take as a primary target the improvement of *organization health*—the school system's ability not only to function effectively, but to grow and develop into a more fully functioning system."[9] He listed six interventions aimed at improving organizational health: (1) team training; (2) survey feedback of information about attitudes, opinions, and beliefs of members of the system; (3) work-conference on roles of all people in a particular role; (4) target setting and supporting activities; (5) organizational diagnosis and problem solving; and (6) organizational experiment.

It seems apparent that every state and local school system, educational institution, and organization must develop defensible plans for effecting appropriate changes if it is to be prepared to meet future needs. (See Chapters 3 to 7 for further discussion of basic theory, research, and concepts.) These plans should be based on considerations such as those listed below.

1. Appropriate steps should be taken to attempt to ensure that the organizational health is good and that the climate is conducive to the introduction and implementation of defensible innovations.
2. There should be a conscious effort to include, as members of the organization, competent people who are interested in new ideas and procedures and who are sufficiently well balanced that they are not likely to be seeking change for the sake of change.
3. There should be a continuing search within each institution for ideas that seem worthy of consideration and that can be used to develop an inventory and categorization of especially promising concepts.
4. Appropriate procedures should be developed for analyzing and evaluating the ideas and concepts that seem most promising. Findings of pertinent research studies, analyses of experiences elsewhere, and value judgments should be utilized in an effort to distinguish between defensible concepts and those that have little merit.
5. From time to time, the most promising concepts should be selected, with the concurrence of the people who should be involved, for introduction in some school or aspect of the educational program. There should be assurance that all conditions are as favorable as possible for the successful introduction and implementation of these concepts.

EDUCATIONAL ADMINISTRATION AND THE BEHAVIORAL SCIENCES

While educational administration differs in a number of respects from other types of administration, there are some common elements.

---

[9]Matthew B. Miles, "Planned Change and Organizational Health," in *Change Processes in the Public Schools* (Eugene, Ore.: Institute for the Advanced Study of Educational Administration, University of Oregon, 1965), pp. 11–32.

14 BASIC PRINCIPLES, CONCEPTS, AND ISSUES

Lazarsfeld commented on four major tasks faced by all administrators, which vary chiefly in relative emphasis:[10]

1. The administrator must seek to achieve the *goals* of the organization.
2. The administrator must utilize *other people* in fulfilling these goals, not as if they were machines, but rather in such a way as to release their initiative and creativity.
3. The administrator must also face the humanitarian aspects of the job. He should want people who work with him to be happy. This is *morale*—the idea that under suitable conditions people will do better work than they will under unsuitable conditions.
4. The administrator must try to build into his organization *provisions for innovations*, for needed change, and for development. In a changing world, people must adapt to changing conditions.

Administration has been discussed as a common-sense approach to and method of dealing with problems, as an art, and as a series of techniques that can best be transmitted from one administrator to another. While some of these elements will undoubtedly persist, the study and practice of administration is becoming more scientific from year to year. But, as Gross has pointed out, "... although administrative thought has made tremendous advances the greatest advances still lie ahead."[11]

The practice of educational administration, as well as of administration in general, is becoming more scientific because the body of pertinent knowledge is being increased by scientific study. Progress in the development of a theory or theories of administration, increases in the volume and quality of research and other developments have brought new knowledge and understanding that provide sounder bases for improvements in various aspects of administrative operation. (See Chapter 3.)

Both education (including teaching and learning) and educational administration are much more complex and have many more facets than were formerly recognized by most people. Through research by psychologists, social psychologists, anthropologists, sociologists, political scientists, economists, and others—as well as by educational researchers—many of the dimensions of the educational and administrative process have been discovered. These findings have resulted in many significant improvements in the curriculum and in methods, materials, organization, and ad-

[10]Paul F. Lazarsfeld, "The Social Sciences and Administration: A Rationale," in *The Social Sciences and Educational Administration,* Lorne Downey and Frederick Enns, eds. (Edmonton: University of Alberta, 1963), pp. 3 and 4.

[11]Bertram M. Gross, "The Scientific Approach to Administration," in *Behavioral Science and Educational Administration,* Daniel E. Griffiths, ed., The Sixty-third Yearbook of the National Society for the Study of Education, Part II (Chicago: University of Chicago Press, 1964), p. 33.

ministration. It is important to recognize that many of these advances would not have been possible without the contributions made by the behavioral sciences (often referred to as the social sciences). These sciences are as concerned with the behavior of man and the organizations he develops as are people in the field of education. However, each is concerned with different aspects of man's behavior, or with analyzing the same item of behavior in terms of different concepts.[12]

These sciences hold that the behavior and products of men can best be understood on the basis of three concepts: (1) *goals* (end states or conditions), (2) *functions* (activities by which men achieve goals), and (3) *arrangements* (structures and mechanisms for arranging activities). Psychology has been primarily interested in the study of individualistic attributes of people and other organisms; the other disciplines, with collective attributes that grow out of group interaction. Fortunately, during recent years a number of behavioral and other scientists have become interested in various aspects of education ranging from board-superintendent relations, communication, and decision making to the economics of school finance, and have made studies that provide needed insights and knowledge. Not only several of these studies but also emerging planning and management technologies and similar developments that have important implications for educational administration are discussed at appropriate places in subsequent chapters. The major point to be emphasized here is that not only students and professors of educational administration but also practicing administrators need to be familiar with and make use of these contributions as a basis for effecting improvement in education and in educational administration.

UNIQUE FEATURES OF EDUCATION IN THE UNITED STATES

The policies and plans that have been developed for the organization and administration of education in the United States have a number of unique features. These features grew out of the beliefs, attitudes, and experiences of the people who have helped to develop the nation and its institutions.

Neither the schools nor other institutions of a nation can be understood merely by studying them as they are at present. Back of any institution is a long and complex history involving many conflicting ideas,

[12]See Fred Fosmire and Richard A. Littman, "The Behavior Sciences—an Overview" in *Social Sciences View School Administration* (Englewood Cliffs, N.J.: Prentice-Hall, Inc., 1964), pp. 36–53.

struggles among and within various groups, a variety of experiences, and many other factors.[13] Thus, origins of the system of education in this country are found in European culture, but the schools were not transplanted in the form in which they had developed in any other nation. Concepts and practices that seemed to have value were tried out, and either modified or discarded. New ideas that were developed in this country went through a similar process. As pointed out by the Educational Policies Commission some years ago, "Every system of thought and practice in education is formulated with some reference to the ideas and interests dominant or widely cherished in society at the time of its formulation."[14] In every case the crucial but often unrecognized test applied was: *Was the practice or proposal consistent with, and did it contribute to the attainment of, the ideals and value systems that were developing in America?*[15]

Some of the unique features of education in the United States are discussed briefly in the paragraphs that follow.

The system of education is relatively decentralized. The people in the respective states (not the federal government) have the basic responsibility for the organization and control of education (See Chapter 2). Each state, in fact, has developed a system of education which differs in some respects from that developed by other states. In most states, much of the responsibility for the organization and administration of public schools has been delegated to local school districts. However, the increasing concern of the federal government about education has been indicated by provisions for financial assistance, by United States Supreme Court decisions concerning the implications of constitutional provisions, and in many other ways. The extent of decentralization in the United States contrasts sharply with the marked centralization of control found in many other nations.

The people, rather than educators or government officials, are ultimately responsible for all basic policies relating to education. Although in practice many policies are cooperatively developed, the decision as to what policies are to be adopted and followed is usually delegated to the legislature and state board of education (for state policies) and to local lay boards of education selected by the

---

[13]For a thorough discussion and analysis of the forces and factors that influenced the development of schools and other educational institutions and the provisions for the organization, administration, and control, see R. Freeman Butts and Lawrence A. Cremin, *A History of Education in American Culture* (New York: Holt, Rinehart & Winston, Inc., 1953), especially Chaps. 7, 8, and 16.

[14]Educational Policies Commission, *The Unique Function of Education in American Democracy* (Washington, D.C.: National Education Association, 1937), p. 6.

[15]For discussion of sociological background and meanings, see George S. Counts, *The Social Foundations of Education* (New York: Charles Scribner's Sons, 1934); also Emile Durkheim, *Education and Sociology* (New York: Free Press of Glencoe, Inc., 1956).

people (for local policies) or, in some cases, the decision is made by the people themselves. The recommendations of educators are usually considered and often followed. In many countries, most operating policies are determined nationally.

A system of education open freely to all has been established. This system, contrasting sharply with the dual systems formerly found in many countries, is one logical outgrowth of the concept of equal opportunity in and through education for all citizens. Thus, every person, regardless of his social, economic, political, religious, or racial background, has a constitutional right (not yet fully recognized in practice) to an equal opportunity to develop his talents fully so he may become a socially and economically productive citizen. These opportunities are provided primarily through a system of public education extending in many states from early childhood or kindergarten education through comprehensive secondary schools and higher education.

Although primary emphasis is placed on public schools, provision is also made for private and parochial schools. Most people believe that public schools have a special and necessary contribution to make to the development and unity of the American way of life. Provision is made for these schools supported by public tax funds to be available to all, and special efforts are being made to ensure that they are organized and operated in the interest and for the benefit of all people. Parents may, however, send their children either to public or to nonpublic schools. Private and religious agencies have been given considerable freedom to establish, control, operate, and support schools and other educational institutions in accordance with their own beliefs and concepts.

The public schools and educational institutions are safeguarded insofar as possible from partisan political control. Control of the schools or other public educational institutions by any partisan political group is considered not only undesirable but potentially dangerous. Therefore, provision has generally been made for the schools to have a comparatively independent status, so there is an opportunity to resolve educational issues separately from other issues and so school boards and educators can be relatively free from domination or control by partisan political agencies or groups, and even by other governmental agencies.

Education in the public schools and educational institutions is nonsectarian. No religious creed or doctrine may be taught in the public schools. Special provisions are made to ensure that these schools on all levels are safeguarded against domination or control by any religious organization. Such provisions make it possible for the public schools to "teach" about religions and to instruct in moral and ethical values, but not to present these matters from the point of view of any sect or religious organization.

Most citizens believe that those who are responsible for the administration of their schools, as well as those who teach in the schools, should be especially prepared to meet their responsibilities. The idea that educational administrators should have special preparation has developed slowly but is now accepted in practically all states.

Purposes, Policies, and Values

As the nation developed, despite many sharp disagreements and controversies, most people began to recognize the need for certain purposes and goals to be achieved and to agree upon some of the basic policies and characteristics of programs of education suitable for all citizens. These agreements grew out of the beliefs, judgments, and experiences of the people.

Statements of purposes and policies that are acceptable must reflect the values and aspirations of the people and therefore should:

Be consistent with the concept that education should help the people of the nation approach the democratic ideal. Although this ideal has never been defined to the satisfaction of all, practically everyone believes in the democratic way of life as the one most suitable for this nation and agrees that the schools should help to ensure that it is achieved.

Make clear that the schools must provide for the education of all as a basis for national stability and progress. It is generally recognized that democracy cannot function satisfactorily unless all members are sufficiently well educated to participate intelligently and constructively in the democratic processes and their improvement.

Ensure that provisions will be made for each individual to have the opportunity to realize fully his own potential and, thus, be prepared to contribute to the improvement of his community, state, and nation. When the potentialities of each individual are fully and properly developed, he should become the type of citizen needed to contribute to the improvement of the nation and, indirectly at least, of the world in which he lives.

Recognize that education constitutes one essential key to a better life for all. Although some people are concerned primarily with abundance in a material sense, most recognize that the lives of people will be most meaningful and the improvement of civilization will proceed most satisfactorily when the "abundant" life is interpreted to include cultural, spiritual, and ethical values, as well as material qualities.

Be developed through intelligent participation, discussion, and understanding by the people. In matters pertaining to education, Americans are not willing to leave vital decisions such as those involving purposes and policies for education to their leaders or to any one segment of the population. They believe that education is so basic and potentially so significant for the future of the nation and of the world that everyone should be encouraged to attempt to understand the problems, think through the issues, and cooperate in arriving at sound conclusions.

Purposes and Social Policy

The generally accepted statements of purposes of education in the United States constitute the guidelines for one major aspect of social policy that must be fully implemented if the democratic way of life is to function satisfactorily. Such statements have become the basis for a program of action in establishing, organizing, and operating educational institutions designed to serve as one means of satisfying the imperatives for socialization and individualization in modern society. Whether these purposes are classified under self-realization, human relationships, economic efficiency, and civic responsibility, as suggested by the Educational Policies Commission,[16] or under other defensible headings, may not be important as long as the goals are defensible and can be agreed upon.

One of the problems at present confronting the people of each state and the nation arises from the fact that there are substantial minorities who either do not agree with some of these purposes or goals or are not willing to make the effort to provide the kind and quality of schools and programs needed to attain them. At times, differences of opinion may serve to stimulate further thinking and discussion, but long-continued and emotionally supported differences may result only in confusion and inaction. Unless some way can be found to resolve major differences, it will probably be impossible to effect some of the needed changes. The problem has been complicated by the organization of vigorous groups of extremists who seem to be more interested in attempting to mold the educational institutions to suit their own purposes than in seeking to understand the educational problems and needs of the nation.[17] Moreover, as Willis Harman[18] has observed, there are some dangerous gaps between what most people say they believe about education (for example, providing equality of opportunity for all students and equity for taxpayers who support the schools) and the provisions that are actually made. These differences tend to result in confusion, frustrations, and loss of confidence in the schools.

The process of serious discussion—attempting to understand, taking into consideration the pertinent evidence and the points of view of others,

[16]Educational Policies Commission, *The Purposes of Education in American Democracy* (Washington, D.C.: National Education Association, 1938), pp. 45ff.
[17]See Roald F. Campbell, Luvern L. Cunningham, and Roderick F. McPhee, *The Organization and Control of American Schools* (Columbus, Ohio: Charles E. Merrill Books, Inc., 1965), Chap. 13.
[18]Willis W. Harman, "The Nature of Our Changing Society: Implications for Schools." Paper prepared for the ERIC Clearinghouse on Educational Administration, Eugene, Oregon, October 1969.

20   BASIC PRINCIPLES, CONCEPTS, AND ISSUES

and striving to find common ground as the basis for agreement—which has been so significant in the past must be pursued vigorously in the future if the schools and other educational institutions are to continue as a vital force in American life.

In considering purposes and goals of education, four important observations should be kept in mind: (1) any educational program or procedure (including the stated or implied purposes and goals) tends to be continued or perpetuated even after changes have occurred in the society that established the purposes, or after evidence from research has shown the need for modification; (2) because education is so important and because of its inherent potentialities, a constant struggle may be expected with those who would use it to enchance their own power, privileges, or prestige, or that of their group; (3) continuing studies and discussions are necessary to ensure that there is agreement on purposes and goals of education consistent with the needs of a changing society and with the desires and needs of the people, and that schools are dynamic rather than static institutions; and (4) constant vigilance is essential to ensure that the educational program is developed for the benefit of all and not controlled by or in the interest of any one group or class.[19]

PROVISIONS FOR ORGANIZATION AND ADMINISTRATION

The general plan for organizing and administering schools in the United States had to be evolved by the American people somewhat as they evolved purposes and goals. In the early days, a relatively simple organization sufficed. However, as communities became larger and the nation developed, more thought had to be given to problems of organization and administration. Since the educational programs that were being developed had some unique features, it is not surprising that the provisions for organization and administration of education that eventually emerged would also be unique in certain respects. The major features are: (1) the people in each state are responsible for developing and establishing plans and making provisions for the organization and operation of public schools and institutions of higher learning designed to meet the needs of the state (see Chapters 2 and 9); (2) the people in each *community*, during the early days, and now the people in each *school district* created as an administrative unit of the state are responsible for establishing and operating schools designed to meet the needs in accordance with policies and standards established by the state (see Chapters 10, 11 and 12); (3) the federal

[19]Adapted from statements in Malcolm MacLean and Edwin H. Lee, *Change and Process in Education* (New York: Dryden Press, 1956), Chap. 1.

government constitutionally has no direct responsibility for controlling, organizing, or operating schools or institutions of higher learning established by a state but is expected to encourage and assist the states in developing adequate and effective programs. However, the interest of the federal government in education has increased sharply and its role seems to be changing (see Chapter 8).

The plans and provisions for the organization and administration of education in this country vary considerably from state to state and, to some extent, among school districts within the state. But there are more basic similarities than differences. These similarities have grown out of the commonly accepted purposes of education, of experiences with various types of organization, and of studies relating to the subject. As a result, some of the least satisfactory provisions have been discarded, and an increasing similarity is found in basic provisions that are considered desirable on the basis of purposes, experiences, and the conclusions from numerous studies. For example, the small school districts established in the early days have generally been found to be inefficient and unsatisfactory and have gradually been replaced in many parts of the country by larger districts. (See Chapter 10.)

As the people have learned from various types of experiences and have had an opportunity to develop realistic concepts regarding educational administration, they seem to have reached general agreement on the following characteristics of a sound plan for the administration and operation of local school systems: (1) the local policies and goals for education should be established by a lay board of education representing the people of the area; (2) the educational program and the schools should be administered by professional personnel prepared for that purpose; (3) the professionally prepared administrator of the district, with the assistance of his staff, should be expected to recommend policies and goals for consideration and approval by the board, and to execute those that are approved; and (4) the schools should be adequately staffed by professionally prepared teachers and other educational specialists, whose work is facilitated by competent operation and service personnel.

Many of the early concepts relating to organization and to the administration of education have been considerably modified during the past few years as a result of changes in society, in governmental functions, and in insights based on research studies and findings. Further modifications seem inevitable, because the evidence, some of which is discussed in subsequent chapters, points clearly to the need for such changes.

The system (or systems) of education in this country should be viewed as constituting a (presumably) coordinated unit or part of the system of government. The organization comprises a staff that is selected and organized for the purpose of achieving the purposes and goals of education. The development and modification of the organization is a function of administration that attempts to relate and fuse the purposes of the schools, of the staff, and of society. "It is the continuously developing plan which defines the job and shows how it can be efficiently and effectively accomplished by the people functioning in a certain social environment."[20] All organizations are affected to some extent by the prevailing forces and factors in the society and culture in which they operate. Most large organizations, especially, tend to develop some of the characteristics of what has come to be called a bureaucracy.

Four fundamental concepts have commonly been used as a basis for studying, attempting to understand, and proposing improvements in organization: the task (or job); the position (relates to a grouping of tasks); the authority (who may initiate action for whom); and the administrative unit or department. For educational organizations, Charters proposed an analysis of the *work flow* (sequence in which work operations are performed and techniques used in order to effect results) and the *division of labor* (manner in which tasks in the school's work flow are broken up and distributed among instructional and noninstructional personnel).[21] He considered "organizational maintenance" as comprising input-output functions and work-coordinating functions. Lonsdale explained organizational maintenance as ". . . sustaining the organization in dynamic equilibrium through a developing integration of task-achievement and needs-satisfaction."[22] He observed that this is a complex process which involves achieving the tasks of the organization and meeting the needs of the individual.

During recent years, the concepts of administration have moved far from the old idea of "scientific management" and "efficiency" as primary concerns to a much greater emphasis on consideration of factors involved in human relations and in the interactions among components of the system. In some respects, an interpretation given sixty years ago is still appropriate: "Administration is the capacity of coordinating many, often conflicting, social energies in a single organization so adroitly that they shall operate as a unity."[23]

---

[20]Daniel E. Griffiths, David L. Clark, D. Richard Winn, and Laurence Innaccone, *Organizing Schools for Effective Education* (Danville, Ill.: Interstate Printers and Publishers, Inc., 1962), p. 10.

[21]W. W. Charters, Jr., "An Approach to the Formal Organization of Schools," in *Behavioral Science and Educational Administration,* Daniel E. Griffiths ed., The Sixty-third Yearbook of the National Society for the Study of Education, Part II (Chicago, University of Chicago Press, 1964), Chap. 11.

[22]Richard C. Lonsdale, "Maintaining the Organization in Dynamic Equilibrium," in *Behavioral Science and Educational Administration,* Daniel E. Griffiths ed., The Sixty-third Yearbook of the National Society for the Study of Education, Part II (Chicago, University of Chicago Press, 1964), Chap. 7.

[23]Brooks Adams, *The Theory of Social Revolutions* (New York: The Macmillan Company, 1914), p. 207.

Griffiths, after emphasizing and explaining the value of the tridimensional concept (the job, the man, and the social setting) for educational administration, analyzed the human-relations aspects of the motives of man, perception, communication, power, authority, morale, group dynamics techniques, decision making, and the human-relations approach to leadership.[24] Simon also gave considerable attention to the use of fact and value in decision making (both are usually involved), as well as to rationality in behavior.[25]

Modern authorities are concerned with the development of a unifying theory as a way of looking at organization and administration, procedures for examining these areas, and the implications of findings from research studies. These and other basic concepts and principles of organization and administration and the major implications for education are discussed in Chapters 3 and 4.

SOME IMPORTANT PROBLEMS AND ISSUES

As indicated by the discussion in this chapter, there are many unresolved issues relating to the systems of education that have been or are being developed in nations around the world. A few of the major issues are discussed briefly on the following pages; others are considered in subsequent chapters.

How Should Education Contribute to Community, State, and National Development?

Two major problems that should be of concern to educators as well as to all other citizens are: (1) How can the educational program best be adapted to the needs of a rapidly changing civilization? and (2) How can and should education contribute to community, state, and national development (improvement) and help to ensure that the direction and results of change will be beneficial rather than harmful?

A group of social scientists from the United States and one of the Latin American countries has proposed several assumptions for guidance in considering certain aspects of these problems, a few of which are given below.

[24]Daniel E. Griffiths, *Human Relations in Social Administration* (New York: Appleton-Century & Appleton-Century-Crofts, 1956).
[25]See Herbert A. Simon, *Administrative Behavior: A Study of Decision-Making Processes in Administration*, 2d ed. (New York: Free Press of Glencoe, Inc., 1957).

- From a long-range point of view, the best way to assure that needed improvements will be effected in any society is to improve the education of the people. Thus improving the knowledge, insights, understanding, and skills of the people becomes a key to the improvement of a community, state, and nation.
- Insofar as practicable, improvements should be carefully and systematically planned, rather than left to chance or caprice. Plans should be developed on the basis of scientific studies and research; goals and objectives should be established by agreement among informed and competent people who should cooperate in their attainment. However, there must be an awareness that social change may occur (1) through a process of evolution, (2) through a revolution, (3) through diffusion, and (4) through planned action.
- National plans should include policies for national, state, and community development. They should provide for the national government to (1) implement directly only those aspects of the general plan which must be undertaken at that level, and (2) stimulate and encourage state and local planning in those aspects which are appropriate for state and local decisions and which, if undertaken nationally, would retard or discourage local creativity and initiative and tend to increase and to perpetuate needless centralization and control.
- The process of planning involves many little-understood aspects and factors and, therefore, should be continuously studied and improved as a means of safeguarding against mistakes or correcting them. Optimum safeguards are provided when competent people who are genuinely interested in bona fide community, state, and national improvements cooperate in the process of developing and appraising plans.
- All plans should incorporate procedures for evaluation designed to ensure that imperfections will be discovered as promptly as possible, so steps can be taken to assure needed adjustments and to avoid undesirable developments and outcomes.[26]

In what respects should these assumptions be supplemented or modified? What are some of the implications for programs and procedures for preparing teachers, administrators, and technicians who are concerned with aspects of community, state, or national improvement? For educational programs and for the organization, administration and support of education?

How Much Centralization Is Desirable?

There are many people who believe in considerable centralization in an effort to promote efficiency. Many others vigorously resist this concept. One difficulty is that the terms "centralization" and "efficiency" mean different things to different people. It is, therefore, difficult even to discuss these concepts without giving some attention to definitions and interpretations. Centralization in education is often used to mean the organization of larger schools or larger school systems. On the other hand, it may mean

[26]Developed by the Staff, Instituto de Estudos Rurais, Fundação Escola de Sociologia e Política de São Paulo (Brazil).

that an increasing number of things are done—and decisions made centrally—that is, by the central office of the school system, by the state, or even by the federal government.

What would be the effect on the educational program of assigning additional functions to a more central organization? The following criteria have been suggested for general guidance in resolving such questions: (1) *those things should be done (or decisions made) centrally that do not require or involve local initiative and responsibility and which can be done more efficiently and economically on a centralized basis; (2) those things should be decentralized and carried out at the local level which require decisions relating especially to local needs and which, if done centrally, would prevent or limit desirable initiative and handicap the development of effective local leadership and responsibility.* How should these be revised or supplemented?

How can issues such as the following be resolved if some of the disadvantages of extreme decentralization or extreme centralization are to be avoided: What aspects of the educational program should be centralized and to what extent? How can the state, intermediate or regional service unit, and local school systems best cooperate in improving educational programs without creating a situation in which desirable local initiative and responsibility are discouraged?

Who Should Control Education?

One of the major concerns of the American people has been to ensure that public schools and educational institutions are not directly subject to control by groups or organizations that might seek to use them for their own purposes. In no other country have the people provided the safeguards sought in most sections of this country. However, the schools are always in some danger. Certain individuals and groups are constantly seeking to influence or even to control education for their own advantage. Control of education offers one promising opportunity to control the thoughts and destinies of the people in the community, state, or nation.

Most people apparently believe that education is so basic and has such tremendous possibilities for good or evil as far as community, state, and national progress are concerned, that special provisions are essential to ensure that the schools will not be diverted from their major purposes. But the people are not yet fully agreed on how this can best be accomplished.

In almost every community and state, there are some individuals or organizations who are constantly seeking to keep the schools from doing certain things or to see that they do other things that would be contrary

26 BASIC PRINCIPLES, CONCEPTS, AND ISSUES

to the basic purposes of education. Bitter attacks have sometimes been made on boards of education and school administrators who resisted these efforts. Certain groups would, if they could, prevent students from studying about UNESCO, about evolution, about family relationships; in fact about many other matters that must be studied if they are to learn to understand and think through some of the problems of the modern world. Groups that have "axes to grind" sometimes deliberately set about to control the board of education and consequently the school program by supporting candidates who are openly or secretly committed to their particular point of view. What steps can be taken to ensure that no group can control the schools for its own purposes? How can attempts to get the schools to do something that is contrary to their proper functions best be resisted?

How Can Greater Agreement Be Reached on Purposes and Goals of Education?

Among the distinctive features of the educational program as developed in many of the democratic nations of the world, Kandel pointed out one that seems especially significant:

> A system of administration conceived as it is in England and the United States is itself educative; it demands intelligence and it elicits intelligence; it relies for the progress and success of education on public opinion and that public opinion must be enlightened; it calls for cooperation and participation of all who are concerned with education but it also creates that concern.[27]

At no time has there been adequate understanding of this unique role of education, nor has there been agreement on purposes and goals. Complete agreement probably should not be expected. Yet, when there are significant differences of opinion, there are bound to be controversies regarding the schools, criticisms, and difficulties in developing defensible programs of education. The public schools need the support of the people. To the extent that this support is not forthcoming from any substantial number, the schools will be handicapped.

There are marked differences of opinion concerning the tasks of the public schools, "the fundamentals," the nonsectarian nature of public schools, adult education, career education, preparation of teachers—in fact, about almost every significant aspect of the educational program. What procedures can be utilized to bring about greater agreement than

---

[27] I. L. Kandel, *Types of Administration* (New York: Oxford University Press, Inc., 1938), p. 43.

exists at present on purposes and goals and in establishing priorities? In areas where substantial agreement is impossible, what should the schools do?

What Kind of Organization Is Needed to Facilitate the Attainment of Acceptable Purposes?

All citizens should have a direct concern about education. If it is seriously neglected or perverted in any state or in many communities, the nation may be handicapped. The fact that a good program of education is essential for the development and continuation of a sound democratic form of government has been recognized by many from the beginning. If the federal government had been given more responsibility for education when the nation was organized, could some of the mistakes and weaknesses found in various parts of the country have been avoided? Are there any respects in which steps should be taken to develop a national system or program of education?

A few states have left public school education to be developed primarily by communities, with comparatively little state direction or influence. In fact, schools throughout the country are often thought of as "local" schools. Would it be feasible to consider education as a local rather than a state responsibility? What should be the major responsibilities of a state for educational provisions and programs? What kind of local organization for schools is needed to facilitate the attainment of purposes and goals generally agreed upon?

What Should Be the Place of Nonpublic Education in American Life?

A majority of parents representing most religious denominations apparently prefer that their children attend public schools. Many Catholics also take this point of view. In fact, there is currently a vigorous debate within the Roman Catholic Church in this country about the future of Catholic elementary and secondary schools. Some contend the policy, "Catholic children must not attend non-Catholic, neutral or mixed schools . . ." except with special permission,[28] should be continued; others insist that it be materially revised. Several writers have strongly supported the latter point of view.[29] Proposals relating to financial support for nonpublic schools have helped to bring this problem into clearer focus.

[28]From Title XXII, "Concerning Schools," Catholic Canon Law.
[29]See, for example, Mary Perkins Ryan, *Are Parochial Schools the Answer?* (New York: Holt, Rinehart & Winston, Inc., 1964).

Let us assume that the time may come when a majority, rather than a small minority, of all students attend nonpublic schools of one type or another. What will be the effect on American life and attitudes? Will the ability to look at problems from a common background and point of view, and to resolve most differences of opinion satisfactorily, be decreased? Would the divisive influences in American life tend to become more serious than they are at present?

There are communities in some states where a majority of the people support nonpublic schools and send their children to them. In certain cases, these people have elected representatives to the board of education who, for one reason or another, have failed to support the public school program. In some of these communities the children who are attending public schools are being denied the opportunities to which they should be entitled. What is likely to happen to the public schools and to their contribution to American life in those communities or states in which a majority of the citizens send their children to and support nonpublic schools? Do some of the developments in Holland have any implications for people in America?[30]

Some competition between public and nonpublic schools in unavoidable and may to a certain extent be beneficial. However, Americans have learned that competition in any phase of life may have its unwholesome as well as its wholesome aspects. There has been some unfair criticism of nonpublic schools by public school supporters. Criticism of the public schools by some supporters of nonpublic schools has also, on occasion, been not only unfair but misleading. For example, the charge has frequently been made that the state is attempting to establish a monopoly of public schools even though the Supreme Court has held that that cannot be done. Another criticism charges that there is an unfair system of "double taxation" on those who send their children to nonpublic schools, in spite of the fact that this is a voluntary choice.

In what respects has the American public generally been unfair in its attitude toward or criticism of public schools? Of nonpublic schools? What would be the "best" solution to these problems?

SELECTED REFERENCES

BEREDAY, GEORGE Z. F., ed., *Essays on World Education: The Crisis of World Supply and Demand.* New York, N.Y.: Oxford University Press, 1969.

COOMBS, PHILIP H., *The World Educational Crisis: A Systems Analysis.* New York, N.Y.: Oxford University Press, 1968.

[30]See Reller and Morphet, *Comparative Educational Administration,* Chap. 4.

HACK, WALTER G., et al., *Educational Futurism 1985: Challenges for Schools and Their Administrators.* Berkeley, Calif.: McCutcheon Publishing Corporation, 1971.

HIRSCH, WERNER C., et al., *Inventing Education for the Future.* San Francisco, Calif.: Chandler Publishing Company, 1967.

KEBER, AUGUST and WILFRED R. SMITH, eds., *Educational Issues in a Changing Society,* 3d ed. Detroit, Mich.: Wayne State University Press, 1968.

MCHALE, JOHN, *The Future of the Future.* New York, N.Y.: George Braziller, Inc., 1969.

MANN, JOHN, *Changing Human Behavior.* New York, N.Y.: Charles Scribner's Sons, 1965.

MICHAEL, DONALD, *The Unprepared Society: Planning for a Precarious Future.* New York.: Basic Books, 1968.

MORPHET, EDGAR L., and CHARLES O. RYAN, eds., *Prospective Changes in Society by 1980,* (1966); and *Implications for Education of Prospective Changes in Society,* (1967). Denver, Colo.: Designing Education for the Future. (Republished by Citation Press, Scholastic Magazines, Inc., New York, N.Y.)

RELLER, THEODORE L., and EDGAR L. MORPHET, eds., *Comparative Educational Administration.* Englewood Cliffs, N.J.: Prentice-Hall, Inc., 1962, Chaps. 1, 18, 19, 20, and 21.

2

The Legal Basis for Education*

In this chapter, major attention is devoted to the origin, evolution, and implications of constitutional provisions, laws, board policies, administrative regulations, and court decisions relating to education. There must be a rational authority—that is, a legal basis—for all major decisions in or relating to formal education. In this country the legal basis for education, as well as for other aspects of government, has been developed and modified from time to time by the people or their representatives. The Constitutional and other legal provisions, as interpreted in many instances by court decisions, determine the kinds of educational programs that can be provided and of provisions that can be made for organizing, administering, financing, and operating these programs. Of course the perceptions and attitudes of state and local school board members and the competencies and points of view of the educational personnel they employ also have an

*Prepared with the collaboration of M. CHESTER NOLTE, Professor of Educational Administration, University of Denver.

important and often a significant influence on the effectiveness and quality of the programs provided. An understanding of the major legal provisions is important for all who are concerned with education and is essential for those who have administrative responsibilities.

BASES FOR LEGAL PROVISIONS

In all nations the legal provisions (ranging from those incorporated in the constitution—if there is one—through enactments of a legislative body, decrees, or other official policy statements, administrative regulations, and court decisions) grow out of the values, beliefs, and concerns of the people or their rulers. The legal system may be designed primarily to protect the privileges of the governing group and its supporters, to ensure the perpetuation of certain customs or practices, or to provide the basis for orderly progress. In the United States, the federal and state provisions that relate to education are a direct outgrowth of the value systems and beliefs of the citizens of the nation and of the various states regarding the place and role of education in the lives of people and in the governmental structure. These provisions are an integral part of a comprehensive legal system that constitutes a body of guides and rules for many aspects of human conduct and relations that are prescribed and enforced by legally authorized representatives of the organized society.

The Conceptual Design

In general, the legal provisions for education are based on what Hamilton and Mort have termed the "conceptual design" for education which is an outgrowth of the beliefs, values, and aspirations of the people.[1] This conceptual design is based on the stated or implied purposes to be achieved through education and includes, by implication, the generally accepted perspectives and concepts concerning the place and role of education in society and government, the scope and major goals, and the basic guidelines or policies considered necessary to ensure adequate and effective provisions and programs. These legal provisions are organized into a more or less consistent and rational system that provides for policies and practices considered "good" or desirable, and a basis for rejecting those that are considered "bad" or undesirable. Although the conceptual design for education is not static, many of the basic elements are relatively constant.

The evolving design is influenced by changes in society that have

[1] Robert R. Hamilton and Paul R. Mort, *The Law and Public Education,* 2nd ed. (New York: Foundation Press, Inc., 1959), Chap. 2.

implications for education and by new information, ideas, and concepts relating to education. Basically, the design is affected by such factors as the following, which are often interrelated: (1) a new or revised theory concerning education and its organization and administration, (2) findings and conclusions based on important research studies in areas ranging from learning through finance, (3) the evaluation of experiences resulting in conclusions as to what works well and what does not, (4) new and challenging ideas and concepts which seem to hold promise, and (5) the changing beliefs and aspirations of the people.

Histories of education have directed attention to the differences in purposes and provisions that developed in the New England area, in the Middle Colonies, and in the South. Had some of the original elements of the "design for education" in any one of these areas been accepted, the nation might have developed primarily parochial or church-controlled schools, fee or tuition schools to which many children of poor families would not have had access, public pauper schools for the poor and private schools for the more wealthy, or some other kind of school system based on purposes quite different from those generally accepted and incorporated in the current design. However, the purposes accepted were those that seemed best suited to meet the needs of the new nation. If different purposes had been accepted, the legal structure for education would necessarily have differed in basic respects from that found at present.

Apparently only a few of the early leaders (notably Jefferson) had much insight into the place and significance of education in a government of, by, and for the people. The process of thinking through and envisioning the kind of educational program and structure needed by the evolving democratic nation presented many problems and difficulties. While conflicting views and important differences of opinion have continued throughout the history of the nation and will undoubtedly continue into the future, a majority of the people eventually began to agree upon concepts such as the following:

1. All citizens must be reasonably well educated if a democratic form of government is to survive and to function satisfactorily.
2. The citizens themselves are responsible and must make provisions primarily through public schools for the opportunities that are necessary to ensure that everyone will be educated (since education cannot satisfactorily be left to parents, to church groups, to private institutions, or even to the discretion of local communities).
3. The people of the entire nation should be concerned about education and should be interested in helping to provide for and stimulate the development of satisfactory provisions and programs.
4. The people of each state should directly assume the responsibility for education (as implied by the Tenth Amendment to the federal Constitution) and should recognize and provide for the implementation of that responsibility by appropriate provisions in the state constitution and laws.

Neither the people of the nation nor those in the areas that later became states began with laws relating to education. They started with beliefs, attitudes, and ideas—with the elements of a conceptual design—that constituted the basis for legal provisions. Some of their aspirations for education became statutorily sanctioned; others resulted in, or were the result of, decisions by courts of law—a process still in use today. This conceptual design is still evolving with some differences noted from state to state, continues to be inconsistent and irrational in some respects, moves at inconstant rates within the nation as a whole, and some aspects continue to be controversial. To the extent that standards are set by the courts—and especially by the United States Supreme Court—the process tends to be relatively uncontrolled by state interests except in those areas not subject to constitutional strictures.

As a result of having to design education without a fully developed model to guide them, early citizens and educators tended to grope idealistically toward a future system of education that no one really envisioned, but which began to be expressed in purposes and goals to be attained and ends to be achieved. For example, Horace Mann wrote in the 1840s:

> I believe in the existence of a great, immortal immutable principle of natural law, or natural ethics—a principle antecedent to all human institutions, and incapable of being abrogated by any ordinance of man—which proves the *absolute right* to an education of every human being that comes into the world, and which, of course, proves the correlative duty of every government to see that the means of that education are provided for all.[2]

This aspiration of Mann's (universal education at public expense) has become the cornerstone for most of the state systems of education since the 1840s and continues to challenge citizens and state planning agencies or commissions in the 1970s.

The Sources of Law

It is precisely because of the deep and abiding faith of the people in universal education at public expense that the states were able to obtain the cooperation of parents and students in attempting to implement Mann's concept. Through compulsory attendance, compulsory taxation, and related statutes, the legislative bodies preempted some aspects of the field of personal liberties (now considered essential for individuals) on the grounds that the American way of life depended on an enlightened citi-

---
[2] Horace Mann, *Tenth Annual Report to the Massachusetts State Board of Education,* 1846, pp. 177–180.

zenry, and that such measures were necessary in order to achieve the "great American dream." The states controlled these aspects of public education until 1954, when the "Warren Court" was requested, and attempted, to bring about a better balance *between the responsibility assumed by the states and individual freedoms* under the Constitution.

Prior to the Warren Court decisions, the courts had hesitated to act on appeals to intervene in order to support an individual's rights in or for education—doing so only when a board of education clearly acted outside its legal powers or in an arbitrary or capricious manner in denying individual rights. But the United States Supreme Court in 1954 warned that any such power by the state, desirable as it might seem, nevertheless posed a clear and present danger to individual liberties. Instead, it said that in order to limit individual rights in schools, the school officials must show "an overriding public purpose to be served" which made such limitation necessary.[3] As a result of its decisions relating to educational policy, the Warren Court wielded considerable power in shaping some important aspects of current policy.

The fact that some important educational policies have been determined by the courts, however, does not minimize or eliminate the need for increased emphasis in the states on determining needs and planning better educational futures for their citizens. If anything, the need for such planning is heightened by the Court's attempts to balance the interests of the state against those of each individual teacher, student, and lay citizen. Continuing or periodic study and review of the basic purposes and goals of education should be considered essential in every state and community. To the extent that agreement can be reached, there is an acceptable basis for developing legislation and for planning educational programs. New purposes and goals or new emphases will emerge from time to time, and these, of course, will have implications for developments throughout the state.

There must also be policies or general guides for action that are agreed upon as useful in attempting to attain the purposes and goals of education. Policies may either be expedient devices which provide for some immediately acceptable steps, or guides for carefully planned courses of action designed to facilitate the attainment of goals. Soundly conceived policies should result in programs of legislation and education that are consistent with statements of purposes and goals and should promote their attainment.[4]

[3] *Brown v. Board of Education of Topeka,* 347 U.S. 483 (Kans. 1954).
[4] See James Bryant Conant, *Shaping Educational Policy* (New York: McGraw-Hill Book Company, 1964), Chaps. 2 and 3.

The Structural Pattern

Since public education is "one instrumentality of society for the carrying out of a function which society has decreed to be a desirable one,"[5] it is not surprising that the basic provisions for the organization and operation of education are determined by the society in which it operates. Thus, the society determines not only the conceptual design for education but also the structural pattern. Educators, through their concepts, ideas, and studies, undoubtedly influence both the design and the structure in many ways, but they do not necessarily determine what either is to be. This means that educators need to recognize that they are operating to some extent in the public domain and in the political arena and cannot go much beyond what the people will accept. In other words, educators cannot expect to be successful in attempting to preserve the status quo when the people want progress, or to institute changes the people or their representatives are unwilling to accept. Effective two-way communication is essential. Educators must communicate and interpret research findings and new concepts and their implications, and the people must communicate effectively their own concerns and concepts. Understanding and agreement should constitute the basis for progress.

Ideally, the structural pattern for education should emerge from the conceptual design and be consistent with it. Actually, the structural pattern often is determined basically by the legal system that establishes the plan for organization and operation by creating the agencies to be utilized in attaining the desired goals and allocating functions among them within prescribed limits. However, the legal system is often supplemented or extended by practices and procedures in areas not closely defined or restricted by law.

The structural pattern tends, in certain respects, to lag behind the evolving conceptual design for education. In other words, constitutional provisions, laws, and even court decisions are based on elements of the conceptual design *at a particular time.* As the design changes, the legal system usually retains some practices and concepts that are outmoded. Many illustrations can be given: the continuation of small obsolete school districts, the county as an intermediate unit with an elected superintendent in areas where districts have been reorganized, the apportionment of funds on bases found by research to be unsound, and so on. Moreover, the structural pattern, for one reason or another, often omits important elements of the conceptual design or includes nonrational aspects that prevent the development of an effective program of education, at least in

[5]Hamilton and Mort, *Law and Public Education,* p. 3.

certain parts of the state. For example, Section 183 of the Kentucky Constitution of 1891 requires the general assembly to "provide for an effective system of common schools throughout the state." However, Section 186, until significantly revised some sixty years later, required that all state school funds be apportioned to districts on the basis of the number of children of school census age, thus making an adequate and effective system of education impossible in many sections of the state.

Such inconsistencies and limitations should not be surprising. Constitutional conventions and legislatures often include some people who do not subscribe to the generally accepted conceptual design for public education or do not understand the implications of some of the provisions they advocate. The problem is likely to be particularly acute in states in which there are sharp differences of opinion concerning elements of the conceptual design, the design itself is vague or poorly formulated in certain respects, or the people are relatively uninformed or indifferent about changing needs and the characteristics of an effective program of education.

Some steps that might well be taken in any state in an effort to ensure that the structural pattern is as consistent as possible with the evolving conceptual design include the following:

1. Educational and lay leaders should systematically review, and if necessary revise, the conceptual design for education periodically in an effort to ensure that it will facilitate the attainment of the desired purposes of education, that it is internally consistent, and that it is clearly stated.
2. Legislators and other citizens in all parts of the state should be encouraged to discuss this tentative statement and to propose revisions or clarification. This procedure should result not only in improving the statement and making it more meaningful but also in facilitating understanding, agreement, and support.
3. All major legal provisions should then be reviewed as a means of identifying any handicapping constraints, lags, or inconsistent aspects, and as a means of proposing revisions.
4. The legislature should be encouraged to incorporate into the legal structure all basic elements that seem to be substantiated by evidence and experience, so as to make the structure as consistent as possible with the design.
5. The legislature should be expected to refrain from mandating any aspect of structure that is inconsistent with the design or is based on an emerging concept that has not yet been adequately tried out or tested.
6. As a basis for ensuring greater flexibility in introducing locally promising innovations, the legislature should provide for considerable local discretion and should refrain from restricting local boards to those educational policies and practices that are specifically authorized by statute.

CONSTITUTIONAL PROVISIONS

The basic legal provisions relating to or having implications for education are found in the federal and state constitutions. Those in the federal

Constitution are of significance for education throughout the nation, whereas provisions found in each state constitution are applicable only to the educational program within the state.

The Federal Constitution

As far as education is concerned, one of the most significant provisions of the federal Constitution is found in the Tenth Amendment, which —like other sections of the Constitution—does not even mention education. This amendment reserves to the states or to the people all powers not delegated to the federal government by the Constitution. The power of each state to provide and maintain public schools is thus inherent in the state responsibilities established by this amendment but, as noted previously, it is not an unlimited power. The provision of education for all citizens is one important means the state may use to facilitate its own progress. Without such a system, which should help to provide for the development of citizens who can act rationally and intelligently on matters of public concern as well as in their own affairs, the progress of a state might be jeopardized. The system of education provided by the state, therefore, is to be considered legally as a service to the citizens for the benefit of the state and society, rather than as a service to the individual primarily for his own benefit, or as a charitable or philanthropic service.[6] However, as explained later, the courts have held that education is a fundamental right of every child and, consequently, no state can deny that right.

Four other provisions in the federal Constitution and its amendments noted below and commonly recognized as having considerable significance for education are discussed in Chapter 8. Most of them are concerned with the protection of what is often referred to as the inherent rights of individuals. Sections 8 and 10 of Article I prescribe, respectively, that Congress shall have power to provide, among other things, for the general welfare, and that no state shall pass any law imparing the obligation of contracts. The First Amendment prohibits Congress from making any law "respecting an establishment of religion, or prohibiting the free exercise thereof." (Later, the Bill of Rights, including the First Amendment, was held to apply to the states as well as to the Congress.) One clause of the Fifth Amendment, which is concerned with the protection of individuals against self-incrimination in criminal cases, has been invoked in cases in which investigation committees have sought to inquire into connections teachers and others may have had with what some people may consider to be "subversive organizations." The Fourteenth Amendment prohibits any state from making or enforcing any law abridging "the privileges or immu-

---

[6]Lee O. Garber, *Education as a Function of the State* (Minneapolis: Educational Test Bureau, Inc., 1934), p. 21.

nities of citizens of the United States," or from depriving any person of "life, liberty, or property, without due process of law," or from denying "to any person within its jurisdiction the equal protection of the laws." Each of these provisions has been the basis for a number of controversies and challenges involving education, as will be pointed out later.

Although each state has the responsibility for developing its own public school program, it cannot through its constitutional provisions or laws violate (without the probability of challenge in the courts) any of the provisions of the federal Constitution including its amendments. There are thus important controls on what states may do in certain respects, but as long as these limitations are observed, the people of each state are free to develop their own education program as they see fit.

State Constitutional Provisions

The people of each state have incorporated in their constitution some of their basic beliefs about, and policies for, education as well as other aspects of government for which they are responsible. However, as new information has become available, insights and points of view have gradually changed. Some of these changing concepts have tended to be reflected in most states either in new constitutions adopted by the people or in amendments to the original constitution.

The constitution should include only the fundamental policies and basic provisions concerning education and other aspects of government. The more specific and detailed provisions are usually included in the statutes, policy statements, and regulations. All of these, as supplemented or modified by court decisions, constitute the presumably rational—and legal—authority for organizing and operating school systems and schools. Constitutional provisions are usually more difficult to revise or repeal than statutes. For that reason, it is generally considered wise to include in the constitution only those fundamental expressions of policy that guide but do not handicap the development of the educational program and are not likely to need revision in a relatively short time.

One of the policies that has found expression in some form in every state constitution is that the state legislature must provide for a uniform and effective system of public schools. Thus the people generally have not left the legislature any discretion as to whether public schools shall be established. Usually, however, it has had considerable discretion as to steps and procedures that may be used in establishing such schools. Other policies relating to education that have been expressed in the constitution of nearly every state include the following: the permanent school fund is to be kept sacred and inviolate, and only the income from the fund may be used for public school purposes; public schools are to be provided at public expense; and public tax funds made available for educational purposes are to be used only for the support of public education.

Although one objective of the people in each state seems to have been to incorporate in their constitution those provisions that require and facilitate the development of an adequate program of public education, experience has shown that restrictive or handicapping provisions have from time to time been included. For example, constitutional provisions in some states prescribe such rigid limits on taxes or bond issues for school purposes that the people in many communities have not been permitted to make the effort they would be willing to make to support schools. Thus the provisions relating to education that are incorporated in a state constitution have vital significance. They may either stimulate and facilitate the development of an adequate program of public education or make such a program difficult, if not impossible, to attain until they are repealed.

The legislature of a state has full power, commonly referred to as *plenary* power, to enact laws regarding the schools as well as other aspects of government. However, such legislation should not conflict with provisions of the state or federal Constitution. If any such conflict exists and the matter is taken to the courts, the statute will be declared unconstitutional. The following statement in a New York court decision is significant:

> The people, in framing the constitution, committed to the legislature the whole law making power of the state which they did not expressly or impliedly withhold. Plenary power in the legislature for all purposes of civil government is the rule.[7]

LAWS AND ADMINISTRATIVE POLICIES RELATING TO EDUCATION

Laws as well as constitutional provisions relating to education vitally affect the provisions for education and should be of concern to everyone interested in education or government. Statutes (commonly referred to as "laws") enacted by the legislatures of the respective states have the "color" of law as long as they are not in conflict with the state's constitution or the federal Constitution and its amendments. Such statutes presumably express the majority beliefs and intent of the people of the state, and in certain respects may be as significant as constitutional provisions in deter-

[7] *The People v. Draper,* 15 N.Y. 532.

mining the scope and adequacy of the educational program that can be provided. Narrowly restrictive or unwise statutes may be as serious as limiting constitutional provisions.

Majority rule must give way, however, where the courts indicate that the state has overstepped its authority and infringed upon the individual rights of any citizen. The philosophical question as to whether "majority rule should predominate in all things" is too involved to be treated here. Suffice it to say that our "law" comes from two sources, neither of which is exclusive: (1) enactments of public policy by majority legislative decision; and (2) decisions by the courts and administrative bodies upholding the rights of individuals or minorities as contrasted with those of the state. The model, an apothecary's scale, sees justice in this framework as balancing the interests of the individual in relationship to those of the state (all the other individuals).

Federal Laws

Since education has been established as a function of the respective states, the basic laws relating to the organization, administration, and operation of schools are state rather than federal laws. However, the people of the entire nation have always been interested in education and, as a consequence, from the time of the early land grants there have been federal laws relating to one aspect or another of education (see Chapter 8). Although some of these laws are concerned with direct responsibilities of the federal government (for education of the military forces or wards of the federal government, education in certain federal areas and territories, and educational services provided by the federal government through various agencies), others are designed to aid or stimulate education in and through the states. These laws have provided for grants and services to the states for various educational purposes.

The chief problems from the point of view of many people have arisen over the narrow categorical financial provisions and the requirements or controls that have been incorporated in some laws relating to financial assistance. Congress undoubtedly has a right to establish requirements that are not inconsistent with provisions of the federal Constitution. The issue is basically one as to the kind of policies and the extent of controls that seem to be needed and are prudent. Usually, states have been given the right (theoretically, at least) to decide whether they will accept the funds authorized. However, if a state is willing to accept the funds authorized by any law, it must observe the conditions attached to the acceptance.

State Statutes

State statutes supplementing the constitutional provisions presumably express the will and policy of the people of the state regarding education and its operation. The number and complexity of laws (statutes) relating to education have increased rapidly during the last few years in practically every state. Compilations of statutes relating to education that could be included in not more than fifty printed pages a few decades ago have, in some instances, grown into a volume (or several volumes) of more than a thousand pages. In some states several hundred bills relating to education are introduced at each session of the legislature and many may be enacted. A large proportion of these bills usually are concerned with minor amendments or with relatively brief proposals for new sections (some of which may conflict with earlier laws), but others may require several printed pages and incorporate many details regarding some one aspect of the educational program.

A basic issue that persists comes from the legal question, "How can the interest of the state in providing for an adequate system of public education and an enlightened citizenry be made compatible with the right of the individual to be himself or herself—that is, to be free from domination by the state?" This issue leads to questions such as: Should compulsory attendance laws be modified or eliminated? How should schools be supported financially? To what extent or how should students be entitled to participate in decisions relating to education that may significantly affect their lives?

Proponents of statutory relief for educational inequities tend to say that such problems can be solved "by passing a law." On the other hand, those who advocate minority rights tend to agree with the Supreme Court's declaration that "state-operated schools may not be enclaves of totalitarianism," that children are "persons" under our Constitution and do not "shed their rights" at the schoolhouse door. The latter groups do not believe that the majority is always right, nor that merely enacting a statute will solve the problems of education. In many recent court decisions, some minority points of view have been upheld and the power of the state in educational matters has been eroded in certain respects. Whether local boards of education have, or may have in the future, enough remaining power to solve their real-life problems is paramount among the legal questions that are of concern to many people.

Two major questions underlying educational legislation in each state are: What kinds of statutes are essential to provide for the development of an adequate and effective program of public education? What procedures can be utilized to help to ensure that changes in statutes or new legislation are as carefully planned as most legislators would expect changes in educational programs or procedures to be? Appropriate statutes are those that facilitate the attainment of these goals; those that do not should be challenged. Undoubtedly, every state has some statutes that, properly assessed, would be found indefensible.

The process of evaluating the statutes is constantly taking place in every state. Sooner or later, unwise or hastily enacted statutes are likely to be found unsatisfactory on the basis of studies and experiences in various parts of the state and may be repealed or materially modified. Unfortunately, however, once statutes are enacted, the process of evaluation often tends to be slow or ineffective. Many inappropriate or restrictive laws tend to be continued indefinitely.

Some state legislatures have accepted quite literally the concept that education is a function of the state, and tend to assume that local school systems should have no responsibility or authority unless it is specifically granted by the state. Such states have developed very detailed statutes because such detail has been considered necessary in order to enable school systems to operate satisfactorily. A system of statutes prepared on the basis of this premise is referred to as a "mandatory" system or code. California is a good example of a state that has had (but has recently abandoned) a mandatory system of school legislation, since school districts have been prohibited from doing anything that is not authorized or clearly implied by legislation. Some years ago, the state attorney general advised that:

> The question is not whether the payment of expense [as proposed by a school board] would contribute to the education of pupils, but whether the authority is vested in the board to make such an expenditure. ... School districts are *quasi* municipal corporations of the most limited power known to law.[8]

Such a system results in a vast volume of detailed legislation that places a burden not only on the legislature but also on school officials who are attempting to observe the provisions of statutory law. Perhaps even more significant, it tends to stifle local initiative and may prevent local school systems from experimenting or instituting some promising innovations until the legislature has authorized the action. Especially during this

[8]California Attorney General Opinion 47–38, 1947.

period of rapid change and search for helpful innovations, such a policy can be defended only on the basis of tradition.

Several states have attempted to observe the principle that, while basic policies and responsibilities must be prescribed, some discretion should also be granted to local school systems to assume responsibilities not inconsistent with law that are found necessary for an effective program of education. Provisions of this type, sometimes called a "mandatory-discretionary" system of laws, seem to be favored by an increasing number of states. In a study of the powers and duties of local school boards in selected states with "mandatory" and others with "mandatory-discretionary" types of school codes, Hall found the difference in wording to be small but significant.[9] In the latter group of states, a clause, worded somewhat as follows, was added to the section listing the powers and duties allocated to local school boards: ". . . and in addition thereto, those which it may find to be necessary for the improvement of the school system in carrying out the purposes and objectives of the school code." After analyzing court decisions in these states, Hall concluded that, in the absence of abuse of discretion, the courts generally ruled in favor of the board in its use of the discretionary authority granted.

Most states have found it necessary, especially during the past half-century, to organize their statutes relating to education into a code. When many different statutes are enacted at each session of the legislature, some provisions are likely to be inconsistent with provisions in older statutes. Under these conditions, it may become difficult or impossible for school officials or even lawyers to determine what the law on a given subject may mean in terms of responsibilities of local school officials. A plan for codification of the statutes on any subject means in essence a plan for organizing them logically so that they can be more readily located and understood. In many states the school code (or education code) is one of a series of codes comprising statutes on different subjects or aspects of government.

Studies show that there is considerable variation in the progress states have made in organizing and codifying their statutes relating to education. Although many state codes met reasonably well almost all standards and criteria used in a 1954 study, some of them met none satisfactorily.[10] Statutes pertaining to schools, unlike those on many other subjects, have to be used for guidance by both professional educators and laymen serving on boards of education. Few of them have had much legal

[9]Donald Ellis Hall, "Discretionary and Mandatory Provisions of State Education Law" (Ph.D. dissertation, University of California, Berkeley, 1959).
[10]National Education Association, "The Codification of School Laws," *NEA Research Division, Research Bulletin,* **32**, No. 1 (February 1954), 45.

training. Even well-drafted statutes may have relatively little meaning for laymen unless they are well organized, written so they can be readily understood, presented so they can be easily located, and properly indexed. For this reason, many states are giving increasing attention to standards for codification.

Several plans have been proposed for organizing and codifying the statutes relating to education. One of the simplest of these provides for a code comprising two or three major parts. The first part would include statutes that have implications for all aspects of education, with appropriate divisions, chapters, and sections; the second part would include the more specific provisions with divisions, chapters, and sections incorporating statutes dealing with personnel, students, program, plant, finance, and so on; a third part, or a separate code, would include statutes relating to institutions of higher learning and other aspects of education.

Board Policies, Standards, and Regulations

Some legislation has included details that have resulted in needless handicaps to the educational program. An extreme illustration is afforded by a statute enacted some years ago in one of the states providing that a course on safety education be "taught by lectures." A more common illustration is found in statutes providing that a designated number of minutes each day be devoted to a certain subject in every school.

Experience has shown that it is not practicable and usually not desirable to include minor policies or details in legislation. In every state, therefore, provision is made for the development and adoption by some state agency (usually the state board of education) of policies, standards, and regulations that have the effect of law. Similarly, local boards are authorized to adopt policies and regulations that are not inconsistent with state laws or regulations and which, if properly developed and adopted, have the effect of law in the local school system.

If the legislature were to attempt to grant unlimited powers to a state board of education or to a chief state school officer, the courts could be expected to hold that the legislature cannot delegate its responsibilities, that the powers granted are too broad and, therefore, null and void. When the legislature prescribes the general policies and establishes definite limits within which administrative policies or regulations must come, difficulties should be avoided. But the policies and regulations adopted as authorized by law must be consistent with the provisions of law and must be reasonable.[11]

[11] Newton Edwards, *The Courts and the Public Schools,* rev. ed. (Chicago: University of Chicago Press, 1955), p. 31.

A good example of legislation that requires the adoption of administrative policies and regulations can be found in the field of teacher certification. In many states the statutes set forth the purposes of certification, the general procedures to be used, and perhaps, the major kinds or classes of certificates authorized. The responsibility for prescribing detailed policies, standards, and regulations is usually delegated to the state board of education. The state board should establish application procedures and prescribe requirements to be met before a certificate can be issued. These regulations, however, would have to be reasonable and consistent with the purpose of the statutes to assure fair treatment for all applicants.

All major policies and directives should, therefore, be incorporated in legislation but details that might retard improvements in education or may need to be changed from time to time should be avoided. The statutes should clearly delegate responsibility, when appropriate, for administrative policies and regulations but should carefully define the limits. Boards or agencies to which such responsibilities are delegated should take steps to ensure that their actions are authorized by and consistent with provisions of law, are reasonable, and do not constitute an impulsive or arbitrary exercise of delegated power.

The process of developing policies in a local school system often involves some difficulties. Each proposed policy must be considered in relationship to other policies; otherwise, there may be conflicts and crosscurrents with resultant confusion, dissension, or inefficiency. Studies by a competent and representative committee in advance of board consideration should mean that if the board adopts the recommended policy, it is not only likely to be sound and defensible but also to have a reasonably good prospect of being accepted by the staff and by the community. Adoption of the policy by the board means that the board then has a guide for action in that field, subject to possible revision on the basis of further studies. Once a policy has been adopted, a board should not need to spend time in considering individual problems that arise in that area. Nor should it have to risk the possibility of inconsistent action while attempting to work out a solution for each problem without reference to previous decisions.

As pointed out in Chapter 11, the board should not enact, nor should the administrator prescribe, restrictive or detailed rules and regulations governing the implementation of board policies. Unless reasonable flexibility is provided for management, there will be little innovation in a school system. It is not good policy for the legislature, the state board of education, the local board of education, or the administrator to prescribe in detail the activities of principals and teachers. Better educational programs tend to be found in those systems which provide for a considerable amount of decision making at the operating level.

COURT DECISIONS

Any statute or any board regulation may be constitutional or unconstitutional. When a question arises, either the statute or the board regulation bears the presumption of constitutionality unless or until a court of competent jurisdiction has declared otherwise. This means that any untested statute or regulation must be presumed to be valid until such time as it has been declared unconstitutional and all appeals to higher courts, including the United States Supreme Court, have been exhausted or abandoned.

Ordinarily, courts will not of their own volition test the constitutionality of a statute or public law: they interpret only *concrete* examples of the applicability, or misapplicability, of the statute or public law in question. Inasmuch as each case differs in some or perhaps many respects from other cases, a school administrator needs to be familiar with related adjudicated cases of recent vintage in order to develop a reasonably defensible position for dealing with legal problems that arise in his work, and should seek to work closely with the board's legal counsel on all major legal problems with which the school system is or may be concerned.

The Role of the Courts

Since education affects practically all people in one way or another at some time during their lives, there are many differences of opinion regarding the rights, privileges, and obligations of people relating to schools. As society becomes more complex, as attempts are made to adapt education to the rapidly changing needs, and as laws relating to education increase in number and scope, more and more questions regarding the purposes and intent of those laws are likely to arise. Thus, the courts in every state and, in some cases, federal courts, are called upon from time to time to interpret one aspect or another of the laws relating to schools.

The courts have been established to attempt to resolve the many controversies that are certain to arise in a pluralistic society. They function in accordance with established rules or criteria in an effort to assure equity and justice for all in every aspect of life, including education. Fortunately, courts do not always decide issues merely by precedent or weight of evidence. As the United States Supreme Court stated in a landmark decision holding that the Social Security Act was not in conflict with the Tenth Amendment, "Nor is the concept of general welfare static. Needs that were narrow or parochial a century ago may be interwoven in our day with the well being of the Nation. What is critical or urgent changes with the times."[12] On the basis of this decision it should be apparent that Congress

---

[12] *Helvering v. Davis,* 301 U.S. 619, 57S. Ct. 904 (1937).

has considerable discretion in establishing or modifying national policies relating to education.

In this way, controversies are rationalized in the legal and judicial frame of reference. The result has been a slowly changing conceptual pattern to which the courts have made significant contributions. At times, they have helped to free education from some outmoded legislative constraints, and, in a way, have served as an adapting agency between legislation and educational administration.[13]

In addition to the federal system of courts (to which recourse may usually be had only when a constitutional issue or a federal policy or statute is involved) each state has its own judicial system. Practically all educational controversies except those involving federal questions are resolved in state courts.

During most of our nation's history, public education was controlled largely by statutes and state and local board of education rules and regulations, with comparatively little weight being exercised by courts of law. Rapidly changing civil liberties beliefs and attitudes, however, led in the 1950s to an enlarged role for the courts in setting educational policy. Today, the courts have assumed a role considered by some people to be "legislative" in nature rather than strictly judicial. How this came about is an interesting study in social change and some of its implications.

Since the Constitution of the United States is the supreme law of the land, no law can be contrary to its provisions. The statement concerning the supremacy of the Constitution (Article VI) presupposes the power of some agency or body to declare acts of the President and the Congress unconstitutional. Such power is vested in the United States Supreme Court. The Supreme Court, which is the court of final appeal in the system, is given final jurisdiction over all constitutional cases that arise. When the United States Supreme Court exercises its granted jurisdiction by accepting a case (often from a lower federal or a state court) involving an interpretation of the Constitution, and this Court finds that a law—federal or state—is contrary to the Court's interpretation, this law is declared void for that reason. This is what is meant by declaring an act "unconstitutional."

There is a common misapprehension that the Supreme Court frequently declares acts of the Congress unconstitutional. However, throughout its history, the Supreme Court had held only 82[14] acts of the Congress unconstitutional in whole or in part through 1971. Considering the immense volume of congressional legislation enacted during this long period in the nation's history and the limited number of restraints imposed on congressional power, it seems evident that the highest court in the nation has exercised considerable "judicial restraint" and self-control.

---

[13]Hamilton and Mort, *Law and Public Education,* pp. 1 and 11.
[14]Paul C. Bartholomew, *Summaries of Leading Cases on the Constitution* (Totowa, N.J.: Littlefield, Adams & Co., 1972), p. 13.

The controversy over whether a court is "legislating" when it is deciding legal controversies undoubtedly will continue for some time to come. An important issue, however, is whether or not this way of regulating the power of the other two branches of government is likely to remain. There is no doubt that basic public policy, including that pertaining to the public schools, will continue to be determined to a large extent by the courts of law. This fact in no way minimizes the necessity for adequate planning by the states and the federal government in matters relating to public education. In fact, if there were more state-level planning and leadership, the role of the courts in educational decision making probably would be somewhat more limited than it is at present.

During recent years, the chief concern of the courts has been with those problem areas related to the rights of individuals—teachers, students, administrators, and others—vis-à-vis the schools as an agency of government. As our society becomes more pluralistic, the need for judicial interpretation and review tends to become more evident. Through a system of *stare decisis* (let the decision stand), landmark cases are accepted as precedents to be followed in future cases of the same kind. The courts, however, can and often do overrule prior decisions, so the doctrine of *stare decisis* is by no means ironclad.

State courts are also charged with judicial review responsibility, especially with respect to the state constitutionality of statutory enactments by legislatures, and often act as screening devices in the early stages of litigation. For example, the *Serrano*[15] case in California in 1971 contributed significantly to the development of cases and court decisions relating to provisions for financing schools in a number of other states. The issue was whether the state's plan for funding public education denied "to the child in a poor district equal protection of the laws because it makes the quality of that child's education a function of the wealth of his parents and neighbors." The California Supreme Court held that the provisions being challenged did deny equal protection. However, a somewhat related decision by the U.S. District Court in San Antonio, concerning the Texas provisions for financing schools in the state, was reversed in a 5 to 4 decision by the United States Supreme Court, March 21, 1973 *(San Antonio Independent School District* v. *Rodriguez).*

In the light of a 1972 New Jersey Supreme Court decision *(Robinson* v. *Cahill),* which is similar to the California decision, and of recent developments in several other states, it seems apparent that most progress in improving provisions for financing schools is likely to be made in those states in which the constitution and laws clearly require reasonable equity for taxpayers and equality of educational opportunities for students.

[15]*Serrano v. Priest,* 487 P.2d 1241 (Calif. 1971).

United States Supreme Court Decisions

Since education is not mentioned in the federal Constitution, it is never involved directly in questions that come before the United States Supreme Court. The involvement is always incidental, and comes through other questions, but often is quite significant.

According to Spurlock, 45 cases involving education to a rather significant extent came before the Supreme Court between the time the Constitution was adopted and 1954.[16] Most of these cases were concerned with questions relating to: (1) state or federal power and functions, (2) civil rights under the First and Fifth Amendments, and (3) due process of law and equal protection of law under the Fourteenth Amendment. The cases were classified under the following headings: (1) contests involving rights of parents and students, (2) contests involving rights of teachers and touching on property rights and personal freedoms, (3) contests involving rights of races in schools in states maintaining segregated schools, (4) contests involving powers of school authorities in fiscal matters or in matters involving rights of citizens and (5) contests involving rights of nonpublic schools.

It is interesting to note that most of these cases occurred after 1925. Before that time, only eighteen cases had important implications for education. Of these, only nine occurred before the beginning of the present century. Between 1925 and 1954, however, there were 27 cases. Many of these touched on conflicts between individual rights and state requirements and conflicts relating to separation of church and state.

During the period 1953 to 1969, the "Warren Court" decided 33 cases involving education (8 relating to religion in the public schools, 13 relating to segregation of the races, and 12 to academic freedom).[17] Of the eight cases dealing with separation of church and state, five concerned the practice of bible reading and/or prayers in the schools' opening exercises. The remaining three cases dealt with lending textbooks to children in parochial schools, teaching Darwin's theory of evolution, and allowing individuals to contest the expenditure of federal funds for related purposes.

The thirteen decisions concerning segregation-integration included the landmark case of *Brown v. Board of Education*[18] which established the controlling legal principle that *racial discrimination in the public schools is in violation of provisions of the Constitution*. Significantly in this decision the court also emphasized the *importance of education:*

---

[16]The authors are indebted to Clark Spurlock, *Education and the Supreme Court* (Urbana: University of Illinois Press, 1955), for much of the basic information presented in this section.
[17]H. C. Hudgins, Jr., *The Warren Court and the Public Schools* (Danville, Ill.: Interstate Publishers, 1970), p. 155.
[18]*Brown v. Board of Education of Topeka*, 347 U.S. 483 (Kans. 1954).

> Today, education is perhaps the most important function of state and local government. . . . in these days it is doubtful that any child may reasonably be expected to succeed in life if he is denied the opportunity of an education. Such an opportunity, when the state has undertaken to provide it, is a right which must be made available to all on equal terms.

Subsequent decisions have clarified to some extent this area of the law, but much remains to be decided on the integration issue.

Between 1953 and 1969, the Supreme Court dealt with freedom of speech and association (seven cases) and loyalty oaths for teachers and other state employees (five cases). The five loyalty oath laws were declared to be unconstitutional, teacher affiliation with certain organizations was decided on the narrow issues in each case, and free speech protection was upheld for both teachers and students in two separate cases. Later statutes reinstating a loyalty oath were subsequently upheld, and the scope of teachers' freedom of speech widened by the Burger Court. Since many of the decisions of the Warren Court were the result of a divided court, later courts might reverse any of them. The school administrator should keep abreast of the latest decisions involving education handled by the Supreme Court as the scene changes.

Two landmark cases involving students' rights are noteworthy. In 1967,[19] the Supreme Court held that the state may not maintain two legal standards, one for adults and another for children. In declaring that "due process [of law] is not for adults alone," the Court established the principle that children are entitled to the constitutional guarantee of due process despite juvenile codes to the contrary in many states. In 1969[20] the Court widened and clarified its window on student rights by declaring that:

> In our system, state-operated schools may not be enclaves of totalitarianism. School officials do not possess absolute authority over their students. Students in school as well as out of school are "persons" under our Constitution. They are possessed of fundamental rights which the State must respect, just as they themselves must respect their obligations to the State. . . . In the absence of a specific showing of constitutionally valid reasons for regulating their speech, students are entitled to freedom of expression of their views.

Thus, the Supreme Court has set a new standard by which the courts will judge the propriety of a local board's rules and regulations. In the future if a local board attempts to restrict personal freedoms of its students in any way, *it must show that there is an overriding public purpose to be served*

---

[19] In the matter of *Gault,* 87 S. Ct. 1428 (Ariz. 1967).
[20] *Tinker v. Des Moines School Board,* 393 U.S. 503 (Iowa 1969).

thereby. In the absence of such a showing, the courts will intervene to uphold individual rights where denial of a guaranteed constitutional freedom is involved.

In some cases the Supreme Court has indicated that it is reluctant to consider matters that might pertain to state educational policies, in view of the fact that education is clearly recognized as a function of the respective states. Nevertheless, it is apparent that the Court has exercised significant influence in a number of respects on the design and pattern for American education. Without such decisions, the American system of education would undoubtedly have been different in many respects than it is today. Thus the federal government, through Supreme Court decisions, has controlled more aspects of the development of education in the various states than many people realize. This control has been in the direction of stabilization and of unification in certain aspects of the conceptual design for education.[21]

In a case some years ago, one of the justices expressed concern that the Supreme Court might be tending to become a national board of education. However, it seems apparent that the Supreme Court, in its expressed philosophy underlying decisions, has uniformly tended to avoid questions involving state policy except where provisions of the federal Constitution are at issue.

State Supreme Court Decisions

United States Supreme Court decisions, by implication at least, affect education throughout the United States. On the other hand, a decision by a state supreme court is of direct significance for education only in that state, although it may have indirect significance in other states if it is used or cited by courts in those states. Courts do not legislate, but their decisions have the effect of law. Consequently, reference is frequently made to *statute law* or law enacted by legislature, and to *case law* or law interpreted in specific instances through court cases.

Ordinarily, the role of the state courts is to interpret state statutes in the light of the state's constitution. A state court, however, is not responsible for determining the *wisdom* of the particular law, but is concerned instead with the *reasonableness* of the law. The court will not intervene unless there is some clear or present danger, or the board has acted outside its legal powers or in an arbitrary and capricious manner. Reasonableness is often considered a matter for a jury to decide, since the interpretation may differ from community to community. What would be reasonable in

[21]Spurlock, *Education and the Supreme Court,* p. 238.

a rural setting would perhaps not be reasonable in an urban environment. Also, one jury might hold reasonable a law in one state while another in a different state might decide just the opposite. Thus there have been variations in decisions regarding similar laws among the different states, and from time to time state court decisions have been modified or reversed.

Almost every aspect of the educational program has at some time been involved in court decisions in each of the states. The laws among the states differ so widely and there are so many different types of court decisions that generalization would seem to be difficult if not impossible. Yet there are many basic similarities in state laws and, likewise, many basic similarities in court decisions relating to fundamental issues. Although it is necessary to consult the laws and court decisions of a particular state before authoritative statements can be made regarding many aspects of the educational program, there are certain legal principles that have become sufficiently well established to permit generalization. Among the most important are the following:

- The courts are generally agreed that education is a function of the state and that the control and management of the public schools is an essential aspect of state sovereignty.
- The legislature has full and complete power to legislate concerning the control and management of the public schools of the state, except in respects in which that power is restricted by the state constitution or by the federal Constitution.
- The legislature may delegate certain powers and responsibilities for education to designated state and local agencies, but it may not delegate all its powers. It must establish reasonable limits that are required to be observed by state or local agencies as they exercise their delegated responsibilities.
- Public schools are state, not local, institutions. In reality the public school program is a partnership program between the state and the local unit created by the state. The state may create and reorganize local school districts and delegate to them definite powers for the organization, administration, and operation of schools. These districts may be especially created for school purposes or may be municipal or county districts. However, the municipality or county has no authority or power over the schools within its boundaries except as such authority or power is definitely granted by the state.
- On the basis of an old common-law principle, school districts are not liable for the negligence of their officers or agents acting in their official capacity unless there is a state law imposing such liability, or liability has been imposed by the state supreme court. However, there has been a tendency during recent years for the courts to recognize increasingly the responsibility and liability of the state and its agencies.[22]

SOME IMPORTANT PROBLEMS AND ISSUES

A few of the many important issues relating to the legal aspects of education are discussed briefly in this section.

[22] Adapted from Garber, *Education as a Function of the State*, pp. 68–70.

How Much Educational Policy Should Be Incorporated into Law?

Although it may not be possible in any state to get complete agreement on educational policies, majority concurrence on all or most aspects of the conceptual design for education is both feasible and desirable. Without such concurrence, some policies and laws would probably be likely to deviate sharply from a rational pattern, and the educational program could be seriously handicapped.

One of the first concerns of many who want to change educational policies or practices seems to be to incorporate their "idea" into law. Some apparently believe that when a "law" has been enacted, the problem has been solved. However, those who understand the situation recognize that laws do not necessarily solve problems. A statute requiring counseling in all schools, providing for environmental education or even for accountability, does not necessarily mean that all local school boards, administrators, or teachers are in a position to implement rationally the intent of the law, or will do so.

Laws, of course, are necessary if local school systems are to operate, because their basic authority and responsibilities must be established by the state. For example, because of differences in wealth among school districts, legal provision must be made for equitable financial support. Beyond such basic provisions, what other laws are necessary? How can the number of laws be kept to a reasonable minimum when there are so many demands by different groups for laws designed to protect or promote their interests?

What Criteria Should Be Utilized in Evaluating Proposals for Legislation?

Laws originate in many different ways. Sometimes they grow out of careful studies by some appropriate group concerned with the conceptual design and with needs and ways of meeting those needs. In other cases, some individual or group may become concerned because school expenditures have increased rapidly, because some board has inaugurated a controversial type of program, or for some other reason, and may seek legislation designed to prevent the schools from doing those things the person or group considers undesirable. Ignorance, selfishness, and provincialism are likely to lead to bad legislation in any state. While there is probably no way to prevent some unwise or handicapping laws, there are some important safeguards. The most fundamental safeguard is widespread understanding of the role and significance of high-quality education. However, even this understanding needs to be supplemented by effective political activity by those who believe in and support public education, and by vigorous leadership by competent leaders who understand the conceptual design and appropriate means of achieving it. This kind of climate should contribute to the development of a "conscience" by the people and in the legislature that will be favorable to sound legislation for education. What criteria should be used in determining whether proposed legislation is needed?

When educators fail to agree, the legislature finds itself in the position of having to decide what it believes to be the best educational policy. In several states, reasonably effective plans have been developed for coordinating the interests and efforts of major lay and educational groups. What steps should be taken to avoid serious conflicts concerning legislation among lay and educational groups?

The point of view and attitude of the public and of the legislators they select is usually a decisive factor in determining the kind of legislation relating to education that is enacted in each state. Hamilton and Mort suggested the need for a legislative "code of ethics" with reference to education.[23] Would such a code be feasible and helpful? If so, how should it be developed and what should be included?

How Can the Responsibilities of School Boards and the Rights of Individuals Involved in Educational Programs Be Reconciled?

The Supreme Court's mandate that "state-operated schools may not be enclaves of totalitarianism" suggests that individual students and teachers of the future will be protected in their right to speak and write freely, to associate with groups of their choice, and otherwise to conduct themselves as first-class citizens while in attendance or teaching in the public schools. Nevertheless, these rights, like all other constitutional freedoms, are relative and not without limits: there must be a proper balance between the right of a state or local school system to operate "orderly" schools and the right of an individual student or teacher to be himself, to dress and conduct himself in an individualized manner, and otherwise to enjoy his constitutional rights while in school.

A clue to possible future court rulings may be gleaned from these statments by the Supreme Court in the *Tinker* case[24] in 1969:

[23] Hamilton and Mort, *Law and Public Education*, pp. 619–620.
[24] *Tinker v. Des Moines School Board*, 393 U.S. 503 (Iowa 1969).

Under our Constitution, free speech is not a right that is given only to be so circumscribed that it exists in principle but not in fact. . . . It can hardly be argued that either students or teachers shed their constitutional rights to freedom of speech or expression at the schoolhouse gate.

Undifferentiated fear or apprehension of disturbance is not enough to overcome the right to freedom of expression. Any departure from absolute regimentation may cause trouble. Any variation from the majority's opinion may inspire fear. Any word spoken, in class, in the lunchroom or on the campus, that deviates from the views of another person, may start an argument or cause a disturbance. But our Constitution says we must take this risk. Our history says that it is this sort of hazardous freedom—this kind of openness—that is the basis of our national strength and of the independence and vigor of Americans who grow up and live in this relatively permissive, often disputatious society.

What are some guidelines that should be used in attempting to resovle these issues? What, if any, steps should be taken by student organizations, parents, the school board and staff, the legislature, or the courts? An individual not only has rights, he also has obligations. What are some of them?

To What Extent Should the Judiciary Be Involved in Making Educational Decisions?

Some people have expressed considerable alarm about the propensity of the judiciary to hand down educational decisions affecting the public school systems of the nation. Yet it seems fair to say that many of the changes the courts have made in school interrelationships would not have occurred without the intervention of the courts. Improving education is everybody's business, so everyone has a right to "get into the act." "Everybody" includes, but is not limited to, the legislatures in the various states, other lay citizens including taxpayers, educators, *and* the courts (who have a stake in balancing the interests when controversies arise). This is not to say that "judge-made" law is best—it only occurs when any failure or cessation of the leadership by the governor, the legislature, or others in a state raises the need for judicial intervention.

Judges are no more interested in solving education's problems than they are in resolving other social issues—welfare, abortion, and similar problems. In fact, the courts in the *Serrano* and related controversies have practiced what has been called "fiscal neutrality"—hesitating to hand the states any set program to follow, preferring instead to put their stamp of approval on those proposals which the states themselves originated and the courts thought fell within the constitutionally permissible area of state funding. In general, this policy has been observed by the courts in the *Brown* progeny cases. Where the local districts have made good-faith attempts to resolve integration problems, the courts have been cooperative. On the other hand, the courts will not approve a plan which clearly violates the constitutional protection of individual rights.

The issue of judicial involvement in educational decision making will continue to prove challenging to educators in the future even though they may take a more active part in educational planning in their respective states. The reason for this is that the judiciary is a viable and much-needed member of the team without which orderly development of the school system would be impossible.

Should the courts ever attempt to give the "answers" to educational problems (such as finance and student rights)? Have they attempted to do so? What are the best safeguards against such a possibility?

Is the Concept of "Equal Educational Opportunity" for All America's Children Practically or Legally Attainable?

Horace Mann's dream—his belief in the *absolute right* of every human being to an education and in the duty of every government to see that the means of that education are provided for all—has been only partly realized. Although his belief that education is a "fundamental interest of every citizen" has been declared valid by many courts, the duty of the government to see that the means of that education are provided for all remains largely unfulfilled. Should the government seriously attempt to equalize educational opportunity, or are the states only obligated to live up to their own constitutions, which in the main guarantee only "a uniform system" of public education at taxpayer expense? Although education is considered a responsibility of the states, what does "equal protection of the laws" mean for those students who happen to live in the poorer districts? What are the implications for state policies and provisions for school support? For other kinds of provisions for education?

Perhaps no more pressing issue has presented itself in this century than the question, "How can the state system for school district organization, for funding schools, or other provisions for education be designed to ensure every child equal protection of the laws?" What steps should be taken in a serious effort to attain this goal?

SELECTED REFERENCES

ALEXANDER, KERN and K. FORBIS JORDAN, "Constitutional Alternatives for School Finance," Chap. 13 in Roe L. Johns, Kern Alexander, and K. Forbis Jordan, eds., *Financing Education: Fiscal and Legal Alternatives.* Columbus, Ohio: Charles E. Merrill Publishing Company, 1972.

BOLMIER, EDWARD C., *Teachers' Legal Rights, Restraints and Liabilities.* Cincinnati: W. H. Anderson Co., 1971, Chaps. 4 and 9.

DORSEN, NORMAN, ed., *The Rights of Americans: What They Are—What They Should Be.* New York: Random House, 1971. Essays commemorating the 50th anniversary of the American Civil Liberties Union.

DRURY, ROBERT L., and KENNETH C. RAY *Principles of School Law with Cases.* New York: Appleton-Century-Crofts, 1965.

EWARDS, NEWTON, *The Courts and the Public Schools,* rev. ed. Chicago: University of Chicago Press, 1971, Chaps. 1, 7, and 21.

GAUERKE, WARREN E., *School Law.* New York: Center for Applied Research in Education, 1965.

HAMILTON, ROBERT R., and PAUL R. MORT, *The Law and Public Education,* 2d ed. New York: The Foundation Press, 1959, Chaps. 1, 2, 4, and 17.

LAMORTE, MICHAEL, HAROLD GENTRY, and D. PARKER YOUNG, *Students' Rights and Responsibilities.* Cincinnati: W. H. Anderson Co., 1971, Chaps. 5 and 6.

NOLTE, M. CHESTER, ed., *Law and the School Superintendent,* (2d ed.), Cincinnati: W. H. Anderson Co., 1971. Legal Problems of Education Series, National Organization on Legal Problems in Education.

NOLTE, M. CHESTER, *School Law in Action: 101 Key Decisions with Guidelines for School Administrators.* West Nyack, N.Y.: Parker Publishing Co., 1971, Part One, Landmark Cases.

REUTTER, E. EDMUND, JR., and ROBERT R. HAMILTON, *The Law of Public Education.* Mineola, N.Y.: The Foundation Press, 1970, Chap. 1.

Yearbook of School Law. Topeka: National Organization on Legal Problems of Education. Published annually (Lists leading cases from year to year since 1923).

3

Theory and Research Relating to Educational Administration

Some executives have been inclined to scoff at the use of theory in educational administration. The expression "That is all right in theory but it won't work in practice" has been frequently used by self-styled "practical" school administrators. The myth that theory and practice are incompatible has been attacked by Coladarci and Getzels. "Theorizing is not the exclusive property of the laboratory or the ivory tower. Everyone who makes choices and judgments implies a theory in the sense that there are reasons for his action. When an administrator's experiences have led him to believe that a certain kind of act will result in certain other events or acts, he is using theory."[1] The authors also state that when an administra-

---

[1] Reprinted with permission of the publishers from *The Use of Theory in Educational Administration,* by Arthur P. Coladarci and Jacob W. Getzels (Stanford: Stanford University Press, 1955), p. 5

tor learns from experience, he is theorizing, ". . . it may be poor theorizing, but it is theorizing nevertheless."[2]

Much progress has been made in recent years in laying the foundations for a science of educational administration. No systematic science in any discipline has ever been developed by the trial-and-error process; however, until comparatively recently that was the principal method used to develop our knowledge of educational administration. Progress in the physical sciences was very slow as long as knowledge was derived primarily from trial-and-error methods, folklore, and superstition. When the scientific method was applied, our knowledge of the physical sciences developed at an astounding rate.

In recent years, we have begun to apply the scientific method to develop knowledge in the social and behavioral sciences. The scientific method involves the conceptualization of theories from which hypotheses may be formulated and tested. The development of theory and research in the disciplines of psychology, sociology, social psychology, anthropology, political science, and economics has provided a number of useful theoretical bases for developing a science of educational administration. Some of these theories will be presented and discussed briefly in this chapter. These theories and some other concepts will be applied to organizations in Chapter 4 and to leadership in Chapter 5.

GENERAL SYSTEMS THEORY

One of the most significant innovations in the study of the social and behavioral sciences during the last half of the twentieth century is the application of general systems theory to those sciences. Ludwig von Bertalanffy, an Austrian biologist, is generally considered the original proponent of the application of general systems theory to all the sciences. He noted that the sciences were being split up into narrower and narrower specialized fields with little intercommunication. He also observed that the same general formulas were being derived to explain phenomena in many diverse fields by experimenters who were usually unaware that they had been previously stated in another field. He then set about to formulate general systems theory to describe systems in general in order to provide a framework for unifying the sciences. Bertalanffy stated

> . . . the aims of general systems theory can be indicated as follows: (1) There is a general tendency towards integration in the various sciences;

[2] *Ibid.*

natural and social; (2) Such integration seems to be centered in a general theory of systems; (3) Such theory may be an important means for aiming at exact theory in the non-physical fields of science; (4) Developing unifying principles running vertically through the universe of the individual sciences, this goal brings us nearer to the goal of the unity of science and (5) This goal can lead to a much needed integration in scientific education.[3]

It is now generally recognized that there is a discernible linkage among all the sciences and that systems theory provides an important part of that linkage. According to Hearn:

> General systems theorists believe that it is possible to represent all forms of animate and inanimate matter as systems; that is all forms from atomic particles through atoms, molecules, crystals, viruses, cells, organs, individuals, groups, societies, planets, solar systems, even the galaxies, may be regarded as systems. They are impressed by the number of times the same principles have been independently discovered by scientists working in different fields.[4]

The journal *Behavioral Science* is devoted to general systems theory. The following statement was made in an editorial appearing in the first issue published in January 1956.

> Our present thinking—which may alter with time—is that a general theory will deal with structural and behavioral properties of systems. The diversity of systems is great. The molecule, the cell, the organ, the individual, the group, the society are all examples of systems. Besides differing in the level of organization, systems differ in many other crucial respects. They may be living, nonliving, or mixed; material or conceptual and so forth.[5]

Griffiths defines a system as follows:

> A system is simply defined as a complex of elements in interaction. Systems may be open or closed. An open system is related to and exchanges matter with its environment, while a closed system is not related to nor does it exchange matter with its environment. Further, a closed system is characterized by an increase in entropy, while open systems tend toward the steady

---

[3]Ludwig von Bertalanffy in *General Systems: Yearbook for the Society for the Advancement of General Systems Theory,* Vol. 1 (Ann Arbor, Michigan: Braun-Brunfield, Inc., 1956).
[4]Gordon Hearn, *Theory Building in Social Work* (Toronto: University of Toronto Press, 1958), p. 38.
[5]*Behavioral Science,* 1, No. 1 (1956).

state. (Given a continuous input, a constant ratio among the components is maintained.) All systems except the smallest have subsystems and all but the largest have suprasystems, which are their environment.[6]

Each system and subsystem is conceptualized as having a *boundary*. There is more interaction among the units included within the boundary of a system than between units within the boundary and units outside it. It also requires more energy to transmit energy across the boundary from within to without or from without to within than to exchange matter or information among the units included within the boundary of a system.[7]

The environment of a system, subsystem, or suprasystem is everything external to its boundary. There are numerous factors both within a system and its environment that affect the behavior, structure, and function of both the system and its environment.[8]

In Chapters 1 and 2, considerable attention was given to the value structure of our society. There has been much controversy concerning whether scientific research should be "value free." Since values are factors both in a social system and in its environment, the social scientist cannot ignore values. But he will treat a value in the same manner as he would treat any other factor affecting a system or its environment.

Some Characteristics of Social Systems

Following are some important characteristics of social systems.

ORGANIZATIONAL EQUILIBRIUM. Any system has a tendency to achieve a balance among the many forces or factors operating upon the system and within it.[9] Chin distinguishes between different types of equilibriums as follows: "A *Stationary equilibrium* exists when there is a fixed point or level of balance to which the system returns after a disturbance.... A *dynamic* equilibrium exists when the equilibrium shifts to a new position of balance after disturbance."[10] Current literature on systems theory usually refers to stationary equilibrium as "equilibrium," and to dynamic equilibrium as "steady state." In this chapter, steady state and

---

[6]Daniel E. Griffiths, ed., *Behavioral Science and Educational Administration.* Sixty-third Yearbook of the National Society for the Study of Education (Chicago: University of Chicago Press, 1964), p. 116.
[7]James G. Miller, "Toward a General Theory for the Behavioral Sciences," *American Psychologist,* 10 (1955), 516–517.
[8]Hearn, *Theory Building,* p. 42.
[9]Robert Chin, "The Utility of Systems Models and Developmental Models for Practitioners," in *Planning of Change,* eds. Warren G. Bennis, Kenneth D. Benne, and Robert Chin (New York: Holt, Rinehart & Winston, Inc., 1969), pp. 297–312.
[10]*Ibid.,* p. 205.

dynamic equilibrium will be used as synonymous terms. Chin theorized that a system in equilibrium reacts to outside impingements by: "(1) resisting the influence of the disturbance, refusing to acknowledge its existence, or by building a protective wall against the intrusion, and by other defensive maneuvers. . . .; (2) By resisting the disturbance through bringing into operation the homeostatic forces that restore or re-create a balance. . . .; (3) By accommodating the disturbance through achieving a new equilibrium."[11] Strategies 1 and 2 are designed to attain a stationary equilibrium without making changes; strategy 3 is designed to attain a dynamic equilibrium or steady state by making changes.

The concepts of stationary equilibrium and dynamic equilibrium or steady state are of great significance to educational administrators because of the consequences of alternate strategies to the social system called the school system, which is at the present time receiving more signals from its environment than ever before.

The concept of "feedback" is closely related to the concept of equilibrium. "Cybernetics" is the study of feedback control. Lonsdale defines feedback as follows: "As applied to organization, feedback is the process through which the organization learns: it is the input from the environment to the system telling it how it is doing as a result of its output to the environment."[12] It is hypothesized that if any social system (including the school system) fails to learn from its environment, it will eventually fail to survive in that environment or the environment will force changes in the system. If research sustains this hypothesis, what will be the eventual fate of a school system that makes continuous use of strategies 1 and 2?

There are other concepts of equilibrium which are of great importance to administrators. As has been pointed out already, every living system strives to maintain a steady state. It will resist a disturbance if it can and adjust to it if it must. Every system produces entropy, but at a minimal rate when the system is in a steady state. *Entropy* in a social system is a tendency toward disorganization or chaos. When a system is under such stress or strain that its components cannot bring it back into a steady state, the system may collapse. Systems under threat will usually use first the most available and least costly processes to relieve the strain on the system by removing the variable disturbing a steady state. Later, the less quickly available and more costly processes will be utilized if necessary to restore the equilibrium of the system.[13] Thus, any living system, including

[11] *Ibid.*

[12] Richard C. Lonsdale, "Maintaining the Organization in Dynamic Equilibrium," Chap. 7 in *Behavioral Science in Educational Administration,* ed. Daniel E. Griffiths, Sixty-third Yearbook of the National Society for the Study of Education, Part II (Chicago: University of Chicago Press, 1964), p. 173.

[13] See James G. Miller, "Living Systems: Cross-Level Hypotheses," *Behavioral Science,* **10**, No. 4 (1965), 394–397.

such social systems as the school system, has a precarious existence. It needs feedback in order to receive the information necessary for the system to serve the environment and to adjust to it, if the system is to survive. But the feedback disturbs the equilibrium and if the steady state cannot be restored, the system will break down. Change is necessary for the survival of the system, but it usually causes stress and strain. These times, which require a rate of change greater than ever before, present an unparalleled challenge to the educational administrator to provide leadership for making desirable innovations and at the same time maintain a dynamic equilibrium in the school system.

ENTROPY. One of the limitations of general systems theory is that the concept of entropy varies for different types of systems. Systems can be classified in many ways, such as open and closed, living and nonliving, social and nonsocial, mechanical and nonmechanical, material and conceptual, and so forth. The impact of entropy differs for open and closed systems. Immegart has pointed out that open systems can combat entropy and remain in a dynamic life state by exchanging matter and energy with their environment. Closed systems are isolated from their environment and inevitably move toward entropy, a death state.[14]

The tendency of an open living system to combat death or disorganization (entropy) is called *negentropy.* Thus, the living animal maintains a steady state (dynamic equilibrium) by receiving energy inputs in the form of food and air. The social system (including a school system) maintains a dynamic equilibrium by negentropy inputs from its environment in the form of feedback needed for survival. Furthermore, the social system usually includes actors who move the system toward entropy and also negentropy actors who move the system toward the steady state.

As pointed out above, entropy in a social system such as a school system can be defined as the tendency toward disorganization or chaos. The engineer considers entropy as the amount of energy generated in a system which is not available for producing useful work and is lost to the system or dissipated by some means, such as heat loss or friction.[15] In communications theory, noise is considered as entropy. In thermodynamics, entropy may be considered as the tendency toward homogeneity or static equilibrium. Although the concepts of entropy vary for different types of systems, there is a general thread of similarity running through all these concepts.

[14]G. L. Immegart. "Systems Theory and Taxonomic Inquiry into Organizational Behavior in Education," in *Developing Taxonomies of Organizational Behavior in Education Administration.* D. E. Griffiths, ed., (Chicago: Rand McNally & Co., 1969).

[15]Some of the concepts of this section were adapted from an unpublished paper entitled, "General Systems Theory: The Implications for Educational Administration" presented by John M. Turner at a seminar at the University of Florida in March 1972.

EQUIFINALITY. Open, self-regulatory systems have the property of equifinality. According to Granger ". . . in such systems identical output conditions appear to be derived from different initial inputs, and identical inputs appear to achieve different results."[16] This condition is common in complex social systems such as school systems which have many variables both within the social system and within the environment. Those developing management information systems for school administrators should study the concept of equifinality. Frequently, the school system may obtain substantially equal outputs in the form of measurable learning objectives from different inputs of money, teaching methods, and instructional delivery systems. Furthermore, widely different outputs may be obtained in different schools from substantially the same inputs of money, teaching methods, and instructional delivery systems. Therefore, useful management information systems should include information on all factors both within the school system and in its environment that affect output.

The School as a Social System

The system theory discussed in this book deals only with open living systems. A school system is an open, living social system which can be conceptualized in a number of ways in terms of system theory. For example, an individual school might be conceptualized as a system; its departments, sections, and divisions as subsystems; and the central staff, the board of education, the state education agencies, and, if present trends continue, even federal education agencies may all in the order listed be conceptualized as suprasystems. The environment of any given system consists not only of its subsystems and suprasystems, but also of all the other systems in the society with their attendant beliefs, values, and purposes.

Parsons has suggested a useful conceptualization of the formal school organization.[17] He proposed that the hierarchical aspect of school organization be broken down according to function or responsibility. Using this concept, Parsons classified the hierarchical levels of authority in school systems as the "technical" system, the "managerial" system, and the "community" or "institutional" system. The teaching function is in the technical system, the management system controls the technical system, and the community legitimizes the management system through creating agencies for the control of schools or by direct vote.

[16]Robert L. Granger, *Educational Leadership: An Interdisciplinary Perspective* (Scranton, Pa.: Intext Educational Publishers, 1971), p. 12.
[17]Talcott Parsons, "Some Ingredients of a General Theory of Formal Organization," Chap. 3 in *Administrative Theory in Education,* ed. Andrew W. Halpin (Chicago: Midwest Administration Center, University of Chicago, 1958), p. 41.

Systems theory can also be used to conceptualize informal organizations in social systems. This topic will be treated more completely in Chapter 4.

Research and Systems Theory

Systems theory has proven to be extremely useful for conceptualizing and organizing research dealing with organization and administration. It provides a systematic method for utilizing research from the social and behavioral sciences to understand and control organizational and administrative phenomena. Research on administration and organization conceptualized on meaningful theoretical bases will bring that research into the mainstream of valid research in the social and behavioral sciences and should eventually produce a science of administration.

Miller, after making an exhaustive study of research based on systems theory, listed 165 hypotheses which had been proposed by various researchers including himself.[18] He noted that some of these hypotheses had been confirmed by research but that some were probably entirely wrong or partially wrong and needed to be modified. Miller also observed that, undoubtedly, many other hypotheses relating to living systems could be formulated. His work is highly significant for practicing educational administrators and for researchers in educational organization and administration. Because of their significance, a few of the 165 hypotheses listed by Miller are quoted below and their significance for educational systems indicated.

1. "In general, the more numbers or components a system has, the more echelons it has."[19] The larger the school system, the more pupils and teachers and the longer the chain of command. As we lengthen the chain of command, it can be hypothesized that we retard communication and increase the internal friction of the system. There are many economies of scale that can be obtained by making school systems larger. If, however, as we make school systems larger, we must increase the echelons of control, how large can we make school systems until the disadvantages of internal friction and difficulty of communication arising from increasing the echelons of control outweigh the advantages of economy of scale gained by increasing the size of school systems? Available research on educational administration has not yet provided the answer to that question.

2. "System components incapable of associating, or lacking experience which has formed such association, must function according to strict

---

[18]James G. Miller, "Living Systems: Cross-Level Hypotheses," *Behavioral Science,* **10,** No. 4 (1965), 380–411.

[19]*Ibid.,* p. 383.

programming or highly standardized operating rules."[20] The armed services are sometimes criticized for the regimentation inevitably arising from "highly standardized operating rules." However, when consideration is given to the situation facing officers dealing with recruits and constantly changing personnel, it is probable that the armed services could not function efficiently by any other plan. Is the school system similar to or different from the army? Does the fact that the school system and the army have different purposes affect the validity of the processes of control of each? Those who believe that the purposes of a school system can best be achieved by strict programming and highly standardized rules probably assume a set of purposes for the schools different from those who disagree with them. If research sustains the hypothesis, then the educational administrator who wishes to avoid strict programming or highly standardized operating rules in any system or subsystem he is administering should select as components of that system or subsystem persons who are capable of working with each other and provide them with opportunities to do so in group situations.

3. "The larger a system is and the more components it has, the larger is the ratio of the amount of information transmitted between points within the system to the amount of information transmitted across its boundary."[21] A number of the largest city school systems in the United States have experienced serious crises in recent years. Is it possible that these large school systems have lost some public support because of failure to transmit sufficient information across their boundaries? It might also be hypothesized that the larger the school system, the greater the difficulty in getting information from the environment across the boundary into the school system.

4. Miller presented several hypotheses, supported by some research, concerning communication channels. Following are two examples: "The further away along channels a subsystem is from a process, the more error there is in its information about that process."[22] "The probability of error in or breakdown of an information channel is a direct function of the number of components in it."[23] The implications of these hypotheses to educational organization and administration are obvious. The further the teachers are removed from contact with the central administration and the more the echelons placed between the teacher and the central administration, the greater the chance of error in the teachers' perceptions of the actions of the central administration and the greater the number of errors in the factual information reaching the teachers. The same is true for the central administration.

[20] *Ibid.*, p. 384.
[21] *Ibid.*, p. 385.
[22] *Ibid.*, p. 388.
[23] *Ibid.*, p. 389.

SOME THEORETICAL MODELS

In the remainder of this chapter, some theoretical models will be presented and applied to problems of organization and administration.

Toward A General Theory of Action

A bold attempt was made in 1951 by a group of psychologists, sociologists, and anthropologists to develop a general theory of the social sciences.[24] Their frame of reference for a theory of action was based on personality, social system, and culture. Personality was defined ". . . as the organized system of the orientation and motivation of action of one individual actor."[25] A social system was defined as "Any system of interactive relationships of a plurality of individual actors . . ."[26] Although culture can be conceptualized as a body of artifacts and systems of symbols, it is not organized as a system of action and, therefore, is on a different plane from the personality and social systems. However, cultural patterns tend to become organized into systems.

The personality is viewed as a relatively consistent system of need dispositions which produce role expectations in social systems. Roles rather than personalities are conceptualized as the units of social structure.

Cultural patterns may be internalized both by the individual personality system and by the social system. These patterns are not always congruent, and the integration of personalities in social systems with different cultural patterns frequently presents serious difficulties.

Rewards, roles, and facilities in a social system are scarce and must be allocated. Therefore, the social system, or organization, must deal with the problems of allocation and integration. Furthermore, "The regulation of all of these allocative processes and the performance of the functions which keep the system or the subsystem going in a sufficiently integrated manner is impossible without a system of definitions of roles and sanctions for conformity or deviation."[27]

The formulation presented by Parsons and his associates seems highly general and abstract. But the conceptualization of the reciprocal integration of the personality, the social system, and the culture through interaction processes stimulated much creative thinking by other social scientists.

Can the theories of Parsons and his associates be applied to the development of solutions of educational problems? From what theoretical

---

[24]Talcott Parsons and Edward S. Shils, eds., *Toward a General Theory of Action* (Cambridge: Harvard University Press, 1951).
[25]*Ibid.*, p. 7.
[26]*Ibid.*
[27]*Ibid.*, p. 25.

bases will we develop solutions to the problems of integration of the races in the schools? From what theoretical bases will we develop educational programs to accomplish the purposes of the Economic Opportunity Act of 1964 and Titles I and III of the Elementary and Secondary Education Act of 1965? The educational provisions of these acts both deal with the educationally and culturally disadvantaged. It may be inappropriate to refer to pupils as "culturally disadvantaged." It may be more appropriate to use the term "culturally different." For example, a child reared in a slum develops a culture which enables him to cope with his environment in a slum. A child from the middle class has acquired a culture that ill equips him to survive in a slum environment but serves him well in his own environment. The problem of developing educational programs for culturally different children and adults and educationally disadvantaged children and adults is one of the greatest challenges to the educational leadership of the nation. Solutions to this problem by trial-and-error methods will be very slow. The intelligent application of appropriate theory should greatly speed up the development of education programs to alleviate this problem.

The Organization and the Individual

Perceptive administrators have long recognized that every administrator must deal with the organization, the individual, and the environment. The organization and the environment must come to terms with each other—the organization establishing and attaining purposes wanted by the environment, and the environment supporting the organization that satisfies its wants. Similarly, the individual and the organization must come to terms with each other by the individual accepting and facilitating the attainment of the purposes of the organization, and the organization satisfying the wants of the individual.

One of the earliest writers placing these propositions in theoretical form was a business executive, Chester Barnard.[28] He conceived of an organization as a system which embraced the activities of two or more persons coordinating their activities to attain a common goal. He considered organization as the binding element common to all cooperative systems. According to Barnard's theoretical formulation, the continuance of a successful organization depends upon two conditions: (1) the accomplishment of the purposes of the organization, which he termed "effectiveness," and (2) the satisfaction of individual motives, which he termed "efficiency." Two types of processes were required for meeting these con-

---

[28]Chester I. Barnard, *The Functions of the Executive* (Cambridge: Harvard University Press, 1938).

ditions: (1) those relating to the cooperative system itself and its relationship to its environment, and (2) those related to the creation and allocation of satisfaction among individuals.[29]

Getzels has developed a model for explaining social behavior which has been extremely fertile in producing hypotheses and stimulating research.[30] He started with the assumption that the process of administration deals essentially with social behavior in a hierarchical setting: "... we may conceive of administration *structurally* as the hierarchy of subordinate-superordinate relationships within a social system. *Functionally,* this hierarchy of relationships is the locus for allocating and integrating roles and facilities in order to achieve the goals of the social system."[31]

He conceived "... the social system as involving two classes of phenomena which are at once conceptually independent and phenomenally interactive."[32] Those two phenomena are the institution with roles and expectations fulfilling the goals of the system, and the individuals with personalities and need dispositions who inhabit the system. The observed interaction he termed social behavior. He asserted that "... social behavior may be understood as a function of these major elements: institution, role, and expectation, which together constitute what we shall call the *nomothetic* or normative dimension of activity in a social system, and individual, personality, and need-disposition, which together constitute the *idiographic* or personal dimension of activity in a social system."[33]

Getzels summarized this theoretical formulation in a simple model, which he presented pictorially as follows:[34]

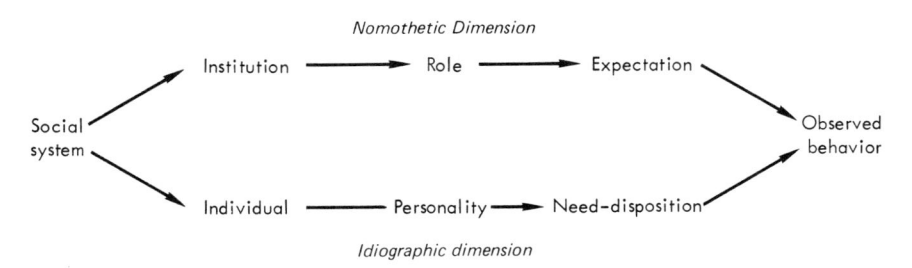

```
                        Nomothetic Dimension

                 Institution ──────▶ Role ──────▶ Expectation
               ╱                                              ╲
    Social  ╱                                                   ▶  Observed
    system                                                          behavior
               ╲                                              ╱
                 Individual ──────▶ Personality ──▶ Need-disposition

                        Idiographic dimension
```

---

[29] *Ibid.,* Chap. 1.
[30] Jacob W. Getzels, "Administration as a Social Process," Chap. 7 of *Administrative Theory in Education,* ed. Andrew W. Halpin (Chicago: University of Chicago, Midwest Administration Center, 1958). NOTE: Getzels credits Egon Guba with assisting him in developing his theoretical formulations.
[31] *Ibid.,* p. 151.
[32] *Ibid.*
[33] *Ibid.,* p. 152.
[34] *Ibid.,* p. 156.

This model has already become a classic because of its simplicity and seminal properties. It clearly demonstrates the utility of models in presenting abstract theoretical concepts. A number of empirical research studies have been based on hypotheses originating in Getzels' formulation.[35]

Compliance Relationship

It is assumed that any formal organization must fulfill its purposes at least to the extent required by its environment or it will cease to exist or be substantially restructured. It is also assumed that the actors in an organization must accept the organizational roles assigned to them and comply with the directives of superordinates, if the organization is to accomplish its purposes. Etzioni has formulated a middle-range theory of organization, utilizing compliance as the primary variable for the classifications in his typology. He defines compliance as "a relation in which an actor behaves in accordance with a directive supported by another actor's power, and the orientation of the subordinated actor to the power applied."[36] Etzioni assumed that the exercise of power involved the manipulation of physical, material, and symbolic means to secure rewards and deprivations, depending upon a person's perception of the legitimacy of the exercise of power by his superordinate and the need disposition of his subordinate. These factors determine the involvement of the individual in the organization, ranging on a continuum from positive to negative. The term "alienative" was used to refer to an intensely negative orientation; "calculative" to a low-intensity involvement, either positive or negative, and "moral" to a high-intensity commitment.[37]

Another basic assumption of Etzioni's theory was that social order in an organization was accounted for by three sources of control: coercion, economic assets, and normative values. He constructed the following typology of compliance relations based on these assumptions.[38]

The terms coercive and remunerative in his typology are self-explanatory. Normative power depends upon the regulation of symbolic rewards and deprivations involving esteem, prestige, social acceptance, ritualistic symbols, and other factors associated with values.

[35] *Ibid.*, pp. 159–165.
[36] Amitai Etzioni, *A Comparative Analysis of Complex Organizations* (New York: Free Press of Glencoe, Inc., 1961), p. 3.
[37] See Douglas Richard Pierce, *An Analysis of Contemporary Theories of Organization and Administration* (Unpublished doctoral dissertation, University of Florida, 1963), for an interesting analysis of Etzioni's theories as well as a number of other contemporary theories.
[38] Etzioni, *Complex Organizations*, p. 12.

A Typology of Compliance Relations

Kinds of power	Kinds of involvement		
	Alienative	Calculative	Moral
Coercive	1	2	3
Remunerative	4	5	6
Normative	7	8	9

The numbers in Etzioni's typology model are used to identify the types of possible involvement resulting from the use of a kind of power. That is, Type 1 is alienative involvement from the use of coercive power, Type 2, calculative, and Type 3, moral. Each number identifies a different type of power-involvement response.

Etzioni further theorized that organizations exhibiting similar compliance structures exhibit similar goals. Goals were classified as follows: (1) order goals to control actors considered deviant, (2) economic goals to provide production and services to outsiders, (3) culture goals to institutionalize attempts to preserve and create culture and to create or reinforce commitments to these ends. A prison would be an example of an organization with an order goal, a factory, an organization with an economic goal, and a school system, an organization with a culture goal.

Following are some other hypotheses Etzioni derived from his formulation: (1) organizations tend to emphasize only one means of power, and when two means of power are used on the same actors in an organization simultaneously, they tend to neutralize each other; (2) organizations exhibit all three kinds of power but emphasize only one kind or segregate the application of different kinds of power; (3) Types 1, 5, and 9 from the preceding model represent the responses most likely to be received from the application of the different means of power.

Etzioni's theories have many applications to educational administration. Should the same means of power be used on all classes of personnel in an educational organization to obtain compliance? For example, should there be any differences in the types of power used with teachers, custodians, secretaries, and students? Assuming that the goal of the total school system is cultural, can it be assumed that the goal of each subsystem is cultural? If a new principal uses normative power at the first meeting of his faculty, coercive power at the second meeting, and normative power again at the third meeting, what kind of involvement on the part of the faculty can he anticipate at the third faculty meeting?

Innovation and Change

Numerous theoretical formualtions have been developed to account for innovation and change. Only a few examples are discussed here.

Presthus has developed an interesting theory relating to the individual's reaction to the organization in which he finds himself.[39] He assumes that organizations have manifest as well as latent goals. The manifest goals are in terms of the organizational purposes, particularly productivity. The latent goals are in terms of the need dispositions of members for security, recognition, and self-realization. He hypothesized that the attainment of the manifest goals would be promoted by recognition of the legitimacy of the latent goals of the actors in the organization. It is noteworthy that Presthus' formulation bears a close resemblance to the assumption on which Getzels' model was based.

Presthus developed a comprehensive analysis of complex hierarchical organizations and hypothesized that there are three types of personal accommodations of actors who remain with the organization: (1) upward-mobiles; (2) indifferents; and (3) ambivalents.

According to this hypothesis, the upward-mobiles become "organization men" and internalize organizational values that become the premises for action. Personal goals are synthesized with organizational goals. The upward-mobiles recognize authority as the most functional value and are sensitive to authority and status differences. They tend to perceive their superiors as nonthreatening models and their subordinates with organizational detachment.

Indifferents adapt to big organizations by withdrawal and redirecting their interest to nonorganizational activities. Since they lack identification with organizational values, they withdraw from organizational activities and decisions.

Ambivalents exhibit dysfunctional behavior in relation to both personal and organizational goals. They depend upon rational values that might be in conflict with the values of the hierarchical organization. The ambivalents are a source of conflict, but they provide the insight, motivation, and the dialectic that inspire change. Therefore, the conflict created by ambivalents is considered as a creative catalyst. Should school administrators deliberately include on a school faculty some ambivalent persons who disturb the "equilibrium" from time to time?

The concepts "local" and "cosmopolitan"[40] have some relationship

---

[39] Robert Presthus, *The Organizational Society* (New York: Alfred A. Knopf, Inc., 1962).
[40] See Alvin W. Gouldner, "Cosmopolitans and Locals: Toward an Analysis of Latent Social Roles," *Administrative Science Quarterly,* **2,** (Dec. 1957), 281–306; **2** (Mar. 1958) 444–480.

to the formulations of Etzioni and Presthus. Local actors tend to identify closely with their organization and to have a stronger allegiance to the vertical institutional subculture than do cosmopolitan actors. The latter tend to have a stronger allegiance to the horizontal subculture of the profession to which they belong than to the subculture of the particular organization in which they are actors. It can be hypothesized that the cosmopolitan actor is more likely to initiate change in an organization than is a local one. He is also more likely to be ambivalent than either indifferent or upwardly mobile. It can also be hypothesized that normative power would be more effective than any other means of power in dealing with a cosmopolitan actor.

Thompson has theorized that the bureaucratic, hierarchical type of organization advocated by Max Weber retards innovation.[41] He hypothesized that "other things being equal, the less bureaucratized (monocratic) the organization, the more conflict and uncertainty and the more innovation.[42] Based on this hypothesis, Thompson proposed that the hierarchical organization be "loosened up" and made less tidy, if innovation and change are desired:

> In the innovative organization, departmentalization must be arranged so as to keep parochialism to a minimum. Some overlapping and duplication, some vagueness about jurisdictions, make a good deal of communication necessary. People have to define and redefine their responsibilities continually, case after case. They have to probe and seek for help. New problems cannot with certainty be rejected as *ultra vires*.[43]

Thompson assumed in his organizational model that some immediate production must be sacrificed in order to assure innovation within the organization.

Carlson has developed a typology of client-organization relationships in service organizations, as opposed to production organizations, from which he has formulated a number of useful hypotheses.[44]

Following is Carlson's typology:[45]

---

[41] Victor A. Thompson, "Bureaucracy and Innovation," *Administrative Science Quarterly*, **10**, No. 1 (1965).
[42] *Ibid.*, p. 4.
[43] *Ibid.*, p. 15.
[44] Richard O. Carlson, "Environmental Constraints and Organizational Consequences: The Public School and Its Clients," Chap. 12 in *Behavioral Science and Educational Administration*, Sixty-third Yearbook of the National Society for the Study of Education (Chicago: University of Chicago Press), 1964.
[45] *Ibid.*, p. 265.

Selectivity in Client-Organization Relationship in Service Organizations

		\multicolumn{2}{c}{Client control over own participation in organization}	
		Yes	No
Organizational control over admission	Yes	Type I	Type III
	No	Type II	Type IV

According to this classification, Type I organizations select their clients and the clients select the organization. Type IV represents the opposite set of conditions under which the organization does not select its clients nor the clients the organization. Private universities, hospitals, and legal firms are examples of Type I, while public schools, state mental hospitals, and reform schools are examples of Type IV.

Carlson designated Type IV organization as "domesticated" for the following reasons: "By definition, for example, they do not compete with other organizations for clients; in fact, a steady flow of clients is assured. There is no struggle for survival for this type of organization. Like the domesticated animal, these organizations are fed and cared for. Existence is guaranteed."[46] (See discussion in Chapter 1.)

He classified Type I organization as "wild" because: ". . . they do struggle for survival. Their existence is not guaranteed, and they do cease to exist. Support for them is closely tied to quality of performance, and a steady flow of clients is not assured. Wild organizations are not protected at vulnerable points as are domesticated organizations."[47]

It was hypothesized "that domesticated organizations because of their protected state, are slower to change and adapt than are wild organizations."[48] Following are some of the hypotheses that Carlson formulated from his model concerning how an organization adapts itself to unselected clients: (1) An adaptive response of domesticated organizations to not being able to select its clients is segregation. Example: "dumping" students unsuited to academic programs into vocational areas, special sections, or even special schools. (2) Segregation may lead to goal displacement, which is the replacement of the original goal by some other goal. Example: discipline may be substituted for learning. (3) Preferential treat-

[46] Ibid., p. 266.
[47] Ibid., p. 267.
[48] Ibid.

ment may be given the clients that accommodate themselves to the purposes of the organization. Example: research has shown that preferential treatment is frequently given in the public schools to middle-and upper-class children in such matters as discipline, punishment, and curriculums.[49]

It was also hypothesized that the inability of the student client to select his organization resulted in the following adaptations: (1) receptive adaptation, (2) dropout adaptation, (3) situational retirement, (4) rebellious adjustment, and (5) side-payment adaptation.

There is much interest at the present time in innovation and change in education. Griffiths has identified some propositions aiding or inhibiting change which have been derived from the system theory model. They are as follows:

> The major impetus for change in organizations is from the outside.
> The degree and duration of change is directly proportional to the intensity of the stimulus from the suprasystem.
> Change in an organization is more probable if the successor to the chief administrator is from outside the organization than if he is from inside the organization.
> When change in an organization does occur, it will tend to occur from the top down, not from the bottom up.
> "Living systems respond to continuously increasing stress first by a lag in response, then by an over-compensatory response, and finally by catastrophic collapse of the system."[50]
> The number of innovations expected is inversely proportional to the tenure of the chief administrator.
> The more hierarchical the structure of an organization, the less the possibility of change.
> The more functional the dynamic interplay of subsystems, the less the change in an organization.[51]

In this chapter, we have presented only an introduction to some of the theoretical formulations which are useful in studying the phenomena of change. Some additional concepts relating to innovation and change are applied to organizational and leadership problems in the chapters immediately following.

[49] *Ibid.*, pp. 269–273.
[50] James G. Miller, "Toward a General Theory for the Behavioral Sciences," *American Psychologist,* **10** (1955), 525.
[51] Daniel E. Griffiths, "The Nature and Meaning of Theory," Chap. 5 in *Behavioral Science and Educational Administration,* Sixty-third Yearbook of the National Society for the Study of Education (Chicago: University of Chicago Press, 1964), pp. 117–118.

Community Power Structure

Kimbrough and Johns and their research assistants have developed a typology of community power structure and related it to community decision making.[52] It was assumed from existing research that a small minority of elite influential persons in each school district had more influence on the political decisions made in that district than did the unorganized majority. It was hypothesized that this elite formed informal organizations in order to communicate and exercise influence. It was also hypothesized that different communities had different types of power structures. Kimbrough and Johns and their assistants in their investigations formulated the following typology for community power structures:[53] Type I: the *monopolistic-elite* single-group power structure described by Hunter as existing in Regional City;[54] Type II: *multigroup noncompetitive elite* consisting of two or more overlapping groups of elite members who generally agree on community issues with little regime conflict; Type III: *multigroup competitive elite* consisting of two or more groups of elite members with limited overlapping, who disagree on some community issues and engage in some regime conflict; Type IV: *segmented pluralism,* a segmented or diffused structure with numerous competing groups which have very little overlapping, but with regime conflicts among many groups.

It will be noted that this typology of power structures constitutes a continuum ranging from a single-group monopolistic structure to the political scientists' ideal of pluralism.

The following hypotheses were developed from this formulation: (1) that school districts with Type I and II power structures tended to make less financial effort in relation to ability than districts with Type III and IV structures; (2) that the influential persons in districts with Type I and II power structures tended to be more conservative in their civic and economic beliefs than those in districts with Types III and IV; (3) that educational innovations and change were less likely to occur in districts with structures of Types I and II than in districts with structures of Types III

---

[52]Ralph B. Kimbrough and R. L. Johns, Co-directors of Cooperative Research Project 2842, *Relationship Between Socioeconomic Factors, Educational Leadership Patterns, and Elements of Community Power Structure and Local School Fiscal Policy* (Gainesville, Fla.: College of Education, University of Florida, 1967).

[53]This typology was first described by William Robert Marsh, a research assistant for Cooperative Research Project 2842, in his unpublished doctoral dissertation: *Characteristics of the Power Structures of Six Florida School Districts Selected on the Basis of Population, Educational Effort, and Elasticity of Demand for Education* (Gainesville, Fla.: College of Education, University of Florida, 1965).

[54]Floyd Hunter, *Community Power Structure* (Chapel Hill: University of North Carolina Press, 1953).

and IV. At this writing, research has not confirmed or rejected these hypotheses, although it has confirmed that these types of power structures (and perhaps others) do exist.

These different types of conditions existing in the environment of the social system called the school system undoubtedly require different strategies on the part of the school administrator if he is to succeed in obtaining political decisions favorable to the public schools. There are no recipes available to the administrator for dealing with each situation. Even if there were, the situation might change with great rapidity. The administrator is more likely to develop a successful strategy if he conceptualizes his problem theoretically and develops his solution in accordance with sound theory. Bailey and his associates,[55] Kimbrough,[56] and others have amply demonstrated that public school administrators are inevitably participants in political decision making when public school issues are decided by the political process.

Theories From Economics

There are many theoretical formulations from economics that have significance for educational organization and administration. Theories of investment, input-output, division of labor, economic growth, the allocation of resources, marginal utility, taxation, and credit are only a few examples. Fortunately, in recent years a number of economists have directed their research toward a study of the economics of education. For example, Fabricant in 1959 presented estimates showing that a large portion of the economic growth of the nation between 1889 and 1957 could not be explained by increased inputs of land, labor, and capital.[57] The classical economists had long used an economic model that included land, labor, and capital as the only factors for explaining production. Fabricant hypothesized that investments in education, research, and development and other intangible capital might account for the unexplained difference in economic growth. In 1961, Schultz tested this hypothesis and found that approximately one half of the unexplained increase in national income could be attributed to investment in education.[58] He concluded that a large part of the resources allocated to education could be classified as an investment, because it resulted in the formation of human capital.

[55]Stephen K. Bailey, Richard L. Frost, Paul E. Marsh, and Robert C. Wood, *Schoolmen in Politics* (Syracuse: Syracuse University Press, 1962).
[56]Ralph B. Kimbrough, *Political Power and Educational Decision Making* (Skokie, Ill.: Rand McNally & Co., 1964).
[57]Solomon Fabricant, *Basic Facts on Productivity Change,* Occasional Paper 63 (New York: National Bureau of Economic Research, 1959).
[58]Theodore W. Schultz, "Education and Economic Growth," Chap. 3 in *Social Forces Influencing American Education,* Sixtieth Yearbook, National Society for the Study of Education (Chicago: University of Chicago Press, 1961).

The educational literature on school finance is beginning to include numerous concepts based on theories from economics.[59] Space does not permit discussion of these concepts.

Mathematical Models of Theory

Economics is the first of the social and behavioral sciences in which theoretical models were developed and utilized for formulating hypotheses to be tested by scientifically acceptable methods of research. Economists discovered that many concepts in economics could be expressed in mathematical form. This was a great advantage. The preciseness of the language of mathematics made it possible for researchers to express hypotheses exactly in mathematical equations and to test these hypotheses by valid methods. The extensive use of this approach to the study of economics gave rise to a new specialty in economics called econometrics.

Recently, there has been a trend toward the use of mathematical models in research on organization and administration. Simon was one of the first social scientists to make extensive use of mathematical formulations for expressing theoretical concepts in administration and organization. For example, Simon expressed in mathematical form Homans' theoretical system of group relationships.[60] Subsequently, March and Simon made extensive use of mathematics in presenting a comprehensive theoretical approach to organization.[61] Miller used a considerable number of mathematical formulas in presenting 165 cross-level hypotheses on living systems.[62] Griffiths has been the pioneer among professors of educational administration in using mathematical formulations of organizational theory.[63] It is probable that mathematical formulations for research in educational organization and administration will be used even more extensively in the future. Furthermore, mathematical formulations adapted to computers are already used widely in decision making by the armed services and some types of business and industry. It is anticipated that a considerable amount of middle-management decision making may be

---

[59]See Charles S. Benson, *The Economics of Public Education* (Boston: Houghton Mifflin Company, 1961), Chaps. 1, 2, 3, 11; and Roe L. Johns and Edgar L. Morphet, *The Economics and Financing of Education,* second ed., (Englewood Cliffs, N.J.: Prentice-Hall, Inc., 1969), Chaps. 3 and 4.

[60]Herbert A. Simon, "Some Strategic Considerations in the Construction of Social Science Models," in *Mathematical Thinking in the Social Sciences,* ed. Paul F. Lazarsfeld (New York: Free Press of Glencoe, Inc., 1954).

[61]James C. March and Herbert A. Simon, *Organizations* (New York: John Wiley & Sons, Inc., 1958).

[62]James G. Miller, "Living Systems: Cross-Level Hypotheses," *Behavioral Science* **10**, No. 4 (Oct. 1965).

[63]Daniel E. Griffiths, *Administrative Theory* (New York: Appleton-Century-Crofts, 1959).

done by computers in the near future. Thus, as so often happens, theoretical mathematical formulations, which were originally applied primarily to pure research problems, are now being applied to day-to-day operations.

However, there are certain dangers in using computer simulation models for evaluation of educational outputs and the determination of accountability.

SOME IMPORTANT PROBLEMS AND ISSUES

In this chapter we have presented only a sampling of the rich body of significant theory already available. No general field theory of educational organization and administration has yet been formulated. Nor is this likely to occur soon. However, system theory does provide an extremely useful means by which it is possible to tie together much significant research in educational organization and administration. In the following paragraphs, some further applications of theoretical formulations to educational problems and issues are presented.

Can Theory Be Used as a Basis for Obtaining Support for a Bond Issue?

The board of education of a large, rapidly growing urban school district employed a firm of educational consultants to make a school plant survey. It was a competent firm, and it made a thorough and accurate engineering-type, school plant survey. The technical report was submitted to the board, which accepted the major part of the recommendations. Among those recommendations was the proposal that a bond issue of $30 million be submitted to the electorate for approval. The evidence in support of the bond issue seemed overwhelming. At the time the issue was submitted, 10,000 pupils were on double session and thousands of other children were in overcrowded rooms or housed in substandard facilities. The school population was increasing at the rate of 6,000 per year, but current revenue was sufficient to provide new housing for only approximately 2,000 pupils per year. The district had very little outstanding indebtedness, and the legal limit on indebtedness was more than adequate to cover the proposed issue. There had been no school bond issue for fifteen years.

The board voted to call a special election for a referendum on the bond issue. Numerous news releases on the bond issue were given by the superintendent to the press and to radio and television stations. Great quantities of mimeographed material explaining the bond issue were sent to parents through the pupils. The superintendent and individual board members made frequent speeches to service clubs, parent-teacher associations, womens' clubs, and other organizations. The superintendent and board members also were frequently on radio and television programs.

When the bond election was held, it was soundly defeated. What theoretical formulations could help explain the defeat of this bond issue? What strategies based on these concepts might be used to pass such a bond issue?

How Can Change Be Initiated in a Junior College Faculty?

The public junior college in a thriving, growing city of 100,000 has been in existence for seven years, but it was started by taking over the facilities and staff of a private junior college. That college had been in existence for thirty-seven years when it was changed to a tax-supported institution. The private junior college had selective admissions and a good academic reputation, but it was designed to provide only a two-year program equivalent to the first two years of a four-year college. The board of trustees of the private junior college was willing to turn the institution over to a new, publicly elected board of trustees for operation as a public institution because of financial difficulties.

When the institution became a public junior college, the new board continued the president, his administrative assistants, the deans, and the faculty in their positions. However, additional faculty members were provided because of a large increase in enrollment.

When the publicly elected board of trustees assumed responsibility for the junior college, it inaugurated nonselective admissions and defined the purposes of the junior college as including vocational, technical, and general adult education as well as the two-year college parallel program. It requested the president of the junior college to change the curriculum of the institution to include these purposes, and it provided the necessary funds for staff and facilities.

The broad-purpose program and the open-door policy were privately opposed by the president of the junior college and most of his staff. The new facilities were constructed and some staff members provided for implementing the additions to the program. But the new programs in vocational, technical, and general education for adults did not flourish. The new faculty members added for these new purposes were not accepted by the other faculty members as peers. The president, instead of promoting the new programs, seemed to apologize for their existence. No effort was expended to inform the pupils and to recruit students for these new programs.

A new situation developed when the president of the junior college resigned and accepted the presidency of a senior college. He took two of his deans with him. When the president resigned, he recommended one person on his staff to succeed him and two other persons on his staff to succeed to the vacant deanships. His recommendation, submitted to the board, was accompanied by a petition signed by 85 percent of the faculty.

The board desired some substantial changes in the program and in the general climate of the junior college. What theoretical concepts would help the board to bring about change in this junior college? What are some strategies that would be consistent with these formulations?

How Can the Recent Increase in Teacher Unrest be Explained?

During recent years, classroom teachers in the public schools have become increasingly vocal, active, and aggressive. The membership of teachers in labor unions has increased, and many local education associations have adopted some of the tactics of labor unions, such as collective bargaining and withholding of services for certain functions. Sanctions have been imposed on entire states as well as on a number of local school systems. Teachers have been demanding a more aggressive professional leadership at local, state, and national levels. In one school system of 400,000, the classroom teachers by a majority of 90 percent voted to censure their superintendent, their board of education, their legislative delegation, the state superintendent of schools, the state legislature, and the governor, and then voted to impose sanctions on their local school system.

What theories can be used to conceptualize this problem? What hypotheses can be derived from these theories to explain this phenomenon?

What is the Present Role of Theory in Research on Administrative Problems?

Griffiths, one of the principal leaders in building abstract theories of educational administration, has concluded that there is little theory building at present in educational administration but considerable useful theorizing.[64] Following are his insightful conclusions concerning the use of administrative theory in education.

[64]Daniel E. Griffiths, "Theory in Educational Administration: 1966," in *Educational Administration: Internal Perspectives*, George Bacon, Dan H. Cooper and William G. Walker, eds. (Chicago: Rand McNally & Company, 1969), p. 154.

1. The emphasis now is on theorizing, not on theory building. Studies are being done in which concepts are developed, related to each other, and tested against empirical data.
2. Theorizing is proceeding in a variety of ways—a highly desirable development. The study of administration should proceed through as many methodological approaches as possible.
3. There appears to be little theorizing concerning some of the major problems of educational administration: collective negotiation, integration, and more effective ways of organizing to provide education. The realm of public policy making has received little attention.
4. Significant bits of research, theory, and theorizing are not being "followed-up." Much research which opens an area gets no further because no one picks it up.
5. The search for one encompassing theory (if anyone is searching) should be abandoned. There is need for a number of theories concerning the various aspects of administration. Just as there is no one theory of anatomy, but theories of circulation, the nervous system, etc., similarly there should be theories of decision-making, personal relations, structure, etc., etc. Each theory may help in the understanding of the totality.
6. We have learned that a modest approach to theory pays off. Theorizing in terms of basic understanding of administration is proving more fruitful than did the highly abstract and formal theories of a decade ago. ....[65]

It has been alleged that educational administration as taught in many universities is not very relevant to the solution of problems of practicing school administrators. Will the use of theory in the solution of administration problems make the science of educational administration more relevant or less relevant to the solution of problems in the field?

SELECTED REFERENCES

BARNARD, CHESTER I., *The Functions of the Executive.* Cambridge: Harvard University Press, 1938.

BENNIS, WARREN G., KENNETH D. BENNE, and ROBERT CHIN, *The Planning of Change.* New York: Holt, Rinehart & Winston, Inc., 1961.

BERELSON, B., and G. A. STEINER, *Human Behavior: An Inventory of Scientific Findings.* New York: Harcourt, Brace & World, Inc., 1964.

[65] *Ibid.,* pp. 166–167.

BERTALANFFY, LUDWIG VON, "General System Theory—A Critical Review," in *Modern Systems Research for the Behavioral Scientist,* W. Buckley, ed. Chicago: Aldine Publishing Co., 1968.

BLALOCK, HUBERT M., *Toward a Theory of Minority Group Relations.* New York: John Wiley & Sons, Inc., 1967.

BUCKLEY, WALTER, *Sociology and Modern Systems Theory.* Englewood Cliffs, N.J.: Prentice-Hall, Inc., 1967.

———, *Modern System Research for the Behavioral Scientist.* Chicago: Aldine Publishing Co., 1968.

BURKHEAD, JESSE, *Input and Output in Large City High Schools.* Syracuse: Syracuse University Press, 1967.

CHURCHMAN, C. WEST, *The Systems Approach.* New York: Dell Publishing Co., 1968.

CULBERTSON, JACK A., and STEPHEN P. HENCLEY, *Educational Research: New Perspectives.* Danville, Ill.: Interstate Printers and Publishers, Inc., 1963.

ETZIONI, AMITAI, *A Comparative Analysis of Complex Organizations.* New York: Free Press of Glencoe, Inc., 1961.

GETZELS, J. W., J. M. LIPHAM, and R. F. CAMPBELL, *Educational Administration as a Social Process.* New York: Harper & Row, 1968.

GRIFFITHS, DANIEL E., *Administrative Theory.* New York: Appleton-Century-Crofts, 1959.

GRIFFITHS, DANIEL E., ed., *Behavioral Science and Educational Administration* Sixty-third Yearbook of the National Society for the Study of Education. Chicago: University of Chicago Press, 1964.

———, *Taxonomies of Organizational Behavior.* Skokie, Ill.: Rand McNally & Company, 1967.

JOHNS, R. L., Chapter 4 in *Emerging Designs for Education,* E. L. Morphet and D. L. Jesser, eds. Designing Education for the Future, and New York: Citation Press, Scholastic Book Services, 1968.

MILLER, JAMES G., "Living Systems: Basic Concepts," *Behavioral Science* **10**, No. 3 (July 1965).

———, "Living Systems: Structure and Process," *Behavioral Science,* **10**, No. 4 (Oct. 1965).

———, "Living Systems: Cross-level Hypotheses," *Behavioral Science,* **10**, No. 4 (Oct. 1965).

PARSONS, TALCOTT, *Structure and Process in Modern Society.* New York: Free Press of Glencoe, Inc., 1960.

PARSONS, TALCOTT, and EDWARD A. SHILS, eds., *Toward a General Theory of Action.* New York: Harper & Row, Publishers, 1962.

PRESTHUS, ROBERT, *The Organizational Society.* New York: Alfred A. Knopf, Inc., 1962.

Thompson, Victor A., *Modern Organization.* New York: Alfred A. Knopf, Inc., 1961.

Tope, Donald E., *et al., The Social Sciences View School Administration.* Englewood Cliffs, N.J.: Prentice-Hall, Inc., 1965

Wagner, Harvey M., *Principles of Operations Research with Applications to Managerial Decision.* Englewood Cliffs, N.J.: Prentice-Hall Inc., 1969.

Weber, Max, *The Theory of Social and Economic Organization,* Trans. A. M. Henderson and Talcott Parsons, ed. Talcott Parsons. New York: Free Press of Glencoe, Inc., 1947.

White, D. J., *Decision Theory.* Chicago: Aldine Publishing Company, 1969.

4

Concepts and Principles of Organization and Administration

A number of authorities on organization and administration have insisted that most, if not all, of the currently accepted principles of administration are unscientific. For example, Simon wrote in 1950 that the currently accepted principles of administration are "little more than ambiguous and mutually contradictory proverbs."[1] He found many so-called principles of administration to be mutually incompatible when applied to the same situation. For example, it had been stated as a principle that administrative efficiency is improved by keeping the number of persons supervised (span of control) at any given level to a small number. It had also been stated as a principle that administrative efficiency is improved by keeping to a minimum the number of levels through which a matter must pass before it is acted upon. Simon considered these two

[1] Herbert A. Simon, *Administrative Behavior* (New York: The Macmillan Company, 1950), p. 240.

principles contradictory. He asked, how is it possible to keep the span of control at any given hierarchical level to a small number and at the same time hold the number of hierarchical levels to a minimum? One can agree with Simon that current statements of principles of span of control and number of hierarchical levels leave much to be desired. Nevertheless, every administrator of an organization, especially a large complex organization, must make decisions on how many persons to place under the control of one administrator at each level in the organization, how many persons for each type of task to place under the control of one administrator, and how many hierarchical levels to establish in the organization. Perhaps research based on systems theory discussed in Chapter 3 might develop a principle (or perhaps valid criteria) incorporating both the concept of span of control and number of hierarchical levels, which would be useful in making decisions on these matters.

Another example of contradiction is the statement of principles presented by a number of writers relating to "flexibility" and "stability." These two concepts seem to be contradictory. Actually, many concepts of administration and organization are like some mathematical functions that are valid only within certain limits. Unfortunately, the limits of the applicability of many concepts of administration and organization have not yet been determined. When these limits are defined, it should be possible to state more generalizations in the form of principles that can be used as reliable guides for decision making.

Griffiths wrote in 1957, "At the present time, there appear to be no established principles of administration."[2] He generally agreed with the point of view expressed by Simon.

Blau and Scott commented as follows concerning the development of principles:

> The object of all science is to explain things. What do we mean by a scientific explanation? An observed fact is explained by reference to a general principle, that is, by showing that the occurrence of this fact under the given circumstances can be predicted from the principle. To first establish such an explanatory principle as theoretical generalization, many particular events must be observed and classified into general categories that make them comparable. To explain a principle requires a more general proposition from which this and other specific principles can be inferred.[3]

[2]Daniel E. Griffiths, "Toward a Theory of Administrative Behavior," Chap. 10 in *Administrative Behavior in Education,* ed. Roald F. Campbell and Russell T. Gregg (New York: Harper & Row, Publishers, 1957), p. 368.
[3]Peter M. Blau and W. Richard Scott, *Formal Organizations: A Comparative Approach* (San Francisco: Chandler Publishing Co., 1962), p. 10.

Very few (if any) principles of administration have been developed in strict compliance with the standards proposed by Blau and Scott. Nevertheless, the literature on administration contains many statements of principles of administration.[4] In this chapter, some of the most commonly accepted "principles" will be presented and discussed. These cannot be considered as scientifically determined but rather as operating rules of thumb which have been developed largely from experience. They constitute a part of the "folklore" of administration and should be studied because they point to the areas in which principles of administration are needed.

Principles of administration developed in accord with the standards proposed by Blau and Scott are value-free. That is, such principles should be equally applicable in authoritarian and democratic societies. However, values are variables and, since democratic administrators and authoritarian administrators have different value structures, administrative processes and organizational structures will vary even though the same principles are applied. The implementation of principles of organization will vary widely in different countries and different communities, depending largely upon the philosophical assumptions and values of those in a position to make decisions. The administrator holding an authoritarian philosophy will make many assumptions concerning the implications of theories of administration and organization that differ from those made by the person holding a democratic philosophy. Therefore, some of the assumptions underlying contrasting philosophies of administration will be presented.[5]

No attempt is made in this chapter to distinguish between the principles of organization and the principles of administration. In accord with systems theory, the school administrator is conceptualized as an actor in a social system interacting with the environment. Since the administrator is always an actor in an organization, it is extremely difficult to distinguish between principles of organization and principles of administration.

SOME CHARACTERISTICS OF ORGANIZATIONS

In this chapter, we are concerned primarily with the administration of certain types of formal organizations, although certain propositions and theories are probably applicable to all types of organizations. It is difficult

[4]One of the earliest of these statements of principles was made by Frederick Taylor in *The Principles of Scientific Management* (New York: Harper, 1911).
[5]Some of the concepts presented in the following pages were adapted from Chap. 9 of of *Better Teaching in School Administration* (Nashville, Tenn.: Southern States Cooperative Project in Educational Administration, George Peabody College for Teachers, 1955).

to define a formal organization in precise terms. March and Simon observed that "It is easier, and probably more useful to give examples of formal organizations than to define them."[6] Thus, a business firm and a public school system are examples of formal organizations, as contrasted with such face-to-face groups as work groups in a factory or office and groups of interacting influential persons in the community power structure, which are examples of informal organizations.

Classification of Organizations

With reference to formal organizations, Blau and Scott stated, "Since the distinctive characteristics of these organizations is that they have been formally established for the explicit purpose of achieving certain goals, the term 'formal organization' has been used to designate them."[7] These authors have developed a useful typology for classifying organizations. They started with the assumption that the following four basic categories could be distinguished in relation to any formal organization: the members or rank-and-file participants, the owners or managers, the clients and the public-at-large.[8] The following typology was then developed in terms of who benefits from the organization: "(1) 'mutual benefit associations' where the prime beneficiary is the membership; (2) 'business concerns' where the owners are the prime beneficiary; (3) 'service organizations' where the client group is the prime beneficiary; and (4) 'commonweal organizations' where the prime beneficiary is the public at large."[9] Examples of mutual benefit associations are unions, teachers associations, and clubs; examples of business concerns are factories, stores, and private utilities; examples of service organizations are public schools, hospitals, and social work agencies; and examples of commonweal organizations are the armed services, police forces, and fire departments.

Crucial Problems of Different Types of Organization

Blau and Scott made the following observations concerning the crucial problems of these different types of organizations:

> Thus the crucial problem in mutual benefit associations is that of maintaining internal democratic processes—providing for participation and control by the membership; the central problem for business concerns is that of

---

[6]James C. March and Herbert A. Simon, *Organizations* (New York: John Wiley & Sons, Inc., 1958).
[7]Blau and Scott, *Formal Organizations*.
[8]*Ibid.*, p. 42.
[9]*Ibid.*, p. 43.

maximizing operating efficiency in a competitive situation; the problems associated with the conflict between professional service to clients and administrative procedures are characteristic of service organizations; and the crucial problem posed by commonweal organizations is the development of democratic mechanisms whereby they can be externally controlled by the public.[10]

Attention is directed to the fact that these observations concerning the crucial problems of the different types of organizations are applicable only to organizations located in countries with a capitalistic economy and a democratic value system, such as the United States. These are not the crucial problems of the same types of organizations in a country with a socialist economy and an authoritarian value system.

It seems that all these problems for different types of organizations are crucial in a public school organization, with the possible exception of "maximizing operating efficiency in a competitive situation." However, a crucial problem of public school administration is competition with other governmental services and also with the private sector of the economy for allocation of the national product. Furthermore, public school administrators are under pressures quite as severe as administrators of private firms to make efficient use of resources.

Relationship of Informal Organizations to Formal Organizations

Attention has already been directed in Chapter 3 to a number of other typologies by which organizations may be studied. It is obvious that the study of organization is a very complex matter. Since we are concerned primarily in this chapter with the phenomena of formal organizations, it would seem that our problem should be simplified. However, numerous authorities have pointed out that it is impossible to ignore informal organizations in the study of formal organizations, because informal organizations of actors are factors in the functioning of formal organizations. Therefore, considerable attention will be given to informal groups in Chapter 5.

One of the important distinctions between formal and informal organizations is that formal organizations usually have a longer life than the actors in the organization, while the informal organization usually has a shorter life than the actors in it. In a formal organization such as a school system, the organization will continue after the services of a particular group of teachers are terminated, but the informal organization of a particular group of teachers ceases to exist when that group of teachers severs

[10] *Ibid.*, p. 43.

its connection with the school system. The formal organization has long-term purposes which must be continuously met, and the personnel of the organization must be replenished to do this. The informal group usually has a short-term purpose directed toward satisfying the personal needs of the actors in the informal organization. When those needs are met, the group may disappear. Differences between formal and informal organizations that affect organizational structure are discussed in the sections that follow.

Need for Organizations

The purpose of an organization is to provide the means by which the actors in the organization may cooperate. An organizational structure is necessary when any group has a common task.[11] This is true for gregarious animals as well as human groups.[12] An unorganized group is only a mass of people. It can neither determine its purposes nor accomplish its ultimate objectives. Therefore, in order to survive, the group must organize. The organization, no matter how simple, must provide for at least the following procedures for making decisions and taking action:

1. A procedure for selecting a leader or leaders;
2. A procedure for determining the roles to be played by each member of the group;
3. A procedure for determining the goals of the group;
4. A procedure for achieving the goals of the group.

Advocates of democratic procedures sometimes infer that organization and administration are less necessary in a democracy than in an authoritarian government. Thomas Jefferson's statement, "The least governed is the best governed," is sometimes quoted as authority for that belief. Even Plato, who was not an advocate of democracy, contemplated in *The Republic* the idea of a simple communistic society without government. He rejected the idea, because he believed that man was naturally ambitious, acquisitive, competitive, and jealous. The researches of social psychologists, anthropologists, political scientists, and authorities in business and educational administration do not reveal less necessity for organization and administration in democratic than in authoritarian

[11]George C. Homans, *The Human Group* (New York: Harcourt, Brace & World, Inc., 1950), Chaps. 4 and 5.
[12]W. C. Allee, "Conflict and Cooperation: Biological Background," in *Approaches to National Unity, Fifth Symposium,* ed. Lyman Bronson, Louis Finkelstein, and Robert MacIver (New York: Harper & Row, Publishers, 1945).

government. Patterns and procedures of organization and administration will differ, of course, but organization and administration are equally necessary in all forms of human society.

Decision Making

Every organization must make provisions for decision making. Decisions must be made concerning what goals, purposes, objectives, policies, and programs will be accepted by the organization as legitimate. Decisions need to be rendered continuously with respect to the implementation of policies and programs. Therefore, every organization, in order to be effective, must have the ability to make decisions. These decisions may be made by the leader, by the group, by authorities external to the group, or by a combination of methods. Regardless of how decisions are made or who makes them, an organization cannot operate unless decisions are rendered.

The processes of decision making are so vital to the understanding of administration and organization that significant progress has been made in their theoretical analysis. Simon has suggested that the understanding of the application of administrative principles is to be obtained by analyzing the administrative process in terms of decisions.[13] He theorized that the effectiveness of organizational decisions could be maximized by increasing the rationality of organizational decisions. He assumed that there are limits to human rationality and that this creates a need for administrative theory. According to Simon:

> Two persons, given the same possible alternatives, the same values the same knowledge, can rationally reach only the same decision. Hence administrative theory must be concerned with the limits of rationality, and the manner in which organization effects these limits for the person making the decision.[14]

Griffiths has formulated a theory of administration as decision making based on the following assumptions:

1. Administration is a generalized type of behavior to be found in all human organization.
2. Administration is the process of directing and controlling life in a social organization.

[13]Simon, *Administrative Behavior*, p. 240.
[14]*Ibid.*, p. 241. Also see Daniel E. Griffiths, *Administrative Theory* (New York: Appleton-Century & Appleton-Century-Crofts, 1959), pp. 57–60, for a discussion of Simon's theories.

3. The specific function of administration is to develop and regulate the decision-making process in the most effective manner possible.
4. The administrator works with groups or with individuals with a group referrent, not with individuals as such.[15]

He presented a set of concepts on decision making, perception, communicaiation, power, and authority, and formulated the following major propositions:

1. The structure of an organization is determined by the nature of its decision-making process. . . .
2. If the formal and informal organization approach congruency, then the total organization will approach maximum achievement. . . .
3. If the total organization is not approaching maximum achievement, then, in all probability, the formal and informal organization are divergent. . . .
4. If the administrator confines his behavior to making decisions on the decision-making process rather than making terminal decisions for the organization, his behavior will be more acceptable to his subordinates. . . .
5. If the administrator perceives himself as the controller of the decision-making process, rather than the maker of the organization's decisions, the decision will be more effective. . . .[16]

Using these concepts, Griffiths presented the view that the central process of administration is decision making, which is composed of the following aspects:

1. Recognize, define, and limit the problem.
2. Analyze and evaluate the problem.
3. Establish criteria or standards by which solution will be evaluated or judged as acceptable and adequate to the need.
4. Collect data.
5. Formulate and select the preferred solution or solutions. Test them in advance.
6. Put into effect the preferred solution.
   a. Program the solution.
   b. Control the activities in the program.
   c. Evaluate the results and the process.[17]

---

[15] Griffiths, *Administrative Theory*, p. 91.
[16] *Ibid.*, pp. 89–91.
[17] *Ibid.*, p. 113.

Griffiths' approach to the study of administration is an example of the modern scientific methods being used in the study of administration, as contrasted with the work of Fayol[18] and Gulick.[19] Gulick saw administration as the processes of planning, organizing, staffing, directing, coordinating, reporting, and budgeting. Griffiths presented his assumptions, stated his hypotheses, which can be tested, and stated his conclusions in the framework of a theoretical formulation. Fayol and Gulick did not really present any theoretical formulation. They only described what they had observed about administration in accordance with certain functional classifications of administrative processes. The work of Griffiths and other similar theorists is seminal *for the creation of new knowledge;* the approaches of Fayol and Gulick, terminal.

Miller has proposed a number of significant hypotheses of decision making in social systems.[20] Further research on these and other hypotheses related to the processes of decision making will undoubtedly produce significant advances in understanding principles of administration and organization.

Selecting a Leader

There are many methods by which a group may be provided with leadership. The leader (here not distinguished from the administrator) may be selected by instinct, as in the case of bees, or by a test of physical strength, as in the case of the wolf pack. The leader may be selected by force or chicanery, in accordance with the patterns usually followed in dictatorships. The leader may be selected by the group itself or by representatives of the group, as in a democracy or a republic. Regardless of the method of selection, an effective group will always have leadership. The role of the leader will vary widely in different types of groups, depending upon the goals and values of the group, the leader's perception of his role, the group's perception of the leader's role, and other factors.

The group cannot attain its maximum productivity and the maximum satisfaction of individual members unless functions, activities, interests, and assignments are coordinated. That is one of the principal functions of executive leadership. The executive head of an organization, in order to be of maximum usefulness to the organization, must also be a leader. The functions of leadership are many and varied. The definition of

[18]Henri Fayol, *Industrial and General Administration,* trans. J. A. Courborough (Geneva: Industrial Management Association, 1930).
[19]Luther Gulick, "Notes on the Theory of Organization" in *Papers on the Science of Administration,* ed. Luther Gulick and L. Urwick (New York: Institute of Public Administration, Columbia University, 1937).
[20]James G. Miller, "Living Systems: Cross-Level Hypotheses," *Behavioral Science,* **10.** No. 4 (Oct. 1965), 394–397, 406.

the term "leadership" itself is an involved undertaking. This subject is discussed in detail in the following chapter.

Determination of Roles

The organization must also provide for the determination of the roles of each member of the group. Again, the method of determining these roles will vary widely among different groups, depending upon the nature of the group. In the lowest order of animals, the individual role of a group member may be assigned largely by instinct. In a higher order of animals, such as human beings, the roles of individual members may be determined arbitrarily by the leader, or largely by the choice of individual members of the group, or by various combinations of these methods. Regardless of how roles are determined, each member of the group or organization must have an appropriate role for the social system to function with maximum efficiency.

Determination of Goals and Purposes

An organization such as a school system must provide some method by which a group may determine its common goals. This is very easy in the case of some groups, such as the wolf pack. The common goal of obtaining food was the reason the group was formed. Even in animals of a higher order, such as human beings, common goals are usually the basis of group formation. When human beings are arbitrarily forced together, they cannot become an effective group until common goals have been determined. This phenomenon is sometimes observed in faculties of schools which do not have common purposes. Conflicts sometimes develop within a group over the determination of purposes. If these conflicts are not resolved, the group will either disintegrate or break into two or more factions.

Miller has stated the following two hypotheses concerning the determination of goals and purposes which have been supported by some research:

1. Lack of clarity of purpose or goals in a system's decisions will produce conflict between it and other components of the suprasystem.
2. If a system has multiple purposes and goals, and they are not placed in clear priority and commonly known by all components and subsystems, conflict among them will ensue.[21]

[21] *Ibid.*, pp. 404–405.

Attainment of Goals

All groups must develop procedures for taking action to attain goals. If these goals are not attained, the group will either disintegrate or be reorganized. The goals must include the goals of individual members as well as those of the organization if it is to maximize its production possibilities (see Getzel's model presented in Chapter 3). It is impossible to attain organizational goals with efficiency if there is a crucial conflict between organizational goals and the goals of the actors in the organization.

A distinction should be made at this point between goal attainment of formal organizations and of informal organizations. An effective organization must be an active one. In fact, activity is essential for organizational survival. Since formal organizations usually have long-range goals which must be continuously met, the need for activity is continuous. But informal organizations usually have short-range goals arising from the needs of the actors in the informal organization. If the goal is attained and no other goal is substituted for it, activity ceases and the organization disappears. The same thing is true even of some types of formal organizations, such as a political organization formed to elect a particular candidate at a given election. After the election, the goal is either attained or abandoned, activity ceases, and the organization dissolves. Thus, we have the paradox of the necessity for the organization to attain its goals in order to succeed but the probability of nonsurvival once it attains its goals.

Fortunately, the school organization does not face this kind of dilemma because each year, each class or grade has new inputs of students with fresh goals to be attained for those students. A school organization is a dynamic system continuously seeking to attain its goals and at the same time continuously assuming responsibility for assisting maturing students and new entrants to attain their goals. Therefore, no school system has failed to survive because it attained all its goals. The critical problem with school organizations is failure to adopt goals relevant to the needs of students and the community or inadequate attainment of relevant goals.

Nature of Organizational Structures

The tendency in formal organizations is to develop pyramidal, hierarchical structures with superordinate-subordinate relationships among the actors in the organization. This phenomenon has been observed in all societies, regardless of stage of civilization, economic system, or political philosophy. The larger and more complex the organization, the more bureaucratic and hierarchical the structure of the organization tends to become. For example, the organizational structure for a rural elementary school district that provides educational services for only 150 pupils in a six-teacher school is far less hierarchical and bureaucratic than the organizational structure for a municipal district with a population of 500,000 providing numerous elementary and high schools, a junior college, and many special educational services. Further attention will be given to the structure of formal organizations later in this chapter.

Informal organizations are usually small in size and have a very simple structure with few organizational hierarchies. Berelson and Steiner have reported that most informal groups have an upper limit of fifteen to twenty persons.[22] Informal organizations usually have face-to-face relations in small groups.

CONCEPTS OF ORGANIZATION AND ADMINISTRATION

In the following sections of this chapter, a number of concepts of organization and administration are presented. Although each of these "principles" is stated in terms of its relationship to the effectiveness of the organization in surviving in its environment and attaining its goals, it could just as readily be stated in terms of "administrative efficiency." For example, the proposition concerning the single executive could be stated: (1) administrative efficiency is increased by having a single executive head of an organization; or (2) the effectiveness of an organization is enhanced by having a single executive head. These two statements illustrate the relationship of principles of administration to principles of organization. However, the ultimate purpose of an organization is not to establish conditions that increase administrative efficiency but to establish conditions that will enhance the effectiveness of the organization in attaining its goals. Sometimes this important point has been forgotten by an administrative hierarchy snarled in red tape. *Administrative efficiency is valid only to the extent that it contributes to the attainment of the goals of the organization, the goals of the actors in the organization, and the extent that it meets the requirements of the environment for the survival of the organization.* In the future, more meaningful and useful principles of administration and organization than those presented here will no doubt be developed from current and future research, much of it based on systems theory. Educational administrators administer social systems usually comprising a complex of suprasystems

[22]Bernard Berelson and Gary A. Steiner, *Human Behavior—An Inventory of Scientific Findings* (New York: Harcourt, Brace & World, Inc., 1964), p. 325.

and subsystems. Therefore, useful principles must deal with cross-level factors as well as factors at one system level.[23]

The generally recognized "principles" of organization are presented in the following paragraphs. As pointed out above, some theorists insist that there are no principles in the scientific sense. That may be true. Perhaps they should be called criteria or guides. Regardless of what they are called, they are concepts useful for the study of organization and administration.

Single Executive

THE EFFECTIVENESS OF AN ORGANIZATION IS ENHANCED BY HAVING A SINGLE EXECUTIVE HEAD. The executive must provide central coordination for the activities of an organizaion. Although an organization may have a number of leaders, one of these leaders must serve as the coordinating head of the group. Unless this is done, no organization can achieve its purposes, because division of central leadership will prevent the coordination of its activities. The necessity for the recognition of this principle becomes more imperative as the size of the organization's membership increases. This principle of administration was among the earliest generally recognized. Despite the fact that numerous experiments in divided central executive leadership have failed, proposals are still being advanced to provide an organization with two executive heads. In educational administration numerous attempts have been made to divide the executive functions for education into educational and business administration. Boards of education have sometimes employed two superintendents, one for educational and one for business administration, each directly responsible to the board and neither responsible to the other. These experiments have almost invariably resulted in friction and in the failure of the organization to attain its goals effectively. The activities of any effective organization must be coordinated, and this can best be achieved through a single executive head.

Unity of Purpose

THE EFFECTIVENESS OF AN ORGANIZATION IS ENHANCED BY CLEAR DEFINITION OF GOALS AND PURPOSES. The processes of determining goals and purposes may be formal or informal. The members of a simple

[23]See Miller, "Living Systems."

organization may have tacitly agreed upon its purposes before the organization was formed. However, a complex organization such as an educational structure has many purposes and goals. In such an organization these must be carefully determined. Unless that is done, the organization is likely to operate with conflicting purposes. Such an organization will almost inevitably end in conflict among members of the group or between the group and the official leadership. Unresolved conflicts will eventually destroy informal organizations and "wild" formal organizations (defined in Chapter 3). The members of a public school organization are members of a "domestic" organization. Such a group, with undetermined or conflicting purposes, may legally continue in existence past its period of usefulness. The turnover in such a group is high and the group is ineffective. Therefore, it is vital that any organization determine its purposes and goals if it wishes to continue serving a useful function.

Unity of Command

THE EFFECTIVENESS OF AN ORGANIZATION IS ENHANCED WHEN EVERY PERSON IN THE ORGANIZATION KNOWS TO WHOM AND FOR WHAT HE IS RESPONSIBLE. This principle, as its name implies, was first recognized by the armed services. As pointed out later in this chapter, there is much disagreement concerning the validity of this proposition. Following are some of the assumptions underlying it.

The organization should provide for the definition of the role of each individual. It is demoralizing to the individual and destructive to the productivity of the organization to have individuals uncertain of their duties. Whether the individual is assigned his duties by the status leader or participates himself in their selection, he will not be an effective member of the organization unless he knows what his obligations are. Unless the lines of responsibility and authority are clearly defined, chaos is inevitable. It follows that no individual in the organization should be compelled to take direct orders from more than one person, because conflicts will inevitably arise.

Delegation of Authority and Responsibility

THE EFFECTIVENESS OF AN ORGANIZATION IS ENHANCED WHEN SUPERORDINATES DELEGATE AUTHORITY TO SUBORDINATES. It would seem that this is a self-evident fact rather than a principle. However, the problem of delegation of authority and responsibility has plagued mankind since the development of organizations. One of the assumptions back of this principle is that when an administrator delegates responsibility for a task to a subordinate, he should at the same time delegate to the subordinate the necessary authority to accomplish the task.

As is true with many principles of organization and administration, there are limits to the operation of this principle. Miller has hypothesized that segregation (compartmentalization) increases conflict among subsystems.[24] He cited in support of that hypothesis the observation of March and Simon that the delegation of authority to departments in firms increased the disparity of interests and created conflict among them.[25]

Division of Labor

THE EFFECTIVENESS OF AN ORGANIZATION IS ENHANCED BY THE DIVISION OF LABOR AND TASK SPECIALIZATION. Provision for an appropriate division of labor in order to increase productivity was the basic reason private firms were established. Adam Smith presented an excellent illustration of this principle in his famous book, *The Wealth of Nations,* published in 1776. In his illustration, he demonstrated that if a group of men making pins divided the labor and each specialized on a task, the same number of men could greatly increase their production of pins in a given length of time.

Much of the increase in the productivity of the economy of Western civilization during the past two centuries has been due to the formation of large numbers of complex organizations which have applied the division-of-labor principle. The growth in technology and the industrialization of society have greatly increased the emphasis on division of labor and specialization during the past twenty-five years. This trend has created some critical problems which will be treated later in this chapter.

Miller has hypothesized that the segregation of functions in a system is increased by structurally increasing the types of its members or components.[26]

Standardization

THE EFFECTIVENESS OF AN ORGANIZATION IS ENHANCED BY THE DEVELOPMENT OF STANDARDIZED PROCEDURES FOR ROUTINE ADMINISTRATIVE OPERATION. Standardized procedures are applicable to such operations as accounting, data gathering, statistical reporting, and record keeping. Standardization of routine operations saves labor on the part of

[24] *Ibid.,* p. 403.
[25] March and Simon, *Organizations,* pp. 41–42.
[26] Miller, "Living Systems," p. 384.

all members of the organization. Such procedures are also essential to collecting much of the data necessary for establishing management information systems.

Span of Control

THE EFFECTIVENESS OF AN ORGANIZATION IS ENHANCED BY ASSIGNING TO EACH ADMINISTRATOR NO GREATER A NUMBER OF PERSONS THAN HE CAN DIRECTLY SUPERVISE. This is an extremely controversial principle, as will be shown later. However it is a time-honored principle, generally accepted by military and business organizations. Perhaps this principle is applicable to some types of organizations and not applicable to others. Or perhaps the most efficient span of control differs for different types of organizations and for different types of tasks within an organization.

Stability

THE EFFECTIVENESS OF AN ORGANIZATION IS ENHANCED BY CONTINUING POLICIES AND PROGRAMS UNTIL RESULTS CAN BE EVALUATED. An organization that changes its policies or programs capriciously is almost certain to be an ineffective organization. If policies and programs are carefully defined and given a thorough trial before being abandoned or changed, "sunk costs" are minimized and the probability of establishing a favorable ratio between input and output is increased.

Flexibility

THE EFFECTIVENESS OF AN ORGANIZATION IS ENHANCED WHEN IT MAKES PROVISION FOR INNOVATION AND CHANGE. Innovation and change are facilitated when policies are stated in broad enough terms to permit reasonable flexibility in management. The principle of flexibility also implies that, once a program or policy has been continued long enough for evaluation, provision should be made for needed changes. Therefore, the principle of flexibility might be interpreted as a contradiction of the principle of stability. However, these two principles do not contradict each other as much as they tend to balance one another. What is sought in effective administration is an appropriate balance between stability and flexibility. The need for flexibility of administration and organization increases in these times of rapid change.

Security

The Effectiveness of an Organization is Enhanced When the Organization Provides Security for Its Members. Different members of the group have many different individual needs, but the need for security is universal. This universal craving for security makes it essential that this need be met in any group, regardless of its political philosophy. As a matter of fact, security itself is frequently the goal or purpose for which informal groups are formed. The need for security is no less present in formal groups, such as educational organizations, than in informal groups.

Personnel Policies

The Effectiveness of an Organization is Enhanced By Personnel Policies, Which Include Selecting the Competent, Training the Inexperienced, Eliminating the Incompetent, and Providing Incentives for All Members of the Organization. Even informal organizations such as street gangs follow these procedures. Personnel policies in formal groups, such as school faculties, must be carefully defined. Selecting the competent is essential to recruiting potentially effective group members. Training the inexperienced is essential to obtaining maximum productivity from individual members of the group. Eliminating the incompetent is essential to maintaining the integrity, cohesiveness, and effectiveness of the group. Providing incentives by meeting the individual needs of group members is essential to maintaining group morale and assuring maximum productivity.

Evaluation

The Effectiveness of an Organization is Enhanced When Provision is Made for Evaluating Not Only the Products of the Organization But Also the Organization Itself. Activity without evaluation may be fruitless. The ability to evaluate is one of the characteristics which distinguish the human species from lower orders of animals. Evaluation is provided not only by actors within the organization, but also by the environment of the organization if evaluation is effective. Evaluation by the environment is obtained by making provision for the organization to receive feedback, as pointed out in Chapter 3.

Leavitt has presented evidence indicating that two-way communication in an organization providing feedback reduces error.[27] Feedback provides one means of continuous evaluation.

There are numerous technical and scientific methods available for evaluation of the material products of an organization. The instruments available for the evaluation of the nonmaterial products of the educational system are far less precise. This does not relieve the educational system of the necessity for evaluation. It only makes the problem more difficult.

TRADITIONAL AND EMERGING CONCEPTS OF ORGANIZATION AND ADMINISTRATION

There are two principal competing concepts of organization and administration, which we will call the traditional monocratic, bureaucratic concept and the emerging pluralistic, collegial concept. The use of the terms "traditional monocratic, bureaucratic concept" and "emerging pluralistic, collegial concept" should not be interpreted as suggesting that we have a clear dualism in types of administration and organization. As Bennis has said, "So we hear of 'Theory X vs. Theory Y,' personality vs. organization, democratic vs. autocratic, task vs. maintenance, human relations vs. scientific management, and on and on. Surely life is more complicated than these dualities suggest, and surely they must imply a continuum—not simply extremes."[28]

Therefore, in this section we will describe not dual concepts of administration and organization but the extreme ends of a continuum. The principles of administration discussed in the previous section are equally applicable throughout this continuum. However, as will be shown in this chapter, the structure of the organization and administrative procedures will vary greatly, depending upon the assumptions made and the value systems of those applying these principles.

The Traditional Monocratic, Bureaucratic Concept

The traditional monocratic, bureaucratic concept of organization and administration is defined as a pyramidal, hierarchical organizational struc-

[27]Harold K. Leavitt, *Managerial Psychology* (Chicago: University of Chicago Press, 1958), p. 123.
[28] Warren G. Bennis, "Theory and Method in Applying Behavioral Science to Planned Organizational Change," *Journal of Applied Science,* 1, No. 4 (1965), 356.

ture, in which all power for making decisions flows from superordinates to subordinates. This concept has been described by Weber.[29]

We are indebted to Abbott for the following succinct description of Weber's monocratic, bureaucratic model:

> For Weber, the essential and distinctive characteristics of a bureaucracy were somewhat as follows:
>
> 1. The regular activities required for the purposes of the organization are distributed in fixed ways as official duties. Since the tasks of an organization are too complex to be performed by a single individual, or by a group of individuals possessing a single set of skills, efficiency will be promoted by dividing those tasks into activities which can be assigned to specific offices or positions. This division of labor makes possible a high degree of specialization which, in turn, promotes improved performance in two ways. First it enables the organization to employ personnel on the basis of technical qualifications; second, it enables employees to improve their skills by limiting their attention to a relatively narrow range of activities.
> 2. The positions in an organization are arranged on the principle of office hierarchy and of levels of graded authority. This means that there is a firmly ordered system of superordination and subordination in which the lower offices are supervised by the higher ones. Although specialization makes possible the efficient performance of specific tasks, specialization also creates problems of coordination. To achieve the required coordination, it is necessary to grant to each official the requisite authority to control the activities of his subordinates.
> 3. The management of activities is controlled by general rules which are more or less stable, more or less exhaustive, and which can be learned. These rules are general and abstract, and they constitute standards which assure reasonable uniformity in the performance of tasks. They preclude the issuance of directives based on whim or caprice, but require the application of general principles to particular cases. Together with the hierarchical authority structure, rules provide for the coordination of organizational activities and for continuity of operations, regardless of changes in personnel.

---

[29]Max Weber, *The Theory of Social and Economic Organization,* trans. A. M. Henderson and Talcott Parsons, ed. Talcott Parsons (New York: Free Press of Glencoe, Inc., 1947). NOTE: Max Weber (1864–1920) was a remarkably productive German scholar. He began with the study of law but soon went on to study economics. After writing a number of outstanding works on economics, he turned to the development of a science of sociology. Every serious student of administration should read *The Theory of Social and Economic Organization.*

4. Bureaucracy develops the more perfectly the more completely it succeeds in eliminating from official business love, hatred, and all purely personal, irrational, and emotional elements which escape calculation. The essence of bureaucratic arrangements is rationality. A spirit of formalistic impersonality is necessary to separate organizational rights and duties from the private lives of employees. Only by performing impersonally can officials assure rationality in decision making, and only thus can they assure equitable treatment for all subordinates.

5. Employment in a bureaucracy is based upon technical competence and constitutes a career. Promotions are to be determined by seniority, or achievement, or both; tenure is to be assured; and fixed compensation and retirement provisions are to be made. Since individuals with specialized skills are employed to perform specialized activities, they must be protected from arbitrary dismissal or denial of promotion on purely personal ground.[30]

Weber wrote as follows concerning the superiority of his model for human organization:

> Experience tends universally to show that the purely bureaucratic type of administrative organization—that is, the monocratic variety of bureaucracy—is, from a purely technical point of view, capable of attaining the highest degree of efficiency and is in this sense formally the most rational known means of carrying out imperative control over human beings. It is superior to any other form in precision, in stability, in the stringency of its discipline, and in its reliability. It thus makes possible a particularly high degree of calculability of results for the heads of the organization and for those acting in relation to it. It is finally superior both in intensive efficiency and in the scope of its operation, and is formally capable of application to all kinds of administrative tasks.[31]

Weber was definitely at one end of the continuum. He insisted that, considering the needs of mass administration, the only choice was between bureaucracy and dilettantism in the field of administration. His opinion of "collegiality"—the formal requirement that legitimate acts of a body require the participation of all its members in decision making—was expressed as follows:

[30]Max G. Abbott and John T. Lovell, eds. *Change Perspectives in Educational Administration* (Auburn, Ala.: School of Education, Auburn University, 1965), pp. 42–43.
[31]Weber, *Social and Economic Organization*, p. 337.

Furthermore, it divides personal responsibility, indeed in the larger bodies this disappears almost entirely, whereas in monocratic organizations it is perfectly clear without question where responsibility lies. Large-scale tasks which require quick and consistent solutions tend in general, for good technical reasons, to fall into the hands of monocratic "dictators" in whom all responsibility is concentrated.[32]

Strangely enough, Weber did not consider his idealized bureaucracy as authoritarian. On the contrary, he thought that it foreshadowed mass democracy, because according to his model, technical experts would be placed in the executive, decision-making positions in the hierarchy, instead of staffing these positions through the traditional methods of patriarchalism, patrimonialism, and charisma. Viewed from this standpoint, the development of the modern bureaucracy was considered a step toward democracy because, theoretically, positions of power in the hierarchy would be opened to experts who could come from the masses.

Thompson has pointed out, however, that at the present time one of the crucial problems in modern organizations is the reconciliation of conflicts between specialists on the staff of an organization who know and executives in the power structure of the line organization who do not know.[33]

Weber's monocratic, bureaucratic model has been severely criticized in ways discussed later in this chapter. Despite such criticism, the monocratic, bureaucratic concept of administrative organization is the prevailing model of organization found in every advanced country of the world, regardless of its political philosophy or economic organization. It has been the basic model for organizing the public school systems of the United States, especially the larger systems.

In the following section, some of the assumptions underlying the monocratic, bureaucratic concept are presented. It will be noted that a number of these assumptions are not value-free.

Some Assumptions Underlying the Traditional Monocratic, Bureaucratic Concept

Administrators differ widely in theory concerning the application of the principles of organization and administration to: first, those activities

[32] *Ibid.,* p. 399.
[33] Victor A. Thompson, *Modern Organization* (New York: Alfred A. Knopf, Inc., 1961), pp. 81–113.

relating to the formulation of goals, programs, and policies; second, those activities relating to goal attainment through the implementation of programs and policies; and third, those activities relating to maintaining the group. There is no recognized field theory of administration. Furthermore, it is difficult for the student to find anywhere in the literature of educational administration a coherent statement of theory on how the principles of organization and administration should be implemented.

Critics of administrators, sometimes administrators themselves, have tended to categorize administration as good or bad, efficient or inefficient, without attempting to differentiate carefully between different concepts of administrative theory. In this chapter, an attempt is made to distinguish between the traditional monocratic, bureaucratic and the emerging pluralistic, collegial concepts of administration and organization, but for many people even these words, unfortunately, have good and bad connotations.

Sometimes the arbitrary classification of administrative theory by labels that have value connotations retards a scholarly analysis. It is better to assume that administrators are neither good nor bad but that they differ in their assumptions concerning these concepts. In the following paragraphs, an analysis is made of some of the important assumptions underlying the monocratic, bureaucratic concept.

LEADERSHIP IS CONFINED TO THOSE HOLDING POSITIONS IN THE POWER ECHELON. Those accepting such a premise generally assume that the population is divided into two groups, the leaders and the followers. The leaders should be assigned to power positions in the hierarchy, where it is their responsibility to exercise leadership. If persons other than power holders exercise leadership, conflicts are bound to arise. A capable person should obtain a power position if he wants to be a leader. If such a persons attempts to exercise leadership when he does not hold a power position, he will become a troublemaker and interfere with the administrative leadership of the person holding the superordinate position. If the superordinate permits leadership outside of the power structure to develop, his own position is threatened. If a person does not exercise his authority, he will lose it. The superordinate must carefully protect his prerogatives, or he is likely to lose his leadership position.

GOOD HUMAN RELATIONS ARE NECESSARY IN ORDER THAT FOLLOWERS ACCEPT DECISIONS OF SUPERORDINATES. The decisions of the officials in the power hierarchy must be accepted and implemented, or the enterprise fails. The power holder can use force on his followers and require them to accept his decisions, but force requires rigorous inspection and supervision, which is expensive in time and energy. Therefore, he should establish good relations between his followers and himself so that they will voluntarily follow him without question.

AUTHORITY AND POWER CAN BE DELEGATED, BUT RESPONSIBILITY CANNOT BE SHARED. The top executive may delegate power and authority to subexecutives, and he may hold them responsible for the proper exercise of the power and authority he has delegated to them. Nevertheless, all responsibility is ultimately his if things go wrong.

FINAL RESPONSIBILITY FOR ALL MATTERS IS PLACED IN THE ADMINISTRATOR AT THE TOP OF THE POWER ECHELON. The top executive in the organization is ultimately responsible for everything that happens. He should receive the credit and he should receive the blame. This assumption logically follows the assumption with respect to responsibility. Certainly, if the executive is ultimately responsible for everything, he should have the authority to veto any decision of his subordinates.

THE INDIVIDUAL FINDS SECURITY IN A CLIMATE IN WHICH THE SUPERORDINATES PROTECT THE INTERESTS OF SUBORDINATES IN THE ORGANIZATION. The person holding the top position in the power echelon should defend his subordinates, right or wrong, so long as they take his orders and are loyal to him. This assumption is similar to the assumptions of feudalism, whereby a person made himself a vassal of a feudal lord for protection. The success of the feudal system was based upon the loyalty of vassals and on the effectiveness with which the feudal lord protected his vassals.

Thompson made the following comment concerning this point:

> Bureaucratic hierarchy has inherited the rights and privileges of the early charismatic leader and his retainers, the traditionalistic king and his nobility, and the entrepreneurial owner-manager and his family protégés. Consequently, to be socially defined as "successful" in our culture, one must proceed up some hierarchy.[34]

UNITY OF PURPOSE IS OBTAINED THROUGH LOYALTY TO THE ADMINISTRATOR. Since the administrator will protect his subordinates, right or wrong, his subordinates owe him their undivided loyalty. This loyalty requires that subordinates defend him and also accept his decisions without question. This, too, is an essential assumption of the feudal system.

THE IMAGE OF THE EXECUTIVE IS THAT OF A SUPERMAN. According to Thompson, "The impression is fostered that occupants of hierarchical positions are, of all people in the organization, the ablest, the most industrious, the most indispensable, the most loyal, the most reliable, the most

---

[34] *Ibid.*, p. 96. Reprinted from *Modern Organization* by Victor Thompson by permission of Alfred A. Knopf, Inc. Copyright (c) 1961 by Victor Thompson.

self-controlled, the most ethical, which is to say the most honest, fair, and impartial."[35]

Since money is one of the most important factors in determining prestige and status, the person occupying the top position in the hierarchy should be paid the highest salary. For example, a requirement for accreditation of high schools by the Southern Association of Schools and Colleges is that no person in the school system may be paid a salary higher than that of the superintendent of schools.

MAXIMUM PRODUCTION IS ATTAINED IN A CLIMATE OF COMPETITION AND PRESSURE. People excel in their efforts when they compete with each other. Life is a competitive struggle for survival, and greater rewards should be given to the persons who are successful. This competition should be supplemented by pressure, taking the form of either rewards or punishment. Competition and pressure are good for production.

THE LINE-AND-STAFF PLAN OF ORGANIZATION SHOULD BE UTILIZED TO FORMULATE GOALS, POLICIES, AND PROGRAMS, AS WELL AS TO EXECUTE POLICIES AND PROGRAMS. Since the best leadership is placed in the line-and-staff structure, this leadership is most competent to formulate goals, policies, and programs. That structure has the responsibility for implementing the goals, policies, and programs, and therefore should have the responsibility for formulating them.

AUTHORITY IS THE RIGHT AND PRIVILEGE OF A PERSON HOLDING A HIERARCHICAL POSITION. Authority is inherent in the position itself. The authority should be given to the person who has the greatest ability. Administrators have the greatest ability, or they would not be in positions of power in the hierarchy. This assumption can be traced back to the divine right of kings theory.

THE INDIVIDUAL IN THE ORGANIZATION IS EXPENDABLE. The purpose or goal of the organization is more important than the individual. For that reason, the individual should be sacrificed if necessary to accomplish the goals of the organization. The individual exists in order to serve the organization, rather than the organization to serve the individual.

EVALUATION IS THE PREROGATIVE OF SUPERORDINATES. Since the superordinate is finally responsible for everything, logically he should have the exclusive authority to evaluate persons and production. Evaluation is one of the means by which he enforces discipline in the organization.

[35] *Ibid.*, p. 143.

THE EMERGING PLURALISTIC, COLLEGIAL CONCEPT

Unfortunately, no scholar with the brilliance of a Weber has attempted to describe the model for the pluralistic, collegial concept of administration and organization. Many writers have described in detail the defects of the bureaucratic model, but none has suggested its complete abandonment.[36] The emerging pluralistic, collegial concept of organization can perhaps best be described as a modification of the monocratic, bureaucratic concept, providing for a pluralistic sharing of power to make policy and program decisions on a collegial basis. Under this concept, the organization is structured hierarchically, as in Weber's bureaucracy, to implement programs and policies, and is structured collegially on an egalitarian basis for making policy and program decisions. Perhaps the best example of this model is a college which: (1) emphasizes academic freedom, scholarship, and the dignity of the individual; (2) provides that the faculty, and not the administrative hierarchy, shall make major policy and program decisions, and (3) pays distinguished professors salaries as high as or higher than those of persons holding positions in the administrative hierarchy. This is not a hypothetical case. This concept of organization and administration is actually found in many of the leading colleges and universities of the nation.

Thompson noted that the monocratic, bureaucratic organization is not innovative.[37] Following is a summary of his proposals for making a bureaucratic organization more innovative: (1) the organization will be more loosely structured, with less emphasis on a precise definition of duties and responsibilities; (2) jobs will be described in terms of professional responsibilities, as contrasted with duties; (3) communications will be freer; (4) appropriate types of decisions will be decentralized; (5) there will be less stratification in the organization, and salary scales will no longer reflect chiefly "awesome status differences"; (6) greater use will be made of group processes and less emphasis made of authority; (7) work assignments will be made broader; (8) more opportunities will be provided for multiple group membership and interpersonal communication; (9) departmentalization will be so arranged as to keep parochialism to a minimum; (10) the organization will not be as tidy as the monocratic

---

[36]For example, see Victor A. Thompson, *Modern Organization* (New York: Alfred A. Knopf, Inc., 1961); Chris Argyris, "The Individual and Organization: Some Problems of Mutual Adjustment," and Wallazz B. Eaton, "Democratic Organization: Myth or Reality" in *Educational Administration:* Selected Readings, ed. Walter G. Hack, *et al.* (Boston: Allyn & Bacon, Inc., 1965).

[37]Victor A. Thompson, "Bureaucracy and Innovation," *Administrative Science Quarterly,* **10,** No. 1 (June 1965).

bureaucracy, because some overlapping of functions and vagueness concerning jurisdictions promote interdepartmental communication.[38] While Thompson did not attempt to conceptualize the pluralistic, collegial organizational model, he made the following proposals, which take us a considerable distance on the continuum toward this model.

> If formal structures could be sufficiently loosened, it might be possible for organizations and units to restructure themselves continually in the light of the problem at hand. Thus, for generating ideas, for planning and problem solving, the organization or unit would "unstructure" itself into a freely communicating body of equals. When it came time (as opposed to stimulation of novel or correct ideas), the organization would then restructure itself into the more usual hierarchical form, tightening up its lines somewhat.[39]

Thus, Thompson has recommended a major modification in Weber's model in order to promote innovation.

Argyris has presented an extremely interesting analysis of the conflict between the healthy human personality and a monocratic bureaucracy established in accord with the principles of formal organization already discussed in this chapter.[40] He did not accept the arguments of some advocates of formal organization that the choice is between the monocratic, bureaucratic organization or no organization at all. Nor did he accept the arguments of some human-relations researchers that formal structures are "bad" and that the needs of the individual actors in the organization should be given priority over organizational goals. He assumed that, to date, no one has defined a more useful set of formal organizational principles than those discussed in this chapter. He then proceeded to demonstrate how each of the formal principles of organization, such as division of labor, unity of chain of command, unity of purpose, and span of control, is in conflict with the psychological needs of a mature, healthy human personality. He cited research showing that the self-actualizing personality through the process of growth passes from a state of being passive as an infant to a state of increasing activity as an adult, tends to develop from a state of dependency upon others as a child to relative independence as an adult, tends to develop from being able to use only a few of his capacities as an infant to the ability to use many capacities as an adult, tends to grow from a subordinate position as an infant toward an equal position as

---

[38] Adapted from Victor A. Thompson, "Bureaucracy and Innovation," *Administrative Science Quarterly*, **10**, No. 1 (June 1965).

[39] *Ibid.*, p. 16.

[40] Chris Argyris, "The Individual and Organization: Some Problems of Mutual Adjustment," Chap. 14 in *Educational Administration: Selected Readings*, ed. Walter G. Hack, *et al.* (Boston: Allyn & Bacon, Inc., 1965).

an adult, and tends to grow and mature in many other ways.[41] After comparing the needs of the human personality with the requirements for strict application of the principles of formal organization, Argyris observed:

> If the principles of formal organization are used as ideally defined, then the employees will tend to work in an environment where (1) they are provided minimal control over their work-a-day world, (2) they are expected to be passive, dependent, subordinate, (3) they are expected to have a short-time perspective, (4) they are induced to perfect and value the frequent use of a few superficial abilities, and (5) they are expected to produce under conditions leading to psychological failure.[42]

Argyris concluded that these conditions lead to conflict. He made no proposals for major changes in the bureaucratic organization. But he stated that the basic problem is the reduction in the degree of dependency, subordination, and submission required of the employee, and suggested that "job enlargement and employee centered (or democratic or participative) leadership are elements which, if used correctly, can go a long way toward ameliorating the situation."[43]

Some Assumptions Underlying the Emerging Pluralistic, Collegial Concept

Some of the assumptions underlying the pluralistic, collegial concept of administration differ sharply from those underlying the traditional monocratic, bureaucratic concept. Under the headings that follow an analysis is made of some of these assumptions.

LEADERSHIP IS NOT CONFINED TO THOSE HOLDING STATUS POSITIONS IN THE POWER ECHELON. Any person who helps a group to formulate goals, programs, and policies, any person who assists a group to attain its goals, or any person who helps maintain the group, is providing leadership. Therefore, leadership is not a narrow or restricted function, exclusively reserved to superordinates, but leadership potential is widely dispersed throughout the organization. The person holding authority will be more effective if he develops, rather than restricts, this leadership potential throughout the group. Instead of losing his leadership by sharing

[41] *Ibid.,* pp. 161–162.
[42] *Ibid.,* p. 176.
[43] *Ibid.,* p. 182.

it, he will increase his own potential. He can prevent conflicts from multiple leadership by the appropriate use of the coordination function of executive leadership.

GOOD HUMAN RELATIONS ARE ESSENTIAL TO GROUP PRODUCTION AND TO MEETING THE NEEDS OF INDIVIDUAL MEMBERS OF THE GROUP. Good human relations improve group morale, and high group morale generally facilitates production. Individual members of the group feel the need for acceptance by other members. When individual needs as well as group needs are met, the organization is more productive.

RESPONSIBILITY, AS WELL AS POWER AND AUTHORITY, CAN BE SHARED. If leadership can be shared, responsibility can be shared. If potential leaders in the organization are permitted to exercise their leadership potential, they will voluntarily accept responsibility as well as authority and power. Since all responsibility is not placed in the executive at the top of the power echelon, he should not receive all the credit or all the blame.

THOSE AFFECTED BY A PROGRAM OR POLICY SHOULD SHARE IN DECISION MAKING WITH RESPECT TO THAT PROGRAM OR POLICY. This assumption is stated as follows in the Declaration of Independence: "... Governments are instituted among men, deriving their just powers from the consent of the governed. ..." Lincoln stated basically this same assumption in the following words: "... Government of the people, by the people, for the people. ..." Perhaps traditional and emerging administration theories differ more on this assumption than any other. Due to the development of large, complex educational organizations, not all members can participate directly in all types of policy decisions. But all members can participate through their representatives.

THE INDIVIDUAL FINDS SECURITY IN A DYNAMIC CLIMATE IN WHICH HE SHARES RESPONSIBILITY FOR DECISION MAKING. A person is more secure in implementing goals, policies, and programs if he understands them. He will understand them better if he helps to formulate them. A person is more secure if he helps to determine his own fate. A free man is more secure than a vassal.

UNITY OF PURPOSE IS SECURED THROUGH CONSENSUS AND GROUP LOYALTY. When members of a group participate in the formulation of goals, policies, and programs, the group is more likely to accept them than if they are handed down through the hierarchy. As the group works together, interactions occur which make the group more cohesive. If the leader works effectively with the group, he will be accepted by the group as a member. When the group develops goals, policies, and programs, they tend to be the property of the group, and the group will be loyal to what it has developed and to the members who have shared in that process. Unity of purpose is secured through these interactional processes.

MAXIMUM PRODUCTION IS ATTAINED IN A THREAT-FREE CLIMATE. The by-products of competition and pressure may ultimately reduce, rather than increase, production. A threat-free climate does not mean a problem-free situation.

> The solution of problems promotes the growth of the individual and also gives him a feeling of satisfaction. External pressures are sometimes exerted on an individual in order to force him to accept a value or achieve a goal. A pressure is a threat if it is resented by the individual concerned and is destructive of his personality. A threat is particularly destructive to the individual if the pressure is exerted to force him to accept a value or attain a goal which he does not believe is valid. If the individual participates in the determination of acceptable values and goals and they become his own values and goals, he will be under pressure to attain goals that are consistent with his values, but the pressure will be internal rather than external. This internal pressure will then become a felt need of the individual. As he meets his needs, he will solve problems which promote his growth and give him satisfaction.
>
> The emerging theory of administration provides a climate which avoids the use of external pressures that are destructive of human personality. The traditional theory of administration does not hesitate to use external pressures in order to attain production.[44]

THE LINE AND STAFF ORGANIZATIONS SHOULD BE USED EXCLUSIVELY FOR THE PURPOSE OF DIVIDING LABOR AND IMPLEMENTING POLICIES AND PROGRAMS DEVELOPED BY THE TOTAL GROUP AFFECTED. It will be noted that the emerging collegial concept, as well as the traditional monocratic concept of administration, accepts the necessity of a line-and-staff organization. However, these two concepts differ in the way the line-and-staff organization is used. Under the monocratic concept, it is assumed that the line-and-staff organization determines and also executes policies and programs. The emerging collegial concept of administration calls for group participation in decision making. Therefore, the line-and-staff organization alone will not meet the requirements of emerging theory. Two structures are needed under the emerging theory of administration: one structure for determining goals, policies, and programs, and another structure for executing policies and programs. Under the emerging theory of

[44] *Better Teaching in School Administration,* pp. 92–93.

administration, the structure for implementing policies and programs is usually a line-and-staff organization. The structure for developing policies and programs is usually some type of a committee organization in which all members of the organization have a peer status, regardless of position in the power echelon.

THE SITUATION AND NOT THE POSITION DETERMINES THE RIGHT AND PRIVILEGE TO EXERCISE AUTHORITY. Authority arises out of the situation, rather than out of the position. The point of decision making should be as near the scene of action as practicable. The situation itself demands that authority be exercised by someone. The administrator finds himself in a situation in which he must exercise authority in order to meet the needs of the group. Therefore, he exercises that authority due to the necessities of the situation not due to the prerogatives of his position. The teacher is in a situation which requires that authority over certain matters be exercised. He exercises that authority, not because of privileges he holds by reason of being a teacher, but because the situation demands authority.

THE INDIVIDUAL IN THE ORGANIZATION IS NOT EXPENDABLE. The ultimate purpose of an organization is to meet the needs of individuals in human society. The individuals in the organization are a part of that society. Government was created to serve people, and not people to serve government. Therefore, the worth of the individual should not be ignored by the organization. Furthermore, the organization can better achieve its own purpose by conserving and improving the members of the organization.

EVALUATION IS A GROUP RESPONSIBILITY. If there is broad participation in the formation of goals, policies, and programs, then there must be broad participation in evaluation. Participation in evaluation by the group is necessary to develop the competencies of the group. Collegial group evaluation is more valid and reliable than evaluation by one individual. Furthermore, broad participation in evaluation provides valuable feedback.

SOME CONTRASTS BETWEEN THE MONOCRATIC, BUREAUCRATIC AND THE PLURALISTIC, COLLEGIAL CONCEPTS

As has already been pointed out, the assumptions made and the values held by those in a position to formulate the structure of an organization and to administer it determine largely the point on the monocratic, bureaucratic–pluralistic, collegial continuum (hereafter shortened to monocratic-pluralistic continuum) on which an organization can be located. Although the principles of formal organization are generally applicable to all types of formal organization, there are vital differences between school systems on one end of the monocratic-pluralistic continuum and those on the other end. Some of those differences are discussed under the headings that follow.

Climate

The climate of human relations is different in school systems operating under the monocratic and pluralistic concepts of administration. The absence of fear of the hierarchy, the feeling of equality, and the knowledge that one is master of his own fate beget different personalities in systems at the opposite ends of the monocratic-pluralistic continuum. The monocratic school system tends toward a *closed climate,* as contrasted with the tendency toward an *open climate* in a pluralistic system.[45]

Structure

It has already been pointed out that there are wide differences in organizational structures developed in accordance with the assumptions underlying the monocratic concept and with the pluralistic concept. Structures based on the monocratic concept of administration emphasize centralized authority for planning, controlling, and decision making. Such structures also usually exercise a close inspectional type of supervision. Since the executives in such organizations are responsible for all decision making and planning and, at the same time, for exercising highly centralized control over all operations, the span of control or the number of persons supervised by the executive in the monocratic organization is usually less than the executive span of control in the pluralistic organization. Therefore, the monocratic organization requires more echelons of authority and tends to have longer chains of command supervised by each executive.

There has been some misunderstanding concerning the line-and-staff structure. Some writers have even inferred that the line-and-staff structure is outmoded and should be abandoned. This reasoning seems to be based on the assumption that structure is inherently undemocratic. Actually, the line-and-staff structure is not at fault; the fault lies with the way in which

---

[45]See Andrew W. Halpin and Don B. Croft, "The Organizational Climate of Schools," *Administrators Note Book,* 2, No. 7 (Mar. 1963). These researchers did not specifically study the variations in climate of school systems at opposite ends of the monocratic-pluralistic continuum; they did define carefully the characteristics of schools with open and closed climates. Although not intended to do so, those descriptions rather accurately distinguish between the climates of school systems at opposite ends of the continuum.

it is used. For instance, in one organization the line-and-staff structure may be so used as to require that all decisions, even routine ones, be cleared with the executive head of the organization before action is taken. This method of operating ignores the possibility of increasing the efficiency of the organization by a judicious delegation of authority. Furthermore, it violates the principle that *a decision should be made as near the point of action as practicable.* In another organization, line-and-staff structure for the implementation of programs and policies is accompanied by proper delegation of authority and supplemented by machinery for broad participation in decision making with respect to policy and program. Both organizations use a line-and-staff structure, one inappropriately and the other appropriately.

Structures for pluralistic, collegial administration emphasize wide sharing of authority for planning, controlling, and decision making, and such centralized authority as is necessary for coordinating the total organization. The organizational structure may actually be more complex than that for the monocratic, bureaucratic organization. However, this additional complexity is introduced for the purpose of making the arrangements necessary for broad participation in decision making.

It is sometimes said that there is less emphasis on structure in pluralistic than in monocratic organization. It is probably true that the skeleton of monocratic structure is more stark, because of its constraints, than the skeleton of pluralistic structure. On the other hand, the structure for pluralistic organization is designed to give maximum freedom to the individual; therefore, the individual is less conscious of the structure itself.

Communication

The communication patterns differ widely in monocratic and pluralistic organization. The communication pattern for monocratic organization is quite simple. It goes up and down a vertical line organization. A communication from the top must pass through all *intermediate echelons* of authority before it reaches the bottom, but no *intermediate echelon* can stop the communication from the top down. A communication from the bottom to the top must also pass through each *intermediate echelon,* but any *intermediate echelon* can stop the communication from a lower level from reaching the top. Therefore, the channel of communication is not strictly a two-way channel. Furthermore, great emphasis is given to "going through channels," and any communication from the bottom to the top which does not go through channels is frowned upon. The administrator in the monocratic hierarchy uses his control over communications to increase his status, power, and prestige.

There are many channels of communication in pluralistic organizations. Such organizations have provisions for communicating through a vertical channel, but it is a two-way channel. Communication is also circular and horizontal in pluralistic organization. The organization provides for a committee structure or some other arrangement whereby members at the bottom of the line structure may communicate in a face-to-face relationship with the top executives. Since communication is much freer among all members of the organization in a pluralistic structure, the opportunity for beneficial interactions is much greater.

Administrative Behavior

For want of better terminology, we have already referred to democratic and authoritarian administration. The assumptions underlying traditional monocratic, bureaucratic concepts of administration are largely authoritarian, and the assumptions underlying emerging pluralistic, collegial concepts of administration are largely democratic by popular definition. It should not be inferred, however, that democratic administration is *ipso facto* good and that authoritarian administration is *ipso facto* bad. History provides numerous examples of successful and unsuccessful democratic administration and successful and unsuccessful authoritarian administration. Furthermore, it is not strictly accurate to classify administration as democratic and authoritarian. It would be difficult, if not impossible, to find an administration which is completely authoritarian or completely democratic. It is more accurate to think of democracy and authoritarianism as part of the same continuum. Democratic and undemocratic behavior were defined in a series of studies at the University of Florida of school principals. The definitions are as follows:

Democratic behavior:
(a) Action involving the group in decision making with respect to policy and program.
(b) Implementation in line with democratically determined policy.
(c) Action promoting the group or individual creativity, productivity, and satisfaction without harm to other groups or individuals.
(d) Behavior or attitude respecting the dignity of individuals or groups.
(e) Action that indicates that the principal seeks to become an accepted member of the group.
(f) Action that indicates that the principal seeks to keep channels of communication open.

Undemocratic behavior:
   (a) Action that indicates that decision making is centered in the status leader or his inner circle.
   (b) Implementation that ignores democratically determined policy.
   (c) Action that frustrates group or individual creativity, productivity, and satisfaction.
   (d) Action that indicates that the principal attains objectives by pressures that jeopardize a person's security.
   (e) Action that indicates that the principal considers himself above or apart from the group.
   (f) Action that indicates that the principal discourages or blocks free communication.[46]

These definitions were developed to describe the behavior of school principals, but they are equally applicable to other types of administrators. According to these definitions, the words "undemocratic" and "authoritarian" are synonymous terms.

Innovation and Change

Attention has already been directed to the fact that a number of investigators have found that monocratic, bureaucratic organizations are not as innovative as pluralistic, collegial organizations. This is not surprising, because monocratic control limits feedback both from the environment and from the subsystems of an organization. Furthermore, in monocratic organization the upwardly mobile person must become an organization man; follow the chain of command, observing closely all rules, regulations, and norms of the organization; and above all things, avoid becoming a threat to his superordinates by being an innovator. Consequently, innovation and change, when it does come, usually comes from the top of the hierarchy downward.

In pluralistic, collegial organization, there is more feedback from the environment and from subsystems in the organization. Leadership which promotes change is encouraged at all hierarchical levels. Therefore, in the pluralistic organization, there tends to be more change and innovation, and it may come from the bottom of the hierarchy as well as the top.

[46]Carroll D. Farrar, *Refinement of an Instrument to Determine Certain Characteristics of the Working Patterns of School Principals* (Doctoral Dissertation, University of Florida, 1956), pp. 14–15.

Assumption Concerning People

McGregor,[47] one of the leaders of the human relations movement, developed an interesting theory of management which he called Theory X and Theory Y. He distinguished these two theories by analyzing the assumptions behind each theory. According to McGregor, Theory X is based on the following assumptions:

1. The average human being has an inherent dislike of work and will avoid it if he can.
2. Because of this human characteristic of dislike of work, most people must be coerced, controlled, directed, threatened with punishment to get them to put forth adequate effort toward the achievement of organizational objectives.
3. The average human being prefers to be directed, wishes to avoid responsibility, has relatively little ambition, wants security above all.[48]

Following are the assumptions upon which Theory Y is based:

1. The expenditure of physical and mental effort in work is as natural as play or rest.
2. External control and the threat of punishment are not the only means of bringing about effort toward organizational objectives. Man will exercise self-direction and self-control in the service of objectives to which he is committed.
3. Commitment to objectives is a function of the rewards associated with their achievement.
4. The average human being learns, under proper conditions, not only to accept but to seek responsibility.
5. The capacity to exercise a relatively high degree of imagination, ingenuity, and creativity in the solution of organizational problems is widely, not narrowly, distributed in the population.
6. Under conditions of modern industrial life, the intellectual potentialities of the average human being are only partially utilized.[49]

[47] Douglas McGregor, *The Human Side of Enterprise* (New York: McGraw-Hill Book Company, Inc., 1960).
[48] *Ibid.*, pp. 33-34.
[49] *Ibid.*, pp. 47-48.

It is noted that there is a marked similarity between the assumptions upon which Theory X is based and the assumptions upon which the monocratic bureaucratic concept of organization and administration is based. The assumption behind Theory Y and the assumptions behind the pluralistic collegial concept are also very similar in nature.

SOME IMPORTANT PROBLEMS AND ISSUES

A summary of some of the most commonly accepted concepts and principles of organization and administration was presented in the first part of this chapter. It is apparent that many of these concepts and principles are not sure guides to administrative action because of possible wide differences in interpretation and application. Perhaps what is needed is a unifying theory of administration which will make possible a rational interpretation and application of principles. Additional problems associated with the interpretation of these concepts and principles are presented in the following paragraphs.

How Can Principles Be Validated?

It has already been pointed out that principles of organization and administration have been developed largely by practical experience. How can these principles be scientifically tested? Griffiths has tentatively suggested the following steps for theory development in administrative behavior:

1. A *description* of administrative behavior in one situation.
2. A *definition* of certain basic concepts.
3. A more *general statement* which is descriptive of the average behavior in a limited number of situations.
4. A statement of one or more *hypotheses*.
5. An *evaluation* and *reconstruction* of the hypotheses in accordance with later observations.
6. The statement of one or more principles.[50]

It would seem that some procedure, such as that suggested by Griffiths, should be used to test principles of organization and administra-

[50]Daniel E. Griffiths, "Toward a Theory of Administrative Behavior," Chap. 10 in *Administrative Behavior in Education,* ed. Roald F. Campbell and Russell T. Gregg (New York: Harper & Row, Publishers, 1957), p. 379.

tion. The scientific approach would certainly sharpen the statements of those principles, define the operating limits of a principle, and might reveal that some are not even principles. *A principle should serve as a guide to action.* If these guides are invalid or crudely defined, they are not of much use to school administrators. Therefore, research on theory is probably one of the most needed types of research. Can the so-called principles of administration presented in this chapter be validated by the procedures recommended by Griffiths?

How Can Assumptions Be Tested?

It has already been pointed out that traditional monocratic concepts are based on somewhat different assumptions than emerging pluralistic concepts of administration. How can these assumptions be tested? Some are philosophical in nature and cannot be tested by objective research. Philosophical assumptions must be tested against the value system of the society in which the organization finds itself. This test of philosophical assumptions would yield somewhat different results in the United States of America than in Russia. For instance, the assumptions underlying traditional monocratic administration are fairly consistent with the assumptions of Plato and Nietzsche. Emerging concepts of administration, however, are fairly consistent with the philosophy of John Dewey and the philosophy expressed in the great political documents of this country, such as the Declaration of Independence and the Constitution with its amendments.

Assumptions dealing with such factors as production, group morale, and human relations can be tested by objective research. As a matter of fact, a considerable body of research dealing with these assumptions is already available.[51] The weight of available evidence indicates that the assumptions underlying pluralistic, collegial concepts of administration relating to production, group morale, and human relations are more valid than the assumptions of monocratic concepts. Some of that research is reviewed in the following chapter. However, this research has been done largely in the United States, a country with a democratic orientation. Whether the same research would yield the same results in a country such as Russia with an authoritarian orientation is unknown. Much additional research needs to be done on identifying the assumptions underlying different concepts and theories of administration. Furthermore, those as-

---

[51]See, for example, Bernard Berelson and Gary Steiner, *Human Behavior: An Inventory of Scientific Findings* (New York: Harcourt, Brace & World, Inc., 1964), and Darwin Cartwright and Alvin Zander, *Group Dynamics: Research and Theory* (New York: Harper & Row Publishers, 1960).

sumptions should be subjected to much more rigorous testing and examination than has been the case up to the present time. This will involve the development of more precise theoretical models than have yet been developed, from which appropriate hypotheses may be formulated and tested.

The testing of assumptions is not as simple a matter as it might seem. For instance, before assumptions with respect to production can be tested, production itself must be defined. Production may be defined solely as the output of the organization, or the definition may include what happens to members of the organization along with the output. If one accepts the first definition, process and product are separable, because members of the organization are expendable. If one accepts the second definition, process and product are inseparable, because members of the organization are not expendable. To state the problem in another way, if one accepts the second definition, production will be measured not only in terms of the quantity and quality of production over a definite period of time, but it will also include the future production potential of the organization. Similar difficulties will no doubt be encountered as other assumptions are tested. Can values be ignored when testing assumptions?

How Can Individuals and Minorities Be Protected from Group Domination?

The group can be quite as authoritarian as the executive in suppressing individuals and minorities. The group itself, if it so chooses, can exercise powerful sanctions against its members to force compliance with group norms, values, and goals. The rights of individuals and minorities are likely to be jeopardized if the administrative group shifts suddenly from the benevolent, paternalistic, directive authoritarian style to a permissive, democratic style. A sudden change from monocratic decision making to pluralistic decision making is likely to create a power vacuum. Group members with authoritarian tendencies are likely to rush into this power vacuum and take over. Thus, a group inexperienced in democratic group operation will hardly become democratic overnight, simply because the administration is changed. There is no assurance that the group will act democratically, unless group members are dedicated to democratic values. Even such dedication does not always protect individuals and minorities from capricious group action. The government of the United States is based on a constitution with amendments that incorporate a bill of rights protecting individuals and minorities from capricious group action. Should educational organizations also develop constitutions incorporating a bill of rights and an internal judicial system for protecting the rights of individuals and minorities?

How Much Collegiality in Decision Making Is Practicable?

When large numbers of people are involved, it is impracticable to submit all matters to the total group for decision. The government of the United States is a republic rather than a pure democracy. Nevertheless, certain matters are submitted to a vote of the total electorate.

In large school systems and even in large schools, it is impractical to submit all matters to the total faculty. The problem that arises as to what matters should be decided by the total faculty, what matters should be decided by committees respresenting the faculty, and what matters should be decided by the executive head.

There are also problems relating to lay participation in decision making. Boards of education are selected to represent the people. But the existence of thousands of citizens committees and parent-teacher associations throughout the nation is evidence that present legal means of lay participation in decision making with respect to the schools do not meet the demand for wider participation. This problem is so important that it is treated more extensively in other chapters of this book.

What criteria could be used to determine the matters that should be decided by the faculty or its representatives and the matters that should be decided by the hierarchy?

Are the Monocratic, Bureaucratic and Pluralistic, Collegial Concepts of Administration Equally Suitable for All Types of Organizations?

Earlier in this chapter, reference was made to Blau and Scott's typology of organization based upon who benefits.[52] These authors classified organizations as mutual benefit, business concerns, service organizations, and commonweal organizations.

A public school system is a service organization operated for the benefit of its clients, as contrasted with a business concern operated for the benefit of its owners, and a commonweal organization operated for the benefit of the general public. Will organizations with such widely different functions as a labor union serving its members, a factory making automobiles to provide profits for the stockholders, a school system serving children, or an army protecting the general public be equally effective in

---

[52]Peter M. Blau and W. Richard Scott, *Formal Organization, A Comparative Approach* (San Francisco: Chandler Publishing Co., 1962), p. 43.

utilizing either the monocratic, bureaucratic concept of organization or the pluralistic, collegial concept?

Teachers are becoming "cosmopolitans" rather than "locals" in their orientation.[53] Therefore, teachers may be oriented to the goals of the profession quite as much as to the goals of an organization. Most college professors are also cosmopolitans. There is considerable evidence that teachers and professors are more productive in pluralistic, collegial organizations than in monocratic organizations. Would the same thing be true of army personnel? Would the type of organization that is most effective for producing automobiles be equally effective for educating students?

SELECTED REFERENCES

Argyris, Chris, *Interpersonal Competence and Organizational Effectiveness.* Homewood, Ill.: Richard D. Irwin, Inc., 1962.

Berelson, B., and Gary A. Steiner, *Human Behavior: An Inventory of Scientific Findings.* New York: Harcourt, Brace & World, Inc., 1964.

Blau, Peter M., and W. Richard Scott, *Formal Organizations: A Comparative Approach.* San Francisco: Chandler Publishing Co., 1962.

Blau, Peter M. and Richard A. Schoenberr, *The Structure of Organization.* New York: Basic Books, Inc., Publishers, 1971.

Carzo, Rocco and John W. Yanouzas, *Formal Organization, A Systems Approach.* Homewood, Ill.: Richard D. Irwin, 1967.

Etzioni, Amitai, *A Comparative Analysis of Complex Organizations.* New York: Free Press of Glencoe, Inc., 1961.

Golembiewski, Robert T., *Behavior and Organization.* Skokie, Ill.: Rand McNally & Co., 1962.

Griffiths, Daniel E., ed., *Behavioral Science and Educational Administration.* Sixty-third Yearbook of the National Society for the Study of Education. Chicago: University of Chicago Press, 1964.

March, James C., and Herbert A. Simon, *Organizations.* New York: John Wiley & Sons, Inc., 1958.

March, James G., *Handbook of Organization.* Skokie, Ill.: Rand McNally & Co., 1966.

Miller, James G., "Living Systems: Cross-Level Hypotheses," *Behavioral Science,* **10,** No. 4 (Oct. 1965).

Morphet, Edgar L. and Charles O. Ryan, eds., *Implications for Education of Prospective Changes in Society.* Denver, Col.: Designing Education for the Future,

---

[53]Alvin W. Gouldner, "Cosmopolitans and Locals: Toward an Analysis of Latent Social Roles," *Administrative Science Quarterly* **11** (Dec. 1957), 281–306, **11** (Mar. 1958), 444–480.

1967. (Republished by Citation Press, Scholastic Magazines, Inc., New York, N.Y.).

MOUZELIS, NICOS P., *Organization and Bureaucracy: An Analysis of Modern Theory.* Chicago: Aldine Publishing Co., 1968.

PRESTHUS, ROBERT, *The Organizational Society.* New York: Alfred A. Knopf, Inc., 1962.

THOMPSON, VICTOR A., *Modern Organization.* New York: Alfred A. Knopf, Inc., 1961.

TOFFLER, ALVIN, *Future Shock.* New York: Random House, 1970.

TOWNSEND, ROBERT, *Up the Organization.* New York: Alfred A. Knopf, Inc., 1970.

5

Role of Educational Leadership

Concepts of leadership and administration are rapidly changing. Since 1925, hundreds of research studies on group characteristics, leader behavior, human relations, and formal and informal organization have been creating a new and exciting body of knowledge. The implications of these studies are so significant that the demand for new theoretical concepts of administration and organization is widespread. Such interest is not limited to educational administrators. In fact, much of the significant research in these areas has been conducted by business and industry, the armed services, the National Training Laboratories, and university research centers such as the Personnel Research Board at Ohio State University, the Research Center for Group Dynamics at the University of Michigan, the Graduate School of Business Administration at Harvard University, and the Yale Labor and Management Center.

This movement has had a significant impact on educational administration. An organization called the National Conference of Professors of Educational Administration was formed in 1947 primarily to improve preparation programs for school administrators. The Cooperative Program in Educational Administration, sponsored by the American Association of School Administrators and supported in part by grants from the W. K. Kellogg Foundation, was established in 1950 to improve the theory and practice of educational administration.

The National Conference of Professors of Educational Administration in 1954 approved a project involving the preparation of a book to synthesize research findings of significance to educational administration and to preparation programs for educational administrators. A committee of eighteen professors prepared this synthesis, which was published in 1957.[1] The findings of this study indicated clearly that many traditional concepts of leadership or leader behavior are not supported by recent evidence.

An organization called the University Council for Educational Administration was formed in 1956. The council encourages basic research and the dissemination of important research findings through seminars and publications including the *Educational Administration Quarterly*. It has also fostered the use in educational administration of theoretical concepts developed in the social and behavioral sciences. This policy has contributed significantly to the beginnings of a science of educational administration, because most of the significant research on leadership, organizations and social systems has been done by social and behavioral scientists.

SOME CONCEPTS OF LEADERSHIP

In Chapter 3, major attention was given to systems theory and the value of theory and research in dealing with problems of organization and administration. In Chapter 4, systems theory was applied to the examination of concepts and principles of organization. In this chapter, attention will be given to the leader and his role in the social system. This is not a simple task for a number of reasons. In the first place, there is no general agreement among researchers and writers on the meaning of the word "leader." For example, some writers, especially historians, do not distinguish clearly between a leader and the holder of a position with status in the organizational hierarchy. These persons, as well as lay persons generally, assume that the holder of an important position in the hierarchy is, by virtue of his position, a leader. Most behavioral scientists do not hold that view.[2] Lipham has attempted to solve this problem by suggesting in

---

[1] Roald F. Campbell and Russell T. Gregg, eds., *Administrative Behavior in Education* (New York: Harper & Row, Publishers, 1957).
[2] James M. Lipham, "Leadership and Administration," Chap. 6 in *Behavioral Science and Educational Administration*, ed. Daniel E. Griffiths, The Sixty-third Yearbook of the National Society for the Study of Education, Part II (Chicago: University of Chicago Press, 1964).

effect that the term *leader* be restricted to the role of change agent and the term *administrator* to the role of maintaining the organization. Some valid reasons exist for accepting this definition, but it is not the concept of leadership utilized in the research designs of most behavioral scientists. It is the position of the authors of this book that leadership can be provided by an administrator in his acts of maintaining an organization as well as in his acts as a change agent. Furthermore, leadership can operate to prevent change as well as to facilitate it. Therefore, Lipham's typology is not used in this book.

Cartwright and Zander in 1953 wrote:

> It is not possible at the present stage of research on groups to develop a fully satisfactory designation of those group functions which are peculiarly functions of leadership. A more promising endeavor, at least for the present, is to identify the various group functions, without deciding finally whether or not to label each specifically as a function of leadership, and then to discover by empirical investigation such things as what determines this distribution within the group and what consequences stem from various distributions among members.[3]

Since 1953, considerable research has been based on role differentiation in a social system. Many behavioral scientists now conceptualize leadership in that context.[4] In this chapter *we conceptualize leadership as the influencing of the actions, behaviors, beliefs, and feelings of one actor in a social system by another actor with the willing cooperation of the actor being influenced.* The top leader in any system, subsystem, or suprasystem is the actor who most often influences in critical matters the actions, behaviors, beliefs, and feelings of the greatest number of other actors in that system with the willing cooperation of the actors being influenced. Under this concept, there are many leaders with different degrees and kinds of influence in a social system, and a leader may or may not hold a position in the hierarchy of the formal organization.

We are confining ourselves in this chapter to leadership in formal organizations and in informal groups. There are other types of leaders which are worthy of study, but they are beyond the scope of this book. Some examples are: (1) opinion leaders such as interpreters of news events, (2) intellectual leaders such as Albert Einstein, and (3) societal leaders such as Marx and Engels.

[3]Darwin Cartwright and Alvin Zander, eds., *Group Dynamics-Research and Theory* (New York: Harper & Row, Publishers, 1960), p. 494.
[4]See Paul F. Secord and Carl W. Backman, *Social Psychology* (New York: McGraw-Hill Book Company, 1964).

In examining the leadership phenomena of educational organization and administration, we are concerned primarily with concepts and theories of leadership that are applicable to those who hold decision-making positions in the various hierarchies of educational organizations and in informal organizations that interact with formal educational organizations. These persons include state and local superintendents of schools, school principals, college and university presidents, leaders in teacher organizations and federations, leaders in parent-teacher organizations, and leaders of informal organizations. Educational organizations commonly include suprasystems, subsystems, and numerous informal organizations or groups. Educational administrators deal not only with a complex of systems within the educational organization but also with a complex of social systems in the environment of the school system, all of which are exchanging inputs and outputs of information, energy, and matter with each other. Unfortunately, most research on leadership has been confined to leadership in small face-to-face groups. Most of the literature on group dynamics is based on research with small groups. Lipham commented on this situation: "Leadership roles in structure organizations are, indeed, complex. Thus, the methodology and findings of leadership studies concerned with small, unstructured, randomly selected groups are likely to be of only limited value when transplanted indiscriminately to large, complex, hierarchical organizations."[5]

Berelson and Steiner published a comprehensive review of the research relating to human behavior in 1964.[6] They compiled from the research available in the behavioral and social sciences 1,045 propositions or hypotheses of moderate generality dealing with groups, organizations, social processes, and other phenomena of human behavior. Most of the propositions they advanced concerning leadership are based on research in small face-to-face groups.[7] Their propositions relating to leadership in organizations did not seem to be based on much research.[8]

Miller has pointed out that a hypothesis or proposition which does not apply to two or more levels of systems does not have much generality.[9] He listed 165 cross-level hypotheses (applicable across different levels of suprasystems and subsystems within a social system) which could reasonably be supported by available research. He did not list a single cross-level hypothesis on leadership.

[5]Lipham, "Leadership and Administration," p. 125.
[6]Bernard Berelson and Gary A. Steiner, *Human Behavior: An Inventory of Scientific Findings* (New York: Harcourt, Brace & World, Inc., 1964).
[7]*Ibid.*, pp. 341–346.
[8]*Ibid.*, pp. 372–377.
[9]James G. Miller, "Living Systems: Cross-Level Hypotheses," *Behavioral Science,* **10,** No. 4 (1965).

130 BASIC PRINCIPLES, CONCEPTS, AND ISSUES

How many of the conclusions concerning leadership that have been reached from research in small face-to-face groups are applicable to administrators of complex, bureaucratic, hierarchical organizations such as medium and large school systems, colleges, and universities? We will not know until more cross-level research is carried out, and this will require sophisticated designs conforming to rigorous standards.[10] With the above limitations in mind, we present certain generalizations and phenomena relating to leadership in the remainder of this chapter.

TRENDS IN STUDIES OF LEADERSHIP

Leadership is very highly valued in human society, so it is not surprising that many books have been written and many studies conducted concerning leaders and leadership. Classical literature is filled with references to leaders and leadership. The need to lead and the need to be led is a pervasive characteristic of the human animal. Some approaches to the study of leadership are presented next.

Studies of Traits

Prior to 1945, most of the studies of leadership were devoted primarily to the identification of the traits or qualities of leaders. These studies were based in part on the assumption that human beings could be divided into two groups—the leaders and the followers. Therefore, leaders must possess certain traits or qualities not possessed by followers. Some persons in each generation since the dawn of recorded history have believed that "leaders are born, not made."

In 1948, Stogdill examined 124 studies on the relationship of personality factors to leadership. A summary of his findings follows:

1. The following conclusions are supported by uniformly positive evidence from fifteen or more of the studies surveyed:
    A. The average person who occupies a position of leadership exceeds the average members of his group in the following respects: (1) intelligence, (2) scholarship, (3) dependability in exercising responsibilities, (4) activity and social participation, and (5) socioeconomic status.
    B. The qualities, characteristics, and skills required in a leader are determined to a large extent by the demands of the situation in which he is to function as a leader.

[10] *Ibid.*, pp. 382–384.

2. The following conclusions are supported by uniformly positive evidence from ten or more of the studies surveyed:
   A. The average person who occupies a position of leadership exceeds the average member of his group to some degree in the following respects: (1) sociability, (2) initiative, (3) persistence, (4) knowing how to get things done, (5) self-confidence, (6) alertness to and insight into situations, (7) cooperativeness, (8) popularity, (9) adaptability, and (10) verbal facility.[11]

Stogdill, however, after further study of the evidence, concluded:

> A person does not become a leader by virtue of the possession of some combination of traits, but the pattern of personal characteristics of the leader must bear some relevant relationship to the characteristics, activities, and goals of the followers. Thus, leadership must be conceived in terms of the interactions of variables which are in constant flux and change.[12]

Therefore, leadership is not a matter of passive status, nor does it devolve upon a person simply because he is the possessor of some combination of traits. Rather, the leader acquires leader status through the interactions of the group in which he participates and demonstrates his capacity for assisting the group to complete its tasks.[13]

In 1954, Myers analyzed more than two hundred studies of leadership that had been made in the previous fifty years.[14] Following is a summary of some of Myers' conclusions concerning the relationship of personality traits to leadership:

1. No physical characteristics are significantly related to leadership.
2. Although leaders tend to be slightly higher in intelligence than the group of which they are members, there is no significant relationship between superior intelligence and leadership.
3. Knowledge applicable to the problems faced by a group contributes significantly to leadership status.
4. The following characteristics correlate significantly with leadership: insight, initiative, cooperation, originality, ambition, persistence, emotional stability, judgment, popularity, and communication skills.[15]

---

[11] Ralph M. Stogdill, "Personal Factors Associated with Leadership, A Survey of the Literature," *Journal of Psychology*, 25 (1948), 63.

[12] *Ibid.*, p. 64.

[13] *Ibid.*, p. 66.

[14] Robert B. Myers, "The Development and Implications of a Conception for Leadership Education" (Unpublished doctoral dissertation, University of Florida, 1954).

[15] *Ibid.*, pp. 105–106.

Myers observed the following concerning the characteristics just enumerated:

> These characteristics denote qualities of an interactional nature. They are present in leadership situations much more often than are characteristics that denote status or qualities of more individualistic nature. Some characteristics of the latter kind are socioeconomic background and self-confidence.
>
> The research indicates, however, that the personal characteristics of leaders differ according to the situation. Leaders tend to remain leaders only in situations where the activity is similar. No single characteristic is the possession of all leaders.[16]

Thus it is seen that Stogdill and Myers are substantially in agreement concerning the relationship of personality traits to leadership. The study of personality traits alone will not explain leadership. These studies have shown clearly that the assumption, "leaders are born, not made," is largely false. The only inherited trait that has been identified as having some relationship to leadership is intelligence. Even this relationship is frequently quite low.

Stogdill investigated 33 separate research studies on the relationship of intelligence to leadership.[17] He found that the average of the coefficients of correlation between intelligence and leadership was only 0.28. A coefficient of correlation this low is only slightly better than a chance guess. Hopper and Bills made a study of the relationship of the intelligence of school administrators to success as administrators.[18] They reported that the school administrators studied were considerably above average in intelligence but that there was very little correlation between intelligence and success within the group of administrators studied.

All the other personality traits identified as being related to leadership are acquired traits and, as such, are subject to modification by training and experience. Actually, most of the personality traits or characteristics that have been found to be associated with leadership should be classified as skills or competencies rather than personality traits. Therefore, it should be possible within limits to attain these skills and competencies through an appropriate program of learning experiences. This emphasizes the importance of preparation programs for school administrators.

It must not be assumed that the many studies of personality traits in relation to leadership have been totally unproductive. Although the traits

---

[16] *Ibid.*, p. 107.
[17] Stogdill, "Leadership Literature."
[18] Robert L. Hopper and Robert E. Bills, "What's a Good Administrator Made Of?" *The School Executive*, **74** (1955), 93–95.

approach has not provided a comprehensive description of leadership, it has opened the way for further research that gives promise of great significance. Researchers in this area have had great difficulty in defining and measuring leadership and the traits being studied. Different researchers have used different definitions and different instruments. Situational factors have been ignored in most studies. It is not surprising that the conclusions of a number of studies have been contradictory. With sharper definitions, improved instruments, and better control of conditions, researchers in the future will undoubtedly contribute additional knowledge needed in this area.

The "Times Make the Man" Approach

When it became apparent that the traits approach to the study of leadership had limited value, other approaches were sought. The "times make the man" approach captured the imagination of some people about 1940. Hitler, Mussolini, and Stalin were certainly leaders. Yet each lacked many of the qualities that rationally should be associated with leadership. Perhaps they were products of their times. Historians in other days have frequently speculated on that point with respect to other figures in history. This approach produced much speculation but little research. Perhaps its principal contribution was to give emphasis to the need for studying the leader in relation to his social environment.

The Interactional or Group Approach

Another approach is known as the interactional or group approach to the study of leadership. It is generally accepted as being the most productive to the understanding of leadership. Although the individual leader is still an important object of study, it is now generally recognized that he cannot be studied in isolation. The focus of most research on leadership is now on "leader behavior" in a social system, rather than on "leader traits."

The remainder of this chapter presents some generalizations concerning leadership that have been derived principally from studies of leadership in relation to a social system.

Some Definitions and Concepts

Before we proceed further, it is advisable that a few definitions be given of some of the concepts and terms used in this chapter. Leadership has already been defined in terms of the influence of one actor in a social system on another actor in that system with the willing cooperation of the actor being influenced. But the many concepts of leadership cannot be encompassed by a single definition. Following are some additional concepts necessary to the understanding of leadership.

LEADERSHIP ACTS. A person performs leadership acts when he: (1) helps a group to define tasks, goals, and purposes; (2) helps a group to achieve its tasks, goals, and purposes; or (3) helps to maintain the group by assisting in providing for group and individual needs.

ATTEMPTED LEADERSHIP, SUCCESSFUL LEADERSHIP, AND EFFECTIVE LEADERSHIP. Hemphill has defined these terms as follows:

1. Attempted leadership acts are acts accompanied by an intention of initiating structure-in-interaction for solving a mutual problem.
2. Successful leadership acts are acts that have initiated structure-in-interaction during the process of mutual problem solution. An attempted leadership act may or may not become a successful leadership act depending upon subsequent observation of its effect upon the structure of interaction.
3. Effective leadership acts are acts that have initiated structure-in-interaction and that have contributed to the solution of a mutual problem. An effective leadership act is always also a successful leadership act, but a leadership act may be successful without being effective for solving mutual problems.[19]

SOME INFORMAL GROUP CHARACTERISTICS. The informal group, sometimes called an informal organization, has the following characteristics:

1. Each member of the group is able to interact with every other member of the group.
2. The group develops its own structure and organization.
3. The group selects its own leader or leaders.
4. The group has been voluntarily formed to achieve certain common tasks, goals, and purposes.
5. It does not have an officially prescribed hierarchical structure.

[19]John K. Hemphill, "Administration as Problem Solving," Chap. 5 in *Administrative Theory in Education,* ed. Andrew W. Halpin (Chicago: Midwest Administration Center, University of Chicago, 1958).

SOME FORMAL ORGANIZATION CHARACTERISTICS. The formal organization, sometimes called the formal group, has the following characteristics as contrasted with the informal group:

1. Each member of the organization usually is not able to interact with every other member.
2. The formal organization is usually structured by external authority or by a suprasystem.
3. The holders of positions of status in the organization are usually determined by external authority or by the suprasystem.
4. The tasks, goals, and purposes of the group may be determined in part by authority external to the group.
5. It usually has an officially prescribed hierarchical structure.

There are many variations in types of human groups other than those identified above. For example, a state education association is a voluntary group with some of the characteristics of an informal group and some of a formal organization. Attention was directed in Chapter 4 to four types of formal organizations based on who benefits. It would require an extensive treatment to present a comprehensive analysis of all types of human groups. Much of the research on leadership has been done in small informal groups and only a limited amount in large formal organizations. However, all educational administrators deal with informal groups as well as with a formal organization. Furthermore, if the assumptions back of general systems theory are valid, it is possible that more of the findings concerning leadership in small groups are applicable to leadership in formal organizations than has been assumed by some behavioral scientists. Therefore, in the next section we will examine some group phenomena that are important to an understanding of leadership.

THE GROUP

School administrators spend much of their time working with groups. The most effective administrators are leaders as well as holders of "headships." Effective administrative leadership involves an understanding of the behavior of people in groups. Many studies of group behavior and structure have been made. Some principal findings of one of the most significant of these studies, that of Homans, are presented in the following paragraphs.[20]

[20]George C. Homans, *The Human Group* (New York: Harcourt, Brace & World, Inc., 1950).

The Human Group

Homans, after studying numerous small groups sometimes called "face-to-face groups," concluded that the underlying human relationships differ from group to group in degree rather than kind. This concept is of great significance because, if it is valid, it is possible to make a systematic analysis of group behavior.

Each group is conceived of as having a boundary, outside of which lies the group environment. Each person may belong to many different groups, and large groups may be subdivided into smaller groups and cliques. Each group has an external environment that differs for every group, and the behavior of each group must be such that it can survive in its environment.

The elements of the behavior of a group are sentiment, activity, and interaction. These elements are all mutually interdependent. Homans analyzed these elements of behavior with respect to the external and internal systems of the group, these two systems together being conceived of as making up the total social system.

The sentiment, activity, and interaction of a group are conditioned by the external environment of the group. That is why Homans calls it the external system. Sentiment in the external system is defined as the motives, drives, and attitudes that individual group members bring to the group from the external environment. Activity in the external system is defined as the activities demanded by the job. The environment conditions the behavior of the group, but the group will in turn attempt to change its environment in order to survive. For instance, the behavior of a school faculty is certainly affected by its environment. But the faculty will attempt to change its environment with respect to salary, tenure, community attitudes, and working conditions if it feels this to be necessary for survival. Thus, in the external system of the group, the elements of sentiment, activity, and interaction are mutually dependent and are in constant flux. These elements are being conditioned by the external environment, and the group is changing its environment. Therefore, the entire external system of the group is constantly changing.

Homans then examined these same three elements of behavior in the internal system of the group. He defines the internal system as "group behavior that is an expression of the sentiments toward one another developed by members of the group in the course of their life together."[21] The life together of the group could be considered the internal environment of the group as contrasted with the external environment. Sentiment, activ-

[21] *Ibid.*, p. 110.

ity, and interaction are also mutually dependent in the internal system. Sentiment in the internal system is defined as the feelings that people develop toward each other and their group as they work together. As a group works together, it develops norms as part of the internal system. A norm is "an idea in the minds of the members of a group, an idea that can be put in the form of a statement specifying what the members or other men should do, ought to do, are expected to do, under given circumstances."[22] Since norms and the various elements of behavior in the internal system are all mutually dependent, the internal system of a group is constantly changing. But this is not all, because the total internal system of the group affects the total external system, and vice versa. Therefore, the total social system of a group is constantly changing.

Homans presented some hypotheses concerning these interactions that are of great significance to the understanding of leadership. Some of these hypotheses are as follows:

1. If the frequency of interaction between two or more persons increases, the degree of their liking for one another will increase, and vice versa.
2. If the interactions between the members of the group are frequent in the external system, sentiments of liking will grow up between them, and these sentiments will lead in turn to further interactions over and above the interactions of the external system.
3. A decrease in the frequency of interaction between the members of a group and outsiders, accompanied by an increase in the strength of their negative sentiments toward outsiders, will increase the frequency of interaction and the strength of positive sentiments among the members of a group, and vice versa.[23]

Let us apply these hypotheses to a school. We might generalize as follows:

1. The more all people—faculty, students, and parents—interact with each other, the more opportunity they have to like each other.
2. Sentiments of liking grow up between teachers and administrators who work on the job together, and these sentiments will lead to other activity beyond the requirements of the job.
3. If the communications between a faculty group and a community group are reduced and this lessening of communications is accompanied by an increase in the negative sentiments of each group toward the other, then the members of each group are drawn closer together, but intergroup hostility is increased.

[22] *Ibid.*, p. 123.
[23] *Ibid.*, p. 112–113.

Let us apply this same reasoning to the relationships between the superintendent or principal and the teacher group. If the administrator is not accepted by the teachers as a member of the teacher group, then he is an outsider and a part of the external environment of the group. As already pointed out, a group has sentiments and norms in its internal system. A group endeavors to survive in its environment. In order to do so, it protects its norms and sentiments. Any attack on these norms and sentiments, especially from an outsider, solidifies the group and develops negative group sentiments toward the source of the attack. If a member of a group violates or offends the norms and sentiments of the group, the group itself disciplines the group member. The group may discipline the administrator by making him an "outsider."

But group norms and sentiments are not likely to be positively changed by interaction unless the sentiment climate is positive. This seems to be a defect in Homans' hypotheses. He assumes that the liking of group members for each other will always increase as interactions increase. It is conceivable that the negative sentiments of group members for each other might increase with an increase in interactions if the climate of the group is such as to stimulate negative sentiments.

Summarizing: Human society is composed of innumerable groups, each with a different environment. But all groups have certain common elements of behavior, and those elements are sentiment, activity, and interaction. The elements of behavior differ in degree in each group, but they are always present and mutually dependent. In the external system of the group, each element of behavior conditions the other; the external environment conditions the elements of behavior, and the group conditions its environment. In the internal system, each element of behavior conditions the other; interactions produce group norms, and the internal and external systems of the group are mutually dependent. Within a formal organization such as a large school system, groups tend to increase in number. For instance, the board, the superintendent and his central staff, the principals, and the teachers might each be a tight, separate group. This is especially true if interactions between these groups are minimized. In addition, there will be innumerable informal groups.

Homans' remarkable work has become a landmark in the study of leadership. He was the first to make extensive use of systems theory in the study of groups. There have been numerous studies of groups since Homans' original study, but that study has had more influence on the conceptualization of group phenomena than any other study.

Research on Group Characteristics

Behavioral scientists have formulated a number of hypotheses based on evidence produced by research on group behavior. Following are some hypotheses proposed by Berelson and Steiner, which they derived from their inventory of scientific findings in the behavioral sciences:

1. A small group after discussion finds a more satisfactory solution to a problem than individuals working alone when the problem is technical rather than attitudinal, when a range of possible solutions is available, when the task requires each member to make a judgment, when rewards and punishments are given to the group as a whole, when the information and skills needed are additive, when the task can be subdivided, and when the task includes "traps" that might be missed by individuals.[24]
2. Active participation in the communicating itself is more effective for persuasion and retaining information than is the passive reception of information.[25]
3. The more people associate with one another under conditions of equality, the more they come to share values and norms and the more they come to like one another.[26]
4. The more interaction or overlap there is between related groups, the more similar they become in their norms and values; the less communication or interaction between them, the more tendency there is for conflict to arise between them. And vice versa; the more conflict, the less interaction.[27]

SOME GENERALIZATIONS ON LEADERSHIP

A number of generalizations and hypotheses concerning leadership have developed from studies in this area. Although these propositions have not all been fully confirmed by research, they are worthy of study.

Generalizations Proposed by Myers

As has already been pointed out, a great number of studies have been made of leadership and the relationship of leadership to the group. Myers, after making an extensive analysis of these studies, proposed the following generalizations which are supported by two or more studies:

1. Leadership is the product of interaction, not status or position.
2. Leadership cannot be structured in advance. The uniqueness of each combination of persons, of varying interactional patterns and of varying goals and means, and of varying forces within and without impinging upon the group will bring forth different leaders.
3. A leader in one situation will not automatically be a leader in another situation.

---

[24] Adapted from Bernard Berelson and Gary A. Steiner, *Human Behavior: An Inventory of Scientific Findings* (New York: Harcourt, Brace & World, Inc., 1964), p. 355.
[25] *Ibid.*, p. 548, adapted.
[26] *Ibid.*, p. 327.
[27] *Ibid.*, p. 331.

4. Leadership does not result from a status position, but rather [from] how a person behaves in the organization.
5. Whether a person is a leader in a group depends upon the group's perception of him.
6. The way a leader perceives his role determines his actions.
7. Most groups have more than one person occupying the leadership role.
8. Leadership fosters positive sentiments toward the group activity and persons in the group.
9. Leadership may be democratic or autocratic but never laissez-faire.
10. Leadership protects the critical group norms.
11. Leadership is authority rendered to some who are perceived by others as the proper persons to carry out the particular leadership role of the group.
12. Program development that involves only persons of a single position (such as principals, or supervisors, or teachers) is not as comprehensive or lasting as that which involves people of various positions in the organization.[28]

Although each of these generalizations is supported by some research, it must not be assumed that each generalization is completely valid. Much additional research needs to be done for the further validation of these and other generalizations.

Some Hypotheses Formulated by Berelson and Steiner

Berelson and Steiner made an extensive survey of the scientific findings in the behavioral sciences and formulated a number of propositions and hypotheses. Following are a few of their most important formulations related to leadership in small groups:

1. The closer an individual conforms to the accepted norms of the group, the better liked he will be; the better liked he is, the closer he conforms; the less he conforms, the more disliked he will be.
2. The higher the rank of the member within the group, the more central he will be in the group's interaction and the more influential he will be.
3. In general, the "style" of the leader is determined more by the expectations of the membership and the requirements of the situation than by the personal traits of the leader himself.

[28]Robert B. Myers, "A Synthesis of Research in Leadership" (Unpublished paper presented to A.S.C.D., Mar. 1957), pp. 4–9.

4. The leadership of the group tends to be vested in the member who most closely conforms to the standards of the group on the matter in question, or who has the most information and skill related to the activities of the group.
5. When groups have established norms, it is extremely difficult for a new leader, however capable, to shift the group's activities.
6. The longer the life of the leadership, the less open and free the communication within the group and probably the less efficient the group in the solution of new problems.
7. The leader will be followed more faithfully the more he makes it possible for the members to achieve their private goals, along with the group's goals.
8. Active leadership is characteristic of groups that determine their own activities, passive leadership of groups whose activities are externally imposed.
9. In a small group, authoritarian leadership is less effective than democratic leadership in holding the group together and getting its work done.[29]

Berelson and Steiner also formulated some hypotheses concerning leadership in organizations. However, these authors did not distinguish between leaders as defined early in this chapter and holders of power positions in the hierarchy of an organization. But their formulations do point up some of the difficulties of an executive in the hierarchy when he attempts to provide leadership. They point out that holders of intermediate positions in the hierarchy are under pressure from their superiors for productivity and under pressure from their subordinates for human consideration, and this cross-pressure is the source of actual or potential conflict in their behavior.[30] Following are a few of the hypotheses proposed by Berelson and Steiner relating to leadership (more properly, headship) in formal organizations:

1. The leader's style of leadership tends to be influenced by the style in which he is led.
2. The more the member holds to the organization's professed values, the more likely he is to be promoted within the organization.
3. The requirements for organizational leadership change with the life of the organization: at the start the leader is characterized more by doctri-

---

[29]Bernard Berelson and Gary A. Steiner, *Human Behavior: An Inventory of Scientific Findings* (New York: Harcourt, Brace & World, Inc., 1964), pp. 341–344. NOTE: This important work should be read by every serious student of administration.
[30]*Ibid.*, p. 372.

nal loyalty, aggressiveness, and personal quality ("the charismatic leader"); later, when the organization is well established, by administrative skills ("the bureaucratic leader").

4. Within an organization, conflict between leader and subordinates tends to increase the number and the concreteness of the organization's regulations, and vice versa—i.e., regulations go along with conflict.[31]

Although these hypotheses relate to management rather than leadership, they are quite provocative.

Homans' Exchange Theory of Leadership Determination

Homans has developed an interesting theory of exchange for explaining social behavior.[32] It can be used to explain when a person decides to lead and when he decides to follow. The exchange theory is a complex formulation. Homans attempts to explain behavior in terms of costs incurred and rewards exchanged by actors interacting in a social system. He incorporates some of the market exchange concepts from economics and reinforcement concepts from psychology. Exchange theory incorporates four basic concepts: reward, cost, outcome, and comparison level.

Let us apply these concepts to a leadership situation. Let us assume that an actor in a group is contemplating initiating a leadership act in a problem situation. He considers what rewards he may receive if he provides leadership in terms of increased status, need for dominance, desire to see the problem solved, etc. He then considers the cost in terms of loss of status if the group rejects him or his solution fails, increased effort and responsibility on his part, etc. He then attempts to determine the outcome by subtracting the costs from the rewards. If the outcome is positive, it is a profit, and if negative, a loss. His decision to act will also depend on the comparison level. The profit must be sufficiently above a "break-even" point, and his past experiences in comparable situations must have been successful often enough for him to take the chance of leadership. The more frequently he has succeeded in leadership attempts in the past, the more likely is he to attempt another leadership act (reinforcement).

In a similar manner, the actor in a social system who decides to follow also seeks a fair exchange. He weighs the costs against the rewards, considers the qualifications of the person offering to lead, and how successfully he has led in similar situations in the past. He then decides whether there is a fair profit for him if he follows rather than leads.

[31] *Ibid.*, pp. 376–377.
[32] George C. Homans, *Social Behavior: Its Elementary Forms* (New York: Harcourt, Brace & World, Inc., 1961).

LEADERSHIP IN EDUCATIONAL ADMINISTRATION

An understanding of leadership, group phenomena, and systems theory is of vital importance to educational administrators. The job of the school administrator is much more complicated than the process of dealing with a primary group. He deals with many groups, both formal and informal, within and without the school system. Many of these groups have conflicting goals and purposes. In addition, he must operate within the limitations of statutory and constitutional law, both state and federal, and within the regulations of the state board of education and his own board of education. He is far from autonomous.

Campbell has described the conflicting expectations faced by administrators.[33] Different groups within the community and within the school system have different perceptions of the role that should be played by the administrator. The board of education also has its perception of the administrator's role. Individuals even within the same group have different perceptions of the role of the administrator. The administrator has his own perception of his role, and somehow he must reconcile all these differences in role perceptions. Therefore, many situational factors condition the behavior of the educational administrator.

The following paragraphs indicate the relationships of some of the concepts of leadership to educational administration presented earlier in this chapter.

A Model for the Study of Administrative Behavior

Halpin has proposed a model or paradigm for the study of administrator behavior in education.[34] He developed this model to facilitate research in administrative behavior and to contribute to the development of a theory of administration. This model has been useful in examining leadership theory as related to educational administration.

Halpin defines administration as a human activity with at least the following four components: (1) the task, (2) the formal organization, (3) the work group (or work groups), and (4) the leader (or leaders).[35]

Halpin points out that the Office of Strategic Services, Cartwright and Zander, Barnard, and others have defined the fundamental group goals as group achievement and group maintenance.[36] They also find that the group leader must be committed to these goals. Halpin then reasons that

---

[33]Campbell and Gregg, *Administrative Behavior in Education,* Chap. 7.
[34]Andrew W. Halpin, "A Paradigm for the Study of Administrative Research in Education," in *Administrative Behavior in Education,* ed. Campbell and Gregg (New York: Harper & Row, Publishers, 1957), Chap. 5.
[35]*Ibid.,* p. 161.
[36]*Ibid.,* p. 170.

leader behavior associated with group goals must be delineated. He accepts as the two major dimensions of leader behavior "initiating structure in interaction" and "consideration," dimensions that were identified by the Ohio State group.[37] A study was made by Halpin of the relationship between the two leader-behavior dimensions, initiating structure and consideration, and the two group goals, group achievement and group maintenance.[38] He found that effective leaders are those who score high on both dimensions of leader behavior.

Using these concepts, Halpin developed a paradigm for analyzing leader behavior.[39] He presented the paradigm in a series of diagrams. In brief outline form, the paradigm or model follows:

Panel I Organizational task
Panel II Administrator's perception of the organization's task
  1. Behavior as decision maker
  2. Behavior as group leader
Panel III Variables associated with administrator's behavior
  1. Administrator variables
  2. Intraorganization variables
  3. Extraorganization variables
Panel IV Criteria of administrator effectiveness
  1. Evaluation of administrator as decision maker
    a. Organization maintenance
    b. Organization achievement
  2. Evaluation of administrator as a group leader
    a. Organization maintenance
    b. Organization achievement[40]

This scheme was designed for studying the organization at Time A and Time B, and the change is used as a measure of leader effectiveness. This brief description does not do justice to the implications of the paradigm for the study of leader behavior, but it is sufficient to suggest the following relationships between the concepts of leadership presented earlier in this chapter and the job of educational administration:

[37]John K. Hemphill, et al., "Relation Between Task Relevant Information and Attempts to Lead," *Psychological Monographs*, 70, No. 7 (1956).
[38]Andrew W. Halpin, "Studies in Aircrew Composition III: The Combat Leader Behavior of B-29 Aircraft Commanders," HFORL MEMO No. TN–54–E (Washington, D.C.: Bolling Air Force Base, Human Factors Operations Research Laboratories, Air Research and Development Command, 1953).
[39]For a complete description see Andrew W. Halpin, "A Paradigm for the Study of Administrative Research in Education," in *Administrative Behavior in Education*, ed., Campbell and Gregg (New York: Harper & Row, Publishers, 1957), Chap. 5.
[40]*Ibid.*, adapted from Fig. 6, p. 190.

1. The school system's task may be largely defined by authorities external to the group by means of laws and regulations.
2. The administration's perception of the school system's task may be different than the perceptions of other members of the organization. This is a potential source of conflict.
3. Different groups within the system may have goals that are in conflict with the task of the organization. This is a potential source of difficulty.
4. The administrator, in order to be effective, must be a group leader, and this may be difficult if the goals of primary groups are in conflict with the goals of the formal organization. When such a situation occurs, informal organizations develop in order to achieve the goals of primary groups. The task of the administrator-leader is then to bring the formal and informal groups into congruence with respect to goals, if he is to be an effective leader.

Although Halpin developed his model some years ago, it is still useful for the study of administrative behavior when adapted to take into consideration the basic concepts of systems theory.

Coffey and Golden have made the following observations concerning the formal and informal structures:

> Along with the formal structure are the informal functions which have much less structure, are characterized by more spontaneous flow of interpersonal relationships, and are often effective in either aiding the formal structure in reaching goals or working as a very antagonistic core and in a private way against the public goals of the institution. An institution is likely to function more effectively and with greater satisfaction to its employees if the needs which are expressed in the informal social relationships are dealt with in the formal structure.[41]

The Administrative Process

Gregg has made an excellent analysis of the administrative process.[42] He describes the administrative process in terms of the following seven components: (1) decision making, (2) planning, (3) organizing, (4) communicating, (5) influencing, (6) coordinating, and (7) evaluating.

In describing each of his seven components, Gregg dealt with some of the concepts of leadership, group process, and human behavior. As he observed, "Leadership and group processes as well as the whole matter of human relations, are unquestionably important aspects of the administrative process."[43]

---

[41]Hubert S. Coffey and William P. Golden, Jr., *In-Service Education for Teachers, Supervisors, and Administrators,* Fifty-sixth Yearbook of the National Society for the Study of Education, Part I (Chicago: University of Chicago Press, 1957), pp. 101–102.
[42]Campbell and Gregg, *Administrative Behavior in Education,* Chap. 8.
[43]*Ibid.,* pp. 273–274.

There has been less emphasis in recent years on studying administrative processes as separate entities. As Gregg pointed out, these processes are all interrelated.[44] Fortunately, systems theory provides a framework by which the interrelationships of administrative processes may be studied. Gregg complained in 1957 that "Empirical research relating to the administrative process is notably lacking."[45] Unfortunately, the research in this area is still very meager. With greater use of systems theory, especially hypotheses that cut across various levels of social systems, more useful generalizations concerning administrative processes will surely be developed.

Power and Authority

There has been a tendency on the part of some to reject the terms "power" and "authority" as being inconsistent with democracy. Those who hold that belief seem to assume that if proper leadership is provided, power and authority are not essential to the social system. Let us take a look at power and authority.

For the purposes of this chapter, it is best to conceive of power in terms of behavior. Hunter has presented such a definition. Power, according to Hunter, is "the acts of men going about the business of moving other men to act in relation to themselves or in relation to organic or inorganic things"[46]

Dubin defines authority as "institutionalized power."[47] Simon defined authority in behavioral terms. According to him, "a subordinate may be said to accept authority whenever he permits his behavior to be guided by a decision reached by another, irrespective of his own judgment as to the merits of that decision."[48] Authority is always backed by power. Therefore, it might be said that a person has authority when he is perceived by the group to have the institutionalized right to "move other men to act in relation to themselves or in relation to organic or inorganic things."[49]

Griffiths has presented a thoughtful analysis of power and authority as affecting human relations.[50] Following are two of his conclusions con-

[44] *Ibid.*, p. 274.
[45] *Ibid.*, p. 316.
[46] Floyd Hunter, *Community Power Structure* (Chapel Hill: University of North Carolina Press, 1953).
[47] Robert Dubin, *et al., Human Relations in Administration* (Englewood Cliffs, N.J.: Prentice-Hall, Inc., 1951), p. 188.
[48] Herbert A. Simon, *Administrative Behavior* (New York: The Macmillan Company, 1951), p. 22.
[49] Hunter, *Community Power Structure.*
[50] Daniel E. Griffiths, *Human Relations in School Administration* (New York: Appleton-Century & Appleton-Century-Crofts, 1956), Chaps. 5 and 6.

cerning power which are of particular significance to the study of leadership:

1. Power is the cement which holds our society together as well as the societies of totalitarian states such as Soviet Russia and Nazi Germany. . . .
2. A democratic society is one in which the power command is held by a large number of people and is subject to the will of all of the people.[51]

We see that power cannot be ignored in a democracy any more than in an authoritarian state. School administrators certainly are not the only wielders of power in the school systems of the United States. Back of the superintendent is the board, and back of the board are the people. Teachers and pupils also have power in certain situations.

Wiles has pointed out that power is used differently by persons with different concepts of leadership.[52] He distinguishes between "power over" and "power with" the group. "A "power over" approach decreases the possiblities of releasing the full power of the group. It limits the potential accomplishment of the group."[53] Wiles states his concept of "power with" the group as follows:

> Under the group approach to leadership, a leader is not concerned with getting and maintaining personal authority. His chief purpose is to develop group power that will enable the group to accomplish its goal. He does not conceive of his power as something apart from the power of the group. He is concerned with developing the type of relationships that will give him "power with" the group.[54]

Wiles insists that there is greater control over group members under the "power with" approach, because the group itself will bring pressure to bear on individual group members to achieve group goals.[55] It should not be assumed, however, that Wiles is advocating a system in which the official leader of the group has nothing to do with power. On this point he states: "The official leader administers the controls the group imposes on itself."[56] This is perhaps the ideal for which to strive. However, as has

---

[51] *Ibid.*, p. 105.
[52] Kimball Wiles, *Supervision for Better Schools,* 2d ed. (Englewood Cliffs, N.J.: Prentice-Hall, Inc., 1955), pp. 161–167.
[53] *Ibid.*, p. 163.
[54] *Ibid.*, p. 164.
[55] *Ibid.*, p. 167.
[56] *Ibid.*, p. 223.

already been pointed out in this chapter, informal group goals are sometimes inconsistent with the goals of the total organization. In that event, the administrator may be compelled to resort to the "power over" approach, but this will reduce his acceptance as a leader. Therefore, one of the primary objectives of the administrator-leader must be to bring informal group goals and organizational goals into congruence.

Since authority in an organization is backed by institutionalized power, it cannot be exercised effectively unless the person exercising the authority is perceived by the members of the organization as having the right to do so. There are further limitations on authority. Griffiths makes this point:

> Although there is a line of authority in each organization, there are also modifying conditions which change the effectiveness of the power being exerted. We note that the authority of an administrator is affected and modified by the board of education, the teachers, non-teaching staff, parents, students, patrons, the state school law, the customs and traditions of the community, and the authority of the profession.[57]

This concept is also extremely important to each group within the school faculty. No school group is completely autonomous in authority. All school groups, both formal and informal, are subgroups of the total organization. The ultimate "group" that has the final authority to determine school goals is the people. Therefore, no group within a school system has the legal or moral right to consider itself a completely autonomous primary group. Participation in decision making by all groups and individuals concerned is now being widely advocated. As groups participate in decision making, it is vital that the limits of authority of each group be clearly defined. The administrator-leader must also make clear to groups and individuals participating in decision making the decisions that he reserves for executive decision making and the decisions in which they can share. To do otherwise would result in chaos. These implications are important for state school administration as well as for local school administration.

Areas of Critical Behavior

The School-Community Development Study Project, coordinated by the College of Education of the Ohio State University, identified nine areas of critical behavior of educational administrators.[58] Those areas are as

[57] Griffiths, *Human Relations,* p. 142.
[58] John A. Ramseyer, *et al.,* "Factors Affecting Educational Administration," Monograph No. 2 (Columbus, College of Education, Ohio State University, 1955), p. 20.

follows: (1) setting goals, (2) making policy, (3) determining roles, (4) appraising effectiveness, (5) coordinating administrative functions and structure, (6) working with community leadership to promote improvements in education, (7) using the educational resources of the community, (8) involving people, and (9) communicating.[59]

These nine areas were identified for the purpose of classifying observations of administrator behavior with respect to interpersonal and environmental factors that have been found to make a difference in administrator behavior. A conceptual scheme for studying administrator behavior was then developed, based upon these nine critical areas. This approach is contrasted with an approach to the study of administration based upon the application of learned technique. It has facilitated the development of research on administrator behavior. It is interesting to note that these nine critical areas of administrator behavior are closely related to several of the administrative processes identified by Gregg.

EXECUTIVE BEHAVIOR

The behavior of the executive (who may or may not be a leader) in the hierarchy is influenced by his own values or beliefs and by the values and beliefs of his superordinates. His behavior is also influenced by his environment and interaction with other actors in his organization and perhaps other factors. We are interested here, however, primarily in the values and beliefs of the executive and his superordinates and subordinates in the hierarchy. If his values and beliefs are in conflict with the values and beliefs of the mass of actors in the social system which he administers, conflict in the system is inevitable and the executive no longer is a leader in the social system. He may continue to hold a command position because of his institutionalized power but he is not a leader as defined in this chapter. At the present time many school superintendents and boards of education are in conflict with the classroom teachers in their systems. A number of college presidents are also in conflict with either their faculties or their students or both. In Chapter 4 we have already discussed McGregor's[60] Theory X and Theory Y relating to differing assumptions with respect to the nature of workers in the organization. If the executive of an organization assumes that Theory X describes the nature of most of the workers in his organization and the majority of these workers are more like Theory Y, destructive conflict will surely arise and the executive cannot be a leader in that organization. In the following paragraphs, a number of concepts and beliefs are presented which may affect favorably or unfavorably the leadership potential of the executive.

[59] *Ibid.*
[60] Douglas McGregor, *The Human Side of Enterprise* (New York: McGraw-Hill Book Company, Inc., 1960).

Scientific Management Theory

The public school system made great strides between 1900 and 1925. Public elementary and secondary education was well on its way to becoming available everywhere in the United States. Professional school administrators were employed to serve most of the larger school districts. A literature on school administration was being written. The words "efficient" and "businesslike" appeared frequently in that literature. The dynamic, bustling, aggressive administrator was confident that he could use the proven methods of business and industry to solve all the important problems of educational administration.

The "gospel of efficiency" dominated the thinking in the first third of the twentieth century.[61] Frederick Taylor, Henri Fayol, Luther Gulick, and Lyndall Urwick were all influential promoters of administrative and organizational efficiency. All these men, with the exception of Gulick, were identified primarily with engineering. The efficiency formulations developed by these men did not conceptualize human beings as living systems but rather as inanimate parts of an organization. Consequently, these men gave little emphasis to human relations and the interactions of social systems. They were concerned primarily with getting more from the workers, the managers, and the organizational structures, without giving much consideration to what happened to the human components of organizations.

Callahan[62] made a brilliant analysis of this movement in his study of the social forces that have shaped the administration of the public schools. He was particularly intrigued with the concepts of Taylor.[63] He described Taylor's system as follows:

> When Taylor introduced his system into any shop, his first step was to make a careful, detailed, and exhaustive study of the various aspects of the jobs being done. For example, in a machine shop Taylor would observe, time with a stop watch, and record the times of various motions of a group of the most skillful men in the shop. After studying his data, he would then select a worker he regarded as being potentially a first-class man, offer him a bonus for working faster, and experiment. He would combine what he regarded as the best and fastest movements for each phase of the work that he had observed, and eliminate all useless motion. The experimental first-class man would then be taught all the proper motions and Taylor would have him

---

[61]See Bertram M. Gross, "The Scientific Approach to Administration," Chap. 3 of *Behavioral Science and Educational Administration,* The Sixty-Third Yearbook of the National Society for the Study of Education (Chicago: University of Chicago Press, 1964).

[62]Raymond E. Callahan, *Education and the Cult of Efficiency* (Chicago: The University of Chicago Press, 1962).

[63]Frederick Taylor. *Scientific Management* (New York: Harper, 1912).

repeat the process until he had satisfied himself that the job was being done in the best and fastest manner. This procedure would then be standardized and one by one the other workers would be taught and required to use this system. His belief was that there was one best way of doing any job and this method could be determined only through the scientific study of that job by experts with proper implements, i.e., a stop watch and recording card.[64]

There was much resentment among factory workers both here and abroad to "Taylorism." These workers were relatively uneducated. Nevertheless, there have been attempts in school systems to establish teacher rating and merit pay for persons who were relatively well educated. Teachers generally have associated this practice with "Taylorism" and deeply resented it. This resentment has usually bred unproductive conflict and impaired or destroyed the leadership potential of the school executives responsible for inaugurating that policy.

Today there is a widespread demand for "accountability" and management by performance. Is this a revival of Taylorism? This question will be dealt with in more detail in Chapter 19.

The "Survival of the Fittest" Theories

The "survival of the fittest" theory of life reached a high point of acceptance during the latter part of the nineteenth century. It was even held by many to be the law of life. In fact, this theory has a powerful influence on the social thinking and actions of many people on the contemporary scene.

Malthus laid the foundation for the "survival of the fittest" theory in his famous *Essay on Population*, written in 1798. In that essay he stated the theory that poverty and distress were unavoidable, since population increases in geometric ratio whereas the food supply increases in arithmetic ratio. He accepted war, famine, and disease as necessary to human survival because the population must be kept in balance with the food supply.

Darwin, stimulated by the work of Malthus, wrote his *Origin of the Species* in 1859. He started with the assumption that more of each species are born than can possibly survive. The surplus starts a struggle for existence, and if any individual in the species varies in any way profitable to itself, it has a better chance of survival. Thus, the surviving individual has been "naturally selected."

[64]Callahan, *Education*, pp. 28–29.

The scientist Huxley supported and advanced still further the theories of Darwin in his *Struggle for Existence,* written in 1888. But the theories of Darwin and Huxley needed philosophical justification. This was done in masterly fashion by Nietzsche in *The Will to Power,* written in 1889. He looked upon life as a battle in which strength rather than goodness, pride rather than humility, unyielding intelligence rather than altruism, and power rather than justice are needed. He concluded that theories of equality and democracy had been disproven by the laws of selection and survival; therefore, democratic procedures were decadent.

The "survival of the fittest" theories gave rise in the latter part of the nineteenth century to a school of thought known as Social Darwinism.[65] Herbert Spencer, a brilliant English thinker, was the intellectual leader of this movement. His *First Principles,* published in 1864, *The Study of Sociology,* published in 1872–1873, as well as his other publications, were widely read in the United States.

The Social Darwinists applied Darwin's theories of biological evolution directly to social institutions and the life of man in society. The "struggle for existence" and "survival of the fittest" concepts suggested that natural law demanded that these factors be permitted to operate in human society or that society would degenerate. Competition would eliminate the unfit, and this would assure continuing improvement.

Is the school executive of a large, urban school system, with a concentration of disadvantaged minority groups, likely to provide the leadership needed to raise the educational level of these disadvantaged groups if he and his board hold a Social Darwinist point of view?

Ricardo, a close friend of Malthus, accepted Malthus' population theory (though not most of his economic theories) and published in 1817 a brilliant exposition of economic theory in *Principles of Political Economy.* Of interest here is Ricardo's "iron law" of wages. According to Ricardo, a worker should be paid only a subsistence wage, defined as a wage sufficient for the worker to survive and reproduce a sufficient number of workers to meet the needs of the economy. If a worker were paid wages above the subsistence level, the reproduction rate would increase to the point where a surplus of workers would be produced, which would drive wages back down to the subsistence level. At that level, poverty, misery, disease, and reduced reproductive activity would hold the number of workers down to the number needed. Ricardo saw little need for cooperation of workers with the managers and owners because, in his view, their interests were conflicting.

[65]Richard Hofstadter, *Social Darwinism in American Thought* (New York: George Brazeller, Inc., 1959).

Is an executive holding Ricardo's views likely to be perceived as a leader by the teacher and other employees of the school system?

Mutual-Aid Theories

It should not be thought that the "survival of the fittest" theory went completely unchallenged. Many voices were raised against the sweeping conclusions being drawn from this theory. Many religious leaders opposed the doctrine because of its association with the theory of evolution, which they considered atheistic. The fact of evolution could not be refuted, so the opposition of the ministry was not very effective.

Some intellectuals soon began to reveal the fallacies of Social Darwinism. The early pragmatists were among this group. In 1867, William T. Harris started the *Journal of Speculative Philosophy,* in which he and others attacked many of Spencer's propositions. The pragmatists accepted evolution but rejected Social Darwinism. William James, the famous philosopher and psychologist of Harvard University, first accepted Spencer, but by the middle 1870s he was exposing the fallacies of Spencer's theories.[66] The influence of John Dewey and his *Democracy in Education,* published in 1916, has already been mentioned. Dewey was greatly influenced by Harris and James.

Kropotkin, an anthropologist, wrote a series of essays between 1890 and 1896 in which he attacked some of the theories of Darwin and Huxley.[67] He rejected the Darwinian concept that the struggle for existence pitted every animal against every other animal of the same species. He contended that competition within the same species was of only limited value and that mutual aid was the best guarantee for existence and evolution. Kropotkin's conclusions were based on studies of conditions for survival of animals, savages, barbarians, a medieval city, and of the times in which he lived. He found that the unsociable species were doomed to decay. But the species that reduced to its lowest limits the individual struggle for existence and developed mutual aid to the greatest extent were the most numerous, the most prosperous, and the most likely to develop further. His studies of human beings, regardless of the stage of civilization, led to the same conclusions.

Montagu, another anthropologist, has also boldly challenged the Darwin-Huxley thesis that the nature of man's life is a conflict for the survival of the fittest. He assembled an array of evidence from the investi-

[66]*Ibid.,* p. 128.
[67]Peter Kropotkin, *Mutual Aid, A Factor of Evolution* (London: William Heinemann, Limited, 1902).

154 BASIC PRINCIPLES, CONCEPTS, AND ISSUES

gations of many scientists and concluded that the true nature of man's life is cooperation. He stated his position as follows:

> Evolution itself is a process which favors cooperating groups rather than dis-operating groups and "fitness" is a function of the group as a whole rather than of separate individuals. The fitness of the individual is largely derived from his membership in a group. The more cooperative the group, the greater is the fitness for survival which extends to all its members.[68]

He studied the researches of Allee on lower order animals[69] and concluded that animals confer distinct survival values on each other. For Montagu, the dominant principle of social life is cooperation and not the struggle for existence. The findings of Montagu are particularly significant because they are based on the researches of biologists, anthropologists, physiologists, psychologists, and many other scientists. He accepts the theory of evolution but insists that, for the human animal, the fitness to survive is based more on the ability to cooperate than on "tooth and claw." It is interesting to note that both Darwin and Huxley recognized in their later years the importance of cooperation in the evolutionary process, but many of their followers would have none of it. Nietzche died holding firmly to his thesis.

LaBarre, an anthropologist, has presented a synthesis of the sciences of man, an integration of human biology, cultural anthropology, psychiatry, and their related fields.[70] According to LaBarre, man is a polytypical anthropoid and not a polymorphous anthropod. The polytypical anthropoid is a species in which all individuals have essentially the same characteristics. A polymorphous anthropod is an insect species that has been structured into many physical castes by evolution. Each of these castes is a proper slave to the codified instincts of the hive. Since man is a polytypical anthropoid, he cannot grow maximally under a rigid caste or class system. Biologically, all men are brothers; therefore, man can grow best in a society of peers or equals.

He also concluded that racial traits have nothing to do with the survival of the individual or the races. Therefore, the ultimate survival of societies depends primarily on "what the people in them believe," and not

[68] Ashley Montagu, *On Being Human,* 2d ed. (New York: Hawthorn Books, 1966), p. 45.
[69] Ward C. Allee, *Animal Aggregations* (Chicago: University of Chicago Press, 1931).
[70] Weston LaBarre, *The Human Animal* (Chicago: University of Chicago Press, 1954), p. 225.

on physical differences. Social organisms are the means of survival of mankind. The findings of LaBarre support the thesis that the evolution and growth of mankind is primarily dependent on cooperative procedures which assume that all members of human society are essentially equal.

The executive who believes in the essential equality of all people and their potentiality for growth will tend to develop a cooperative organization in which he is a leader as well as an executive.

SOME IMPORTANT PROBLEMS AND ISSUES

The emerging concepts of leadership described in this chapter have great significance for administrative action. Some of the problems and issues associated with the application of these concepts are discussed in the following paragraphs.

Can a Person Be a Leader and at the Same Time Hold an Executive Position in an Organization?

Attention has already been directed to the fact that the executive holding a position in the hierarchy of an organization is under pressure from his superordinates to attain the goals of the organization, and he is under pressure from his subordinates to meet their personal needs (the nomothetic versus idiographic dimensions of the social system). Thompson commented as follows concerning this dilemma:

> Modern social scientists are coming to the conclusion that headship and leadership are incompatible or that their consolidation in the same hands is very unlikely. Leadership is a quality conferred upon a person by those who are led, and in this sense the leader is always elected. An appointed person on the other hand, must work to advance the interests of his sponsors. He cannot be a leader for his subordinates and still serve his sponsors, unless there is complete harmony between the two, an unlikely event.[71]

Is the situation as hopeless as Thompson implies? Would the application of the emerging pluralistic, collegial concepts of organization and administration help to resolve this dilemma? How does the exclusion of administrators from the AFT and NEA relate to this issue?

[71] Victor A. Thompson, *Modern Organization* (New York: Alfred A. Knopf, Inc., 1961), Reprinted by permission of Alfred A. Knopf, Inc., Copyright (c) 1961 by Victor Thompson.

Is There a Need for Role Differentiation Among Leaders?

Leadership acts include those acts intended to help meet group goals and also acts intended to maintain the group by meeting group and individual needs. Berelson and Steiner have pointed out that even in small face-to-face informal groups the "intellectual leader" who structures the group and initiates action to attain group goals is usually not the same person as the "social leader" who meets group and individual needs by promoting mutual acceptance, harmony, liking, etc.[72] That is, the top position in an informal group on both "liking" and "ideas" is not frequently held by the same person. If this hypothesis is sustained by research on informal face-to-face groups, can it be assumed that the same findings would be applicable to different leadership roles in formal organizations? Some organizations have placed a "tough" man to say no as a second man to the top executive. Is the purpose of this arrangement to give a better image to the top executive, so that it will be possible for him to play a leadership role when the situation seems to require it? Despite the myth that the top executive in an organization must assume final responsibility, sometimes a subordinate in the executive hierarchy is sacrificed when a serious mistake has been made, in order to preserve the favorable image of the top executive. This policy has been justified because "it was for the good of the organization." What would be the long term effect of this policy on the leadership potential of the top executive?

What Officials Should Be Elected by the Group?

Research indicates that if a group elects its head, the person elected is perceived by the group as being its leader. He is accepted by the group as a group member, and he is in a strategic position to provide leadership for the group. But research has also shown that the person chosen by a group to be its leader is likely to be the person who most nearly is representative of the norms of the group. Rate of production is one of the norms in a factory group. The production norm is the average rate of production that the group believes ought to be maintained. If a group member produces considerably more or considerably less than the group norm, he is not likely to be accepted by the group as its leader.

A school faculty is a formal school group, but the elements of behavior of a face-to-face formal group are similar in some respects to the elements of behavior of a primary or informal group. The executive officer

---

[72] Berelson and Steiner, *Human Behavior*, pp. 244–245.

of the faculty is the school principal. The almost universal practice in the United States is for the principal to be appointed by the board of education upon the nomination of the superintendent. Considering the concepts of leadership presented in this chapter, should the present practice be continued, or would it be better for the principal to be elected by the faculty?

In some large high schools and in some institutions of higher learning, department heads are elected by the members of the department concerned. Is this good practice?

In some states the county superintendent of education, who is the executive officer of the board, is elected by the people. What are the advantages and disadvantages of this procedure?

The prevailing practice in the United States for the selection of board members is election by the vote of the people. The board of education is a legislative and policy-forming group. Do the concepts of leadership and group dynamics presented in this chapter justify that practice?

Committee members in school faculties are sometimes appointed by the principal and sometimes elected by the faculty. What criteria should be used to determine whether members of a committee should be elected or appointed?

When the Goals of Two Groups Are in Conflict, How Can They Be Harmonized?

Cooperative procedures involving group operation will very frequently result in conflict both within a group and among different groups. This is especially true if the membership of a group was deliberately selected to represent different points of view. However, conflict itself, if properly understood and dealt with, may present an opportunity for growth. Therefore, conflict can be either constructive or destructive. This point of view was originally presented by Mary Parker Follett in 1925.[73] Miss Follett was one of the pioneer thinkers in the field of human relations. In her great paper on constructive conflict, she advanced the point of view that the three main ways of dealing with conflict are domination, compromise, and integration.[74] Domination, the victory of one side over the other, is the easiest and quickest but the least successful method for dealing with conflict. Compromise, the most commonly used method, involves each side moderating its demands in order to have peace, neither side obtaining all its objectives. If the ideas of both sides are integrated into a solution

---

[73]Henry C. Metcalf and L. Urwick, eds., *Dynamic Administration, The Collected Papers of Mary Parker Follett* (New York: Harper & Row, Publishers, 1940).
[74]*Ibid.*, pp. 30–49.

that encompasses the desires of both sides, the highest level of dealing with conflict is reached. Miss Follett's illustration of her point is worthy of repetition here.

It seems that a dairymen's cooperative league was on the point of breaking up over the question of precedence of unloading. The creamery was located on the side of a hill. The men who came uphill thought that they should have precedence, but the men who came downhill thought their claims to precedence were stronger. If the method of domination had been followed, one side or the other would have been given precedence. If the matter had been compromised, the uphillers and downhillers would each have been given precedence on alternate days. But a consultant suggested that the platform be so arranged that unloading could be done on both sides, in order that the uphillers could unload on one side and the downhillers on the other. This solution was adopted. Each side got what it wanted, and the conflict was resolved. She pointed out that thinking is too often confined between the walls of two possibilities. The integrator is inventive and examines all possible alternatives, not just the ones being advocated by the parties in conflict.

Unfortunately, more differences are settled by compromise than by integration. Undoubtedly, conflicts have been resolved many times by compromise when the possibilities of developing integrated solutions had not been fully explored. Incidentally, Nehru once suggested that compromise that represents a step toward attaining a desirable objective may be good; compromise that results in abandoning an objective or substituting an inferior principle may be bad. The most effective groups, however, will not resort to compromise to resolve conflicts without first attempting to find an integrated solution.

Conflict is destructive when it continues or increases social disorganization or is damaging to individual personalities. Conflict is constructive when it can serve as the impetus for growth in human relations and for bringing about desirable change.

What should be the role of the administrator in resolving conflicts? What procedures can be used to help groups grow in their ability to resolve conflicts constructively? Under what conditions are destructive conflicts likely to be encountered in educational organizations?

What Is the Relation Between Group Morale and Task Achievement in the Formal Organization?

Let us first consider informal groups that are subgroups of the formal organization. Each informal group, as has been pointed out, has two principal goals: group achievement and group maintenance. Each group defines its own achievement goals. The group maintenance goal is attained when both group and individual needs are substantially met and members get satisfaction from group membership. When a group continues to attain its two primary goals, the morale is high; but if it fails, the morale is low. An informal group with high morale is more productive in terms of its own standards of measuring production than a low-morale group. However, a high-morale group may not be productive as measured by the achievement of the tasks of the organization.

Let us now consider the formal organization of which the informal groups are subparts. The formal organization also has two principal functions: achievement of its goals and organizational maintenance. Let us assume, for example, that we have a formal organization such as a school faculty that has no real achievement goals accepted by its members. Let us assume further that the formal organization has been ineffective in meeting group and individual needs. In fact, the formal organization is not an entity, but rather a collection of individuals subdivided into primary groups and cliques. The informal organization, rather than the formal organization, holds the real power and authority. The morale of the actors in this organization is low.

What can the administrator-leader do to make the formal organization a real group?

How Can the Administrator-Leader Bring About Change and Innovations?

The public school system must constantly change its tasks, goals, and purposes if it is to meet the changing needs of society. This involves changes in the curriculum, the organizational structure, and the services provided. But the administrator always encounters some resistance to change. This is especially true if the changes conflict with critical group norms or threaten the status roles of individuals in the organization. But the administrator, if he is to be a leader, cannot assume a laissez-faire role and avoid change, because change is inevitable. On the other hand, if the administrator in bringing about change ignores certain vital factors of human relations, he will lose the leadership of his group. Under what conditions can institutional changes be made? Coffey and Golden, after an extensive review of applicable research, suggested the following conditions for facilitating organizational change:

> (a) When the leadership is democratic and the group members have freedom to participate in the decision-making process; (b) when there have been norms established which make social change an expected aspect of institutional growth; (c) when change can be brought about without jeopardizing

the individual's membership in the group; (d) when the group concerned has a strong sense of belongingness, when it is attractive to its members, and when it is concerned with satisfying member needs; (e) when the group members actually participate in the leadership function, help formulate the goals, plan the steps toward goal realization, and participate in the evaluation of these aspects of leadership; (f) when the level of cohesion permits members of the group to express themselves freely and to test new roles by trying out new behaviors and attitudes without being threatened by real consequence.[75]

Recently, there has been much interest in planned change. Bennis, Benne, and Chin and their associates have presented a design for planned change.[76] Under this concept there is "... the application of systematic and appropriate knowledge to human affairs for the purpose of creating intelligent action and change."[77] The process involves the deliberate collaboration of the change agent and the client system. These authors objected to the conceptualization of a change agent exclusively as a "free" agent brought in as a consultant from outside the client system. They comment on this issue as follows:

> For one thing, client systems contain the potential resources for creating their own planned change programs under certain conditions; they have inside resources, staff persons, applied researchers, and administrators who can and do act as successful change agents. For another thing, we contend that a client system must build into its own structures a vigorous change-agent function, in order for it to adapt to a continually changing environment.[78]

Is the change-agent role a leadership role when the change is made with the "willing cooperation" of the members of the client system? What theoretical concepts discussed in this chapter can be used to predict the by-products of imposing change on a group against its will? Should outside consultants be used as change agents as well as personnel within an organization?

[75]National Society for the Study of Education, pp. 101–102.
[76]Warren G. Bennis, Kenneth D. Benne, and Robert Chin, eds., *The Planning of Change* (New York: Holt, Rinehart & Winston, Inc., 1961).
[77]*Ibid.*, p. 3.
[78]*Ibid.*

SELECTED REFERENCES

Annese, L. E., "Principal as a Change Agent," *The Clearing House,* Vol. 45, Jan. 1971, pp. 273–277.

Bennis, Warren G., Kenneth D. Benne, and Robert Chin, *The Planning of Change.* New York: Holt, Rinehart & Winston, Inc., 1961.

Berelson, Bernard, and Gary A. Steiner, *Human Behavior: An Inventory of Scientific Findings.* New York: Harcourt, Brace & World, Inc., 1964.

Blanchard, K. H. and P. Hersey, "Leadership Theory for Educational Administrators," *Education,* Vol. 90, April 1970, pp. 303–310.

Carlson, Richard O., Art Gallaher, Jr., Mathew B. Miles, Roland J. Pellegrin, and Everett M. Rogers, *Change Processes in the Public Schools.* Eugene, Ore.: Center for the Advanced Study of Educational Administration, University of Oregon, 1965.

Cartwright, Darwin, and Alvin Zander, *Group Dynamics: Research and Theory.* New York: Harper & Row, Publishers, 1960.

Eagly, A. H., "Leadership Style and Role Differentiation as Determinants of Group Effectiveness," *Journal of Personality,* Vol. 38, Dec. 1970, pp. 509–524.

Fantini, Mario and M. A. Young, *Designing Education for Tomorrow's Cities.* New York: Holt, Rinehart & Winston, Inc., 1970.

Granger, Robert L., *Educational Leadership.* Scranton, Pa.: Intext Educational Publishers, 1971.

Griffiths, Daniel E., ed., *Behavioral Science and Educational Administration.* The Sixty-third Yearbook of the National Society for the Study of Education. Chicago: University of Chicago Press, 1965.

Hare, A. Paul, Edgar F. Borgatta, and Robert F. Bales, *Small Groups: Studies in Social Interaction.* New York: Alfred A. Knopf, Inc., 1965.

Homans, George C., *The Human Group.* New York: Harcourt, Brace & World, Inc., 1950.

_____, *Social Behavior: Its Elementary Forms.* New York: Harcourt, Brace & World, Inc., 1961.

Innaccone, Lawrence and F. W. Lutz, *Politics, Power, and Policy: The Governing of School Districts.* Columbus: Charles E. Merrill, 1970.

Johns, R. L. and Ralph Kimbrough, *The Relationship of Socioeconomic Factors, Educational Leadership Patterns and Elements of Community Power Structure to Local School Fiscal Policy.* Washington, D.C.: Office of Education, U.S. Department of Health, Education and Welfare, May 1968.

Kimbrough, Ralph B., *Political Power and Educational Decision-Making.* Skokie, Ill.: Rand McNally & Company, 1964.

Nunnery, M. Y. and R. B. Kimbrough, *Politics, Power, Polls, and School Elections.* Berkeley: McCutchan Publishing Corporation, 1971.

Petrullo, Luigi, and Bernard M. Bass, eds., *Leadership and Interpersonal Behavior.* New York: Holt, Rinehart & Winston, Inc., 1961.

Secord, Paul F., and Carl W. Backman, *Social Psychology.* New York: McGraw-Hill Book Company, 1964.

6

Planning and Effecting Improvements in Education*

Most people would probably agree that the schools and other educational institutions have made many significant contributions to the development of this nation. But several writers have noted recently that there seems to be a growing feeling of frustration—what some have called a *crisis of confidence* in public education—apparently partly because some important needs of this complex and rapidly changing society are not being met satisfactorily, and the inequities and inadequacies are being more clearly recognized than at any previous time. Many people have reached the conclusion that some major improvements in education are urgently needed, and that merely continuing to increase expenditures for present provisions or programs will not resolve basic problems. In most states and communities, however, there seem to be wide differences of opinion con-

*Prepared with the collaboration of DAVID L. JESSER, Associate Director, Improving State Leadership in Education, Denver, Colorado.

cerning what changes should be made in education; how needed changes should be made; and whether some of the changes that have been proposed would actually result in significant improvements. Such differences in perspectives and opinions cannot be resolved either quickly or easily in a pluralistic society.

As noted in Chapter 1, the leaders and usually most of the people in every society and nation recognize some important purposes and goals that should be attained through education. In this country these include: (1) helping to transmit to the children and youth the major concepts and elements of the cultural heritage in a manner that will enable them not only to understand and respect earlier traditions and values but also to recognize that some of these have been modified, and that others will need to be modified to meet the needs of a changing society; and (2) helping the present and future generations to learn to make the constructive adjustments that will enable them to live creatively in a changing society and to contribute effectively to any changes that are made.

Many people seem to be convinced that present educational policies and procedures are not contributing effectively to the achievement of these or similar purposes. The evidence available seems to support this point of view, as indicated by these generally accepted observations:

- Some young people are progressing through their school years without learning even to read perceptively, and many are not prepared to become productive members of society.
- Not enough of the educational effort is being directed to those who need it the most—the poor and disadvantaged.
- The methods of financing education in most states are grossly inequitable and indefensible for many taxpayers and often result in discrimination against students in the less wealthy areas.
- Many parents and other lay citizens are seeking—but have not yet found— meaningful ways to participate effectively in the decision-making processes relating to education.

In terms of what is now known about social systems (see Chapter 3), leadership (see Chapter 5), provisions for relevant learning (see Chapter 14), and deficiencies and problems in education—many of which have existed for some time and cannot easily or quickly be resolved—everyone should recognize that some major changes are urgently needed in many aspects of education. However, these changes *should be coordinated* (not made just in one aspect without considering the implications for other aspects) *and systematically planned.* They should not be made merely because they are proposed by a prestigious group or person, or seem to make some minor improvements possible. In the planning process, appropriate attention will need to be given to long-range goals and priorities as well as to goals and objectives that can and should be attained within a relatively short period of time. Finally, those concerned with planning improvements in education need to recognize that competent lay as well as educational leaders must be involved at least in the process of determining goals and major policies because these goals and policies must be accepted by the public before they can be utilized for guidance in effecting any significant changes in education.

RATIONALE AND BASIC CONSIDERATIONS

If educators, board members, legislators, and other concerned citizens are to cooperate effectively in planning and effecting changes that will result in significant improvements in education, it will be necessary for all of them to understand and be willing to utilize appropriate processes in planning for and effecting those improvements. They need to know, for example, that:

- Modern planning is a logical and systematic process that differs significantly from the elementary kinds of procedures utilized during earlier years;
- In a *planning society* the people cooperatively determine their goals and appropriate ways of attaining them, whereas in a *planned society* the goals are determined for the people by their rulers or government;
- The goals of a democratic society are or should be social and economic goals concerned with the welfare and progress of all citizens, rather than selfish goals designed to promote or protect the concerns and privilieges of special-interest groups; and
- Cooperation means or implies the bona fide involvement of representative and perceptive lay citizens as well as educators in studying problems and needs and in agreeing on appropriate goals and optimum ways of attaining them, rather than merely accepting the goals and policies developed by a few educators or lay citizens.

Those involved in the processes of planning also need to understand that:

- Changes will occur with or without planning. However, by anticipating probable developments, we can prepare to facilitate needed changes and to avoid or mitigate some that might be harmful; and
- With appropriate planning procedures it is possible to identify maladjustments or deficiencies that are causing—or are likely to cause—educational problems, and thus enable those in decision-making roles to determine in advance what adjustments are necessary.[1]

[1] Adapted from Edgar L. Morphet and David L. Jesser, "The Future in the Present: Planning for Improvements in Education," in *Cooperative Planning for Education in 1980* (New York: Citation Press, Scholastic Magazines, Inc., 1968), p. 3.

Another important concept concerning the development of a defensible rationale for planning in and for education relates to the rather common practice of reacting primarily to crisis situations. Legislation has often been enacted in an effort to deal with some acute problem or to remedy some inequitable situation; school board regulations have often been formulated for similar reasons. Obviously, changes should be made when they are needed. But when changes are made on a piecemeal basis to deal with "crisis" situations and there is little or no recognition of the interrelationships between *present and future* needs, or the interrelatedness of the various components of the societal and educational systems are ignored, significant improvements in education are not likely to result from a long-range point of view.

Some Important Concepts and Guidelines

Some of the important and still relevant concepts and guidelines relating to educational planning developed three decades ago by the Council of Chief State School Officers are given below:

- The responsibility for leadership in planning educational programs properly belongs to and should be assumed by the regularly constituted educational agencies and authorities at the proper level.
- The planning procedure and process should be carefully formulated, unified, and systematically carried out.
- Educational planning should be recognized and carried out as an integral aspect of community, state, and national planning.
- Definite provision for planning must be made in educational agencies in order that planning may proceed satisfactorily and attain tangible results.
- One phase of educational planning should provide the basis for organized research; another should be built on and utilize fully the results of research.
- Educational planning must be thought of and established as a continuous process requiring constant adaptation of plans to meet emerging needs.
- Educational planning to be functional must be realistic and practical but should not be needlessly limited by existing situations.
- All educational planning should involve the active and continuing participation of interested groups and organizations.
- The planning process should result in specific recommendations which are understood and accepted by those who are participating.
- Provision for continuing evaluation of the planning process [and products] is basic.[2]

[2]From report on *Planning and Developing Adequate State Programs of Education* by the Study Commission on State Educational Problems, as approved by the National Council of Chief State School Officers. Published in *Education for Victory*. Dec. 20, 1944, pp. 15–16.

In 1947 representatives from 14 Southern states with the cooperation of several national consultants prepared and published a comprehensive volume concerned with planning and effecting improvements in education that included the following pertinent comments:

- A better world [and] a better nation ... can be built through education. But that must be an education which is geared to change. It must be an education which is deliberately designed to meet the needs of the people.
- More attention should be given to the development of comprehensive and well integrated plans [for the improvement of education].
- Planning should be projected in terms of the aims [and goals] of education and of society and therefore must take into consideration the [needs and interests of all] groups in the planning area.
- [State and local education agencies and every] planning committee should differentiate between plans for possible immediate attainment, those that should be implemented in the near future, and those that may require several years for accomplishment.
- The program of each[state and local] school system or educational institution should be evaluated in terms of its goals as related to valid goals for the state, region and nation.[3]

In 1949 the National Citizens Commission for the Public Schools was organized under the chairmanship of Roy E. Larsen of Time, Life and Fortune to encourage and assist lay citizens and educators throughout the nation to cooperate in improving the schools in their communities and states. A few years later, the National Society for the Study of Education, with the cooperation of members of the National Citizens Commission and educators who had worked with the commission, published the yearbook *Citizen Cooperation for Better Public Schools*[4] that included numerous suggestions relating to cooperative procedures for improving education.

As one result of these efforts, during the decade beginning about 1945, nearly one fifth of the states and numerous local school systems utilized these or similar conceptual guidelines as a basis for conducting cooperative studies and developing plans that, in most cases, resulted in important improvements in their provisions for education.

[3] *Building a Better Southern Region Through Education:* Southern States Work Conference on Educational Problems, Edgar L. Morphet, Executive Secretary and Editor. (Tallahassee, Florida: State Department of Education, 1947), pp. 57–60.
[4] *Citizen Cooperation for Better Public Schools,* Fifty-third Yearbook of the National Society for the Study of Education, Part I. Edgar L. Morphet, Chairman (Chicago: University of Chicago Press, 1954).

PREPARING TO PLAN SYSTEMATICALLY

With some notable exceptions, most educational planning until recently has been of the short-range type (usually for one or two years except for population and related projections), often has been closely related to the traditional annual or biennial budgets, and has been concerned primarily with certain aspects of education. But this situation has changed significantly during the past few years as a result of several developments including: (1) many more people are interested in and understand the importance of systematic planning; (2) the kinds of information essential for effective planning can now be more readily obtained; (3) more competent personnel are available to assist with the technical as well as the human relations aspects of planning; (4) there is a better understanding of the need for clearly stated and acceptable goals; and (5) better means are available for selecting and utilizing the best alternatives for attaining those goals.

In recent years state and local boards and administrators have been confronted with many demands and pressures for changes in the curriculum, instruction, provisions for financial support—in fact, in almost every aspect of education. Such demands by various and diverse publics obviously reflect areas of concern that must be seriously and carefully considered by administrators and board members. However, if changes are effected only in response to crisis-type situations, some of the basic problems may not be resolved. Moreover, unless serious consideration is given to organizational structures and procedures that are conducive to effective planning, these changes are not likely to result in significant long-range improvements. If constructive and lasting improvements are to be effected, it is essential that a conscious and concerted effort be made by every state and local education agency to develop (1) an organization that will facilitate bona fide planning, and (2) procedures that will support effective planning processes. In other words, these agencies will need not only a properly staffed unit concerned with planning, but also the resources needed to ensure effective planning.

In a changing society everyone interested in planning and effecting improvements in education must be concerned not only with current problems and needs but also with the implications for education of prospective changes in society. Although many aspects of the future cannot be accurately *predicted,* it is possible to utilize appropriate information and insights as a basis for *forecasting* and considering the effects of probable and alternative developments in society[5] and some of the major implications for

---

[5]For example, see discussion by Richard C. Lonsdale in Edgar L. Morphet and David L. Jesser, eds. *Preparing Educators to Meet Emerging Needs,* (New York: Citation Press, 1969), pp. 19–31, and the footnote references at end of the chapter.

education. For example, Harman[6] has utilized this macro-view approach as a basis for considering some of the implications for education if society during the next few decades (1) merely moves into a later stage of industrialization, or (2) becomes increasingly concerned with individuals and their development (as seems probable on the basis of recent developments).

Kinds of Planning

Many of the recent controversies about various aspects of education (including the limited progress made by some students, integration, and school finance) have tended to divert attention from the basic issue: *What kind and quality of education is essential to meet present and emerging needs, and how can it best and most effectively be provided?* The most promising procedure for resolving this issue seems to be through perceptive leadership and systematic, comprehensive, long-range planning *with* rather than *for* people.

Culbertson[7] has noted that there are essentially two interrelated kinds of systematic planning, each of which has different purposes: strategic planning and management planning. Each of these may be utilized for both long- and short-range planning, as well as for comprehensive planning or planning concerned with some aspect of education. Moreover, each includes the concept of contingency planning (developing defensible alternatives that can be utilized if unanticipated circumstances arise).

Strategic planning, which fosters and requires productive relations and linkages with public agencies and groups other than those directly responsible for education, should receive primary attention because it involves the determination of policies and the establishment of new or revised goals and objectives. This concept should be of special interest to educational leaders who have a major responsibility for developing and implementing plans because, if properly utilized, it will help to ensure the commitment and support that is essential to facilitate needed changes.

Management planning, on the other hand, is concerned with the effective and efficient attainment of goals and objectives that have been agreed upon and accepted. It may, therefore, be conceptualized as that portion of the planning process that is implemented *after* the basic decisions relating to goals and policies have been made. Through appropriate management planning, those responsible for the implementation of these decisions should be able to ensure that all goals and objectives are achieved.

[6]Willis W. Harman, "The Nature of Our Changing Society: Implications for Schools" (Prepared for the ERIC Clearinghouse on Educational Administration, Eugene, Oregon, October 1969).
[7]Jack A. Culbertson, *et al., The Simulation of an Urban School System* (Columbus, Ohio: University Council for Educational Administration, 1971).

Everyone concerned with education needs to understand that strategic and management planning are interrelated in many ways and that, from a long-range point of view, the effectiveness and meaning of each will be determined primarily by the effectiveness and meaning of the other. Unless appropriate goals and policies are identified and accepted through strategic planning, even the most effective management planning will have limited significance. On the other hand, unless management planning ensures that the goals are effectively achieved and policies implemented, many of the potential dividends from strategic planning will be lost.

The Politics and Economics of Planning

As Bowles[8] has observed, when the problems of education are not solved within the system they are appealed to the public and the decision is ultimately in favor of the majority—that is, it is made through the political processes. Strategic planning involves political as well as other processes that can and should provide a rational and defensible basis for major decisions and, therefore, an opportunity for everyone concerned to consider most controversies and issues from a broader and more appropriate perspective or frame of reference than might otherwise be feasible.

Strategic planning should be considered a nonpartisan—rather than a partisan—political process. For example, there must be substantial agreement among the citizens of a state or local school system that such planning is essential if adequate resources are to be provided or utilized for that purpose. However, management planning and such essential matters as the collection and analysis of data should be considered primarily technical and nonpolitical in nature.

Planning requires funds and other resources that have seldom been available in adequate amounts to local school systems and state education agencies for that purpose. If such resources were available and utilized wisely in all school systems (1) the long-range social and economic benefits of gains in student learning and progress and in the more effective utilization of staff would probably exceed the planning costs, and (2) the meaningful involvement of competent citizens in the planning and decision-making processes should result in broadening the base for the support of education in some areas.

Fortunately, through some of the provisions of Title V of the Elementary and Secondary Act of 1965, rather substantial funds from federal sources have been made available to assist and encourage state education agencies and local school systems to improve their planning capabilities.

[8]Frank Bowles, *Educational Opportunity and Political Reality* (New York, N. Y.: Academy for Educational Development, Inc. Paper No. 2, 1965), pp. 2 and 11.

Moreover, several states have provided funds for that purpose. The purpose of one of the first federally funded projects under Section 505 of Title V (Designing Education for the Future) was to assist the people in the Rocky Mountain and Great Basin area to

> ... anticipate the changes that are likely to take place in this country, in the eight-state area, and within each state during the next ten to fifteen years, and to plan and implement changes and improvements that should be made in the educational organization and program during that period.[9]

Another project among several funded under the same section (the Comprehensive Planning Project) was authorized to assist six states and Puerto Rico to cooperate in developing strategies for bringing together dispersed planning functions in an effort to develop a comprehensive and integrated educational program in each state, and especially to effect "the maximum utilization of resources in the development of the state educational program and for providing optimum services and leadership to the local school districts."[10]

Initiating the Planning Process

It is not easy to initiate comprehensive long-range strategic planning in a state or local school system in which the only experience has been with short-range planning primarily concerned with establishing or complying with minimum standards or with minor changes in one or a few aspects of education. In the first place, many people (probably including a substantial number of those involved in education) may not understand the value or importance of long-range planning. Moreover there may not be anyone in the system who is competent or has the insights and skills needed for successful cooperative planning. However, a number of states and local school systems, even with limited resources and many competing demands, have made substantial progress with planning.

In some states the planning has been initiated by action of the legislature or by the governor. In others, sometimes with the stimulus provided by federal funds available for planning, the state education agency has taken the initiative. In most states significant progress has been made in

---

[9]See Edgar L. Morphet, David L. Jesser, and Arthur P. Ludka, eds., *Emerging State Responsibilities for Education* (Denver, Colorado: Improving State Leadership in Education, 1970), p. 161.

[10]An account of the activities and programs in each of the seven participating states is given in Bernarr S. Furse and Lyle O. Wright, eds., *Comprehensive Planning in State Education Agencies* (Salt Lake City, Utah: Utah State Board of Education, 1967).

developing staff competency, in planning, and in helping local school systems with planning.

In any state that undertakes comprehensive, long-range strategic planning, it is important that the governor, the legislature, or preferably both the governor and the legislature, give full support. Without such support little progress is likely to be made. In local school systems the initiative may come from the administration and the board or from an influential group of interested citizens. Under optimum conditions, the proposal would have the support of the board, the staff, and leading lay citizens.

Developing an Organizational Structure

Every state education agency, regional service agency or intermediate unit and local school system should include in its organizational design appropriate provisions for planning and other related services. Unless this is done there probably will be little or no attention to long-range planning.

If a state or local system has not previously been involved in strategic planning, or if plans developed earlier have not recently been revised and updated, there are several alternatives available. For example, the agency or school system may: (1) employ some organization or group of consultants to develop the plans; (2) organize its own staff to do the planning with or without the assistance of consultants; or (3) arrange or help to arrange for the organization of a competent committee that—with the assistance of well-qualified staff members provided by the agency or school system and of consultants as needed—will determine the basic policies for the study, analyze the materials and information, and agree on the conclusions and the details of the comprehensive plan.

In view of the previous discussion and what is known about cooperative procedures, it would seem that in many school systems the third alternative listed above, with appropriate adaptations, would have many advantages over the others.[11] Many states, including those involved in the Designing Education for the Future project, and a number of the larger local school systems have utilized this approach.

The committee or group responsible for policy determination should be composed of well-qualified lay citizens and educators. Membership may be determined in a variety of ways. At the state level, appointment may be made by the governor, a legislative committee, or the state board of education. At the local level, appointment is usually made by the school

---

[11]For a more detailed discussion of this and related topics, see Chaps. 3, 4, and 5 in Edgar L. Morphet, David L. Jesser, and Arthur P. Ludka, *Planning and Providing for Excellence in Education,* (New York: Citation Press, Scholastic Magazines, Inc., 1971).

board or by the board and the superintendent. At the state or local level, the policy committee should be responsible for appointing a director, staff members, consultants, and perhaps special study committees, as explained in a later section. In most states and local school systems that have planning and other related specialists on the staff, continuing studies are conducted to provide a basis for determining when revisions in the basic plans are needed. All decisions concerning basic policies are or should be made by the board and administration rather than by the specialists.

THE NATURE AND PROCESSES OF PLANNING

As indicated in an earlier section, there are wide differences in opinions about what the term "planning" means or implies. Howsam has observed that, "There is much semantic looseness among educators where change is concerned."[12] There seems to be as much or perhaps more "semantic looseness" among educators and lay citizens about what planning means. Among educators it is almost impossible to identify anyone who is willing to admit that he does not plan. However, in many instances educators plan to do tomorrow that which they did yesterday, and as a consequence fail to give serious consideration to: (1) determining what the future may or should be like; and (2) selecting from various alternatives the procedures that are best designed to facilitate attainment of the future state or condition that is needed. Huefner has commented:

> Everyone plans—but not very well. Most of our actions are influenced by expectations of the future and a written—or at least a mental—"plan" of how that future can be improved. *But seldom have these plans been subjected to a critical evaluation of assumptions and objectives, or a careful coordination with other plans to which they must relate.*[13]

Some people prefer to describe or define planning as "to make plans"; that is, they emphasize the plans as the *product* of planning. In this context, planning presumably has taken place when a teacher develops lesson plans, or when an administrator develops a budget which is considered a *plan* for controlling expenditures. Most, however, prefer another definition: planning is the process that is utilized to attain some goal or goals.

---

[12]Robert B. Howsam, "Effecting Needed Changes in Education," in Edgar L. Morphet and Charles O. Ryan, eds., *Planning and Effecting Needed Changes in Education,* (New York: Citation Press, Scholastic Magazines, Inc., 1967), p. 71.

[13]Robert P. Huefner, "Strategies and Procedures in State and Local Planning," in Morphet and Ryan, eds., *Planning and Effecting Needed Changes in Education,* p. 16.

Perceived in this manner, planning means more than the development of plans; it is viewed as *a process* or a method that is developed to achieve some purpose and, therefore, is *future oriented*. Thus, by utilizing appropriate planning procedures and processes it is possible to gain some control over future developments. This concept has prompted many planning projects and efforts in education during recent years and has contributed to the idea that many aspects of the future can be, in large measure, the kind of future for which we plan.

Technologies of Planning

Some people may consider use of the word "technology" inappropriate in the context of a discussion relating to the processes or techniques of planning. This is understandable because that term is often used to refer to *products* rather than *processes*. However, "technology" can be used to describe a process or processes and, because this section deals with some technical processes, the authors have used the phrase "technologies of planning" to describe them.

Each of the various planning technologies has its own unique charcteristics but also has elements in common with other technologies. Each, when properly used, will contribute significantly to the attainment of appropriate goals pertinent to any plans that may be developed. Moreover, each in its own way will contribute to the development of a total process that makes it possible to: (1) ascertain and analyze existing conditions with respect to needed conditions; (2) design, develop, and test strategies or procedures that are likely to achieve the conditions needed; and (3) implement, evaluate, and modify as needed those strategies that are developed. There are two elements or characteristics that every planning technology, regardless of its specialized approach, should have: planning, to be effective, must be *systematic,* and it should be *comprehensive.*

SYSTEMATIC PLANNING. The concept of systematic (and usually long-range) planning has been an integral component of the planning efforts of various segments of society for some time. The military, for example, has utilized the concept to solve perplexing problems since the beginning of World War II; scientists have utilized it in their quest for solutions to problems of medicine, biochemistry, and space travel. Planners in these fields have recognized the existence and interrelationship of the many microsystems or subsystems that contribute to the effective and efficient functioning of the macrosystem or total system. It has only been relatively recently, however, that many educators have begun to understand the significance of the facts (discussed in Chapter 3) that: (1) education is a macrosystem with many subsystems that operates in some relationship to numerous other macrosystems, each of which also has subsystems; (2) the many important interrelationships among educational subsystems and between the educational system and other social systems must be recognized and understood; and therefore (3) educational and other planners need to utilize the concepts of systems and systematic planning, as a basis for developing more effective plans.

COMPREHENSIVE PLANNING. Most planning in education has been concerned primarily or exclusively with one level or with some aspect of education, and frequently has given little attention to other agencies and services (such as health and similar service agencies and programs) that may have many important implications for education.

Bona fide comprehensive strategic planning concerned with all levels and aspects of education is complex and difficult but should be undertaken in every state probably about once every decade because all levels and aspects of education are interrelated in many important, but often ignored, ways. At least periodic comprehensive planning for each major level of education should be considered essential and serious efforts made to ensure that the goals and procedures proposed are interrelated. Such questions as the following should be considered by every group involved: What will be the impact or effect of each proposed change on other aspects or levels of education? What forces and factors are likely to facilitate implementation of the desired change? To retard or prevent it?

When planning is comprehensive, it is essential that: (1) values and goals be clearly defined; (2) policies relate effectively to the changes that are planned; and (3) every important and relevant factor be considered.

In addition to its systematic and comprehensive aspects, planning should relate to certain time frames. Nix[14] has identified three interrelated time-frames or spans for planning:

1. *Futuristic-span.* The planning group or agency looks ten or more years into the future, and from what it perceives, derives broad directions for development—that is, long-range goals.
2. *Development-span.* Each unit in the agency then sets developmental goals for itself to be reached in three, four, or five years. Operational strategies and project-type endeavors are devised and implemented to bring about goal achievement. With large margins for contingencies, resources are earmarked for the endeavors and the plans provide the basic direction for the organization.
3. *Short-span.* This is the mode of management by objectives. A division of project management sets down in writing what it will have accomplished six months, or twelve months hence. It also identifies the operations it will undertake to produce these accomplishments, and concurrently distributes, by budget, resources to the respective operations.

[14]Charles Nix, *Planmaking Capabilities in State Education Agencies* (Denver, Colorado: Improving State Leadership in Education, 1972), p. 4

176   BASIC PRINCIPLES, CONCEPTS, AND ISSUES

SPECIALIZED PLANNING TECHNOLOGIES.   As the need for more systematic planning to effect needed changes has become increasingly apparent, a variety of specialized and interrelated (although seemingly discrete) technologies has been developed. These include the "system approach," the planning-programming-budgeting system (PPBS), operations research (OR), the educational resources management system (ERMS), the program evaluation and review technique (PERT), the critical path method (CPM), and others that are less well known. Each technology is most useful for certain tasks or aspects of planning. Educational planners, therefore, should identify and utilize the specific technology or combination of technologies that best suits the purposes of the planning effort. These technologies have been discussed in numerous articles and books.[15]

THE SYSTEM APPROACH TO PLANNING.   One technology that should have special consideration in educational planning is commonly referred to as the "system approach to planning." It encompasses components included in most of the planning technologies and therefore seems to provide a sound base for all planning efforts in education. In its basic form, the system approach provides for three fundamental activities: (1) analysis; (2) planning and design; and (3) implementation and evaluation. This process makes it possible to examine any problem in a systematic manner and to systematically identify the best way or ways of solving it. When utilizing the system approach, those involved in planning can: (1) identify the problem; (2) analyze the problem and set goals; (3) determine the best strategy or strategies for solution; (4) implement the solution strategy; and (5) determine the effectiveness of the strategy selected.[16]

Because experts are most familiar with and attach high value to the techniques commonly utilized in their area of specialization, one caution seems appropriate for those who are involved in educational planning: the best techniques or technologies do not necessarily solve complex problems such as many encountered in education; these problems can only be resolved by people who understand the needs and concerns of society and the role of education in a dynamic society. The various technologies should, therefore, be viewed as essential tools and procedures that must be used intelligently and perceptively by competent people who are responsible for attempting to solve these problems.

[15]For example, see Morphet and Ryan, eds., *Planning and Effecting Needed Changes in Education,* Chap. 12, and Edgar L. Morphet and David L. Jesser, eds., *Planning for Effective Utilization of Technology in Education,* (New York: Citation Press, Scholastic Magazines, Inc., 1968).
[16]Donald W. Johnson and Donald R. Miller, "A System Approach to Planning for the Utilization of Technology in Education," in Morphet and Jesser, eds., *Planning for Effective Utilization of Technology in Education,* p. 210.

The Processes of Planning

As previously indicated, the development of plans should always be recognized as an essential *means* to make it possible to accomplish some important purposes. The ultimate purpose of all planning in education is to help to ensure not only that that provisions, programs, and procedures will effectively and efficiently meet the learning needs of all who can benefit from education, but also that those who benefit are prepared to contribute to the orderly and wholesome development of a dynamic society.[17] It is essential for everyone who is engaged in or concerned about planning to understand that it (1) is a systematic *human* process that usually involves many kinds of people, (2) has essential technical aspects, and (3) requires a series of logical steps and procedures. The major steps and procedures are discussed briefly in the paragraphs that follow; those that have special significance for planning improvements in educational programs and learning opportunities are discussed more fully in that context in Chapter 14.

AGREEMENT ON PURPOSES. In any cooperative effort that involves representatives of several different publics, there are likely to be divergent views about the purposes of the endeavor. If each participant perceives the purpose of the planning effort as serving primarily the ends of any group to which he belongs, it is probable that little or nothing will be accomplished. Thus, it is essential at the beginning that the leader and all members of the group agree on a common purpose and on major goals. Moreover, as anyone who has worked with committees or other groups knows, there may be a tendency for the group to want to move rapidly in the direction of specifics and to avoid consideration of broadly conceived goals and concepts. If this occurs—that is, if details are dealt with in the absence of any agreement on purposes and procedures—a built-in mechanism may be developed for rejection by individual members of any proposals that are not consistent with their major interests or concerns. Therefore, as preparations are made for meaningful planning efforts, it is essential that there be a commonality of understanding and acceptance of the major purposes of planning.

ORGANIZATION AND PERSONNEL. Some of of the basic considerations relating to the development of an organizational structure for strategic planning are discussed earlier in this chapter. When an appropriate structure has been established by or for a state or local school system, the

---

[17]For a rather comprehensive discussion of this concept, see Morphet and Jesser, *Cooperative Planning for Education in 1980.*

commission or agency responsible should: (1) agree upon the purpose, scope, and time span, and determine the resources allotted or available; and (2) decide upon the basic policies, the kinds of studies and personnel needed, and the organization and relationships considered essential. Some of the important guidelines usually observed are:

- A competent executive director, who understands education as well as the planning processes, is selected to guide and coordinate all studies and activities;
- A special study committee, and perhaps a consultant, is appointed for each major aspect (such as educational programs, personnel, organization and administration, and finance) and its responsibilities and relationships are made clear; and
- The sponsoring commission or agency studies all findings and recommendations of these committees and assumes the responsibility for developing (with any assistance that is needed) defensible and well-coordinated plans.

As noted earlier, the services of a variety of technicians and other types of experts are essential in developing defensible plans. It is necessary, however, that they as well as others involved in the planning process clearly recognize and understand that the specialists should not attempt either to develop the plans or to make the basic policy decisions. On the other hand it is essential that those responsible for developing policies and plans carefully consider all suggestions, findings, and conclusions of these specialists.

NEEDS AND GOALS. The determination of needs and the formulation of goals, from one point of view, are separate steps. In reality, however, they are interrelated in so many ways that they cannot be completely separated in practice. Few of the broad statements of goals that are based on the long-accepted beliefs and value judgments of the citizens about the place and role of education in each state and in the nation are likely to be changed significantly; in fact, many of them have not yet been attained in most parts of the nation as shown by studies of needs. On the other hand, systematic studies will provide empirical evidence regarding unsolved problems and unmet needs and will help to direct attention to previously unrecognized—or at least unstated—goals relating to provisions for organization, financial support, and other matters, as well as to educational programs and instructional procedures. Identification of and agreement on appropriate goals not only makes it possible to devise and implement optimum ways of achieving them, but also provides a sound basis for establishing accountability as noted in other chapters.

Any realistic identification and assessment of needs is a complex and difficult undertaking in a state or large local school system. Although much information can be obtained through an adequate management information system, if one has been developed, considerable supplementary data will almost always have to be obtained and carefully analyzed if all needs are to be determined.

PRIORITIES. Some goals are more important and certain needs are more serious than others. Since it will be impossible to attain all goals and, in the process, to meet all needs in a relatively short period of time, it will be necessary for every group involved in planning to agree on short- and long-range priorities. Appropriate criteria for determining priorities should be identified and accepted as a basis for making the necessary decisions. In all situations the basic criterion should probably be: the highest priority should be given to those goals which, when achieved, will result in the maximum educational benefits for students at a reasonable cost. In some states this might mean that reorganizing districts, revising provisions for support of schools, or removing restrictive provisions in the constitution or laws should have highest priority. In some local school systems, improving the curriculum, instructional procedures, or even the administrative organization and policies might receive high priority.

ALTERNATIVES. Frequently there are several feasible ways of achieving a desired goal or a series of related goals, and of meeting certain needs in the process. After needs have been determined and goals agreed upon it is essential to (1) identify these alternatives, and (2) ascertain the advantages and disadvantages—the probable implications or consequences—of each as a basis for selecting on a rational basis one that seems to be the most promising and defensible. (See Chapter 14 for a more detailed discussion relating to educational programs.)

IMPLEMENTATION, EVALUATION, AND REVISION. The development of plans has little meaning unless the plans are implemented—that is, are utilized as a basis for effecting improvements. As indicated earlier, the strategic planning process should be designed to facilitate implementation. The plans will (or should) specify what is to be done and provide some indications as to how certain things can best be accomplished, but should not attempt to specify the policies and details that will be required for effective implementation. The management planning team should be expected to assume this essential but difficult responsibility. It can most effectively do so when (1) some of the members have been involved in the entire planning process, and (2) those who will be most affected by the policies and procedures have an opportunity to participate in the development of these plans.

Regardless of the approach utilized, all plans are likely to include some proposals that, for one reason or another, do not work out satisfactorily. Provisions should therefore be made for continuous study and monitoring to determine the extent to which goals are being met, whether any conflicts or disharmonies are encountered, and so on, in order to provide a basis for needed revisions. The process of monitoring and modification may be conceived as a series of "feedback loops" that provide for the recycling of any modification that may be found necessary, either for the discrete steps or for the overall planning endeavor.[18]

EFFECTING NEEDED CHANGES

Change in one form or another is an inevitable fact of life and of the world in which we live. However, as many educators as well as others will attest, the inevitableness of change has not reduced the tendency of many people to resist changes—to assume that life and the institutions that have been established can continue without any significant changes in traditional patterns or procedures.

Although most people, including educational leaders, recognize that changes in some form are inevitable, many seem reluctant to make any serious effort to determine what changes are needed or are likely to take place, when or why they may occur, and the probable implications for people and the institutions they have established. Many educators have tended to consider educational problems and needs in terms of the more comfortable present, or even of the past, rather than on the basis of the needs of a rapidly changing society.

The fact that change does—and will—occur has many important implications for all members of society. The advent of technology, the population explosion, the increasing pollution, the discovery of new ways of harnessing and utilizing previously untapped sources of energy, and many other developments have had dramatic, sometimes tragic, consequences for society. They offer mute testimony to the fact that change does occur, *with or without coordinated planning*. Educational leaders, together with others concerned, urgently need to recognize this fundamental concept relating to change.

Interrelations of Planning and Change

It is, therefore, important for everyone to understand that by appropriate systematic planning: (1) many of the harmful and potentially disastrous changes in society that have been occurring or are likely to occur can be avoided or at least mitigated; (2) the future prospects for society can be

[18]For a more detailed discussion of this concept, see Johnson and Miller, "A System Approach," pp. 207–211.

greatly improved; and (3) it is possible to prepare to control many aspects of an uncertain and potentially disastrous future.

It is equally important, however, for everyone to understand that planning is only one essential step in the process of effecting improvements in education or society. Unless plans are effectively implemented—that is, the needed changes are made—the established traditions will tend to continue with only minor adjustments and the major problems will persist. It is, therefore, essential that at least the leaders understand the strategies and processes of change and cooperate in ensuring that plans are implemented. In education, as in other aspects of society, this step involves many problems and difficulties because of the tendency of people to continue in their accustomed ways until they realize that some change is imperative.

It should be clear that, if planning and change are to be effective and meaningful, there should be a close relationship between the two processes. Obviously, there should be a reason (or a series of reasons) why a needed change should take place; in similar fashion, there should be a reason (or a series of reasons) for any planning that is undertaken. Each process—that of planning and that of change—may have separate or discrete purposes or reasons. However, this should not be interpreted to mean that each process should exist independently of the other. Yet many educational planners have neither considered nor developed viable strategies that are based on an understanding of the processes of change.

Change can occur without meaningful planning; conversely, planning can take place without resulting in an identified needed change. When change occurs without meaningful planning the result—the change—will probably be viewed as something that "just happened." In similar fashion, when "planners" formulate a *plan* that is never (or cannot be) implemented, the result may be perceived as being something that "didn't happen." In neither case can there be effective and meaningful change. If, however, proper attention is given to the interrelationships between planning and change, the total process—from initial planning to implementation of change—can become operational, and there will be greater assurance that a desired change will be effected.

Strategies for Effecting Changes

If needed changes are to be effected and have much long-range significance in the educational system (or any aspect of the system) it is essential that every proposed change be purposeful—that is, be designed to help to achieve some desirable goal or goals. Moreover, (1) there must be defensible and clearly stated reasons for any change that is proposed, and (2) these reasons must be understood and accepted by those who should be involved in, or would be affected by, the change. In other words, not only the changes that should be made in education, but also the procedures or strategies that should be utilized in effecting those changes need to be systematically and perceptively planned.

Many kinds of strategies have been used in efforts to prevent or discourage social systems (or the people involved in those systems) from changing, as well as to encourage them to change. Some of these have been crude or ruthless and are no longer defensible. The major strategies currently considered appropriate for use in facilitating needed changes in education are discussed briefly in the paragraphs that follow. It is important, however, for everyone to understand that these strategies should be utilized perceptively and constructively rather than as a means to manipulate people to do what someone or some group considers desirable.

CREATION OF A FAVORABLE CLIMATE. Unfortunately many excellent plans that have been developed for improving major aspects of education have not resulted in any significant changes either because the climate (environment) has not been favorable, or because inadequate attention has been given to the development of appropriate policies and procedures for implementation. As Howsam has observed, "An important general strategy is to approach change in such a way that there results a climate hospitable to continuous adaptation and change."[19] Moreover, Evans has noted that ". . . social systems and institutions rarely include mechanisms for facilitating change."[20] Improvements in education are most likely to be made when both the attitudes and expectations of lay citizens (the external climate) and those of educational personnel (the internal climate) are favorable. This climate (or environment) may be influenced by many factors including the processes utilized in planning.

INVOLVEMENT OF PEOPLE. When both lay citizens and educators, or at least their leaders, have had an opportunity to become involved in studying, or to become informed about, educational problems and needs in a changing society, they tend to gain new perspectives and insights and to be more willing to support needed changes.

DEMONSTRATION AND DIFFUSION. When people have an opportunity to see in operation, or perhaps even to learn about, some new practice or procedure that seems to facilitate learning or provide an effective way of resolving some important problems in education, they may be convinced that similar changes should be made in their own schools.

---

[19]Robert B. Howsam, "Needed Changes," p. 72.

[20]Richard I. Evans, "Resistance to Educational Technology: Some Psychological Observations," in Morphet and Jesser, eds., *Planning for Effective Utilization of Technology in Education,* p. 346.

POWER AND AUTHORITY. When sufficient power or pressure is applied in an effort to effect certain changes, there are likely to be at least some temporary adjustments. Whether any real changes are effected from a long-range point of view will be determined by many factors.

Each basic strategy for effecting change has obvious advantages and disadvantages.[21] The education and involvement process is probably the "best" strategy in terms of *long-range effectiveness,* but the wise use of power and authority may sometimes be needed for *short-range efficiency.* In every instance, the apparent advantages and disadvantages of a proposed strategy for effecting change should be carefully considered in the context of the ultimate goal or goals. *The optimum strategy, in terms of achieving a goal or a needed change, is the one that can most effectively reduce resistance to the proposed change.* More often than not, the best strategy will probably be some appropriate blend or adaptation of the strategies listed above.

SOME IMPORTANT PROBLEMS AND ISSUES

Although most people probably would agree that many changes in education are urgently needed, there are sharp disagreements about what changes should be made as well as about how and by whom they should be made. Some people apparently believe all changes should be made by educators, but Nyquist has commented, "Education is too important to be left solely to educators."[22] In fact, in this country, the decisions relating to major educational policies have always been determined by the citizens or their representatives. Moreover, unless a majority of the citizens in a state or community understand the need for making major changes in education and are convinced that these changes will result in improvements, they are not likely to be made. What are the most important changes that should be made in education? Why? What policies and practices in education should not be changed? Why not?

How Can the Kinds of Cooperation Needed for Strategic Planning Be Facilitated?

In any group, and perhaps especially in a group concerned with educational planning that includes both lay citizens and educators, there may be some people who insist that others cooperate with them—that is,

---

[21] A detailed discussion of advantages and disadvantages of various change strategies may be found in Morphet *et al., Planning and Providing for Excellence in Education,* Chap. 8.

[22] Ewald B. Nyquist, "State Organization and Responsibilities for Education," Edgar L. Morphet and David L. Jesser, eds., in *Emerging Designs for Education,* (New York: Citation Press, Scholastic Magazines, Inc., 1968), p. 154.

184 BASIC PRINCIPLES, CONCEPTS, AND ISSUES

help them to get their own proposals adopted. When this happens, sharp controversies may develop or some of the decisions may be based on extraneous factors rather than on serious consideration of the evidence, or on what would best meet the needs of education in a changing society. What should the chairman (leader) or members of the group do to help to ensure bona fide cooperation in developing constructive and defensible proposals for improving education? Some suggested guidelines relating to cooperative procedures are given below:

- All cooperative efforts to improve education should utilize and observe the basic concepts or principles pertaining to satisfactory human relations, including (1) there should be respect for each individual, yet continuing recognition of the fact that the common good must always be considered, (2) the talents and abilities of all persons who can make a contribution should be utilized, and (3) the thinking and conclusions of two or more persons with a good understanding of the problems and issues are likely, in most cases, to be more reliable than the conclusions of one individual;
- The procedures used in any cooperative effort should be designed to ensure that conclusions will be reached on the basis of pertinent evidence and desirable goals; and
- The leaders understand and believe in cooperative procedures.[23]

Are any of these guidelines inappropriate? If so which ones? What are some others that should be helpful?

What Are Some of the Major Problems in Effecting Improvements in Education?

Although most people apparently agree that major improvements are urgently needed, many seem to underestimate the need and pressures for change. On the other hand, some educators and lay citizens either seek to continue traditional programs and procedures with minor changes, or tend to support what seem to be promising proposals for change in some aspect of education without considering either the implications for other aspects or feasible alternatives. If they become involved in planning they may assume that the problems in the future will be essentially the same as those encountered in the past, except perhaps more effort may be required to resolve them. In fact, they may find themselves in the posiiton of planning for education in the kind of society in which they have been living, rather than for education to meet the needs of a dynamic and rapidly changing

[23] Adapted from Edgar L. Morphet, *Cooperative Procedures in Education* (Hong Kong: Hong Kong University Press, 1957), pp. 5–9; and Edgar L. Morphet, Chairman, *Citizen Cooperation for Better Schools* (Chicago: National Society for the Study of Education, Fifty-third Yearbook, Part I, 1954), Chap. 10.

society. What are some of the other problems and hazards or pitfalls in planning improvements in education? How can they be avoided or minimized?

Under What Conditions, If Any, Should Changes in Education Be Mandated?

It may be fortunate that some people involved in organizations, agencies, and institutions tend to resist some proposals for change. If they sought change indiscriminately, life and society could soon become chaotic. When changes in education come too slowly to meet the needs, however, many people become critical and may either react in ways that would tend to handicap the students in a school system, or seek to have the legislature or the board mandate the changes they consider desirable. Some people seem to think that when a law has been passed or a regulation adopted the problem has been solved. But many legal mandates (for example, those relating to equality of educational opportunity and integration) have resulted only in superficial changes, or the mandate has sometimes been ignored. Some standards or requirements seem to be essential, but most people apparently believe the emphasis in education should be on helping and encouraging staff, students, and lay citizens to seek to achieve excellence, rather than relying on laws or standards.

Should some changes in education be mandated by law or board policy? If so, what kinds of changes and under what conditions? How can undesirable kinds of mandates best be avoided?

What Is Implied by the Term "Cooperation"?

Although the term "cooperation" means to work or associate with others for mutual benefit, some "leaders" seem to think it can be interpreted to mean manipulation of other people for their own benefit—that is, to help the leaders achieve their own purposes and goals. From this distorted perspective there seem to be three kinds of "cooperation": authoritarian, controlled, and voluntary.

> *Authoritarian* cooperation is essentially the master-slave concept of human relations. The leader or leaders do all the thinking and give all the instructions. The followers or workers cooperate by carrying out all instructions.
>
> *Controlled* or pseudodemocratic cooperation is the same in principle as authoritarian cooperation. The leader decides what he wants done and uses subtle and clever means to ensure that the "right" decisions are made by the group. The "leader" may attempt to manipulate a group into agreeing with

his previously determined conclusions by using any or all of the following devices: (1) encouraging the appointment of members who agree with his own purposes and goals; (2) appearing to encourage bona fide thinking and discussion, but attempting to limit or slant the information to which they have access; or (3) commending certain suggestions, and ignoring or passing lightly over others. A leader of this kind must be very clever because most members would be resentful if they realized he was attempting to control their thinking and conclusions. It is surprising, however, how often the techniques of attempting to secure controlled cooperation are used in the United States by authoritarian leaders who insist that they are using democratic processes.

Voluntary cooperation tends to be facilitated when people are not only free to think for themselves but are encouraged to do so. It is the opposite of the master-slave relationship, because all citizens are recognized as peers. People are not manipulated and each person is encouraged to contribute to the thinking of the group.

How can the schools and colleges prepare citizens who not only understand and support bona fide cooperative procedures, but also can detect and discredit the kind of leaders who attempt to manipulate the thinking of members of a group? How can members of a group best cope with a leader who seems to be attempting to control their decisions?

How Can Leaders Facilitate Needed Changes in Education?

One of the characteristics of an effective leader is that he helps to establish and facilitate the attainment of appropriate goals. This often means that he must help people prepare to effect needed changes. Argyris has observed that "effective change occurs when the changes are long lasting, when they are self-monitoring, and when they are reinforcing of system competence and lead to further system development."[24] As he has noted, some people believe that change may be more effective when attention is centered first on structural changes; others believe it should begin with interpersonal relationships. What criteria should leaders concerned with improvements in education use to determine when and under what conditions a proposed change (1) would be likely to meet the tests listed in the quotation above; and (2) should be initially concerned with structure or with people?

Significant changes in a social system such as education usually are not made easily. Careful planning can help to minimize, but will not eliminate, the inevitable feeling of insecurity on the part of many people,

---

[24]Chris Argyris, *Management and Organizational Development* (New York: McGraw-Hill Book Company, 1970), p. 164.

some of whom may become resentful or antagonistic. Some perceptive "interventionists" may be necessary to facilitate stability and ensure progress. The purpose of any such intervention should be to find ways of utilizing the tensions to motivate individuals to seek more information, to design appropriate procedures, and to develop a commitment to the goals as well as to procedures. In education, who should play the role of interventionist? How? Should the interventionists be authoritative or authoritarian? What criteria should they utilize to facilitate cooperation in attaining the goals and, in the process, effecting the needed changes?

How Can the Best Alternatives for Improving Education Be Determined?

Whether or not the educational provisions and procedures throughout a state will be more adequate and effective within ten years than they are at present will be determined by many factors including decisions that are made in the meantime. If most changes result from pressures or haphazard developments, some may be beneficial; others may have little significance or could actually be harmful from a long-range point of view. If, however, changes are systematically planned—utilizing the most competent leaders and the best information, insights, and procedures available—the prospects for improving all aspects of education for everyone who could benefit should be greatly enhanced. The kind of systematic cooperative planning needed, however, is not likely to occur unless it is given high priority by political and other lay and educational leaders and is strongly supported by most citizens. What steps should be taken to help to ensure that this is done?

In this complex process many important and difficult decisions will need to be made at every stage and for every aspect. The matter of selecting the best and most defensible alternatives, for example, is vital but has often been given inadequate attention. Although agreement on goals is essential, it may have little practical meaning unless the best or most defensible procedures for attaining each goal and effective ways of measuring progress are agreed upon and utilized. To be more specific, let us assume that in a certain state one goal is to ensure that during his first three years in school every normal student will have learned to read sufficiently well that, with minimum assistance thereafter, he will not be seriously handicapped by reading difficulties. Is this goal desirable and feasible, as some authorities contend? Is this proposal based on value judgments or on valid evidence? If on the latter, what is the evidence?

There probably are several conceivable ways that could be utilized to achieve this goal. Which ones seem to be best? What does the evidence indicate about the short- and long-range costs and benefits of each? What procedure or combination of procedures (alternatives) should be recommended? Why?

SELECTED REFERENCES

ARGYRIS, CHRIS, *Interpersonal Competence and Organizational Effectiveness.* Homewood, Ill.: Richard W. Irwin, Inc., 1962.

———, *Intervention Theory and Method: A Behavioral Science View.* Reading, Mass: Addison-Wesley Publishing Company, 1970.

BENNIS, WARREN G., KENNETH D. BENNE, and ROBERT CHIN, eds., *The Planning of Change* (2d ed.). New York: Holt, Rinehart and Winston, Inc. 1969.

BERELSON, BERNARD, and GARY A. STEINER, *Human Behavior: An Inventory of Scientific Finding.* New York: Harcourt, Brace & World, Inc., 1964.

CARTWRIGHT, DARWIN, and ALVIN E. ZANDER, *Group Dynamics: Research and Theory.* New York: Harper & Row, Publishers, 1960.

ELAM, STANLEY and GORDON I. SWANSON, eds., *Educational Planning in the United States.* Itasca, Illinois: F. E. Peacock Publishers, Inc., 1969.

FURSE, BERNARR S. and LYLE O. WRIGHT, eds., *Comprehensive Planning in State Education Agencies.* Salt Lake City, Utah: Utah State Board of Education, 1968.

HACK, WALTER, et. al., *Educational Futurism 1985: Challenges for Schools and Their Administrators.* Berkeley, California: McCutchan Publishing Corporation, 1971.

HIRSCH, WERNER Z. Et al., *Inventing Education for the Future.* San Francisco: Chandler Publishing Company, 1967.

MARIEN, MICHAEL and WARREN L. ZIEGLER, eds., *The Potential of Educational Futures.* Worthington, Ohio: Charles A. Jones Publishing Company, 1972.

MORPHET, EDGAR L. and DAVID L. JESSER, eds., *Cooperative Planning for Education in 1980,* and *Planning for Effective Utilization of Technology in Education.* Denver, Colorado: Designing Education for the Future, 1968. Republished by Citation Press, Scholastic Magazines, Inc., New York, N. Y.

MORPHET, EDGAR L., DAVID L. JESSER, and ARTHUR P. LUDKA, *Planning and Providing for Excellence in Education.* Denver Colorado: Improving State Leadership in Education, 1971. Republished by Citation Press, Scholastic Magazines, Inc., New York, N. Y.

MORPHET, EDGAR L. and CHARLES O. RYAN, eds., *Planning and Effecting Needed Changes in Education.* Denver, Colorado: Designing Education for the Future, 1967. Republished by Citation Press, Scholastic Magazines, New York, N. Y.

TRUSTY, FRANCIS M., ed., *Administering Human Resources: A Behavioral Approach to Educational Administration.* Berkeley, California: McCutchan Publishing Corporation, 1971.

7

The Environment and the Schools

Throughout history, the relation of the school to the community it serves has been a matter of major significance. To what extent may a faculty teach what it is committed to teach without regard to the wishes of the people? How much support can a school or school system expect if it is pursuing values not accepted with enthusiasm by the community? The historic gown-versus-town conflicts regarding the university have some parallels in every active school community today. The problems have grown more difficult to understand as the nature of the community has grown more vague and the problems of education have become infinitely more difficult.

The rising expectations regarding education which have been noted in many countries of the world add to the problem. The expectations may be so high that they cannot be fulfilled, or at least not as rapidly as desired. Frustration, alienation, and antagonism may then result. Education has become the nation's and the world's most important business; therefore, everyone tends to be involved in it and desires in some manner to contribute to it. Many have rather simple solutions to propose for complex problems. The problem in our society is accentuated by the tendency of many to equate schooling with education.

These rising expectations have been accompanied by a demand for quick action and even quicker solutions. The demand is understandable because of past inequalities, continued problems such as prejudice and racism, and because childhood is experienced only once and passes quickly. While the school, like most institutions, tends to respond much too slowly, the complexity of the problem suggests that a "solution" is not to be found quickly and not without extended research and planning. There is therefore the probability that further alienation may result and that conflict may become endemic—that the energies of even those committed to the educational enterprise may contribute little that is constructive.

Some educators who have sought the participation of the "people" in education (school affairs) and who might indeed be elated over developments have recently at times tended to draw back. The implications of many current developments are difficult to assess, and the road ahead is somewhat unclear. Confronted by an almost incomprehensible power to chart his own destiny—to build or destroy—man may tend to withdraw or to seek quick and "certain" solutions. In such an uneasy world, schools may expect to feel the impact of uncertainty and changes in the society. They must also re-examine their relation to and their impact upon the society. Of this vast arena of the school or school system and its environment, a few issues will be examined as one way of getting a better understanding of the problem which confronts the educator and the citizen interested in education today.

SOME BACKGROUND CONSIDERATIONS

Education in our society has been or is characterized by:

A Great Belief in the Efficacy of Schooling

The people of the United States have long viewed the school as the most important agency of social and economic mobility for the individual. They have assumed that if schools were provided and made accessible, children and youth would avail themselves of the opportunity. To a rather remarkable extent, this has indeed occurred. The mobility which has characterized our society has been highly related to educational provisions. The children of immigrant groups have thus in the second or third generation achieved a status to which they could scarcely have aspired in the countries from which they came. This mobility in our society was, of course, the product of other factors also. However, the point to be noted here is that this concept came to be so widely accepted that there was too little recognition of the extent to which it was not operative, of the individuals and groups which were not involved, of the considerable numbers who did not "see" the opportunity and were not "motivated" to achieve. The society and even many teachers may thus have placed the burden of failure to achieve on the student.

Recent studies and related controversies regarding the impact of schooling have challenged this naive belief in and possibly the myths regarding the influence of schools.[1] The drive for deschooling and for alternate schools also relates to the search for a more meaningful educational experience. In part because of the previous easy acceptance of the value of schooling confusion has been widespread concerning this matter. An adequate response has not occurred. A period of years may be both necessary and desirable to sort out the available data and claims regarding various studies, to conduct additional ones, and to permit educators and the public to arrive at a more valid position regarding this highly significant issue.

A Tendency to Regard Schooling and Education as One

In the commitment of our society to equal educational opportunity, attention has been given largely to the provision of rather formally established opportunities in schools. This concept of equality of educational opportunity has been sharply challenged by the civil rights movement in recent years and by the attack on poverty. Teachers in many instances accepted the achievement of black children and other "lower class" children as being in accord with their potential to a much greater degree than was justified. They found it difficult to think of the kinds of experiences which children had in their homes and communities in the preschool years and while in school as an important aspect of education. They assumed that the formal school opportunity could overcome that which preceded and accompanied it. Actually, of course, in many cases it overcame much,

---

[1] Studies, for example, such as: James S. Coleman, et al., *Equality of Educational Opportunity* (Washington, D.C., Superintendent of Documents, U.S. Government Printing Office, 1966) and Christopher Jencks, et al, *Equality: A Reassessment of the Effect of Family and Schooling in America* (New York: Basic Books, Inc., 1972).

their faith in education (schooling) was an important element in the strength of the school. However, this faith was also a factor which may have prevented educators from seeing the problem of the education of the culturally different in more valid terms. In recent years the society has called for a redefinition of education—one which sees the growth of an individual in light of many factors and forces, only one of which is the school. Thus there is the growing concern about poverty, housing, the community, and the attitudes and aspirations of parents as matters of large importance for the education of the child.

A Tendency to See the School as an Isolated Social Agency Rather Than an Integrated One

The people of the United States have seen the school as an institution which is most unique in their society. Here, long before most other societies, they have attached great importance to the school and have wished to ensure conditions for it which would be strongly supportive. Thus, out of philosophical considerations and as a result of the widespread corruption that characterized city government in the last half of the nineteenth century, they moved toward *ad hoc* boards of education. These boards of education enjoyed a very considerable measure of independence from city government and from the political machines that controlled city government. This development was facilitated by the acceptance of the view that education was a function of the state and thus not the proper concern of the city government.

Very probably, the schools advanced much more rapidly in the United States because of the fact that they were thus isolated from other activities of city government. They enjoyed greater support and lived with higher expectations than other governmental agencies. This removal of schools from the usual political controls gave them a special political position and support of importance. They were removed from politics thus only in the sense of being removed from manipulation by the political bosses. However, the view developed that they were nonpolitical. This and other factors caused them to develop somewhat in isolation from other local governmental agencies and services which were more responsive to political party controls. Teachers and administrators supported the view that they should be independent and that thus they would contribute most to the development of citizens of independence and the advancement of the society.

While, as has been suggested, there were large gains made as a result of this independence, it must also be noted that this was done at certain costs. Among the gains were: the more rapid advancement of education (schooling) than would probably have occurred otherwise, the development of merit plans for appointment of teachers and administrators prior to such developments in other governmental services, the strengthening of the responsibilities of the administrator, the establishment of a plan through which the people could center attention upon the schools and seek their improvement.

On the other hand this independence led to a lack of responsiveness on the part of boards of education to the changing needs of the society; a concern on the part of teachers and administrators with academic learning rather than with the total situation in which the child lived and which had a large impact on his education; an inability of educators and others engaged in public services such as housing, public health, libraries, and social welfare to work together with understanding; a belief that educational services were removed from politics (not recognizing the politics of the nonpolitical), a view which in the long run may have hindered rather than advanced the quality of educational services. This tendency to reagard schools as separate from the home and from other agencies remains and is difficult to overcome. Thus even today most studies of the development of less privileged children center most of their attention upon the school—for presumably it is through the school that change is to be effected. This same tendency may be found in other nations also—though in England, for example, the gulf may be less wide. Studies such as that reported in *From Birth to Seven,*[2] which centers attention not only upon the school but upon the birth and health history, the housing and home experience, the community, the parents and their attitudes and aspirations, ability and attainment, behavior and adjustment, are less likely to be conducted in the United States. Interestingly this comprehensive, longitudinal study involving all children born in one week in March 1958 was conducted by the National Children's Bureau in collaboration with various health and educational institutes and research organizations and associations of educational and medical officers.

This "isolation" may have indeed been justified in the late nineteenth and early twentieth centuries. In rural areas and small towns it was readily understandable because of the limited nature of local government, child, and health services. However, it must be noted that the growing complexity of the society, with its enormous concentrations of population and expanding programs of governmental services, calls for a thorough reexamination of this question. So also does the theory of government which requires a less naive, less simple, and quite possibly a less satisfying concept of how decision making is and probably will be carried on in our democracy.

[2] Ronald Davie, Neville Butler, and Harvey Goldstein, National Children's Bureau (London: Longmans, 1972).

A Commitment to Equality of Educational Opportunity with Relatively Little Understanding or Agreement Regarding Its Meaning

The expansion and improvement of educational services in our society has long been related to a verbal commitment to equality of opportunity. While equality has at times been confused with identity of opportunity, it has been effectively used as a guiding principle which united the society and in light of which advances have been secured. During this century definitions of it have changed in marked fashion. In recent years substantial changes in meaning have occurred and continue to occur. A major change has been from the definition which held that educational opportunities should be provided for all in accord with their ability to the definition which holds that not only must the opportunity be provided but also that the society has the responsibility for ensuring that children and youth can (and will) avail themselves effectively of the opportunity. Possibly there is sharper disagreement in our society regarding the meaning of this concept than there has been for some decades. Some clarification is essential as a base for moving forward in educational services. The search for a new definition—for an adequate one for our times—constitutes a major challenge to the established educational service and the forces in the society related to it.

Ambiguity Regarding Goals Related to the Diversity and Changing Values in Society

Society in the last decade has been deeply troubled in its search for new values. Many have felt deeply that the values of the past have been inadequate and that technological and other developments offer new opportunities for men to build a substantially different world with less competition, tension, uniformity, institutionalization, inequality and economic, racial, and social stratification and differences. This search in society has been paralleled by ambiguity regarding goals in the schools. The old question of what knowledge is of most worth may read in part, "What Are Schools For?"[3] There are calls for the schools to guide youth in learning useful knowledge; to "prophesy urgently, magnetically, and then fulfill these prophecies," an aspect of futurism;[4] "to adopt the affective domain—socialization, democratization, values in education, morality;" or to recognize that "it's the side effects that count." The public and

---

[3] *Phi Delta Kappan,* LIV, September 1972, pp. 1–17.
[4] Walter A. Hack *et al., Educational Futurism 1985* (Berkeley: McCutchan Publishing Company, 1972).

the schools are ambiguous. There are strident calls for accountability. Can sufficient agreement be achieved—and tolerance for diversity—to enable communities and society to move forward effectively?

A Former Tendency Toward Uniformity Challenged by a Concept of "Pluralism"

Public education in the United States was one of the important institutions through which a nation was built out of diverse people. While the melting-pot theory is not fully defensible, it is true that a nation was built with many important and relatively common commitments. In this process and because of the vastness of the continent, limited educational provisions, and the limited supply of prepared teachers, certain procedures such as statewide control of textbooks developed. Later the mobility of the general population and of teachers and administrators as well as ease of communication resulted in a remarkable general similarity of educational provisions in spite of the large number of school districts and the number of states. Many of these arrangements and views have persisted even though challenged by knowledge of individual differences and related matters. In recent years the efforts of minorities to find a reasonable and adequate role in our society and the diversity of values among our people have resulted in a new commitment to pluralism. The more exact delineation of pluralism remains to be worked out—but it is a force challenging the old uniformity. The growing recognition of the legal rights of the individual student also challenges the traditional view.

A Traditional Insecurity of the Professional Educator and a Search for Power by the Professional

The teacher has long had an image marked by insecurity in the United States. This however may be over; teacher groups may find that they have much more power than they believed. They are far from agreed on how or for what ends to use this power. They may become defenders of conservative approaches to educational problems. As they negotiate with the board of education and/or top administration, and especially at the state level, they may become more rigid in positions. Such negotiations may also result in the organization of the principals and other middle groups in order to protect their positions and exert some power. This search for power by professionals is increasingly noticed at the local or district level. As the state becomes more deeply and directly involved in educational practice this power will also be exercised to a much greater degree at the state level. It will not be a return to the fifties when legislatures frequently followed education associations but a period marked by greater controversy. New power relationships will be developing, and this almost inevitably will result in considerable conflict.

A Somewhat Simplistic Belief in "The People" and a Failure to Analyze and Affirm This Belief in Relation to the Rights of Minorities or the Individual

At various times, but especially in the fifties, there was a considerable effort to involve more people in educational decision making. Citizens advisory committees were widely recommended. Generally they brought together representatives of various influential groups and encouraged them to join in securing educational improvements. They commonly did not include those who tended to be little represented in decision-making processes, such as the poor and minorities. Recent demands for community power are not conceptually unrelated to the earlier views regarding people involvement. However they meet other strong power positions including the traditional legal authority of the board of education, the bureaucracy, and the profession. Further, their programs are frequently poorly thought through and lacking competent leadership. Basically no one can seriously oppose the involvement of more people—especially considering the increasing educational influence of forces such as TV outside of the school. However, the issue is an extremely complex one which calls for serious study and careful formulation, development of procedures, and appraisal.

A Belief That Conflict Should (Always) Be Avoided and That It Is the Result of Lack of Communication or Understanding

The optimism, affluence, and commitments of our society have at least in part been the basis for a belief that conflicts on public issues should be avoided at nearly all costs. Thus the board of education election in which the incumbents were reelected with little or no discussion of issues and no serious competitor was not uncommon or unfavorably regarded. There has also been the view that if there is conflict it is the result of inadequate communication. These views are now rejected or at least looked at much more critically. In a pluralistic society—a society in which groups hold sharply different values, a society in the process of change, a painful experience even for our change-oriented society—it is increasingly recognized that differences are inevitable and may indeed offer opportunities for development. This view assumes that attention is not being given to personal conflicts. It also assumes that our society is sufficiently mature to engage in conflict within limits relating to goals, to the common welfare, and with mutual respect for the right of other individuals and groups to hold different views. Clearly the probable inevitability of conflict must be recognized and preparation made for avoiding its quite possible highly destructive features.

An Avoidance of Confrontation Which May Increasingly Become the Method of Seeking Solutions to Problems

The struggle for power and the acceptance of a concept of collective negotiations which involves confrontation as an essential procedure have resulted in considerable change in decision making in many school districts. Related developments may be expected at the state level. The meaning of this development in terms of more established decision-making procedures and in relation to the preparation of administrative personnel for leadership roles has not been carefully explored. It is clear however that both the external and internal environments may be marked by this movement and that analysis and appraisal of its effects are necessary. Possibly it may crest as a movement and recede. Perhaps it will be employed only by certain groups and with reference to certain issues. It is clear however that the past decade has seen a sharp increase in its use and the issues and forces which indicate conflict in the present strongly suggest its continuance.

CHANGED LOCAL CONDITIONS

While the concepts briefly discussed here have persisted, the world in which schools and school systems have existed has been in a process of extremely rapid change. Among the more important of the changes are the following:

From a Rural to an Urban to a Metropolitan Nation

Until relatively recently, the United States has been a predominantly rural nation. From the 24 urban places of 2,500 population or more in 1790, there was a steady population growth in rural and urban areas for more than a century. While the urban growth at times exceeded the rural, it did not make spectacular gains until the early decades of the present century. By 1960 the urban population was approximately 70 percent and it continues to grow far more rapidly than other areas.

Much more striking than the change from rural to urban has been the transformation of the nation from urban to metropolitan. Victor Jones has noted that "The people of the United States became metropolitan before realizing their change from rural to urban."[5] In 1900 approximately one third of the population lived in "metropolitan areas" (according to the Bureau of the Census, a city of at least 50,000, including its county and adjacent counties that are "metropolitan in character" and "economically and socially integrated" with the county containing the city). By 1966 approximately 67 percent were metropolitan dwellers and the expansion was expected to continue.[6] This percent is slightly smaller than the urban percentage because, by definition, the urban figure includes many towns and small cities which are not part of a metropolitan area.

Related to this metropolitan growth was the matter of rapid population growth of the nation. In 1960 the official count of our population was over 179 million. A decade later the federal government estimated that another 25 to 30 million had been added. Further, approximately 90 percent of this population increase was in metropolitan areas. This population growth and concentration was such that during the late sixties the question of population control became a major issue not only in the newly developing countries but in the United States. The question was not one of how many people could be fed but rather what quality of life was likely to be maintained with the population explosion. People began inquiring as to what quality of life now existed in parts of the core cities of the great metropolitan areas.

Before any social policy was accepted regarding population growth the birth rate declined significantly. As a consequence, in the seventies attention had to be given to the problems of the "shrinking" school district. While shrinkage offered opportunities for change it also brought difficult problems. The society was so geared to growth and expansion that it was unsure whether shrinkage offered opportunities for improved quality.

Large Resources and Larger Needs

The metropolitan areas contain enormous economic wealth, scientific and technical skills, and human resources. They are home to a large percent of the great corporations that produce much of the economic wealth of the nation. The income of their people is above that of the nation. Here also

---

[5]John C. Bollens and Henry J. Schmandt, *The Metropolis: Its People, Politics and Economic Life* (New York: Harper & Row, Publishers, 1965) p. 12.

[6]Committee for Economic Development, *Reshaping Government in Metropolitan Areas* (New York, 1970) p. 15.

are found the large financial institutions and the commerical establishments. The accumulation of resources is so great that the metropolitan area achieves ends that were not even sought in a simpler society. It is the golden age of the industrialization and specialization which marks the twentieth century. It acts not only for itself but sets the patterns and trends which substantially dominate the nation.

In its economic life, it too is marked by change. The core city or the downtown area threatens to die and needs major attention. Industries scatter widely over the area. Workers commute long distances and under increasing stress as the transportation system (too often the automobile) breaks down or takes over an increasing land area with far from satisfying results. The distribution of economic resources is often unrelated to the needs of the people or the resources may be more effectively tapped by the state and federal governments. The wealthy center of the metropolitan area can scarcely "afford" to purchase the land for schools and recreation that is absolutely essential to maintain a defensible quality of life.

In the early seventies many people came to understand that the health of the various communities in the metropolitan area was dependent upon the health of the whole. The ecology movement provided more appreciation of the interrelationships of various forces and factors and of the interdependence of components. It constituted another important challenge and opportunity to the educational service.

Local Governments in Great Number and Variety

During the last fifty years, the legal boundaries of cities have not been extended as the city or metropolitan area has grown. In fact there has been very strong resistance to permitting the growth of the city through annexation. As a result, very strong municipal governments have frequently grown up around the city. They have been committed to preventing the expansion of the city. Further, many small municipal governments have either continued or have been established in the metropolitan areas. They have frequently been viewed as a means of avoiding the high taxes of the city and of keeping "undesirable" developments such as factories and low-cost housing out. The boundaries of these local government units are too frequently the result of "cherry-stemming" or similar procedures through which more powerful authorities secure wealthy or otherwise desirable areas. They are not logical, planned, or necessarily in accord with existing community-of-interest patterns.

In addition to the general local governments which are found in the metropolitan area there is an increasing number of *ad hoc* authorities. Some of these exist to meet areawide problems, such as water, sewage, transportation, smog. Others serve to meet special needs or desires of the people in a given area, such as mosquito control or recreation. School districts also continue to be found in large numbers.

The variety and complexity of the local government structure is shown by Bureau of Census reports which indicate that in 1967 the 233 Standard Metropolitan Statistical Areas of the country contained 20,703 local governments.[7] This number included approximately 6,000 school districts, 5,500 special districts, 4,000 municipal governments, and 2,600 towns and townships.

These figures suggest that those interested in school district consolidation have possibly been giving more attention to rural areas than to metropolitan areas. In fact, little has been done to establish minimum standards to be achieved through consolidation in metropolitan areas. It is reasonable to assume, however, that the minimum numbers of pupils, for example, to be accepted as the base for a local district should be considerably larger than is the case in rural areas. The somewhat shocking picture of school districts in metropolitan areas should not be accepted as an indication that the situation in regard to school districts is worse than in the case of municipal governments and other special districts. In fact, because of the interest of the states in education, there has been substantial improvement in the school district situation and there is reason to believe that it will greatly improve in the next few years. This is probably less true of municipal governments and other special districts.

For the school administrator, the situation with reference to municipal governments and special districts other than for schools is of utmost importance. Most metropolitan residents are served by at least four separate local governments. It is with a multitude of districts that the school administrator must work if schools are to be integrated into and developed in light of the life of the metropolitan area of which they are a part. There can be little doubt that in these highly interdependent metropolitan areas there is large need for the coordination of governmental services and great difficulty in achieving it. Further, this proliferation almost certainly has a debilitating effect upon all the local governments involved and tends to reduce the accountability to the public, which has been traditionally regarded as one of the values of local government. Financial disparities and a wide range in standards of service also result. And only in a rather reluctant and stumbling manner do citizens tend to accept the fact that they are indeed citizens of a metropolitan area as well as, probably, of a municipal government and several special districts. If it is true that participation in local government itself is an important educational experience, it would appear that not much progress has been made in making this experience realizable and satisfying.

[7] *Ibid.,* pp. 12–13.

CHANGES IN FEDERAL AND STATE ACTIVITY

The growth in the metropolitan areas in economic power, in population, and in unresolved issues has stimulated the federal government to action in many matters that have hitherto been regarded as matters of state and local responsibility. Establishing the Department of Housing and Urban Affairs in 1965 was one evidence of the growth of this interest in an area with important implications for education. Other extremely significant developments which may be regarded as important aspects of the revolution in education are discussed briefly in the next sections.

The Curriculum Development Programs

The last half of the decade of the fifties and the first half of the sixties was a period in which important changes in the curriculum were effected in fields such as mathematics, physics, and chemistry. Almost as important as the changes themselves were the procedures through which they were brought about. They were effected through federal government grants to private or semiprivate individuals and groups, which brought university personnel and public school personnel together. They involved the preparation of materials by authorities in the academic fields, the development of a plan for the dissemination of the concepts, the development of competence on the part of teachers to use materials, the provision of carefully worked out instructional materials to be employed by the teachers.

In a sense, these curriculum programs became a model illustrating how curriculum change can be effected in a decentralized educational system. These programs reached into a very large percentage of the school districts of the nation and altered matters without creating great concern on the part of local board of education members, teachers, or administrators.

The Elementary and Secondary Education Act of 1965; the Higher Education Act of 1972

The 1965 act may well prove to be one of the more important federal education acts of our country. It broke new ground in its effort to sidestep the parochial-school aid controversy. Developments resulting from this action may influence nearly all local school districts. Of more immediate significance here, however, are its provisions for the establishment of regional educational laboratories. These laboratories were intended to bring the resources of the universities and colleges into close relation to the needs (curriculum development, research, and change) of local and state school systems and private schools. They have failed to live up to what were unrealistic expectations of them. The laboratories testified to a new belief in the significant contribution which could be made to education through research—or more specifically, through research and development. As time passed and "immediate" results of the impact of research in universities and laboratories were not available to legislators, the drive for new arrangements emerged. The establishment of the National Institute of Education through the Higher Education Act of 1972 was a response to this concern. It was intended to greatly strengthen the hand of the federal government in the planning and direction of the research and development effort.

The Elementary and Secondary Education Act provided federal funds to improve the educational provisions for children from low-income groups in public and private schools. The provision of funds for this one group was bound to have large implications for the total school program. It raised in sharp manner the question of what differences should be made in the expenditure of funds and in educational provisions for "poor" children. It raised the question of the meaning of equality of opportunity in new terms.

The Economic Opportunity Act

Not quite as directly or completely seen as an education act but with education (broadly viewed) as its major goal was the Economic Opportunity or Poverty Act of 1964. It was conceived of as a broad attack upon the problems of the relatively uneducated and poor. It proposed to enable them to help themselves. It provided massive programs, such as Headstart, to improve the cultural opportunities of poor children in preschool years and during the years in school. It encouraged the development of councils with substantial representation of the poor to determine the program to be undertaken. It thus challenged the established local government councils and boards, raising the question of the adequacy with which they spoke for the poor or of the extent to which they were seen by the poor as being their representatives. Further, this act provided a direct attack on the problem of employment for youth through job corps centers and related activities. This, too, was a highly important issue which was an educational one in major respects. This act also was important in terms of local school administration in that it brought other local government departments such as those concerned with health, welfare, employment, and libraries much more actively into matters closely related to education. The poor were not going to make their way ahead through the use of the formal school programs only.

Finally, in considering the changing federal program or action in educational matters, attention must be given to the courts. Federal court decisions regarding desegregation, especially when busing was involved, resulted in strong protests in the early seventies. These protests slowed or stopped the movement toward desegregation in many parts of the country. The courts also became deeply involved through a series of court decisions (such as *Rodriquez* in Texas and *Serrano* in California) pertaining to finance. At no previous period were the federal courts so heavily involved in decision making pertaining to the schools. Thus while the impact of the schools was being questioned to a far greater degree than previously, there was also a great struggle going on to ensure through them a more significant equality of opportunity.

OTHER ORGANIZATIONS AND AGENCIES

The great expectations regarding education also had an important stimulating effect on agencies other than public schools. While many others could be identified, such as parent-teacher associations, political parties, research and testing services, taxpayers' associations, associations of school boards, labor unions, business and professional groups, attention will be given here to only three groups.

The Foundations

The number of foundations and the wealth in the hands of the foundations increased greatly in recent decades. Probably it is also true that the foundations increased their interest in education. The largest of the foundations, the Ford Foundation, centered and promises to continue to focus attention on educational developments. A considerable part of the federal action previously described was based at least in part upon programs sponsored in part by foundations. The foundations, being free from the need to support mass programs, were able to exert an influence far beyond that which the dollars they provided would suggest. For theirs was the "venture" money so frequently not forthcoming from the public authorities. While an actual assessment of the influence exerted by the foundations is difficult, it is noteworthy that in recent years it has been sufficient to be the subject of considerable controversy. Some educators have felt that the foundations have not been interested in advancing money to make possible the appraisal of an idea, but rather only to advance an idea to which a commitment existed. The American Association of School Administrators conducted a study of the influence of the foundations because of the concern found among some of its members.[8] Congressional concerns resulted in further regulation and some taxation of foundations in the early seventies.

[8] American Association of School Administrators, *Private Philanthropy and Public Purposes* (Washington, D.C.: The Association, 1963).

Educational Organizations

In recent decades, educational agencies and individuals involved in the educational process have become increasingly organized. Through their organizations, they have gained greatly increased influence in regard to educational matters.

The colleges and universities, for example, have played an increasing role in public education in the last decade. They have had important influence in such areas as curriculum, achievement testing, and accreditation. Through their own admission policies and their concern for the gifted student, they have also influenced secondary schools. The development of research programs in the field of education and the growing interest of psychologists, sociologists, and political scientists in education and the school as an institution suggest that the influence of higher educational institutions and their staff on public education will be felt more significantly in the future.

The growth of organizations of the professional staff of the schools has also been marked in recent years. Related to this growth has been a notable increase in their activity and influence. In this area, reference may well be made to organizations of administrators, curriculum and supervisory staff, guidance personnel, and teachers. The large number of different organizations has reduced the influence which these groups might have had; however, they increasingly accept the view that it is only through organization that they can be effective and correspondingly reject the idea that they should not be a militant group working toward goals which they formulate. Especially noticeable is the growth of militancy among teachers' associations and teachers' unions. They have gained a substantial increase of influence in recent years not only in salary matters but in a wide range of curricular and instructional matters. While teachers and teachers groups have had large influence in many schools and school systems, they are now gaining a new image in this regard and in the public expectations that they have a more explicit and direct role in decision making.

Private and Parochial Schools

Recent decades have been marked by continued action on the part of certain private school groups, notably the Roman Catholic, to which attention is given here, for greater public recognition and for support in one form or another. They have been ably represented by their spokesmen in state legislatures, in the federal Congress, and in the core cities of the metropolitan areas where enrollments in their schools have become quite substantial. During recent years, they have won certain gains in terms of legislation for their students. They have been concerned about the limitations on such aid as have been stipulated or implied by the Supreme Court decisions and are seeking alternative solutions.

More than formerly, the religious schools and their supporters also are troubled, both financially and philosophically. They are far less sure that it would be desirable to have all children of their faith in a separate school system. The results are not conclusive in terms of values achieved. Further, they are in some disagreement regarding the causes of the decline in their enrollments. They have not met the problems of the culturally different or of the gifted more effectively than the public schools. Further, every step such as the release of children from instruction in mathematics and science to the public schools, raises important questions regarding instruction. Many had claimed that all aspects (subjects and textbooks) of instruction should be permeated by the special values of the faith. And each step toward public support must be made at some cost to the values of being private and separate. Fair-employment practice acts do not suggest that religious tests may be employed in selection of teachers, principals, or other staff if there is any public support. The minority status and feeling of being discriminated against which was long a force for the religious school is losing its meaning as change in status occurs. The church also is seeking a new relation to the world outside, and some of its members are unsure that the separate school contributes in this direction. Then, too, its problems are so great with the expansion of educational services, the technological advances in education, the decline in the availability of members of orders to meet teaching needs that it is re-examining its position regarding many educational problems and the relation of education to other religious issues.

It would thus appear that we may be in a new period of "openness" regarding the relations of public schools and various private bodies engaged in education. Quite possibly some of the barriers to communication and development will be reduced when it is more generally recognized that many problems are common to public and private bodies interested in education. Possibly also we are beginning to re-examine the question of pluralism in our society, the form of it we wish to attain, and its relation to the education question.

POWER IN THE LOCAL SCHOOL DISTRICT AREA

The school administrator is in a position of leadership in a district which is but a segment of an area, metropolitan or otherwise. It is not truly a separate unit except legally, and frequently its nature is to be explained by tradition rather than logic. He has responsibilities for a single service, which, however, is expanding and is increasingly linked to a great number of other services that are administered by other bodies. What is done in his unit and service is highly related to what is done in other units providing a similar service and to what is done by local authorities providing related services.

The Power Structures

The power structure of this unit is not always the same or clearly established. Depending upon the nature of the population, the traditions and wealth of the unit, and its relation to the metropolitan or other area, it may appear to be of the Hunter power-elite type. More likely however, it is somewhat of the process-pluralist type, where power and influence on most occasions are dispersed and where decision making involves a measure of bargaining, compromise, conflict, and agreement. If an elite once ruled educational decision making, it is perhaps less likely to do so now because of the growing interest in education on the part of various groups.

The manner in which the power structure in one school district may relate to that in other school districts of the area is unclear. The question of the nature of the metropolitan area power structure and its relation to educational developments in various school districts remains relatively unexplored. This is a matter of importance both because of the fact that a metropolitan or other area is a reality and because many educational services and developments must be conceived in larger terms. The usual school district is greatly handicapped or with extremely limited resources for the development of educational TV, programmed learning, research and development, technical education, adult education, and community college education needed for the area. It may also be extremely limited in its capacity to engage in professional negotiation or bargaining, since it is dealing with agents of groups representing the resources of the whole area.

Impact of Federal and State Activities

In this situation, it is also important to note that the state and federal agencies will be playing an increasingly important role. They have already played a more important one than is generally recognized. For example, the very system of state grants-in-aid to many suburban school districts has made it possible for them to remain independent of the core city or industrial areas of which they are a part. Without such grants, probably the integration of outside areas into a single government unit would have proceeded much more rapidly. But the federal programs in education, court actions, and related matters, previously referred to, will be of far greater significance in determining the decisions made.

This development of federal-state programs will also futher the influence of the professionals, as will the necessary increasing cooperation among the districts of an area. This is not to deny the fact that members of boards of education and other legislative bodies will have a large role in decision making; however, they will be dependent upon the comprehensive information and data development which must occur in the increasingly complex metropolitan and other areas. And it is the bureaucracies of the local, state, and federal governments that will be responsible for the development of these data, for their interpretation and communication regarding them.

Power thus tends to be diffuse, not only in terms of elite or pluralist views regarding the local unit but also in terms of networks of power extending through an area larger than the unit and in terms of federal and state action. And finally, it tends to be diffuse in terms of the inevitable and necessary bureaucracies.

BUILDING AN INTEGRATED SCHOOL COMMUNITY

The educational administrator and the local board of education are thus confronted with the problem of building an integrated school system and community. The people of a school district or of a school system cannot achieve the desired educational program without some cohesion and a measure of *community.* The people must be held together at least in the educational world by some mutual ties that provide a feeling of identity and belonging. Since we may well begin with school communities that are quite heterogeneous and lacking in *community* or integration, this may be among the most important tasks facing the schools.

As a first step in this process, study of factors related to integration may well be essential. Jacob and Teune have suggested that some elements to consider as a possible base for developing an integrated political community are: proximity, homogeneity, transactions, mutual knowledge, functional interest, communal character, political structure, sovereignty, governmental effectiveness, and integrative experience.[9]

Studies of this type may provide the understanding in light of which steps can be taken to develop ties among the people regarding educational issues and goals. Only with some development of this type is the local system likely to be effective, in relation to the larger immediate area of which it is a part, in dealing with the growing organizations of the area, and in working with the stronger state and federal agencies. Unless some

---

[9]Philip E. Jacob and Henry Teune, "The Integrative Process—Guidelines for Analysis of the Basis of Political Community," *The Integration of Political Communities,* ed. Philip E. Jacob and James V. Toscano (Philadelphia: J. B. Lippincott Co., 1964).

community is achieved, the district is likely to be pushed along by external forces. Without clean-cut though not rigid goals, it cannot be a strong unit which melds various pressures and considerations into a constructive organization.

The educator should be aware of facts such as the following regarding the community.

SOCIETY IS CHARACTERIZED BY LARGE POWER ORGANIZATIONS In a community, for example, at least the following power groups of special interest to education will usually be found: the school power structure; governmental structures other than schools (some of which are directly related to political organizations); organizations of businessmen, professional groups, and labor; mass media of communication; and power leaders who may function informally or through recognized organizations.

The term "power" is not used here in the sense that it is something undesirable. Rather, "power" is a word that will be used to describe the "acts of men going about the business of moving other men to act in relation to themselves or in relation to organic or inorganic things."[10] The power of the individual is extremely limited unless structured through an organization or association. Such structuring may be provided for by statute. It may be highly formal or quite informal.

The school system itself may be viewed as a power structure. It coordinates the efforts of the board of education, administration, teaching, and other staff members in the provision and advancement of education. It generally is supported by such groups as the parent-teacher association, which may be regarded as a part of the power structure that exists to further education.

Some other power structures in the community may oppose the school system. But it should be noted that the opportunity that groups have to organize themselves in order to be effective is a fundamental right that a free society must guarantee. In fact, the existence of such groups may be regarded as one measure of the level of maturity of the democratic community.

MANY OF THE POWER ORGANIZATIONS HAVE BEEN CONSCIOUSLY CREATED AND HAVE A DEFINITE PURPOSE. The written statement of purposes, if one exists, may or may not be complete. Possibly it will not reveal some of the purposes. Informal organizations may have greater power than many that are formally organized.

MANY ORGANIZATIONS ARE NATIONALLY ORIENTED. Their members think and act more like members of similar organizations in other

[10]Floyd Hunter, *Community Power Structure. A Study of Decision Makers* (Chapel Hill: University of North Carolina Press, 1953) p. 2.

communities than like other citizens of their own community. This situation is related to the stratification found in the community. It raises the question whether the geographic community is a social community.

INDIVIDUALS ARE FREQUENTLY ASSOCIATED WITH ORGANIZATIONS THAT HAVE CONTRADICTORY PURPOSES. The professional organization to which they belong may oppose the interest individuals have in the education of children and which they demonstrate through work in an association of parents. This lack of consistency suggests the need for involvement of people in an organization if their support is to be secured.

THE COMMUNITY EXISTING OR TO BE DEVELOPED HAS IMPORTANT VALUES, IDEALS, AND CONCEPTS THAT CAN BE SIGNIFICANT LEVERS OF ACTION. The concept of equality of educational opportunity and the understanding that it does not mean identity of opportunity, for example, is extremely powerful. Too little attention is given to such fundamental concepts in many communities, although they also have important implications for education in the state and nation as well as in the community.

THE COMMUNITY WILL NOT ACT IN ACCORD WITH ITS OWN IDEALS, VALUES, AND CONCEPTS UNLESS IT KNOWS THE FACTS AND IS CHALLENGED. It is easy to profess interest in equality of educational opportunity and to behave in ways that deny it. The challenge of facts may be helpful in causing the people of a community to act in accord with their professed values.

THE SCHOOL DISTRICT IS BUT A PART OF A LARGER COMMUNITY. The district cannot and should not expect to move alone. It must be aware of the larger community (both in terms of its own geographical area and with reference to the metropolitan or similar area) and accept a constructive role in it.

STUDIES OF THE COMMUNITY

Methods of Study

An effective, planned program for developing an integrated school community must be based upon the study of the community.

Many methods may be employed to study the complexities of the community and its institutions including the schools. Important methods to be employed are the following:

THE HISTORICAL METHOD. This method, which is too little employed, may reveal how the community has grown, what the nature of population change has been, how the community has been organized, what educational values and issues have been prominent in it, the reasons for the existing school organization, and the relation of community education to other governmental services.

ANALYSIS OF LAWS AND RECORDS. Statutes, minutes of boards of education and of other organizations, press treatment of education, census reports, population data, economic reports, success of high school graduates in college and in employment, and records of dropouts are samples of the large quantities of data pertaining to the community that await analysis. The amount of data available suggests the need for careful definition of purpose and study over a period of time, if a comprehensive picture of the community is to be secured.

SURVEYS OF STATUS AND PRACTICE. What are the existing conditions? Does social stratification mark the community and the school? What have been the objectives, the programs, and the practices of the schools? What is the nature of home life? What is the place of youth, and how are their problems being met? What are the power organizations in the community, who are their members, and how do they operate? Who are the power leaders? Who controls the mass media of communication, and what is the audience and impact of each? How does the school system function as a power organization? What are the community practices and norms? These are a few of the many aspects of status and practice that might be studied as the base for the advancement of the educational system. An approach to these problems will involve the use of many techniques such as observation, interviews, analysis of records, questionnaires, and maintenance of logs and diaries.

STUDIES OF VALUES. These could be regarded as one phase of surveys of status in the sense that one aspect of status would be the values held. They are listed separately, however, because of their significance and because they are not generally thought of as an aspect of current status. The values held are largely ascertained through interviews, but records of elections and previous community actions may also be highly informative.

CASE STUDIES. Case studies are suggested as a method of studying a community because they make it possible to visualize the interaction of various forces and to view the community or any of its organizations or groups as societies in action. They reveal organizations as dynamic structures. This concept of community life must be accepted if one is to be prepared to work with the forces that shape education.

STUDIES OF THE AREA. The school district must be informed regarding the larger geographical area of which it is a part. Therefore, in cooperation with other districts, it must provide for studies of the larger community and of other school districts. Only in this manner can essential cooperative effort be achieved and programs developed which are beyond the resources of any one district.

STUDIES OF STATE AND FEDERAL PROGRAMS AND THEIR INFLUENCE. Too often districts make little or no attempt to determine the influence of federal programs. In fact many districts are small and understaffed to such a degree that they are not prepared to plan effective utilization of the opportunities opened through federal programs. The districts of an area might well plan to attack this problem through a cooperative effort with a staff jointly employed or through the intermediate unit.

Procedure in Community Study

Equally as important as the methodological approaches used in the study of the community are the procedures by which the study is conducted. Although certain of the suggested methods would need to be carried on individually by highly trained specialists, this would not be true in the great majority of instances. Competent specialists or consultants would, of course, need to participate in planning, formulating hypotheses, constructing the instruments used, preparing research workers, analyzing data, and formulating findings. But many people residing within the community could participate in the work. Local personnel need to do much of the work, not only for reasons of greater economy and a consequent expansion of the program, but because the knowledge gained would more likely result in action.

It would, therefore, be desirable to plan considerable action research. This would involve using available resources under competent leadership. It means systematically collecting and using many data that presently go unused. It would involve many teachers, parents, older students, and other citizens of the community interested in any organization that impinges on education.

In organizing such a program no one form is to be preferred in all situations. Provision should generally be made to involve the following:

1. Both laymen and teachers;
2. Lay leaders of status and laymen representative of a wide variety of groups;
3. Consultants;
4. Resource people and assistants to carry out the routine and data collecting and analysis operations, and to relate data to community values;
5. Research and development staff to design and appraise the work undertaken and to advise regarding implementation.

Consultants and research and development staff may be supplied by a metropolitan or other intermediate or areawide unit.

Implications of Community Study

Frequently, questions are raised regarding the use of data pertaining to the community. For example, does the administrator become subservient to the power structure when elements of it are known to him? Or is he then in the position to become a manipulator? Or in a better position to provide constructive leadership?

The administrator, board of education, and others are in a position to act with intelligence and with reference to accepted values only when the power structure is known to them. Certainly the administrator and the board of education need to avoid becoming the tools of any single power group that may or may not have knowledge of and belief in the potential of education. At times, permitting such a group to make decisions may appear to be the easy road, but it would scarcely be consistent with the purposes of public education in a democracy.

If being a manipulator is interpreted to mean concealing facts, seeking personal power, controlling or making decisions for others, this concept or role must be rejected. However, if by being a manipulator reference is made to providing leadership and helping the community determine what its status is, how status differs from values held, and how the community can achieve what it seeks for its children and youth, the role should be welcomed. The role of manipulator might well be sought if it means helping a community reconsider and clarify its purposes. In reality, this is leadership, not manipulation.

In serving in a leadership role the school administrator needs also to recognize his power in relation to the decision-making process and the effect of the values he holds upon the processes and action to be taken. Too frequently, he may see his views (values) as objective and the only defensible ones. He may indeed re-examine his values and modify or hold fast to them, but it is important that he understand them in explicit terms. This understanding will provide him with a much more adequate base for analyzing the situations which present themselves, for seeing himself in interpersonal relationships, for suggesting processes, for relating to role expectancies. Then he may see and understand the possible importance of deviant values—their potential for new integration or for disintegration. He must provide for them, though unfortunately, contrary to the American dream, there is no assurance that they inevitably will produce a desired integrated school community.

ACTION BASED ON COMMUNITY STUDY

A knowledge of the community is an essential background of action in the school-community relations area. Without this knowledge, any program developed must be based upon various assumptions regarding the community-assumptions that may or may not be sound.

A knowledge of the community includes a knowledge of the school, for the school is one of the institutions of the community. It can be understood only by considering various other conditions existing in the community. Without a thorough knowledge of the school and its relations to the community, the development of a program cannot be carried on in an effective manner.

The study of the community, including the school, should supply answers to such questions as: What have been the media of communication between school and community? What are the areas of ignorance between the school and community? What "publics" exist in the community? What resources are available for use in the program? How competent are school personnel to participate in the program? What mass media of communication service the community, and what contribution can they be expected to make? What power structures and what organizations exist in the community? What are the major limitations of the public education power structure in the community? What are the values of the community? What are the major strengths and weaknesses of the schools?

When data of the types suggested are available, it becomes possible to give careful, considered thought to the development of a program for achieving an integrated school community. In developing the program, it should be recognized that a most difficult task is being undertaken. Fundamentally, the problem is one of communication and of education. It is a matter of assisting the community in gaining knowledge of the schools, of the schools' potential, and of the procedures through which the potential may be realized. Given the diversity of backgrounds, interests, and activities of citizens however, and the variety of media that may be employed, the problem of communication is an exceedingly complex one. A good medium of communication with a few people may have no value with many others. It must be remembered that in communication what is heard may be very different from what is spoken. And, of course, behavioristic communication may be much more effective than verbalistic.

The inevitability of communications in the school-community relations area must be recognized. A visit to a school, a meeting with children going to school, a child's report regarding events in school, the role of teachers in community organizations, a school building—an infinite number of situations exist through which some type of communication occurs.

The problem is whether a sufficient number of media of high validity can be utilized to improve the understanding of school and community and enable them to progress together. If this can be achieved, a substantial benefit will result for the school and community and for education itself, since much of it goes on in the home and in the community outside the school. Thus, although the best school program is central in any school-community relations program, it also must be remembered that education is most likely to achieve significant goals through a high level of school-community understanding and action. The parent or community organization for youth with little understanding of the school is not prepared to contribute in a highly effective manner to the education of youth. But the parent and the youth group are inevitably "educating" youth.

Suggestions Regarding School-Community Action

In developing a program to promote school-community cooperation the following guidelines should be kept in mind.

MULTIDIRECTIONAL COMMUNICATION IS ESSENTIAL AND MUST BE BOTH THE BASIS OF THE PROGRAM AND ONE OF ITS PURPOSES. Two-way communication is mentioned frequently. It is necessary but not likely to be effective unless accompanied by communication within the school staff and within various other agencies.

A POLICY STATEMENT REGARDING SCHOOL-COMMUNITY INTERACTION SHOULD BE ADOPTED BY THE BOARD OF EDUCATION, MAKING CLEAR THE PURPOSES OF THE PROGRAM AND THE ROLE OF SCHOOL PERSONNEL. Failure to establish adequate policies in this area sharply reduces the opportunity for effective leadership by school administrators.

THE PROGRAM MUST BE PLANNED. The difficulty of the task as well as the variety of possible ends and media demand careful planning. Without such planning, achievement will probably be extremely limited. A committee of laymen familiar with the organizational life of the community and with the media of communication within it can be of great assistance in this planning. Studies to determine the extent of information about and attitudes toward various aspects of the educational program are an essential base for planning.

AN EFFECTIVE PROGRAM CAN ONLY BE DESIGNED WITH SOME CLEARLY DEFINED GOALS IN MIND. Are there particular problems to be met, groups to be communicated with, or areas of ignorance on the part of the school or community? A planned program can be integrated with the more routine work in the field of school-community relations that is established with reference to legal requirements, events in the school calendar, and seasonal opportunities regarding aspects of the total educational program. While the vision must be large, steps toward it should permit observable progress.

REPORTING IS AN ESSENTIAL ELEMENT OF THE TOTAL PROGRAM AND NEEDS TO BE DEVELOPED IN AN EFFECTIVE MANNER WITH REFERENCE TO THE VARIETY OF GROUPS TO BE REACHED. It may involve report cards or conferences with parents; press relations; the preparation of brief, attractive, and well-illustrated annual or special reports; and reports on achievements and needs of the schools. Above all it must offer satisfaction through achievement by participants.

INVOLVEMENT OF MANY CITIZENS IS DESIRABLE. It facilitates a higher level of understanding and more action than is likely to result from reporting. It avoids the tendency of school people to have the "answer" to the problem and then to attempt to win acceptance for it. Rather, it places the problem in the hands of many more people for consideration and the formulation of tentative solutions. It reveals large, unused personnel resources. It should lead to more sound solutions and to earlier implementation. It is likely to be developed effectively only if the board has adopted policies encouraging it.

A WIDE VARIETY OF MEDIA SHOULD BE EMPLOYED. The error of utilizing only one medium, such as the press or the parent-teacher association, should be avoided. This is not to underestimate the significance of such media, but rather to suggest that consideration should be given to the many that are available. Different media may involve or reach different groups, or may have a different impact.

THE SIGNIFICANCE OF THE INDIVIDUAL SCHOOL IN SCHOOL-COMMUNITY RELATIONS SHOULD BE RECOGNIZED. The most impressive contact that parents will have with the school system will be at the school that their children are attending. They will inevitably think of the system in terms of their personal experiences with teachers and principal at the school they know. If many are going to be involved in working through problems and policies, it is likely to be done at the individual school level. The communities or neighborhoods served by schools vary widely in many systems, and consequently the programs at the school level need to be characterized by variation. The movement toward decentralization should substantially increase the contribution of the individual school in this program.

THE CENTRAL OFFICE SHOULD TAKE RESPONSIBILITY FOR A FEW SYSTEMWIDE SCHOOL-COMMUNITY RELATIONS ACTIVITIES AND SHOULD

CONCENTRATE ITS ENERGIES ON THE DEVELOPMENT OF A STAFF FOR MORE EFFECTIVE PARTICIPATION IN THE WORK. Principals need help in developing programs for their schools. Teachers need assistance in developing competency for utilizing parent-teacher conferences effectively. Many staff members need to develop more competency in working as a member of a lay-professional committee or in serving on a panel. Staff members are frequently lacking in group process skills, which are most important if problems are to be worked through cooperatively. Many groups in the community remain relatively uninvolved.

RESPONSIBILITY FOR COORDINATION AND LEADERSHIP IN SCHOOL-COMMUNITY RELATIONS SHOULD BE FIXED UPON SOME ONE PERSON. Formerly, this person probably would have been drawn from the press. With the broader concept of the work, however, he needs to have much more than press experience-though this would still be desirable in terms of mass media of communication. Today, however, he needs to be skillful in techniques of community analysis and in communication, able to help others develop competency in working with laymen in a wide variety of ways, and competent in the field of education. He must be an expert in public participation and action.

EVALUATION OF THE PROGRAM AND OF ITS VARIOUS ASPECTS IS OF VITAL IMPORTANCE. Many activities are carried on without any systematic attempt at collecting available data and at evaluating the work done. Many parent-teacher associations carry on programs for years without critically constructive evaluations being made. A citizens committee is formed, operates for several months or a year, submits a report, and dissolves without anyone's studying its procedures and its strengths and limitations. When another committee is formed, there is too little knowledge available as a result of past experience. What are the results of the program of reporting through the press, or through special reports? What coverage of vital issues is offered? Various people have judgments regarding the effectiveness of various techniques and procedures, but all too rarely are they based upon a planned evaluation. Just how is desirable educational change effected?

THE COMMUNITY AND ITS SCHOOLS

In concluding this section, attention is called to the fact that the community (the state, the local school system, or the area served by the individual school) substantially determines the quantity and quality of educational provisions. Its understandings, values, ability to organize its efforts and to act are central elements in the decisions that it inevitably makes.

In making these decisions the community must have concern for children and youth and also for various staff members connected with the schools. It must be aware of the organizational structure of the community and of the schools. It must be familiar with legal structure pertaining to schools and function in accord with it, effecting changes when needed. It must constantly seek facts so that it may make sound decisions. It must periodically re-examine its philosophical commitments and use them as standards for evaluating its practices.

In all of these activities the community should be able to regard the school administrative staff as its agent, providing leadership in its relentless search for a more adequate educational program—a program involving the aspirations and practices of schools, community, and parents. The community must have an understanding of the conditions under which leadership can function effectively, and it must scrupulously protect those conditions. The leader must no less scrupulously respect the competency of the community to make decisions.

Under these circumstances, the community and its educational leaders cooperate in planning, in formulating policy, in implementing programs, and in evaluating. School-community relations are not then essentially matters of reporting or interpreting. Rather, they are carrying forward a public enterprise with laymen and educators playing the respective roles that are most rewarding in terms of the education of men. Action now builds mutual understanding in depth.

SOME IMPORTANT PROBLEMS AND ISSUES

In the following pages, consideration is given to a few of the major issues pertaining to the community and its schools.

May Public Opinion or a Pressure Group Be Too Large a Determiner of Educational Practice?

There is danger that uninformed public opinion or perhaps a small but highly vocal group will have too large an influence on educational practice. Occasionally, a meeting is reported where a vote is taken on a rather technical subject about which the voters are uninformed. The individual or group with the greatest pressure potential does not necessarily have the sound answer.

The school administrator should not abdicate his leadership responsibility, a responsibility that includes presenting the facts and the results of studies that have been carried on regarding the problem, presenting proposals for a more thorough study, and presenting suggestions for essential research. The administrator must assist groups in recognizing that there are important ways to get information regarding a matter other than asking opinions about it. Public interest in an issue needs to be seen as an opportunity for its fuller study—an opportunity for many to learn more about the issue.

This is not to suggest that public opinion should be ignored on many issues. It is an important factor in many situations and must be considered. However, this interest may be of more value in suggesting communication, clarifying goals and practices, or re-examining values than in pointing the way in regard to practice. If public opinion differs widely from the views or understandings of school personnel, an excellent opportunity would appear to exist for some planned research and a cooperative study of the problem.

The development of sound educational practices demands that there be recognition of the limitations of the expert. Often he may be so deeply immersed in the subject that he misses some of the broader implications. It also requires that the contribution of the expert be recognized and capitalized upon. Closer attention to many educational problems will increase the awareness of laymen regarding the complexity of the issues. It will reduce the demand for simple solutions—especially those involving a return to some practice that may have worked reasonably well in a far simpler and quite different society. It may also result in the development of a more soundly based public opinion, that could be a most important element in controlling the influence of groups not seeking constructive ends.

What are the strengths and limitations of the expert? How can a community best use the expert? What types of issues require research rather than a survey of public opinion in order to arrive at sound solutions?

Does the Closeness of the School to the Community
Subject the School to the Narrowness of the Community?

Will not the school merely reflect the prejudices of the community if it works closely with it? Will not community lack of concern for human values limit the school in the attention it can give to them? Will the administrator become a part of the business group with which he associates, largely a reflector of its concepts? Or the captive of a pressure group?

In response to these queries, a number of observations may be made. The community may of course contain a wide variety of groups and individuals, some of whom may have better vision regarding educational objectives than the administrator and the teaching staff. Then, too, it is assumed that the administrator has the competence to work with groups without being enveloped by them. His own values and commitments with reference to society and education are an important source of strength. Although leadership is recognized as having a relationship to various situational forces, the assumption must not be made that the administrator is without influence, adrift in a nondescript public-opinion or pressure-group sea. Rather, knowledge of the complexity of the leadership role enables the administrator to be more effective.

The community also has values that if brought to public attention may be important levers through which it can raise its vision and activities. The administrator has responsibilities in this sphere.

Finally, in the case of the community that does not seek or attain even desirable minimum levels of educational provision, whether in terms of what is taught or how it is taught, there is recourse to the state and to constitutional rights. In general, the state should be seen as a stimulating agency, an agency of cross-fertilization challenging communities with the pollen gathered over the nation. Regrettably, however, there will also be times when the state must make attempts at enforcing minimum standards. This role of the state should remain a minor one, one that is exercised less and less frequently as competent communities seriously contemplate and act upon educational problems. Therefore, there would seem to be much reason for seeking the close integration of the community and the school, recognizing, however, that neither local community nor the local school system will always take a sound position. The interaction of the two, with contributions to thought and practice from school and community leaders and at times from the outside, offers much promise.

Can the schools rise above the community? How can the administrator avoid becoming the instrument of the more reactionary forces in the community? Of a militant, pressure group?

Is a School Public Relations Program Consistent with the Educational Purposes of Our Society?

Some educators have doubted the desirability of devoting large energies to various aspects of the school-community relations program. They have been suspicious of publicity. This concern is quite understandable in a society in which much publicity has not sought the enhancement of the citizen but rather has sought to make him an unthinking captive of some group. This publicity has sought to influence through offering the half-truth or through hiding essential facts and thus distorting. The fear that man may become merely the dupe of those with the resources to control the mass media should not be discarded without thought.

On the other hand, it must be recognized that unless the facts and the case for public education are put forth vigorously through the most effective instruments employed in our society, the gap between the people's desires and practice in education will widen. And even their values and desires may shift farther away from interest in children and young people and concern for the dignity and worth of the individual. In the fierce struggle for the minds and commitments of men the administrator cannot default and remain an educator.

The educator may consider this program as one of adult education regarding the schools. In an age when the school may be playing a less significant educational role than at times in the past—because of the great impact of the mass media of communication—it is especially fitting that fuller consideration be given to educational goals in our society and the relationship of various agencies to them.

Furthermore, if the ability to govern is related to experience in governing, then the public schools may constitute one of the most important opportunities to develop the skills of self-government. In a period of growing central control, decision-making opportunities close to the people take on added significance. Carrying on a public relations program should facilitate rather than militate against the cooperative solution of educational problems.

For these various reasons it appears clear that public relations per se are not inconsistent with the purposes of education in a democracy but are an important factor in achieving those purposes.

Is there a danger that the school system will reveal only the facts that reflect favorably upon it? How can this be avoided?

The fear that government officials may engage in propagandizing and not present the facts in the light of which the people can make decisions, should not be dismissed lightly. However, the growing complexity of the educational enterprise and of the society of which it is a part demands increased expenditure of time and money for the promotion of understanding. Without such understanding the possibility of intelligent citizen action or of sound action on the part of educators is greatly reduced. A sound approach to the problem will recognize these facts and give attention to the manner in which the work can be most desirably carried forward. There are standards regarding the programs of public relations that need to be established. The development of closer working relationships between citizens and educators will in itself constitute an important barrier to the development of undesirable practices.

Are present statutory provisions regarding the expenditure of funds for public relations purposes sound?

How Much Concentration upon School-Community Relations in the Local School or School System Is Desirable?

Our society is marked by large organizations. The federal government plays a larger and larger role in our lives. The nation is economically one unit. Is it not rather self-deceptive to be so greatly concerned about the local situation?

Conceivably such concern could be self-defeating. Intense interest and concern about the local school might result in a lack of interest in the utilization of the federal tax power for educational purposes, even though the economic organization of the society would indicate the desirability of this.

Similarly, the local system might be quite incapable of fending off the attacks of a national organization with large resources that is devoted to the weakening of public education. Such a national organization might choose to strike at a few local organizations at any one time and shift its energies to best achieve its ends.

Although there is no completely satisfactory safeguard against these dangers, it must be observed that the local school is probably the most readily available base for interesting and activating the citizen. The citizen is interested in education both within the school and outside. His children are involved and his devotion to their development is as great as that of the educator. From this base his concern for more adequate education in other areas can be developed. The bringing together of strong local forces of different communities could result in the striking advancement of education in the state or nation.

It is not suggested that strength at the local level is sufficient. Increasing attention must be focused upon the organization of those interested in education at the state and national levels. Local forces need the assistance of national organizations. Concentration upon the local situation should be desirable if accompanied by the development of an understanding of the nature of our society and of the ability to function effectively in it.

How can the tendency of many laymen and educators to be concerned with education only in their own area be overcome?

Can the PTA or Other Group Be a Part of the Educational Power Structure and Yet Enjoy Independence of Thought and Action?

In some communities the parent-teacher organization is one of the more important parts of the power structure devoted to the advancement of education. Some people hold that in too many instances the parents' group or citizens' group may become merely a mouthpiece of professional educators. Some "educators" may desire to have parents' groups play this role.

It is surely proper and desirable that the parents associated with the school should be part of the organization of the total forces devoted to education. It must be recognized, however, that the total structure related to education will be better and stronger if various parts of it enjoy a very real measure of independence and initiative. The parent group that does not think for itself is not one of great strength. Neither is it, in the long run, one that contributes significantly to education.

Educators and other citizens need to develop stronger belief in the desirability of honest differences in judgment, in the expression of different points of view. The submissive power structure is not one that will grapple effectively with large issues. Groups motivated by common purposes can gain much through the utilization of all the capacity found in them—and by developing their potential capacity through attacking important issues.

Does the PTA enjoy adequate independence of action in most communities? How can a strong, nonsubservient PTA be developed? Would the same proposals apply to other citizen groups?

What Are the Limits of Involvement as a Practice Designed to Improve Educational Services?

There are limits to involvement in terms of available time, in terms of the contribution of those involved, and in terms of the abilities of the various parties to work together in a satisfactory manner.

Development of plans for and working with large numbers of laymen is time consuming for the educator. He cannot work with too many groups at once without neglecting other responsibilities. This may be remedied in part as more members of the professional staff develop competency in working with lay groups. Laymen also have many demands upon their time and unless adequate resources are available to facilitate the collection of essential data, committees either fail to do the job or do it without adequate knowledge. The limits of time for involvement therefore need to be considered carefully.

Limitations may also exist in terms of the competency of various people to work together and to contribute to the specific issue under consideration. Laymen may be profitably involved in a consideration of the uses to which the school buildings will be put in evenings and for which provision should be made in the plans, but there would be little point in having them consider details of structural safety. Various factors have to be considered when determining whether or not there will be involvement and what the nature of the involvement will be.

Finally, it should be noted that participation must be carried on in such a manner as not to hamper the operation of the organization. Many decisions need to be made in the operation of a school or school system. Involvement is essential in broad policy and procedural determination but scarcely in the details of administration resulting from the application of the policy. Citizens may, however, be involved in preliminary screening for a principalship provided the limits of their role are clearly established in guidelines.

Unless there is a realization of the limits of involvement, it is conceivable that it will result in increasing the insecurity of the teacher and administrator and in reducing the effectiveness of the educational program. On the other hand, its possible contribution to the teacher, to the administrator, and to the education of children and young people is large. With careful consideration the dangers should be largely avoided while the benefits are secured. Fruitful utilization of involvement requires time and analyzed experience.

Why must much of the participation occur at the school level? How can staff and citizens be prepared for participation in the school-community relations activity? Are teachers prepared to work on studies in cooperation with citizens? What are the practical limits of involvement?

SELECTED REFERENCES

BANFIELD, EDWARD C., *Big City Politics.* New York: Random House, 1965.

BOLLENS, JOHN C., and HENRY J. SCHMANDT, *The Metropolis: Its People, Politics and Economic Life.* New York: Harper & Row, Publishers, 1965.

CAMPBELL, ROALD F., LUVERN L. CUNNINGHAM, and RODERICK F. MCPHEE, *The Organization and Control of American Schools.* Columbus, Ohio: Charles E. Merrill Books, Inc., 1965.

CAMPBELL, ROALD F., and JOHN A. RAMSEYER, *School-Community Relationships.* Boston: Allyn & Bacon, Inc., 1955.

DAHL, ROBERT, *Who Governs?* New Haven: Yale University Press, 1961.

HAVIGHURST, ROBERT J. and BERNICE L. NEUGARTEN, *Society and Education,* 3d ed. Boston: Allyn and Bacon, Inc., 1967.

HAWLEY, WILLIS D. and FREDERICK M. WIRT, eds., *The Search for Community Power.* Englewood Cliffs, New Jersey: Prentice-Hall, Inc., 1968.

HUNTER, FLOYD, *Community Power Structure. A Study of Decision Makers.* Chapel Hill: University of North Carolina Press, 1953.

KAUFMAN, HERBERT, *Politics and Policies in State and Local Governments.* Englewood Cliffs, New Jersey: Prentice-Hall, Inc., 1963.

KIMBROUGH, RALPH B., *Political Power and Educational Decision Making.* Skokie, Ill.: Rand McNally & Co., 1964.

KIRST, MICHAEL W., ed., *The Politics of Education.* Berkeley: McCutchan Publishing Corporation, 1970.

LUTZ, FRANK W. and JOSEPH J. AZZARELLI, *Struggle for Power in Education.* New York: The Center for Applied Research in Education, Inc., 1966.

ROSE, ARNOLD M., *The Power Structure: Political Processes in American Society.* New York: Oxford University Press, 1967.

part II

THE ORGANIZATION FOR EDUCATION

8

The Federal Government and Education

Despite the fact that most people have assumed that the states are responsible for education, the federal government is also deeply involved in education. A 748-page volume was required to publish 88 federal statutes relating to education[1] in the *Compilation of Federal Education Laws* prepared for the Committee on Education and Labor of the House of Representatives in 1971.

The United States Office of Education listed 132 programs administered by the Office in a publication entitled *Guides to OE Administered Programs, Fiscal Year 1970*. The involvement of the federal government in education has increased dramatically since the early 1950s. In 1952–53, the federal support for all education totaled $1,417,000,000, more than half of which was expended on the education of veterans. In 1971–72, federal

---

[1]Committee on Education and Labor, House of Representatives, *A Compilation of Federal Education Laws* (Washington, D.C.: U.S. Government Printing Office, 1971).

support for all education and related activities totaled approximately $12,-812,000,000. In this chapter, we will present a brief history of federal relations to education, describe some of the major issues, and analyze some of the recent major changes in federal educational policy.

The relationship of the federal government to public education is one of the most controversial and yet one of the most important issues before the American people. This issue has been debated since the adoption of the Constitution in 1789, but during the past 25 years, interest in this issue has been greatly intensified. In 1951, Quattlebaum listed 42 governmental commissions, advisory groups, and voluntary organizations as having made studies and issued recommendations concerning federal educational policies during the preceding twenty years.[2] Since that time, the number of such studies has greatly increased.

The relationship of the federal government to public education has become the battleground for testing many important principles of law, theories of government, and philosophical values. Issues concerning states' rights, the general welfare, the police power, federalism, freedom of speech and press, freedom of religion, separation of church and state, impairing the obligation of contracts, equal protection of the laws, civil rights, the due process of the law, the power of Congress to tax and spend, and other vital matters have become involved in this problem. Decisions on public education made by the federal government serve as precedents defining the relationship of the federal government to the states and to the people on many other important issues. Fundamental changes in the economy of the nation and in international relationships are bringing about many changes in the respective roles of the federal government and the states. Changes and proposals for changes naturally become political issues in a democracy. Therefore, it is not surprising that interest in the relationship of the federal government to public education is increasing.

A comprehensive treatment of this problem would require a formidable volume. Therefore, this chapter presents only some of the more important facts and issues that will serve as a basis for the further study of the relationship of the federal government to public education.

FEDERAL CONSTITUTIONAL AUTHORITY[3]

The powers of the government of the United States are delegated rather than inherent. The Tenth Amendment provides: "The powers not

[2]Charles A. Quattlebaum, *Federal Educational Activities and Educational Issues Before Congress* (Washington, D.C.: U.S. Government Printing Office, 1951), pp. 69–128.

[3]The authors are indebted to Newton Edwards, *The Courts and the Public Schools* (Chicago: University of Chicago Press, 1971), for many of the concepts set forth in this section.

delegated to the United States by the Constitution, nor prohibited by it to the States, are reserved to the States respectively or to the people." The federal government, therefore, has no powers other than those specifically conferred on it by the Constitution or such as can reasonably be implied from those specifically granted.[4] On the other hand, the governmental powers of the states are plenary except for the powers that have been delegated to the federal government or withheld from the states by some specific provision of the Constitution.

The Constitution of the United States makes no reference to education. Therefore, under the Tenth Amendment the states have assumed the basic responsibility for public education. Any authority of the federal government to finance, to control, or to regulate education must be found in the implied powers delegated to the central government in one or more clauses of the Constitution. But the Constitution is a very broad statement of principles, and numerous judicial interpretations of these principles have greatly extended the application of the implied powers of the federal government since the adoption of the Constitution.

The General Welfare Clause

Clause 1 of Section 8 of Article I of the Constitution provides that "The Congress shall have the power to lay and collect taxes, duties, imposts and excises, to pay the debts and provide for the common defense and general welfare of the United States...." This clause of the Constitution, although it deals with many other important matters, is commonly known as the "general welfare clause." It has been one of the most controversial provisions of the Constitution since the very beginning. It was the center of the famous controversy between Alexander Hamilton and James Madison. It was argued by Madison that this clause conferred no additional powers on the Congress to tax and spend, and therefore it was meant only to be a reference to powers that were specifically granted to Congress by the Constitution. Hamilton held, however, that this clause conferred upon Congress the power to tax and spend for purposes in addition to those specifically enumerated by the Constitution and in fact conferred on Congress the power to tax and spend for any purpose that it deemed to be for the general welfare.

This controversy has continued for more than 175 years, but the battleground has shifted from constitutional authority to wisdom of policy. The Supreme Court, in ruling upon the Agricultural Adjustment Act, declared that "the power of Congress to authorize expenditures of public money for public purposes is not limited by the direct grants of legislative

[4]*Ibid.*, p. 1.

power found in the Constitution."[5] The Supreme Court, in an opinion relating to the Social Security Act, held that the descretion of determining whether some purpose of federal expenditure was for the general welfare laid with the Congress and not the Court, provided it was not clearly a display of arbitrary power. The Court further declared that the concept of general welfare is not static because what is critical or urgent changes with the times.[6]

It seems clear that the constitutional authority of the Congress to appropriate money for public education has been clearly established by the principles of law enumerated by the Supreme Court in other cases before it. Therefore, the controversy now centers on whether it is good public policy for the federal government to take positive action with respect to public education and what the nature and extent of such action should be rather than on the constitutional authority of Congress to act.

Limitations on the States

Opposition to federal control of education is widespread in the United States. The term "federal control" is interpreted in various ways by different people. Actually, the federal government from the beginning of the nation has exercised substantial control over certain aspects of the educational activities of the states, as will be explained later. Many of these controls are so well accepted that the people have seldom thought of them as controls. Actually, if a movement were started to eliminate them, there would be as much opposition as there is to more federal control of education. Such is the force of custom and propaganda.

The educational policies and activities of the states are profoundly affected by limitations on the powers of the states contained in the Constitution. Some of these limitations are discussed in the following paragraphs.

SEPARATION OF CHURCH AND STATE. The power of the federal government to control the relationship of the public schools to religion was clearly established by the First and Fourteenth Amendments. The First Amendment provides: "Congress shall make no law respecting an establishment of religion, or prohibiting the free exercise thereof. . . ." The Fourteenth Amendment provides in part: ". . . No state shall make or enforce any law which shall abridge the privileges or immunities of citizens of the United States. . . ." The Supreme Court has held that this amendment makes the First Amendment applicable to the states in defining the relationship between church and state. In the case of *Illinois ex rel. McCol-*

---

[5] *United States v. Butler,* 297 U.S. 1, 56 Sup. Ct. 312.
[6] *Helvering v. Davis,* 301 Dr. S. 619, 57 Sup. Ct. 904.

lum v. *Board of Education*[7] and in *Everson* v. *Board of Education*[8] the Court declared the First Amendment was intended to erect a "wall of separation between church and state." The Court has made it clear in these two opinions and in other opinions that tax-supported property cannot be used for religious instruction and that neither a state nor the federal government can set up a church or levy a tax, large or small, to support any religious activities or institutions.

In recent years, a number of states have attempted to give financial assistance to parochial schools from public funds. Up to the present time, the federal courts have declared these measures to be a violation of the First Amendment.[9]

A case involving Bible reading in the public schools was brought before the United States Supreme Court in October 1962. The Court ruled in 1963 that Bible reading in the public schools was a violation of the First Amendment.[10]

EQUAL PROTECTION OF THE LAWS. Neither a state nor an agency of the state, such as a board of education, can deny a citizen of the United States equal protection of the law. The Supreme Court on May 17, 1954, in dealing with five cases before it, ruled that segregation in the public schools was unconstitutional because it denied equal protection of the laws. The Court stated:

> We conclude that in the field of public education the doctrine of "separate but equal" has no place. Separate educational facilities are inherently unequal. Therefore, we hold that the plaintiffs and others similarly situated for whom the actions are brought are, by reason of the segregation complained of, deprived of the equal protection of the laws guaranteed by the Fourteenth Amendment.[11]

This ruling reversed the position of the Court on *Plessy* v. *Ferguson* in 1896, when it ruled in a transportation case that separate but equal facilities were constitutional.[12] The educational policies of seventeen states and the District of Columbia were vitally affected by this decision. The *de facto* segregation by race in the large cities of many other states has also been affected by this decision. It will be noted that this decision controls not only the educational policies of the states with respect to segregation by race but also the policies of boards of education wherever

---
[7]333 U.S. 203.
[8]330 U.S. 1.
[9]Examples of such cases are: *Lemon v. Kurtzman*, 403 U.S. 602; 91 S. Ct. 2105, 1971; and *Leeman v. Sloan* 340 F. Supp. 1356, 1972.
[10]*School District of Abington Township v. Schempp*, 374 U.S. 203.
[11]*Brown v. Board of Education*, 347 U.S. 483, 74 Sup. Ct. 686.
[12]163 U.S. 537, 16 Sup. Ct. 1138.

situated. The states' rights theory, insofar as it applies to segregation of the races, was also overthrown by this decision.

Since 1954, numerous orders have been issued by federal courts requiring boards of education to take measures to desegregate the school systems under their control. Up to the present time, all such orders providing for the implementation of *Brown* v. *Board of Education,* when appealed, have been upheld by the United States Supreme Court.

The Civil Rights Act of 1964 greatly increased the power of the federal government to eliminate discrimination in public education. Title VI of this act states: "No person in the United States shall on the ground of race, color, or national origin, be excluded from participation in, be denied the benefits of, or be subject to discrimination, under any program or activity receiving Federal financial assistance." This act gives any federal agency disbursing federal funds the power to withhold such funds if the recipient agency or institution violates this act. The United States Office of Education has used this act in recent years to force racial integration by withholding federal funds from both public and private schools and colleges that fail to comply with the provisions of the act. Since federal grants are now quite substantial, this is a powerful control designed to force racial integration. The enforcement of the Civil Rights Act has greatly speeded up this movement.

CONTRACTUAL OBLIGATIONS. The Supreme Court in a large number of cases has ruled that neither a state nor a board of education could take action "impairing the obligations of contracts" as provided in Section 10 of Article I of the Constitution. This provision of the Constitution has frequently been applied to settling controversies between states and colleges or universities over contractual provisions of charters and to controversies between teachers and governing authorities over tenure and retirement rights. The Supreme Court has held that "a legislative enactment may contain provisions which, when accepted as a basis of action by individuals, become contracts between them and the state or its subdivision. . . ."[13] Thus, the federal Constitution itself provides substantial control over the actions of the states and boards of education, insofar as those actions involve the impairment of obligations under contract.

THE DUE PROCESS OF LAW AND THE POLICE POWER. The Fourteenth Amendment provides in part ". . . Nor shall any state deprive any person of life, liberty, or property, without due process of law. . . ." But the police power is inherent in every state, and this power frequently must be balanced against the due-process-of-law clause that protects an individual. Edwards states: "The police power is that power of the state to limit

[13] *State ex rel. Anderson v. Brand,* 313 U.S. 95.

individual rights in the interest of the social group."[14] The limits of the states in exercising the police power are continually being redefined by the courts. Prior to 1860 the Supreme Court placed almost no restrictions on the states in the exercise of this police power except those restrictions specifically set forth in the Constitution. Since the adoption of the Fourteenth Amendment with its due-process-of-law clause, the Supreme Court has had much greater authority to restrict the police power of the states, but it did not begin to exercise that power until after the case of *Muller v. Oregon*[15] in 1908. In that case the Court took cognizance of physiological and social facts bearing on the employment of women. This case set the precedent for considering psychological and social facts in the five segregation cases ruled on in 1954. It is now apparent that the Supreme Court, when making a decision involving a determination of a proper balance between the due process of law and the police power, will make the decision not so much in terms of abstract legal concepts as in terms of psychological, economic, and social facts.

Space does not permit adequate illustrations of these limitations on the educational powers of the states and their subdivisions. Attention has already been directed to the case of *Brown* v. *Board of Education* in which it was ruled that segregation itself was unequal.[16] Psychological and social facts and not abstract legal concepts were the bases for the decision.

On the other hand, the Supreme Court has upheld the constitutionality of the Smith Act.[17] This act makes it a crime punishable by fine and imprisonment to advocate the overthrow of the government by force. This act clearly comes within the police power of the federal government. It is definitely a federal control over one aspect of what may be taught in a public or even a private school. Therefore, those who insist that the federal government should have no control whatsoever over the curriculum of the public schools seem to be unaware of the inherent police power of the federal government relating to matters of national concern.

EARLY HISTORICAL RELATIONSHIPS

Despite wide differences of opinion concerning the role that should be played by the federal government in public education, it has shown an interest in and has participated in the support of public education since before the adoption of the Constitution in 1789. The educational activities of the federal government include (1) financing and administering its own

[14]Edwards, *The Courts and the Public Schools*, p. 12.
[15]208 U.S. 412.
[16]347 U.S. 483.
[17]*Dennis et al. v. United States*, 341 U.S. 494.

educational programs and (2) aiding the states and territories and institutions and agencies therein in financing and otherwise promoting education.[18] A brief review of some of those activities is presented in the following paragraphs.

Land Grants for the Public Schools

The Ordinance of 1785 provided that "There shall be reserved the lot number 16 of every township for the maintenance of public schools in each township." This provision was repeated in the Ordinance of 1787 providing for the government of the Northwest Territory. The interest of the federal government in public education was clearly demonstrated in these words contained in the Ordinance of 1787: "Religion, morality, and knowledge being necessary to good government and the happiness of mankind, schools and the means of education shall be forever encouraged."

Ohio was the first state admitted to the Union under the Ordinance of 1787. The Ohio policy of setting aside the sixteenth section of each township for the public schools was followed for states admitted to the Union up to 1848. Congress set aside two sections in every township for public education when the Oregon Territory was established in 1848. This policy was followed until 1896, when Utah was granted four sections in every township. Similar grants were given to Arizona and New Mexico when they were admitted to the Union in 1912.

The federal government made many other types of early grants for the benefit of the public schools. Some of those were as follows: (1) grants of funds in lieu of land grants in Indian territory; (2) additional land grants under the Internal Improvement Act of 1841; (3) grants of saline lands; (4) grants of 5 percent of the funds received by the federal government from sale of public lands in the states; (5) payment to the states of 25 percent of the income from national forests and 37.5 percent of the income received from the extraction of nonmetallic minerals for the benefit of roads and public schools; and (6) the allocation of surplus federal revenues to the states in 1836.

Swift has estimated that the early grants of land given by Congress to the thirty public land states aggregated an area ten times as large as Maryland and that grants given to the states in whole or in part for the public schools totaled more than 76 million acres.[19]

[18]Quattlebaum, *Federal Educational Activities,* pp. 69–128.
[19]Fletcher Harper Swift, *Federal and State Policies in Public School Finance in the United States* (Boston: Ginn and Company, 1931), p. 59.

Most of the states did not handle these grants very wisely. The land in many states was sold at very low prices. In other states much land was settled by private parties without the state's protesting, and title to the land was lost to the state. In still other states, funds derived from the sale of school lands were lost owing to fiscal mismanagement or misappropriation. However, the income derived from these early land grants is still an important source of revenue in a few states.

Opponents of federal aid for public education almost invariably argue that it is impossible to have federal aid for education without federal control. Nevertheless, the federal government has never exercised any control over these land grants. Perhaps if the federal government had exercised enough control over the land grants to protect them from wastage and misappropriation, these grants would have been of greater benefit to the public schools. Such protection could have been given these funds without any interference by the federal government with the prerogatives of the states to determine the school curriculum, organize and administer schools, and exercise all other legitimate powers with respect to education.

The activities of the federal government in administering the territories and making land grants had other important effects on the public schools. The federal government itself organized school systems in each territory, and when the territory became a state, the federally established school system was taken over by the state. The funds arising from land grants served as precedents for state aid for the public schools.

The Land Grant Colleges

The Morrill Act passed by Congress in 1862 granted 30,000 acres to each state for each representative and senator then in Congress or when a state was admitted to the Union. Provision was made for compulsory military training in the colleges established. The proceeds from the sale of the land grants were required to be used for "the endowment, maintenance and support of at least one college where the leading object shall be, without excluding other scientific and classical studies and including military tactics, to teach such branches of learning as are related to agriculture and mechanic arts." This act also had as one of its purposes "to promote the liberal and practical education of the industrial classes in the several pursuits and professions of life."

This act is of great significance, because it has demonstrated (1) that the federal government, when it deemed it necessary to do so for the common defense or the general welfare, could and would take positive action with respect to education, and (2) that the federal government could and would take positive action with respect to vital areas of education that were neglected by the states. Prior to 1862, most institutions of higher learning catered primarily to the sons and daughters of the wealthy. Cultural and classical education was emphasized. Education in agriculture and engineering was not considered a proper activity for an institution of higher learning. This was a carry-over from European traditions concerning higher education. The Morrill Act might therefore be considered a layman's revolt from the prevailing educational leadership of that day.

Other acts of Congress have supplemented the activities of the land grant colleges. The Hatch Act of 1887, the Adams Act of 1906, the Purnell Act of 1925, the Bankhead-Jones Act of 1935, the Research and Marketing Act of 1946, and subsequent amendments have increased the funds available for agricultural experiment stations. These experiment stations made it possible to develop a scientific knowledge of agriculture which was the basis for the remarkable productivity of American agriculture.

The Smith-Lever Act

The Smith-Lever Act in 1914 provided for extension services by county agricultural agents, home demonstrators, 4-H leaders, and specialists in agriculture and homemaking, and for the professional training of teachers in these subjects. The Coffee-Ketchum Act of 1928, the Bankhead-Jones Act of 1935, the Bankhead-Flannagan Act of 1945, and subsequent amendments have broadened the scope and increased the funds provided by the Smith-Lever Act. The Smith-Lever Act for the first time required the states to match educational funds provided by the federal government.

The extension workers provided by the Smith-Lever Act have made a significant contribution to the education of farmers and housewives. The agricultural agents have been particularly effective in bringing the findings of the experimental farms to the farmers. The extension workers have also made significant contributions to the lives of rural youth. Field demonstrations and the "group process" were first used extensively by these workers. The extension workers were among the first educators to experiment with the techniques of group dynamics and the dynamics of change. They have clearly demonstrated the value of the role of "change agents."

The extension service provided under the Smith-Lever Act is not an integral part of the system of public education. The act is administered on the federal level by the Department of Agriculture. The extension workers are employed by the governing bodies of counties. The state director of extension services is almost always associated with a land grant institution of higher learning, but this is about the only connection between the extension program and the program of public education.

The Smith-Hughes Act

The Smith-Hughes Act of 1917 was the first federal act providing funds for vocational education below college level. This act provided a continuing appropriation for vocational education in agriculture, trades and industry, and homemaking, and for teacher training in those fields. It is administered on the federal level by the U.S. Office of Education. The original act required that the states and local school units match the federal appropriation on a dollar-for-dollar basis. Federal assistance for vocational education was further extended by the following acts: the George-Reed Act of 1929, the George-Ellzey Act of 1935, the George-Deen Act of 1937, the George-Barden Act of 1946, the Vocational Education Act of 1963, and the Vocational Education Amendments of 1968 and 1972.

Public interest in vocational education increased rapidly with the beginning of the twentieth century. By 1909, some 500 agricultural high schools had been established. By 1911, 44 of the 47 states offered instruction in home economics in some high schools. A number of trade schools had been established in city school systems. Nevertheless, comprehensive vocational education opportunities were not available to most high school pupils. Lay organizations such as the American Federation of Labor, the Grange, the National Association of Manufacturers, and the Chamber of Commerce of the United States all urged the expansion of vocational education in high schools. The National Education Association made certain studies of vocational education but did not play a very active role in promoting the development of vocational education. The educational leadership administering the high schools in the early part of the twentieth century was concerned much more with college preparatory education than with education to meet the needs of all pupils of secondary school age. Therefore, the federal acts providing financial support for vocational education represented, in actuality, a lay revolt against prevailing educational policies.

The Smith-Hughes Act provided some federal control of vocational education, but in practice much of the control was delegated to the states. The Smith-Hughes Act and subsequent acts provided a great stimulus for vocational education. All states now spend from state and local taxes far more for vocational education than the amount provided by the federal government, despite the fact that federal funds for vocational education have been greatly increased in recent years.

Relief Measures Affecting Education

The nation was deep in its greatest financial depression by 1933. Franklin D. Roosevelt was inaugurated President in March 1933 and almost immediately he started his New Deal to break the depression. The

New Deal included a large number of new and experimental measures that had as their principal purpose the improvement of the economic condition of the people. Many of these measures affected education, but they were designed primarily as relief measures. Some of the programs are discussed briefly in the following paragraphs.

THE CIVILIAN CONSERVATION CORPS. The Civilian Conservation Corps, or CCC, was created by an act of Congress in March 1933. The purpose of this act was primarily to relieve unemployment through the performance of useful public work and to provide for the restoration of depleted natural resources of the country. The CCC had developed an extensive educational program by 1937. More than 3 million men, most of whom were young, enrolled in the CCC between 1934 and 1941, and more than 2.7 million of this number participated in some type of organized educational activity. Shortly after World War II began, war and defense activities largely eliminated unemployment, and the CCC was abolished in 1943.

THE NATIONAL YOUTH ADMINISTRATION. The National Youth Administration was established by the executive order of the President in 1935. The NYA program provided many benefits to needy college and secondary school students. It carried on a great variety of useful work projects. In the beginning, the young people it aided usually lived at home. Later, an increasing number were housed in NYA residences and dormitories. The NYA even began constructing some special schools in some states. In the later 1930s the educational leadership began to fear that the NYA was beginning to develop a competing federal system of schools. In the defense period prior to 1941, the NYA was charged with competing with defense agencies for manpower. Opposition to the NYA caused it to be placed under the Federal Security Agency in 1939, transferred to the War Manpower Commission in 1944, and liquidated in 1944.

OTHER RELIEF AGENCIES. Many other federal relief agencies carried on programs between 1933 and 1940 that gave significant aid to the public schools and institutions of higher learning. Some of the more important were: the Civil Works Administration, the Federal Emergency Relief Administration, the Works Progress Administration, and the Public Works Administration. The CWA was primarily for the purpose of providing work for the unemployed. Many school houses were repaired and renovated under this program. The FERA distributed many millions of dollars of funds for relief of the unemployed. Thousands of teachers, especially in rural areas, benefited from those funds. The FERA also provided funds for adult education, vocational rehabilitation, and nursery schools. However, the primary purpose of the FERA was to provide work for unemployed persons.

The Works Progress Administration superseded the FERA in 1939. It carried on all the FERA projects, and in addition it provided substantial funds for the construction and repair of school buildings.

The Public Works Administration, established in 1933, made grants for school buildings. Initially, these grants amounted to 30 percent of the cost of construction, but they later rose to 45 percent. The PWA also made loans for part or all of the remaining cost.

All these agencies were liquidated in the early 1940s. It is impossible to make an accurate appraisal of all the educational benefits provided by these relief agencies.

Apparently the only permanent federal aid for the public schools that originated from all the relief measures was federal aid for the school lunch program. The CWA, FERA, and later the WPA provided some aid for the school lunch program in the form of labor. The Federal Surplus Commodities Corporation was established by Congress in 1935. It purchased and distributed surplus commodities to nonprofit school lunchrooms. This was a relief act for agriculture, and it was administered by the Department of Agriculture. Surplus commodities were distributed to both public and private elementary and secondary schools. Some cash was also provided primarily for the purchase of surplus foods to be used in school lunchrooms. School lunch aid for private schools was justified on the grounds that it was an aid to the child and not the school. These policies finally culminated in the National School Lunch Act of 1946, which has apparently made federal school lunch aid a permanent policy. This act was supplemented in 1954 by an act providing special aid for the school milk program and the Child Nutrition Act of 1966 providing for the school breakfast program. Undoubtedly, these acts have greatly stimulated the development of the school food service program.

Federal Educational Activities for Defense and War Prior to 1958

It would require a formidable volume to describe all federal educational activities for defense and war. The federal government has sometimes operated elementary schools, high schools, institutions of college grade, and various other types of educational programs. Some are on service posts, some are in territories, and some are abroad. In fact, all of these activities are still being carried on by the federal government. Furthermore, the federal government has carried on many types of war and defense educational activities through state and local agencies and institutions. Space will permit only a few examples.

THE ARMED FORCES. The Military Academy was established at West Point in 1802, the Naval Academy at Annapolis in 1845, and the Air

Force Academy at Colorado Springs in 1954. The Army Medical School was established in 1893, the Army War College in 1902, superseded by the National War College in 1946, and the Air University in 1947.

The educational system for enlisted men began with an act of Congress in 1866 which provides that "Whenever troops are serving at any post, garrison, or permanent camp, there shall be established a school where all men may be provided with instruction in the common English branches of education, and especially in the history of the United States." Thousands of men have been taught to read and write and also have been given much additional postschool education under this program. The act of 1866 probably set the precedent for the development of the Armed Forces Institute in 1945. This institute now provides very extensive programs of educational opportunities for all career and active duty personnel. It is a voluntary off-duty program.

In summary, the educational activities of Army, the Navy, the Air Force, the Marines, and the Coast Guard now make it possible for all personnel to obtain a wide range of educational opportunities that will not only benefit the armed services but will be of great benefit to the service personnel in civilian life.

THE TRAINING OF WAR PRODUCTION WORKERS. In the period immediately prior to World War II, the federal government initiated a crash program for the training of workers in war industries. This program was administered through the U.S. Office of Education which worked through the state educational agencies in administering the program. Approximately 7.8 million workers were trained through this program. The Office of Education was also authorized to cooperate with degree-granting institutions in organizing short courses for the training of engineers, chemists, physicists, and production supervisors. More than 2 million workers were trained under this program. Other significant programs administered by the Office of Education were the program for training rural war production workers, which benefited 4.2 million students, and the student war loans program.

WARTIME USES OF INSTITUTIONS OF HIGHER LEARNING. When the United States entered World War II, the federal government made wide use of the facilities of institutions of higher learning. By 1943, the Army specialized training program had been established on more than 300 campuses.[20] The Navy V-12 program provided college opportunities of a similar nature for naval personnel. These two programs enabled many thousands of youth to obtain advanced educational training.

[20]Quattlebaum, *Federal Educational Activities*, p. 30.

FEDERAL IMPACT AREAS. The Lanham Act of 1941 provided federal financial assistance to local governments for the construction, maintenance, and operation of community facilities in areas where war-incurred federal activities created financial burdens that the local governments could not bear. Federal authorities worked through the U.S. Office of Education in administering this act insofar as it applied to public education. This act was superseded in 1950 by Public Laws 815 and 874, which continued approximately the same type of federal benefits to areas adversely affected by federal activities.

It is interesting to note that the educational activities of the federal government during the war years affecting the public schools and colleges were carried on largely through the U. S. Office of Education, which in turn worked through state educational agencies as contrasted with the uncoordinated federal relief activities of the 1930s. This newer policy proved to be far more satisfactory from an educational standpoint.

AID FOR VETERANS. Certain postwar but war-related educational activities of the federal government are deserving of mention. The Congress in 1918 provided for the vocational education of disabled veterans of World War I, and the Vocational Rehabilitation Act of 1943 made similar provisions for disabled veterans of World War II. In 1920, the federal government provided funds for the rehabilitation, including training, of disabled civilians. This law required the states to match federal funds. This act was superseded in 1943 by Public Law 113, which provides for federal assistance to the states that develop approved plans for the vocational rehabilitation of injured persons.

The most important postwar educational activity of the federal government was the veterans' training program. Public Law 178 of 1918 provided for the vocational training of World War I veterans at federal expense. Approximately 180,000 veterans received training under this act. Public Law 16 of 1943 provided for the vocational rehabilitation of disabled veterans of World War II. More than 500,000 veterans have received training under this act.

The most important of the veterans' education acts was Public Law 346 of 1944, popularly known as the G.I. Bill. This act provided training for all veterans of World War II, the length of training depending upon the length of service. The educational provisions of this act were very liberal, covering almost every kind of training desired by the veteran from ballroom dancing to advanced graduate research. Approximately 8 million veterans had received some training under this act by 1954. Several millions of veterans were enabled to attend college by this act, and college enrollments more than doubled following World War II. Public Law 550 of 1952 provided educational training for the veterans of the Korean War.

More than a million veterans of the Korean War have received the benefits of this act. In 1966, the Congress extended the benefits of the G.I. Bill to veterans of the Cold War. The Veterans Educational Assistance Act made educational aid for service veterans a permanent federal policy for all veterans who have served 180 days or more since January 31, 1955. The recent veterans' education acts have been administered by the Veterans' Administration.

The various veterans' education and vocational rehabilitation acts have made educational opportunities available to millions of persons who otherwise would not have had those opportunities. Some studies have shown that the increased income taxes paid by veterans and vocationally rehabilitated persons resulting from increased earning power more than reimburse the federal government for the funds expended on their education.

THE NATIONAL SCIENCE FOUNDATION. The National Science Foundation was established by Public Law 507 in 1950. Its purpose is "to promote the progress of science; to advance the national health, prosperity and welfare; to secure the national defense; and for other purposes." The foundation initiates and supports programs to strengthen research in mathematics, the physical and biological sciences and the engineering sciences through contracts, loans, grants, fellowships, institutes, and other means. Of particular interest to the public schools are the new curricula in science and mathematics that have been developed under the sponsorship of the Foundation. These curricula have been widely disseminated by means of institutes for high school teachers which have been financed by the Foundation. The success of the Foundation in changing high school curricula has demonstrated that an adequately financed federal agency can have a powerful influence on curriculum change.

THE COOPERATIVE RESEARCH PROGRAM Public Law 83-531 established the Cooperative Research Program in 1954. This act is administered by the U.S. Office of Education. It authorized the U.S. Commissioner of Education to enter into jointly financed contracts with universities, colleges, and state education agencies for conducting research, surveys, and demonstrations in the field of education. Educational research has received a major impetus from this act. Far more educational research is now being financed under the provision of this act than from all other public sources combined. This act is potentially extremely significant. It may have more permanent effect on the improvement of the educational program than any other federal act. The administration of the Cooperative Research Program was transferred in 1972 to the National Institute of Education discussed later in this chapter.

FEDERAL EDUCATIONAL ACTIVITIES SINCE 1958

The year 1958 marked the beginning of a new era in the relationship of the federal government to education. The scientific success of the Russians in launching the first earth satellite in 1957 jarred the people of the United States out of their complacence. We were carrying on the Cold War with Russia, fully confident of our superiority in science and technology. With the launching of Sputnik I came the realization that our potential antagonist might be gaining on us rapidly. This fear triggered the passage of the National Defense Education Act in 1958, which was the beginning of a large number of subsequent federal acts relating to education. In 1966 Kurth listed what he considered to be the 47 most significant federal acts relating to education or major amendments to such acts.[21] Seventeen of those laws were enacted prior to 1958, and 30 between the years 1958 and 1965 inclusive. A number of very significant education laws have been enacted by Congress since 1965.

The basic federal policies toward education have not changed since 1958. All federal funds provided for education since that date have been earmarked for special purposes. Therefore, the federal government has continued its long-time policy of providing special-purpose grants rather than grants for general purposes. However, the amounts of these grants have been enormously increased since 1958. The federal government no longer takes a laissez-faire attitude toward education. Education is now considered by the federal government as an important means to implement its policies of providing for the common defense, eliminating poverty, promoting economic growth, reducing unemployment, and promoting the general welfare in many other ways.

Although the recent federal grants are all categorical or special-purpose aids, there has been very little coordination in the planning of these acts to prevent duplication of attempts to accomplish a given purpose. Kurth identified 36 major purposes of the 47 acts he studied.[22] However, numerous separate acts have been passed which deal with the same purpose. For example, of the 47 acts Kurth studied, 15 different acts deal with adult education, 19 with educational facilities and equipment, 17 with research, and 10 with guidance.

A few of the more important federal laws relating to education which have been enacted since 1958 are treated briefly in the following paragraphs.

[21]Edwin L. Kurth, *A Chronology Summarizing Important Federal Acts Aiding Education* (Gainesville, Fla.: Florida Educational Research and Development Council, College of Education, University of Florida, 1966).
[22]*Ibid.*

THE NATIONAL DEFENSE EDUCATION ACT OF 1958—PUBLIC LAW 85–864. Congress defined a new role of education as follows in this act:

> ... that the security of the nation requires the fullest development of the mental resources and technical skills of its young men and women. The present emergency demands that additional and more adequate educational opportunities be made available. The defense of this Nation depends upon the mastery of modern techniques developed from complex scientific principles. It depends as well upon the discovery and development of new principles, new techniques, and new knowledge.

The ten titles of this act authorized grants and loans assisting both public and private education from the elementary school through graduate school. The original act provided financial aid primarily for science, mathematics, modern foreign languages, technical and vocational education, and counseling and guidance. This act was amended and broadened in 1964 by authorizing financial assistance for instruction in history, geography, civics, English, and reading. The grants, loans, fellowships, and other forms of financial aids provided under this act have had a significant impact on education in this nation. This act is administered by the U.S. Office of Education.

MANPOWER DEVELOPMENT AND TRAINING ACT OF 1962—PUBLIC LAW 84–415. The basic objective of this act is to reduce the hard core of unemployment by retraining workers whose skills had become obsolete. The costs of training and training allowances for the unemployed were financed under this act. Although the primary purposes of this act were to provide occupational training for unemployed adult workers and to encourage manpower planning based on research, it also provided for "the testing, counseling, and selection of youths, 16 years of age or older, for occupational training and further schooling." This act is administered jointly by the U.S. Department of Labor and the Office of Education in the U.S. Department of Health, Education and Welfare.

HIGHER EDUCATION FACILITIES ACT OF 1963—PUBLIC LAW 88–204. This act authorized $230 million a year for three years beginning in 1964 for the construction of facilities for higher education. Of this amount 22 percent was earmarked for construction of public community colleges and public technical institutes. Public or other nonprofit higher institutions are eligible for financial assistance under this act. This act was subsequently amended and extended for an additional number of years. It is administered by the U.S. Office of Education.

THE VOCATIONAL EDUCATION ACT OF 1963—PUBLIC LAW 88–210. This act more than quadrupled the federal appropriations for vocational and technical education. It has much broader purposes than the original Smith-Hughes Act for vocational education. The major purposes of the 1963 act are to provide occupational training for persons of all ages and achievement levels in any occupational field that does not require a baccalaureate degree, to provide for related services which will help to ensure quality programs, to assist in the construction of area vocational facilities, and to promote and to provide financial assistance for work study programs and residential schools. The federal provisions for vocational education were greatly extended by the amendments to the 1963 act in 1968.

THE ECONOMIC OPPORTUNITY ACT OF 1964—PUBLIC LAW 88–452. The major purpose of this act was "to mobilize the human and financial resources of the Nation to fight poverty in the United States." Section 2 of the act declares, "that it is the policy of the United States to eliminate the paradox of poverty in the midst of plenty in this Nation by opening to everyone opportunities for education, training, work, and a life of decency and dignity, and the purpose of the act is to strengthen, supplement, and coordinate efforts in furtherance of that policy." This act, probably more than any other act of Congress, clearly recognized the social value of education as well as its economic value. Education was recognized not only for its value to the individual but also for its contribution to production and to the distribution of the fruits of production.

The Office of Economic Opportunity in the Executive Office of the President was established by this act. This office was headed by a director who coordinated all the programs supported by this act. The director operated some programs directly and other programs through the following federal agencies: the Office of Education, the Department of Agriculture, and the Small Business Administration. The operation of this act was discontinued by executive order in 1973.

THE ELEMENTARY AND SECONDARY EDUCATION ACT OF 1965—PUBLIC LAW 89–10. This was the most important federal act affecting the elementary and secondary schools passed by Congress up to 1965. It provided, at that time, approximately $1,300,000,000 annually to support the programs included in the act. It doubled the federal aid available for elementary and secondary schools, increasing the total revenue receipts provided by the federal government for public elementary and secondary schools from 4 to 8 percent in 1966.

There are five major titles of this act. The financial aid under the first three titles is allocated to the elementary and secondary schools and under Titles IV and V to institutions of higher learning and state departments of education. Of the appropriations, 90 percent is earmarked for elementary and secondary schools.

Title I provides financial assistance for educational programs especially designed to benefit the children from families with an income below a specified level per year or who are receiving welfare aid for dependent children; Title II provides funds for libraries, textbooks, and audiovisual materials; Title III provides funds for supplementary education centers for students in both public and private schools; Title IV provides funds for regional educational research and training laboratories; and Title V provides funds for strengthening state departments of education. This act is administered by the U.S. Office of Education.

THE HIGHER EDUCATION ACT OF 1965—PUBLIC LAW 83–333. This act contained twelve titles dealing with such matters as community service, library assistance, strengthening developing institutions, student assistance with loans and fellowships, improvement of undergraduate instruction, improvement of facilities, networks for knowledge, education for public service, improvement of graduate programs, and other programs. This act was substantially amended in 1966, 1968, and 1972.

Analysis of Recent Developments

Practically every important statute dealing with education enacted by Congress since 1958 has been amended in each succeeding session of Congress. For example the Ninety-second Congress in 1972 enacted Public Law 92–318 which substantially amended the Higher Education Act of 1965, the Vocational Education Act of 1963, the Elementary and Secondary Education Act of 1965, Public Law 874, the General Education Provisions Act, and related acts. Therefore, federal provisions for education are in a very fluid state and are difficult to administer at all levels—federal, state, and local.

Jackson and Steinhilber reported in 1960 that "Over 50 major administrative units in 22 federal departments and agencies reported expenditures in programs which provided funds for educational activities of the States and of educational institutions, or which provided educational services or funds for financing the education of individuals."[23] Even more federal agencies were involved in administering federal funds for education by 1972. Despite this scattering of federal responsibility for the administration of educational funds, considerably more than half of all the federal funds, exclusive of contract research, allocated to elementary and secondary schools and higher institutions in the United States in 1972 were

[23]Penrose B. Jackson and Delores A. Steinhilber, *Federal Funds for Education: Fields, Levels, Recipients 1959 and 1960,* U.S. Department of Health, Education and Welfare, Office of Education (Washington, D.C.: U.S. Government Printing Office, 1962), p. 5.

administered through the U.S. Office of Education. Furthermore, most of the recent federal appropriations to elementary and secondary education are allocated through the U.S. Office of Education. Therefore, the problem of the control of federal educational funds by noneducational agencies is not as serious as it might seem.

The critical problem is the earmarking of all federal appropriations for special purposes. Although the public elementary and secondary schools were receiving more than $5 billion in federal funds by fiscal 1972, many boards of education could not provide educationally balanced budgets because of this earmarking policy. This problem will not be solved until a substantial amount of general-purpose funds is made available annually by the federal government or until the number of federal special-purpose grants is increased sufficiently to cover all major educational needs. In this latter event, the difficulty of administering so many funds might result eventually in their consolidation into a general-purpose fund. However, despite this pressure there are no signs at the present time that the federal government intends to substitute general-purpose grants for special-purpose grants in the near future. Instead of the federal government adopting policies to avoid or reduce federal control of education, recent federal acts all extend federal control of education. This is apparently due to the fact that education is now seen as a major instrument for accomplishing national purposes. Therefore, the Congress enacts legislation which controls educational objectives to the extent deemed necessary to attain national purposes. An administration bill proposing the consolidation of a number of categorical appropriations into a partially earmarked "revenue sharing" appropriation was being considered in 1973. However, at the time of this writing, Congress had taken no action on that bill.

Table 8-1 shows the federal outlays for elementary and secondary education for fiscal 1971 and estimates for 1972 and 1973.[24] Although in 1972, federal funds for elementary and secondary education totaled $5,762,000,000, grants to states and school districts totaled a little less than one-half that amount, and all these grants were in the form of categorical grants. This has greatly reduced the options available to boards of education for optimizing the educational returns from federal funds. There are some who argue that this is not to be deplored because the federal government provides financial assistance to education not to attain educational purposes but primarily for such federal purposes as providing for the common defense, improving the economy, improving the equity of taxes, reducing poverty, improving nutrition, providing the skills needed to reduce unemployment, improving the health of the nation, and so forth. However, educators argue that most of these are purposes of education as

[24] Executive Office of the President, Office of Management and Budget, *Special Analyses, Budget of the United States Government, 1973* (Washington, D.C: U.S. Government Printing Office, 1973) p. 121.

TABLE 8-1. *Federal Outlays for Elementary and Secondary Education by Agency and Program (in millions of dollars)**

Agency and Program	1971 Actual	1972 Estimate	1973 Estimate
Agriculture: Child Nutrition	928	1,309	1,374
Defense: Education of overseas dependents	156	172	197
Health, Education, and Welfare:			
Office of Education			
Emergency school assistance	51	103	381
Grants to states and school districts	2,551	2,660	2,737
Demonstration projects	361	433	428
National Institute of Education	—	2	50
Office of Child Development: Head Start	366	376	387
Social Security Administration: Student benefits	160	177	189
Interior: Indian education	180	182	206
Labor: Neighborhood Youth Corps in-school	64	75	75
Housing and Urban Development: Model Cities	52	71	99
National Science Foundation: Science education	36	31	35
Other Federal agencies	154	171	187
TOTAL	5,059	5,762	6,345

*Executive Office of the President, Office of Management and Budget. *Special Analyses, Budget of the United States Government, 1973*. Washington, D.C., United States Government Printing Office, 1973, p. 121.

well as national purposes and that there is no real conflict between educational purposes and national purposes. It is further argued generally by educational leaders that neither national purposes nor educational purposes can be substantially attained until the federal government equalizes educational opportunity throughout the nation by means of a substantial amount of general federal aid. As pointed out in Chapter 18, most authorities on educational finance insist that at least 30 percent of the budget of the elementary and secondary schools should be provided by the federal government.

The federal outlays for higher education are presented in Table 8-2.[25] It is noted that the Office of Education administered only about 20 percent of the approximately seven billion dollars made available to higher education in 1972. The federal financial assistance for higher education is also practically all in the form of categorical grants. An inspection of Table 8-2 will show that half the seven billion of federal aid for higher education

[25] *Ibid.*, p. 127.

TABLE 8-2. Federal Outlays for Higher Education by Agency and Program (in millions of dollars)*

Agency and Program	1971 Actual	1972 Estimate	1973 Estimate
Defense:			
Academic research	198	192	197
Military service academies and Reserve officers training corps	318	343	346
Subtotal, Department of Defense	516	535	543
Health, Education, and Welfare:			
Office of Education:			
Student assistance	745	913	918
Construction of facilities	340	216	140
Institutional and personnel development	303	340	336
Subtotal, Office of Education	1,388	1,469	1,394
Other Health, Education and Welfare:			
Academic research-health and social service agencies	702	780	889
Fellowships and traineeships-health professions	380	397	410
NIH facilities construction	150	142	111
Other health training institutional support	271	376	491
Social security (student benefits)	455	505	537
National Foundation for Higher Education	—	1	30
Other	97	138	156
Subtotal, Other Health, Education, and Welfare	2,055	2,339	2,624
Housing and Urban Development (primarily college housing)	118	69	64
Atomic Energy Commission	101	93	94
National Aeronautics and Space Administration	128	133	136
National Science Foundation	353	413	432
Veterans Administration: Readjustment benefits[+]	1,252	1,706	1,828
Other	243	293	330
Total, higher education	6,153	7,050	7,445

*Executive Office of the President, Office of Management and Budget. *Special Analyses, Budget of the United States Government, 1973.* Washington, D.C., United States Government Printing Office, 1973, p. 127.
[+]G.I. Bill.

in 1972 was earmarked for various forms of student assistance. This policy has enabled many students with inadequate finances to obtain the benefits of a college education. The costs of operating these institutions will continue to increase, and the costs to students will no doubt increase. Therefore, increases in federal aid to institutions of higher education will be necessary to meet these needs.

THE FEDERAL EDUCATION AGENCY

The federal education agency is discussed briefly under the following headings:

THE UNITED STATES OFFICE OF EDUCATION. The present U.S. Office of Education had its origin in an act of Congress in 1867 that established a federal department of education headed by a commissioner. The original purposes of the act were to create a federal service for: (1) "collecting and diffusing such educational information as shall aid the people of the United States in the establishment and maintenance of efficient school systems, and (2) otherwise promoting the cause of education throughout the country.[26] The name, functions, and administrative control of the federal agency designed to serve education have been changed from time to time by acts of Congress or executive orders. For many years, the Office of Education was in the Department of the Interior. It was made a part of the Federal Security Agency in 1939. In 1953 the Office of Education became a part of the newly created Department of Health, Education, and Welfare, where it has remained since that time. The Office is headed by the Commissioner of Education, who is a political appointee of the President. However, for a long number of years, regardless of the political party in power, the appointee has always been an educator. Most of the staff of the Office of Education are selected under the provisions of the federal Civil Service System.

Public Law 92-318 of the Ninety-second Congress, 1972, contains important provisions for the organization and administration of education at the federal level. Following is a summary of those provisions relating to the Office:

> Sec. 401. There shall be, within the Department of Health, Education, and Welfare, an Education Division which shall be composed of the Office of Education and the National Institute of Education, and shall be headed by the Assistant Secretary for Education.

[26]Quattlebaum, *Federal Educational Activities*, p. 8.

Sec. 402. (a) There shall be in the Department of Health, Education, and Welfare an Assistant Secretary for Education, who shall be appointed by the President by and with the advice and consent of the Senate. . . .

(b) The Assistant Secretary shall be the principal officer in the Department to whom the Secretary shall assign responsibility for the direction and supervision of the Education Division. . . .

Sec. 403. (a) The purpose and duties of the Office of Education shall be to collect statistics and facts showing the condition and progress of education in the United States, and to disseminate such information respecting the organization and management of schools and school systems, and methods of teaching, as shall aid the people of the United States in the establishment and maintenance of efficient school systems, and otherwise promote the cause of education throughout the country. The Office of Education shall not have authority which is not expressly provided for by statute or implied therein.

(b) (1) The management of the Office of Education, shall, subject to the direction and supervision of the Secretary, be entrusted to a Commissioner of Education, who shall be appointed by the President by and with the advice and consent of the Senate, and who shall serve at the pleasure of the President. . . .

THE NATIONAL INSTITUTE OF EDUCATION. Congress established the National Institute of Education in Section 405 of Public Law 92–318. In establishing the Institute, Congress made some important declarations concerning federal educational policy. Section 405 (a) reads in part as follows:

> The Congress hereby declares it to be the policy of the United States to provide to every person an equal opportunity to receive an education of high quality regardless of his race, color, religion, sex, national origin, or social class. . . .
> The Congress further declares it to be the policy of the United States to:
> (a) help to solve or to alleviate the problems of, and promote the reform and renewal of American education;
> (b) advance the practice of education, as an art, science, and profession;
> (c) strengthen the scientific and technological foundations of education; and
> (d) build an effective educational research and development system.

Subsection (b) provided that "In order to carry out the policy set forth in subsection (a) that there is established the National Institute of Education . . . which shall consist of a National Council of Educational Research . . . and a Director of the Institute. . . .

Subsection (d) provided that the Director of the Institute shall be appointed by the President, by and with the advice and consent of the Senate, and shall serve at the pleasure of the President. It is interesting to note that the Institute is not a part of the Office of Education and that the Director of the Institute reports directly to the Secretary of Health, Education, and Welfare through the Assistant Secretary. The Director of the Institute is equivalent in authority to the Commissioner of Education. At this writing, there is some uncertainty as to the exact responsibilities of the Assistant Secretary, the Commissioner of Education, and the Director of the Institute and their interrelationships. The organizational structure of the federal education agency as provided in Public Law 92–318 is almost certain to be less than optimum because of potential conflict over authority and responsibility. This is not to suggest that either the National Institute of Education or the Office of Education is an unnecessary governmental agency. Both provide vitally needed educational services at the federal level. But it is suggested that if Congress would observe the principles of organization and administration set forth in Chapter 4, a better coordinated federal agency for education could be provided.

SOME IMPORTANT PROBLEMS AND ISSUES

The problems and issues of federal relationships to education are far from being resolved. As we previously pointed out, general issues of taxation, states' rights, centralization, and other important matters are interwoven with educational issues. Therefore, it is not likely that the issues of federal relationships to education will be speedily settled. A few of the more important problems and issues concerning federal relationships are presented in the following paragraphs.

What Should Be the Role of the Office of Education?

A number of noneducational federal agencies have administered educational programs directly affecting the elementary and secondary educational policies and programs of the states. Sometimes these agencies have bypassed the state education agency and dealt directly with local boards of education. This has frequently caused conflicts between federal and state policies.

It is confusing and frustrating to the states to be compelled to deal with so many different federal departments and agencies on educational matters. Educational authorities generally recommend (1) that when the federal government deals with a state on educational matters it should operate through the central state education agency and not deal directly with local boards of education, and (2) that all federal grants for public education be administered by the U.S. Office of Education. What federal funds now administered by other federal departments and agencies should be transferred to the U.S. Office of Education? See Tables 8–1 and 8–2.

The establishment of a federal Department of Education with a Secretary in the President's cabinet has been advocated for many years by some educational authorities. This issue has come to the front in recent years because of the rapidly increasing federal involvement in education. There is probably more support for this position among the educational leadership of the nation than ever before. It is argued that adequate consideration of educational problems will not be given until education is given cabinet status. It is further argued that the efficiency of administration of federal funds for education would be greatly enhanced by establishing a Department of Education with full responsibility for administering federal funds for education and for coordinating and providing the educational services which can best be provided at the federal level.

The opponents of this policy generally fear that the establishment of a federal Department of Education would lay the base for further increases in federal funds for education and also extend federal control over education. What other arguments for and against the establishment of a federal Department of Education can be advanced?

How Much Federal Control
of Public Education is Desirable?

The issue of federal control of education is a very broad one. Federal control of education has usually, in the public mind, been associated with federal financing of education. However, as pointed out early in this chapter, the federal government under the authority of constitutional limitations on the powers of the states exercises important control over the educational systems of the states. Those controls have no relation to finance.

Furthermore, there seems to be no necessary relationship of federal financing to federal control. In its history, the federal government has made grants for public education with little or no controls. On the other hand, it has made a number of grants with a great amount of federal control. When the Congress desires federal control over a particular appropriation, it writes the desired controls in the act. If it desires to exercise no federal control over a particular appropriation, it writes no controls in the act. There is no evidence of "creeping" federal controls over education. If it can be assumed that Congress represents the people, it can also be assumed that the people from time to time have desired some types of federal controls over education and that at other times they have not. Federal controls over education will be extended or reduced at the will of the people so long as our form of government endures.

What types of federal control are desirable and what types undesirable? What criteria can be used to determine whether a particular educational control should be exercised by the federal government, by the states, or by local school administrative units? Should all federal controls over education be eliminated? Has our time-honored doctrine of state responsibility for education under the Tenth Amendment become obsolete?

SELECTED REFERENCES

ALLEN, HOLLIS P., *The Federal Government and Education.* New York: McGraw-Hill Book Company, 1950.

American Association of School Administrators, *The Federal Government and Public Schools.* Washington, D.C.: The Association, 1965.

CAMPBELL, ROALD F., LUVERN L. CUNNINGHAM, and RODERICK F. MCPHEE, *The Organization and Control of American Schools.* Columbus, Ohio: Charles E. Merrill Books, Inc., 1965, Chap. 2.

GRIEDER, CALVIN, TRUMAN M. PIERCE, and K. FORBIS JORDAN, *Public School Administration.* New York: The Ronald Press Company, 1969, Chap. 3.

JOHNS, ROE L., and EDGAR L. MORPHET, *The Economics and Financing of Education.* Englewood Cliffs, N.J.: Prentice-Hall, Inc., 1969, Chap. 13.

JOHNS, ROE L., and KERN ALEXANDER, eds. *Alternative Programs for Financing Education.* Gainesville, Fla.: National Educational Finance Project, 1971, Vol. 5, Chap. 8.

KURSH, HARRY, *The United States Office of Education; A Century of Service.* New York: Chilion, 1965.

MILLER, VAN, *The Public Administration of American School Systems.* New York: The Macmillan Company, 1972, Chap. 2.

MUNGER, FRANK J., and RICHARD F. FENNO, *National Policies and Federal Aid to Education.* Syracuse: Syracuse University Press, 1962.

PIERCE, TRUMAN M., *Federal, State and Local Government in Education.* New York: The Center for Applied Research in Education, Inc., 1965.

TIEDT, SIDNEY, "Historical Development of Federal Aid Programs," Chap. 7 of *Status and Impact of Educational Finance Programs,* Roe L. Johns, Kern Alexander and Dewey H. Stollar, eds., Gainesville, Fla.: National Educational Finance Project, Vol. 4, 1971.

9

State Organization and Responsibilities for Education

The strategic and significant role of each state in the education of the children and youth of the nation has not been fully understood or appreciated by many American citizens. The people of each state who face their educational responsibilities courageously and make adequate provisions for education are contributing not only to the development of the citizens of their own state but also to the progress of the nation. Shortsighted or unwise provisions not only handicap the development of children and youth in communities throughout a state but also tend to limit national progress.

As pointed out in Chapter 1, the system of education developed by most states is relatively decentralized. In fact, in all states except Hawaii much of the responsibility for the organization and operation of public schools has been delegated to local school systems. For this and other reasons, most people tend to appraise the strengths and weaknesses of local schools without considering the implications of state policies and provisions for the programs that can be conducted in those schools. Actually, adequate and farsighted provisions by a state make it possible for good schools to operate in every part of the state and for an effective program of higher education to be provided for all who should benefit. The adoption of unsound policies or any failure of a state to make adequate provisions inevitably means that the schools and other educational institutions, at least in certain areas, will be handicapped.

EVOLUTION OF STATE SYSTEMS OF EDUCATION

The state systems of education have evolved slowly and with considerable unevenness. Everyone concerned with education should be familiar with the major issues, controversies, and trends, a few of which are summarized in this section.[1]

The beginnings of the present state systems may be traced to the Massachusetts Acts of 1642 and 1647. The adoption of the ordinances of 1780 and 1787 and the provisions incorporated in the Constitution indicated clearly that the American people had begun to recognize that (1) education is a concern of the people of each state and therefore should be a state function, (2) the federal government has an interest in education and an obligation to encourage and aid education in the states and territories, and (3) public funds or resources may not be used to support religious organizations or schools.[2]

When the nation was organized, all the original thirteen states had made some legal provisions for education. These varied from authorization of pauper schools in Pennsylvania and low-cost schools in North Carolina to a strong mandate directing the legislature to encourage public schools and colleges in Massachusetts. These provisions tended to reflect the early attitudes toward education in the different colonies.[3] Soon, however, both Congress and the people began to insist that each new state make some definite provisions for education. Early in the nineteenth century, this concept became accepted as policy. States that adopted new constitutions or made revisions in their original constitutions tended to include stronger and more clear-cut provisions relating to the state responsibility for education. Unfortunately, the legislatures of many states failed to make adequate provisions to implement such directives.

---
[1]See Ellwood P. Cubberley, *State School Administration* (Boston: Houghton Mifflin Company, 1927), and more recent publications dealing with the subject.
[2]Adapted from Lee M. Thurston and William H. Roe, *State School Administration* (New York: Harper & Row, Publishers, 1957), p. 56.
[3]Cubberley, *State School Administration*, Chaps. 1 and 5.

The first state board of education was established in New York in 1784 but was given responsibility only for the colleges and academies authorized during colonial days. Not until 1904 was this board made responsible for the public schools. It was only after Massachusetts established a state board for elementary and secondary schools in 1837 that the movement made any significant headway. By 1870, most states had established boards of education but, among the older states, Georgia, Pennsylvania, and Maine did not do so until after the beginning of the present century.[4]

Before 1830 only three states—New York, Maryland, and Michigan—had provided for the position now known generally as chief state school officer. During the ensuing twenty years, however, another 21 states authorized a position of this type, and by the beginning of the present century all states had provided for a state superintendent or commissioner of education. In many, however, the first state school officers were designated on an ex officio basis; that is, some state official serving in another capacity was given the additional responsibility of serving as superintendent. The movement to provide a chief state school officer in every state was given considerable impetus in the second quarter of the nineteenth century by three developments: (1) the significant contributions of Horace Mann, the first state superintendent in Massachusetts, who was appointed in 1837; (2) the need for some state official to keep a record of the school lands and account for the funds derived therefrom in each of the states; and (3) the growing awareness of the need for someone representing the state to collect information, make reports, and answer inquiries regarding the common schools that were being organized in most communities.[5]

Recognition of the responsibility of the people of each state for devising an adequate and effective system of education has developed slowly in most states but much more slowly in some than in others. There was no pattern to follow and no design that had been agreed upon. Although the people in each state had to develop their own policies and provisions for education, in many cases they were greatly influenced by what had happened in leading states such as Massachusetts. However, society has changed and continues to change more rapidly than the provisions for education and the practices in most schools and other educational institutions. It should be apparent that state systems of education in this country are still in the process of evolution and that this process now urgently needs to be accelerated.

[4]Ward W. Keesecker, *State Boards of Education and Chief State School Officers,* U.S. Office of Education Bulletin No. 12 (Washington, D.C.: U.S. Government Printing Office, 1950), p. 8.
[5]*Ibid.,* p. 25.

STATE PROVISIONS FOR EDUCATION

In some states the constitutional provisions, the laws, and the leadership provided by the people contributed to the development and operation of programs of education that were reasonably adequate and more or less consistent with the ideals, purposes, and goals generally accepted in this country at that time. In others, so many handicaps were inherent in certain policies and legal provisions that some of the stated or implied goals could not be attained.

The State Constitution

The basic provisions for education are found in the constitution of each state, as explained in Chapter 2. Although the phraseology varies considerably, the constitution in most states includes a mandate or directive requiring the legislature to provide an effective system of public education, free of tuition charges and equally open to all who can benefit from education. Other sections in the constitution incorporate additional policies considered essential in the state.

The people of each state, therefore, determine—within limits established by the federal constitution and court decisions—the basic policies for or relating to the operation and support of education within the state. These policies may be sound and future oriented, vague and indefinite, or narrowly restrictive in some respects. The criterion that should be used in evaluating state constitutional provisions relating to education may be stated as follows: *The constitution should set forth the basic policies for the organization, administration, and support of adequate programs of public education; should empower and direct the legislature to establish the basic guidelines for implementing these policies; and should be free from detailed or restrictive provisions that may handicap or prevent the development of adequate provisions for or programs of education.*[6]

State Legislation

The people in each state should expect their legislature to enact statutes (commonly referred to as "laws") that provide for the implementation of the basic policies and provisions incorporated in their constitution. The legislature may act wisely or unwisely and may thus facilitate or handicap the development of the educational program. Serious prob-

---

[6]Adapted from Edgar L. Morphet, ed., *Building a Better Southern Region Through Education* (Tallahassee, Fla.: Southern States Work-Conference on Educational Problems, 1945), p. 173.

lems have developed in some states as a result of the tendency of the legislature to incorporate restrictive details into the law and to preempt a number of functions that should be assigned to the state or local boards of education. The criterion that should be used in evaluating legislative policy may be stated as follows: *The legislature should make a serious effort to implement the constitutional directives by establishing the basic framework for the educational system and the major principles, goals, and policies to be observed in operating that system; the responsibility for developing more specific goals, minimum standards, and the technical requirements consistent with those policies, and for measuring progress, should be delegated to the state agency for education.*[7]

The provisions for the organization of education—that is, the framework within which education operates in any state—are of great importance. Although some good schools and educational institutions can be found in a state with inadequate or limiting provisions, it is likely that even these will be handicapped. Any plan of organization that creates overlapping functions, facilitates the introduction of partisan politics into any aspect of the educational program, discourages meaningful local initiative and responsibility, rewards inefficient organization and operation, or makes appropriate organization and coordination difficult, obviously needs to be improved.

The legislature of each state presumably is elected to represent the people. If many of the people are not seriously concerned about the kind and quality of education provided, if powerful pressure groups are more interested in low taxes than in good schools and institutions of higher learning, if people in the wealthy communities are not concerned about education in the less wealthy areas, or if other similar attitudes and conditions exist, the state design and provisions for education are likely to be defective in certain respects. Moreover, if the educators themselves are sharply divided regarding the purposes and goals of education or means for achieving them, the people and the legislature may tend to become confused and fail to provide for an effective program. Only when a majority of the citizens agree on the goals and the best means for attaining them can significant and continuing progress in improving the design and provisions for education be expected.

THE STATE EDUCATION AGENCY

In every state not only the governor and the legislature but also many other agencies and officials should be deeply interested in and concerned

[7] *Ibid.,* p. 174.

about the provisions for education, many of which have important implications for the progress and welfare of the state. Their decisions and actions may determine, or at least significantly influence, the kind and quality of education that can be provided and the progress that can be made in improving education.

As previously noted, every state has developed some kind of *system* of education. In reality, however, most states have established two or more systems, each of which is primarily responsible for some level or major aspect of education (for example, elementary and secondary education, and institutions of higher learning). These systems tend to function independently in many states with little coordination except that provided by the governor and the legislature. Many people have become convinced that appropriate provisions designed to ensure more adequate coordination are essential in every state if emerging needs are to be met. Some believe this coordination can best be achieved through a properly constituted coordinating council; others believe an agency that is responsible for all levels and aspects of education should be established in every state.

A state education agency (the term commonly used in the literature) usually comprises the state board of education, the chief state school officer, and the state department of education. The manner in which this agency is organized, the functions assigned to it, the way it operates, and the educational responsibilities assigned to other agencies have a rather direct bearing on the kind and quality of educational programs that are or can be provided.

In all but a few states, the existing state education agency is concerned primarily with elementary and secondary education and only incidentally with other levels of education. Traditionally the major responsibilities of these agencies have included collecting and reporting routine information, establishing and enforcing minimum standards, supervision of rural and small-town schools, certification of teachers, and other similar activities presumably designed to ensure stability in the operation of the system. But during recent years it has become apparent that this system has not met many of the needs of a rapidly changing society and, as a result, the role of state education agencies has begun to change significantly along the lines discussed in a later section of this chapter.

The State Board of Education

Because education is concerned with helping every individual to develop his full potential and provides the foundation for many of the beliefs, aspirations, and actions of the people, American citizens have always insisted that the control of education be kept primarily in their hands. To that end, they usually have insisted on and established predominantly lay state and local boards of education that are responsible to them for determining policies, goals, and basic procedures subject to the provisions in the constitution and the laws of the state.

NUMBER AND COMPOSITION. According to a study by Beach and Will, there were 231 state boards concerned with public schools, institutions of higher learning, or other aspects of education in the 48 states in 1954.[8] While some additions and reorganizations have been made, the total has not changed significantly since that time. The number of states having state boards of education for the public schools increased from 30 in 1900 to 49 in 1972. Although Wisconsin has had a state board for vocational education for some years, it has not yet established a board for elementary and secondary schools. There has been a definite tendency to eliminate ex officio state boards of education. In 1890, 20 of the 29 state boards of education were of the ex officio type. By 1940 the number had decreased to 8 out of 39, and by 1973 to 2 (Florida and Mississippi). Not only the ex officio board but also ex officio board members have tended to disappear.

Partly because of the provisions of the Smith-Hughes Act, most states provided for a state board for vocational education shortly after 1920. In a number of states that had already established a state board of education, the two boards were, in effect, merged because the membership was identical. Thus, the state board of education also served as the state board for vocational education. By 1973, only three states still had a separate or independent board for vocational education: Colorado, Massachusetts, and Wisconsin. State residential schools for the blind and deaf are under the state board of education in nearly half the states, under some other state agency in a few, and have their own governing board or boards in the remainder of the states that have such schools. In six states (Florida, Idaho, Maine, Montana, New York, and Rhode Island) the state colleges and universities come under the state board of education (or regents). In a few others the state colleges but not the state universities are under the state board. Various other combinations are found in the remaining states.

SELECTION OF MEMBERS. When the number of ex officio boards began to decrease some years ago, appointment by the governor became the favored method of selecting members for the state board of education. During the past fifteen years several states have changed to popular elec-

---

[8]Fred F. Beach and Robert F. Will, *The State and Education,* Office of Education, Miscellaneous No. 23 (Washington D.C.: U.S. Government Printing Office, 1955), and Robert F. Will, *State Education, Structure and Organization,* Office of Education, Miscellaneous No. 46 (Washington, D.C.: U.S. Government Printing Office, 1964).

tion of state board members or to selection in some other manner than appointment by the governor. The governor now appoints at least a majority of the members of the board in 32 states. In New York the state board is selected by the legislature; in South Carolina one member is selected by the legislators from each judicial circuit; and in Washington the members are selected by local school boards. In 5 states (Nebraska, Nevada—except two who are appointed by the other members—Ohio, Texas and Utah) the board members are elected on a nonpartisan ballot. In 7 states (Alabama, Colorado, Hawaii, Kansas, Louisiana, Michigan, and New Mexico) they are elected on a partisan ballot.

SIZE AND TERM. The state boards for public schools range from 3 ex officio members in Mississippi to 21 popularly elected members in Texas and 23 in Ohio. Only eight states have fewer than seven members and only four more than thirteen. The length of term for appointment or election of state board members ranges from four years or less in fourteen states to thirteen years in New York. The tendency has been to increase the length of term to seven or nine years and to provide for overlapping terms so as to assure some continuity in service of experienced persons.

RESPONSIBILITIES. In some states the differences between the functions of the chief state school officer and those of the state board of education have not been made clear. In most cases an attempt has been made to designate the state board as the body responsible for policies and regulations, and the state superintendent as executive officer of the board. Where the state superintendent is appointed by the board this differentiation seems to work out satisfactorily. In most states where the state superintendent is responsible to the people because he is elected by popular vote, there have been, and probably will continue to be, conflicts and uncertainties from time to time.

It is generally recognized that the state board of education should have the legal responsibility for the general supervision and management of all aspects of the public school program of the state. However the board would not only be ill advised but would be inviting difficulties for itself and the educational programs if it did not expect the chief state school officer and his staff to make studies, prepare reports, and submit recommendations for its consideration in arriving at decisions regarding policies and standards. The major functions of most state boards of education may be listed as follows:

- To appoint and fix the compensation of a competent chief state school officer who should serve as its secretary and executive officer;
- To determine areas of service, establish qualifications, and appoint the necessary personnel for the state department of education;

- To adopt and administer a budget for the operation of the state education agency;
- To authorize needed studies and, with the assistance of appropriate committees and consultants, to develop and submit to the governor and legislature proposals for improving the organization, administration, financing, accountability, and other aspects of education in the state;
- To adopt policies and minimum standards for the administration and supervision of the state educational enterprise;
- To represent the state in determining policies on all matters pertaining to education that involve relationships with other state agencies and the federal government; and
- When authorized to do so, to adopt policies for the operation of institutions of higher learning and other educational institutions and programs operated by the state, or to approve major policies recommended by the board or boards of control for such institutions.

The Chief State School Officer

Potentially the most important educational position in any state is that of a chief state school officer. However, in some states this position has been one of relatively minor significance as contrasted with those occupied by superintendents of some of the larger school districts or presidents of state institutions of higher learning.

Although a few states, primarily in the New England area, adopted from the beginning the concept that the chief state school officer should be selected by and responsible to a state board of education, many states for one reason or another assumed that he should be elected by popular vote, appointed by the governor, or selected in some other manner. In 1896 the chief school officer was appointed by the state board of education in only three states; in 31 states he was elected by popular vote and, in most cases, on a partisan political ballot along with the other officials; in nine the governor appointed the state superintendent and in three he was appointed by the general assembly.[9] Since that time many significant changes have occurred.

In 1973 the chief state school officer was appointed by the state board of education in 27 states and appointed by the governor in five (Maine, New Jersey, Pennsylvania, Tennessee, and Virginia). The number of states in which he was required to be elected by popular vote had decreased to 18. In four of these (North Dakota, Oregon, Washington, and Wisconsin) the election was by nonpartisan ballot. It is interesting that in about one-third of the states the chief state school officer serves ex officio as a member, and in some states as chairman, of the state board of education. This seems to place him in an anomalous position, since as a superintendent he

[9]Adapted from Beach and Will, *The State and Education,* Table 17, p. 30; and Will, *State Education, Structure, and Organization,* p. 26.

would recommend policies and standards to the board, as a board member he would vote on them, and as a superintendent he would implement those that are approved.

Two of the factors that have handicapped the development of the position of chief state school officer in several states have been the low compensation provided and failure to recognize that special qualifications are needed. Generally, as states have changed from popular election to appointment by the state board, salaries have been improved and higher qualifications have been recognized as necessary. Most people in some states now recognize that the person selected for the position as chief state school officer should be the most competent educator who can be found and that the compensation must be adequate to attract such a person.

The duties and responsibilities of the chief state school officer vary considerably from state to state. In the more progressive states they usually include the following:

- To serve as secretary and executive officer of the state board of education;
- To serve as executive officer of any board or council that may be established to facilitate coordination of all aspects of the educational program;
- To select competent personnel for, and serve as the administrative head and professional leader of, the state department of education to the end that it will contribute maximally to the improvement of education;
- To arrange for studies and organize committees and task forces as deemed necessary to identify problems, and to recommend plans and provisions for effecting improvements in education;
- To recommend to the state board of education needed policies, standards, and regulations relating to public education in the state;
- To recommend improvements in educational legislation and in provisions for financing the educational program;
- To explain and interpret the school laws of the state and the policies and regulations of the state board of education; and
- To prepare reports for the public, the state board, the governor, and the legislature that provide pertinent information about the accomplishments, conditions, and needs of the schools.

The State Department of Education

The term "state department of education" includes the chief state school officer and his staff, authorized by and functioning in accordance with provisions of law and policies adopted by the state board of education. The duties and responsibilities of all state departments of education have expanded greatly during the past quarter of a century. For many years these responsibilities were assumed by the state superintendent with the assistance of a secretary or two. In 1900, there were only 177 professional and other staff members in all state departments of education. This number increased to 3,718 in 1940,[10] to approximately 15,000 by 1955, and has increased even more rapidly since that time.

Increases in the number of staff members have been associated with the major stages in the development of state departments of education. At first, these departments were chiefly concerned with accounting and reporting functions. The second stage of development placed considerable emphasis on regulation and inspection. At present, increasing emphasis is being placed on leadership in planning and effecting improvements in education and developing procedures for accountability. As a result of these changes, much more attention is being devoted to the selection of competent professional personnel who can assist educators in the field; organize conferences; plan and conduct studies; lead in facilitating improvements in the state educational program as well as in local programs; and work effectively with the governor, the legislature, and representatives of other state and federal agencies.

In a study of state departments of education, Beach identified three major types of functions, which he classified as leadership, regulatory, and operational responsibilities.[11] The need for greater emphasis on leadership functions in many state departments of education is evident to all who study educational problems. If this need is to be met satisfactorily, it seems apparent that: (1) the chief state school officer who administers the department should be selected because of his ability to provide professional leadership in improving the state provisions for education; (2) the professional members of the department staff should be carefully selected on a basis which will assure that they not only are leaders in their respective areas of specialization but also can work effectively with others in studying and solving educational problems; (3) the department should be so organized and administered that effective functioning is facilitated; and (4) the people and the legislature should insist on and support the kind of services that can be provided through competent and creative leadership in the state department of education.

EMERGING STATE RESPONSIBILITIES AND RELATIONS

Various authorities have directed attention to such basic concepts as the following: education is in the public domain; it is "political" in a broad

---

[10]Fred F. Beach and Andrew H. Gibbs, *Personnel of State Departments of Education,* Office of Education, Miscellaneous No. 16 (Washington, D.C.: U.S. Government Printing Office, 1952), p. 6.
[11]Fred F. Beach, *The Functions of State Departments of Education,* Office of Education, Miscellaneous No. 12 (Washington, D.C.: U.S. Government Printing Office, 1950), pp. 3–17.

sense because it is operated by an agency of the formal political government; its nature and functioning are affected by the political and social climate in which it operates; and, as a formal, specialized structure and organization, education is a subsystem of a complex system concerned with the broader processes of acculturation and socialization in the nation.[12]

In order to understand why a system of education, or an agency for education, is organized and operated in certain ways, it is necessary to identify and understand the beliefs, values, and aspirations of the people and the forces operating in the state as well as those in the national setting. But these have changed in many important respects during recent years and will undoubtedly continue to change. As one result, some of the traditional roles, functions, and priorities of educational agencies and institutions are no longer considered appropriate under modern conditions and are currently being modified in most states in an effort to meet emerging as well as many current needs that have previously been ignored. Some of these modifications have been carefully planned on the basis of systematic studies; others have been haphazard or inadequate.

The most important responsibility of every state education agency in the future will be to provide the leadership and services needed to improve continuously the quality of education in a major effort to achieve excellence in every aspect of education throughout the state. If this effort is to be successful, the agency will need to find effective ways of cooperating with—and obtaining the cooperation of—the governor, the legislature, other state agencies, institutions of higher learning, major organizations, local school systems, and many others, including appropriate representatives from the federal level and perhaps from other states.

The quest for excellence in education will require systematic and comprehensive long-range planning, the utilization of appropriate strategies for effecting needed changes, continuous monitoring and appraisal of progress, and the periodic revision of plans to deal with new or unrecognized problems and needs (see Chapter 6). It will also necessitate, in many states, a different plan of organization, new attitudes and approaches, and different roles for most members of the state department staff.

The major responsibilities of the state education agency, in addition to developing and maintaining an appropriate structure and operating procedures for the staff, will include services and procedures designed to:

---

[12]See, for example, J. K. Galbraith, *The Affluent Society* (Boston: Houghton Mifflin Company, 1958), p. 355; and Howard Dean, "The Political Setting of American Education," in *The Social Sciences View School Administration* (Englewood Cliffs, N.J.: Prentice-Hall, Inc., 1965), pp. 213–217.

1. Increase the adequacy and effectiveness of educational policies in the state as authorized or required by existing laws, regulations, and professional standards; and
2. Identify, develop, and encourage promising new or improved policies, procedures, and practices in the organization, administration, operation, and support of education (encourage continuous educational renewal).

Relations with Other State and Federal Agencies

STATE AGENCIES. In a number of states, responsibilities for certain functions or services involving or related to the public schools have been assigned to agencies other than the state agency for education. Some of these assignments have been made capriciously and unwisely. In such cases, local school officials have often become involved in red tape and delay because they were required to attempt to work with a variety of state agencies whose roles and services were not satisfactorily coordinated.

The following criteria are generally recognized as desirable for guidance in planning state services and developing coordination in education:

1. Services primarily educational in nature should be provided by the state agency for education, and those chiefly noneducational should be provided by other state agencies.
2. The state education agency or some other appropriate educational agency established by the state should be charged with the responsibility of coordinating the entire state program of education. It should work in close cooperation with other appropriate agencies of state and local governments in planning and providing services in areas of joint concern.
3. When two state agencies are concerned with policy matters involving the schools, any minimum standards or regulations that are found to be necessary should be jointly approved and adopted by both agencies. For example, in matters involving school health the standards should be jointly approved by the state board of education and the state board of health.
4. The state department of education should serve as a coordinating agency and clearing house for matters involving formal relations or contracts with—or applications from local school systems to—other state or federal agencies. For example, in the school plant field, the state department of education should be able to save local school systems much confusion and delay if it has the responsibility for obtaining approval of plans by the state fire marshal, the state health department, and any other state agency that is responsible for approving any aspect of the plant program.[13]

FEDERAL AGENCIES. Many agencies of the federal government have been concerned with one or another aspect of education for some years (see

[13] Adapted from National Council of Chief State School Officers, *The State Department of Education* (Washington, D.C.: 1952), pp. 25–26; and Beach, *The Functions of State Departments of Education*, pp. 7–8.

Chapter 8). Important problems of federal-state-local relations have been encountered from time to time. Although the increased national interest in education and the additional funds for education provided by Congress during the past few years have helped to stimulate all states to make important changes in their provisions for certain aspects of education, some of these developments have resulted in serious problems and concerns. Because most of the federal funds have been categorical in nature (can be utilized only for the purpose designated), the requirements for participation result in considerable detailed work in preparing applications and reports, the state's provisions for financing schools have largely been ignored, and the funding has often been so late or uncertain that realistic planning is often impossible, *state priorities in some cases have been seriously distorted.* Fortunately there are many indications that at least some of the most indefensible federal policies will be abandoned in the near future and that a bona fide federal-state partnership will emerge.

On the basis of a recent study, Milstein concluded that the impact of federal grants on state policy may be as dependent, or almost so, on the leadership qualities of the state education agencies as on the stipulations for the grants. He noted that:

> With strong leadership, the state education agency can do much to further its own objectives. Without strong leadership it can be led by the "carrot" of the dollar and the "stick" of regulations and guidelines to become the purely regulatory agency which critics of federal aid portend.[14]

Many people are seriously concerned that an increasing number of important decisions regarding education may continue to be made at the federal level. Some realignment is probably inevitable, but this does not mean that the concept of state responsibility for education is outdated. What it does mean is that *all states must face up to their responsibilities and prepare promptly to meet them realistically.* The people in every state will need to reevaluate their existing policies and procedures as a basis for developing better ways of meeting their responsibilities for education in the future. Such improvements will not only provide needed safeguards against inappropriate federal encroachments but will also establish a basis for constructive cooperation that should assure more adequate programs of education.

[14] Mike M. Milstein, "Federal Aid and State Education Agencies," *Administrators Notebook,* Vol. XVI, No. 7 (March 1968).

State Policies and Standards

Since the legislature should not attempt to prescribe by law all details of policies and standards that may be needed for education, an important question that arises is: How much responsibility or discretion should be delegated to state or local boards of education? A generally recognized principle of law provides that *limits or boundaries should be established for any discretionary authority that is granted.* Thus, the legislature should prescribe only the basic state policies, goals, and standards, and should authorize the development of more specific policies, goals, and standards by an appropriate administrative agency, such as the state board of education.

Some minimum standards have been found necessary in every state as a means of helping to ensure adequate educational opportunities. However, states have learned by experience that the establishment of minimum standards alone will not solve the problem. Those standards cannot substitute for adequate state and local leadership and planning, nor can they result in satisfactory programs of education unless the state plan ensures that sufficient funds will be available to finance these programs.

Among the important criteria relating to standards and regulations that have generally been accepted by authorities are the following:

1. Although a major responsibility of the state should be to provide adequate leadership and services, it should, when necessary, establish those minimum standards and only those that are universally applicable, that are designed primarily to assure adequate educational opportunities for all children and youth, and that in no way limit the freedom of local school systems to go beyond the established standards.

2. In making decisions regarding the desirability of minimum standards or other controls, preference should be given to retaining control locally, especially for those elements concerning which there is no certainty that central authority will provide the best long-term results.

3. The advantages of local responsibility for educational programs should be protected and promoted by avoiding inhibiting controls over local boards of education, school programs, or school funds by the state, the state education agency, or by noneducational authorities.[15]

State Leadership and Coordination

Among the most important functions of state leadership are planning and coordination. Planning, to be effective, must be based on carefully

[15] Adapted from National Education Association, Committee on Tax Education and School Finance, *Guides to the Development of State School Finance Programs* (Washington, D.C.: The Association, 1949), pp. 5–10.

developed studies, research, and bona fide cooperation in determining purposes, goals, and objectives and agreement on steps to be used in attaining them. Improvements in the state provisions for education cannot safely be left to chance developments. Failure to formulate defensible plans and proposals for improving educational programs may result in unfortunate changes sponsored by groups with vested interests, perpetuation of inefficiencies that handicap the entire program, or even failure to obtain the support of the people and the legislature in providing funds to meet emerging school needs. Cooperatively developed and well-formulated plans should, on the other hand, result in constantly improving programs that are strongly supported by the people.

Few people realize the amount and extent of coordination needed in any state if education is to be developed satisfactorily. In addition to coordination involving state agencies and institutions, there must be coordination and cooperation *within* the state department of education. No member of the staff can operate satisfactorily without relating his work to what others are doing. No bureau or division can function in isolation. Most educational problems are interrelated. Finance is not merely a matter of money; it also relates to the provision of necessary services and facilities. Curriculum improvement requires consideration not only of subject matter but also of students and their needs and the relationship of each aspect of learning to other aspects. The need for coordination in research and planning should be obvious. Without coordination, there is likely to be much duplication of effort and failure to give appropriate attention to matters of considerable importance. Competition and rivalry may be disastrous when there is no effective coordination.

Many services provided by the federal government are not well-coordinated and result in some confusion for state and local school systems unless these agencies and groups agree upon a plan and provide the leadership needed to ensure effective coordination. In most situations the state education agency is necessarily involved in developing plans for such coordination.

PREPARING FOR THE FUTURE

Unless or until there are significant pressures for change, every social organization tends to continue to do what it was established to do, holding itself relatively stable and resisting attempts at reorientation or restructuring (see Chapter 4). The pressures to change may come from new leadership, new insights, changes in society or societal expectations, or from other similar developments including major court decisions. This concept applies not only to state legislatures and education agencies but also to other educational agencies, institutions, and organizations concerned with social progress.

Some of the most obvious pressures to effect significant changes in state and local policies and provisions relating to education have come from recent state or federal court decisions holding that: (1) a child's education cannot be a function of the wealth of the district in which he lives; (2) some state aid formulas, for this and perhaps other reasons, violate the equal protection clause of the Fourteenth Amendment to the Constitution; (3) laws that require segregation of students solely on the basis of race are unconstitutional because they deprive children of minority groups of equal opportunities; and (4) the traditionally recognized constitutional rights of students must be considerably expanded. (See discussion in Chapter 2.) It should be obvious that changes in policies and provisions in these and similar areas must be made primarily through the political processes because state laws and traditionally accepted policies are involved.

Kimbrough has perceptively observed:

> In past years many educators were enamored with the idea that education should not be in politics ... [But] studies of ... power structures have demonstrated that education is—and indeed ought to be—in politics. ... Through the interaction of influentials with each other and with other leaders and politically active citizens, important channels of communication crystallize. ...
>
> Political action must be based on commitment to attainable legislative goals. ... Every great movement in education has been based upon some purposeful goals that captivated the minds of those who led the movement. ... There are limits to how much educators can improve schooling unless attention and power are focused upon improving the political power system in which the schools function ...
>
> State education agencies need to furnish aggressive leadership and coordinative services in the planning of long-range goals for education in the states ... State leaders must be effective (strong) enough to motivate and assist local educators to bring about changes ... Local leaders need to "stand and be counted" when political strength is needed in the state education agency.[16]

A major problem in most states arises from the fact that many people who give "lip service" to the commonly expressed purposes and goals of education apparently have reservations about some of them. Moreover

---

[16]Ralph B. Kimbrough, "Power Structures and Educational Change" in Edgar L. Morphet and Charles O. Ryan, eds., *Planning and Effecting Needed Changes in Education* (New York: Citation Press, Scholastic Magazines, Inc., 1967), Chap. 6.

there are sharp differences of opinion as to how these goals can best be achieved. Such differences complicate the problem of developing an effective and viable state agency for education and ensuring that it is properly organized and assigned appropriate roles. They also may make it difficult for the agency to provide the leadership required to redefine or reorient purposes and goals, conduct needed studies, and develop policies, plans, and procedures for attaining them. A primary problem in many states, therefore, is to obtain majority agreement on the need for an effective state agency for education, get it established on a sound basis, and define its functions realistically in terms of emerging needs.

Relatively few state education agencies seem to have been seriously interested, until recently, in developing a strongly supportive educational or political clientele. For example, few people in institutions of higher learning have been constructively interested in sponsoring pertinent research, preparing students for service in the agency, or collaborating in other appropriate ways in helping state agencies to modernize their role and improve their services. Moreover, most local school systems and educational organizations apparently have been so concerned with their own problems and attempting to obtain help for short-range solutions, or with safeguarding their traditional rights and prerogatives that they have tended to view with suspicion proposals for modifying significantly the role of the state education agency. Even many legislators have tended to view the primary responsibility of this agency as that of establishing and enforcing standards and regulations. But fortunately new insights and developments have resulted in some promising breakthroughs.

Some Encouraging Developments

Several recent studies and reports have focused attention on the state role in facilitating needed changes in education. Proposals have been made for major reorganization and new roles for the state education agencies to involve them more directly and aggressively in research and the development and dissemination of new policies and practices.

A few years ago four political scientists who made studies of the dynamics of educational policy making at the state level were concerned with the role of educators in initiating and formulating public school policy in eight Northeastern states.[17] This study brought out clearly the importance of leadership from the ranks of professional schoolmen and state department personnel, as well as of other key personnel, in helping to effect changes in state educational policy. Three other political scientists studied the processes of arriving at decisions affecting public schools in

---

[17]Stephen K. Bailey, Richard T. Frost, Robert C. Wood, and Paul E. Marsh, *Schoolmen and Politics: A Study of State Aid to Education in the Northeast* (Syracuse, N.Y.: Syracuse University Press, 1962).

three Midwestern states.[18] They noted that much of the state politics in those states has been concerned with public schools and that ". . . the ways in which the state is involved in education vary and so do the political processes."

All volumes in the Designing Education for the Future and the Improving State Leadership in Education project series, as well as a number of other recent publications, have been concerned directly or indirectly with the role and relations of the states in improving education (see Selected References at end of chapter). In fact, all projects sponsored and at least partly financed under the provisions of Title V, Section 505 of the Elementary and Secondary Education Act of 1965 have been designed to help the participating states plan and effect improvements in important aspects of their provisions for education.

Practically every state has been involved in and benefited from participation in one or more of these projects which range in focus from comprehensive planning through curriculum, teacher education, school finance, and accountability. Funds are also available under other sections and titles of this act to help state education agencies and local school systems to upgrade and improve the competencies of their staffs not only in planning and effecting needed changes but also in other appropriate ways.

Among the recent promising state developments are some in Florida that are briefly summarized below:

> In 1968 the legislature established a unique incentive plan (with substantial state funding) that was designed to facilitate and encourage comprehensive state and local long-range planning (with lay participation) for improvements in all aspects of education. A related legal mandate for educational renewal directed the Commissioner of Education, as rapidly as feasible, to "expand the capability of the Department of Education in planning the state's strategy for effecting constructive educational change and providing and coordinating creative services necessary to achieve greater quality in education" (Section 229.551 Florida Statutes, 1968).
>
> During the process of planning improvements, several local groups became seriously concerned about a number of provisions in earlier laws that made it impossible for them to implement some of the changes they considered essential. As a result of systematic studies of the laws relating to educational programs and procedures by members of the state department of education staff, legislators, and others, all such restrictive provisions were identified and repealed at the 1972 legislative session. Thus, a major breakthrough was made in facilitating planned innovation and bona fide accountability for progress.
>
> As one result of these developments, the state department staff and many

---

[18]Nicholas A. Masters, Robert A. Salisbury, and Thomas H. Eliot, *State Politics and the Public Schools* (New York: Alfred A. Knopf, Inc., 1964), Chaps. 2–4.

local staffs have been reorganized and the roles reoriented. Since the incentive plan was merged with the comprehensive foundation program at the 1972 legislative session, systematic participatory planning has tended to become an accepted way of life in the state education agency and in most local school systems. Several carefully developed policy statements and guides (including an explanation of the state strategy for educational renewal and accountability, planning models, and school district comprehensive educational planning responsibilities and procedures) serve as one basis for staff improvement at district and area work conferences, and for developing understanding and support for the state strategy for educational renewal.

During the past few years all state education agencies have made considerable progress in developing planning and other related competencies, but some are still handicapped by legal constraints or a political climate that is not favorable to the assumption of urgently needed new roles and functions. Several state agencies have begun to utilize at least some aspects of the systems approach not only in comprehensive planning but also in adapting the planning-programming-budgeting and other similar systems for utilization in education, in devising provisions and procedures relating to accountability, in developing adequate management information systems that are so essential under modern conditions, and in many other ways.

Although changing the traditional rural-small town orientation of state education agencies has been difficult for many reasons (including the noncity background and interests of most staff members, and the position of relative independence of the big cities that developed during their earlier, more affluent decades), this orientation has begun to change. In several states, the big cities have decided they can not only benefit from services that should be provided by the state education agency, but can also contribute to the development of a more adequate and viable state system of education. Florida, New Jersey, New York, Ohio, and Texas are among the states in which substantial progress has been made in this respect during the past few years.

SOME IMPORTANT PROBLEMS AND ISSUES

A few of the problems and issues relating to state educational organization, administration, and responsibilities are discussed briefly on the following pages. What others are important?

How Should Members of the State Board and the Chief State School Officer Be Selected?

The way each aspect of this issue is resolved in a state should be considered of vital importance. The kinds of decisions made and the manner in which they are implemented over a period of years are likely to influence significantly the kind and quality of provisions for education and the prospects for continuously improving every aspect of education.

Although each of these decisions is of great importance, perhaps the most fundamental decision relates to the kind and quality of members selected to serve on the state board. If most of them have low aspirations for education, are satisfied with existing provisions, or are more concerned about political prestige than about the quality of education, the educational system is not likely to make much progress. The citizens of each state, therefore, need to insist—even demand—that members of the board be highly competent individuals who are dedicated to the achievement of excellence in education throughout the state. Unless this expectation is fulfilled, no method of selection is likely to result in the kind and quality of board members needed under modern conditions.

If the chief state school officer is selected by the state board, this board can and should hold him responsible and accountable for improvements. If he is elected by the people he can, if he chooses to do so, practically ignore or thwart the board except for legal formalities—as has occurred in some states. If he is appointed by the governor, as advocated by some political scientists, he can make the role of the board almost meaningless.

How can some of these dilemmas best be resolved for the benefit of education? Assuming that some coordination among all levels and aspects of education in a state is essential, how can this best be achieved?

How Should the Staff of the State Education Agency Be Organized and Function?

Procedures for selecting and appointing professional personnel for state education agencies (which may include social scientists, economists, systems analysts, computer programmers, and similar kinds of specialists as well as leaders and specialists in many aspects of education) are usually influenced or restricted by established state policies that may be roughly classified as follows: (1) personal or political appointments made and terminated by the decision of the chief state school officer in some states in which he is elected by popular vote; (2) appointments based on legally established civil service specifications that may or may not be adapted to the competency or salary levels needed to attract competent professional personnel from any state for service in the department; or (3) the establishment of an "institutional status" for the state education agency (similar to that authorized for institutions of higher learning) that will enable the board to establish appropriate qualifications and salary levels within limits set by the authorized budget.

Traditionally, most state department staffs have been organized into semiautonomous divisions or units, each of which was directly responsible to the chief state school officer for some level or aspect of education. Frequently there has been relatively little communication or cooperation among these units. Many departments are currently being reorganized in an effort to assure maximum coordination and cooperation in planning and effecting needed changes in education. Several have established an administrative or coordinating council, reorganized existing divisions to meet modern criteria and needs, created temporary task forces for special purposes, and taken other steps designed to ensure effective communication and more rational decision making. But communication across the boundaries of a social system, such as the state education agency, is even more difficult than communication among the units within that system. Few state or local education agencies have made satisfactory progress thus far in communicating effectively with lay citizens, many organizations, or other units of government.

What kinds of policies, provisions, and procedures will be most helpful in facilitating adequate staffing, organization, and functioning of a state department of education? In facilitating meaningful communication within the department and with other people and groups outside the department?

What Responsibilities Should the State Education Agency Have for Research?

Although research is essential to identify problems and needs and to provide a basis for assessing progress, few state education agencies have the personnel or resources needed to undertake significant research studies. The development of long-range goals and plans for achieving them will be facilitated by utilizing appropriate data and the findings from related research studies as bases for the carefully considered value judgments that must be made.

There is serious doubt as to whether state departments of education should undertake basic research since this usually can be done better and more appropriately by universities or independent research agencies. State departments, however, should be interested in encouraging such research and seeking to identify practical implications.

The state department probably should have a research or a research and reference unit that is concerned with the development of a statewide research plan and program, with facilitating coordination and cooperation, and perhaps with undertaking certain projects on its own initiative. Many of these studies might well be concerned in one way or another with procedures and innovations designed to effect improvements in the educational program or organization. The permanent staff should probably be small, but funds should be available for extensive use of consultants and for assisting institutions and other agencies to plan and conduct special studies as needed.

The research functions of the state department of education should probably include: (1) helping to create a favorable climate not only for research but also for utilizing the findings of research; (2) identifying major problems and issues concerning which research is especially needed; (3) stimulating ideas for research and the development of research projects; (4) helping to coordinate the research efforts in the state and to focus attention from time to time on certain problems that need special study; (5) assisting, or locating qualified consultants who can assist, with research design; (6) developing, organizing, and keeping up-to-date a "library" of research findings in areas that would be of interest and value in the state; (7) developing a plan for ensuring that the research findings in appropriate areas are summarized, synthesized, and interpreted in such a way that they will be of maximum benefit to educational leaders in the state who should utilize them.

How can the state agency help universities and local school systems in the state to encourage and cooperate in studies that would be especially helpful to the state department and to local school systems? Would a research coordinating council be helpful?

What Procedures Should be Utilized in Improving State Provisions for Education?

Most state education agencies are almost always under some pressure to improve certain aspects of education, such as finance, the curriculum, or the preparation and certification of teachers. Yet all aspects of education are interrelated and piecemeal changes, even though they may result in some improvements, are not likely to resolve some of the basic educational problems. Sooner or later, in almost every state the need for a systematic study of all major aspects of the state provisions for education seems essential. A comprehensive study of all provisions and programs may direct attention to imbalances and problems that might be overlooked in studying only certain aspects. (See discussion in Chapter 6.)

Under what conditions should a comprehensive study be undertaken? What should be the respective roles of the state education agency and of lay citizens and educators in planning and conducting any studies that may be needed and in developing proposals for improvements in education? How should such studies be financed, organized, and conducted? What problems are likely to be encountered and how can these best be avoided or resolved?

What Should Be the Role of the State Education Agency in Providing for Accountability?

Several state legislatures have recently taken steps designed to establish procedures and responsibilities for accountability in education. Accountability, however, has many facets, some of which have implications for legislators, parents, and students as well as for educators at all levels.

It seems apparent that every state education agency should be responsible for the development and utilization of appropriate procedures for continuous evaluation of: (1) its own role, functions, operations, and relationships and its plans for, and progress in, effecting improvements; (2) the organization, programs, and accomplishments of local school systems and area service units; (3) the plans for improving education in the state and the progress in implementing plans (as a basis for making needed revisions); (4) the progress and accomplishments of all kinds of students at various levels; and (5) various kinds of programs and procedures in terms of cost-effectiveness and other pertinent factors. (See Chapter 19.)

It should also be apparent that the state agency will not be in a strategic position to provide the leadership and services needed to assume this role unless: (1) the people and the legislature want it to do so and make appropriate provisions; and (2) the agency makes a serious and continuing effort to define its appropriate role and functions relating to evaluation and accountability in the light of emerging needs, evaluates realistically its current strengths and deficiencies, and develops and implements appropriate plans and procedures for providing the essential leadership and services in the area of evaluation and accountability.[19]

Why is accountability in and for education important? What are some of the pitfalls or dangers? How can they be avoided?

SELECTED REFERENCES

Annual Reports of the Advisory Council on State Departments of Education. Washington, D.C.: U.S. Office of Education, series beginning in 1967.

CAMPBELL, ROALD F., GERALD E. SROUFE, and DONALD H. LAYTON, eds., *Strengthening State Departments of Education.* Chicago, Ill.: Midwest Administration Center, University of Chicago, 1967.

CONANT, JAMES BRYANT, *Shaping Educational Policy.* New York: McGraw-Hill Book Company, 1964.

---

[19]Edgar L. Morphet, David L. Jesser, and Arthur P. Ludka, eds., *Emerging State Responsibilities for Education* (Denver, Colo.: Improving State Leadership in Education, 1970), p. 81.

Council of Chief State School Officers, *State and Local Responsibilities for Education,* 1968, and *State & Federal Relationships in Education,* 1971. Washington, D.C.: The Council.

Designing Education for the Future Series, especially: *Implications for Education of Prospective Changes in Society* (1967); *Planning and Effecting Needed Changes in Education* (1967); *Cooperative Planning for Education in 1980,* (1968); and *Emerging Designs for Education* (1968), Edgar L. Morphet, David L. Jesser, and Charles O. Ryan, eds. Denver, Colo.: Designing Education for the Future. Republished by Citation Press, Scholastic Magazines, Inc., New York, N.Y.

FULLER, EDGAR and JIM B. PEARSON, eds., *Education in the States: Nationwide Development Since 1900.* Washington, D.C.: National Education Association of the United States, 1969.

HARRIS, SAM P., *State Departments of Education, State Boards of Education, and Chief State School Officers.* Washington, D.C.: U.S. Government Printing Office, 1973.

Improving State Leadership in Education Series: *Emerging State Responsibilities for Education,* (1970); *Planning and Providing for Excellence in Education,* (1971), (Republished by Citation Press, Scholastic Magazines, Inc., New York, N.Y.); and *Revitalizing Education in the Big Cities,* (1972); Edgar L. Morphet, David L. Jesser, and Arthur P. Ludka, eds., Denver, Colo.: Improving State Leadership in Education.

THURSTON, LEE M. and WILLIAM H. ROE, *State School Administration.* New York, N.Y.: Harper & Row, Publishers, 1957.

USDAN, MICHAEL D., DAVID W. MINAR, and EMMANUEL HURWITZ, JR., *Education and State Politics.* New York: Teachers College Press, Columbia University, 1969.

WRIGHT, LYLE O. and BERNARR S. FURSE, *Developing Comprehensive Planning Capability in State Departments of Education.* Salt Lake City, Utah: Utah State Board of Education, 1969.

10

School Districts and Area Service Agencies

Instead of directly administering and operating all schools and educational programs, every state except Hawaii[1] has established local school districts and delegated to them (within limits prescribed by the state constitution and legislature) the responsibility for organizing and operating schools and other related provisions for education. Traditionally these districts have also been responsible for providing most of the funds they utilized not only to operate the schools and programs but also to finance the necessary services and facilities. But some of these traditions have begun to change in a number of states and can be expected to change even more significantly in the near future. Some commonly used terms relating to state provisions for local organization and operation of schools that

[1] Although in Hawaii the state operates and finances all schools and programs, district superintendencies have been established with headquarters on the four larger islands: Oahu, Hawaii, Kauai, and Maui.

sometimes have been misunderstood or misinterpreted by both lay citizens and educators are discussed briefly in the paragraphs that follow.

A *local school district* (or local school administrative unit) is a quasicorporation[2] authorized or established by a state for the local organization and administration of schools. It is comprised of an area within which a single board (or officer) has the responsibility for, and commonly has considerable autonomy in, the organization and administration of all public schools and related educational programs. It has certain powers, usually including limited power to specify tax levies for school purposes, that have been delegated by the state.

A *local school* (or educational center) is any one of several places or locations in a district at which educational programs are authorized by the governing board to be conducted for children, youth, and/or adults. The term is also used to refer to the group of students and staff members participating in the educational processes at any such location, or to the facilities used for that purpose. Thus, there may be a school for early childhood, elementary, intermediate, high school, or adult education, or for any authorized combination of these groups or of learning activities.

A *local school attendance area* is usually that portion of a school district whose population is served in part at least by a single school. During recent years, however, some students in many of the larger districts have been transported from beyond the customary attendance area boundaries in order to facilitate integration or to enable them to benefit from programs designed to meet their special needs.

An *intermediate unit* or a regional service agency is a unit or agency established by a state to provide some educational services for the state education agency and for the districts within the region or area it is expected to serve.

A *decentralized district* or school system is one in which several subunits (or subdistricts) have been established within a district—usually a large city— and authorized to assume designated responsibilities for education (but not for tax levies or financial support) in their respective areas.

LOCAL SCHOOL DISTRICTS

The early settlers and leaders in this nation could have made an assumption similar to the one made by those who went to Australia: each state should be responsible for organizing and operating all schools and

[2] As defined by Newton Edwards, "A Quasi-corporation . . . is purely a political or civil division of the state; it is created as an intrumentality of the state in order to facilitate the administration of government. . . . A municipal corporation proper is a city or town incorporated primarily for purposes of local government." *The Courts and the Public Schools* (Chicago: University of Chicago Press, 1955), p. 63.

programs of education. However, the people who settled in this country made a different assumption: each state should be responsible for the education of its citizens, but school districts should be organized as needed, and the responsibility for providing, organizing, administering, and operating schools and programs of education in accordance with state policies and requirements should be delegated to them. Each of these assumptions had many implications for the development of education. Each also has resulted in some problems. For example, in the United States many of the originally organized school districts proved to be too small to provide an effective program of education; the people in some districts did not take their responsibilities seriously; and in many areas the local resources were so inadequate that only limited education could be provided. In Australia, although inequities in financial support have been minimized, some leaders have concluded that the state agencies for education have tended to become somewhat bureaucratic and inflexible and, as a result, often have difficulty in adapting to modern needs.[3]

In this country, some of the units created by states for local governmental purposes (for example, cities, towns, townships, or counties) were also assigned considerable responsibility for organizing and operating schools. In most states, however, special districts (frequently with the same boundaries) were established for the local governance of education. These districts usually were not subject to control by other local governmental agencies. However, in some states a local government agency was either granted some authority over the school district or was even organized to encompass education within its framework of responsibility (as in some cities with special charters).

The provisions for the organization and operation of local school districts within each state developed out of the political philosophy and the geographic circumstances of the growing nation. Although early Massachusetts legislation placed local educational responsibility and control in the town (township), the people were not long satisfied. As the colonists spread out and new communities developed, the residents wanted their own institutions, such as churches and schools, and the townships were divided into school districts. This seemed appropriate at a time when population was sparse, when communication and transportation between communities were difficult, and when isolation was the condition of life. As the frontier moved westward, this tendency continued. The concept of "home rule" in education is historical.[4] As one result, in most states the legislatures authorized small settlements and rural areas to be organized as

[3]S. D'Urso, ed., *Counterpoints: Critical Writings on Australian Education* (Sydney: John Wiley & Sons Australasia Pty. Ltd., 1971).
[4]American Association of School Administrators, *The American School Superintendency,* Thirtieth Yearbook (Washington, D.C.: The Association, 1952), p. 103.

local school districts. Many districts in some states still have the same limited boundaries established under frontier conditions.

For many years the small district, with its school in close physical proximity to the students and controlled by residents of the community, was looked upon as the epitome of educational organization. Every community came to look upon itself as independently competent to choose its teachers, determine the conditions and program of learning, and govern and finance its school. It was this extremity of provincialisam and isolationism that caused Horace Mann to refer to the Massachusetts law establishing small independent local school districts as "the most unfortunate law on the subject of education ever enacted by the State of Massachusetts."

Some Factors Affecting District Organization

Since frontier days, the people in each state have been attempting more or less seriously to adapt their schools and school district organization to new and changing circumstances. However, as pointed out in Chapter 1, a local school system in one sense is a domesticated organization which has been slow to change. Some factors that continue to require serious consideration are discussed briefly in the following paragraphs.

IMPROVEMENTS IN TRANSPORTATION AND COMMUNICATION. The time and distance limitations on communication and the movements of man have been greatly extended. Each person now has contact with persons, places, and organizations that are much farther removed from his place of residence, and they in turn have impact on him. As one result, school districts in many areas have been expanded or reorganized to meet the needs of rapidly growing communities and other related developments in society.

EXPANDING EDUCATIONAL PROGRAMS. The citizens have made continually increasing demands on the public schools. Most schools that offered only the rudiments of instruction to a limited number of children or youth have been gradually replaced by institutions that offer a broad scope of learning experiences to nearly every segment of society. Efforts to provide adequate educational opportunities, to avoid duplication of offerings, to facilitate articulation involving different grade levels and programs, and to meet many other needs have stimulated the development of larger districts.

CHANGING ECONOMIC CIRCUMSTANCES. As long as schools remained small and the basis of economic wealth was largely the land from which man produced his sustenance, the matter of financing education was considered to be a local problem. However, the economy and sources of income have changed greatly. Other types of wealth have come into existence or increased in importance and consequently the economic resources are much more unevenly distributed than during pioneer days. As a result of the rapidly growing industrialization and urbanization, differences in the ability of local districts to support schools have increased significantly in many areas.

CHANGING PATTERNS OF EDUCATIONAL LEADERSHIP. In face of the increasing complexities encountered in organizing and administering programs of education, the lay school boards in smaller districts, with increasing frequency, have either operated with evident inefficiency or have had to turn to state or other educational leaders for advice and direction. Well-prepared and competent administrative leaders and supporting staff have been available generally only to the larger districts. Increasingly, the fact has been recognized that only districts of sufficient size and ability to attract, support, and retain competent lay and educational leadership are able to assume bona fide local responsibility in and for their school systems.

Thus, many school districts (and schools) that were organized to meet a pioneer situation have become inadequate in terms of needs arising from changes in transportation and communication, expanding educational programs, the changing economic situation, the necessity for competent educational leadership, and other factors.

Some Significant Trends

As early as 1837, Horace Mann advocated the abolition of the newly created common school districts and reestablishment of the township system in Massachusetts. Since then most states have been concerned from time to time with matters relating to school district reorganization including proposals for permissive legislation, compulsory reorganization, semicompulsory plans, or legislation embodying some financial incentives for reorganization. Many states have relied chiefly on educational leadership at state and county levels to facilitate reorganization. Several have created state commissions on district reorganization to provide criteria and guidelines.

NUMBER OF DISTRICTS. As a result of these and other related developments, there has been a significant decrease in the total number of school districts during the last 40 years. In 1932 (the first year reasonably complete information was assembled) there were 127,244 local school districts in the

United States; in 1942 there were 115,384 districts; in 1952, 70,933; in 1962, 26,800 (2,420 of which did not operate any schools); and in 1973 approximately 17,000. Nearly 70 percent of all districts in the nation, however, still have fewer than 1,800 students (many have fewer than 50 students), and some do not operate any schools. On the other hand, more than 80 percent of all students in the nation are in districts that have an enrollment of more than 1,800. The evidence available indicates that from 3,000 to 5,000 properly organized districts could more adequately meet the needs of education in modern American society and provide opportunity for more meaningful local responsibility for the operation of schools than would be possible under the present district structure.

KINDS OF DISTRICTS. There are many kinds of types of school districts. For example, in Florida, Maryland (except the city of Baltimore), Nevada, and West Virginia, all counties are organized as school districts. In most Southern states and Utah, all county areas are organized as school districts, but the major cities usually constitute school districts that are not included in the county units in which they may be geographically located.

Arizona, California, Illinois, Wisconsin, and a few other states have distinctly different prevailing patterns. A wide variety of districts is found within each state. Only the unified districts have a single board of education responsible for all education, kindergarten through high school. In other areas of each of these states, and in many rural areas in some other states, there are separate districts for elementary and for secondary school students with separate governing boards and administrative officers for each level. However, the separately organized elementary and high-school districts are gradually being replaced by unified districts.

The basic types of school districts can be classified, for the most part, into six main categories: (1) the common school district, most frequently found in the rural areas of several states, is generally relatively small both in area and in enrollment, frequently has a single school, and usually provides education only on the elementary level; (2) county-unit districts with boundaries coterminous—or nearly so—with county lines; (3) city school districts that are usually coterminous—or nearly so—with city boundaries; (4) county districts in which the cities constitute separate districts; (5) special "independent" districts organized by legislative act in some states to provide education on an elementary or high-school level or both; (6) town or township districts found in several of the New England states as well as in some areas in Indiana. To this list should be added high-school districts, usually encompassing two or more elementary school districts, found in several states, and separately organized junior or community college districts that have been created in some states. Most county-unit, city and town or township districts, and many of the county districts in which the cities constitute separate school districts, are unified —that is, include grades K through 12.

ORGANIZATION AND RELATIONS. In most instances the local school district is a relatively autonomous unit operating by authorization of the state and not responsible to other governmental units except in specified instances. Each district has a governing board that is usually elected by the people. Except in small districts and in some county districts where the superintendent is elected, a superintendent is appointed by the governing board as its chief administrative officer and policy consultant. Under his professional leadership the local district has the opportunity, subject to minimum requirements established by the state (and in certain respects by the federal government), to develop its own program of education. This near autonomy of the local school district is uniquely American, and the preservation of what is commonly called "local control" is a rallying issue in many public debates about a variety of school problems.

Nevertheless, as already pointed out, school districts are instruments of the state for the accomplishment of the state's educational function. The state legislature, subject to state and federal constitutional limitations and court decisions, has complete authority over such districts and may instruct, advise, direct, create, or abolish them in accordance with its judgment regarding the welfare of education in the state. A statement by the State Supreme Court of Washington gives the commonly held legal point of view regarding the relationship of school districts to the state:

> Local subdivisions of the state can be created by the sovereign power of the state without solicitation, consent, or concurrent action by the people who inhabit them. This being so, it follows that legislative authority over school districts is unlimited except as that limitation is found in the state constitution.[5]

Characteristics of Effective School Districts and Schools

The chief function of a school district is to make it possible for the citizens of the area to provide for the organization, operation, and administration of an adequate, economical, and effective educational program for those who should be educated in and through the public schools. Any district that fails to carry out this function satisfactorily is an ineffective district. The ineffectiveness may be due to the attitude of the people, to

[5] 18 Washington (2d) 37, or 137 Pacific (2d) 1010, 1943.

the limited size of the area, to inadequate human or economic resources, to failure to recognize or meet emerging needs, or to any combination of these factors.

Since some of the major characteristics of a satisfactory program of education and of provisions for its organization, administration, and support are discussed elsewhere in this book, major attention will be centered here on other criteria, including size (number of students) that must be observed if a district is to be in a position to operate effectively. However, the number of students should not be the only determining factor, because an adequate number of students does not assure effectiveness; it only makes it possible when other conditions are favorable.

When an area is too small in terms of population, it cannot provide an adequate program at an economical cost. When it is too large in terms of distance or population, the citizens may have difficulty in communicating, agreeing on goals, and cooperating in developing policies and plans. Largely for this reason some people have advocated that districts be organized to encompass communities whose residents have been accustomed to cooperating in certain matters of common interest. However, "homogeneous" districts, especially in metropolitan areas, may tend to result in economic or even racial segregation. It seems evident that in school districts, as well as in other aspects of government, people with widely divergent backgrounds will need to find effective ways of cooperating in developing solutions for problems of mutual interest.

Authorities are agreed that every district should be in a position to provide an educational program that extends through at least the high-school grades. Separate districts for elementary and for high schools, even though they may be fairly large, are not considered desirable because education should be a continuous process, unhampered by unnecessary complications for voters, for children, or for the educational staff.

Research findings show that reasonable economy of scale cannot be attained in districts with a school population of fewer than about 10,000 students. Districts that are smaller in size are faced with higher unit costs for an adequate educational program as the number of students decreases. In districts with fewer than 1,800 the unit costs become so great that adequate opportunities can seldom be provided. Many people, therefore, believe the minimum acceptable size for a school district should be 10,000 students in all except the most sparsely settled areas where the minimum probably should be 5,000. These minimum sizes should not be confused with optimum sizes, which in many areas should probably be between 25,000 and 50,000 students.

The organization of districts that meet the criteria suggested above would make it possible to resolve the small-school problem in all except isolated and sparsely populated areas where such schools may have to be continued regardless of higher costs. However, the continued existence of small districts usually means that the small school in each district is likely to be perpetuated even when it should be consolidated.

Reorganization of School Districts

On the basis of experiences in the various states and other developments, the following criteria have been proposed for guidance in developing state plans and laws relating to district reorganization:

- Legislation relating to district reorganization should be kept as simple as possible and should make it easy for districts to effect defensible reorganization.
- All state laws, regulations, and financial provisions should be reviewed periodically to determine their effect on district reorganization. Those that encourage the continuance of inadequate districts or retard needed reorganization should be revised or repealed.
- All reorganization proposals should be based on careful studies and planning. Many reorganizations based on the desires of local groups have been found to be unsatisfactory because facts pertinent to the situation were overlooked or ignored.
- The people in each state should agree upon, and the legislature should prescribe, basic criteria or minimum standards to be used for guidance in planning reorganization of districts.
- In all states with a large number of small districts the law probably should provide for a state reorganization commission. This commission must be properly financed and staffed if it is to function effectively.
- The responsibilities of any reorganization commission and of all groups and persons officially involved in the reorganization program should be clearly defined.
- Provision should be made for the participation of lay and educational leaders who will work cooperatively for effective district reorganization. Only when the people involved in developing a plan for reorganization understand all the pertinent facts are they in a position to make wise decisions.
- A favorable vote by a majority of the electors in an area proposed for a reorganized district (or both in a major center of population and in the remainder of the area) should suffice to make the proposal effective.
- Needed funds for adequate educational programs, buildings, and transportation should be assured for any properly reorganized district.
- A three or four-year deadline within which reorganization is scheduled for completion on a voluntary basis should be established by the legislature which should also provide that, for any reorganizations not completed by that time, the state education agency or a district reorganization commission is to develop a reorganization plan for approval by the legislature.[6]

[6]Adapted from Edgar L. Morphet *et al.*, "State Laws Can Aid District Reorganization," *Phi Delta Kappan,* **32** (Mar. 1951,) 319–320.

Problems and Prospects

While considerable progress has been made in reorganizing school districts in many states, the pace in some states has been too slow to meet the needs. Few legislatures have adopted a harmonious set of laws that have removed all obstacles and afforded effective incentives for reorganization. A piecemeal approach, involving only minor changes in existing laws or failure to provide effective machinery, has commonly been used. The reluctance of legislatures to deal realistically with this problem can be understood (but not defended) in light of the pressures frequently exerted by local and sometimes statewide groups to maintain a traditional system that seems to many to have worked reasonably well in the past. However, the evidence clearly indicates that much more reorganization is needed in most states in the immediate future. Some of the problems and prospects are considered briefly below.

NONOPERATING DISTRICTS. As noted earlier, several states still have a number of districts that exist legally but do not operate any school. Some also have areas not included in any district. The reason these situations are permitted to exist is that citizens and their legislators have been lax in dealing with them, perhaps because they have failed to recognize the inequities and the unfair tax advantages that are usually provided.

SMALL DISTRICTS. Most of the existing districts that are too small to be effective are for elementary schools, but a rather substantial number of high school and unified districts (some of which are county districts in Southern states in which separate city districts have been organized) should be included. Yet every study that has been made shows that these districts are costly to operate and most provide inadequate programs. Hanson, for example, reported higher costs ranging from $19 to $96 per student in districts of 1,500 than in districts of "optimum" size in nine states from the East to the West Coast.[7] The average difference was $27 per student.

Morphet and Ross directed attention to what seems to be one of the most serious shortcomings of the smallest school districts in California (unified school districts with fewer than 1,500 students, elementary school districts with fewer than 900, and high school districts with fewer than 300).[8] They pointed out, on the basis of an analysis of the laws relating

[7]Nels W. Hanson, "Economy of Scale in Education: An Analysis of the Relationship Between District Size and Unit Costs in the Public Schools" (Unpublished Ph.D. dissertation, Stanford University, 1963).
[8]Edgar L. Morphet and John G. Ross, *Local Responsibility for Education in Small School Districts,* Legislative Problems No. 1 (Berkeley, Calif.: Bureau of Public Administration, University of California, 1961), pp. 23 and 33.

to the districts and county services, "that small school districts are not expected to assume full responsibility for the nature and quality of the educational program." They also made a study of the operations of small school districts and concluded that

> ... local responsibility and control in small school districts is not as complete or as vigorous as has often been assumed. ... These findings do *not* support any conclusion that the elimination of small districts would reduce local responsibility for education. On the contrary, the findings suggest that the *elimination of small districts may increase the potential for effective local responsibility and control of education.*

SEPARATE DISTRICTS FOR ELEMENTARY AND HIGH SCHOOL PURPOSES. This pattern began to develop in some states as high schools were established, partly because existing elementary school districts were too small to include the attendance area for a high school. A high school district that included two or more elementary districts was then established with a separate board, tax levies, and so on. In spite of the complexities and confusion, the lack of coordination, and other problems, the pattern, once established, was continued, expanded, and vigorously defended by some educators and lay citizens in a number of states. This plan of organization has persisted even in some cities and suburban areas, although the deficiencies have been pointed out by numerous authorities. Such districts are all too slowly being replaced by a more defensible plan of organization.

LARGE DISTRICTS. The evidence available indicates that costs per student tend to be lowest in districts having more than 10,000 students and fewer than 40,000 to 50,000. Beyond 50,000 costs tend to rise again and may increase as much as $10 or more per student in much larger districts; however, this could result from increased services or quality. When factors other than costs are considered (e.g., adaptability and adoption of defensible innovations) the evidence seems to indicate that special problems are encountered in large districts for a number of reasons. In very large as well as very small districts, conditions relating to school quality tend to become less favorable. In both kinds of districts, special arrangements seem to be necessary to achieve the best possible quality of education.[9]

On the basis of such evidence and for other reasons, some authorities have advocated that the large city districts should be divided into smaller autonomous districts. However, if that were done, some of the districts would be much more wealthy than others and serious inequalities would

[9] *Relations Between Community Size and School Quality,* Institute of Administrative Research (New York: Teachers College, Columbia University, **2**, No. 1 (Oct. 1961), 1–3.

result. This seems to mean that the large city base should be retained for overall planning and financial purposes, and that districts should be organized within the city for administrative and operating purposes. Further studies and adjustments are undoubtedly needed to provide a sound basis for resolving the problems inherent in such situations.

DISTRICTS IN SUBURBAN AREAS. Many suburban areas present especially troublesome problems. If districts are organized about "communities" some are likely to be quite wealthy, others (especially tract housing bedroom communities) will have limited tax bases and other kinds of problems. The optimum plan for school district organization in such areas will probably have to ignore subdivision boundaries; yet, this will present special problems of coordination and cooperation. The development of a defensible plan for district organization in urban and suburban areas will require high-quality statesmanship on the part of educators as well as lay citizens.

DISTRICTS IN RURAL AREAS. The problems of district organization in rural areas are quite different from those in urban and suburban communities. In most rural communities the people have been accustomed to the "idea" that they are responsible for operating their own schools. When districts are reorganized, many people are concerned that local responsibility will be lost, even though they may never have assumed much real responsibility. Ways need to be found to continue this concept of responsibility in a different context. Although many reorganized districts will necessarily be fairly large in area, most will not have a large population.

JUNIOR OR COMMUNITY COLLEGE DISTRICTS. Special districts for junior or community college purposes have been organized in a number of states; in some, they are operated by the larger local school districts as a part of the public school system; in others, these institutions are operated by the board for higher education; in a few states no definite plans for junior or community colleges have been implemented thus far. The need for each state to develop a plan in the near future to provide for the orderly development of junior or community colleges should be apparent.

FURTHER REORGANIZATION. Many of the reorganizations that have occurred in rural areas, and some in suburban areas, have been inadequate from a long-range point of view. Further reorganization involving new combinations of reorganized districts will be needed in many states. However, the fact that reorganization is not a panacea should be clearly recognized. But reorganization does make it possible to solve problems that could not otherwise be solved. For example, neither equality of educational opportunities for students nor equity for taxpayers in providing funds for support of schools is feasible in many states under present conditions.

When any district in a state has even 25 times the ability of another district in the same state to support schools (and the ratio is much higher in a number of states) it will be difficult or perhaps impossible to implement the intent of some of the recent court decisions discussed in Chapter 2 without district reorganization or full state and federal funding of education.

FISCALLY INDEPENDENT SCHOOL DISTRICTS. Although more than 90 percent of the school districts in the United States are fiscally independent from a legal point of view, none is autonomous in any fundamental sense. In four states—Hawaii, Maryland, North Carolina, and Virginia—and in some districts in a number of other states, the fiscal needs and resources to be provided are determined primarily by an agency other than the school board. As a matter of fact, in all states some limits of one kind or another have been placed on what school boards may do in terms of finance, either on the basis of constitutional or legislative provisions, or by a requirement for approval by vote of the citizens under certain conditions. Moreover, no district is entirely politically independent or autonomous. School district officials must, if they are realistic, cooperate with other officials and agencies of government in developing plans and proposals. To fail to do so would mean sooner or later isolating themselves from some of the support they need and perhaps even failing to win the approval of the voters in an election involving needed school funds.

LOCAL RESPONSIBILITY. Although the people in most school districts insist that they believe in local "control" of education, in far too many instances they have failed to exercise much responsibility. Often only a minority has participated in elections for board members and many boards have failed to meet some of their responsibilities for developing an effective program of education in the district. During recent years control of some aspects of education has gradually moved toward the state, and in some respects, toward the federal government. Some assumption of state control in certain respects (especially provisions for financial support) is probably inevitable and may be desirable from a long-range point of view, but the process may be in danger of being carried too far in some states. Only when districts are properly organized and vigorously supported by citizens who demonstrate that local responsibility can be met can a wholesome local-state-federal partnership be assured. As districts are reorganized, the leaders, with the cooperation of the citizens, should identify and clearly define the responsibilities that can and should be assumed at the district and at the individual school levels, as well as those that should be assumed by the state, and develop appropriate procedures designed to ensure that these responsibilities are met. If this is done properly and wisely—even with full state and federal funding—the cherished tradition of local responsibility for education can become a reality (rather than a gradually eroding myth) from which both the students and the adult citizens of the nation will benefit.

SCHOOLS AND OTHER EDUCATIONAL CENTERS

Some people apparently believe that within the next few years the school district structure will be abolished in most states and that these states will then assume full responsibility for the organization and operation of all schools. They assume that strong local resistance will make it impossible for realistic district reorganization to be effected in many areas, and that, as states provide increased funding from state tax sources, state control and operation will be necessary to ensure economy and efficiency.

Although the authors of this book are convinced that increased funding from state and federal nonproperty tax sources is desirable in most states for reasons discussed in Chapters 2 and 18, they do not accept state control and operation of all schools as the best and most defensible solution for many of the problems confronting education in this country. They believe the concept of local responsibility for education has considerable merit and should not be abandoned without seriously exploring all feasible alternatives for making it more meaningful and effective.

Any large state that undertakes to operate all schools and other educational centers would face many difficult problems that would challenge the skill and ingenuity of the most capable leaders. Among these would be locating and assigning competent and appropriate personnel not only for the state education agency itself but also for every school and classroom in the many different kinds of communities in the state. Undoubtedly, as in Hawaii, the state would need to be divided into regions or areas to each of which some administrative and perhaps other responsibilities would have to be assigned. But a major concern would be the size and complexity of the state agency itself, especially in the more populous states, and its almost inevitable tendency to become a relatively inflexible bureaucracy that would be slow to adapt to changing needs. A major issue would be how, or whether, the agency could avoid this tendency.

Most states have already established minimum enrollment standards for schools except those that are isolated because of distance or other factors that make transportation impractical. It is generally recognized that an elementary school, if feasible, should have sufficient students to justify at least two teachers per grade or age group, and that a junior or senior high school should have at least 100 students in each grade or age group. However, elementary and high schools enrolling at least twice this minimum are usually in a position to provide a more adequate program at a somewhat lower cost per student. Similar standards or criteria would need to be established for any state-operated system of schools, as well as special requirements for other learning centers such as have been developed recently in an attempt to meet the needs of some groups, including potential dropouts. Most authorities seem to agree that schools that become too large and impersonal tend to create some special problems that urgently need attention. (See Chapter 13 for further discussion of these and other related issues.)

INTERMEDIATE UNITS AND REGIONAL SERVICE AGENCIES

The intermediate unit of school administration began to develop primarily in the Midwest when most school districts were small and communication was slow and difficult. The need for some agency to perform certain services both for the small, relatively isolated districts and for the state soon became apparent. Since counties had been established by most states as local units of government (following somewhat the pattern in England) it seemed logical for them to be designated as the intermediate units for schools in many states. However, the township was actually the first intermediate unit established in some of the Midwestern states, notably Michigan and Indiana. The need at that time seemed to be for an agency to oversee small districts, to enforce certain state regulations, to gather information for the state, to direct the distribution of state funds within the area, and to provide certain services for the districts.

The primary concern and responsibility of these intermediate units was for rural schools, although at first they were also legally responsible for some general oversight of town and small-city schools. As cities began to increase in population in many states, they tended to develop separate organizations for government and for schools, to bypass or ignore the intermediate units, and to insist on an independent status. Thus the intermediate unit in most states became predominately an organization for limited control of and service to rural schools and also for service to the state.[10] In some instances, the intermediate organization was resisted as an unwanted arm of the state; in others, it was considered at times as a protector of the local district against unwanted state-level control. But in all instances, the intermediate unit, when established, was created by state action and was a political subdivision of the state, organized in part to assist in carrying out the state's educational function.[11]

[10]William P. McLure, *The Intermediate Administrative School District in the United States* (Urbana: University of Illinois Press, 1956), p. 3.

[11]Shirley Cooper and Charles O. Fitzwater, *County School Administration* (New York: Harper & Row, 1954), Chaps. 4 and 5.

Intermediate Unit Organization and Role

According to a study by Hooker and Mueller,[12] 30 states had established by 1969 some type of intermediate or regional units for education. Each of the six New England states utilized what they called "supervisory unions;" 19 other states had established the county as the intermediate unit for some or all areas; and five had created regional service agencies that were not coterminous with county boundaries. However, five of the states in the latter two groups were in a transitional stage from county to regional units and consequently had some units of both types.

Those who have studied the evolving intermediate unit structure seem to agree that under modern conditions the county is not a logical or defensible type of intermediate unit in most situations. Many counties have a relatively small population, and the boundaries established during an earlier period are frequently not appropriate in the light of recent population developments and trends. Moreover, in many states the county superintendent is still elected by popular vote and may not be the best qualified person to direct the development of an adequate intermediate unit program. Many people are concerned that, for various reasons, the establishment of county intermediate units may tend to perpetuate small and inadequate school districts and thus delay urgently needed reorganization.

In several states the role of the intermediate unit has not been clearly defined and, perhaps for this and other reasons, the limited financial support available has made it impossible for most of them to provide much more than rather routine services. On the other hand, the regional Boards of Cooperative Educational Services (BOCES), established in New York in 1948, have attracted generally favorable attention throughout the nation because of the kind and quality of services many of them provide. During recent years several other states have begun to develop somewhat similar regional service agencies rather than the more traditional type of intermediate unit.

In the report of a study of intermediate units and regional service agencies, Chambers[13] identified the following control and organizational patterns that are utilized singly or in some combination by states that have established such units:

- They are branch offices of the state department of education;
- They are independent locally controlled service agencies;

[12]Clifford P. Hooker and Van D. Mueller, *The Relationship of School District Reorganization to State Aid Distribution Systems: Part 1, Patterns of School District Organization* (Minneapolis: University Minnesota, 1970), pp. 59–60.
[13]Ernest W. Chambers, *Planning for Regional Education Services in a State* (Denver, Colo.: Improving State Leadership in Education, 1971).

- All public local education agencies in the state are included in the system of regional service agencies; or
- Participation in regional service agencies is voluntary and some areas and districts are not included.

Emerging Concepts and Policies

Hooker and Mueller, after observing that intermediate units are changing from primarily regulatory to service functions, commented:

> Coupled with this change is a restructuring of the boundaries of the intermediate units to reflect the socio-economic areas that exist irrespective of county lines. . . . The service function has reshaped the intermediate unit. The states that have not shifted to this idea have seen the intermediate unit [begin to] drop out of a significant place in the educational structure in their state.[14]

Unfortunately, needed changes will probably come slowly in many states. For example, the county will tend to persist as an intermediate unit in a number of states partly because of tradition but, perhaps equally important, because powerful vested interests may seek to prevent or delay the development or implementation of realistic alternatives. The changing socioeconomic situation, the elimination of small districts through reorganization, and the emergence of new concepts and points of view relating to what is required to ensure adequate educational opportunities, however, are resulting in new perspectives concerning provisions for the organization and operation of educational institutions and programs.

Even when all districts in a state have been reorganized, there will probably be a need for regional educational agencies that can provide a number of special services for component districts that could not be provided economically or effectively by the state education agency. These services would vary somewhat from state to state and among the regions in a state, but probably would include a media and communications center, a computer and data processing center, and a center to assist with needs assessment, and perhaps some responsibilities for planning and appraisal of progress, for special projects, and for assistance with other programs and services. These agencies should probably be financed primarily by funds from state and perhaps federal sources and governed by a competent board that would be responsible for developing appropriate policies. As Haskew[15] has perceptively observed, a basic question is: "How can states use

---

[14]Hooker and Mueller, *Patterns of School District Organization,* p. 58.

[15]Lawrence D. Haskew, "Leadership Through State Systems of Service Centers: Some Strategic Considerations," Supplementary Statement in *Planning for Regional Education Services in a State,* p. 25.

to advantage extra-district entities to achieve enhanced productivity for the schools?"

Provisions for district organization and regional educational services in the metropolitan areas in every state need much more careful consideration than they have received thus far. Neither reorganization of existing districts nor additional funding will suffice to resolve some of the complex educational problems in these areas.

On the basis of a study of public education in the San Francisco Metropolitan Bay Area, Reller proposed that the number of school districts be reduced from 164 to 30 or 40, each of which would be prepared to meet certain basic needs more effectively.[16] He concluded that, even after reorganization, these districts would not be in a position to provide effectively for all aspects of the educational program. He, therefore, recommended the creation of a regional or metropolitan district for education that in certain respects would serve as a regional service agency for the districts in the area. This proposed metropolitan district would have its own board and administrative staff and would be responsible for financial matters, for providing educational assistance for the component districts, for special educational services for certain types of students such as the severely handicapped, perhaps for community college programs, and for the development of programs for older youth and adults.

Hooker and Mueller,[17] after studying the hodgepodge of school districts in the Kansas City and St. Louis metropolitan areas, directed attention to serious and indefensible inequities in educational opportunities and in the progress of students, in funds available for support of schools, and in other respects that resulted from existing district boundaries and financing policies. On the basis of these and other related findings, they recommended that: (1) each metropolitan area be established as a district or agency for purposes of obtaining and apportioning to the component operating districts on an equitable basis all funds for support of schools, for coordination of planning, and for providing special services needed by the districts; (2) the component districts be reorganized with more realistic and defensible boundaries; and (3) each component district be primarily responsible for developing and implementing programs and policies designed to meet the needs of its students.

It should be apparent that no state should attempt to deal with existing problems relating to education and financial support in rural, small-city, and metropolitan areas merely by enacting legislation that mandates reorganization of districts or establishes regional educational

[16]Theodore L. Reller, *Problems of Public Education in the San Francisco Bay Area* (Berkeley Calif.: Institute of Government Studies, University of California, 1963).

[17]Clifford P. Hooker and Van D. Mueller, *Equal Treatment to Equals: A New Structure for Schools in the Kansas City and St. Louis Metropolitan Areas* (Report to the Missouri School District Reorganization Commission, June 1969).

service agencies on the basis of "ideas" and compromises that have enough support to win acceptance at the time. Instead, all such legislation should be based on carefully planned and systematic studies of present and emerging problems and needs and the advantages and disadvantages of feasible alternatives for dealing with them. These studies should result in the identification of, and substantial agreement on, appropriate policies and procedures needed to effect proposed changes.

In developing plans and legislation for regional educational service agencies, therefore, each state should make the studies and utilize procedures that would help to resolve satisfactorily a number of major issues including the following: Are such agencies needed for all parts of the state or only in certain areas? What criteria should be utilized in establishing the service area for each such agency? What should be the major roles and functions of these agencies? How should these agencies be organized, governed, administered, and staffed? What should be their relations to the state education agency and to the districts they are expected to serve? How should these agencies be financed on a basis that will enable them to function effectively?

DECENTRALIZATION OF LARGE DISTRICTS

Although most school districts throughout the nation are too small to provide adequate educational opportunities and programs at a reasonable cost, it should be evident that some have become so large and bureaucratic that they have not functioned effectively. The fact that serious problems have arisen in many large districts, however, should not be interpreted to mean that these problems resulted entirely from size (in area or population). Perhaps a more defensible conclusion would be that the most serious problems developed primarily because these districts continued with traditional patterns of organization and operation that were not modified or adjusted to meet changing conditions and needs—that is, they failed to accept or utilize a concept that is essential for any organization that continues to remain functional in modern society.

Delegation of responsibility is not a new idea in education. It has been customary for boards and administrators to delegate some responsibilities (often vaguely defined) to principals and teachers. But in a large organization (especially in a collegial type of organization) any such delegation must be systematically and cooperatively planned to meet changing needs, to ensure accountability, and to minimize bureaucratic tendencies, if major problems are to be avoided. This is an essential part of the process of planning for meaningful decentralization in all large school systems.

In 1966, the New York State Legislature mandated the development of a plan for decentralization in the ponderous New York City school system. On the basis of this plan, 31 "community" school or subdistricts were created, each of which has a board and an administrator responsible for employing staff, developing the curriculum, and preparing and administering a budget. Consultants and other resource personnel are provided by the central staff and the state department of education. In some of these districts, decentralization seems to have worked reasonably well; in others there have been major problems. At least these developments constitute one interesting attempt to provide for decentralization.

Other approaches to decentralization, frequently involving the appointment of administrators for areas within a large district, have been developed in Atlanta; Chicago; Dade County, Florida; Detroit; Los Angeles; Montgomery County, Maryland; St. Louis, and several other large districts, but the best solutions to these problems are obviously still being sought.

The purpose of decentralization is not to divide large districts into smaller autonomous districts with authority to levy their own taxes for support of schools (and thus increase differences in local ability to support schools) but rather to encourage and facilitate the development of programs and procedures designed to meet the needs of students. For that and other related reasons, the policies and provisions for decentralization should be carefully planned with the cooperation of lay citizens as well as educators. Such questions as the following should be adequately considered in the process of reaching agreement on proposals: Would decentralization be likely to result in better and more appropriate educational opportunities for students? What should be the optimum size for each subdistrict and how should the boundaries of each be established? Should each such district have a policy or advisory board, an administrator, and a staff? If so, how should the board be selected and what responsibilities should it have? What should be the responsibilities of the central board and staff of the original or parent district? How can major conflicts or differences best be avoided or resolved? If substantial agreement on the "answers" to such questions can be reached, the propects that decentralization will result in improved educational programs and opportunities should be enhanced.

SOME IMPORTANT PROBLEMS AND ISSUES

The report of the first national conference on reorganization of local school units (sponsored by the U.S. Commissioner of Education in 1935) observed that many of the problems facing the schools "... are inherent in our systems of administering and financing schools through a multiplicity of small school districts.... The way to permanent improvement is believed to be through large-scale, generally state-wide, reorganization of school units."[18] The first nationally financed study of local school units (districts), begun the following year, concluded: "In no state is the present organization adequate in every respect ... a well rounded educational program will be practically impossible of attainment either in localities or in the state as a whole."[19] In what respects would these observations need to be modified if a similar study had been made during the past year or two?

If there were no small school districts, unnecessary small schools, or ineffective or outmoded intermediate units in any state, the quality of education might be considerably improved over that found in many areas at present. What steps should be taken to improve the unsatisfactory aspects of the present situation? Why have they not already been taken?

What, If Any, Responsibilities Now Delegated to Districts Should be Assumed by the States?

Since districts have only the powers and responsibilities delegated to them by the state in which they are located, the legislature would have the right to abolish them or to withdraw some or all of these powers. For example, the legislature could prescribe salaries for school personnel; establish uniform standards for testing, grading, and promotion of pupils; reorganize all school districts, and take other similar steps. Many people favor more state control on the assumption that it would result in greater efficiency and improved quality of education throughout the state.

Many local school boards (perhaps partly because of lack of interest on the part of citizens in the area or of leadership by the administrative staff) have been lax about meeting some of the responsibilities delegated to them. Some have shown little interest in developing high-quality programs of education for their area.

A number of authorities believe that the solution to many of the present problems can best be effected by organizing districts of adequate size and delegating even greater responsibilities to them. They contend

---

[18] Katherine M. Cook, ed., *Reorganization of School Units* (Washington, D.C.: U.S. Office of Education Bulletin, 1935, No. 15, United States Government Printing Office, 1936), p. 1.

[19] Henry F. Alves and Edgar L. Morphet, *Principles and Procedures in the Organization of Satisfactory Local School Units* (Washington, D.C.: U.S. Office of Education Bulletin, 1938, No. 11, United States Government Printing Office, 1939), p. 1.

that withdrawing more responsibilities from properly organized districts would only weaken them further and discourage local leadership. This in turn would encourage the state to assume even more responsibilities and further weaken local districts.

There is almost certain to be at least some further realignment of state and local responsibilities during coming years. It is important that the implications of such shifts in power be carefully thought through in each state so wise decisions may be made. What criteria should be used in determining responsibilities that should be assumed by the states and those that should be assigned to the districts? What kinds of responsibility shifts to the states would be advantageous from a long-range point of view? What kind would be disadvantageous?

How Can School District Reorganization Best Be Effected?

The people of each state are responsible for determining the basic policies to be followed in providing for the organization of school districts and schools. It seems evident that the district structure in a state is not likely to be materially altered unless most citizens believe a change would be beneficial. Voluntary reorganization in any area is likely to occur only when a majority of the citizens are convinced that the proposed plan would be an improvement. Therefore, popular understanding of the major educational needs and how they can be met most satisfactorily is of considerable importance.

Many contend that reorganization must be permitted to proceed voluntarily. However, experience shows that in many situations the people in districts with considerable wealth hesitate or refuse to join with districts having limited wealth. Moreover, residents of one or more districts have often prevented reorganization in situations where state laws require a favorable vote in each district. Some people believe that a time should be set by which all districts should reorganize voluntarily, and after that, needed reorganization should be effected by the legislature on the basis of a plan prepared by the state education agency or a state commission.

What is the best policy for bringing about needed reorganization of districts? How can unwise reorganization be avoided?

What Can Be Done to Encourage Local Interest and Initiative in Large Districts?

Research has reasonably well established the minimum size for an effective school district, but there has been inadequate attention to the maximum size or to some of the problems of the largest districts that are particularly difficult to resolve, such as (1) What can be done to prevent the staff from becoming enmeshed in a web of impersonal relationships, red tape requirements, and prescribed procedures that tend to discourage initiative and responsibility and to place a premium on conformity? (2) What can be done to help citizens keep in close touch with their schools, to demonstrate to them that the educational program is designed to meet the needs of the area in which they live, and to eliminate the feeling that they and their children are insignificant factors in a vast educational machine?

Various proposals have been made for solving these problems. Some have suggested that the largest districts and especially the large cities should be divided into smaller districts. However, such a step might create other problems. Others have proposed that the city or metropolitan district should be retained as a basic planning, taxing, budgeting, and bonding unit, but special subdistricts should be organized for the operation and administration of schools. Thus, the original district would continue to have a policy board and an administrator with a staff that would include competent consultants. Each subdistrict would also have a board elected by the residents of the area, a superintendent, and a staff for its schools. The large district would thus become primarily an agency that would provide basic support, services, and coordination, and the subdistricts would become basic units for the operation of the educational program in their respective areas.[20] What should be done to solve the unique problems confronting some of the largest and most populous school districts?

How Much Local School Autonomy Should Be Preserved When Districts Are Reorganized?

Some small districts have more board members than teachers. In such districts almost every citizen knows every board member personally. When these districts are reorganized, the board usually has from five to seven members elected from the entire area in which from two to a dozen or more small districts may have previously existed. Thus, the number of school board members representing the area is usually considerably reduced. People who live in the outlying rural areas may not know a single member of the new board. They tend to feel they no longer have much of a voice in school affairs. Not much has been done to help to solve this problem in many reorganized districts.

[20]See, for example, McLure *The Intermediate Administrative School District,* p. 153.

Several districts have experimented with the idea of an informal advisory board or committee for each school. Members of each such committee may be elected informally, usually for three-year overlapping terms, at an annual meeting of the patrons of the school. Of course, such advisory boards or committees cannot be given legal responsibilities that conflict with those of the central board. However, it seems logical that the advisory board should be encouraged to work with the principal and his staff in studying problems and needs, in developing policies for the school, and in presenting to the central staff and board proposals that have implications for improvements in the program of the school. The concept of such advisory boards seems to have considerable merit, but has not gained wide acceptance because the idea is relatively new to most people, some central boards are afraid they might run into conflicts or competition that would weaken their authority, and many principals are concerned as to how it would work. Some have frankly stated they are afraid they would not have a "free hand" to run their schools if they had an advisory board.

Is the concept of advisory boards or committees for individual schools worthy of careful consideration? Would this be appropriate for city districts? If so, how should such committees be selected and what should be their responsibilities? What problems must be faced in developing and implementing such a plan?

Should All Local School Districts Be Eliminated?

During the past few years several writers and speakers have contended that all local school districts should be abolished and that the states should operate the schools. They are disturbed by the inequities existing at present and by the complexities and problems found in what they consider to be a cumbersome and out-dated system. Most people in this country would probably be opposed to any proposal for the state to operate all schools. Although they recognize some of the weaknesses in district operation, they contend that the advantages greatly outweigh the disadvantages. They believe that the state-local partnership plan that is still evolving is best adapted to meet emerging needs. They point out that the farther decision making is removed from local schools, the greater the danger of developing a cumbersome and slow-moving bureaucracy that ignores local needs and discourages innovations. What would be the advantages and disadvantages of a state-operated system of schools in any or all states? Does social sytems theory support or justify the establishment of local school districts?

Under What Conditions Are Intermediate Units or Regional Service Agencies Needed?

In a number of states the intermediate unit has been changed to a regional service agency that has developed on a professional basis. These agencies are attempting to meet the needs of rapidly growing districts in metropolitan areas as well as districts in many rural areas. Some of the larger districts, perhaps because they believe they can provide all the services needed by the schools, have tended to ignore established intermediate or regional units. Some of the smaller districts have sought more "independence," whether or not they are prepared for it. It should be apparent that the role of the regional service agency, the manner in which it should be organized, and the services it should render need careful study.

How should regional service agencies be organized, administered, and financed? What services should they provide for what kinds of districts? For the state?

SELECTED REFERENCES

Advisory Commission on Intergovernmental Relations, *Alternative Approaches to Governmental Reorganization in Metropolitan Areas.* Washington, D.C.: Government Printing Office, 1962.

American Association of School Administrators, *School District Organization.* Commission on School District Reorganization. Washington, D.C.: The Association, 1958.

FITZWATER, C. O., *State School System Development: Patterns and Trends.* Denver, Colo.: Education Commission of the States, 1968.

HOOKER, CLIFFORD P. and VAN D. MUELLER, *Equal Treatment to Equals: A New Structure for Schools in the Kansas City and St. Louis Metropolitan Areas.* (Report to the Missouri School District Reorganization Commission, June 1969).

———, *The Relationship of School District Reorganization to State Aid Distribution System: Part I, Patterns of School District Organization.* Minneapolis, Minn.: University of Minnesota, 1970. (Report of a special study for the National Educational Finance Project.)

———, in *Planning to Finance Education,* Roe L. Johns, Kern Alexander, and K. Forbis Jordan, eds. Gainesville, Fla.: National Educational Finance Project, 1971, Chap. 11.

PURDY, RALPH P. (Director), *Guidelines for School District Organization.* Lincoln, Nebr.: The Great Plains School District Organization Project, 1968.

WISE, ARTHUR E., *Rich Schools, Poor Schools.* Chicago: University of Chicago Press, 1968.

ZIMMER, BASIL G. and AMOS HAWLEY, *Metropolitan Area Schools: Resistance to District Reorganization.* Beverly Hills: Sage Publications, 1968.

11

The Local Education Agency

In previous chapters it has been emphasized that the educational system in the United States is legally a state system. Decisions of the courts establishing this fact have been cited. Considerable attention has also been given to the structure of education at the state level and to the manner in which the state discharges its responsibilities.

THE SIGNIFICANCE OF THE LOCAL AUTHORITY

This chapter has been titled "The Local Education Agency" rather than "The Local School System" in order to more appropriately label the local unit. It could also have been called "The Local Education Authority."[1]

---

[1] The term "local education authority" has been employed in England for several decades and generally is referred to as the LEA. It has been an authority with rather broad responsibilities in the areas of elementary, secondary, and further education and an authority with close working relationships to other agencies such as those involved with health, delinquency, child care, youth employment, and library services.

This title implies a different local orientation, organization, and responsibility from the traditional one. It escapes the rather narrow connotation of the local *school system* and suggests that the local education authority may indeed provide for a much wider range of educational services. Many school systems are providing services for children, youth, and adults beyond the operation of schools and more will be doing so in the future. It should be noted that the provision of schools would remain the central responsibility of the local education agency as it has been of the school district.

This wider range of educational services is indicated by many practices and proposals pertaining to education. Examples are: preschool provisions; industry-based vocational or technical education; youth services; library services; child health services; performance contracts; voucher plans; placement and follow-up of youth in employment; and community-based rather than school building-based schools. A local education agency may be engaged in these or other programs which are part of the educational service but which may not be regarded specifically as a part of a school system. They, or some of them, however, would clearly be seen as appropriate areas of service by a local education authority. The development of a rather more diverse range of programs and services would appear essential in the building of an adequate public education program in the future. This change in title appears fitting as we move toward a local agency with broader powers and greater responsibility for meeting diverse educational needs in a highly complex society. This title also suggests that some eduational services may be rendered by other agencies under contract, for example, or in cooperation with the local education authority. The local education authority would thus be the responsible agency for educational services in the local area though it would not directly provide all of them. It should, however, provide the essential coordination of these services and leadership in the development and evaluation of them.

The sharp decline in the number of school districts in the last decades might be interpreted to indicate that the local school authority is of decreasing importance. The growing national and state interest and action in education could be used to support this thesis. Further, the tendency of states to pass legislation which sharply limits the scope of the decisions to be made at the local level would also seem to support this view. In fact, the significance of the local agency may seem to be declining.

It is the view of the authors, however, that this should not necessarily be the inference to be drawn from these and other factors that may be cited. Rather, it is our view that the decrease in the number of school districts creates the potential for much more vigorous initiative and responsibility on the part of the local agency. Most of the systems which have been eliminated were too small to have the resources essential for the development of adequate educational services. The states and the federal government have generally not expected initiative and innovation to be shown by most local authorities because of a lack of confidence in their competence. The growing belief in or recognition of dependence upon education in our society, as in other societies, indicates that the role of the local authority needs to expand sharply in the years immediately ahead.[2] This should occur concurrently with the increase in state and federal action in education.

The traditions and myths of our society regarding local control of education as well as present societal needs constitute an impressive base upon which to develop local school authorities of great vitality and unique characteristics.

If this is to be accomplished, it will be necessary not only to avoid restrictive state regulations but also to recognize that a local educational agency is a political and social system, closely related to external and internal traditions, needs, and forces. Provision will need to be made to facilitate change within it as a result of planning, experimentation, and research. Its own differences from other authorities and the variety within it will be greatly valued. Then it may become the instrument of its staff and its people to achieve to the fullest basic values drawn from the past struggles and experiences in the development of men. Whether the society achieves these values with the aid of education will depend upon the vision and action which is found within local authorities. There would be less reason to except them to be achieved in a monolithic system, which would dominate a state or the nation, and which was not continuously rebuilt utilizing the resources, energies, inspirations, and initiatives of the people (staff and citizens) in local units or authorities. The movement toward a local authority from a system is believed to be an essential step through which the call for greater variety in educational provisions can be responded to in a constructive manner while maintaining a cohesive, vigorous local agency committed to the educational interest of all people. This view, of course, does not deprecate the essential role of the state and federal government in establishing guidelines to attain minimum standards, in ensuring the rights of all people, in providing leadership, in

[2] In this regard see Jesse Burkhead, *Public School Finance Economics and Politics* (Syracuse: Syracuse University Press, 1964), p. 284. "The consideration of who would lose power in such a new working arrangement—the local school board, state department of education, the professional, academic, or layman adviser—is a meaningless one because a new institutional framework for the educational process would increase the responsibility of all and would make the tasks more difficult, but surely more interesting, provocative, and meaningful. As institutions grow in size and complexity, the challenge of all concerned increases. To be sure, individuals who are unwilling to accept change or different ways of doing things are bypassed and become disgruntled. But the persons and groups accepting change and challenge usually find the new situation brings greater responsibility."

facilitating experimentation and local initiative, and in providing financial resources. The case for a stronger, more vital partnership appears to be unassailable.

THE STATE-LOCAL PARTNERSHIP

Even though the educational system has been a state operation in accord with statute and judicial interpretation, it has also been a service characterized by partnership. In the early years of the nineteenth century the state did not exercise its interest in education vigorously. Some local areas established schools and developed them, but other communities provided little in the way of educational opportunity. Whether a community had good schools or not was probably more the result of local forces and factors than because of any special activity on the part of the state. This is not to deny that general or special state laws existed with reference to education or that there were some state leaders such as Mann and Barnard who supplied much encouragement. But education actually developed as a local activity. State educational personnel was exceedingly limited and quite unable to serve the great number of local districts in a direct manner.

When the state did become more interested in the development of an educational service that would meet the needs of children and youth, it generally chose to do so through local school districts. Thus the partnership was strengthened. The state offered certain financial aid and stimulated local districts by making available trained state personnel who could work with them in meeting their problems. The direct provision and management of the schools was a responsibility of local authorities. Thus it could be said that the school system was actually a local one. It was a state system marked by variety, by wide differences in opportunity, and by excellent provisions in some cases and extremely inadequate ones in others. In later years the state became much more active and sought to guarantee all children and youth at least a minimum level of opportunity. Even this, however, was done through local districts. The system was scarcely a decentralized one, for it had never been centralized. It was rather a partnership with the state rendering much assistance and giving attention to the development of more competent and responsible local partners.

A system was achieved in which it was hoped that desirable experimentation and innovation would result from the independence of local districts in developing schools to meet needs. Many of the advances that have marked education have come from the exercise of initiative by local districts. After the worth of these practices was demonstrated in some communities, they gradually spread to many other communities. In some instances the spread of the practices was aided by the state department personnel—in other cases by the enactment of legislation supporting them financially. Our state system of education is also a local system and a partnership.

The nearness of the schools to the people has always been a distinguishing feature of the school system. In few other countries has there been such a close relationship between the schools and the people. This has had both advantages and disadvantages. It has been a major factor in the strong interest that the people have had in their schools. The development of the schools has been closely related to this interest. It has stimulated the making of adaptations in educational practice. It has resulted in a school system of remarkable vitality and excellence, though also with serious shortcomings and with relatively little exercise of rigid controls by state and federal governmental agencies.

On the other hand, it resulted in the continuance of many small school districts that did not provide reasonable adequate educational opportunity even though their costs were high. Furthermore, the "interest" of certain pressure groups in education has at times known no bounds, and interference with the schools has harmed them. Materials have been introduced or eliminated from the curriculum as a result of pressure by some group—not always one interested in or competent to judge "what education is of most worth." Teachers also have been subjected to pressure or even discharged without adequate reason or even the opportunity to be heard. The responsibility of the trained educator has at times been seriously hampered by the unsound action of citizens.

Despite the difficulties that have been encountered, few desire to increase the distance between the schools and the people. The desire is to move in the other direction, especially in larger communities where the distance separating them may be greater than is generally recognized. In this development, however, there is a growing awareness that some guidelines need to be established. Such guidelines should facilitate close relationship and high public interest without undesirable interference.

In recent years the people of our society have been reexamining their values to an unusual degree. Consequently they have been seeking greater diversity in educational practice and have grown sharply critical of the educational *system.* Many have come to regard it as a rather rigid bureaucracy which meets the needs of those operating it more than the needs of children; as an institution which suffers from serious hardening of the arteries and which finds innovation and change unpalatable or even impossible. One of the results of these views has been the demand for decentralization and for greater variety in schools with more parental choice regarding types of schools.

THE BOARD OF EDUCATION

While, generally, there has been a close relationship of the citizenry to the schools, there has been a legal structure for the establishment and development of the local school authority. The legal responsibility has rested upon the education committee of the town in New England and in other sections of the country upon the board of school trustees, school directors, or board of education.

Selection of Board Members

The members of boards of education are generally elected by popular vote. In the majority of instances they are not sponsored by political parties and are not elected as members of a political party. In some of the larger cities, board of education members are appointed by the mayor. In a few cases they have been appointed by another agency such as judges of common pleas courts. The appointment procedures have been employed in some cases to effect a closer relationship between the education service and local government services. In other cases appointment reflects some lack of belief in the ability of citizens to elect competent school board members. Opinion in general, however, strongly supports popular election, though it is recognized that board members of a wide range of competence are found under any plan of selection.

Formerly, many boards of education members were elected as representatives of wards or areas within the district. This tended to result in board members representing the ward from which they were elected. Consequently, there has been a long-term trend toward election at large. Despite this trend some boards continue with election of members for subdistricts or areas within the school district, and a few have turned to it recently. This arrangement may be necessary where people in certain parts of the district or from certain ethnic groups feel they will be completely overshadowed by a more populous section. In some instances members are required to be residents of specified areas though elected by vote of all the people of the district. Election from subdistricts should be viewed as a somewhat temporary expedient to be replaced when the confidence of the people in the district as a unit has been established.

Board members are generally elected for overlapping terms of three to six years. In order to ensure reasonable continuity, the longer term (with no more than one or two members elected in any one year, or two elected every second year) appears to be preferable.

Size of Boards

The size of boards has varied greatly. Many small rural districts have had only three members. In some of the cities the boards grew as the city added territory, until late in the nineteenth century some boards had several hundred members. During the current century, with the elimination of many of the smaller districts and with an awareness of the problems resulting from extremely large boards, the trend has been toward boards of five to seven or possibly nine members.

Board Duties

The board of education is responsible for the establishment and operation of the local public school system. This usually includes responsibility for kindergartens and grades one through twelve. In some states, depending upon the size of the district, the board also makes provisions for adult education, various special education offerings, and junior college education. Statutes fix this responsibility upon local boards of education either by mandating broad and implied powers or by specifying in more detail the duties and powers of the local board of education. In either case it should be clear that the local board derives its power legally from the state. It thus is an agent of the state and also of the people of the district whom it serves. It serves the people of the district in accord with the mandate of the powers vested in it by the state. With the recognition that equality of opportunity can be achieved only through a social action program broader than the school system it may be expected that the board of the local authority will be granted larger powers pertaining to the development of children and youth. Some federal grants have stimulated action in this direction.

Among the many powers of the board of education the following are of outstanding importance:

1. The selection of a chief administrator, the superintendent of schools;
2. The establishment of policies and procedures in accord with which the educational services are administered and a range of programs are developed;
3. The establishment of policies relating to planning improvements and to accountability;
4. The adoption of the budget and the enactment of provisions for the financing of the schools;
5. The acquisition and development of necessary property and the provision of supplies;

6. The adoption of policies regarding and the appointment of necessary personnel to staff the varied services;

7. The appraisal of the work of the schools and adoption of plans for development.

Board Organization and Functioning

When boards of education were large, dependence upon administrative staff limited, and board members represented subdistricts, the practice of administering schools through the standing committee system was widespread. It was not uncommon for individual board members to get deeply involved in the details of administration. They individually interviewed applicants for teaching positions and selected instructional materials.

Today, it is agreed that board members need to recognize that they as individuals do not have powers regarding the schools. Statutes fix responsibility upon the board of education, rather than upon individual members. Furthermore, the standing committee is not favored, though boards may from time to time appoint temporary committees to consider a special problem and report back to the board. The desirability of having the board recognize the establishment of policies and procedures, rather than involve itself in administrative details as a major responsibility, is increasingly clear. This, of course, assumes that the board has competent leadership and staff to develop and provide it with the data that are essential as the basis for the determination of policies and procedures. It also assumes that the board has an administrative staff that can administer the schools in accord with the policies and can report results, including the inadequacies of established policies and procedures.

Thus, the board of education is or should be a unified body devoted to the provision and advancement of the educational service with the cooperation of the teaching, administrative, and other groups of personnel and the cooperation of parents and various other agencies concerned with the development of children, youth, and adults. Its cooperative relationship with the administrative and teaching staff is especially important because of the close understanding that must exist among them if the organization is to function properly.

If the board of education is to discharge these difficult responsibilities in an effective manner, it needs to give attention to and make provision for procedures to be followed at board meetings and to records regarding board actions. Otherwise, it will spend its time in the discussion of details rather than policies, and it will frequently engage in lengthy discussions of matters about which it does not have essential data.

The successful board of education meeting is dependent upon a number of factors such as preparing the agenda and related materials effectively, planning the meeting, giving adequate hearings to individuals and groups, and reviewing the meeting.

The agenda should be prepared several days before the meeting and should be submitted to the members of the board along with various reports containing the essential data that must be studied by the board members if they are to be prepared to make decisions. At the opening of the meeting, brief consideration should be given to the plans for the meeting, with tentative allocation of time made to different matters on the agenda. The rules of the board should establish procedures for getting items on the agenda. The rules should provide that under certain circumstances brief presentations may be accepted from individuals or groups regarding matters not on the agenda. The time for such presentations, however, should be limited, and discussion and action generally should be delayed until essential related data may be gathered and presented to the board. At the conclusion of meetings, at least occasionally, the procedures followed should be reviewed. If considerable time was wasted through lack of planning, this should be recognized and plans made to avoid similar situations at later meetings. Meetings can be made fruitful and effective if adequate attention is given to the manner in which they are conducted. Attention can and should be given to important instructional issues frequently overlooked because of lack of time. Many boards in recent years have given more attention to developing plans for a consideration of these matters. Otherwise, the details of buildings, finance, and business administration will consume the total energies of the board.

The successful functioning of the board is largely a result of the assistance it has in planning the agenda and the conduct of its meetings. No other person can render as large a measure of assistance as the superintendent of schools. Partly in recognition of his central relation to sound board functioning many boards designate the superintendent to serve as their secretary.

The politics of confrontation and the vigorous challenge by teacher and community groups is causing many boards of education to carefully reexamine their own organization and policies. This would appear to be imperative if they are to discharge their responsibilities effectively. For the power of the board may be eroded—and while this could be desirable, surely it should be done with an awareness of what is occurring.

THE SUPERINTENDENT OF SCHOOLS

The importance of the position of the superintendent of schools has already been implied in the consideration of the work of the board of education. The position is at least the equal in significance to any other position in the community. If schools are to contribute to the development of the values of the people and not just reflect the community, it will in no small part be because of the leadership furnished by the superintendent.

While the role of the superintendent and the type of leadership needed may vary from community to community and over time, there is little reason to question the view that environmental factors such as "the widespread sense of social and educational crisis" and the "waves of conflict within and without school systems" call for the best leadership talent available in society. Further, the challenge may be sufficient to attract or produce more charismatic and even prophetic leaders.[3] Later in this chapter the importance of the structure or organization of the educational service is emphasized. While organizational development and organizational health are of large significance it should not be assumed that they lessen the imperative need for a much greater effort to identify, select, and prepare men and women for leadership roles in the educational service. The profession of educational administration and the universities need to respond to this challenge cooperatively.

Selection of Superintendent

No single act of the board of education is more important than its selection of a superintendent. If one is chosen who provides the needed leadership and who is an excellent administrator, the work of the board can be far more effective. An inadequate administrator will make it virtually impossible for the board to render excellent service. The board therefore should devote great care to the selection of the superintendent.

It may do this by first clarifying the role and competencies that it desires of a superintendent and then indicating the personal characteristics and educational background and experience that it believes relate significantly to this role. It may also want to assess the local school and community situation as a basis for defining the role. Many boards desire the assistance of professional educators in doing this job. The retiring superintendent, members of the state department of education, or professors in neighboring colleges or universities may be able to render valuable assistance to the board in the work of defining the position and the type of man needed and in doing at least preliminary screening of applicants.

After the position has been defined, recommendations of persons for the position should be sought from colleges, universities, and leading school administrators. The position is too important to be filled merely by receiving applications of those who by chance hear of it and apply. In the

---

[3]See Jack Culbertson, et al., *Preparing Educational Leaders for the Seventies* (Columbus, Ohio: University Council for Educational Administration, 1969), Section III.

last analysis the board itself will have to choose the person—but it can do a far better job if it has followed procedures such as those suggested here and does not find its energies consumed an interviewing large numbers of persons who hold administrative certificates but vary widely in competence.

The quality of person secured will, of course, be dependent in part upon the situation. Important considerations in the local situation will be the board and its procedures and attitudes, the quality of the professional staff, the community attitudes toward education, and the nature of the contract and the salary. The initial contract should be long enough to give the superintendent the opportunity to study the situation, to develop plans, and to have a chance to test them through application. This suggests that a four-year contract is a minimal one. After the first contract it would be desirable for the superintendent to hold a continuing contract during satisfactory service.

Responsibilities of the Superintendent

Another important factor related to the quality of superintendent who will accept the appointment is the concept of the position held by the board. Few excellent people will go into a situation in which they are denied opportunity to perform the duties they regard as those properly vested in the superintendent. In this respect, it should be noted that the duties of the superintendent are largely determined by action of the board —except in a few large cities where a charter or statute partially defines the duties. There are relatively few powers conferred on the superintendent by statute. Although some strengthening of the powers of the superintendent through statute is probably desirable, most laymen and educators favor keeping major responsibility for defining the responsibilities of the superintendent in the hands of the board of education.

Among the important duties of the superintendent are:

1. To serve as chief executive officer of the board of education and thus to be responsible for all aspects of the educational service;
2. To lead the board in the development of policies;
3. To provide leadership in the planning, management, and evaluation of all phases of the educational program;
4. To select and recommend all personnel for appointment and to guide staff development;
5. To prepare the budget for submission to the board and to administer it after its adoption by the board;
6. To determine building needs and to administer building programs—construction, operation, and maintenance;
7. To serve as leader of the board, the staff, and the community in the improvement of the educational system.

If the superintendent is to render superior service, it is important that his duties be clearly defined, but this should not be done by stating a multitude of details that tend to limit his activity and produce a rigid administration lacking vision and initiative.

Again it should be noted that the role of leadership is now more "demanding and formidable" than in any previous period. Bennis in his consideration of postbureaucratic leadership has said that it involves

> four important sets of competencies: (1) knowledge of large, complex human systems; (2) practical theories of intervening and guiding these systems, theories that encompass methods for seeding, nurturing, and integrating individuals and groups; (3) interpersonal competence, particularly the sensitivity to understand the effects of one's own behavior on others and how one's own personality shapes his particular leadership style and value system; and (4) a set of values and competencies which enables one to know when to confront and attack, if necessary, and when to support and provide the psychological safety so necessary for growth.[4]

Staff Organization

The growth in responsibility and the larger size of local school systems as a result of the elimination of many of the small districts, the growth in population, the changing concept of what constitutes an adequate education, the increasing aspirations of the people regarding education, and the growing relations with the state and federal governments—all have led to substantial increases in size of administrative staff. These increases have at times resulted in sharp criticism of administrators and in the charge that too large a percentage of the budget is devoted to administration. Most of this criticism is probably unjustified. However, it should be recognized that the organization of staff, the determination of special competencies needed, the definition of responsibilities, and the appraisal of administrative functioning are highly essential in what is more generally becoming a large-scale organization.

Consideration of the responsibilities of the superintendent listed here suggests the importance of an administrative staff of adequate numbers and high quality. The administrative staff consists of not only the assistant superintendents, directors, and administrative assistants found in the central office but also those in area or divisional offices and the principals and assistants located in the respective schools. In a small system the superintendent will need to discharge many responsibilities with very little ad-

---

[4]Warren G. Bennis, *American Bureaucracy* (New York: Transaction Book, Aldine Publishing Company, 1970), pp. 185–186.

ministrative assistance. In a large system his work may be largely the identification of needed development and leadership in stimulating it, the coordination of the work of others and the direction of the growth of other administrators in the discharge of their responsibilities.

A few decades ago, there was some question as to whether the school system should be organized on a unit or dual or even multiple basis. This was fundamentally a question of whether the superintendent of schools should be the chief executive of the system or whether there should be no one chief executive. It is almost universally agreed today that the organization should be a unitary one and that, since the superintendent of schools is basically concerned with instruction (the educational program), he should be the chief executive. It is also widely accepted that the organization should facilitate development and satisfaction of organizational expectations and individual needs.

The superintendent of schools has an important decision to make regarding the manner in which the staff is organized. A few decades ago the line-and-staff organization was generally accepted as the most desirable type. With changing concepts of the meaning of educational leadership, this concept of organization has undergone further examination. Can the school principal be effective, both as a line and a staff officer? Or is the term "officer" acceptable? Does the line-and-staff organization facilitate the cooperative effort that the school administrator seeks in the school system today? Is there some other type of organization that is more in accord with present-day concepts of leadership and that has larger potential? (See discussion in Chapter 5.)

To what extent should the new administrative staff be located at the central office? At the school level? At selected secondary schools which serve as centers for a number of schools? Or in large systems should there be area superintendents with an office and staff located in the area served? If so, which services shall be decentralized and which centralized?

Fundamental also is the question of the staffing pattern of the local school district. Rapid change in education demands new personnel or reassignment of those with other responsibilities. An old organization is called upon to meet new challenges, to plan, to provide new services, to coordinate services. The organization is frequently subjected to criticism by legislative committees and by teachers' organizations. Teachers' organizations criticize the type and amount of supportive help provided for them.[5] The growing specialization of staff and range of services provided in a school system as well as the increasing rate of change emphasize the need for developing staffing patterns and defensible staffing ratios. With-

---

[5] Arthur D. Little, Inc., *Guidelines for Staffing School Districts to Facilitate Constructive Change* (San Francisco, 1965), p. 20.

out such guidelines, essential staff provisions to facilitate planning, appraisal, and constructive change are not likely to be made.

A central question regarding the staff is whether it should be functional (traditional) or organic. Bennis has predicted that in the future, organizations

> will be adaptive, rapidly changing *temporary systems,* organized around problems to be solved by groups of relative strangers with diverse professional skills. The groups will be arranged on organic rather than mechanical models; they will evolve in response to problems rather than programmed expectations. . . . Organizational charts will consist of project groups rather than stratified functional groups, as is now the case. Adaptive, problem-solving, temporary systems of diverse specialists, linked together by coordinating executives in an organic flux—this is the organizational form that will gradually replace bureaucracy.[6]

Probably the most important and difficult of the chief administrator's responsibilities is that of selecting and stimulating the development of the members of the administrative team. If his staff in the central and area offices are highly competent in their respective fields and if they can work effectively as a team and with other people, the superintendent's burdens are greatly reduced. If the principals of the schools are competent and provide leadership in the study of children and youth, the development of the educational program, the stimulation of student growth, and in the area of home-school coordination, then a superior school system should result. In a large system the superintendent cannot hope to work directly with large numbers of the teaching staff, but he can influence them greatly through the organization evolved and the administrative staff he develops.

THE POLICY AND PROCEDURE GUIDE

As a way of summarizing this conception of the role of the board of education and the superintendent of schools, attention will be turned briefly to the significance of developing an administrative or policy and procedure guide. It should contain policy statements that guide the board, the superintendent, and other staff in the administration of schools in the system, and it should outline procedures regarding some of the more important activities. It can be of great value for the orientation of new board members and new staff. It serves to give to each party involved a

[6]Bennis, *American Bureaucracy,* p. 166. See also E. G. Bogue, "Disposable Organizations," *Phi Delta Kappan,* 53 (October 1971), pp. 94–96.

better understanding of his responsibilities and thus lessens misunderstandings. It aids the public in understanding how the schools are operated. It facilitates getting the work of the schools done and helps center attention upon the various phases of work that need to be planned and carried through. In the development of a guide all those who are affected by it should be involved. The past practices of the board and system should be analyzed as one basis for it. In the preparation of the guide it is very important that attention be given not only to the specific duties to be discharged by each party but also to the fact that many of the activities can be effectively discharged only through the cooperative action of a number of parties.

The guide should, for example, help the principal to understand the major responsibilities that are his—and also the extent to which he should serve as a leader of others in decision making rather than just as a decision maker. The development of too detailed a code that would result in rigid organization and operation should be avoided. A rigid organization which fails to recognize that the informal organization may be as important as the formal one is not likely to result in an effective educational system.

SOME IMPORTANT PROBLEMS AND ISSUES

In the following pages, consideration will be given to some of the more important issues pertaining to the local administration of schools.

How Can a Community Ensure
the Most Competent Board of Education?

Election to boards of education is on a nonpartisan basis in most states. It has been held that the education service should be carried on independently of the usual political organizations through which the people make choices regarding many questions of public policy. This question is one which may desirably receive further consideration in the next decade. The increasing interrelatedness of school programs and other public services may suggest further involvement of political parties in establishing public policy regarding schools.

Everyone would probably agree that a spoils system would not be desirable in education. However, the attempt at avoiding political relationships may have resulted, in some cases, in the concept that education is and should be noncontroversial—that there are no major public policies regarding education that can best be resolved through extended discussion. This may have resulted in the practice of reelecting board of education members without opposition and thus without the vital debate of policies that should take place. It is not the view here that controversy per se is desirable and that elections of school board members should always be contested. Instead, education is considered a service of great public significance. In the long run, educational advances are likely to be related to the extent to which there is public discussion and decision making on important issues. One of the ways to facilitate this discussion is through contests for board of education positions.

There is of course the danger that the contest may not pertain to public policy matters but rather to details of practice or to personalities. This can probably be avoided through careful planning and by developing through public understanding a situation in which a change in board members does not inevitably or even generally mean a change in the chief administrator. The tendency to change the administrator frequently may be related to our spoils tradition, and especially to the immaturity of our communities in the procedures they employ in electing board members and the expectations that they have of them.

If the community is going to secure outstanding board members, it is not likely to do so through inaction. Rather, interested citizens and groups, preferably in a cooperative manner, need to take various steps. They need to define the qualifications that board members should have, to attempt to identify men and women who have good potentials, to encourage such individuals to run for office and to offer them assistance, to stimulate citizen interest in voting, to take steps to avoid the view that contested elections are undesirable, and to avoid the thought that the new board member is or should be the instrument of the group that supported him. One of the qualifications for the board member should surely be the ability to study objectively the facts and participate in decision making in the interest of those served through education. Prior fixed pledges to some group regarding what will be done about specific services and personnel must therefore be scrupulously avoided. How can a competent citizen make a commitment without a knowledge of the situation, which knowledge can only be gained in full measure after election? Such study and encouragement of persons to serve as members of boards of education should be applied to incumbents as well as to other citizens.

Through the development of attitudes and practices such as are briefly outlined here it is believed that more outstanding boards of education could be elected in many communities, desirable public discussion of policies related to education could be greatly increased, some of the tendency of the new board member and of the community to expect a quick radical turnover of practices and staff could be eliminated, and the problems confronting the public schools could be met in a more intelligent and effective manner.

Unless the public accepts responsibility for providing excellent board members, minorities may control. How can citizen action regarding board member selection be increased and improved?

Should Boards of Education be Organized with a Number of Standing Committees, or Should the Board as a Whole Be a Standing Committee?

When boards of education were large and when they still engaged in direct administration, standing committees were generally used. In some cases, there were many standing committees organized to care for various services or to look after the schools in different sections of the community. It was one way to get the business completed when the administrative staff was extremely limited. Through standing committees it was also believed that the talents of the respective members could be utilized most effectively. The banker chaired the finance committee; the retired contractor, the maintenance committee; the exathlete, the committee on athletics. The standing committee did give some members of the board an opportunity to learn a considerable amount regarding some phase of the work.

On the other hand, standing committees led too frequently to the exercise of large influence and even participation in the details of administration by individual board members. In extreme cases they became administrators. Then, too, as a result of the amount of board business and the number of standing committees, the board as a whole came too often to have little time for or interest in major policy matters. Its energies were spent in receiving and generally approving with little discussion the reports of numerous committees. Thus the board came to be less informed than it would have been had it devoted its energies to considering the major issues that confronted it. Another of the problems resulting from the standing committee system was that in effect it resulted in decisions in reality being made in committee—the meetings of which were not open to the public.

The organization of the board as a committee of the whole probably resulted from the desire to have all members involved in decision making and to avoid having board meetings marked by the public presentation of conflicting views. The board could make its decisions in committee and at the board meeting quickly and harmoniously transact its business.

With the growing acceptance of the idea that individual board members should not engage directly in the administrative process and that public business should be conducted in open meetings, the case for standing committees has declined. Approaching the matter positively, it can be said that boards have come increasingly to see the desirability of acting upon major policy matters in public session after adequate data have been collected and analyzed to constitute a base for intelligent action. Of course, it is recognized that in some matters such as certain personnel problems it is in the public interest as well as the interest of individuals to act in closed session. Such matters, however, constitute a very small part of the total activity of the board.

Under what circumstances, if any, are board of education committees desirable?

How Can the Board of Education Appraise the Results of the Educational Service?

Probably the most difficult of the responsibilities of the board of education is that of appraisal. It has selected its staff, provided resources to carry the program through, devoted long hours to a consideration of many policies and procedures, and now it must evaluate. For without evaluation it lacks the basis for decision making regarding future planning and development. Several steps are suggested. They assume that board members are competent.

Each board member should, with the help of the state association of school boards and that of the local staff, develop considerable knowledge about education. He will not be an educational expert—and must avoid assuming that he has become one. But he must become familiar with schools, educational practices, alternatives, problems, and issues. Unless he does so, he cannot exercise that judgment that appraisal requires on his part. Some of this knowledge he can get through planned visits to schools. For such visits he must have some background and assistance in order that he may understand the significance of what he observes.

Considerable knowledge can be gained through board of education meetings that are planned with this purpose. Materials need to be developed regarding the services or issues under consideration and distributed prior to the meeting. Various staff members may make presentations. Alternative policies and practices need to be presented. Board of education meetings that greatly increase the board members' knowledge of the educational service are not likely to occur unless the need for them is recognized, plans are made for them, and specified times are set for them.

The development of more adequate research provisions and the conducting of continuous evaluation programs are other essential steps. Regrettably, prior to the federal programs developed in the sixties, few resources were provided for research in most school systems. Also, too little is done in planning for a continuing evaluation program which over a period of years would collect large amounts of data about the variety of programs and services that are provided in the schools. The board that will insist upon the development of such plans has taken a long step in the direction of developing a base in the light of which appraisals can be made.

Finally, the board may periodically seek a more comprehensive appraisal. It, too, like the continuous appraisal referred to above, may be carried forward under the direction of the administrative staff. It also may involve the assistance of consultants. It generally should be cooperative—involving teachers and citizens—in many of its aspects. Further suggestions regarding the manner in which such a study can be carried forward are contained in Chapter 19 dealing with evaluation and accountability.

Board of education members and the staff associated with them should recognize that appraisals are inevitably going to be made. Attention therefore needs to be centered upon the problem of ensuring that appraisals have a real measure of validity and avoiding the too readily available alternatives of making appraisals on the basis of few or no facts, on the spur of the moment, or in consideration of personalities.

Boards of education need also to recognize that the emphasis in recent years upon the development of a systems approach which requires a serious planning effort, the clarification of goals, the development of specific instructional and instructional support programs, the development of objectives cooperatively by staff involved, and the establishment of evaluation procedures offers an approach of significant promise.

What is the role of the superintendent of schools in assisting the board of education to appraise the educational service?

Can and Should the Work of the Board of Education and That of the Administrator Be Sharply Separated?

In an effort to assist individual board members to avoid getting involved in the details of administration it is frequently pointed out that the individual board member, except when the board is in session, has no legal powers not possessed by all other citizens. Further, it is held that the board should see its role as that of policy maker, and the administration should administer in accord with established policy. This view may be sound enough. However, it is unrealistically simply. Consider, for example, the question of the selection of personnel.

A desirable policy would doubtless be that the most competent personnel should be secured—that personnel which can render the greatest service to children. The board however would probably wish to go well beyond such a general policy statement in discharging its responsibility in this area. It would probably wish either to adopt procedures that were judged most likely to implement the policy effectively, or to ask the administration to submit to it the regulations and procedures proposed to be employed. In the consideration of the policy and especially in the consideration of procedures related to it, the board needs the assistance of the administrative staff. Studies would be required outlining various possible procedures and indicating their probable results. The administrative staff would seek the assistance of members of the instructional staff in formulating such proposals. Periodically, also, the board would wish the assistance of the executive arm in evaluating the procedures in the light of results produced and in effecting modifications. Thus, although the board would adopt the policies and the procedures through which they are to be implemented, it generally could not hope to do the job without very important assistance from its administrative staff. In a sense, therefore policy making is engaged in by board, administrator, teachers, and other interested parties. Only policies developed through cooperative effort are likely to be sound and have genuine promise of implementation.

Approaching the issue from the other side it can be observed that policy making is a part of administration. Furthermore, such actions as approval of plans, adopting the budget, fixing the tax rate, and authorizing borrowing for capital outlay purposes are important phases of administration. Regarding all these matters, the administrative staff has a highly significant role to play, though the final decision is legally that of the board. In these matters, both the board and administrators are significantly involved in reaching a decision. Other groups such as the teachers and community groups may also play important roles. With the increase in community interest in education and the growing strength of the organized educational profession, it is likely that the problem of determining "who makes the decision" may be more difficult in the future. The growing complexity of the situation, however, demands that attention be given to fixing the responsibility for initiation, for example, and clarifying the expectations of the various groups involved. What thus appeared to be a rather simple problem—the separation of the powers of the administrator and of the board—is a very complex one, one that will be satisfactorily resolved only through extended cooperative effort based upon mutual confidence and respect among the parties involved.

All this is not to suggest that the board or its members should again become involved in the details of selecting teachers. The procedures employed should outline clearly the steps to be followed by a competent professional staff in making the selection. The board would confirm the appointments, maintain an interest in the results, and receive reports regarding them. This it would need to do in order to meet its legal responsibility regarding the employment of personnel and in order to be enabled to discharge its appraisal function.

How can the essential cooperative relationship and the recognition of the respective responsibilities of the superintendent and board be attained?

Is the Superintendency a Defensible Position, or Are the Expectancies of the Position Too Great?

The superintendency which has long had a reputation for insecurity, short tenure, and being an anxious profession, is in one of its most troubled periods. This is a result of many factors, including the growing expectations for education, the increased role of teachers in administrative and policy decisions, and the view that educational leadership must mean community leadership. Thus de facto segregation, an important community problem, has become a major challenge to the school system and to the superintendent.

With the growing awareness of the great variation in the expectancies regarding the superintendency, the question has been raised whether the position is not an impossible one. Should the administrative organization be changed to reduce the varying "demands" on the superintendent? Has there been a tendency to regard the superintendent as the one who can resolve inevitable conflicts—and then to condemn him when they are not resolved?

The board of education looks to the superintendent as its chief executive and perhaps even more importantly as its adviser, guide, and leader. Many teachers may expect the superintendent to reflect their point of view in his work with the board. Various groups of citizens have widely varying views regarding education and they expect the superintendent to represent their respective views. He also must keep children and youth in mind and decide what would be in their interest. This decision will, of course, be related to his philosophy of life and of education. He has a loyalty to these innermost convictions as well as to the groups just mentioned.

It also should be noted that in an organization the point of view of the chief executive is extremely important. Many individuals are influenced by it, because in a sense the viewpoint of the chief executive sets the tone of the organization or system. His views or attitudes even though not verbalized are known or assumed to be known and rapidly communicated.

Certainly it is true that the superintendency is one of the most difficult positions conceivable because of the impact of expectancies. And even boards of education and individual members, for example, may have widely varying views regarding the superintendency and may over a period of time change their expectancies. In communities in which the local superintendent is largely an administrator and not a leader, the position is a much simpler one to fill. However, it is probable that neither our society nor administrators themselves would choose a system that might be easier for the individual but would lower the vision of the system, for out of the conflict of expectancies may come much desirable educational change.

Thus, the continuance of the present system in its essentials appears likely. Recognizing this, we see that certain things might be done. The varied expectancies might well be more clearly determined. The administrator can make greater effort to understand the perspectives of those with different expectancies. With better understanding of the perspectives of others, communication is more likely to occur. With greater involvement of others in the process of decision making, more common understanding can be developed between and among the various parties, including the superintendent. Administrative guides should emphasize the extent to which cooperation marks administration (if it truly does), rather than rigid, fixed definitions of individual responsibility. Recognition that many decisions that must be made are neither right nor wrong but merely best judgments, and a further willingness to examine carefully all proposed solutions, can also make the superintendency more desirable. Knowledge of processes through which sound answers may be found will frequently be better than answers.

Further, the emphasis upon alternative educational programs encourages research, experimentation, and development regarding many issues in education. The superintendent should take the initiative in formulating problems for study and experimentation, in utilizing research facilities which may become available, and in seeking answers through carefully planned development and evaluation. This emphasis may avoid or blunt both unsound attacks and plans and too much dependence upon past experience.

Acceptance by the superintendent of the fact that others may be equally desirous of serving youth and the society may be helpful. The superintendent must recognize that to be helpful to others—to be a leader of others—he must be perceived by others as one who is helpful, one who is a leader.[7] This perception on the part of others has to be earned through demonstrated ability to understand and to work with others and through demonstrated commitments to the purposes of public education.

Finally, the superintendent must recognize that in the very large difficulties of the position are to be found large opportunities. His position is a highly influential one and he may play a negative role, as Callahan has indicated.[8] He can, however, recognize that it is not too unlike other leadership positions in a vital democracy. Kerr has written of the univer-

---

[7]Harriet O. Ronken and Paul R. Lawrence, *Administering Changes: A Case Study of Human Relations in a Factory* (Cambridge: Graduate School of Business Administration, Harvard University, 1952), p. 305.

[8]Raymond E. Callahan, *Education and the Cult of Efficiency* (Chicago: University of Chicago Press, 1962).

sity presidency in terms not at all unlike the experiences of many superintendents. As Kerr has stated, the position of the leader-initiator is rarely a happy one. But there are goals beyond happiness. "Some abuse" is to be expected. "He wins few clear cut victories; . . . He must find satisfaction in being equally distasteful to each of his constituencies; he must reconcile himself to the harsh reality that successes are shrouded in silence while failures are spotlighted in notoriety." But in return for this he has the satisfaction of knowing that he is "in the control tower helping the real pilots make their landings without crashes even in the fog."[9] He is in an enviable position to both guide the planning and monitor the flight.

Would it be desirable to state more fully the duties of the superintendent in statutes or in board policy? If so, what duties?

Should the Superintendent of Schools Have Greater Security?

The school superintendency has developed into one of the most important positions in our society. Few, if any, men in other professions discharge a role that has a larger impact upon the development of individuals and of our society. The values that he holds as well as his knowledge impinge upon many people. Quite possibly we have developed an administrative situation that fixes too large a responsibility upon one man. Generally, it has been held that the superintendent should be given large powers by the board of education and then held responsible for the effectiveness of the educational system—and not reemployed if he does not "produce." This was a simple, rather clear-cut arrangement and contributed much.

However, it is quite possible that the situation needs to be carefully examined and possibly revised. Increasingly, it is being recognized that effective administration is related not only to the administrator but also to many other factors in the situation. Concerning some of these situational factors the administrator may be able to do little or nothing. The very insecurity that he has known has tended to reduce his ability to cope with some of the situations in an effective manner. Improved administration would thus appear to be probable if the situation surrounding the administrator were improved. Insecurity is unlikely to enable the administrator to function well in the interest of the board, the teachers, the children, or the community.

Certainly the role of the superintendent is changing. The growth of collective negotiations in the educational scene raises many issues regard-

[9]Clark Kerr, *The Uses of the University* (Cambridge: Harvard University Press, 1963), p. 40.

ing the superintendent's role. The tendency to seek solutions to problems through confrontation rather than through careful open analysis is of large importance regarding the functioning of an educational service. Opportunities for leadership could be significantly reduced through such procedures.

Much larger acceptance of responsibility for leadership in the community on major policy issues by the president of the board of education may also be desirable. It may reduce the too-prevalent view that the superintendent makes decisions regarding policy. It could also result in emphasizing the superintendent's responsibility for offering and analyzing two or more alternatives and thus assisting the board greatly in making decisions on policy questions. The superintendent of schools would thus have a role somewhat more like that of the director of education in local education authorities in England—and possibly the base for a bit of essential security.

Greater security is not a matter of protecting incompetency. Because of the nature of the administrator's role it is not at all certain that "tenure" in the sense it is applied to teachers is desirable. Rather, it may be found in a growing understanding on the part of boards of education, of teachers' groups, and of community groups that they must act in relation to some of the situations found and not attribute all difficulties to the administrator alone. They need to come to recognize that in this way they may best advance both their own interests and that of education.

On the other hand, administrators should move to overcome some of the situational difficulties themselves and not turn back the movement toward client-centered administration, even if they could. This is but recognition of the fact that general principles regarding personnel which have come to be widely accepted in government, business, and education also have application in the case of school administrators. When administrators are perceived (and accepted) by themselves and others as having certain strengths and limitations, they will be enabled to render more outstanding service.

Should the superintendent of schools have a tenure status similar to that of teachers? What would be the advantages and disadvantages?

Can a "System" Be Achieved if Individual Schools or Area Subdivisions Have Large Leeway and Opportunity for Initiative?

As local school systems have developed in the United States, considerable attention has been given to the development of the system as a whole. Citizens' groups have frequently been quite vocal in demanding that similar programs be offered in all schools as a way of attempting to provide what they have regarded as equality of opportunity. Boards of education and administrators also have not been adverse to developing the central office staff in order that needed data regarding the schools may be readily available and that planning may be done in any part of the system in which it is needed. The availability of information resulting from the use of modern data collecting and processing equipment has now altered this situation.

Emphasis upon the development of the system can have the unfortunate effect of reducing the significance of the school or of a small number of schools that may serve a part of the district. All schools may tend to look toward the central office for leadership, rather than utilize the opportunity which is theirs either individually or in cooperation with other schools of their neighborhood. Similarly, the specialized staff may be housed largely at the central office rather than at the schools where the instruction is carried on. Such developments can lead to the view that the central office is apart from the schools and is the place where decisions are made. Complaints by school personnel regarding the "downtown" office then are not uncommon.

The view offered here is that the best system can only be achieved by fixing large responsibility upon individual schools or groups of schools serving an area and challenging them to develop the program that best meets the educational needs of the children involved. This does not mean that systemwide goals should not be established or that central purchasing is not advantageous. The adoption of the philosophy and practice which holds that the strong system is the system composed of outstanding schools, each having distinctive achievements, is strongly urged.

The great interest in the decentralization of school systems which has developed in recent years is indeed encouraging. It must be recognized however that it may not be easy to achieve. Teachers' groups may exercise their growing power to block it. Further, it is possible to have illusory decentralization [10] —deconcentration of power from the central office to divisional offices or schools—but with decision making in all important matters remaining at the central office and with little involvement of people (staff and citizens) at the division or school level. This decade should be an extremely important one in developing and testing decentralization programs.

Teachers generally will support that system in which they have strong commitments to the school of which they are a part. They will have strong commitments to the school if they have been able to develop pride

[10]James W. Fesler, "Approaches to the Understanding of Decentralization," *Journal of Politics,* **27** (1965), 536–566.

in the manner in which the school meets its educational problems. Thus, the unity that should characterize the strong system is developed by affording opportunity for diversity, which appears to be essential if education is to develop in consideration of the needs of children and youth.

How Can Initiative Be Fostered within the Local School System?

As has been indicated in Chapter 10, larger local school systems are being achieved as the result of district organization and because increases in population tend to be centered in metropolitan areas. However, many exceedingly small systems remain. On the other hand, some of our local systems are extremely large—larger, in fact, in student population than many states.

With larger units, communication becomes more difficult. Decision making may occur at increasing distances from the scene of action. The system may remove itself farther from the many communities it encompasses. With the drives toward conformity that mark our society and the desire to be sure of what happens in each school, there might be more of a tendency toward decision making at the center. "Efficiency" in the narrow sense argues for a well-structured, rigid system.

However, one of the main strengths of the public school system has been its nearness to the people. We have sought adaptation through a noncentralized system—anticipating the bubbling up of experimentation and variation in light of needs. The continuance of local taxes for public education has been advocated in part because of the belief that this will facilitate a "local" system of schools.

Perhaps it has been too easily assumed that adaptation, experimentation, and development in the light of needs of children and youth will occur somewhat inevitably. If the local system is to be characterized by initiative it will be the result of opportunities being provided for initiative within the system—probably largely at the individual school level.

Attention should be turned to the restraints that may exist within school systems and to steps that should be taken to stimulate the exercise of initiative. Study may reveal that individual schools are not moving forward because of factors such as the distance between the school and its community, certain state laws, the policies and practices of the board of education or central office staff that reward conformity, positions taken by the teachers' union or association, the attitudes of principals (the peer group) or teachers in other schools within the system, rigid rules and regulations, the difficulty of developing sound educational programs, and the qualities that are valued when principals are selected.

As systems grow larger, there appears the need to develop a plan by which each school may achieve a life, a uniqueness, and a vitality of its own. In this manner, staff and community can be energized, and the feeling of inability to effect changes in policy and practice that too often marks teachers in extremely large systems can be overcome. Basic to this type of development is a philosophy of administration that seeks high standards through the development of all people involved, rather than through the imposition of uniform practices. This does not mean that there should be no broad common goals and guidelines to practice that are applicable throughout the system. It does mean, however, that the efficiency of practices must be determined in light of the development of people (principals, teachers, pupils, parents) that occurs under these goals and guidelines, rather than in terms of arbitrary standards. It emphasizes the central role of the principal as a leader of school and community and suggests that the main efforts of the central office should be in the direction of rendering assistance in the growth of that leadership.

In regard to what matters are schools encouraged to and aided in taking initiative in most local systems? Is this desirable?

How Should Educational Services Be Coordinated with Related Services such as Library, Social Welfare, Public Health, Youth Agencies, Private Schools, Housing, and City Planning?

The growing concentration of population in metropolitan areas and the growing complexity of society point to the need for closer coordination of the efforts of the educational services and other public and semipublic services concerned with individual and community development.[11] This appears necessary and inevitable if education and the other services are to be administered effectively. Closer coordination among the services should lead to better understanding of children by the various agencies. It also should result in the strengthening of each agency, because greater understanding would result between and among the lay and professional personnel who are associated with the various agencies including the schools.

Decades of development have tended to separate education from other public and private services in the United States. Public education has been uniquely valued as the road to equality of opportunity and the progress of the society. Thus, it has had its own separate government in our society to a far greater degree than in most societies. Federal educational legislation and other developments, stimulated by the problems of

[11]Theodore L. Reller, ed., *The Public School and Other Community Services,* Annals of the American Academy of Political and Social Science, **302** (Nov. 1955).

the great cities and the recognition of inadequate achievement of goals, has called for a reexamination of the relation of public education to other agencies involved with the development of children and youth. It calls also for a rethinking of the relation of education and schooling. Research has also made increasingly clear the fact that equality of opportunity can only be achieved with a change in parental attitudes and aspirations and the contribution of all agencies which have an impact on the social and economic level of families and children.

Fiscal independence for schools has created some misunderstanding on the part of some people concerned with other community services. Without reopening the question of fiscal dependence or independence at this time, there is little question but that much more coordination of effort could be effected. The school system having a responsibility for the development of youth and legally having a relationship with more of them than any other agency should accept responsibility for initiating and facilitating such coordination.

In a middle-sized city or other large district, some effort at coordination must be made through the central office of the school system and that of other agencies. Here the criteria for such coordination should be developed in coordination with the other agencies concerned. New patterns of coordination need to be developed and tested during the present decade.

The heart of the effort at coordination, however, must be at the secondary-school attendance area or neighborhood level. The education of a child or youth is greatly influenced by the home, the community, and the school. It is essential that these parties know one another and know something of the efforts of each other. The necessity of home-school cooperation has been emphasized. There has not been a similar emphasis upon school-community cooperation, even though the school is spoken of frequently as the community school, and improved community living looms as one of the major objectives. The effort at coordination should be related to the neighborhood that may contain three or four elementary schools, a couple of junior high schools, and a senior high school. It may also contain private schools, a public library, youth clubs, state employment offices, and a public health center. The area may be larger or smaller than this, depending upon the area organization of related agencies and upon existing feelings of community or neighborhood. It needs to be large enough to involve some resources in terms of personnel from various agencies, yet small enough to make it possible to know youth and resources well.

The nature of the organization for coordination found in various sections of a large school district will vary widely because of their different needs. Although coordination of existing resources is essential, it should be noted that the identification of needs and the securing of more adequate provisions will be the major challenge to both lay and professional personnel.

What factors make it difficult for the schools to achieve the cooperation of other agencies working toward community improvement and equality of educational opportunity?

SELECTED REFERENCES

American Association of School Administrators, *Professional Administrators for America's Schools.* Thirty-eighth Yearbook. Washington, D.C.: The Association, 1960.

———, *Profile of the School Superintendent.* Washington, D.C.: The Association, 1960.

———, *School Board-Superintendent Relationships.* Thirty-fourth Yearbook. Washington, D.C.: The Association, 1956.

ARGYRIS, CHRIS, *Management and Organizational Development.* New York: McGraw-Hill, 1971.

ARTHUR D. LITTLE, INC., *Guidelines for Staffing School Districts in California.* San Francisco, 1965.

BENNIS, WARREN G., ed., *American Bureaucracy.* Transaction Book, Aldine Publishing Co., 1970.

BIRLEY, DEREK, *The Education Officer and His World.* London: Routledge and Kegan Paul, 1970.

CALLAHAN, RAYMOND E., *Education and the Cult of Efficiency.* Chicago: University of Chicago Press, 1962.

CARLSON, RICHARD O., *School Superintendents: Careers and Performance.* Columbus, Ohio: Charles E. Merrill Publishing Co., 1971.

CASTETTER, WILLIAM B., *The Personnel Function in Educational Administration.* New York: The Macmillan Co., 1971.

CULBERTSON, JACK, ROBIN H. FARQUHAR, ALAN K. GAYNOR, and MARK R. SHIBLES, *Preparing Educational Leaders for the Seventies.* Columbus, Ohio: University Council for Educational Administration, 1969.

Educational Policies Commission of the National Education Association and the American Association of School Administrators, *The Unique Role of the Superintendent of Schools.* Washington, D.C.: The Commission, 1965.

GOLDHAMMER, KEITH, *The School Board.* New York: The Center for Applied Research in Education, Inc., 1966.

GRIFFITHS, DANIEL E., *The School Superintendent.* Englewood Cliffs, N.J.: Prentice-Hall, Inc., 1966.

KERR, CLARK, *The Uses of the University.* Cambridge: Harvard University Press, 1963.

MILES, MATTHEW B., *Innovation in Education.* New York: Bureau of Publications, Teachers College, Columbia University, 1964.

National School Boards Association, *New Dimensions in School Board Leadership.* Evanston, Ill.: The Association, 1969.

SCHMUCK, RICHARD A. and PHILIP J. RUNKEL, *Handbook of Organization Development in Schools.* Palo Alto: National Press Books, 1972.

SERGIOVANNI, THOMAS J. and FRED D. CARVER, *The New School Executive: A Theory of Administration.* New York: Dodd, Mead and Co., 1973.

SPALDING, WILLARD B., *The Superintendency of Schools: An Anxious Profession.* Cambridge: Harvard University Press, 1954.

12

Organization and Administration of Education in Metropolitan Areas

The question may well be raised as to whether the organization and administration of education in metropolitan areas should be given separate or special consideration in this volume. Clearly this subject has not been analyzed carefully in most books dealing with the general organization and administration of elementary and secondary education. Is educational administration in metropolitan areas sufficiently different to justify this special attention? It is our view that the metropolitan area and components of it indeed have a uniqueness in problems and issues. Further, while the inner cities have lost the leadership role in education which they held for decades, it is possible that the severity of issues confronting them may stimulate educational responses through which they may become more innovative and thus regain a significant measure of leadership.

THE INNER CITY
AND THE METROPOLITAN AREA

Before analyzing the problems of the metropolitan community it is necessary to make clear some facts about the area with which we will be concerned. Until about three or four decades ago, as the population of a city increased and as housing or industry extended beyond the legal boundaries of the city, these areas were often annexed. Thus the city grew and in many instances it included all or most of the population and the commerical and industrial developments which were an integral part of it. However, a few decades ago this situation changed. Greater ease of transportation enabled people and plants to be farther removed from the central city and in fact to be removed from the boundaries of the city. To a degree, then, there were economic and what appeared to be social advantages in continuing to be a part of the city for certain purposes but removed from it for others. Suburban communities then desired to maintain their independence and eventually organized into cities or townships which resisted annexation to the city and which did not work cooperatively with one another or with the central city. Thus the crazy quilts which are metropolitan America today came into existence.

Approximately two-thirds of the population of the nation is located in metropolitan areas if the definition of the U.S. Bureau of the Census of metropolitan areas is accepted. This definition holds that each standard metropolitan statistical area (SMSA) must contain one city of at least 50,000 population or two contiguous cities which together constitute a single community with a minimum population of 50,000. Generally a SMSA includes the entire county in which the central city is located and adjacent counties if they are *metropolitan in character* and *economically and socially integrated* with the central city or county surrounding it. This definition, it will be noted, sets only approximate limits and causes some people to believe that it results in the inclusion of too much area. Others believe that the resulting population figure is too small to describe true "metropolitanism."[1]

It must be noted that metropolitanism does not imply exactly the same type of growth or development in different states or regions. Some metropolitan areas are spread out far more than others. Some are characterized by far more rapid growth than others. The artificial barriers between the central city and suburbs vary considerably as does the percent of population found respectively in the suburbs and core city. Some are intracounty and others intercounty. Variations exist with respect to per-

---

[1] John C. Bollens and Henry J. Schmandt, *The Metropolis: Its People, Politics and Economic Life* (New York: Harper & Row, 1965), pp. 7–10.

centages of population from various ethnic groups. However, while differences among metropolitan areas should be recognized, it is important to recognize "that metropolitan areas have numerous major characteristics in common, characteristics which weld them together to form a category of phenomena that can be validly called 'metropolitan.'"[2]

As indicated previously, the metropolitan areas have roughly two-thirds of the population of the country. Until the early 1960s the larger part of this population lived in central cities. Today, however, the population of the suburbs exceeds that of the central cities.[3]

In terms of the economic life of the nation, metropolitan areas are even more impressive, having a percentage in terms of almost any measure exceeding that of population. Thus this worldwide phenomenon has a significance which is difficult to appreciate—metropolitan areas tend to dominate regions and nations. In examining these facts Bollens and Schmandt conclude

> Metropolitan areas therefore have most of the people, most of the jobs, and most of the public and private financial resources (as well as most of the debt, it should be added) of the United States. Consequently, they are the primary centers of population, industry, commerce, labor, and government; but they are more, too. They are the major centers of education, art, music, literature, drama and entertainment. They provide ways of life and ideas that pervade the entire nation. They are the magnets of hope, not alone economic but also social of many people. They also have most of the critical domestic problems, some governmental and others social or economic. Some involve deficiencies of public services or gross inequities in financing them; others concern the ability of people of different racial, ethnic, educational, and social backgrounds to get along with one another, the ability of newcomers and the metropolitan community to adjust adequately to one another, and the ability of metropolitan areas to prosper in face of continued growth.[4]

"A Mosaic of Social Worlds"

The simplicity of the structure of the former town with its "other side of the tracks" is in marked contrast to the metropolitan area. It is described as

> ... heterogeneous, constantly changing, fragmented;
> ... arranged spatially in an often confused and seemingly incompatible pattern;

[2] *Ibid.*, p. 19.
[3] Committee for Economic Development, *Reshaping Government in Metropolitan Areas* (New York: The Committee, 1970), p. 12
[4] Bollens and Schmandt, *The Metropolis*, pp. 27–28.

> ... numerous neighborhoods and suburban groupings of varying social, ethnic and economic characteristics scattered throughout the metropolitan complex;
> ... the luxury apartment casts its shadow on the tenement houses of workers. The Negro ghetto is ringed by a wall of white neighborhoods. The industrial suburb lies adjacent to the village enclave of the wealthy.[5]

Thus, the metropolitan area is a balkanized one. Homogeneity characterizes many neighborhoods. Some neighborhoods are affluent, others are populated heavily by refugees of a rapidly changing society. Many live where they do partly because of financial resources, others because of a type of enforced segregation. These neighborhoods have vastly different educational needs and expectations of a school system, and differ in their participation. These different neighborhoods may be described by such factors as social rank, urbanization, and segregation.

In terms of social rank, the range is from the neighborhoods composed largely of broken homes, minorities, considerable unemployment, and unskilled workers, to those made up largely of professionals, business executives, and college graduates. Urbanization refers to the family and home situations which prevail. They range from the suburban area marked by single family units, no or few working mothers, and young families with small children, to the rooming house and apartment areas with many single men and women, and married couples with few children, both of whom are working. The factor of segregation relates to the ethnic composition. The segregation may be an imposed one, as is frequently the case of the Negro, or it may result from other forces such as the tendency for a religious group to settle around a school. The tendency for segregation to increase in metropolitan areas is one of the major challenges to our society. Only recently has serious consideration been given to its fuller implications. Even today, the middle and upper economic classes continue to escape from the core city and to settle in a suburb, perhaps hoping to avoid the problems of the metropolitan area. Thus, in spite of the expressed desire of the society to have less segregation, it may have more. This situation poses major problems for education and its governmental structure and raises the question as to whether men are or will be citizens of a metropolitan area or only of a neighborhood.

Further analysis of the metropolitan area and of its neighborhoods can well be done regarding such matters as mobility of the people, age structure of the population, changing ethnic composition, percentage of youth in the population, fertility of the population, recreational needs and opportunities, occupational patterns, and occupational mobility. Regard-

[5] *Ibid.* p. 83.

ing all these matters, attention must also be given to changes which are still occurring, for the metropolitan areas are especially characterized by rapidity of change.

In this mosaic of ethnic and social worlds major issues and directions of the society are being determined. The desegregation struggle in the metropolitan areas poses many problems. Central issues are the questions concerning (1) how to achieve the social justice to which we are legally and ethnically committed for economic and ethnic groups; (2) to what extent and in what manner should (can) the school lead or succeed in this effort; and (3) would a coordinated effort of agencies such as those related to school, welfare, housing, family-life planning and development and employment have greater promise of achievement than thrusts by one or more of these programs alone? If so, how can such coordination be achieved?

The City Versus the Surrounding Area

Any consideration of education in the metropolitan area must give attention to the core city and to the surrounding area. The central city which was formerly in a leadership role in education has now lost that position in almost all cases. Its facilities and staff are no longer outstanding. Rather it is torn by strife. Its board of education, no less than its general government, is being challenged to overcome difficulties which appear almost overwhelming. Many of its citizens do not believe the board of education acts in the interest of their children and youth. The financial advantage which it formerly enjoyed has disappeared—in fact in many cases it now may be financially disadvantaged, considering the nature and quality of educational services it must develop if it is to make a claim to being effective. The short tenure of the superintendent appears to be increasingly found also for principals. In an effort to regain creditability and effectiveness it seeks increased participation by staff and citizens. It also explores the concept of decentralization and makes attempts to move in that direction—hoping thereby to win that understanding and support which must be regained if it is to move forward. Except for a few cities it tries administrative decentralization rather than political decentralization.[6]

[6]Decentralization is employed here as "the generic term to describe all types of power distribution, with the adjective 'administrative' tacked on to identify instances of internal allocation and 'political' to cover the transfer of authority to officials who are responsible to a subjurisdictional electorate or clientele." This is in accord with James W. Fesler, "Centralization and Decentralization," *International Encyclopedia of the Social Sciences,* Vol. 2 (New York: Macmillan, 1968), pp. 370–377, as cited by Henry J. Schmandt, "Municipal Decentralization: An Overview," *Public Administration Review,* Vol. XXXII, Special Issue (October 1972), p. 572.

In the meantime the suburban area and the small municipalities surrounding the central city struggle to remain independent of the city. Many of them are too small to develop highly effective programs. They vary widely in wealth and in human resources. They discover that they are not cut off from the city to the degree they desire. The problems of youth in our culture pervade them. Still they resist the development of closer relations to the city and the thought that the metropolitan area must attack its problems in a more cooperative, planned manner. New ad hoc authorities are created to make it possible for them to provide more adequately some services such as vocational-technical and aspects of special education. In many instances however they continue to be rather insulated pockets and to provide an educational service which is not well attuned to the realities of the metropolitan area of which they are a part. The intermediate unit assists them in some measure to provide for the staff development and instructional improvement which is essential.

In some instances through a council of superintendents or other staff an effort is made to bridge the gap between the districts. In many others the level of understanding and especially of cooperative effort is regrettably very limited.

Any effort to develop a metropolitan feeling or government is muted by the reluctance of the area surrounding the core city to move in that direction. In some instances this reluctance is also supported by leaders of the "minority" group or groups in the central city. They have gained some power, or at least see it in their grasp in the central city, and regard any move toward metropolitanism in government as a move to deny them that opportunity to govern which they have won so recently. They fear that a metropolitan organization would once more submerge them and destroy leadership opportunities to them.

DISTRICT STRUCTURE IN THE METROPOLITAN AREA

Serious inadequacy characterizes the district structure in metropolitan areas. This is true for local government purposes as well as for education. In 1967 the metropolitan areas in the United States had almost 21,000 local governments (including those for education) of all types. The average number of local governments per metropolitan area was over 90. Thus the Chicago metropolitan area had 1,113; the Philadelphia area 871; and the Pittsburgh area 704.[7]

[7]Committee for Economic Development, *Reshaping Government in Metropolitan Areas*, p. 13.

Many of the local governments in metropolitan areas are small in population and geographically. Approximately two-thirds of these municipalities had a population under 5,000, and one-half covered a land area of less than a single square mile. Residents of metropolitan areas are generally served by four local governments including a school district, at least one special purpose district, a county, and a municipality or township. In addition an increasing number are served by special-purpose authorities or districts which involve a major portion of the metropolitan area such as those for water, sewage, transportation, air or smog control, and environmental development.

Many small school districts also continue to exist in metropolitan areas. They may be pockets of wealth, pockets of poverty, segregated social or economic units, or racial enclaves. Generally relatively little attention has been given to the problem of school-district structure in metropolitan areas. In fact policies of the state—such as state financial arrangements—frequently have encouraged the development and maintenance of quite inadequate units. Commissions on school-district organization have devoted their energies largely to rural areas. They have seldom noted how different and more difficult to justify is a district of 1,000 or 5,000 population which is a part of a major metropolitan area from a district of the same size in a mountainous area with extremely sparse population. Few if any states have set up significant guidelines for school-district structure in metropolitan areas.

A variety of arrangements other than the crazy quilt pattern which is now widespread might be considered both for school and for general local government. Among them are (1) a one-tier system, (2) a one-tier system with extended administrative decentralization, (3) a two-tier system, and (4) a federation of local units.

A *one-tier system* could be achieved by having one large unit or in larger metropolitan areas several somewhat equally sized smaller ones—all of which are independent units directly responsible to the state. If the one-tier system results in an extremely large district, many people would probably favor provisions within it for extended administrative decentralization. The *two-tier system* would provide a government for education for the entire area but would probably provide limited powers for the central or first tier and place very substantial responsibility for decision making, operation and management upon the second tier. In the plan to have a *federation of local units* covering the metropolitan area, the local units would be the basic ones and the federated unit would be granted most of its powers by the local units. In this plan it would be desirable to have the local units reasonably equivalent in size and all of such size as would facilitate or ensure substantial competence in providing and administering important services.

All these proposals suggest that the county or traditional intermediate unit may have little or no place in the metropolitan area. In fact the first tier of government in a two-tier system might indeed be a very adequate intermediate unit in a number of metropolitan areas. Such a first-tier unit might well be the regional unit for the metropolitan area if the state were divided into regions as intermediate units.

It must be recognized that a major issue related to any of these plans is the size of the unit—whether first or second tier. In larger metropolitan areas no unit can probably be justified with a minimum of less than 100,000 population—for no unit smaller than this is likely to be able to provide services extending from preschool through secondary or community college, and including special education, vocational and technical education, except at an extremely high unit cost. Further, smaller units are unlikely to obtain the administrative leadership essential for staff and program development. On the other hand, there is a basis for the argument that a unit, especially a second-tier or operational one, should not be so large that citizens may have the belief or may experience a unit which eludes responsiveness to them. This same concern need not exist regarding the first-tier unit if it is a government of limited powers and if the operation and management of schools is the responsibility of the second tier.

If our society should move in the direction of having a local education authority,[8] the second-tier units would probably have full responsibility for operation of schools while the first tier might be more directly involved in some of the extraschool educational services which would serve the metropolitan area or a substantial part of it. It would also probably have significant responsibility with reference to planning, to finance (achieving greater equality of opportunity in the metropolitan area), to staff development including administrative staff, to research and development, to technical areas such as computer-assisted instruction, and to physical facilities and capital outlay.

Planning for Reorganization

The question as to how such reorganization of government for educational purposes in metropolitan areas can be achieved may properly be raised. It is unlikely to result from the application of procedures heretofore followed with reference to school district reorganization. It is likely to occur only if the people (including educators) of the metropolitan areas recognize how inadequately they are organized to provide essential educational services and even to make their case heard in state legislatures. No

---

[8] As suggested in Chap. 11.

one speaks for the metropolitan area today—and frequently through silence or direct action various parts of it speak against one another. Further, a more rational governmental organization for education in metropolitan areas is likely to occur only if state legislatures recognize that the planning for and establishment of an adequate structure for the development and administration of education is one of their most fundamental responsibilites—and that the continued neglect of this responsibility can only result in having the legislature make more and more decisions regarding the details of the educational service and processes—in matters regarding which they have minimal competence.

The inadequacy of district structure must be recognized as a highly important element in the federal court decisions pertaining to the Richmond and Detroit areas and desegregation. Whatever the final outcome of these cases, they need to be seen in this context. Further, the *Rodriguez* and *Serrano* cases pertaining to district ability to provide educational opportunity unrelated or less related to local district wealth are substantially the result of legislative inaction in terms of developing a more adequate governmental structure for education. Conceivably our society will move in the direction of state-operated systems of education and replace local government authorities with district offices of the state department of education. If we move this way, however, we should do so knowingly— with an awareness of the possible or probable costs. Given the commitments and traditions of our society, the direction here suggested is believed to be one which might well be highly preferable even though it might not be quite as tidy.

Some Encouraging Developments

In concluding this brief statement on district structure for educational government in the metropolitan area it should be noted that a few metropolitan areas in the United States have moved in this direction. Further, the development of the two-tier system in Toronto should be recognized as one model—though as should be expected, not one without problems. Finally, the effect and achievements of the English Parliament along these lines is worthy of careful study. Through the local government act of 1972 the Parliament provided for a two-tier system of local government in metropolitan areas but fixed responsibility for the operation of schools upon second-tier authorities. The second-tier authorities have a minimum population of 250,000. While some consideration was given to fixing certain responsibilities for education upon the first tier, it was found too difficult to draw a clear line between those educational responsibilities which were to be exercised by the first- and second-tier authorities respectively. A principle which was followed was that the small city (roughly 400,000 or under) and surrounding area should be a one single-tier local unit while the large conurbation should have two-tier government with a metropolitan county (first tier) divided into a number of boroughs (second tier) of at least a quarter-million population each. This major local government act, designed to produce strong local authorities with important taxing (rate) power, resulted in the creation of 101 local authorities in the nation with educational responsibilities. These local authorities are general purpose. However, 60 to 80 percent of their expenditures are for education, and the education committee is widely regarded as the most important. Further, the local authorities receive a large general grant (not specifically for education or other designated services) from the Parliament which is based upon a number of factors involving need and ability. Thus an attempt is being made to preserve and strengthen local government responsibility in one nation marked by metropolitanism.

STATE AND FEDERAL GOVERNMENTS AND THE METROPOLITAN AREA

One of the most serious group of problems pertaining to the large city (and the metropolitan area) is that of the images held regarding it and related views and practices.

Looking first at the large city school district, it must be observed that historically it enjoyed a large independence from the state. It was in the forefront in educational matters and did not depend upon state standards or guidelines or even heavily upon state financial aids. As a result state departments of education rendered few services to it and in fact were not staffed or otherwise prepared to serve it in a substantial manner. Such state departments were heavily involved with the many small and poor districts which were below state minimum standards. The big city expected little from the state department of education, and the state department of education did not interfere with that expectation. Only during the last decade have state departments seriously considered their obligations to the big cities. A number have now made staff and other provisions to enable them to be of more assistance. However, in spite of the nature and extent of the problems confronting the big city in the last decade, the state department of education is not generally today seen as a source of substantial assistance.

Because of the traditional state-big city relationship and because of the plight of the big cities and the power and financial resources of the federal government there has been a strong tendency in recent decades for the big cities and the federal government to develop a special direct relationship. At times this relationship has avoided involving the state. An extremely strong statement regarding the desirability of such an arrangement is that of Shedd, who suggests *"that the federal government nationalize the big city school systems of this country:* that their operation and their funding be taken over by the government."[9]

He states further that he sees "a national system in the big cities, totally federally funded, as the only solution" by which the Nations's urban schools can be rescued from disaster. This drastic solution would separate the big city from the metropolitan area of which it is an integral part and would challenge the tradition of state responsibility for education. The fact that it has been offered, however, must be seen as an indication of the seriousness of the problem of education in the big cities and of the "failure" to meet it through local and state action.

Another important aspect of the problem of the metropolitan area is that it generally has not been seen by the people themselves as a unit with common problems and that it has not been so regarded by state and federal bodies and authorities. As indicated previously, state legislatures have not generally grappled seriously with the problem of district structure in metropolitan areas. Rather through legislation they have encouraged and facilitated the continuation of many small school districts surrounding the city. In the legislature no one speaks for the metropolitan area. Most citizens and educators see themselves as citizens of school district or village X rather than as citizens of a metropolitan area. Perhaps as the metropolitan area grows larger and more difficult to cope with, they cling more desperately to the village—except in such matters as water, sewage, air, and transportation where they cannot hold to the boundaries of an earlier day. They hope to escape the problems of the big city even though economically they are an integral part of it and even though problems related to education cannot be confined to the big city boundaries.

When the extent to which the tone and quality of education in the nation is set in the metropolitan areas is recognized, the extremely serious implications of the inadequate governmental structure for education in these areas can be better understood.

DECENTRALIZATION IN THE METROPOLITAN AREA

No concept is receiving more widespread approval in this decade than decentralization. This is partially in response to the demand for more

[9]Mark R. Shedd, *National Policy and Urban Schools* (New Haven: Yale University, Institute for Social and Policy Studies, 1972), p. 13.

participation by the citizenry. Other related factors are the fear of the power of the educational bureaucracy and the growth of governmental centralization or federal power in many aspects of life. The traditional American belief in local government or local autonomy is also a factor which arouses support because of the fear that it has slipped or is slipping away. Another matter of importance has been the realization or belief that the big city systems have been notably unresponsive to the needs of the children or the people of large sections of the city—namely the minority or culturally different.

Although Cillié[10] pointed out a considerable number of years ago that our big city systems had indeed become highly centralized, this viewpoint has not been widely accepted. Rather, we have held fast to the belief that our system of administration of education is highly decentralized, as Kandel[11] indicated so effectively in comparing it with other systems. Both were correct. While the general situation in the nation was properly characterized as one with much responsibility at the local level—since state centralization had never existed, and with many of the local units very small—nevertheless, the large cities had become highly centralized in their organization and operation. When the percentage of children of the nation found in the large cities is considered, a surprising number of our children were in rather centralized units while the mythology or reality of a highly decentralized system persisted.

Any serious consideration of decentralization in the large city requires careful definition if it is to be meaningful. For it can be applied to a variety of situations or can describe widely varying practices. Further, it is possible to widen participation in various ways while increasing centralization through further strengthening central decision-making power. The illusion of decentralization can thus be achieved. The meaning of decentralization is rather different when applied to the metropolitan area, which has lacked centralization to a striking degree, from its meaning when applied to the core city, which has probably been highly centralized. If an adequate structure is achieved for the metropolitan area to enable it to function as a unit at least for major limited purposes, such development should very probably be accompanied by a carefully developed plan of political decentralization. Unless this concurrent decentralization occurs, the development or acceptance of any metropolitan authority is highly unlikely.

Decentralization is being used here to describe the movement of decision-making power to a unit nearer the place of action and the fixing

---

[10]F. S. Cillié, *Centralization or Decentralization* (New York: Teachers College, Columbia University, 1940).

[11]I. L. Kandel, *Types of Administration,* (Wellington: New Zealand Council for Educational Research, 1938).

of responsibility for decision making upon the people of the unit. Accordingly the establishment of divisional or field offices to represent or act for the central administration is not considered decentralization. On the other hand, if such offices become responsive to the staff and citizenry of the unit or district and if the staff and citizens of the unit share substantially in the decision making, it may properly be regarded as a decentralized system. Decentralization thus involves the attainment of a measure of centralization or ability to act in the interest of the whole area followed by the delegation of certain specified powers and responsibilities to a subunit.

There are many constraints on the achievement of a high degree of decentralization in big city school systems. Many of these are not fully recognized by some of those who speak easily and positively of decentralization. Among them are:

- *Legal barriers.* Statutes fix responsibility upon the board of education of the city and generally do not provide for subunits with significant powers.
- *Tradition.* The organization of the system has been toward a growing centralization. Economics, communication, the pursuit of efficiency, technological advances are all seen as forces favoring the continuance of the traditional organization. In fact some of these, such as the development of more adquate information (data) systems, may make decentralization more viable.
- *Difficulty of developing a new structure.* The determination of adequate subunits and the delineation of the powers which should remain with the central body and the subunits respectively is exceedingly difficult. Subunits with a "community identity" may indeed be unacceptable because of their economic or ethnic imbalance.
- *Opposition of teacher groups.* While this is not inevitable, it is highly probable, for many teachers and teacher organizations will find less security and considerably more effort needed to maintain certain positions if they can be negotiated at subunit levels. Further, at the subunit level they may come into sharper disagreement with groups seeking "community power."
- *Difficulty of developing a responsible subunit.* While the idea of subunits is enthusiastically endorsed, few have given attention to the problems of developing leadership in a new unit or to achieving citizen participation and representativeness. Most institutions have a history which undergirds their functioning. The building of a new institution quickly is a major challenge and one for which too little provision is generally made. Thus early enthusiasm can quickly turn to disillusionment.
- *The delegation of decision making to the individual school.* This may appear to make unnecessary the establishment of an administrative unit between the central office and the school. If the individual school has large powers, the subunit must be an authority with important firmly delegated or established responsibilities or it will be seen only as an undesirable buffer for the central administration and a further bureaucratic invention to delay action.

These constraints are not offered to discourage attacks on the problem of centralization. Rather they are offered in the hope that they may be considered in the development of a strategy to achieve an effective metropolitan structure with political decentralization.

PLANNING AND DEVELOPMENT IN THE METROPOLITAN AREA

In recent decades there has been a sharply increased awareness of the possibilities of planning and a recognition that planning in fact is one of the major responsibilities of the educational administrator. It is suggested here that the metropolitan area offers special opportunities in this regard. The crisis which exists regarding education and other public services provides an increased willingness on the part of many who would otherwise be complacent to approve and to participate. The rapidity of change also suggests the greater field for planning educational development. Further, it is in the metropolitan area that the greatest resources for planning are found.

In examining the problem of recognition of the potential but also the limitations of planning, Reller has observed that

> We have slowly come to recognize the necessity for planning, and to understand and appreciate its possible contributions as well as its limitations. The vast, complex, interrelated changes in urban life, which continue with or without planning, urgently demand more careful study than has been common. Unless there is systematic planning for improvements, the very stability of our society is seriously threatened. In the light of the growing evidence, there has also developed a more humble expectation from planning.

Walsh has noted that:

> ... plans that purport to be holistic grand designs, vast and comprehensive models of future society, are interesting, but usually utopian. Moreover, man is as capable of planning himself into misery and ugliness as he is of stumbling into them.[12]

Reller also noted:

> However, man cannot afford to fail to use his intelligence in formulating comprehensive policies, harmonizing goals, seeking greater agreement among the many actors in the metropolitan scene, and in establishing an agenda to focus and organize debate, examining activities not only in terms of an annual budget and incremental changes but also in terms of long-range needs and resources, broadening the available base of information as the

---

[12] Annamarie Hauck Walsh, *The Urban Challenge to Government*, (New York: Praeger Publishers, 1969), p. 181.

basis for decision making, identifying alternative plans and their probable results, and introducing innovation into the metropolitan government scene which may be heavily laden with inertia.[13]

Planning and development in the metropolitan area provide a number of especially inviting opportunities. They include the opportunity:

- To involve state and noneducational local planning staff in educational planning. One of the barriers to more effective work in the metropolitan area is the lack of common goals and understanding, cooperation, and mutual acceptance among professional staff engaged in various services. Planning is an area where the professionals, each with his own limited vision, may come together with less threat than in direct administration. Further, staff in a number of agencies, planning and otherwise, may be more experienced in planning than most of those directly involved in education.
- To involve those engaged in services which have a large impact on education but which may not be directly involved with schools. These include such services as land use, housing, youth programs, social welfare, health, library, and environmental development. Thus education rather than schooling may be advanced.
- To enable educators to contribute more significantly to the "quality of life" in the metropolitan area and to facilitate the improvement of the contribution of the school to this end. To examine again the question of whether environment can be controlled or whether it is the controller. While relevancy of the instructional program can be unintelligently or inappropriately pursued and with too little recognition of its limitations, it warrants serious consideration.
- To facilitate the development of an effort or a structure involving a number of governmental agencies at the state, local, and federal level to carry forward the educational program, and thus to overcome such simplistic views as "education is the province of the board of education and the administration of education in the metropolitan area is a local responsibility." Planning should ensure a more complex and potentially more promising and realistic view and structure.
- To manage educational (including schooling) costs.

As Coombs and Hallak have said:

To get at this whole problem of education change and innovation, new types of planning are needed that penetrate beneath the outer "macro" dimensions of educational systems to their internal affairs (which economists, perhaps understandably, have hesitated to grapple with). Unlike most educational planning to date, this new generation of planning, yet to be elaborated, must extend beyond the goal of linear expansion of the educational *status quo* and become a positive force for redesigning entrenched and now inappropriate educational processes. Its emphasis must be on systems design—on educational processes designed to fit relevant objectives for each

---

[13]Theodore L. Reller, "Developing a revitalized Educational System," in Edgar L. Morphet, David L. Jesser and Arthur P. Ludka (Eds.), *Revitalizing Education in the Big Cities*. (Denver, Colorado: Improving State Leadership in Education, 1972), p. 102.

place and time and learning clientele in an efficient and effective manner. To achieve that sort of "design approach" to educational planning, economic research and analysis must join hands with pedagogical and sociological research and analysis. Only then will the vital concepts of cost effectiveness and cost benefit acquire their full meaning and receive more realistic application.[14]

To achieve very much in this direction, resources (financial and human) greater than those of school districts (even those of metropolitan areas) must probably be involved. This could be a challenge to metropolitan area authorities with specialist staffs. They could test theories of educational change and development and regain for the metropolitan area the leadership role once held by the cities. The problems of educational processes in the metropolitan area—involving as they do issues such as alienation of youth, low achievement and dropout, opportunities to develop positive attitudes toward the society, language and dialect problems, perceptions of the school as an institution, drug culture and violence, and staff development—constitute some of the most difficult educational issues confronting the society. Congressional concern regarding these problems has been a major stimulus to federal activity in educational research and development in recent decades. Regrettably during this period most metropolitan areas have not been organized and staffed adequately to enable them to grapple with these problems directly. Conceivably a direct attack on problems such as these by the metropolitan areas with the cooperation of universities, educational laboratories, and other resources is one of the more promising approaches. Clearly, more adequate authorities must exist in metropolitan areas with responsibility for research and development if a vigorous effort is to be made to understand such issues and to plan and test proposed steps to meet them. Such metropolitan area authorities, if properly constituted, would have important advantages over existing institutions and agencies in attacking many of the major educational issues of our society.

SOME IMPORTANT PROBLEMS AND ISSUES

Should the Metropolitan Area Be Reorganized for Educational Purposes with a Two-Tier District Structure?

No definite answer has emerged to this question. However, there is much evidence available that for various matters the metropolitan area

---

[14]Philip H. Coombs and Jacques Hallak, *Managing Educational Costs,* (New York: Oxford University Press, 1972), p. 270.

needs to be organized to enable it to meet educational needs more effectively. Provisions for technical, vocational, and special education are important cases where this is true. Adult education and community college education are also significantly dependent upon this development. If essential planning, research, and development is to be carried forward, a relatively large authority will be needed to provide the necessary staff competencies. Programs of staff development—of the middle management group, for example—also call for resources well beyond those of the great majority of school districts in the metropolitan areas. The effective development and utilization of computer-assisted instruction also requires competencies not found in the small school district.

On the other hand, there is no doubt that many of the people desire to have an increased opportunity to participate in decision-making and even in the processes of education. The apparent importance of the attitudes and aspirations of parents with reference to the educational development of children supports this desire. The impact of community alienation upon the schools also points to the need for genuine communication between the schools and the public. It would therefore appear highly desirable that there be recognition of the desirability of keeping the schools "close to the people."

These facts and judgments suggest that a structure must be developed which will facilitate planning and utilization of resources available only to a large unit while providing for more participation. This can be done through a two-tier system, a decentralized large unit, or a federation of competent local units. Basic to it, however, is the development of much more knowledge regarding decentralization, a minimum population size for local operation units, the achievement of a metropolitan citizenship.

Can a school district (second tier) of less than 100,000 population be justified in a metropolitan area of one million? Why or why not?

How Can a Reorganization of School District Structure Be Achieved in Metropolitan Areas?

Certainly the adequate reorganization of school districts in metropolitan areas is extremely difficult and is not likely to occur unless change takes place in a number of directions. Among needed conditions for such a development are:

- A recognition that state and federal educational finance plans have been a major contributor to present structure or to the maintenance of present structure. This needs to be coupled with an awareness that new major state finance proposals need to be examined in terms of their impact on district structure and need to be formulated in such manner that they will facilitate a more

adequate structure rather than the maintenance of the status quo. Regrettably many such plans, perhaps unintentionally, freeze inadequate structures.
- The development of more adequate governmental structure for general local government purposes. More adequate provisions for educational government may indeed precede those for general government. However, significant movement in regard to general government would facilitate similar developments involving education. What is reasonably adequate governmental structure in the metropolitan area has meaning both for general purposes and for education. Further, if that coordination of general government and education which is imperative is achieved, it will be substantially facilitated by somewhat parallel developments in structure. What school district will coordinate its planning or recreation or health programs through a dozen cities?
- Metropolitan educational authorities need to be developed concurrently with regional educational units throughout the state. Otherwise they are unlikely to receive general support. The regional units should either replace or become the intermediate units. The need for regional units in the parts of the state other than those that are metropolitan may not appear quite as pressing. However, they can play a highly significant role in the development of the education service and in making less likely a drift toward state operation of schools. Such regional units need to be highly responsive to adequately sized and competent local units.
- Educators of the metropolitan areas need to develop common understandings regarding the problems of education in the metropolitan area and greatly increased ability to cooperate and coordinate the efforts of their respective districts. Too frequently educators of suburbs and city have little understanding of their respective problems and see no or few common metropolitan education problems. Such understanding should be expected to precede the development of cooperation among the citizens of the respective districts. The development of a high level of cooperation among the educators (administrators and teachers) is essential not only to achieve essential reorganization. It is also an important element in the operation of a reorganized metropolitan area. This has been clearly illustrated by the work of the superintendents of the respective cities which constitute metropolitan Toronto. A similar informal organization of directors of education in Greater London has been a major force in the operation of schools in that metropolitan area.
- The respective powers of the central metropolitan board of education and those of the operational units need to be defined by a commission responsible to the legislature. In general, in accord with the traditions of our society the central board should have only a few limited powers—though very important ones—and the base units (second tier) should have large and relatively untrammeled responsibility for operating the educational system. Accordingly the staff of the central unit should remain small. The second-tier authorities must be large enough to be competent to provide a wide range of educational services at a defensible cost. They and schools within them should be encouraged to develop diversity in their programs and practice.
- Public understanding and opinion must be developed in support of the more adequate, responsive, and responsible structure.

Can voting by the people of the many school districts of the metropolitan area be regarded as a viable method of achieving the essential structure for educational government? Why or why not?

In the Metropolitan Area Have the Advantages of One Type of Governmental Structure for Education Over Other Types Been Demonstrated?

Although in this chapter a preference has been indicated for a two-tier system, it must be acknowledged that the case for it over other plans is not clearly established. Efforts to overcome the "failure" of schools in core cities may be made and substantial improvement may be effected through different organizations. They range from the plan whereby the metropolitan office is a field division of the state through a modified field division, a coterminous field division and local government, to a substantially independent local government.

Probably there could be agreement on such matters as the following:

- Present structure in most metropolitan areas is inadequate and legislatures have been extremely slow in responding to the challenge.
- Schools alone cannot bear the burden of providing educational service. Many other agencies must be involved.
- Financing of schools and other educational services in most metropolitan areas, especially in core cities, has been quite inadequate.
- The resources of the metropolitan area must be utilized in the interest of the children of the area to a much greater extent than is usual.
- Accountability, more adequate management, efficiency, and effectiveness must be strengthened.
- Development and evaluation are essential areas which must receive greatly increased attention.
- Decentralization should be sought within the big city and within a metropolitan framework. In the finance area, *"the guiding principle is to allow a maximum of control over, and responsibility for, expenditures at the local or building level while using the central or regional level for revenue raising and perhaps certain special services."*[15] Somewhat similar guiding principles can be developed for areas such as curriculum and instruction.
- Considerable tension may be expected as issues are worked through regarding the roles of the central unit and its bureaucracy, the new local units, the teaching staff, and the communities which seek to participate in a substantial manner. This tension may well be the basis upon which a new and vital structure and operating system may be developed.

Is the metropolitan area governable? Can it govern itself in educational matters? If so, how?

[15] John W. Polley, "Improving Provisions for Organization, Housing, Financial Support and Accountability," in Edgar L. Morphet, David L. Jesser, and Arthur P. Ludka, eds., *Revitalizing Education in the Big Cities,* p. 75.

What Form of Decentralization of the Large City System Will Most Likely Facilitate Balancing of Roles of the Professionals with Parent and Community Participation?

Experience in recent years suggests that political decentralization is more promising than administrative decentralization if some shift in power is sought. Some shift in power may be essential if the underlying alienation is to be countered and if participation is to have much significance. It must also be recognized that the turn to administrative decentralization may be in part an attempt to avoid the demand for political decentralization. Certainly political decentralization is generally more threatening to a bureaucracy than is administrative decentralization. Political decentralization calls for greater change, for greater mutual understanding and trust, and for a higher level of creativity. These facts also may support moves toward administrative decentralization rather than political.

If decentralization is sought which goes beyond "administrative restructuring,"[16] in what manner, to what extent, and with what community participation can this be sought? What are the values of administrative decentralization? How can administrative decentralization be employed effectively?

SELECTED REFERENCES

ALTSHULER, ALAN A., *Community Control: The Black Demand for Participation in Large American Cities.* Indianapolis: Pegasus, 1970.

BOLLENS, JOHN C. and HENRY J. SCHMANDT, *The Metropolis: Its People, Politics and Economic Life.* New York: Harper & Row, Publishers, 1965.

Committee for Economic Development, *Reshaping Government in Metropolitan Areas.* New York: The Committee, 1970.

Curriculum Essays on Citizens, Politics and Administration in Urban Neighborhoods, Public Administration Review, Vol. XXXII, Special Issue, October 1972.

MERANTO, PHILIP, *School Politics in the Metropolis.* Columbus, Ohio: Charles E. Merrill, 1970.

MORPHET, EDGAR L., DAVID L. JESSER, and ARTHUR P. LUDKA, eds., *Revitalizing Education in the Big Cities.* Denver, Colorado: Improving State Leadership in Education, 1972.

[16]Marilyn Gittell, "Decentralization and Citizen Participation in Education," in *Curriculum Essays on Citizens, Politics and Administration in Urban Neighborhoods,* (*Public Administrative Review,* Vol. XXXII, Special Issue, October 1972), p. 682.

National Society for the Study of Education, *Metropolitanism, Its Challenge to Education.* Chicago: University of Chicago Press, 67th Yearbook, Part I, 1968.

RHODES, GERALD, Ed., *The New Government of London: The First Five Years.* London: Weidenfeld and Nicolson, 1972.

WALSH, ANNAMARIE HAUCK, *The Urban Challenge to Government.* New York: Frederick A. Praeger, 1969.

13

The Administration of the Community Education Center*

It is not possible to know whether the present turmoil in public school education is transitory, evolutionary, or revolutionary in nature. Within this context of turmoil, there are two trends which make the individual school an incipient community education center. First is the trend to extend education below the age of five-and-a-half and above the age of 18, so that the school could become an educational center for everyone. Second is the increasing participation of members of the community in assessing the educational needs of their children; in questioning the curricula and instructional strategies used to meet those needs; in demanding educational options or alternatives to what they see as the traditional type of schools; and in becoming actively involved in the school's activities as volunteers, paid aides, critics, supporters, learners,

*Prepared in large part by JOHN P. MATLIN, Assistant Dean, School of Education, University of California, Berkeley.

teachers, and change agents. The future of the public school has contradictory potential directions; on the one hand the school could become the intellectual center and educational catalyst of the community; on the other, it could endure profound crises endangering its very survival. Whatever the future, there is no doubt that the community school center, as the operating unit of the school system and the critical component which produces the educational services, is in sharp public focus.

Other chapters in this book give major emphasis primarily to the suprasystems of the school center. However, the basic function of the superstructure of board of education, superintendent, and his central staff is to provide the facilities, staff, and services that should facilitate the production of educational services at the school center. But a study of the area of the administration of the school center shows little agreement in either policy or theory as judged both by prevailing practices and by the growing body of literature critical of public schools. There are many reasons why this is true; some reasons stem from the historical development of the public schools while other reasons lie in the current social context.

Our schools started on an extremely decentralized basis. Even in city systems, during the first half of the nineteenth century the school center was usually a ward school governed by ward trustees. It was not until shortly before the middle of the nineteenth century that the practice of giving citywide boards responsibility for the schools of a city was initiated. At about this same time, these boards began the practice of employing a professional superintendent to administer the schools. By the middle of the twentieth century, the large majority of public school pupils attended school in multiple-school districts. Rural schools emerged in much the same way. These schools originally were typically one-teacher schools governed by local trustees. In most states, rural schools were largely reorganized during the first half of the twentieth century. The number of one-teacher schools in the country diminished from 196,037 in 1917-18 to only 4,146 in 1967-68.[1]

These trends can properly be described as trends in the direction of centralization of the administration, supervision, and financing of public schools. As recently as 1967 it seemed that the advantages of centralization of local school systems had been demonstrated and that we could expect this plan to continue. But there is growing evidence that the local school community members have seen centralization as a loss to themselves of control of their community school center, as an assumption by the professional educators of all aspects of educational decision making and instructional implementation, and as an alienation of the school and its staff from the community. There has grown a thrust toward decentralization, com-

[1] NEA, *Research Bulletin* (Vol. 49, No. 2, May 1971), p. 53.

munity control, and community participation. Decentralization includes the delegation by central authority to subunits of the local school system of functional responsibility and some decision making. Community control implies the assumption by elected community representatives of decision making and responsibility concerning the educational program and the expenditure of money for a school or group of schools. Community participation implies formal and systematic methods to involve members of the school community in advising and assisting in the decision-making process on the local school level. There is evidence that many large school districts are moving in one or all these areas.[2]

The position of school principal changed as the schools moved from a basis of decentralization to one of centralization. One-teacher schools required no principal. As small multiple-teacher schools were formed, one teacher was named head teacher. As these multiple-teacher schools grew larger, the practice of employing nonteaching principals emerged. When school districts were small, the duties of principal and superintendent were discharged by the same person. As multiple-school districts were formed, it became necessary to employ principals for multiple-teacher schools and superintendents for multiple-school districts. Thus two major types of school executives have evolved in the American school system, the executive of the individual school and the executive of the administrative district. However, it should not be assumed that all schools in the United States are organized according to this pattern. Actually, almost every stage of the evolution of the organization of American education is still found in existence somewhere in the nation, although observers on the national level are also impressed by the remarkable uniformity found in the classroom atmosphere and educational environment of the American public schools.

The primary purposes of this chapter are to explore and describe the decision-making roles of the community school center; the relationships of the school principal to the central administration, to the school staff, to the students, and to the community; and the problems and issues which apparently are vitally affecting these relationships. This exploration and description will be conducted partially in the context of some major concepts which have been developed in the study of organization and administration; partially in the context of the organizational structure of the individual school; and partially in the context of current phenomena relating to the public schools.

[2]NEA, *Research Bulletin* (Vol. 48, No. 1, March 1970), pp. 3–7.

THE DECISION-MAKING ROLES
OF THE COMMUNITY SCHOOL CENTER

The decision-making role of the school center is determined largely by the board and the superintendent although increasingly the school staff and the community are also affecting that role. This determination by the board, superintendent, staff, and community is based on the theories of administration and organization accepted and the assumptions that are made in accord with them. These theories usually are not formally stated; nevertheless, especially the policies of the board and the actions of the superintendent reveal concepts of theory, either stated or unstated.[3] Some emerging theories of modern administration are described in Chapter 4. That these theories are not universally accepted is clearly revealed by wide divergence in the roles assigned to school centers in different school systems; that they are not widely implemented is evident in the mounting criticism of the operation of the local school center.

Silberman contrasted the role of the British headmaster or head teacher with that of his American counterpart. He found that, "Once appointed, a head has almost complete autonomy over his school's organization, time-table, and curriculum," whereas "No American principal experiences that degree of independence."[4] In some school systems, the area of decision making assigned to individual schools is very narrow. The rules and regulations of the board with respect to individual school administration are written in great detail. The course of study for each grade level and the curriculum generally also are prescribed in great detail. The principal in such systems usually has little to do with the appointment of either instructional or noninstructional personnel and he must seek the approval of the superintendent on all but the most trivial matters. He and his faculty often have little opportunity for leadership.

It is also necessary to differentiate between the extent of decision making which is assigned to elementary and secondary school principals. A stratified sample of 300 elementary principals drawn from all states was surveyed for their opinions concerning a number of areas in educational administration.[5] The study concluded that the elementary principals believed they were increasingly being isolated from involvement in group decision making that affected leadership and the operation of their schools. They believed they had little or no opportunity to participate in district-

---

[3] Arthur R. Coladarci and Jacob W. Getzels, *The Use of Theory in Educational Administration* (Stanford: Stanford University Press, 1955), pp. 4–8.
[4] Charles E. Silberman, *Crisis in the Classroom* (New York: Vintage Books, 1970), p. 273.
[5] Keith Goldhammer, *et al., Elementary School Principals and Their Schools* (Eugene: University of Oregon Press, 1971), pp. 4–5.

wide decision-making processes and had become just one more subadministrator as school districts increased in size. They also believed that in addition to being generally the lowest paid administrative personnel in the school district they also did not have the independence in the operation of their schools which the secondary school principals had.

In contrast with the school systems that exercise rigid control over the educational activities of individual schools, there are other school systems that give school centers a considerable degree of freedom in decision making. Following are some of the characteristics of the school systems that fix important responsibilities on school centers:

- Board actions with respect to the education program are expressed in terms of broad policies and objectives rather than in terms of detailed specific regulations.
- The principal and his staff are expected to take the primary responsibility for the development of the educational program at the school center.
- The principal, in accordance with policies approved by the board, recommends to the superintendent for appointment all personnel, both instructional and noninstructional, employed at the school he administers. This does not mean that the principal should have complete autonomy in the matter of appointments. All persons recommended for appointment by the principal should meet the qualifications set forth in board policies. Further, especially in large systems, the principal cannot possibly do all the necessary recruiting. These systems normally establish a personnel department. This department usually conducts initial interviews, obtains records of college training and experience, writes for recommendations, and performs such other services required to provide a roster of qualified personnel available for appointment.
- Representatives from the principals, teachers, the central staff, and others advise with the superintendent concerning any regulations of systemwide application before he presents such regulations to the board for adoption.
- The budget is based on an educational plan, but that plan is not developed exclusively by the superintendent and his central staff. The overall educational plan is based on an analysis of the educational needs at each individual school center. Therefore, the principal and his staff at each school are given important responsibilities for participating in developing the educational plan upon which the budget is based. The principal and his staff are expected to work closely with the citizens of their school community in developing the educational plan.

Elsewhere in this book, attention is directed to the fact that one of the most important problems of educational administration is the determination of the appropriate level of government at which a particular decision should be made. Education is a state responsibility; therefore, the legislature has extremely broad powers with respect to public education. Sometimes legislatures exercise those powers unwisely by enacting too many specific laws regulating the curriculum. Laws or regulations of the state board of education that are too detailed and specific with respect to the curriculum sometimes handicap local school systems and individual schools. As pointed out, boards of education sometimes handicap individual schools by rigid rules and regulations.

However, the development of education depends on more than adequate financing, administrative efficiency, and the elegance of organizational structure. Development implies change but change does not always mean evolution or growth. Dozens of theories of learning and methods of teaching and curriculum organization are being advocated vigorously by their proponents. But most inventions originate outside a given school system.[6] Changes in a school system and in the school center are usually adoptions or adaptations of innovations. If the school program at the operating level of the school center would change in accordance with the needs of the times, then not only must the central administration give the school center the freedom to change but it must also stimulate and encourage desirable change.

There is reason to be pessimistic about the innovations which have been proposed in the last decade, the theoretical framework of those innovations, and the changes initiated by central administration and by school centers. The decade of the sixties saw many innovations stimulated by federal and private foundation money, but there is increasing evidence that little change has taken place as a result of the millions of dollars invested in the school systems. Does this mean that the emerging theories of administration, organization, leadership, and cooperative action described elsewhere in this book as well as the procedures suggested have not been adequately understood or used? Does the school center only need greater freedom and the possibility of more productive initiative than now prevails in many large centralized school systems? There is still much work to be done by the organizational theorist in education. Related severe problems for the practicing educational administrator remain. For example, in the psychology of administration there are limited data on the thought processes of educational administrators and the significance of those thought processes for later decisions.[7]

THE PRINCIPAL

The possible roles for both elementary and secondary school principals are determined largely by the principal's perceptions of those roles, by the roles assigned by the central administration, and by the perceptions of the principal's roles as held by the school staff and local school commu-

[6]Matthew B. Miles, ed., *Innovation in Education* (New York: Bureau of Publications, Teachers College, Columbia University, 1964), p. 640.
[7]Louis M. Smith and Pat M. Keith, *Anatomy of Educational Innovation: An Organizational Analysis of an Elementary School* (New York: John Wiley & Sons, Inc., 1971), pp. 238–239.

nity. The principal and the staff are expected to develop and administer the educational program at the school center within the broad framework of policy established by the people through the legislature and their local board of education. However, the implications of this charge for the roles of the principal are still not resolved. Is the principal mainly an administrative manager or an institutional leader; an implementer of educational policies or a leader in education? Although the preceding questions are of great concern to theorists as well as practitioners in educational administration, it is not clear whether the answers are being sought in the area of theory and research or in the area of philosophy and educational ethics.

Answers have been sought to the related question of the specific competencies that are needed by principals. This question was explored during the 1950s by comparing the competencies needed by principals, superintendents, and supervisors of instruction. Woodard made an extensive study of competencies needed by these three groups.[8] He reviewed the professional literature and identified 203 competencies as essential for superintendents, principals, or supervisors. Of these 203 competencies, 188 were listed as essential for the superintendent, 171 as essential for the principal, and 163 as essential for the supervisor. But he found that 70 percent of these competencies were common to all three types of positions. Furthermore, he found that 84 percent of the competencies listed as essential for the principal were also listed as essential for the supervisor. The major differences in competencies needed according to the professional literature are as follows:

- Superintendents need a greater knowledge of finance, buildings, public administration, and how to work with the board than do the principals or supervisors.
- Supervisors need to know more about curriculum and supervising teachers than do superintendents.

Woodard also selected juries of superintendents, principals, supervisors, and professors of administration to identify the competencies needed for each position. The findings derived from the jury studies were practically identical with the findings derived from the study of the professional literature.

Several conclusions were drawn from this and similar studies. One conclusion was that although there were some important differences between the job of the superintendent and the job of the principal, the differences in the nature of the critical tasks performed were not great.

---

[8]Prince B. Woodard, "A Study of Competencies Needed by School Administrators and Supervisors in Virginia with Implications for Pre-Service Education" (Doctoral dissertation, CPEA Project, University of Virginia, 1953).

Another was that the philosophical concept of "responsible educational executive" in conjunction with concepts from modern theories of organization, administration, leadership, and cooperative action, implied that the preservice training program for principals should include many of the same features included in the preparation programs for superintendents. A further conclusion was that since principals often became superintendents or were given important executive and leadership responsibilities in large school districts they should be competent to discharge those responsibilities, and this competence implied similar training. The conclusions thus seemed to focus upon the area of similarities without considering that the area of differences might be crucial to the performance competencies of the principals.

There is evidence that preparatory programs for principals are inadequate; that they do not differentiate between the superintendency and the secondary and elementary school principalships; that generalized preparation programs are provided which are based upon the advance of administrators through the ranks and hence which emphasize the terminal job rather than the intermediate jobs; and that there is little consideration given to experiences which might develop knowledge, skills, and critical insights in the prospective principals.[9] Although the study cited dealt mainly with the elementary principalship, it included comparisons with the secondary principalship and has implications for the latter.

A recent study reported by Daniel E. Griffiths[10] indicates the need for considering further the competencies needed by the principal and the matters which his preservice training should include. Four elementary schools were selected on the basis of whether they had an open or closed organizational climate and a high or low socioeconomic setting. Each of the four principals' offices was videotaped for fourteen days, six-and-a-half hours daily. An analysis was then made of the problems recorded in terms of frequency, types, and the initiators of the problems. One startling finding was that a total of 12,062 problems, each with an initiator, was derived from the videotapes. Griffiths concluded that this sheer weight of problems indicated the need for a principal's office with a completely different form as well as the need for training which would prepare the principal for this incomprehensible task. Was this finding unique to the four elementary schools studied or to just the elementary principalship? Are the numbers of problems and initiators of problems growing, particularly in urban schools? How does the principal perform his other tasks and exert educational leadership in the face of the magnitude of the problems?

[9]Goldhammer, *Elementary School Principals,* p. 7.
[10]Daniel E. Griffiths, "What Happens in the Principal's Office?" (*UCEA Newsletter,* Vol. XIV, No. 1, October, 1972), pp. 4–7.

Some writers in the field of secondary school administration are concerned that many secondary school administrators are projecting a low-level image of their profession because they are concerned with organizational management and maintenance rather than with educational and institutional leadership. Secondary school principals are said to be neglecting their role of instructional leader if they spend most of their time on the relations of students and teachers, reports, schedules, athletic events, and the like. Secondary principals are caught in the same context of reality as the elementary principals as indicated above, and the definitions of their required competencies and preservice training should reflect that reality. If the preceding is the context of reality for the principal how will educational leadership be provided in the community school center? The new position in some school districts of "Educational Leader," a position superior to the high school principal in authority and status, may be an indicator of one solution to the need for educational leadership as well as for administrative management.

RELATIONSHIP OF THE PRINCIPAL TO THE CENTRAL STAFF

Reference has already been made to the fact that an executive in the line organization is in a position of potential role conflict because he is under pressure from his superordinates to attain the goals of the organization and he is under pressure from his subordinates to assist them in attaining their individual goals. The principal holds a position in the line organization which is vulnerable to this type of role conflict because he is closest to the teachers. In fact, he frequently is perceived by the teachers as a leader in the informal organization as well as the holder of status in the hierarchy. This enhances the leadership potential of the principal. But when the teachers expect the principal to express their norms, sentiments, and needs, even when they are not congruent with organizational purposes, he is placed in a situation of role conflict which can be dysfunctional as well as personally painful.

Another potential source of conflict is lack of clear definition of the role of the principal in relation to the central staff. The relationship of the principal to the central staff of the school system should be clearly defined and understood by all parties concerned. The nature of that relationship varies in different school systems, as has been pointed out above. In school systems that provide a considerable degree of freedom for school centers and that expect the principal to be a real rather than a nominal leader, the relationships are somewhat as follows:

- Lines of communication between the principal and the superintendent are direct rather than circuitous. District superintendents or supervising principals who serve as line officers between the superintendent and the building principal sometimes retard action rather than facilitate it. In large school systems, the superintendent will have deputy or assistant superintendents who may serve as line officers for certain matters. The operating arrangements should be so designed that these officers facilitate rather than retard the development and operation of the educational program.
- There is direct functional communication between the principal and the business office, the maintenance department, the central film library, and similar central services where the matters concerned are within the established policy or within the budget for that school. On matters outside the budget or established policy, the principal communicates with the superintendent or his designated representative, and he does not act without approval.
- The principal is recognized by the central staff as the executive head of the school he administers.
- No one from the central staff has direct control over the employees at a school. The principal has that responsibility.
- The principal and not the supervisory staff of the central office is administratively responsible for the educational program of the school he administers. The supervisory staff of the central office are staff officers and not line officers. Therefore, they act in an advisory rather than administrative capacity.
- The principal is responsible for executing board policies at his school center. If he does not believe that a particular policy is sound he has the right and the responsibility to seek a change in policy. However, until the policy is changed he either executes it or resigns from his position.
- The board of education does not adopt a policy or educational program until it has been carefully studied. Such studies should involve principals, teachers, lay citizens, and others when appropriate.
- The relationship between the principal and the central staff is friendly and cooperative. The principal is not an isolate but rather a member of a team that has the characteristic of an effective group.

This may seem a somewhat formal statement of relationships. There is considerable evidence that some of the relationships described are not commonly accepted. Elementary principals feel imposed upon by the demands of central-staff personnel and are uncertain of their relative position with respect to the teachers in their schools and in the district administrative structure. They feel unjustly left out of contract negotiations that determine their obligations to their teaching staff and, perhaps most critically, see their positions in the educational community as being generally ambiguous.[11] In the fourth ten-year survey[12] the Department of Elementary School Principals found that the percentage of supervising principals who believed that their central offices looked upon them as leaders dropped from 59 percent in 1958 to 55 percent in 1968, while those who

[11] Goldhammer, *Elementary School Principals*, pp. 4–6, 21–23.
[12] Department of Elementary School Principals, NEA, *The Elementary School Principalship in 1968* (Washington, D.C.: DESP, NEA, 1968), pp. 54, 143.

thought that the central office looked primarily upon them as supporters rose from 39 percent in 1958 to 41 percent in 1968, and as followers from 2 percent to 4 percent in the same decade.

Are elementary principals discriminated against and do secondary principals enjoy a better relationship with the central office? Although secondary school principals are also criticized for being administrative managers rather than institutional leaders, do they see themselves as being more autonomous and as members of the school-district team?

ORGANIZING THE STAFF

The organizational structure of the community school center is influenced by a number of factors, including the size of the school, the available facilities, the goals of the school, the variety of programs, the school level, the community involvement, and the organization of the program. As schools become larger the organizational structure becomes more complex and more critical in carrying out the educational functions. Elementary schools of 600 to 800 pupils, junior high or intermediate schools of 1,000 to 1,500 pupils, and senior high schools of 1,200 to 2,000 pupils have become common in urban and suburban areas. Much larger schools are found in many school systems.

Size is not the only factor creating organizational problems. A wide variety of types of grade organization is found in the public schools. A 1,000-pupil senior high school presents very different organizational problems than does a 1,000-pupil school including grades 1–12 or a 1,000-pupil school including only grades 4–6. The type of facilities available is also important in determining the organizational structure. A high school with traditional facilities has organizational possibilities different from a high school which uses the community resources and has multisized instructional spaces, instructional materials centers, learning laboratories, banks of automated instructional devices, or movable walls. Elementary school facilities have similar implications for organizational structure.

The local school staff can be roughly classified as follows: (1) the instructional staff, (2) the clerical and secretarial staff, (3) the custodial staff, and (4) the lunchroom staff. The instructional staff in a large elementary or high school may include the following types of instructional personnel: regular classroom teachers with many specializations, teachers of exceptional children, resource teachers, adult education teachers, itinerant teachers, assistant principals, curriculum consultants, administrative assistants, deans, counselors, librarians, psychologists, teacher and community aides, coordinators of community resources, and physiotherapists. This staff reflects the variety of programs found in the school as well as the goals of the school.

There are a number of variations in the way the work may be divided for administering an elementary school. One teacher may teach children in two or three grade levels in a small school, while in a large school there may be a number of sections at each grade level or each teacher may have a multigraded or multiaged classroom, similar to that in the smaller school. The elementary school may be organized on a self-contained classroom basis, a departmental basis, a team teaching basis, a learning center basis, an upgraded basis or some other basis. During the decade of the 1960s it was believed that a considerable number of innovations and new concepts were being developed and introduced.

Surveys of actual operations of the elementary public schools do not indicate the realization of the expectations listed above. One such survey was made of 158 classrooms of 67 schools in 26 school districts in the major cities of 13 states in a nationwide geographic spread.[13] Classrooms were observed and teachers interviewed on the K–3 level in schools that were considered to be average, special, or innovative, and some with a large proportion of environmentally disadvantaged children. In general, the data for the three different types of schools presented the same configurations. It was found that in spite of claims to innovations, such as nongrading, with very few exceptions the schools and classrooms functioned actually as did traditionally graded classrooms. Where team teaching was claimed —as it was by a substantial number of schools—only occasional instances of team planning and other team activities were actually found. The study found that almost all the schools observed a course of bland uniformity regardless of school setting or pupil population. Are elementary schools actually organized and operating in a large variety of ways?

Large high schools are commonly organized on a departmental basis, each subject area making up a department. This plan has the advantage of providing for vertical articulation of subject matter but it does not facilitate interdisciplinary coordination. This type of organization has sometimes developed into a monocratic bureaucracy. There are hopes that the high school of the future will move from rigid mass instructional practices to provisions for individual differences among learners such as independent study, individual library research, self-instruction with autoinstructional devices, vertical and horizontal enrichment, large-group and small-group teaching, programmed materials, new instructional materials and media, and many others. However, it is too soon to make a survey of the spread

---

[13]John I. Goodlad, M. Frances Klein, and Associates, *Behind The Classroom Door* (Worthington, Ohio: Charles A. Jones Publishing Company, 1970), pp. 33–34, 39, 86–87.

of such practices in the high schools since they are still mainly in the process of discussion. There is no specific plan of organization that is useful for all types of schools. The principal and the staff at each school should have the freedom to develop the particular plan of organization that best meets the needs of that school.

WORKING WITH THE STAFF

The organizational plan lays the basis for the procedures by which the principal works with his staff, both instructional and noninstructional. Ideally, all members of the staff would participate in the development of the plan of organization. No better method of achieving acceptance and understanding has been devised than the method of participation.

One of the major differences between a school that is a monocratic bureaucracy and a school that is characterized by collegial pluralism is observable in faculty meetings. Following are some of the characteristics of faculty meetings in the latter type of school:

- Faculty members and not the principal usually preside at meetings. The principal is the chief executive officer of the faculty but that responsibility does not require that he preside at all meetings.
- The agenda is prepared by a committee of the faculty. The principal has the same right as other members of the faculty to place matters on the agenda.
- The major amount of time at faculty meetings is spent on program development and policy formation, and only a minor portion of time is spent on announcements and routine matters.
- Ad hoc study committees frequently make reports to the faculty on matters being considered.
- The principal participates in faculty discussion on a peer basis with other members of the faculty.
- The faculty strives to reach consensus before taking action.
- The faculty considers the recommendations on appropriate matters from the parent-teacher association, citizens' committees, and student groups before taking action.
- When the faculty is making decisions on matters involving noninstructional employees, those employees are involved in the decision-making process.
- The principal does not veto actions of his faculty unless the actions are in conflict with state law or with the regulations of the board. The principal should avoid having to make this type of veto by making clear to the faculty the limits of their decision-making authority. There is nothing more frustrating to a faculty than to be invited to make a decision on a matter and then be advised later that the faculty did not have the authority to make the decision.

A survey of the effectiveness of faculty meetings made in 1971[14] found that 19.2 percent of the elementary teachers and 27.1 percent of the

[14] NEA, *Research Bulletin* (Vol. 49, No. 4, December 1971), p. 106.

secondary teachers indicated that the effectiveness of faculty meetings was a major problem. This contrasted with 16.1 percent of the elementary teachers and 24.2 percent of the secondary teachers who had the same opinion in 1968.

In addition to the characteristics of the faculty meeting, there are other major differences of schools that are moving from monocratic bureaucracy. The creation of a faculty senate has been useful in some schools where the concept of collegial pluralism has been interpreted to include the yielding of some power to various members of the teaching staff although the principal still retains the responsibility with regard to the school. The use of this type of senate is particularly being explored in schools experimenting with new staffing patterns such as team teaching and differentiated staffing.

Further characteristics of a school organized to promote collegial pluralism may include the provision of some type of grievance machinery, particularly for grievances involving such matters as objections to policies set by the principal, department heads or supervisors, staff meetings, assigned duties other than those involving teaching, and methods of evaluating teachers. The preceding and similar characteristics involve the decentralization of authority, the encouragement of staff participation in decision making, the use of small face-to-face groups for planning and communicating, and the creation of an environment supportive of the staff.

THE PRINCIPAL AS INSTRUCTIONAL LEADER

Reference has been made earlier in this chapter to the apparent dichotomy in the principal's role between functioning as an administrative manager and as an instructional leader. But the principal is still mainly regarded as the executive in the line organization at the scene of action and, as such, responsible for the development and implementation of the instructional program at the school. One recurring question is the type of instructional leadership the principal can provide to the teachers who are more expert than he in their particular subject areas.

Gross and Herriott directed a carefully designed research project which explored the effect of the educational leadership of elementary school principals.[15] These researchers found a positive relationship between the amount of professional leadership provided by elementary principals and staff morale, the professional performance of teachers, and the

---

[15]Neal Gross and Robert E. Herriott, *Staff Leadership in Public Schools: A Sociological Inquiry* (New York: John Wiley & Sons, Inc., 1965).

pupils' learning. They also found that the stronger the professional leadership provided by the principal's immediate superior, the greater the professional leadership of the principal. Although this study was confined to elementary principals, it seems reasonable to hypothesize that the findings are also applicable to high school principals.

While it is true that a principal cannot be a technical consultant in each subject matter area taught in the school, he can be a change agent by bringing proposals to the attention of the staff and by encouraging them to plan and experiment with innovations. The principal is also in a strategic position to prevent change. Some principals are seen as staunch defenders of the status quo and the schools they administer are more like "closed, dead systems" than "open, living systems." Some theorists of modern administration believe that the very fact that administrators are concerned primarily with the attainment of established organizational objectives makes it unrealistic to expect them to be innovative. Rather, under this theory it is realistic to expect administrators to prefer stability within the organization and to be lethargic in their attempts to change overall organizational policies. Educational changes would not originate from administrative action but would come from outside the school center.

One resolution of the apparent dichotomy between administrative and instructional leadership roles may lie in the environment of the community school center established by the principal and the manner in which he implements those roles. The principal can support an innovative atmosphere in the school center by using the services of competent instructional supervisors at the system level, by engaging outside consultants with central staff support, by seeking aid in developing extensive in-service training programs for his staff and for himself, and by taking sabbatical leave for advanced study. Fundamental, of course, is the identification and encouragement of the utilization of the many and varied talents of the teaching staff. Principals will be more effective in supervision if they develop the necessary skills and knowledge to build adequate supervisory programs; they will spend more time in program planning and evaluation if they acquire the skills and knowledge to get teachers involved and to accept the results of such planning.

WORKING WITH STUDENTS

If the principal and his staff accept the collegial, pluralistic theories of administration and organization, that commitment must also include students. The teacher is an administrator of instruction in the classroom. the teacher who insists on democracy for himself and is an autocrat with his students is in a strangely inconsistent position. If we accept "education for living in a democracy" as one of the valid purposes of our educational program, then life in the school should provide experiences in democratic living. Those experiences should be provided in the classroom, on the playground, in the principal's office and, in fact, in all phases of school life.

John Walton points out the ambiguous organizational role of students.[16] It is not clear whether they are members of the school center or are customers and clients. The students are not on the payroll; yet, unlike customers, they are required to spend much of their lives in attendance, analogous organizationally to hospital patients, prison inmates, and residents of homes for the aged. There are serious questions about the right of students to participate in academic and management affairs, with increasing evidence that students, particularly in the high schools and junior high schools, are groping with the same questions. There is also indication that students are seeking continually greater involvement in their school center's functioning. The principal and the staff need to make that involvement relevant and knowledgeable.

The ability of students to participate effectively in decision making is frequently underestimated by both teachers and parents. It is often assumed that students cannot participate wisely in decision making until they are fairly mature. But skillful teachers make extensive use of pupil-teacher planning even in the kindergarten. These experiences develop the leadership competencies of students and maximize the conditions for effective learning. They also minimize discipline problems. As students grow in their ability to solve problems and make decisions, they develop competency to participate in many phases of classroom management.

There are many school programs and policies that affect students so directly that they should share in the development of those programs and policies. Some examples are extracurricular activities, school discipline, class and club activities, and similar activities. Many schools have had long and successful experiences with student participation in school government, student councils, student advisory committees, and similar means for student participation in decision making. Students not only participate in planning but frequently administer or participate in the administration of many activities. The basic question that the principal must face in these activities is concerned with whether they are real or contrived.

WAYS OF WORKING WITH THE COMMUNITY

The relationships of the school center to its community formed the basis for the opening paragraph of this chapter and for the conclusion that the school center has the potential for becoming the intellectual center and

[16]John Walton, *Introduction to Education: A Substantive Discipline* (Waltham, Massachusetts: Xerox College Publishing, 1971), pp. 135–138.

educational catalyst of the community. Recent literature on the public school, the community, and community education seems to imply different, important ways for the principal and the staff to work with the community in addition to those traditionally described if the potential for leadership is to be realized.

The way the principal and staff work with the community not only vitally affects the educational program of the school but also has a major influence on the entire school system. Henderson studied school-community relationships in 48 school centers all within one large school system.[17] He found that the quality of school-community relationships improved as principals increased their use of procedures that involved other people in decision making. Community differences in educational level and income were held constant in this study. Henderson found that community attitudes toward the superintendent, the board, and the central staff were affected by the working patterns of principals as well as by community attitudes toward the local school.

One traditional way the principal has worked with the community is implied in the concept of school public relations. This concept emphasizes the "selling" of the school to the community by telling people about the school, bringing parents into the schools, correcting misunderstandings about the aims and activities of the school, and providing other means to develop support for the educational program. The many possibilities for involving the community under this concept include school visiting days for parents, open house programs, sports activities, individual parent-teacher conferences, educational trips to community industries and agencies, the use of the community as resource persons, and many similar activities.

The principal who works well with the community does not neglect publicity. He and his staff make good use of the mass media of communication such as newspapers, the radio, and television. Newsletters and school publications are widely distributed. Not only the principal but members of the staff speak to community groups when requested. The public is interested in school news, both favorable and unfavorable, because it wants to know the whole story. Therefore, school publicity should be honest. The community that really understands its schools will usually cooperate with the principal and the faculty in remedying unfavorable conditions.

The principal who achieves the best community relations uses cooperative procedures whenever and wherever practicable, as described in

[17] Lee G. Henderson, "A Study of Certain School-Community Relationships with Special Reference to Working Patterns of School Principals" (Doctoral dissertation, CPEA Project, University of Florida, 1954).

Chapter 6. Many community groups are ready and willing to cooperate with the principal if given a chance. The parent-teacher association is one of the oldest and has one of the most distinguished records of service. Numerous civic groups, labor organizations, professional groups, governmental agencies, and many private citizens who do not have children in school are able and willing to participate cooperatively in the development of an adequate educational program. In recent years citizens' advisory committes have made many contributions to improvement of the educational program. These committees tend to cut across all organized groups and are particularly helpful in providing for communitywide participation.

But there is a mounting feeling in many communities that the preceding approach provides an information flow which has been primarily one way. There is dissatisfaction with the public school as it functions today and with the community involvement invited by the school as being superficial. The challenge is seen as asking the schools to discharge their responsibilities more effectively, to extend their traditional services not only to the student population but also to all members of the community, and to expand their activities to the identification of community problems and participation in the solutions to those problems.[18] Often the community members demand rather than request that changes be made in their school and the tactics of confrontation are used.

The principal working in the community climate described above will have to augment the traditional ways of working with the community. How will he develop these new understandings, skills, and capacities? Staff members will have to be active in community life and participate in community leadership. Some school districts and some school centers are employing various techniques of "needs assessment" in which the school staff, pupils, and the community join to define the goals of the school and the aspects of the school's programs that they would like to see emphasized. This could well include not only the school program for the children but also the provision of learning experiences for adults and out-of-school youths. It could also include the formation of the school as a true community center in cooperation with other community agencies. Not much is presently known about the nature of the relationships between the school and the community implied in the move from the traditional types of involvement to the community school center but the principal and his staff are being called upon for a new leadership and a new service function in our society.

[18]Jack Minzey, "Community Education: An Amalgam of Many Views" (*Phi Delta Kappan,* Vol. LIV, No. 3, November 1972), pp. 150–153.

SOME IMPORTANT PROBLEMS AND ISSUES

A concomitant of the current turmoil in public school education has been the questioning of and attack upon virtually every phase of the local school operations. The concepts, organizational structure, and current phenomena described in this chapter have reflected what appear to be great social changes, uncertainties, and dissentions. The optimistic applications of even the limited theoretical concepts of the past have not appeared to be congruent with present realities. The projection, just a few years ago, of the rational solution of local organizational problems by the use of research findings and derived general principles has not been validated. The principal and his staff face ever greater problems and issues. There is the belief among some students of public school administration that the future of public school education in America is in serious danger, that there is a great crisis of educational leadership, and that the position of the principal, itself, is in danger.

Some of these problems and issues are discussed in the following pages. Since many of these problems and issues are in the process of developing, some of those omitted will prove to be as vital as those selected, while the unforeseen effects of those discussed may prove to be quite different from how they now appear.

How Will the Role of the Principal Be Defined?

Perhaps the most critical problem faced by the principal today is the general ambiguity of his position. This ambiguity goes beyond the question of whether the principal is an administrative manager or an instructional leader. A solution proposed to clear this ambiguity is that criteria be developed that will define the principal's role explicitly, that the principal be trained to carry out that defined role, and that the principal be given the assistance needed to carry out modern, effective, instructional programs. However, this same source points out that administrators at all levels have the problem of lacking knowledge and techniques for dealing with major social issues, the complex human and organizational relationships within the school systems and the community, and the complexities of educational technology.[19] Who, then, has the knowledge and competency to define the principal's role? When it is further realized that the social issues, the complex relationships, and modern technology, themselves, are in the process of formation and emergence, it can be seen that the task of defining the principal's role is not a simple one of definition or

[19]Goldhammer, *Elementary School Principals*, pp. 17, 166–172.

of deciding between two general viewpoints. Rather, the principal's role is in the process of definition by many forces. There is the further complicating factor that although leadership is displayed within a group, with the various limitations imposed by the group and by the circumstances, there are personal characteristics held in common by those principals who are, in fact, leaders in their schools. Thus it cannot be said what the role of the principal will be but rather what the various trends are and what their implication seems to be for the principal.

How Will Collective Negotiations Help to Define the Principal's Role?

A nationwide survey of school systems enrolling 1,000 pupils or more in 1967–1968, found that 909,976 instructional personnel in 2,212 school systems were represented in negotiation agreements or precedures.[20] The number involved has continued to grow sharply. Items that have been negotiated cover a broad range of subjects including student-teaching programs, student discipline, teacher lunch periods, academic freedom, evaluation of teaching competence, involvement in decision making, and formal grievance procedures. Teacher strikes as a phase of collective negotiations are now so widely used and publicized that it is not necessary to document their occurrence.

These negotiations are generally conducted between the school board and the central office staff on the one side and the teacher organizations on the other side. The principal tends to be excluded from the first group for several reasons, including his distance from the central office, particularly in large school districts, the frequent need for quick action, and the desire of teacher groups to negotiate with top management. The principal tends to be excluded from teacher organizations in their negotiations also for several reasons, including state statutes, ruling of labor and other public boards, and at the preference of some local teachers organizations.

Yet the principal represents middle management, which means he represents the top management (the central office and the school board) in his school. He finds that he must interpret and carry out contractual obligations decided around a bargaining table from which he was excluded, enforcing policies in which he usually has had no voice nor the chance to react to the agreements reached. Further, the scope of the items negotiated, as listed in the first paragraph of this section, often directly affects the principal's discretion in operating the school and involves a close scrutiny of his management by the teacher organizations.

[20]NEA, *Research Bulletin* (Vol. 46, No. 3, October 1968), pp. 84–87.

What are some implications of collective negotiations as they are being carried on for the definition of the principal's role? The principal will find that his power is being eroded and that he is being exposed to pressures from not only the central office but also the teachers groups and the general public. The principal may seek to form his own distinct bargaining unit, to find a position of influence on the top management negotiating team, or to stay out of the negotiating process and rely upon either the central office or the teachers groups to protect his interests and needs. The principal must also seek to gain skills and understandings of the grievance process so that he does not become bogged down in a flood of petty grievances. An important phase of preservice as well as in-service training for principals should include the mastery of informal and formal grievance procedures, including those techniques already worked out by industry, of day-to-day decision making involving formal and informal rules, of communication regarding the constraints of law and negotiated contracts, and of knowing how to satisfy both the needs of the teachers as individuals and the needs of the school as an educational organization.

What Effects May Decentralization Have on Decision Making at the Community School Center?

The relatively recent emphasis upon decentralization in the local school system, community control, and community participation has been noted. What are the implications of this trend for the local school unit, for the school principal, and for the school staff in addition to those already discussed? The implications will be contingent upon the way in which decentralization is accomplished. If smaller school districts are created within the larger system then the principal may find himself closer to his subdistrict superintendent and more accountable to him. At the same time, there may be a local school council which keeps the parents, staff, and students aware of what is going on in the school and hears appeals by parents, faculty, or students from decisions they consider unfair. It may also exert influence at times of decision making concerning curriculum, personnel selection, and other educational matters as well as exert its influence to employ a principal who meets its standards of leadership.

There will need to be some decentralization also of the decision-making process if the principal is to function in a leadership role under the conditions described above. As middle management the principal will need to carry out central policies, conditions of negotiated written contracts, and the rules and regulations of the district office while at the same time working with the parents of the school and the staff in changing the curriculum and instructional strategies for the students in the local situation. The principal will have to administer the school to fit the demands of the local needs rather than try to fit the local needs to the previously existing school.

The principal will need to have skills and understandings in the areas of greater community participation in decision making in the local school, in the allocation of decision-making powers within the school on a functional basis, in encouraging innovations in accordance with the purposes of decentralization, and in the protection of the interests of all the groups involved. The latter will include protection of the teachers' rights and duties to exercise their professional judgment for what they consider to be the good of the student even though other individuals or groups may disagree. The potential for conflict is great in the principal's role in carrying out the preceding functions among the staff members, students, parents, and other community members, and central office staff at both the district and subdistrict levels. What professional training and personal characteristics will be necessary for the principal and the staff not only to survive but to be effective under decentralization?

What Decentralization of Budgeting Should Be Achieved?

Many questions arise if the district budgeting is decentralized to the local school level. Who will develop the educational program which is central in the budget? How much control will the school center actually have over the total allocation to the school? If most of the budget is already committed to relatively fixed costs such as salaries, fringe benefits, building maintenance, and necessary supplies, what real effects will decentralization have? In central office budgeting, the amount of money available per student is often quite small after the preceding costs have been established. On the other hand, if the community school center will have real control over the determination of the staffing pattern, the curriculum, and the selection and purchase of supplies and equipment, another series of questions is raised. What happens to the legal tenure of teachers, their seniority rights, and their right to positions commensurate with their training? How will budget deficits be handled? What will be the authority of the principal and who will determine the priority of needs?

The principal will need to acquire skills and understandings in at least two major areas if the budget is decentralized. The first area will involve training to handle the shifting of the political focus from the central office to the local school as the budgeting decisions are focused, with added difficulties if there is not a concomitant shift in authority or of adequate resources. The second area will include training in the new role expectations of the principal in planning, projecting, and implementing the school budget as well as training in fiscal management and auditing procedures.

Why Are Different Staff Organizational Patterns Being Sought for the Community School Center?

Teachers seem to be dissatisfied with their positions within the local school hierarchy. They see themselves as being at the bottom of a vertical hierarchy although their educational background and technical competence have become close to or equal to that of the principal and other administrators. Teachers also see that promotion means leaving the area of teaching and going into counseling, administration, supervision, or some other nonteaching job.

It is also apparent that both elementary and secondary teachers have a variety of responsibilities to perform in carrying out their major function of teaching, responsibilities which are beyond the capabilities and available time of any one individual. Many of the duties could be performed by persons who do not require the amount of training a teacher receives. In the performance of those duties these persons might also find a career either in steps along the way or ultimately in a teaching position. There are many persons in the local community who are eager and able to serve in some of the many positions implied in the preceding analysis.

Team teaching is one of the different staff organizational patterns suggested to meet some of the needs expressed above. A staff of teachers, with a team leader, plan and implement instructional programs for a common group of students. A more complex staff organizational pattern than team teaching is present in the concept of differentiated staffing. Differentiated staffing is concerned with the use of school personnel in a variety of assignments different from traditional elementary and secondary school line-staff structures. Rather, a variety of teaching roles are created and organized into a teacher hierarchy with differing job responsibilities and with pay commensurate for the differing positions. The position could include a director of learning, senior teachers, master teachers, associate teachers, interns, student teachers, instructional assistants, paid aides, learner aides, high school aides, and volunteer aides.

Under an innovative staff organizational pattern such as differentiated staffing the principal will find added expectations of himself in working with a variety of persons with different training, perspectives, and job functions. The salary schedule may include teachers who have the same salary scale as does the principal. The principal will need to be able to coordinate the activities of experts as well as the use of resources to be the instructional leader and advocate of change and to carry on the more traditional functions of the school at the same time.

The demands made of the principal under this organizational pattern may be too demanding for any one person, just as the teachers believe that the demands made of them are too great. In at least a few high schools, a new position of Education Leader has been instituted. The Education Leader is the person in charge of the high school; the principal operates under his direction to carry out the administrative functions of the school while the Education Leader acts as the instructional leader in its fullest definition. Will the strong demands upon teachers and principals lead to new staffing patterns and a separation of functions with a new set of positions?

How Should the Attendance Area of a Community School Center Be Determined?

Although the capacity of the plant and the accessibility of pupils to the school have traditionally been the most common determinants of which pupils attend a particular school, these have not been the only determinants. Both *de jure* segregation and *de facto* segregation have existed and have been under legal and political attack. School districts are under pressure to modify local school boundaries to desegregate the schools. At present the use of busing to desegregate the public schools has an uncertain political and legal future.

Where the boundaries of the local neighborhood schools are expanded through the use of busing, open enrollment, or similar practices, what are the implications for the principal, the school staff, and the community? What guidelines and what criteria should be used to admit pupils if not solely on the basis of attendance area? Should parents and pupils also have a choice of teachers or of programs and how should the choice of options be made possible? What happens to the concepts of community control and community participation, or to the concept of the community school center itself, when local school boundaries are no longer used?

What Is the Significance of Some of the Newly Emerging Plans for the Organization of Students?

Recent studies show that young people are reaching puberty at a younger age; are more sophisticated socially than were their parents at a similar age; and are more knowledgeable in some subject matter areas such as science, mathematics, foreign languages, and social studies. Society has changed, the modes of communication have become much more sophisticated, information has mushroomed, and the relationships of children and youth to society are changing. Many observers believe that only the schools seem to remain basically unchanged and that the changes claimed are usually not substantive. Thus children today relate to society in a manner significantly different from just a few years ago but seem to be expected to relate to the public school as they did formerly. At the same time, the decade of the 1960s brought together much work in and information about matters of curriculum and instruction. What are some of the emerging trends in the organization of students which may meet the needs listed above and other societal needs?

The trends in organizational patterns of students may be placed into four categories: (1) the relationships of students to academic and school management affairs, (2) organizational changes within the classroom, (3) organizational changes within the school, and (4) organizational changes among schools. Several questions should be kept in mind as these categories are considered. Who should be involved in developing and evaluating the plan of organization? Should it include only the principal and the staff or should it also include the students, the parents, the community, and outside consultants? What changes in the roles of the principal and the staff are indicated? What will training for those new roles involve?

STUDENTS AND SCHOOL PARTICIPATION. There is evidence that in some high schools the participation of students in the traditional activities such as the student council is being supplemented with more vital participation not usually permitted. Recent surveys[21] show that pupils are being asked to participate in school management and academic matters, such as the formal evaluation of teachers, the organization and teaching of student-requested and -designed minicourses, and the participation on subject-matter advisory committees and curriculum councils. Advisory boards of high school students are being organized to make their problems and suggestions known to the principal. Students are being appointed to districtwide or local school ad hoc committees concerned with various curricular matters, educational goals, and policies relating to students.

CLASSROOM ORGANIZATIONAL CHANGES. Organizational changes within the classroom include a wide variety of patterns, including multiage grouping, learning centers, open classrooms, and other movements toward the individualization of instruction. Children of different ages are placed with one or more teachers with the expectation that the instructional programs will be varied for the children who are at different levels of

---

[21]NEA, *Research Bulletin* (Vol. 49, No. 1, March 1971), pp. 13–16.

maturity and experience. Learning centers involve the establishment within the classroom or adjacent classrooms of areas with a considerable variety of materials and approaches to each subject or learning focus, with children moving from one center to another based upon individual needs, interests, and motivation. Open classrooms are based on the philosophy that the child must be an active agent in his own learning while the school provides the climate and learning environment that supports each child's own development. Other methods of individualizing instruction may include the use of programmed materials, learning laboratories, and automated instructional devices.

These classroom organizational changes have many implications for the selection and training of staff, the placement of pupils, the procurement of appropriate and adequate materials, pupil record keeping, and the education of parents. What are the cost factors involved in these new patterns? Should the school center have a certain minimum number of children and teachers per grade or age group? The new patterns of organization require a great diversity of materials to meet individual needs. What is the optimum size for classes and schools within the new organizations and what factors, other than economic ones, need to be considered? What happens to the traditional patterns of staffing and to the traditional hierarchy of administration?

ORGANIZATIONAL CHANGES WITHIN THE SCHOOL. Organizational changes within the school also include a wide variety of patterns. The concept of "schools-within-a-school" has been developing for many years, particularly for use in very large high schools. A large school is divided into several smaller units, each unit having its own administration, group of students, and staff. A central school principal is head of all the subunits and some personnel may serve several or all of the subunits. Questions raised in this type of organization are concerned with whether pupils will be grouped within the subunits by grade level (horizontally) or in groups representing all grade levels (vertically), with variations in the program offerings, the size of the subunits, and the type of staffing and administration needed. There is further concern for the availability of appropriate facilities and materials, for the assignment of facilities among the subunits, for essential cooperation among the subunits, and for the manner of participation of the local community.

A relatively new interpretation of the "schools-within-a-school" concept has been emerging which is concerned with more than the division of a large school into more manageable smaller units. This emerging concept may be variously labeled "educational options," "experimental schools," "alternative schools," "alternative programs," or similar designations. The rationale for such alternative systems within the public school varies considerably but there appear to be some common features. The alternative schools tend to be small, ranging from below 50 pupils to over 300 pupils, with about 100 pupils being common; there is much more participation by students, parents, and the community in all phases of the school's activities; the status of the students is expanding as described earlier in this section, with more voice for the students in both curricular and mangement matters; and there is constant experimentation with subject content, instructional strategies, and class structure. There are also many differences among the alternative schools, even within the same school center, based upon the reason for establishing the optional programs.

What are the implications for the central principal in terms of staff selection and assignment, student placement and participation, community participation and decision making, and the management of budget? What happens when the administrator of a subunit or alternative school carries out policies not in accord with the central principal's wishes but with the strong support of the subunit's pupils and parents?

ORGANIZATIONAL CHANGES AMONG SCHOOLS. Organizational changes are also emerging among schools. One such pattern is concerned with the generally prevalent division of pupils into elementary, junior high, and senior high schools. Attention has focused particularly upon the junior high school, with the opinion by some educators that the junior high school has failed in its purposes or, at least, has become obsolete in light of the changing nature of society and today's youth. Probably the greatest criticism of the traditional junior high school is its seeming reliance upon a high school organizational pattern to solve problems of curriculum and instruction, thus seeming to foster a program which does not meet the needs or help solve the problems of young adolescents. To meet this criticism and other needs, a move toward "middle schools" has developed in which pupils are housed together for grades 5 through 8 or 6 through 8, although other patterns may also be used. This movement raises several significant questions. What challenges are being posed by the middle schools not only for the junior high school but also for the upper elementary grades and the senior high school? What new types of background and training will be required for the principal and the staff in this apparent new look at child growth and development? What facilities and materials are needed? If these questions are not raised or answered, will the changes be in name only or merely in organization and not in substance?

Beyond the discussion possible in this section lies the current interest in alternative schools outside the public schools. Their emergence has vital implications for the community school center. How will such developments affect the roles of the principal and the staff?

SELECTED REFERENCES

Anderson, Lester W., and Lauren A. Van Dyke, *Secondary School Administration*, 2d ed. Boston: Houghton Mifflin Company, 1972.

Baughman, M. Dale, Wendell G. Anderson, Mark Smith, and Earle W. Wiltse, *Administration and Supervision of the Modern Secondary School*. West Nyack, N.Y.: Parker Publishing Company, Inc., 1969.

DeVita, Joseph C., Philip Pumerantz, and Leighton B. Wilklow, *The Effective Middle School*. West Nyack, N.Y.: Parker Publishing Company, Inc., 1970.

Faber, Charles F., and Gilbert F. Shearron, *Elementary School Administration: Theory and Practice*. New York: Holt, Rinehart and Winston, Inc., 1970.

Jenson, Theodore J., James B. Burr, William H. Coffield, and Ross L. Neagley, *Elementary School Administration*, 2d ed. Boston: Allyn and Bacon, 1967.

Jones, James J., C. Jackson Salisbury, and Ralph L. Spender, *Secondary School Administration*. New York: McGraw-Hill Book Company, 1969.

McCleary, Lloyd E., and Stephen P. Hencley, *Secondary School Administration: Theoretical Bases of Professional Practice*. New York: Dodd, Mead & Company, 1965.

Silberman, Charles E., *Crisis in the Classroom: The Remaking of American Education*. New York: Random House, Inc., 1970.

Smith, Louis M., and Pat M. Keith, *Anatomy of Educational Innovation: an Organizational Analysis of an Elementary School*. New York: John Wiley & Sons, Inc., 1971.

Snyder, Fred A., and R. Duane Peterson, *Dynamics of Elementary School Administration*. Boston: Houghton Mifflin Company, 1970.

Walton, John, *Introduction to Education: A Substantive Discipline*. Waltham, Massachusetts: Xerox College Publishing, 1971.

part **III**

DEVELOPMENT AND ADMINISTRATION OF PROGRAMS AND SERVICES

14

Provisions for Learning

The basic purpose of all provisions for education should be to ensure optimum learning opportunities for all who can benefit from education. The adequacy and appropriateness of provisions for financial support, organization and administration, personnel, facilities, services, and programs—of all procedures and activities in or relating to education—should be appraised by determining the extent to which they contribute to the achievement of this purpose by meeting the changing as well as present needs of individuals and society.

Although important changes have been made in some aspects of education during recent years, even greater and more carefully planned changes are essential if present and emerging needs are to be met satisfactorily. All these changes should be concerned directly or indirectly with ensuring adequate and relevant learning opportunities and procedures for every individual—that is, with improving what is commonly referred to as "the educational program." Since the needs of individuals differ in many important respects, however, a more appropriate term would seem to be *educational programs,* or the curriculum, which should be interpreted to encompass all learning activities provided through the schools rather than to refer merely to the subjects taught in the schools.

Educators as well as lay citizens need to keep in mind two important but often overlooked facts in this context: (1) learning begins in infancy and continues throughout the life of every normal individual; and (2) educational programs of various kinds are provided by many different groups and agencies other than the schools. The learning opportunities provided through the homes, by peer groups, and in many other ways may be at least as significant as those provided by the schools in determining the values, aspirations, and even the contributions of each individual. Moreover, some educational programs provided by the schools or other agencies may or may not be relevant in terms of present or emerging needs. Two basic unresolved issues are (1) How can these learning opportunities and programs be improved and effectively coordinated? and (2) What should be the role of the schools in facilitating needed coordination?

If significant progress is to be made in resolving these issues in any state, it is essential that (1) every board of education, with the assistance of the staff, develop and adopt plans and policies that will encourage innovation and progress and discourage complacency—that is, seek to ensure that the school system functions as an open social system; (2) every administrator not only keep informed about major developments and their implications and provide leadership in effecting improvements but also develop a competent staff that is interested in cooperating to ensure progress; (3) every aspect of the environment in each community and its school system be as favorable as possible in order to encourage the schools to develop and provide the kinds of programs and learning opportunities needed under modern conditions; and (4) every person in each community view the child as an "open system" in continuous communication and interaction with his environment, who not only is modified by that environment but also has some effect on it.[1]

THE ENVIRONMENT FOR LEARNING

Although some learning may occur in almost any kind of environment, there are certain settings and conditions that are more conducive to beneficial learning than others. Some of the conditions and factors in the *external environment*—including especially the political and socioeconomic

[1] Adapted from Evelyn Weber, "Conceptions of Child Growth and Learning," in a *New Look at Progressive Education,* James R. Squire, ed. (Washington, D.C.: American Association of Supervision and Curriculum Development, 1972), p. 37.

environment—that tend to facilitate or to retard appropriate educational processes are discussed in Chapter 7. It is generally recognized that little meaningful learning is likely to occur, for example, when conditions in the homes are unfavorable, or when students are undernourished, poorly clothed, handicapped by poor health, or are convinced that they or their families are victims of discriminatory practices. Although educators alone cannot expect to eliminate or neutralize unfavorable factors and conditions in the homes, in the community or in other aspects of the external environment, they cannot afford to ignore them. They urgently need to cooperate with, and obtain the cooperation of, parents and community groups in developing and implementing appropriate strategies for minimizing or eliminating the less desirable or handicapping environmental factors and conditions and for strengthening those that tend to facilitate needed learning.

The *internal environment,* or "climate," in each school and school system affects the attitudes and learning progress of students in important but often unrecognized ways. Among the factors that tend to result in a favorable environment are educational programs, materials and procedures designed to meet the needs of each student; good home, school, and student relations; competent and understanding teachers and staff members who are genuinely interested in helping all students regardless of their limitations; and fellow students who are friendly and cooperative. On the other hand, an unfavorable environment usually includes factors and conditions such as a static and increasingly obsolete curriculum; a rigid and unrealistic emphasis on uniform intellectual accomplishments without adequate consideration of ability or other pertinent factors; and a controlled classroom setting involving the presentation of information primarily from a single source (the teacher) with the criteria for responses and success largely determined by that source.

Although many schools and school systems have been successful in developing a reasonably favorable internal environment, Silberman concluded that most schools he visited in connection with a study sponsored by the Carnegie Corporation were so preoccupied with order and discipline that they tended to neglect bona fide education. He commented:

> It is not possible to spend any prolonged period visiting public school classrooms without being appalled by the ... mutilation of spontaneity, of joy in learning, of pleasure in creating, of sense of self. ... Because adults take the schools so much for granted, they fail to appreciate what grim, joyless places most American schools are ... what contempt they unconsciously display for children as children.[2]

[2]Charles Silberman, *Crisis in the Classroom: The Remaking of American Education* (New York: Random House, 1970), p. 10.

These observations apparently are intended to apply to those schools and school systems that in many unfortunate respects have become tradition-bound and bureaucratic, and to those members of the organization who go through the accustomed rituals associated with learning but fail to consider many of the human factors involved as they attempt to stimulate and challenge individuals who differ in many subtle ways.

It seems apparent that if relevant learning is to be significantly enhanced in many school systems, effective ways will need to be found to improve both the internal and external environments for education. Those who are involved in education must be sufficiently perceptive and creative to find appropriate ways of working with parents, with students, and with various organizations and agencies to improve the standards, expectations, and conditions in the schools, in the community, and perhaps even in the state. Moreover, the citizens in each community can and should help to improve both the internal and external environments for education by selecting for service on the school board only competent people who are genuinely interested in improving education, and by insisting that this board adopt appropriate policies, select competent staff members, provide modern facilities, attempt to ensure adequate financial support, and take other steps that are designed to improve learning opportunities for all students.[3]

NEW INSIGHTS AND CHANGING CONCEPTS

Although most citizens know something about recent developments in society and education, many do not understand their significance or some of the implications. Four major factors seem to be related to the present confusion and uncertainty in and relating to education: (1) many people do not realize that new knowledge and insights and changes in society inevitably require changes in education; (2) some school systems and schools have made changes in one or more aspects of education without adequate study or planning, or without considering or understanding the implications for other aspects; (3) educational leaders in some communities have made relatively little effort to help lay citizens or even teachers and students understand the need for changes in educational programs and procedures or how these can best be implemented; and (4) some lay citizens, school boards, administrators, and teachers have resisted or delayed changes that are urgently needed to facilitate relevant learning for many students.

[3] Adapted from Edgar L. Morphet, David L. Jesser, and Arthur P. Ludka, eds., *Planning and Providing for Excellence in Education,* (New York: Citation Press, Scholastic Magazines, Inc., 1971), pp. 142–143.

As Tumin[4] has perceptively observed, one of the major difficulties in modernizing educational programs and procedures arises because most people tend to think of *ability* primarily as cognitive ability that is assumed to be "undimensional in quality, fixed in level, and unalterable by environmental interventions." Instead, he pointed out, there are many kinds and levels of ability and *"numerous kinds of environmental interventions can and do make a substantial difference in the level and quality of ability that is available for any given task."* He proposed that we always think "of the interaction between a child, the teacher and the experiences called the curriculum as a *process of the continuous creation and re-creation of new domains and dimensions of capacity."*

Among the developments and factors that have resulted in, or contributed to, recent improvements in educational programs and procedures are the following:

- *New studies and information are providing additional insights into the teaching-learning process.* As one result, repetitive drill is no longer considered desirable merely as a mental discipline. The emphasis is on learning experiences that will enable each student to understand relationships among means, ends, and consequences. Knowledge is valued as a means to an end, rather than as an end in itself.
- *Increasing emphasis is being placed on research and the application of scientific methods and findings.* When people know how to find and use pertinent evidence in resolving problems, they are much better prepared to make progress than when they rely primarily on tradition or subjective judgment. The change from reliance on tradition to the use of scientific findings has had tremendous implications for procedures in improving education.
- *Studies have shown that how people learn may be as important as or, in some cases, even more important than what they learn.* With the acceptance of this concept, the emphasis has been changed in many classrooms from formal recitations to group and individual activities organized around problems or topics for study. Teachers and students cooperate in finding out how to study, learn about, and solve these problems.
- *The most meaningful improvements in educational programs are being effected on the basis of cooperative study and agreement.* The concept that educational programs can be revised only by experts or that teaching can be improved primarily on the basis of administrative directives has been discredited. Widespread participation of teachers and students in studying problems and needs has helped to bring about significant improvements in the facilitation of learning. Participation by teacher organizations and lay citizens in studying and agreeing on desirable educational goals and policies is tending to result in better support for needed improvements in education.

Other developments and insights, some of which may be equally or perhaps even more significant for educational programs and learning procedures during the coming years include (1) important discoveries and

[4]Melvin M. Tumin, "Ability, Motivation and Evaluation: Urgent Dimensions in the Preparation of Educators," in *Preparing Educators to Meet Emerging Needs,* Edgar L. Morphet and David L. Jesser, eds. (New York: Citation Press, Scholastic Magazines, Inc., 1969), p. 5.

significant advances that have implications for education are continuously being made in all areas; (2) new information relating to the development of people and especially about the growth and development of children is becoming available each year; (3) most people now recognize that some learnings are much more important than others, and that priorities must be agreed upon and implemented; (4) the development of defensible moral and ethical perspectives and values and of emotional balance probably is at least as important as development of intellectual capacity; (5) the procedures for the preparation of educators urgently need to be redesigned to enable them to deal effectively and realistically with changing educational perspectives, needs, and programs; (6) further major improvements in provisions for the organization, administration, and financing of education are needed in many states in order to facilitate improvements in educational programs and learning opportunities; and (7) as a result of these and other related developments, the concepts and attitudes of parents and other lay citizens are changing in a number of important and helpful respects.

The educational programs and learning opportunities in any school or school system at any time are a result of the interplay of many different factors, including environmental conditions, state and local educational policies, and the attitudes and contributions of the excellent, mediocre, and ineffective teachers and other staff members. Moreover, they cannot, except perhaps in unusual situations, be expected to rise much above the ability and vision of the administrator and the staff, the policies and regulations of the board, or the understanding, expectations, and support of leading citizens.

The educational programs in any school may be appropriate for some students and inappropriate for others. They may help to free the minds of some to be creative and to contribute to the improvement of the society in which they live; for others they may provide major frustrations or give only the knowledge and skills that will help them to become more clever in exploiting their fellow human beings. To a great extent, these programs reflect the culture of the society and of the community in which they are found. They also tend to alter that culture to some extent, either directly or indirectly. Some schools lag behind the needs of a changing society, do little to improve the people they serve, and may even do an unsatisfactory job of transmitting the cultural heritage. Others not only transmit quite successfully the best of the accumulated heritage but also make a substantial contribution to civilization by helping those they serve become better able to solve their own problems and to contribute to the solution of the problems facing their respective communities and the nation.

PLANNING IMPROVEMENTS

In a 1938 lecture John Dewey[5] pointed out that: (1) the subject matter of education consists of bodies of information and skills that have been worked out in the past and the chief business of the schools has been to transmit them to the younger generation; (2) moral training involves forming habits of action in conformity with standards and rules of conduct that have developed in the past; and (3) the general pattern of school organization (including the relations of students to one another and to teachers) has characterized the school as an institution that is sharply marked off from other social institutions. Although there have been changes in most schools during recent years, the basic concepts and rationale utilized by some do not seem to differ significantly from those discussed by Dewey. Moreover, some of the changes that have been made in programs and procedures in many schools may be attributed more to the acceptance of prestigious new "ideas" or to the efforts of strong pressure groups than to careful study and analysis of pertinent research and the implications for educational policies and procedures.

Although changes in educational programs and procedures are urgently needed—and others will be essential during the coming years to meet the needs of a changing society—such changes should not be made fortuitously; they should be carefully and systematically planned to facilitate relevant learning. But if planning is to result in significant improvements, the plans must be promptly and effectively implemented—that is, the needed changes must be made, the impact and implications determined, and the plans revised as necessary to deal with any weaknesses or to provide for newly recognized needs. (See Chapter 6.)

Some Important Considerations

Planning improvements in educational programs and learning procedures is a complex and difficult process in which the state education agency, institutions of higher learning, and local school systems should be continuously and cooperatively involved. Some important considerations relating to planning in this area are discussed briefly below.

The state education agency should assume an important leadership role in planning improvements in educational programs and procedures. This is essential because

---

[5]John Dewey, *Experience and Education* (New York: The Macmillan Company, 1963). Originally published by Phi Delta Kappa.

education is a state responsibility; some statewide goals are needed; state constraints that might prevent local improvements need to be identified and eliminated; and most local school systems can benefit from state assistance in planning improvements in their programs. Local school systems, however, should assume the primary responsibility for improving their own programs and procedures.

All state and local planning should be future oriented. Although planning to meet present needs more effectively is important, it does not suffice in a changing society. Serious efforts should be made to anticipate future developments and needs and to prepare students to live and cope constructively with change.

A broad perspective should be maintained at all times. Any aspect that is studied should be considered in the light of its relationship to, and implications for, the entire curriculum and all aspects of the learning process.

Needed studies should be planned and conducted cooperatively. Those who are involved should be competent, cooperative, have a broad perspective, and be encouraged to increase their insights into and understanding of problems and needs and feasible ways of meeting them. The process of planning itself should help to set the stage for effecting needed changes.

Proposals for improvement should be based on systematic studies of problems, needs, and possibilities. Any changes that are proposed should be based on careful study and evaluation of the situation and needs, of the alternatives available, and on determination of what seems to be the best policy. A well-organized school system has a plan for providing for, encouraging, and assisting with such studies, and for utilizing the findings and conclusions as they become available.

The findings and conclusions should be carefully considered by the board, superintendent, and staff with adequate attention to implications for the total program. If the studies have been properly developed and the interrelationships among all aspects of the program have been kept in mind, the conclusions and recommendations should contribute substantially to the process of developing relevant programs. The board should then be in an excellent position to consider and adopt any policies that are needed to assist in implementing the proposals.[6]

The major steps in developing and implementing goals, programs, and procedures that are designed to meet the present and emerging educational needs of all students and of society are discussed under the headings that follow.

[6]Adapted from Van Miller, *The Public Administration of American Schools* (New York: The Macmillan Company, 1972), Chap. 8.

PURPOSES, GOALS, AND OBJECTIVES

As explained earlier, one of the first but often neglected steps in the planning process is to develop (or revise and update) and attempt to get agreement on a statement of goals for education. A goal is something people want, or should want, to attain as a group or as individuals. The bona fide acceptance of a goal should lead to the accomplishment of a purpose that is determined by the beliefs and values people accept. In this complex and interdependent society there must be national[7] as well as state and local goals for education. Unfortunately, some of these are inconsistent and many are assumed or implied by the actions taken (or proposed and not taken) rather than clearly stated and openly discussed. Moreover, many of these goals apparently have not been accepted by substantial numbers of adults and students.

Opinions about educational programs and procedures grow out of the beliefs and points of view or "frames of reference" people use in looking at education and other aspects of life. Some of these may be based on understanding; others on ignorance or prejudice. These opinions become a part of the value system and philosophy accepted by each person and to which he tends to have a strong emotional attachment. They may be roughly classified under such philosophical positions as realism, idealism, or pragmatism,[8] or perhaps others that are related in one way or another to these major positions. All are concerned with the ultimate nature and purpose of man's relation to the universe and, directly or indirectly, with the nature, purpose, and goals of education. Differences of opinion about purposes and goals (based fundamentally on differences in philosophies accepted) lead inevitably to controversies or criticisms of the schools and the way they are organized and operated. These criticisms and controversies tend to become most widespread following major changes in society or in educational programs.

One major difficulty arises from the fact that although people have many common values and beliefs, there are also marked differences and even inconsistencies in these values. These inconsistencies lead to confusion and sometimes conflict for the individual or group. Every school system and every school within the system needs to face the problem of attempting to reconcile differences in values and beliefs relating to educa-

---

[7]See, for example, *Goals for Americans: Report of the President's Commission on National Goals* (Englewood Cliffs, N.J.: Prentice-Hall, Inc., 1960).
[8]For a discussion of some implications of each of these positions for educational programs, see J. Cecil Parker, T. Bentley Edwards, and Willaim H. Stegeman, *Curriculum in America* (New York: Thomas Y. Crowell Company, 1962), Chap. 2.

tional programs, to resolve inconsistencies, and to obtain agreement on appropriate goals.

The major purpose of education in a free dynamic society should be *to help each and every member of that society to develop fully his capacity and talents and to learn to utilize them creatively and continuously to improve himself and society.* The major goal should be *to ensure excellence in every aspect of life by continuously improving the quality and relevancy of every aspect of education.*

An individual's educational goals, which are determined by many factors (including educational programs and policies), significantly influence not only his progress through formal schooling but also his success in life and his contributions to society. The goals of each student as well as the goals of the schools should include intellectual, or what has traditionally been referred to as academic goals; practical goals concerned with meaningful living in a complex society; personal goals in areas of achievement that are uniquely valuable to him and to society; and appropriate emotional, moral, and ethical goals. Gibson[9] has proposed that *all goals should be concerned with the dimensions of human quality:* the quality of a person as a human being; the quality of the skills he needs; the quality of his knowledge about man and society; the quality of his learning, thinking, and perceiving; and civic quality, concerned with what he should know and do to function as an effective citizen.

As pointed out in Chapters 2 and 8, some national purposes, basic goals, and policies relating to provisions for education have been established by federal court decisions and laws. All states have also developed some state goals and policies. In some states these are incorporated in or implied by laws and court decisions; in others, statements of goals have been developed or supplemented by the state education agency, or by a special group established for that purpose. State goals for education are essential to provide guidance for local school systems, but these should include only the basic goals that are appropriate throughout the state; be developed with the cooperation of competent lay citizens, educators, and students; be widely discussed and agreed upon before they are officially adopted; and be designed to encourage local school systems to develop and obtain agreement on their own supplementary goal statements. *Until clearly stated educational goals are developed and accepted there is no defensible basis for evaluating progress or for establishing accountability.*

Responsible students and teacher organizations should be involved in the process of developing proposals for statements of goals that will affect them in many important ways. They, as well as lay citizens and other

---

[9]John S. Gibson, as quoted in Morphet *et al., Planning and Providing for Excellence in Education,* p. 140.

educators, must agree that any proposed goal is important and appropriate before it can be utilized successfully for guidance in developing programs and learning procedures. The goals accepted by a local school system and by each school should grow out of a number of cooperative studies, including a study of the community in relationship to the state, the nation, and the world; a thorough analysis of the community and its problems and needs to determine the implications for educational programs; and a study of the students in the community and of learners in general, to obtain information that may be used in developing appropriate objectives relating to learning needs and processes.

Most goal statements point to or identify important ends to which efforts should be directed in attempts to achieve the major purposes of education, but do not provide either definite guidelines for developing programs or criteria for measuring progress. It is, therefore, essential that specific objectives relating to each goal be developed to provide useful guidelines for action as well as criteria for determining from time to time what progress has been made by the groups or individuals involved.

During recent years many people have begun to recognize that in order to facilitate meaningful learning and measure progress, it is necessary to develop and to utilize intelligently performance objectives. Although this is a difficult and time-consuming task, it seems essential in the effort to ensure needed improvements in the processes and products of education. There is some danger, however, that a few people will become so involved in, or enamored with, the mechanics of the process that they will tend to overlook the basic purposes indicated above.

Performance objectives should provide a clear and concise description of each desired outcome. Each such objective should be expressed, insofar as feasible, in terms which are so specific that everyone involved can interpret them in essentially the same way. The performance described or the product of any such performance, or both, are observable; hence the extent to which a performance objective has been achieved can readily be measured. The three essential components of any well-constructed performance objective are:

1. The product to be produced and/or the action to be performed;
2. The conditions under which the action must be performed, particularly noting any special aids required or any limitations in availability of aids; and
3. The criteria, or specifications, which describe how well the desired outcome is expected to be performed.[10]

[10]Adapted from Morphet *et al., Planning and Providing for Excellence in Education,* p. 46.

DETERMINATION OF NEEDS

A statement of purposes, goals, and objectives provides one important basis for identifying unmet or unrecognized needs as well as for determining what progress has been made in meeting those needs. On the other hand, a comprehensive study and assessment of problems and needs may also help to direct attention to the fact that new goals should be recognized or that some of the current goal statements should be revised.

A state or local study of educational needs must be systematically planned and conducted if it is to be realistic and helpful. Detailed information should be assembled, analyzed, and utilized in a serious effort to identify and prepare to resolve all problems and deficiencies (including previously unrecognized needs) of individuals and groups that are, and are not, being served by education. This study should also help to direct attention to such matters as handicapping laws, regulations, and policies; weaknesses in organization, staffing, programs, and instructional procedures; problems in school-home-community relations; and deficiencies in supplies, equipment, facilities, resources, and so on. Although the primary focus should be on *needs,* the purpose should be constructive: to ensure that adequate and relevant programs are provided, and appropriate procedures are utilized, to facilitate meaningful learning for all who should be involved.

If a state or local school system has developed and maintains an adequate management information system, a realistic needs assessment can be made periodically without the necessity of obtaining much special information. However, if such a system has not been developed, it will be necessary to devise procedures for obtaining and analyzing all pertinent information which, with careful planning, can and should constitute the basis for establishing an appropriate planning and management information system.

IDENTIFICATION AND ANALYSIS OF ALTERNATIVES

It is generally recognized that many people (including some teachers and administrators) tend to feel more comfortable in continuing to do what they have been doing in the way it has been done in the past. For that and other reasons, one of the first steps in preparing to consider alternative ways of attaining the goals agreed upon probably should be for the group involved to review the findings and conclusions resulting from the needs assessment and also to consider some implications for education of recent and prospective changes in society. If those involved can agree that some changes are needed in educational programs and procedures, they should be prepared to begin seriously to identify, categorize, and evaluate feasible alternatives.

The recent literature includes a bewildering variety of proposals ranging from alternatives *to* public education to alternatives *in* and *for* almost every aspect of public education. Some of these are obviously sensational and impractical; many others merit careful consideration. The following steps are suggested for developing feasible alternatives:

1. Review the literature (books, magazine articles, and special reports) for "ideas" that seem promising, and develop a tentative plan for categorizing and arranging these ideas under what seem to be appropriate headings. Much of this should be done from time to time by state education agencies and universities for their own use and the use of local school systems. The headings or topics relating to educational programs and procedures would include those pertaining to the curriculum; the role of teachers and teacher organizations, parents and others directly concerned with learning processes; the use of various types of media and technologies; ways of identifying and meeting individual needs; and others that seem appropriate.
2. Develop and agree on criteria that should be utilized to identify the alternatives listed under each heading that seem worthy of further consideration, and to select for study and analysis those that seem to be most promising. In connection with this process detailed information will need to be obtained concerning the potential advantages and disadvantages of each of these alternatives in various kinds of situations. Moreover, all proposed alternatives should be carefully reviewed to ensure that they constitute a harmonious and compatible system.
3. Utilize the information assembled to identify the alternative relating to each category (or perhaps the two that seem most promising and could be implemented on a planned experimental basis) that should be recommended for use at least in certain types of schools. Many factors will need to be considered in arriving at this important decision. These will include the personnel, financial, and other pertinent resources available and the costs in relationship to the potential benefits. In determining cost-benefits, however, the initial costs may be high for certain types of students and, in such cases, the benefits should be considered from a long-range point of view.
4. Develop plans and procedures designed to ensure that the proposals will be appropriately and effectively implemented and the progress or outcomes continuously studied and evaluated.

IMPLEMENTING PLANS

There is likely to be some resistance to almost every proposal for change in any major aspect of education. Those who are interested in effecting improvements, therefore, need to understand the dynamics and problems of changes in perspectives and human relations within an educational organization and the community it serves.[11] For example, they

---

[11]Adapted in part from Hubert S. Coffey and William P. Golden, Jr., "Psychology of Changes Within an Institution," *In-Service Education for Teachers, Supervisors, and Administrators,* Fifty-sixth Yearbook, National Society for the Study of Education, Part I (Chicago: University of Chicago Press, 1957), Chap. 4.

should recognize that (1) any change in an institution or organization tends to threaten the roles to which certain persons have been accustomed and in which they find security; (2) people who are complacent and satisfied are usually reluctant to change even when what they are doing is ineffective; and (3) those who become dissatisfied with the results they are attaining or who believe they have not kept pace with progress are likely to be willing to reexamine their perspectives and procedures and to attempt to make some changes.

Any proposal for a defensible change or innovation should be encouraged and supported by the community and the school system. Policies should be adopted that will not only give direction to the program but also provide security and encouragement to members of the staff who are interested in attempting to carry out those policies. When there is substantial agreement, changes can more readily be made than when there are sharp disagreements. When there are marked differences of opinion, proposed changes might best be tried out by small groups instead of being required for all.

Effecting improvements in education may be thought of as *planned social change.* Good human relations tend to facilitate improvements, because the threat to the security of individual members of the staff is far less than when relationships are unsatisfactory. The greatest progress should be expected in those school systems in which (1) effective leadership is provided; (2) there are good relations between teachers, other members of the staff, and the board; (3) teachers and administrators believe that both the community and the board want and expect excellence in education; and (4) satisfactory cooperative procedures have been developed for planning and implementing improvements. In such situations, the teachers and staff members who are contributing to the studies and decisions are likely to be the ones who feel secure when improvements are being made and insecure when there is no progress. The teachers and others who are attempting to hold on to their traditional ways of doing things regardless of the evidence are the ones who are likely to feel most insecure until they can make adjustments.

CHARACTERISTICS OF EFFECTIVE PROGRAMS AND PROCEDURES

All members of a society must share certain common learnings and new insights if that society is to be cohesive and dynamic. In addition, all members will need some more or less specialized learnings to meet their needs as well as those of society. The common learnings are sometimes referred to as "general education," which has been described by Yntema, a prominent industrialist and former university professor, as consisting of "the highest common factors—the parts of education we all need to achieve a full, useful and rewarding life."[12] He listed the main goals of general education as "first, to help the student develop those qualities and abilities that will serve him and the community well, no matter what his calling in life; and second, to foster in him those interests and abilities that will induce and enable him to continue to grow—to learn by himself and in whatever joint activity he may be engaged." He also observed: "There are abilities and skills, generally useful in all fields of endeavor and largely transferable from one to another. These are also the same abilities and skills most durable and useful throughout life." The basic transferable abilities and skills were listed as: (1) the ability to perceive problems and solve them (to be creative and to think); (2) the ability to understand people, to communicate with them, to deal with them well as individuals and in groups; (3) the ability to organize, to structure data into an ordered pattern, and to marshal scarce resources for given ends; (4) the ability to devote full effort to the task at hand; and (5) the development of a good memory. Such statements emphasize the necessity for helping students to develop problem-solving skills, build appropriate attitudes, make defensible decisions, and learn values and develop a willingness to work for a deferred value. Parker, Edwards, and Stegeman noted that: "What keeps people apart are not differences of opinion, but the absence of any common basis for discussion."[13]

For many years, learning opportunities and experiences outside the classrooms were largely ignored by the schools. Studies have shown, however, that learning takes place in a variety of situations. School programs are being adjusted accordingly. Certain learning experiences, by the nature of the situation, must be centered in the schools. This does not mean, however, that they should be restricted to the schools. The concern should be to determine what experiences would be most meaningful and appropriate and to plan procedures that will make it possible to utilize a wide range of such experiences to enhance the learning process.

The Role of Leadership

In some communities most of the leaders tend to be "tradition oriented" while in others they are "progress oriented." Such contrasting

---

[12]Theodore O. Yntema, *The Enrichment of Man*, Benjamin F. Fairless Memorial Lectures (Pittsburgh: Carnegie Institute of Technology, 1964), pp. 54–56.
[13]Parker, Edwards, and Stegeman, *Curriculum in America*, pp. 74–91.

points of view may both reflect and affect the attitude of the citizens about many aspects of life, including schools and educational programs. Partly on the basis of their orientation, the people tend to elect a "conservative" or a "progressive" board, and the board tends to select an administrator whose philosophy is not sharply inconsistent with theirs. However, in every community there are differences of opinion about educational goals and programs. The extent to which needed improvements can be made in a school system will be largely determined by the kind and quality of leadership that influences the decisions affecting education. (See Chapter 5.)

In any school system the professional leaders, including not only the superintendent and members of his facilitating staff but also teachers and others who head up special studies and projects, may either encourage those who want to continue the traditional aspects of the program regardless of their value, and provide encouragement for those who are seeking improvements. Leadership, then, can be considered as providing the stimulation and guidance which is the natural accompaniment of goal-seeking behavior of human beings in any organization.[14] If members of the staff know that the "climate" established by the community, the board, and the administration is favorable, tendencies to participate in planning and effecting needed changes will be encouraged.

Community Education

The concept that people learn from all aspects of their environment —that the total community educates—has been generally accepted in theory but increasingly ignored in practice, especially in many of the big city and suburban school systems. During the earlier years, many of the schools were, in effect, "community schools" with which most of the people were closely associated. During more recent decades formal education has been left increasingly to educators. In many school systems relatively few citizens have had much opportunity, or even been encouraged, to participate in the development of educational goals or policies. Almost their only recourse has been to criticize or complain, with no assurance that their criticisms would have any impact. Thus, there have been few serious attempts in many school systems to relate the education that occurs in the homes and the community (which could reinforce or tend to conflict with the learning in the schools) to the education in the schools.

There have always been some community schools in rural or small-town areas that sought to meet, or to coordinate, the educational needs of

---

[14]Gordon N. Mackenzie and Stephen M. Corey, *Instructional Leadership* (New York: Bureau of Publications, Teachers College, Columbia University, 1954), p. 4.

the community served. Such schools, however, seldom developed in large population centers, perhaps partly because the bureaucratic structure did not encourage or permit such sharp deviations from the established norms. The community education concept began to be revitalized a few decades ago in an urban setting—Flint, Michigan. Stimulated by grants and other assistance, first primarily from the Mott Foundation and more recently from other sources, the movement has spread during the past few years to most parts of the nation. Apparently a contributing factor has been the growing dissatisfaction with the educational organization and procedures, especially in many of the large school systems.

Community education[15] should be viewed as one important process by which the educational needs of the individual and of society can be met. It is designed to provide a workable system for involving people in the community in the identification and solution of their educational and related problems. Moreover, this concept provides a rationale and means for subdividing large cities into smaller community areas and involving the people in the process of identifying and solving their social and especially their educational problems. Obviously any such process, when utilized perceptively, should help to remove many of the present frustrations and handicaps to effective education by providing an opportunity and a challenge for people in the area to begin to develop and provide adequate and relevant educational opportunities.

The Curriculum

Many people still think of the curriculum primarily in terms of the subjects or "disciplines" traditionally taught, rather than as including all the learning activities that should be provided by or through the schools. The traditional curriculum, even in the elementary and secondary schools, has been rather closely related to the disciplines developed by scholars in the generally recognized fields or subjects of study. Curriculum development (planning) for many years consisted largely of a series of segmented operations concerned largely with the subjects to be "taught"—with relatively little attention devoted to the totality (the meaningful relationships among the several segmented parts). Moreover the curriculum at all levels has been primarily a result of the continuation of many long established traditions (some of which are no longer defensible), and of a series of decisions made in a context of conflicting sets of values and interests and in the presence of a multiplicity of competing demands and concerns.

[15]See articles and references in the November 1972 special issue of *Phi Delta Kappan* on "Community Education."

Curriculum revision should be concerned with (1) facilitating the attainment of pertinent purposes, goals, and objectives; and (2) ensuring that appropriate provisions are made for learning experiences designed to meet the needs of *each student* and of the changing society in which he will live. Curricular changes should therefore be systematically planned—not made merely on the basis of revisions in segments of the educational program—and designed to meet emerging as well as present needs.

Moreover, most attention until recently has been devoted to the evaluation of students on the basis of their scores on various kinds of tests and examinations and an appraisal of their class contributions and conduct. Thus, students have been graded or "labeled," often somewhat arbitrarily even early in their school careers. Unfortunately the original classifications have tended to persist. Customarily, students have been held primarily responsible or accountable for their own successes or failures. Most authorities agree that this procedure is neither reasonable nor defensible in the light of what is now known about conditions that affect learning—and that more humane and realistic procedures need to be devised and utilized.[16]

Resources for Learning

Under modern conditions the resources that could and should be utilized to facilitate learning are almost unlimited. Yet, either because some of the elements of earlier traditions tend to persist, or perhaps partly because of the almost bewildering variety of recently developed resources (some of which require special training and new skills if they are to be utilized perceptively and effectively) many schools still tend to rely primarily on more traditional materials and procedures; that is, on a somewhat myopic and "tunnel vision" approach to learning.

Regardless of its source, the subject matter should not determine, but should contribute to, the learning experience. Most teachers have been making effective use for some time not only of encyclopedias, monographs, magazine articles, and other pertinent printed materials found in modern school libraries, but also of film strips, motion pictures, recordings, radio and television programs, and other related community resources of various types. But more recent technological developments (such as instruction by closed-circuit or other educational television, programmed or computer-assisted individualized learning, including in some cases a variety of "teaching machines," language laboratories, team teaching, and flexible scheduling) have brought many new challenges and problems.

---

[16]Adapted from Morphet *et al., Planning and Providing for Excellence in Education,* pp. 144 and 152.

As Katzenbach[17] has pointed out, schools and other educational institutions must plan systematically and prepare personnel for the most effective selection and utilization of technology in education, but many have not done so. He noted that in most schools little thought has been given to the interrelationships among technology, society, and education, and that educators must accept some ideas that are alien to their previous thinking, including the concept that in certain situations "a machine may be more helpful than a person." He emphasized the fact that *'technology must be fitted to curricula—not curricula to technology."*

School systems that select and utilize wisely the "tools" and other resources for teaching and learning now available, as well as others that will almost certainly become available in the future, should be in an excellent position to improve the quality of their programs. In most school systems, however, it will be essential (1) to help teachers and other staff members become well acquainted with, and to understand the advantages and limitations of resources of each type; (2) to identify and arrange to make available those that should make maximum contributions to the teaching-learning processes for students, consistent with their ability, achievement, maturity, and other pertinent factors; and (3) to assist teachers and students to learn how to make optimum use of the resources provided.

Facilitating Personnel and Counseling Services

A major unresolved issue in modern society is: How can parents, teachers, and others best help students to learn and behave in ways that will enable them to become, and function as, effective citizens in a dynamic society? The attitudes and progress of students are influenced by many factors, and especially by many kinds of people in the homes, the community, and the schools. One responsibility of the schools is to help to ensure that the positive and constructive aspects of these influences are maximized. An important step is to help everyone involved in any aspect of the process of education to recognize that his attitudes and actions have some direct or indirect impact on the attitudes and progress of students—that secretaries, food service personnel, and custodians, for example, as well as teachers, counselors, and administrators are or should be members of a team concerned with the facilitation of learning. In other words, a carefully planned and well-coordinated counseling program should be considered essential for every school.

---

[17]Edward L. Katzenbach, in *Planning for Effective Utilization of Technology in Education,* Edgar L. Morphet and David L. Jesser, eds. (New York: Citation Press, Scholastic Magazines, Inc., 1968), pp. 127–129.

Most parents and educators agree, on the basis of evidence now available, that (1) perceptive counseling is needed and should be available to all students beginning in the elementary grades and extending through the colleges and universities; (2) much counseling can and should be carried out by teachers in cooperation with parents, and with the advice and assistance of competent and perceptive counselors; (3) any student may need counseling at one time regarding relations with people, at another regarding habits of study, and at still others regarding health, educational programs, occupational choice, and so on: and (4) a major goal of counseling at all times should be to help students become increasingly able to think through their own problems and work out their own solutions.

SPECIAL PROVISIONS AND PROGRAMS

Although the need for certain essentials (sometimes referred to as common learnings or general education) is common to all students, the program should not be identical for everyone because there are wide differences in abilities and needs. The schools generally are organized to work with students in groups. Such an orientation is appropriate and, within limits, has many advantages and values. However, these limits must be clearly recognized and other provisions made as needed to assure for each child a wholesome and stimulating climate for growth. In other words, individuality must also be encouraged and nurtured. The implications of the comments below should receive careful consideration and lead to appropriate action in all school systems:

> The foundation of our nation is its supreme commitment to the individual human being . . . Now this foundation is threatened because increasing massiveness and complexity have led in many subtle ways toward a great cultural shift . . . With an eye to masses rather than to individuals, the schools are departing from their unique historic character by manipulating pupils and teachers into organizational patterns and by leaning on administrative and mechanical devices that tend to destroy the very quality which has made them great.[18]

While much learning takes place in group situations, supplemented in most schools by individual approaches to learning, it is essential to recognize that *only individuals learn.* The goals accepted and the procedures utilized by administrators, teachers, and students create a climate in all

---

[18] *A Climate for Individuality* (Washington, D.C.: American Association of School Administrators, Association for Supervision and Curriculum Development, National Association of Secondary School Principals, and NEA Department of Rural Education, 1965), p. 9.

schools, colleges, and universities that may favor mass production or individual growth and development.

Most educational authorities in this country believe there should be a reasonable balance between the development of common interests and points of view and the improvement of each person as an individual. If this concept is accepted as a basis for discussing the needs of students, and if the fact is recognized that each student has some needs that differ in certain respects from the needs of others, the foundation for planning and developing programs of general and special education has been established. However, before such programs can be planned in any school system, it is necessary to develop procedures for identifying the needs of individual students and groups of students for whom special provisions should be made. Some of these provisions are discussed briefly under the headings that follow.

Early Childhood Education

Educational, psychological, and medical research during the past couple of decades has directed attention to the crucial importance of what happens, or does not happen, to each child during the first few years of his life.[19] It is now generally recognized that health, environmental, and other related deficiencies during these early years may seriously affect his learning progress. For this and other reasons there has been much discussion and considerable controversy about recent proposals and developments relating to early childhood education.

Most authorities seem to agree that early childhood education should probably begin at about age four for many disadvantaged children, but should not be required for all children; should emphasize wholesome child growth and development rather than cognitive skills; should involve parents and provide for parental education; should provide an environment that reflects the nature and needs of young children; should include appropriate arrangements for meeting medical, dental, and nutritional needs and for social services, day care, and counseling services; should have clearly defined goals so the progress and results can be evaluated; and should be adequately supported by public funds.[20]

The development of programs for early childhood education will necessitate careful long-range planning to identify needs; to ensure public understanding and acceptance; and to provide for the development of staff and facilities, and probably for the reorganization and reorientation of all

---
[19]See, for example, Benjamin S. Bloom, *Stability and Change in Human Characteristics* (New York: John Wiley & Sons, Inc., 1964).
[20]Adapted from *Early Childhood Education* (Sacramento, California State Department of Education, 1972).

primary programs. Several states, including California and New York, have already made considerable progress along these lines.

Provisions and Programs for the Handicapped

Although special programs have been developed for handicapped students in many school systems, substantial numbers who could benefit are not included and some of the provisions are far from adequate in some districts.

THE PHYSICALLY HANDICAPPED. A major concern in each school system should be to identify each child who is physically handicapped and determine the nature of his handicaps, then decide upon any special provisions that must be made to ensure that he has adequate educational opportunities. There is general agreement that students should be assigned to special classes only as long as necessary to enable them to advance satisfactorily and to prepare for resuming work in regular classes.

HEALTH HANDICAPS. In nearly every school system there will be a few students who have serious health handicaps. Some of these will be hospitalized for a while; others may be homebound over an extended period. Teachers who work with such students need to cooperate fully with the teachers responsible for the classes to which these students regularly belong. When the program is properly developed, most students with health handicaps should be in a position to progress nearly as rapidly as those in the regular classes.

THE EMOTIONALLY DISTURBED. All children have some emotional problems from time to time. Fortunately, most of these are only temporary and can be resolved by the child himself, or by the child and his parents and teachers, and do not result in serious handicaps. But the problems of emotionally disturbed children and youth are among the most serious facing society at the present time. School systems generally have made far less satisfactory provisions for meeting and resolving these problems than for many other aspects of the educational program. However, the importance of special services for emotionally disturbed students is now generally recognized by authorities and the better school systems throughout the nation are making more adequate provisions to cope with this problem.

SLOW LEARNERS. Many school systems have organized classes for slow learners with special problems and have assigned to these groups teachers who have had special preparation for working with such students. However, if special classes for slow learners are to meet the needs, (1) the program and procedures should be carefully and cooperatively planned; (2)

the problems of each child should be studied and reviewed continuously to determine whether he is making satisfactory progress under the arrangement that has been made for him or whether he should be reassigned to some other group; and (3) all teachers should accept as a goal for slow learners the development of each to his maximum potential and strive to achieve that goal.

THE CULTURALLY DIFFERENT. During the past years many of the long-ignored problems of culturally different students have been brought into focus as a result of studies by social scientists and a growing awareness by many others of some of the related factors and inequities. School systems and communities across the nation have now begun to face the fact that a culturally different student has little opportunity to benefit from education until some of the handicaps such as those resulting from differences in language and value systems with which he is confronted, through no fault of his own, can be alleviated or eliminated. These concerns and activities have been stimulated by numerous developments, including new federal and state programs recognizing that some of the problems of society and communities cannot be solved by schools alone. A major dilemma arises from the fact that education cannot solve directly many of the basic social and economic problems that result in cultural handicaps for the children, yet many of these problems cannot be solved unless children have better and more meaningful educational opportunities.

Some of the promising steps include: (1) the organization of community groups and agencies that are attempting to resolve some of the problems; (2) programs designed to introduce children to education at an early age (sometimes beginning with the language or dialect used in the homes) and to provide health and other needed services; (3) retraining and rehabilitation programs for youth and adults with provisions for better economic opportunities; (4) provisions for small classes, competent teachers, teaching and community assistants, and appropriate facilities, equipment, and supplies; and (5) programs for in-service training of teachers to help them to understand the value systems, language, and other problems of these students, and to learn to communicate effectively with them.[21]

The Gifted or Talented

A basic consideration is not whether talented students do better work than many others but whether they achieve and progress in accordance with their capacity. Among the steps taken in school systems that have

---

[21] See Benjamin S. Bloom, Allison Davis, and Robert D. Hess, *Compensatory Education for Cultural Deprivation* (New York: Holt, Rinehart & Winston, Inc., 1965), and reports of recent studies and developments.

made substantial progress in meeting the needs of the gifted are the following: (1) each student who is especially gifted or talented in one respect or another is identified on the basis of studies and test results, and an effort is made to determine his needs and make adequate provisions for meeting them; (2) on the basis of conferences involving teachers, a counselor when necessary, the parents, and the student, he is encouraged to undertake special studies and projects in the elementary school and to select appropriate high school courses designed to meet his educational and career needs; and (3) in some schools, especially gifted students are encouraged to enroll in one or two sections that include other students with similar abilities.

Provisions for Vocational-Technical and Career Education

For various reasons (including the fact that traditionally vocational education has not been considered very "respectable" and that the Smith-Hughes Act required the states to establish state boards for vocational education), vocational education has been organized as a separate system in some states. Although a few people still support this point of view, a majority now rejects it as contrary to the basic tenets of a free society and strongly supports the concept of a unified and well-coordinated system of public education in which all aspects are recognized as having some career orientation. Most authorities strongly agree that vocational and career education in the future must differ in many important respects from that provided in the past, and insist that it become an integral aspect of bona fide career education designed to meet modern needs. In the interest of the proper development of the human resources of the nation, it is essential that all school personnel use a positive approach in dealing with the problems and attempting to achieve the potential of vocational or career education. It should never be permitted to become a haven for the academically maladjusted or problem students, or a substitute for other essential aspects of education. It constitutes an important specialized aspect of a comprehensive program of education and should make a definite contribution to the development of effective and economically productive citizens.

There are many kinds of education other than that provided through college preparatory and vocational programs. In many high schools and some community colleges these have tended to be neglected. The required courses, even for collegebound students, should not be permitted to crowd out these specialized aspects of the program. A good secondary school or community college program should be considered one in which provision is made, insofar as possible, for offerings and opportunities that meet the needs and provide for the interests of all students.

Adult and Continuing Education

Laws requiring students who drop out of the regular program to continue their education on a part-time basis until they reach eighteen years of age have been on the statute books of several states for some years. Often they have been almost meaningless, as relatively few local school systems have made any serious effort to provide appropriate programs. It seems clear that every school system should take two important steps in a major attempt to deal more realistically with this situation: (1) reevaluate its program and procedures in an effort to develop more effective ways of providing meaningful learning experiences for the potential dropouts, and (2) develop adequate and effective programs designed to meet the needs of those who do drop out of the full-time program.

Adult education becomes increasingly important as the rate of change increases in society and civilization grows in complexity. If adults are to keep informed regarding many significant developments or to satisfy special interests and needs, a substantial proportion will find it desirable to enroll for special courses or programs provided through the schools or other educational institutions. The evidence points clearly to a great increase in adult education in the near future, since a large proportion of the people are beginning to recognize the importance of some learning beyond the formal educational program.[22] Among the educational institutions conducting programs of adult education are high schools, junior or community colleges, vocational or technical schools, colleges, and universities. Although these schools and institutions cannot expect to meet all educational needs for adults, they have definite responsibilities that should be recognized and met. This means that any institution that has an extensive program in adult education will need staff members who can organize and administer the program and develop a plan for providing special assistance where it is needed, as well as appropriate facilities. Moreover, the problem of financing adult education needs to be resolved in many states and communities. In most states and communities the goal should be to develop plans to ensure that at least a reasonable proportion of the expense will be provided through public funds. Both the community and the individuals involved will benefit when a reasonable proportion of the expense is provided through public funds.

[22] W. C. Johnstone and Raymon J. Rivera, *Volunteers for Learning: A Study of the Educational Pursuits of American Adults* (Chicago: Aldine Publishing Company, 1965), pp. 1–22.

SOME IMPORTANT PROBLEMS AND ISSUES

Since education has such great significance for the lives of people and for the welfare of the nation, it is not surprising that, in a pluralistic culture, many controversies arise about the policies, programs, and procedures. When people accept different values and points of view they are likely to challenge any aspect of education that conflicts with their own values. Most of the issues considered on the following pages are related to this problem. What additional issues should have attention?

How Can the Effectiveness and Adequacy of Educational Programs Be Determined?

Differences of opinion are to be expected regarding what the schools are accomplishing because many people tend to judge them on the basis of their own value systems. There are a number of approaches that may be used in reconciling some of these differences, including (1) attempting to get agreement on revisions in present goals and policies; (2) organizing a committee to study the scope and adequacy of learning experiences and the procedures used in providing them; (3) obtaining pertinent information about students and their progress; and (4) making studies of students who fail to complete the secondary program for one reason or another, and of graduates whose reactions may be helpful in determining the strengths and weaknesses in the program.

What criteria should be used in judging the effectiveness of the educational programs in a school system? What are some important steps that should be taken in every system to provide for a continuous and effective evaluation of these programs? What would be the advantages and disadvantages of using a statewide system of tests?

How Can Innovative Developments Best Be Evaluated?

During the past few years, a number of "experiments" have been concerned with different means of facilitating new kinds of learning experiences for students. Most of these developments have grown out of a genuine interest in improving the effectiveness of education, but some seem to be clever "gimmicks" that the developers hope will become both popular and profitable. Unfortunately some school systems have not planned carefully or developed suitable guidelines for the introduction of new ideas, materials, or equipment. Far too few have helped staff members learn how to evaluate or utilize new materials or procedures effectively. Which of these developments are potentially most significant for improving learning for what kinds of students and under what conditions? What criteria should be developed by a school system to determine which of these should be utilized and how they can be utilized most effectively? What implications would they have for the size and organization of classes, the number of staff members, and costs?

How Can Mediocrity Be Avoided in the Educational Programs Provided by Public Schools?

In this country, the public schools must be prepared to attempt to educate all children except the few who must be cared for in special institutions. There are significant differences in intelligence, study habits, background, emotional stability, aptitudes, and in other important respects. Although not all the extremes are likely to be found in any one classroom, every study has shown that there are pronounced differences, even when students are grouped on the basis of ability or other factors. Some people have charged that the public schools tend to provide a reasonably good program of education for most students but one that, in reality, is mediocre. The fact that the slower learners will probably be below and the more rapid learners above the average in achievement does not mean that the situation is good. In reality, the group may be setting the pace for the fast learners instead of the fast learners helping to challenge others.

Many believe these problems can be solved through better homogeneous grouping of students and insist that such an arrangement would not only facilitate the process of learning for many but would simplify the problems of teaching. Others insist that the problems be solved some other way. Theoretically, schools should be able to adapt the educational program to the needs of *each student,* even when there is a considerable range in ability as well as in other respects in each of the classes. Presumably, teachers should be in a position to give special attention to slower learners in accordance with their needs and at the same time find opportunity to challenge the more capable students and stimulate them to achieve beyond the average level for the class.

What policies should be developed in a school or in a school system that will help to ensure that every student progresses more nearly in accordance with his potential than has been the case on many occasions in the past? How can students best be challenged to make maximum progress?

How Can Tendencies Toward Compartmentalization Be Avoided?

In theory, the comprehensive high school is as indigenous and typical as the public school system. Within many comprehensive high schools, however, certain cleavages and tendencies toward compartmentalization have developed. As a result, some rather difficult problems have arisen. One of these relates to the differences between the college preparatory and other programs. In many communities the college preparatory program has come to be thought of as the program for the "elite," while the noncollege-oriented programs have had only limited prestige. This point of view may be held by teachers as well as by students and their families. In some schools the principal has devoted relatively little attention to vocational programs as long as no problems are encountered. Similarly, some vocational people seem to have relatively little interest in other aspects of the program. However, the tendency toward separateness or compartmentalization exists in other aspects of the educational program. Teachers in one subject area often know little or nothing about what is going on in other related subject areas and do not seem to be concerned, in spite of the fact that learning is not bounded by subject matter areas. One of the serious administrative problems in many school systems is to determine how best to assure coordination and cooperation and to avoid or eliminate tendencies toward separateness in various aspects of the educational program.

What guidelines should be utilized to facilitate the development of bona fide comprehensive secondary schools? How can board or administrative policies help to avoid or to solve the problems in this area? What should be the role of teachers and counselors?

SELECTED REFERENCES

BLOOM, BENJAMIN SAMUEL, *Stability and Change in Human Characteristics.* New York: John Wiley & Sons, Inc., 1964.

BRAMELD, THEODORE, *Education for the Emerging Age: Newer Ends and Stronger Means.* New York: Harper & Row, Publishers, 1965.

GARDNER, JOHN WILLIAM, *Self Renewal: The Individual and the Innovative Society.* New York: Harper & Row, Publishers, 1964.

GOODLAD, JOHN I., and M. FRANCES KLEIN, *Behind the Classroom Door.* Worthington, Ohio: Charles A. Jones Publishing Company, 1970.

HASS, GLEN, and KIMBALL WILES, eds., *Readings in Curriculum.* Boston: Allyn and Bacon, Inc., 1966.

HILGARD, ERNEST R., ed., *Theories of Learning and Instruction,* Sixty-third Yearbook of the National Society for the Study of Education, Part I. Chicago: University of Chicago Press, 1964.

JOHNS, ROE L., KERN ALEXANDER, and RICHARD ROSSMILLER, eds., *Dimensions of Educational Need.* Gainesville, Florida: National Educational Finance Project, 1969.

MORPHET, EDGAR L., and DAVID JESSER, eds., *Emerging Designs for Education.* Denver, Colo.: Designing Education for the Future, 1968, Chap. I. Republished by Citation Press, Scholastic Magazines, Inc., New York, N.Y.

MORPHET, EDGAR L., DAVID L. JESSER, and ARTHUR P. LUDKA, *Planning and Providing for Excellence in Education.* Denver, Colo.: Improving State Leadership in Education, 1971. Republished by Citation Press, Scholastic Magazines, Inc., New York, N.Y.

National Society for the Study of Education, *The Curriculum: Retrospect and Prospect,* Seventieth Yearbook, Part I. Chicago, Ill.: The Society, 1970.

SAYLOR, J. GALEN, and WILLIAM M. ALEXANDER, *Curriculum Planning for Modern Schools.* New York: Holt, Rinehart & Winston, Inc., 1966.

SQUIRE, JAMES REED, *A New Look at Progressive Education.* Washington, D.C.: American Association of Supervision and Curriculum Development, 1972.

WEBER, EVELYN, *Early Childhood Education: Perspectives on Change.* Worthington, Ohio: Charles A. Jones Publishing Company, 1970.

15

Personnel Development and Administration*

The general aim of educational administration is to ensure that school systems function properly, that is, according to preconceived purposes and plans of action. Administrators are needed to convert a variety of resources, such as manpower, funds, facilities, and plans into an effective enterprise capable of achieving the system's mission. Administrators are the activating element in the transformation process.

Of the several major plans which administrators must develop for the operation of an educational institution (such as the organization structure, educational program, logistics, human resources, and external relations), none is as critical to the success of the undertaking as those affecting the people responsible for their implementation. Human resources are the life blood of an institution. They help to conceive the kind of service the

*Prepared in large part by WILLIAM B. CASTETTER, Professor of Education, University of Pennsylvania.

schools can render, to develop and implement plans needed to achieve the goals, and to make adjustments between plans and reality. Formal structure, rules and regulations, courses of study, position guides, and policies may be developed, but they take on significance only as people make use of them.

Administrative activities relating to personnel in the employ of an organization are referred to as the *personnel function.* Plans for and decisions about personnel flow from institutional purposes. Positions evolve from

Chart 1
Emerging Human Problems in Schools Systems and Conceptual Developments Applicable to Their Resolution

Emerging Problems in School Systems with Implications for Personnel Administration	Conceptual Developments Applicable to Resolution of Personnel Problems
Social Increased emphasis on self-realization, freedom, meeting individual needs, new life styles, superior-subordinate relationships, psychological reality, social mobility Discrimination in employment	
Economic Higher standard of living Higher cost of living Higher salaries, wages, benefits Rising financial expectations Employment mobility Emphasis on personal security Imbalances in personnel supply and demand **Organizational** Union ascendancy Larger systems Institutional complexity Increase in staff size Position specialization Increasing professionalization Decentralization Individual-Organization conflict Responding appropriately to social change Organization renewal to meet individual needs and organizational goals Sharing of power	Development of new theoretical systems applicable to personnel administration Emergence of a variety of contemporary schools of administrative thought Contributions of behavioral science concepts, such as satisfaction of human needs, motivation, informal organization, the role of the individual and the group in organizations, participation, power equalization, executive behavior Technological developments, including quantitative analysis, application of computer to staffing process, PERT, personnel practices, manpower planning. New techniques and methods in recruitment, selection, development, performance appraisal.

purposes; positions form the the organization structure. Personnel decisions, including the quality and quantity of manpower needed, recruitment, selection, induction, compensation, development, security, and participation have a significant impact on the budget as well as attainment of organizational purposes, and require considerable thought, planning, time, and effort of all administrative personnel to maintain system stability and viability. The general intent of personnel administration is to develop and maintain a highly motivated and effective school staff.

The past decade has been witness to significant changes in concepts about, cognizance of the need for, approaches to, and increasing complexity of the personnel function in school systems. Contemporary efforts in the area of personnel are directed primarily to its continuing evolution. Most organizations accept the fact that personnel administration is an essential activity. As illustrated in Chart 1, contemporary concerns of those involved in personnel administration are two-fold: (1) how to cope with the human problems emerging in organizations; and (2) how to incorporate into personnel administration the most promising ideas from the rising stream of conceptual developments in order to resolve personnel problems more effectively. In the text which follows we shall examine in turn the nature and importance of the personnel function, as well as organizational designs for its administration which are being brought about by societal, economic, political, and organizational pressures.

STRUCTURING THE PERSONNEL FUNCTION

Chart 2 illustrates the general functions of the superintendency and the homogeneous activities related to each function. Analysis of Chart 2 indicates that the main function of a school organization (instruction) is a *line* function. *Supporting functions,* such as logistics, planning, personnel, and external relations are staff functions. While it is true that there is no universal model for structuring the personnel function in any and all school districts, there is considerable agreement in both theory and practice as to the underlying assumptions involved in organizing the personnel unit. The following assumptions illustrate such points of agreement.

- The major components (minifunctions) of the general personnel function generally fall into the following categories: manpower planning, compensation, recruitment, selection, induction, appraisal, development, maintaining and improving service, security, union relations, and organizational democracy. Each of these major components is subdivided into processes. This type of specialization escalates as the size and complexity of the organization increases.
- While all personnel assigned to administrative roles engage in activities related to the personnel function, it is generally conceded that the personnel function

Chart 2
Illustration of the General and Minifunctions of the Superintendency: A Five-component Model

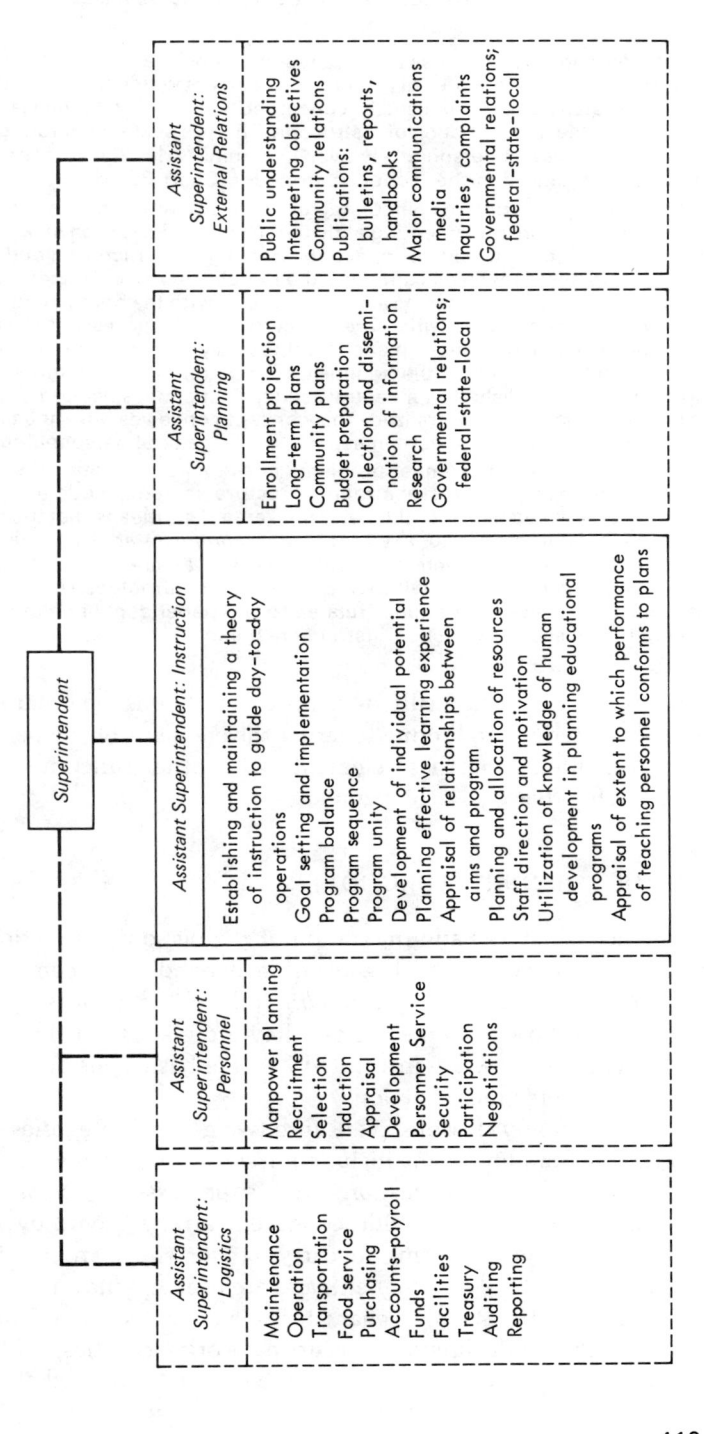

Superintendent

Assistant Superintendent: Logistics

Maintenance
Operation
Transportation
Food service
Purchasing
Accounts-payroll
Funds
Facilities
Treasury
Auditing
Reporting

Assistant Superintendent: Personnel

Manpower Planning
Recruitment
Selection
Induction
Appraisal
Development
Personnel Service
Security
Participation
Negotiations

Assistant Superintendent: Instruction

Establishing and maintaining a theory of instruction to guide day-to-day operations
Goal setting and implementation
Program balance
Program sequence
Program unity
Development of individual potential
Planning effective learning experience
Appraisal of relationships between aims and program
Planning and allocation of resources
Staff direction and motivation
Utilization of knowledge of human development in planning educational programs
Appraisal of extent to which performance of teaching personnel conforms to plans

---

Assistant Superintendent: Planning

Enrollment projection
Long-term plans
Community plans
Budget preparation
Collection and dissemination of information
Research
Governmental relations; federal-state-local

Assistant Superintendent: External Relations

Public understanding
Interpreting objectives
Community relations
Publications: bulletins, reports, handbooks
Major communications media
Inquiries, complaints
Governmental relations; federal-state-local

419

is a staff function. This is to say that personnel is both a responsibility of the entire organization and a special group or department within the central administration. A staff function is usually concerned with activities auxiliary to or supportive of the main function of instruction. There is seldom operating or line authority delegated to personnel involved in administering the personnel function as it is organized in the model illustrated in Chart 2.
- Another way of analyzing the personnel function is to separate it into decision-making and decision-implementing activities. Personnel *decision making*, such as those involving basic courses of action affecting the structuring of the function, or broad personnel plans affecting the system's budget, are generally the province of the superintendency, acting in concert with the board of education. *Decision-implementing* activities are concerned with the essential steps in carrying out major personnel plans developed by upper levels and usually delegated to lower levels of the administrative hierarchy. Recruitment, for example, may be established as a centralized staff function; selection of personnel, however, may be decentralized. This concept conceives both line and staff personnel to be involved in certain aspects of the general personnel function.
- Resolution of modern personnel problems in school organizations is of such crucial importance that the organization structure should include an administrator primarily responsible for the personnel area. This means that the personnel function is formed into a central unit, *administered* by an assistant superintendent, to aid the chief executive as well as line and staff units, in solving personnel problems with which they are confronted. The personnel unit in the central administration is related to and dependent upon other organizational units such as logistics, instruction, planning, and external relations.

In summary, a systematically developed and defensible organization can contribute materially to linking together the elements of the personnel function and to integrating these elements with other functions so that they facilitate effective goal achievement.

PLANNING THE PERSONNEL FUNCTION

The impact which the administration of the personnel function will have on the effectiveness of an organization depends to a considerable extent upon the *plans* and *planning capability* it develops. Types of personnel plans needed, who makes them, how they are made, and the manner in which the who and how are integrated become basic considerations in administering the personnel function.

Planning taxonomy classifies plans into two general categories, *standing* and *single use*. Standing plans include missions, long-range strategies, goals, purposes, policies, programs, procedures, processes, systems, structures, and rules. Such plans provide consistent arrangements by which schools decide to solve problems in carrying out the district mission. Standing plans are relatively permanent, and are used to guide and control the multifaceted functions which characterize a school system. They are especially applicable in dealing with recurring work, activities, problems, and decisions. Single-use plans, on the other hand, are of limited duration.

Personnel Development and Administration 421

Projects, annual budgets, or plans whose lives are of limited duration and designed to accomplish a short-run objective exemplify the single-use plan. Regardless of the plan used, it represents a predetermined course of action.

Types of plans involved in the administration of the personnel function are illustrated in Chart 3. The plans shown in Chart 3 are grouped into three types—those pertaining to the *aims structure,* the *organization structure,* and *personnel processes.* Plans within the aims structure are those designed primarily to establish and maintain *instructional* and *instructional support programs.* Plans contained in the organization structure are especially concerned with *positions* generated by the aims structure. Plans relating to the

Chart 3
*Types of Plans Involved
in the Administration of the Personnel Function*

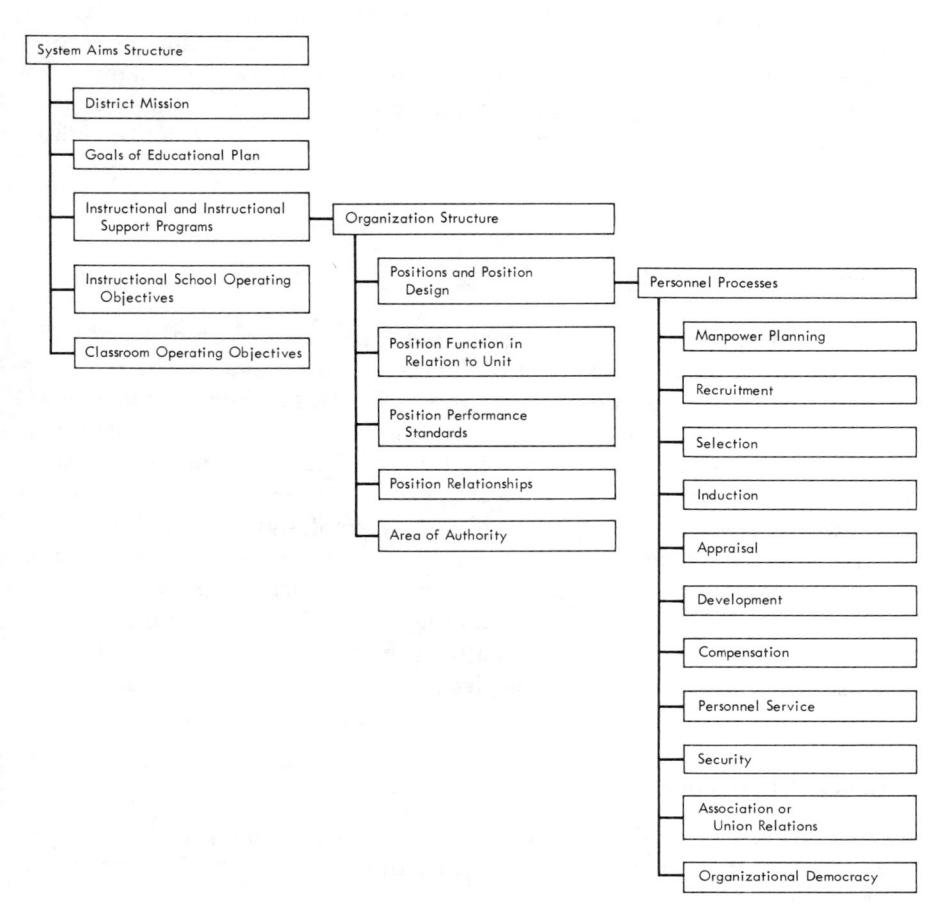

```
System Aims Structure
├── District Mission
├── Goals of Educational Plan
├── Instructional and Instructional
│   Support Programs          ── Organization Structure
├── Instructional School Operating      ├── Positions and Position
│   Objectives                          │   Design                    ── Personnel Processes
└── Classroom Operating Objectives      │                              ├── Manpower Planning
                                        ├── Position Function in      ├── Recruitment
                                        │   Relation to Unit          ├── Selection
                                        ├── Position Performance      ├── Induction
                                        │   Standards                 ├── Appraisal
                                        ├── Position Relationships    ├── Development
                                        └── Area of Authority         ├── Compensation
                                                                      ├── Personnel Service
                                                                      ├── Security
                                                                      ├── Association or
                                                                      │   Union Relations
                                                                      └── Organizational Democracy
```

personnel processes are those designed to attract, develop, and retain *personnel* needed in the manpower system generated by the aims structure.

The personnel processes in operating plans designed to administer the personnel function include manpower planning, recruitment, selection, induction, appraisal, development, compensation, personnel service, security, association or union relations, and participation.

Each of the foregoing personnel operating processes, it should be noted, is further subdivided into sequential tasks essential to achieve the intent of the process and the larger function of which it is a part. This perception of the personnel function is useful in defining tasks of which it will be composed, in fixing responsibility for their performance, and in communicating to the administrative team the information each member needs to carry out those tasks. In addition, breaking down each of the major functions of a school system (instruction, personnel, logistics, external relations, planning) into operating processes not only compels the central administration to clarify organizational expectations, but also assists it in securing consistency among decisions, coordination, and economy of planning efforts. In the sections which follow we shall examine the nature of the several personnel operating processes and consider how each is linked to other personnel processes as well as to other major organizational functions.

STAFFING THE SYSTEM

As noted previously, an organizational structure is composed of various positions designed to accomplish system goals. A variety of administrative activities is essential to keep those positions staffed with personnel who have the knowledge, skills, and motivation to perform the roles effectively. It is becoming increasingly clear that considerable confusion emerges in an organization when these activities are performed independently. What is needed is an integrated system designed to deal with the total array of personnel activities. In the text following we shall examine the first of several processes designed to systematize the personnel function. These include manpower plannning, recruitment, selection, and induction, the intent of which is to attract to and retain in the organization personnel conceptualized in the designs of the various positions to be filled.

Manpower Planning Process

At the core of the personnel function is a planning process which is concerned with resolving major organization personnel problems such as the following:

- How many positions are needed in the school system, both now and in the future, to achieve organizational expectations?
- What should be the design of each position (both present and proposed) in the organization structure?
- What is the relationship of existing manpower to that required in the projected organization structure?

Examination of the foregoing questions relating to the manpower planning process brings into focus a central fact of organization life: manpower plans are determined by the goals of the system. Goals determine the educational plan, the quality and quantity of manpower needed to implement programs comprising the plan, resources to be developed, and the nature of the administrative processes employed to maintain the system.

Operationally speaking, the manpower planning will include the following kinds of activities.

- Forecasting community educational demand (who shall be educated, to what extent, for what purposes?);
- Projecting organization structures and designing positions within the structure;
- Projecting the short- and long-term budgetary impact of manpower plans;
- Reviewing appropriateness of contemporary staff deployment practices within the system;
- Preparing an information system to facilitate manpower planning.
- Estimating the manpower impact of collective negotiations;
- Visualizing the manpower impact of organizational changes; and
- Appraising the results of manpower planning.

While it is important to appreciate that the foregoing description of the manpower planning process conceptualizes a series of sequential and interconnected activities, it is equally important to understand that the process is linked closely to other processes which form the personnel function. The recruitment plan, for example, will be aimless unless it is based on manpower planning decisions indicating the number and types of positions to be filled as well as the specifications designed to guide efforts to match people and positions. How important the interrelation is between manpower planning and other personnel processes may be judged as we consider the process by which the school systems seeks to attract people to positions in the organization structure which need to be filled.

Recruitment Process

One of the assumptions behind the manpower planning process is that it will provide school officials with a view of the flow of personnel into, through, and out of the organization over time. The personnel flow pattern will provide insights into past experience concerning external recruitment, internal promotions, transfers, separations, and terminations. Data such as the foregoing will establish a basis for forecasting personnel needs and set the stage for the initiation of the next step in the personnel function—recruitment.

The recruitment process, as one of the interlocking components of the personnel function, is aimed at bringing into the school system the quality and quantity of manpower needed to fill position openings. The cruciality of a systems approach to the personnel function may be clearly illustrated by the recruitment process. The manpower planning process, for example, should clarify the question of internal promotion versus external recruitment. In addition, data collected in the manpower planning process should shed considerable light on which manpower sources provide the quality of personnel sought by the system. Further, the manpower planning process establishes in advance the extent to which continuing education programs should be provided to enable personnel within the system to move into upper-level positions. Thus, it is clear that personnel recruitment is perceived not as a separate, compartmentalized activity, but as a component linked to many other personnel processes, including manpower planning, selection, induction, and development.

The impact of general personnel policies on the recruitment process becomes clear by analysis of the policy considerations organizations must resolve with respect to:

- Race, creed, national background, age, sex, and physical handicaps of position candidates;
- Internal promotion via career path;
- Personnel development programs; and
- Employment of relatives, veterans, part-time and temporary personnel, mothers and working wives, minors, and rehiring of former personnel.

Once the school system has settled the manpower policy issues alluded to above, as well as decided the manpower sources it wishes to use to fill positions which are currently open, the stage is set to complete the recruitment process. This involves plans for organizing and coordinating recruitment activities.

After the recruitment tasks have been identified, they are assigned to different people at various levels in the organization and coordinated. This includes (1) establishing communication between the school system and potential candidates to provide the information about the position and to secure information about the candidate; (2) recruitment information system; (3) recruitment activities schedule; (4) preparation of recruitment budget; (5) management of recruitment correspondence; (6) systematization of screening procedures; and, (7) tracking recruitment progress of each candidate.

Thus the recruitment process is conceived to be a centrally planned operation, usually under the direction of an assistant superintendent for personnel or equivalent administrator. In order to coordinate the recruitment process effectively, consideration should be given to developing procedures for centralizing recruitment and screening and decentralizing selection. Given this discussion of the recruitment process, let us now examine the collateral process of personnel selection.

Selection Process

The next step in the staffing activity is selection, the process by which the school system goes about matching people and positions. The overall process of matching people and positions resolves itself into a series of subproblems such as the following: (1) what are the requirements of each position to be filled?; (2) what are the main specifications needed to fill the positions?; (3) to what extent does the individual candidate match position expectations?; (4) what is the most feasible and desirable plan for obtaining personnel for the system's short- and long-run needs?

In order to resolve the foregoing problems relative to personnel selection, some type of selection process must be established and maintained. This process includes (1) using a position guide in which essential data regarding the positions and person specifications are written (the position specifications should include facts about position title, primary functions, major responsibility, summary of key duties, special assignments, relationships, area of authority—the person specifications should include facts about such qualifications as education, experience, skills, knowledge, abilities, initiative, judgment, personal characteristics); (2) developing an information system which will yield appropriate data for the selection process; (3) appraising the data and the applicants; (4) preparing an eligibility list; (5) nominating personnel for employment; and (6) appointing personnel formally to positions on the basis of nominations by the chief executive. In this process the role of the school principal as indicated in Chapter 13 needs to be made clear and significant.

The position guide is one of the tools essential to the selection and other personnel processes. It is assumed that for every position in the system there will be a position guide. More than likely, all position guides will be included in the organization manual. This manual then becomes the formal document for use in manpower planning, recruitment, selection, appraisal, and personnel development.

One of the newer approaches to be employed in the selection process, especially as it pertains to administrative personnel, has been described by Odiorne, based upon the objectives of a given position.[1] *The objective approach* to selection starts with the assumption that a position has three types of objectives:

- Innovation or change-making objectives;
- Problem-solving objectives; and
- Regular, ordinary, or routine objectives.

Using the three major categories of position objectives outlined above, the selection process focuses upon uncovering predictors in the individual's history which would point up the probabilities regarding how the candidate would operate at each of the three levels. The routine position objectives are considered to be a must requirement; problem-solving and innovative objectives are on an ascending scale of administrative excellence; the tools of selection are then designed to predict, on the basis of past performance, to what extent a candidate will produce results in terms of position objectives.

No description of the selection process would be complete without making the observation that the division of activities, such as personnel selection, into a series of steps for which designated personnel are responsible is primarily mechanistic. However elaborate the selection process in a school system, it is not a panacea for solving personnel problems. People may meet the criteria but fail in the position for lack of motivation. In short, because people are human and complex, the selection process is fallible. Consequently, other processes are needed to minimize personnel discontent and to assure a high level of performance once they are on the job. The discussion which follows focuses on organizational efforts needed to facilitate the *adjustment* of individuals after a decision has been made to employ them in the school system.

Induction Process

After an applicant has been selected to fill a position in the school organization, it is to the advantage of both the system and the individual that he become adjusted as soon as possible to the position and to the conditions affecting his performance in the position. This process of adjustment is known as induction—a systematic organizational effort to

---

[1] George S. Odiorne, *Personnel Administration by Objectives* (Homewood, Illinois: Richard D. Irwin, Inc., 1971), 270 ff.

minimize problems confronting new personnel so that they can contribute maximally to the work of the school while realizing personal and position satisfaction.

The personnel induction process is designed to resolve the following types of problems which are encountered to a greater or lesser extent by all inductees:

- Problems relating to the *position*—the organizational expectations of the position, the resources needed to perform effectively in the role, and position constraints are illustrative.
- Problems relating to *school system*—mission, policies, procedures, rules, regulations, and services.
- Problems relating to *other system personnel*—colleagues, the superior-subordinate relationship, and the people who will have an impact on his productivity and need satisfaction.
- Problems involved in becoming acquainted with and making adjustments in the *community*.
- Problems of a *personal* nature—finding living accommodations, banking facilities, shopping areas, etc.

The mobility of school personnel, as well as the problem of turnover, emphasizes the need for continuing efforts to maintain and to improve the induction process. The process may take many forms and involve a wide variety of activities throughout the induction cycle which is designed to assist in adjustments during the pre-appointment stage, the interim stage, and the probationary period. The school system and the community need to implement plans to facilitate the attainment of the goals of the induction program.

The induction process is one that contributes to various human goals of the school system, including security, hospitable environment, and placement of personnel in positions in which they will be able to find personal satisfaction and to make effective use of their abilities. The induction process is an organizational acknowledgment that human maladjustment is a prime contributor to system dysfunction. In the text following, our aim is to examine processes in the personnel function designed to improve the performance of personnel once the major problems of induction have been resolved satisfactorily and the inductee is gradually assimilated into the school staff.

IMPROVING PERSONNEL PERFORMANCE

One of the hard realities of organizational life is that the selection process, however perfect, does not ensure that placement of an individual in a position will result automatically in a high degree of man-position compatibility. Every school system is confronted with problems such as the following in order to maintain suitable levels of performance by people in positions to which they are assigned:

- The selection process may produce a mismatch between man and position.
- The requirements of the position may change.
- The behavior of the individual in the position may change.
- The available manpower supply to fill the position may be limited.
- Personnel within the school system can be promoted to a new positions but need training.
- Newly employed personnel need assistance.
- New problems, procedures, knowledge, positions, and developments create a need for continuing education of personnel.
- Social change leads to modification in organizational objectives, which in turn creates a demand for behavioral changes in personnel.

Analysis of the foregoing conditions leads to the conclusion that personnel development has become a major organizational activity and a key process of the personnel function. It is based on the assumption that every organization must apply increasing amounts of its budget to the development of its human resources. Placement of an individual in a position under this assumption means that the organization takes on the task of assisting him, chiefly through two personnel processes, to improve his position performances. These processes are now examined.

Appraisal Process

The nucleus of any organizational plan to assist its members to perform effectively in their present positions and to develop personnel to fill new or existing positions is a program that will identify their strengths and weaknesses. Thus, performance appraisal may be defined as one of the several processes of the personnel function designed to arrive at judgments about the past or present performance and future potential of an individual to the school system against the background of his total work environment. Considered in this way, the appraisal process may be thought of as one of a network of operating processes, each of which is interrelated and interdependent. This observation can be illustrated by examinination of the following activities upon which the appraisal process is focused:

- Place the individual in the system where he can realize his own goals and contribute effectively to those of the organization.
- Motivate personnel toward achieving system as well as personal goals.

- Improve performance.
- Uncover abilities.
- Ascertain the potential of the individual to perform various types of tasks.
- Encourage self-development.
- Point up continuing education needs.
- Provide a guide for salary determination.
- Facilitate mutual understanding between superior and subordinate.
- Transfer, denote, promote, or dismiss personnel.
- Test validity of recruitment and selection processes.

One of the first questions which a school system faces in building an appraisal system is the assumptions on which it will be planned, implemented, and controlled. In effect, to develop a set of premises for an appraisal system is to set forth what the organizations's beliefs or convictions are concerning the appraisal of personnel. The premises form the basis upon which reasoning proceeds relative to what the organization believes the appraisal system should accomplish, and how it should be organized and administered to attain such expectations. The following premises are illustrative:

- The beliefs an organization holds about the nature of man have considerable impact on the design of the appraisal system.
- The effectiveness of a performance appraisal system is dependent upon and influenced by sound structural prerequisites, such as strategies, missions, goals, policies, and programs.
- A performance appraisal system, properly designed, has considerable potential for achieving integration of individual and organizational interests.
- The primary intent of the performance appraisal system is to facilitate the self-development of personnel.
- The appraisal *process* is the core of the appraisal system.
- The quality of the super-subordinate relationship influences to a considerable extent the effectiveness of the performance appraisal process.
- Effectiveness of the performance approval system depends upon plans for the selection and development of competent administrative personnel.
- Maintenance and improvement of the appraisal system are achieved by effective application of the controlling function, i.e., continually evaluating the extent to which results of the appraisal system are in accordance with expectations, and correcting deviations accordingly.

The appraisal *process* involved pre-appraisal and a planning conference, performance appraisal, performance progress and a review conference, post-development program review conference, appraisal process and its recycling. Pressures currently bringing about modifications in the traditional performance appraisal system for school personnel are numerous, including *organizational, social,* and *economic* changes, as well as *client, per-*

sonnel, and *theorist* reaction. Mutual goal setting, counseling, progress review, integration of individual and organization goals, and needs satisfaction of staff members are but a few of the change and reaction contributions to which modern school systems are heir. Let us now turn our attention to the next sequential step in the personnel function designed to improve personnel performance.

Development Process

By definition, development refers to provisions made by the school system for improving the performance of school personnel from initial employment to retirement. There are several dimensions of this definition which need elaboration. The first of these dimensions is organizational responsibility for development. Although personnel can and should improve their effectiveness without formal involvement of the system, development of personnel requires systematic organizational planning.

A second dimension of the definition is that staff development embraces all personnel employed by the system, certificated as well as noncertificated. Every individual on the system payroll, according to this concept of development, will be involved at various stages in his career, in some form of continuing education. A third dimension of the definition is that personnel development is aimed at satisfying two kinds of expectations—the contribution required of the individual by the school system, and the material and emotional rewards anticipated by the individual staff members as performance residuals. A fourth concept of staff development is that deliberate investment in human capital (skills and knowledge of personnel) represents a valuable asset of the system, one which is essential to its stability as well as to its viability.

Of the emerging concepts and practices relating to staff development in a school system, the following are noteworthy:

- One of the realities of school administration is that in all likelihood there will never be an abundant supply of talent to fill every position. Consequently, a plan must be maintained to develop those who are in the system as well as those who are recruited.
- Development is aimed at changing the behavior of personnel toward a predetermined goal. The goal is determined by factors relating to the position, the man, and the organization.
- Performance management is emerging as a replacement of the narrower concept of supervision.
- Performance appraisal is basic to the initiation of plans for improving individual performance.
- School systems of the future will grant much more autonomy to local school

attendance units than is now the case. Consequently, development programs of the future will be highly decentralized, aimed at making each individual effective in his assignment, and enhancing his contribution to the goals of the work unit in which he is located.
- Development programs in the future will be focused upon goals. The prime concerns of the programs will include these questions:
  What behavior do we wish to change?
  What is the present condition or level of behavior we wish to change?
  What is the desired condition we wish to achieve in personnel performance?
  How can we link learning theory to staff development programs?
  What types of training shall be employed (classroom, on-the-job, apprenticeships)?
  What types of newer training technologies shall be employed (computers, projectors, closed-circuit TV, programmed text materials, and video-cassettes?)
  What indicators shall we use to evaluate the effectiveness of development programs?

Staff development, then, is viewed as an essential cyclical plan by which the organization maintains and renews itself. Key concepts in the administration of a staff development program include consideration by school officials of the principle that investment in human resources adds to its capital formation in the form of skills and knowledge; that development means changing human behavior; that learning theory and development plans are inseparable. Having reviewed some of the major concepts of staff development, let us now turn to another process in the personnel function which is equally important in improving staff performance.

Compensation Process

Organizational concern about plans by which personnel are compensated is an ageless problem. A compensation system properly conceived and administered can make an important contribution to attainment of specific objectives of a school system as well as to the individual satisfaction of its members. Goals to which the system can gear its compensation planning include the following:

- Attracting and retaining competent career personnel;
- Motivating personnel to optimum performance in present positions;
- Creating incentives to growth in performance ability;
- Getting maximum return in service for the economic investment made in the compensation plan;
- Developing personnel confidence in the intent of the organization to build *equity* and *objectivity* into the compensation plan;
- Making the plan internally consistent and externally competitive;
- Relating compensation levels to importance and difficulty of positions;

- Making salaries commensurate with the kinds of personnel the organization requires; and
- Establishing a compensation structure conducive to the economic, social, and psychological satisfactions of personnel.

In order to achieve the compensation goals listed above, a systematic process is essential to determine the worth of work and the worth of people who do the work. The compensation process by which this is achieved is shown graphically in Chart 4.

Compensation policy is also an important tool in achieving the compensation goals of the system noted above. The policy guides listed below illustrate their importance to the development and implementation of derivative compensation plans.

- Contemporary thought and practices governing compensation systems embrace a compensation structure consisting of salaries, wages, collateral benefits, and noneconomic benefits (psychic income).
- The compensation structure includes personnel in every capacity, regardless of income level or position responsibility.
- Quality of performance should be rewarded.
- The individual position and the objectives established for it establish a departure from conventional salary administration procedure.

In addition to the foregoing considerations, there are a number of other interrelated factors which affect the amount of the paycheck an individual receives from the school system. These include compensation legislation, prevailing compensation practices, collective negotiations, supply of and demand for personnel, system ability and willingness to pay, as well as the standard and cost of living. While the foregoing capsulization of compensation points up important variables which affect annual compensation levels in a school system, some factor or combination of factors may be more important than others at a given time. In effect, to a considerable extent, compensation is a situational matter.

Chart 4
The Compensation Process

Develop compensation policy → Negotiate with associations, unions → Establish position structure → Set economic value of positions → Judge economic worth of position holders → Devise plan for compensating special personnel → Formalize compensation plan → Control and update compensation plan

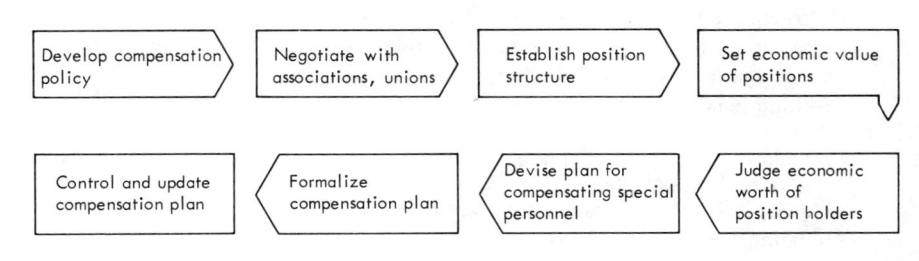

MAINTAINING AND IMPROVING PERSONNEL SERVICE

The flow of personnel into and out of a school system is endless. In order to make it possible for the system to have *uninterrupted and effective* service in each position in the structure, plans designed for this purpose are indispensable. The fact that staff members do become mentally and physically ill, that they do experience work- and nonwork-connected accidents, and that their productivity is affected by physical conditions of employment leads to the inevitable conclusion that organizational plans are essential to keeping the system staffed continuously. Chart 5 has been included to illustrate key goals of personnel service maintenance, as well as the salient provisions needed for achieving the goals.

The process by which problems relating to maintenance and improvement of personnel service are dealt with varies from, but has much in common with, arrangements for making and carrying out other organizational decisions. If the procedures for achieving the objectives of personnel service are analyzed carefully it will be noted that they are to a considerable extent *repetitive*. It is clear, for example, that problems relating to leaves of absence, health, substitute service, and safety are aspects of personnel administration that confront administrators daily. Consequently, the administration of personnel service, as conceptualized in Chart 5, calls for isolation of the recurring elements of these problems and for standardizing, to the extent possible, the manner in which they are treated. The school system can ill afford to wait, for example, until a classroom teacher is hospitalized, or until death in the family of a staff

Chart 5
Personnel Service by Objectives

Objectives of Personnel Service
Improve System Ability to Perform Function
Improve Physical, Psychological, Organizational Environment
Prevent Accidents
Control Personnel Costs
Contribute to Personnel Emotional Security
Comply with Statutory Requirements
Contribute to Personnel Financial Security
Reduce Personnel Turnover
Establish Program Limits
Provide Personnel Opportunity for Development

Procedures for Achieving Goals
Leaves of Absence
Health and Medical Service
Substitute Service
Safety and Working Conditions

member occurs, before deciding what organizational provisions shall govern these events.

Personnel services represent an area of educational administration ideally suited to the application of standing plans such as standard procedures, rules, regulations, and policies, all of which are designed to deal with recurring problems. Standing plans with regard to personnel services not only simplify that task of deciding how a specific personnel situation is to be resolved but also assure a degree of consistency, dependability, and quality of decision throughout the school system as a whole.

The fact should not go unnoticed that the components of personnel service—leaves of absence, substitute service, health and medical service, and safety and working conditions—are usually considered to be items for collective negotiation. As such, they are reviewed annually and considered to be essential provisions to which all organizational personnel are entitled. So viewed, it is incumbent upon school systems to plan personnel services provisions in a way that they are as conducive as possible to the object.

PERSONNEL SECURITY

Throughout history educators have struggled to gain work-related provisions which would protect them against arbitrary treatment; ensure continuing employment; enable them to exercise freedom of thought and expression on and off the job; and protect them against postemployment financial insecurity. The struggle to achieve these ends has been long and difficult. While the principle of personnel security is well established in many nations throughout the Western world, and particularly in the United States, the gap between principle and practice has not been completely eliminated. Chart 6 illustrates the relationship between objectives of personnel security and the tools generally employed to achieve them. The discussion which follows is focused upon five dimensions of personnel security—tenure, academic freedom, protection against arbitrary treatment, retirement, and individual adaptation. Of these dimensions, most are generated by either legislative or system action, such as tenure, retirement, social security, grievance procedures, and academic freedom. One dimension of personnel security which cannot be achieved by legislative or judicial action may be classified as individual adaptation.[2] The latter dimension is the sense of security achieved by the individual when he is able to perform his role effectively in the system. The inner security and self-confidence developed by an individual on the job is generated by a

[2]Other dimensions of the personnel function related to personnel security and discussed elsewhere in this section include collateral benefits, position and financial security, and collective negotiations.

Chart 6
Personnel Security by Objectives

Objectives of Personnel Security	Procedures for Achieving Security Objectives
Academic Freedom	Tenure Provisions
Position Security	Retirement Provisions
Financial Security	Grievance Machinery
Protection Against Arbitrary Treatment	System Personnel Plans
Freedom of Thought, Expression, Action	Transfer, Promotion
Individual Organization Adaptation	

number of provisions which are a part of the design of the personnel function. The nature of position performance management exercised on behalf of the individual staff member, opportunities for development, fair treatment, and general organization climate contribute in varying degrees to the maturation of personnel in the roles to which they are assigned and to the kind of individual-organization fit to which the system aspires.

TENURE OF PROFESSIONAL PERSONNEL. The concept of tenure for professional personnel in education is well established, salient features of which include (1) completion of a specified probationary period; (2) tenure for personnel who meet performance standards during the probationary period; and (3) an orderly procedure for dismissal of personnel.

While it is true that tenure for teachers is accepted in both principle and practice, the decade of the seventies is witness to various challenges to and efforts at the legislative level to eliminate tenure for teachers. The emerging major argument against tenure is that teachers should not be permitted to have the tenure privilege as well as the privilege of negotiating the conditions under which they will work. These two types of privileges, according to legislative reaction, are in conflict with one another. Thus, so the argument goes, teachers must choose one privilege or the other; they should not be permitted to exercise both privileges. It is an issue which will be contested vigorously on both sides as demands escalate for higher salaries and collateral benefits of education personnel.

ACADEMIC FREEDOM. Freedom of thought and expression are crucial concerns in the administration of the personnel function. The right to exercise intellectual freedom in the classroom is basic to freedom of learning. So essential is the concept of academic freedom to the development of free minds for free men that safeguards are needed in local school systems to ensure conditions conducive to the teaching-learning process. Threats to personal and academic freedom of school personnel cannot be dealt with effectively unless protective measures are established by the board of education. Much can be accomplished by the board to ensure academic freedom for its personnel if it develops plans for receiving and examining criticisms relating to the personal and academic freedom of staff members; developing administrative machinery to deal systematically with attacks on personnel, teaching methods, and the educational program; and initiating plans to protect personnel so that they are able to exercise personal and academic freedom in the roles of educator and as citizen.

PROTECTION AGAINST ARBITRARY TREATMENT. Since the dawn of work organizations, some personnel have suffered from arbitrary treatment by their superiors in the form of actual or threatened loss of position, status, power, income, privileges, and freedom of action or speech. Efforts of personnel to minimize arbitrary treatment, as well as social legislation designed to ensure worker rights beyond receipt of pay for services rendered, have brought into being protective arrangements which make organizational exercise of this form of personnel control more difficult. An administrative tool which has been devised and frequently employed to protect personnel against arbitrary treatment is the grievance system. Under this system there is an established procedure for identifying and initiating action to deal with grievances. Systematization of grievance handling is conducive to minimization of discontent and dissatisfaction. The very existence of a grievance system is, in itself, an assurance to the individual staff member that the rights and privileges he has been guaranteed will be protected.

RETIREMENT. The provision of retirement benefits for educational personnel is in keeping with similar arrangements for other groups of public and private employees. Most retirement funds call for contributions to a retirement fund at specified rates by the members as well as by the district and the state. Retirement benefits are based generally upon a predetermined fraction of the average compensation for the last several years of employment. Federal social security arrangements have, on the one hand, supplemented teacher retirement benefits, and on the other, escalated the combined cost of both retirement and social security to the point where the question of the ability of personnel to afford both plans has become an important administrative and social issue. Three criteria are usually employed to test the provisions of a retirement system: (1) Are the retirement funds fully vested? (2) Is the contribution rate adequate; and (3) Are retirement contributions protected against adverse economic conditions, such as inflation and deflation? One of the most valuable services school systems can render to personnel relative to retirement is advice about what needs to be done to prevent the retirement system from drifting into obsolescence. New concepts are constantly emerging regarding the operation of retirement systems, such as the variable annuity, age of retirement, vesting, and relative size of contributions by employee, employer, and the state. Continuous appraisal and modification of retirement systems is an administrative responsibility of high priority, since personnel now consider retirement benefits an important element of their compensation for working, and the equivalent of a property right to which they will become heir in their post-employment period.

PERSONNEL PARTICIPATION

The human goals of a school system, as conceptualized in Chart 7, include organizational citizenship in decision making. The basic assumption behind the concept of personnel participation in shaping the destiny of a school system may be stated as follows: there is a strong, positive relationship between the extent of personnel participation in the affairs of the school system and their willingness to contribute to achievement of organization goals. This relationship extends from performance management involving superior and subordinate to systemwide decisions affecting the status and working conditions of staff members.

The concern of the discussion which follows is to focus upon two personnel processes which have a considerable impact on the extent to and manner in which personnel participation becomes a reality.

Collective Negotiations Process

More than two million teachers in the United States belong to unions or professional education associations. The factual essence of this statistic leads to the inescapable conclusion that such organizations have profound impact on personnel administration. The bonding together of personnel

Chart 7
Conceptualization of the Human Goals of a School System

- Organizational climate conducive to optimum personnel development
- Fair, courteous, considerate treatment
- Absence of discrimination
- Grievance machinery
- Protection against arbitrary treatment
- Equality of opportunity
- Economic security
- Full utilization of personnel talent
- Effective leadership
- Organizational citizenship
- Full information

who seek particular goals (one of which is decision participation), who have assigned tasks to various members, who have employed specialized personnel to carry out the tasks, and who have granted authority to various members to act in their behalf has changed decision making in most school systems from a unilateral to a bilateral or multilateral arrangement. Thus, bargaining has become a way of life in nearly all school organizations, and enlightened educational administration must concern itself with developing union-administration relations so that they are conducive to the purposes for which the school system exists.

Contemporary collective bargaining is conceived as going beyond the willingness of a board of education to hear from, listen to, or be consulted about conditions of employment. The broader concept of collective negotiations is considered to be a joint determination of the terms of employment, which, when mutually agreed to, binds both parties to those terms.

The collective negotiations process in a school system consists of essentially two subprocesses: (1) *agreement negotiation;* and (2) *agreement administration.* This process is considerably different from other personnel processes described earlier, since it transcends the boundaries of the school system by its impact on the political, social, economic, and educational facets of local communities, state, and nation. A collective negotiations agreement in Los Angeles, for example, may have far-reaching consequences on collective negotiation activities in New York City, Chicago, and Honolulu.

The emerging collective negotiations process in education is not without its critics. Demands are increasing to compel unions for educational personnel to engage in compulsory arbitration, and to eliminate the right of teachers' unions to strike. These demands are generally based on the argument that teacher strikes are obstructive to organizational effectiveness and interfere with the right of children to be educated.

The evolution of union-administration relations indicates that problems involved in cooperation are not as distinct, as traumatic, or as unique as they were once assumed to be. Gradually, school systems and unions, despite inevitable conflict in interests, are learning to engage in participative decision making. Slowly there is a realization, especially on the part of boards of education, that a union can exercise a beneficial effect on the viability of the school system if constant and enlightened efforts are made to improve the relationship between the two parties.

Organizational Democracy

No discussion of personnel participation in the affairs of a school system would be complete without reference to the application of democratic ideals to personnel administration.

One of the essential assumptions of institutions which adhere to democratic principles is that those who plan the conditions of work and those who do the work should be involved in determining what the conditions of work ought to be. As illustrated in Chart 8, we may specify two categories of personnel participation: (1) superior-subordinate participation in performance management; and (2) staff participation in matters affecting their own welfare or that of the total system.

The ultimate aim of personnel participation in decision making is to improve the nature of the decisions which are made, either in the manner in which the individual performs his role in the position to which he is assigned, or in the resolution of systemwide problems and issues which affect all personnel. Included in the anticipated by-products of personnel participation are that it will motivate members to cooperate voluntarily in role performance, to exercise greater initiative in performance improvement, to develop more positive attitudes toward superiors and toward the organization, and to engage in a higher level of organizational citizenship. In brief, personnel participation, properly planned, should contribute to both the satisfaction of individual needs and to fulfillment of organizational expectations.

SOME IMPORTANT PROBLEMS AND ISSUES

Some of the salient issues relating to personnel in education include the following:

- Is a tenure law in the best interests of teachers? In the best interests of education?
- Should teachers be allowed to strike? Are existing certification standards obsolescent?

Chart 8
Illustration of Types of Personnel-Organization Participation

Individual Participation in Developing	Group Participation in Developing
Major Goals of Position	District Mission
Position Guide	Educational Goals
Performance Standards for Position	Programs
	General Objectives
Position Relationships	Behavioral Objectives
Performance Appraisal Process	Personnel Goals
Superior-Subordinate Program Review	Personnel Policies, Procedures
Performance Objectives	Union-Organization
Career Path	Relationships

- Is the use of paraprofessional personnel defensible?
- How can the concept of differentiated staffing be employed effectively?
- How should the personnel function in a school system be organized?
- How can a school system deal rationally with the inordinately intense enthusiasm for personnel "accountability"?
- What can be done about the lag in school organizations in developing information systems for better management of manpower resources?

Are Tenure Laws Essential?

As the trend toward collective organization of teaching personnel intensifies, so do demands for the elimination of state tenure laws. The experience under a tenure law in Pennsylvania makes it possible to understand the concerns of legislators, school boards, administrators, and citizens in general about the consequences of tenure laws. The main points made in a study[3] of the Pennsylvania law are:

- Under this law, during the period from 1940 to 1970—*30 years*—only 65 teachers have been dismissed for all the reasons permissible.
- During this same 30-year period, *only 193 tenure cases have been processed* which led to the 65 dismissals.
- In this same period, *only 38 demotions* have been accomplished under the law.
- When averaging these actions *over the 30-year period*, out of a total tenured population of about 100,000 persons, *slightly more than 2 teachers per year* have been dismissed statewide, *and only 1 teacher per year, statewide, has been reduced in salary or position.* Normal personnel standards suggest that the minimum numbers involved in dismissal, demotion, or transfer to other types of work for ineffective work performance should be considerably larger.

The criticisms of tenure laws are numerous, including these: (1) the price a student must pay for such protection against social discipline is inordinately high; (2) good teachers pay a high price for the damage that incompetent teachers do to the operation of the educational program; and (3) the general intent or mission of the school system cannot be achieved under tenure laws. Consequently, the arrangement which teachers are now enjoying—*contractual protection* as well as *legislative protection*—appears to be in for increasing attack and probable modification in the near future.

Should tenure legislation be modified so that it will become a part of the negotiations process between teacher organizations and boards of edu-

[3]Pennsylvania School Boards Association, "Tenure Must Go," *Information Legislative Service,* **X**, 10 (March 10, 1972), 8–9.

cation? Will teacher organizations take essential steps to reduce their ranks of those deemed incompetent?

Teacher Strikes—Compulsory Arbitration?

Another issue affecting indirectly the security of personnel in education is the impact which strikes engaged in by teacher organizations have on the education of children and youth. Within recent years the militancy of teacher organizations has led, in many cases, to the closing of schools and to the embitterment toward education of some segments of society. Demand for teacher accountability, for cessation of increases in local taxes to support teacher salary increases, and insistence upon compulsory arbitration as a surrogate for closing the schools are among the results produced in the harvest of collective negotiations. While these demands for public control over the right of public employees to strike have not been limited to teacher organizations, it is in the closing of schools that citizens perceive most poignantly the "evils" associated with collective negotiations, especially those parents whose children are affected. Consequently, it must be anticipated that there will be continued insistence by the public for the elimination of the right of a public sector of the economy involving at least a fourth of a nation to close its organizational doors. Strikes, it is alleged, endanger the public welfare, and the right to deny a public service such as an education to the citizens who support education through taxation cannot and should not be endured. Is compulsory arbitration a defensible alternative?

How Can Organizational Development and Personnel Administration Be Integrated?

It should be recognized that the demand for more effective personnel management is a strong one. This could be viewed as a direct approach to change the individual. On the other hand, improved management also involves improving organizational health and genuine concern with the "system" as the target of change. Organizational development requires that the members of the system themselves assess and plan the development of their organization—that they seek organizational health. It also assumes that this effort may indeed be the best road to effective personnel development.

Can a plan of organization and operation be developed for your school system or a subsystem of it in which these two theories of invervention are reconciled?

SELECTED REFERENCES

CASTETTER, WILLIAM B., *The Personnel Function in Educational Administration.* New York: The Macmillan Company, 1971.

CASTETTER, WILLIAM B. and RICHARD S. HEISLER., *Appraising and Improving the Performance of School Administrative Personnel.* Philadelphia: Center for Field Studies, Graduate School of Education, University of Pennsylvania, 1971.

CASTETTER, WILLIAM B. and RICHARD S. HEISLER. *Planning the Compensation of School Administrative Personnel.* Philadelphia: Center for Field Studies, Graduate School of Education, University of Pennsylvania, 1970.

GIBSON, R. OLIVER and HEROLD C. HUNT, *The School Personnel Administrator.* Boston: Houghton Mifflin Company, 1965.

MURDICK, ROBERT G. and JOEL E. ROSS, *Information Systems for Modern management.* Englewood Cliffs, N.J.: Prentice-Hall, Inc., 1971.

National Education Association, Educational Research Service, *School Staffing Ratios: Guidelines in Literature, Statute, and Local Policy.* ERS Circular No. 3, 1972. Washington: The Service, 1972.

National Education Association, "New Approaches in the Evaluation of School Personnel," *Research Bulletin* **50**, 2 (May 1972) 40–44.

ODIORNE, GEORGE S., *Personnel Administration by Objectives.* Homewood, Illinois: Richard D. Irwin, Inc., 1971.

PERRY, CHARLES R. and WESLEY A. WILDMAN, *The Impact of Negotiations in Public Education: The Evidence From the Schools.* Worthington, Ohio: Charles A. Jones Publishing Company, 1970.

SCHMUCK, RICHARD A. and MATTHEW B. MILES, eds., *Organization Development in Schools.* Palo Alto, California: National Press Books, 1971.

STRAUSS, GEORGE and LEONARD R. SAYLES, *Personnel: The Human Problems of Management,* 3d ed. Englewood Cliffs, New Jersey: Prentice Hall, Inc., 1971.

16

Facilities for Education*

School facilities are one of the major concerns and opportunities of the school administrator. They are of great importance because of the impact of the plant and equipment on the educational processes and program. While it is generally agreed that the plant should reflect the educational program and needs, it is often true that the educational program bears many evidences of the influence of the plant. This may be the result of a number of factors, such as the tangibility of the school plant and the number of years that it serves.

SCHOOL FACILITIES IN AN ERA OF CHANGE

If it is true that the school facility should reflect educational programs and needs, then it should follow that school plants in an era of change will also reflect the changes.

*Prepared in large part by HERBERT E. SALINGER, Director, Field Service Center, University of California, Berkeley.

While new open-plan schools tend to personify the greatest recent change in school-plant planning, it appears that more educational plant changes are in the offing. The facility planners must be able to take into consideration the push to plan school programs that in terms of space and function (1) are compatible with the environment (the ecology movement); (2) can advance the cause of human understanding by assimilating youth of differing backgrounds (integration); (3) will reflect the needs of younger children (early childhood education); (4) will provide opportunity for a greater understanding and ability to cope with the world of work (career education); (5) will attract children because of unique programs related to specific needs (magnet and alternative schools); (6) will permit the flexible use of professional, paraprofessional, and volunteer aides and staff members (differentiated staff utilization); (7) will permit a wide gamut of curricular approaches (individualized learning including such concepts as individually programmed instruction, computer-assisted instruction, continuous development, mastery learning, variable grouping, etc.); (8) can be used on a year-round basis (the year-round school plans including 45–15, trimester, 4 quarters, etc.); (9) can deal effectively with the knowledge explosion (retrieval systems, computer assisted instruction, media centers); and (10) can meet a varied range of community needs (community education).

Changes in Organization within the School

Change and the opportunity for change within the school also offer a major challenge to the school plant planner. Team teaching and other differentiated staffing patterns including paid and volunteer aides have meaning for the school plant. In many cases this meaning has been translated into large and small group-instructional areas. Related to it are changing staffing patterns such as the development of a handful of professions engaged in teaching as distinct from the teacher, the place of guidance staff, social workers, community liaison workers, and other specialists.

Other internal changes are reflected in the increased use of an all-encompassing media center including a library and multimedia equipment and facilities. The provision of proper facilities for independent study is a challenge. Surely it is not merely a matter of providing more rooms to care for more smaller classes. As classroom walls disappear in a number of new schools, questions are already raised about the need for privacy or "retreat" rooms for the individual child or teacher and pupils.

Technological Change

Technology is ready to facilitate the development of schools with a new organization. Improved construction materials and a systems approach in the planning of school buildings have kept school buildings apace with technological advances.[1] Advances in lighting, heating, and air control also offer new opportunities. In more direct relation to the learning process, developments regarding programming, audiovisual media, and computerized instruction offer the teacher vast new opportunities for securing assistance. So large are the opportunities here that the day may be near when the percentage of the total cost of a new plant which is devoted to instructional facilities or equipment could increase very sharply—but staff members with the Educational Facilities Laboratories indicate that time and cost control methods tied to a systems approach can reduce costs.[2] These reduced overall costs inherent in fast-tracking or PERT systems are already offsetting some increased instructional equipment or facilities costs. These savings are increasingly important during a continuing cost inflation spiral.

More or Less Schools

Summer schools for remediation, acceleration, or enrichment have been the traditional school "stretchers." Recently there has been a national relook at the extended use of the school plant through a twelve-months school year. Hayward and La Mesa Spring Valley in California, Valley View in Illinois, Dade County in Florida, and Utica in New York are examples of districts that have moved in on a partial or districtwide basis to some version of the year-round school.

At the same time there has been a move toward the "non" or "modified" school. Ivan Illich in some of his recent writings talks about the nonschool when he states, "The disestablishment of schools will inevitably happen—and it will happen surprisingly fast. It cannot be retarded very much longer, and it is hardly necessary to promote it vigorously, for this is being done now."[3]

While Illich sees the nonschool outside the "establishment", the nonschools under school-district auspices are exemplified by Philadel-

[1] *Schools: More Space/Less Money* (New York: Educational Facilities Laboratories, 1971), pp. 21–22.
[2] *Ibid.*, pp. 22–24.
[3] Ivan Illich, *Deschooling Society* (New York: Harper and Row, 1970), p. 148.

phia's Parkway Program and Chicago's Metro High School. Alternative schools as found in Berkeley and Alum Rock, California, offer still another choice. While some high schools have work-study programs with pupils on part-time schedules, others such as Lexington (Massachusetts) High School have moved to a home-base school concept with a limited number of pupils in an education-without-walls program.[4]

Changes in the Organization of Schools in the System

For a considerable number of years it appeared that preschool programs would not develop rapidly, that the neighborhood school was an idea which would become increasingly universal, that the 6–3–3 plan of organization would be employed in an increasing number of districts. Further, important forces were emphasizing the use of tests for purposes of grouping either in the school or in the classroom. While there was some discussion of separate schools for the gifted or for vocational purposes, only a few districts made such provisions.

All these questions regarding the organization of schools have been and continue to be reexamined. Is not a K–4–4–4, K–5–3–4, or K–3–4–3–2 organization better than the K–6–3–3 plan? How should any of these plans be altered to accommodate the four-year-olds? Which plan facilitates desegregation? Did we really hold to or utilize the neighborhood school concept to as great a degree as has been assumed? May we not turn to school parks, established in attractive surroundings, containing a number of schools and providing for more effective use of specialized facilities and the growing number of special-technical personnel? Or should school districts move to a cultural-educational cluster as envisioned for the Chicago school system of the future, clusters envisioned "to meet differing needs and to utilize the differing resources available within subareas of the city."[5]

Must we not develop essentially different approaches in the vocational-technical field (career education?) if the needs of youth and society are to be met in this area? If there is to be a new relation to the nonpublic schools, with some of their students coming to the public schools for certain parts of the program, what are the implications for structure?

And with the employment problems before us, are we going to at last grasp adult education in terms of its liberal education values? Perhaps we are in the closing days of the period when it was assumed that school

---

[4] *Schools: More Space/Less Money*, p. 16.
[5] Donald Leu and I. Carl Condoli, *Planning for the Future, a Recommended Long Range Educational and Facilities Plan for Chicago, August 1971* (Chicago: Board of Education, 1971), p. 45.

experience could be ended at sixteen or eighteen. Or possibly we have passed that period but have not yet fully recognized social developments in educational programs.

The Impact of Change

It would appear therefore that the schoolmen confronted with the need for new or different (old) plants are facing the most difficult problem of their careers—difficult because the pace of change is extremely rapid; difficult because many of the old forms are weakened, if not broken, while the new have not been institutionalized; difficult because the opportunity is so great; difficult because the results may be more affected by their knowledge and vision, or lack thereof, than in any recent period.

BUILDINGS AND INSTRUCTION

In many instances the organization of schools has been greatly influenced by the available school buildings. The junior high school was given an important push in many communities by the fact that it was an appealing way to relieve overcrowding in both the elementary schools and the senior high school. Similarly the kindergarten-primary unit has been favored in some communities in recent years because of its ability to relieve elementary schools in areas where remaining sites were few, not primarily because of belief in its educational potential. Action based upon building expediency, rather than upon thorough consideration of educational purposes, may be one explanation of the failure of many junior high schools to develop in accord with the professed educational goals of such schools.

More important than organization are matters of instruction. Many teachers have found themselves extremely limited by the facilities with which they work. To develop a social science or mathematics laboratory (rather than a general classroom) in many existing classrooms is extremely difficult. It is also difficult to team teach or work with large and small group instruction units. It is much easier to settle down to teaching as one was taught. Many who have a vision of instruction more in accord with sound educational principles may lose it rather quickly when confronted with the problems offered by the school building. The building that should be a stimulating agency thus becomes another force for traditionalism. And after a few years, the teacher would not have it otherwise.

Too seldom has the administrator glimpsed his unique opportunity to contribute to the improvement of instruction through leadership in the planning of a new school plant. Too seldom has the administrator had the opportunity to create a new life in an old school. To discuss principles of learning is to deal in abstractions. To discuss the school plant—the design of a learning laboratory or classroom—is to deal with the concrete. By means of the tangible, the more abstract can be envisioned. Many people including teachers and parents can get a better and quicker conception of methodology through consideration of the classroom than through a more direct approach. Where adequate learning space is provided, the administrator also has a responsibility and an opportunity to assist a staff in its effective utilization. It cannot be assumed that the teacher who has had years of experience as a student and teacher in a classroom providing 20 square feet of space per student is prepared to use 30 or 35 square feet effectively, or to use but part of a relatively large open space. Here is an excellent opportunity for the stimulation of staff growth—including growth of the adminstrator.

Not only does the new plant or the prospect of one challenge teachers, it also can challenge parents and help them develop a sounder understanding of educational objectives and of the types of activity and behavior related to the objectives. It may be a better instrument for arousing interest in matters of educational philosophy and method than a direct approach to these matters.

SCHOOLHOUSING NEEDS

Schoolhousing needs are continuing even among the contradictions of rapid growth in some areas of the country and declining enrollments in many other localities. The opportunity that administrators have and will have in the next decade to contribute both directly and indirectly to improved education through schoolhousing will depend on a number of factors. The need to build new school facilities or replace, renovate, or modernize existing facilities is still prevalent throughout the nation. At the same time the administrator is faced with declining support for funding school construction. Less then 50 percent of the school bond elections held nationally during the first quarter of 1971 were approved by the voters. This reduced voter support coupled with the move toward year-round schools as well as trends toward preschool education, career education, and alternative schools will force the administrator to study a number of ways to provide space for students.

In many parts of the country, school facilities planners are considering the potential impact of early childhood education. The planners for the future in Chicago envision small school homes called schomes serving 150 children in an age range of 3–6. These schomes would be operated as "satellites" to an existing elementary school.[6] At the same time the influence of Mott community education programs is spreading, as planners envision even greater shared school-community use of facilities. Schoolhousing needs will also continue to change in urban areas that are going through vast redevelopment and renewal projects.

Planners in many of these areas will need to carefully consider the impact of new rapid transit systems and shifts in population characteristics. The school planner will need to work even more closely with the urban planner. High-rise public housing is being torn down in city after city as planners recognize the need for dispersing public housing in urban and suburban settings. The administrator may no longer base his schoolhouse needs on the traditional school year with the traditional pupil population in traditional settings.

ADMINISTRATIVE-STAFF TIME INVOLVED

Schoolhousing programs will continue to make large demands upon the board of education and the school administrator. The demands will be severe because of the complex issues facing the decision makers. Time for planning will by necessity require thorough analysis of population trends, feasibility of year-round schools, and changes in grade level organization. In addition, there will be a need to evaluate community and staff pressures related to such questions as nonschools, alternate schools, changing internal organization and staffing patterns, changing educational goals, and the relationship of the school to the environment. As the administration involves staff and community and students in the planning process the administration finds additional time required in order to reach consensus prior to making recommendations to the board of education.

In many cases, schoolhousing programs are added to the busy schedule of a superintendent who may not have had the experience gained through the actual working through of successful bond elections to a completed school plant. In large urban districts it is not uncommon to find a number of central office specialists who devote their full time and expertise to facilities planning. The Chicago schools have Directors of Facilities Planning, School Facilities and Population Studies, Building Specifications, and Site Selections. These schools also have an Associate Superintendent, Operations Analysis and an Assistant Superintendent, and Public Building Commission program. These staff members, of course, do not include the

[6]*Ibid.*, p. 37.

support staff including graphic artists and other major staff such as the Associate Superintendent, Education Program Planning.[7]

In some districts the study of population growth, the raising of new funds, the selection of sites, the formulation of educational programs, the employment of architects, the reviewing of plans, and other related problems are always present.

In many instances too little time is provided for the development of the educational program as a base for the needed housing. Attention is diverted from the ongoing educational program in many communities as the schoolhousing program is carried forward.

The schoolhousing program has a certain tangibility that makes it attractive. It also is extremely demanding of time. A large number and variety of decisions must be made with reference to it. Children are waiting to enter the new or renovated or modernized schools, and pressure for quick action is great. Many of the steps such as site selection, review, and rereview of plans by various parties are time consuming.

Many district staffs are finding that the review of existing facilities for possible building renovation is every bit as time consuming as planning a new building from the outset. The review of existing facilities requires the analysis of preconceived short-range solutions versus long-range solutions which could call for abandonment of a building rather than building renovation.

Yet, by its nature, schoolhousing is seen as a somewhat temporary activity, rather than a continuous one. For these many reasons the school administrator must recognize the large opportunity and responsibility he has in the housing field and must seek to establish a plan by which children can be adequately housed for the present and for future years.

DETERMINING NEED AND ABILITY

Attention will now be turned briefly to some of the most important steps that are involved in school plant planning and development.

Estimating Student Population

Student population projection, never an exact science, is going to become further complicated by this country's dips in population growth

[7] *Ibid.*, p. vi.

Facilities for Education 451

rates and shifts in migration patterns. Recent studies have indicated that this country might achieve zero population growth this century. In fifteen years (1957–1972) the fertility rate of almost 3.8 children per family has dropped to 2.08 per family. Demographers state that zero population is a no-growth goal that results when families average out at 2.1 children.

Each school district should have an established plan through which it can continuously or frequently estimate student population for a period of five to ten years. The nature of the plan will vary from community to community. Procedures that are very good for an almost saturated community may have little significance or value for a rapidly expanding suburban community. In addition many areas are experiencing a drop in their student populations. Procedures for student projections in shrinking school districts will differ from those employed in predicting enrollment changes in growth areas. The estimates need to be recognized as such—subject to "error" because of unpredicted changes in social and economic conditions, and subject to probable increase in "error" as the period of years is increased and the size of the area is decreased. Factors to be considered include: births to residents of district by year; past experience of school system as shown by average ratio of students in each grade to preceding one; new construction completed by year and children of various ages per house; mobility of population; preschool census data; enrollments and plans of nonpublic schools; dropout situation in secondary schools; extent to which land area of district is saturated; proposed highway, industrial, and commercial construction projects; zoning; permits secured and planned construction of homes; age of adult population; and size of families. From these factors and with an awareness of the limitations of estimates, student population can be estimated.

The school administrator given the responsibility of estimating student enrollments should be aware of alternative projection methods. The most common method is based on determining cohort survival by advancing the student numbers one year in the grade pattern. Most projection methods, with the exception of a house-to-house census, are variations of the simple cohort survival technique. Many districts use a progression percentage method which reflects total past attendance history. Other planners use a combination of techniques with elaborate weighting systems based on a number of variables for the area including pupil generation formulas from dwelling units (number of children per bedroom in single-family dwellings, town houses, apartments, and so on, employment or unemployment statistics, economic, political, and sociological climate factors.

In making estimates it is important to present ranges of estimates based on most appropriate projection methods and district information, data from utilities, city and county planners, real estate developers, and other applicable sources.

Student population projections by age, grade, and ethnic composition are extremely important for facilities planning and site purchases. The need to periodically reestimate projections at least annually cannot be stressed enough.

Evaluating Existing Plants

Any school district should periodically evaluate existing plants. This is essential for reasons of safety and the elimination of hazards, for the determination of maintenance needs, and for the determination of optimum utilization. The growing district has additional reasons for evaluating existing plants. Before constructing new plants it must determine the capacity and the best use that can be made of the existing plants. This will also frequently involve questions of rehabilitation.

Evaluation of existing plants may well involve the employment of engineers who can determine structural safety. Hazards may also be located with the assistance of the fire marshal or evaluators provided through the firms handling insurance for the district. The alert administrator and teachers may also identify safety hazards.

The evaluation of the plant in terms of educational needs is more difficult. It involves considerable understanding of the nature of a desirable environment for learning. It requires knowledge of space, lighting, heating, and ventilating needs. It requires a genuine understanding of the educational program that is to be carried on. Further, as the word "evaluation" implies, it requires the making of judgments.

Various scorecards and guides for evaluating school plants[8] are available for the use of those undertaking this work. Some of them have been designed for the use of laymen as well as for educators. Participation by laymen in evaluation of school plants is highly desirable. If it is undertaken, however, it is important that laymen and teachers also have the opportunity to develop essential knowledge as a base for making judgments. Such training may be provided by reading, discussions, and pilot evaluations.

When evaluating a school plant it is desirable to determine the capacity of the plant. In many cases plant capacity, particularly in secondary schools, has changed as educational programs have changed. Any evaluation of school plants will need to be made in relation to a number of criteria including such general ones as adequacy for year-round use, educa-

[8]*Profile Rating Wheel, An Instrument to Evaluate School Facilities* (Sacramento, Bureau of School Planning, California State Department of Education, 1972).

tional adequacy (teaching education space, auxiliary education space, and flexibility), and building adequacy (age, expandability, ease of maintenance, cost of modernization and rehabilitation).

Determining Needs

This essentially is a process of bringing the estimated population and the best utilization of existing plant together and determining what additional facilities are needed. This may involve the study of possible use of plants under different organizations such as the 6-3-3, 6-2-4, 5-3-4, or 4-4-4-4 arrangement.

Determining Financial Ability

It is appropriate here only to recognize this problem that is treated in greater detail in Chapter 18. It involves determination of the existing indebtedness and retirement schedule of the debt, the ability and bonding limits of the district, and state or federal grants or loans available.

SELECTING AND EMPLOYING AN ARCHITECT

The selection of the architect for the housing program is one of the most important responsibilities of the board of education and superintendent of schools. Upon it will depend the creativity displayed in meeting the educational needs, as well as the general desirability of the plant secured for the funds expended. The architect becomes essentially a partner of the superintendent, board of education, and staff in carrying the program through. Employment of the local architect because he is local, or the well-known architect because he is well known, must be rejected.

A plan for selecting the architect should be set up. It should supply evidence regarding such things as the ability and willingness of the architect to work with the superintendent, principals, and teachers in clarifying and solving educational needs; the adequacy of the staff of the architect for various essential architectural and engineering studies and plans; past experience of the architect as revealed by the adequacy of plans developed, bids secured, and buildings completed. After data are secured regarding these matters, the superintendent and board may choose to interview the three or four architects who appear to offer the best promise, to visit buildings that they have designed, and to discuss their work with school administrators and boards of education in communities that they have served. In addition boards of education and administrators might plan on studying the extensive architectural exhibits at the annual AASA conventions. Then they should be prepared to select an architect in whom they can develop confidence and work with during the months of close cooperative effort ahead. The contract with the architect also needs to be considered carefully in order that there will not be misunderstanding regarding his work and responsibilities.

SELECTING SITES

The selection of sites is one of the important responsibilities of the superintendent of schools. He may wish the assistance of state department of education personnel or of other consultants in this work. It is important that desirable sites be selected early enough to secure them at reasonable cost. This may be some years prior to the time when the site is needed. To delay, however, frequently results in accepting less adequate sites and paying far larger sums for them. Early action may at times result in the purchase of a site that may later prove unnecessary because of changes in zoning or failure of an area to develop as anticipated. In growth areas, it is possible that such "errors" will not result in financial loss.

Sites should be selected with reference to the location of population to be served. Consideration must also be given to topography, nature of soil, shape, accessibility, convenience to but distance from main highways, utility connections, development potential for beauty and usefulness, and expense involved in purchase and development. Purchase of sites in urban areas is complicated by high cost of land, shifting land use patterns, location of rapid transit stations, and changes in population makeup, including age and ethnic composition of the neighborhood residents. In some urban areas planners are seeking alternatives to the conventional "site." In some cases school facilities are planned in conjunction with commercial buildings and public housing

> ... land and airspace can be occupied jointly by a school and income-producing private enterprise such as housing, retail stores, or office space. Usually joint occupancy results in a single structure or complex of mixed public and private uses, all jointly designed, constructed, and operated. The ideal arrangement is to include enough taxpaying commercial space to carry the cost of the debt service to the school. The school, in this sense, "pays for itself" from the expanded tax base.[9]

[9] *Schools: More Space/Less Money,* p. 30.

Sites should be checked on a scorecard to ensure consideration of all factors of importance. The size of the site will depend upon the type and size of school contemplated. It will also be related to standards for sites that may have been established by the state department of education[10] or recommended by other bodies such as the National Council on Schoolhouse Construction.[11]

Before making the final selection of sites for recommendation to the board of education, the superintendent will want to review the proposals with the city or county planning commission. He also may need to have surveys completed and appraisals made, in order that essential facts are available regarding sites that otherwise appear to be almost equally satisfactory. In selecting sites the superintendent should consult an architect for suggestions regarding the site development and the possible placement of buildings.

EDUCATIONAL SPECIFICATIONS AND ARCHITECTURAL PLANS

Guiding the staff in the preparation of educational specifications is the most important and probably the most difficult of the superintendent's duties in the school housing field.

Educational specifications include a detailed description of (1) all the activities that will take place in the buildings; (2) the curriculum to be provided for; (3) specific architectural characteristics desired; (4) the facilities needed, equipment required and space relationship of these to other facilities; and (5) budget and other governing factors. The community background and history and the educational philosophy of the school district should precede the detailed specifications.[12]

The nature of the varied activities to be provided for in the building must be clear to the architect if he is to design effectively for them. What will class size be? What methods of teaching and learning are envisioned?

[10]*School Site Analysis and Development* (Sacramento: California State Department of Education, 1966).
[11]*Guide for Planning School Plants* (East Lansing, Michigan: National Council on Schoolhouse Construction, 1964).
[12]Texas Education Agency, *How to Prepare Educational Specifications Outline* (Austin, Texas, 1968).

How will space be used? Will the elementary school have full or modified open space? What kind of flexibility will be needed in the secondary school? Are there to be schools within the school? How will the guidance services be related to the instructional program? To what extent will departmentalization be employed? Are provisions to be made for independent study? How broad and varied a curriculum is planned? What new technological provisions are to be included? What learning laboratories and media centers are planned? Is the cafeteria viewed as a feeding station or a service with important educational opportunities in addition to health? Will the plant be used for adult education purposes?

These are suggestive of the many questions that have important implications for the building. Unless the school system has been engaged in considerable curriculum work in recent years, it may find the development of the educational specifications difficult and time consuming. Although some of the specifications need to be formulated by the staff prior to consultation with the architect, there is considerable merit in having the architect share in much of this work.

REVIEWING SKETCHES AND PLANS

A considerable period of time is required for the critical evaluation of proposed solutions to the housing problem. Staff members who participated in the development of the educational specifications should assist in this work. They will need to study the proposed detail of arrangements with great care and through careful inspection make sure that the plans will meet the need as adequately as possible. The administrative staff will need to devote many hours to the careful analysis of plans pertaining to such matters as relationships of various areas, student circulation, and details of various facilities.

Although architects are responsible for the planning, they can make mistakes. They are most likely to avoid doing so if challenged by many intelligent questions. The question might be asked whether this is not intruding on the architect's area of service. Actually, the superintendent's staff and architect must cooperate in finding solutions to many problems. Although the superintendent and staff do not have the technical and design competence of the architect, they may be more able than the architect to anticipate problems that could result from proposed arrangements. Furthermore, the staff members must be as interested as the architect in making sure, for example, that the rooms will have comfortable balanced lighting without glare or contrast that sharply limits the manner in which the rooms can be used. The staff does not need to know the answers, but they surely should be prepared to ask the questions.

In most states, plans need finally to be submitted to and approved by state agencies. They may be checked by a state agency for educational desirability and for safety. Presentation of the plans for approval is made by the architect, though again the superintendent, architect, and school board may be involved.

CONTRACTING FOR AND CONSTRUCTING THE PLANT

Major responsibility for approval of contract forms will rest upon the architect and legal counsel of the board of education. However, the superintendent will need to be familiar with the various provisions of the contracts in order to make sure that the interests of the school district are protected and the needs met. He will also have the responsibility for recommending to the board of education the plans through which the projects are to be financed. As executive officer he will then have the responsibility for carrying through the finance plans with the assistance of specialists as needed. If bonds are to be issued, materials for the prospectus will need to be prepared. A bond attorney should be employed in connection with the issuance of bonds. Concerning contracts and bonding, there are numerous state laws with which the superintendent will need to be familiar if he is to serve as advisor to the board.

In many cases state agencies are involved in some of the final decisions relating to the contract. In most cases the contract approval follows prescribed bidding procedures. The allowable dollar amount for facilities construction in the contract will depend on the amount of local and state funds available for the project.

SUPERVISING THE CONSTRUCTION

During the period of construction, the superintendent will have many duties of a general supervisory nature. The architect will, of course, have responsibility for direct supervision in accord with the provisions of his contract with the board of education. In addition, it is very important that a building inspector be employed by the board who can exercise a more minute supervision under the general direction of the architect. Even with supervision provided, and in spite of the excellence of the plans and specifications, some questions may arise. There will be change orders resulting from the unavailability of materials or the desirability of modifications that become apparent during the course of construction. There will be questions of delays in construction and compliance with the specified construction period. Upon the completion of the construction of the building and a final inspection of all of its aspects by the architect, engineers, contractors, and the superintendent of schools, a recommendation for its acceptance is made to the board of education.

EQUIPPING AND UTILIZING THE PLANT

The superintendent of schools still has many weighty responsibilities beyond the acceptance of the building. Some equipment has been built into the building in accord with the plans. Much equipment and furnishings, however, are still to be determined and installed through separate contracts. Here again, many members of the staff should be involved. Assistance may also be secured from the educational consultant, the state department of education, or from specialists in the various matters under consideration. Many of the questions pertaining to furnishings and equipment should have been partially solved when the plans were developed, since the building had to be designed with reference to the equipment. Decisions had to be reached at that time regarding what was to be built in. However, many final decisions must now be made.

Attention must also be given to the preparation of the custodial and teaching staff for the utilization of the building. Custodians must be instructed about the operation of various technical facilities. They also need instructions for the care of the chalkboards, floors, walls, and equipment. If teachers have been involved in the development of the educational specifications and the selection of the equipment, they have a good background for using the new plant and its equipment effectively. However, many of them will not have been involved, and unless leadership is offered, they may continue to function as they have been accustomed to, rather than in accord with their new opportunity. The open classroom does not just mean greater distances between the rows of desks, as one business manager supposed. Rather, it suggests a different kind of living and learning. What is it to be?

The superintendent thus completes his responsibility with reference to the new plant. He is fortunate indeed if he has been able to provide effective leadership regarding many aspects of the educational program while deeply engrossed in the housing program. He has had to devote much thought and action to housing for a period of two or three years. During all this time he has had to work with many people, become familiar with statutes, and observe and evaluate many proposals. He has had to test all ideas in terms of principles relating to safety, educational desirability, flexibility, expansibility, and initial and operational economy. In addition he has had to plan for the use of equipment and the plant by staffs involved in the programs of the future.

SOME IMPORTANT PROBLEMS AND ISSUES

The following issues among the many in the school plant field have been selected for more extended consideration.

What Kinds of Space for Learning?

The school planner usually bases his decisions on quantitative-square feet and costs and qualitative-climate, esthetics, and tone basis.

Planning decisions are complicated by the need to consider the kind of student population to be served as well as short- and long-range program plans. Staff and community considerations play an important role. The planner must consider the community or staff's acceptance of whatever the facility turns out to be.

As competition for the public dollar grows, school systems throughout the country are looking for alternatives that will provide educational space for the least cost.

The Education Facilities Laboratories in looking at this problem noted,

> This national dilemma has encouraged many school systems to explore a growing range of alternative solutions to provide school space in the most economical fashion. "Economical" in this context can have one of four meanings: providing new or modernized old space at a reduced cost; getting more space or better space for the same amount of money; getting much greater use out of existing space; finding less expensive alternatives to conventional school space.
>
> The search for alternatives has led in many cases to a reexamination of traditional assumptions about how school space can best be provided and used. Out of desperate necessity has come a burst of new thinking about the traditional American schoolhouse.[13]

Some of the Educational Facilities Laboratories suggestions include: found space—finding space in its own school buildings; space not used efficiently; and space in warehouses, factories, industrial plants, and in underused public buildings.

[13] *Schools: More Space/Less Money*, pp.4–5.

Other EFL examples of finding space include: Open Campus Schools, home base schools, nonschool schools, and resource centers.

> A recent study for Educational Facilities Laboratories suggests that barges or floating platforms built as schools can be more economical and constructed in much less time than conventional land-based schools. A prototype design based on conditions in Boston was estimated to cost 15% less to acquire and 43% less time to construct than the most conventional schools, land costs included.[14]

Harold Gores, the President of Educational Facilities Laboratories, in writing about the planning-for-the-future kinds of space for learning, states, "Today, however, prediction with any confidence is more elusive. The future is more obscured than ever because there are so many options and now the places of education themselves are changing fast in response to both educational and technological changes."[15]

Gores, in looking at the future, forecasts a change from the single-purpose schoolhouse to centers that will bring together "all the social service delivery systems."[16] Examples of the new multipurpose service units can be found in Flint, Michigan; Akron, Ohio; Lowell, Massachusetts; Atlanta, Georgia; and Hamilton County, Tennessee.

In looking toward the future, planners envision more use of "nontraditional" space for learning. Some current uses of "found" space include a loft-type factory in the Bronx converted into an open space elementary school; an underused bathhouse in Boston converted into a high school annex; and again in Boston, the conversion of a bowling alley into an open space elementary school. New York City is considering converting a large hotel in the Bronx into a high school.[17]

As educators consider the kind of space for learning they have to continue to raise the question: Space for what kind of learning at what point in the continuum of learning from early childhood to and including adulthood?

What About the Quality of Space for Learning?

Issues related to quality of space are less tangible and more difficult to pin down than issues related to quantitative elements in school planning.

[14] *Ibid.*, p. 25.
[15] Harold Gores, "Schoolhouse of the Future," *National Elementary Principal* Vol. 52, No. 1 (September 1972), p. 10.
[16] *Ibid.*, p. 12.
[17] Evans Clinchy, "The Vanishing Schoolhouse," *National Elementary Principal,* Vol. 52, No. 1 (September 1972), pp. 24–25.

Does the school beckon? Can a building attract? Can a building influence taste? Do the hours spent in a classroom intimately related to the out-of-doors have an effect? What are conditions that stimulate creativity? Does the principal's office have to be an "ogre's den"?[18] Does the classroom invite pursuit of knowledge and truth, or is it a "strait jacket"?

Beyond question we are moving in many schools in the direction of developing more adequate space for learning in the qualitative sense. Too many school buildings, however, continue to be built merely to house children, with little thought or attention given to the quality of the housing in terms of its educational influence. Citizens, educators, and architects must recognize and grapple with this problem more effectively.

It may be objected that all this calls for the use of genuine creative ability; that it costs money. But can a nation with an almost incomprehensible achievement in terms of materials produced do less than devote some of them to the education of its children? Here is an issue that raises questions about the values of our society. Can any state take pride in an "austerity" schoolhousing program—a program that rigidly limits the space available because there are so many children and "the funds are not available" to make more adequate provisions?

Have educators developed a clear concept of the quality of space needed for learning? Are they prepared to lead others in this quest?

How Can School Planning
Serve the Heterogeneous Community?

The provision of a school to serve a heterogeneous group is a recognition of the educational influence of the school itself as an institution. To grow up associated only with children of one race, one religion, or one economic class is limiting. When it is further the result of imposed separation on a group, it may have an additional serious impact. Separate but equal is therefore no longer accepted as equal. While the desirability of these developments should be recognized, it would be a mistake to assume that the educational needs of many of the culturally different (which is not race) are to be regarded as being met through greater heterogeneity in the school population. Rather, it is the hope to establish understandings and a social climate upon which educational opportunity may be built. It would further be an incorrect assumption to believe that the understandings and the climate will result rather automatically. What is provided is but a base for achieving a better educational program.

[18]Lawrence B. Perkins, *Work Place for Learning* (New York: Reinhold Publishing Corporation, 1957), p. 56.

The reexamination of the relation of a school to its neighborhood, particularly as related to the elimination of de facto segregation, has resulted in a number of new approaches to schoolhousing. For a time the educational or school park idea was advanced as an innovative way to integrate urban schools. "In the hypothetical K–4–4–4 park of 16,000 for example, there would be about 5,000 pupils each in the primary and middle school age groups, or enough at each level for 10 separate schools of 500 pupils."[19] The park idea while still present has to some extent been modified by the move toward community school centers. Planners for the future in Chicago envision the educational park as a phase in the evolution of what is termed the cultural educational cluster. The planners state:

> The cultural educational cluster attempts to incorporate all of the advantages of the education park, i.e. large numbers of students and staff to draw from, multiplicity of program opportunity, sophisticated and devious types of equipment and material, heterogeneous population mixes, convenience to and cooperation with other agencies while at the same time avoiding the most obvious disadvantages of the conventional education park, the most glaring of which is the psychological effect of concentrating thousands of students on one congested site.[20]

The community school center already exists in many cities and new centers are being planned for the seventies. The Human Resources Center in Pontiac, Michigan (opened in 1971), typifies the joint use of space and facilities by community and students. The center includes two elementary schools, an adult study center, gymnasium and community field house, preschool kindergarten, parent-teacher counseling center, community offices, medical suite, community lounge, faculty dining and public restaurant, a cafetorium-town hall, and a theater. Although there are distinct student and community levels, some areas in each are shared by students and the community at the same time.[21]

A number of other alternative and experimental school plans have emerged in an attempt to resolve the particular societal problems of urban areas.

The Walt Disney Magnet School (opened in 1973) is an example of one of the alternative approaches. This school is one of seven Chicago schools "designed to increase economic and racial integrations and to develop, evaluate and diffuse innovative curriculum."[22]

[19] John H. Fisher, *The School Park* (Washington, D.C.: United States Commission on Civil Rights, Clearinghouse Publication No. 9, October 1967).
[20] Leu and Condoli, *Planning for the Future,* pp. 45–46.
[21] *Places and Things for Experimental Schools* (New York: Educational Facilities Laboratories, 1972), p. 72.
[22] Leu and Condoli, *Planning for the Future,* p. 40.

The number of alternatives open to school facilities planners increases the need to study the ways that differing needs are being translated into varied kinds of school facilities. The superintendent of schools and staff members should study, describe, and appraise these alternative plans. They could then answer questions about transferability, as well as reasons for adoption of a particular approach.

How Can Adequate Educational Planning as a Basis for Schoolhousing Be Assured?

It is quite probable that the most serious inadequacy of schoolhouse planning is to be found in limited educational planning. This results from factors such as the difficulty of the problem, the intangibility of the process, the lack of adequate time on the part of competent people, and the lack of appreciation of the cruciality of the need. If we are to utilize the creative powers of architects and not build facilities that tend toward obsolescence, some of the following conditions must be more fully realized.

1. The meaning of educational planning must be clarified. It must be clearly understood to be the formulation of the educational philosophy, the nature of the activities to be housed, and the manner in which the activities are to be carried on. It is, in essence, a basic curriculum problem that cannot be grappled with effectively without thoughtful consideration of the needs of children, youth, and adults; without clarification of objectives, without consideration of the organization of learning experience, and without consideration of the organization of the school to meet the accepted needs. It must be agreed that educational planning is *not* a list of rooms with square footages.
2. The educator must recognize leadership in educational planning as his most significant responsibility in the school plant area. He will then insist upon the time and personnel that are essential.
3. Adequate time must be devoted to the formulation of the educational plan. Unless very considerable curriculum work has been done recently in the school system, there are many months of work involved.
4. Provision must be made whereby administrators who are responsible for leadership in this area have sufficient time to do the job.
5. The services of those who can offer leadership in working through the problems in the instructional field must be sought and used. They may be drawn from the school system, the state department of education, universities, and the community. To an extent commitments must be made regarding the kind of educational program and school living envisaged for tomorrow and the years that follow. A concept of function—defined or merely inherited and not thought through—will guide the architect.
6. Even after the best possible educational plan has been developed, thoughts should be given to flexibility and adaptability of the structure. Will it be a constraining or releasing force? Educators must consider the flexibility necessary for individualized instruction—individualized instruction which requires spaces for large- and small-group instruction as well as independent study spaces. In addition, there must be a recognition of programs that require the adaptability necessary to take advantage of technological advances including

computer-assisted instruction, closed-circuit TV, and highly developed media centers.
7. Planners must take into consideration a number of options such as school renewal, revitalization and modernization of existing schools, and a number of nontraditional approaches to schoolhousing including the idea of schools which move students out of the school building directly into the community.

It would be a mistake to believe that educational planning can be done by the architect or the consultant, though they may play roles in it. The possibility of planning well in a few weeks should be rejected. It calls for extended cooperative effort. Effort is needed to tap the resources of literature and the experiences of other schools and persons. Educational planning cannot be done by teachers alone. They may not have had the opportunity to work through the problems and may reflect largely a limited background. But it cannot be done without the involvement of teachers.

How Can School Plant Planning and City-County Planning Be Coordinated?

Coordination and perhaps integration of planning efforts would appear to be increasingly necessary. In a more populous society and one in which an increasing percentage of the people reside in metropolitan areas, land use comes to be of great significance. Without coordination in planning, the probability of achieving an attractive community in which to live and to work appears slight indeed. Furthermore, in addition to the community itself as an educational force, it must be recognized that the library and recreation services, for example, are an aspect of education. We are probably too little aware of the educational impact of the community in which we live. The development of a taste for the beautiful is not unrelated to the opportunity to experience it. We recognize this in our schools. Is it not equally important in our communities?

In addition to the above factors, it must be recognized that there are other arguments strongly favoring coordination. The data collected by a competent city or county planning authority are of great value to the school planner. Data pertaining to highway development, population, land use, zoning, and housing proposals are essential for sound school planning. There is no need to have more than one agency collect these data if through cooperative planning the needs of various public agencies can be met. Furthermore, the schools can render a great service to the planning agency through participation in planning, through assisting in collecting and analyzing data (a project with great educational values), and through a program of education designed to help young citizens develop a knowledge and appreciation of the significance of community planning.

The educator, however, is at times somewhat hesitant to seek the coordination that appears desirable. He has a rather strong attachment to independence—which is related to the struggle for fiscal independence. He draws back when he meets the city planner who may appear to want to "take over" the school planning function rather than to assist in it. And, all too frequently, he finds that the city and county planning office has too little data or staff to be of any considerable assistance, or that it has district boundary lines that confine its interest to only a segment of the school district.

Despite the inadequacies on either or both sides and the frictions that develop at times, there would appear to be no question but that the school and planning agencies should greatly increase their cooperative efforts. This can be to the benefit of both of them, and more especially, to the benefit of the community that they both serve. They share responsibility for improving the quality of community living and are likely to discharge this responsibility most effectively only if they develop a high-level cooperative effort.

What arrangements are likely to result in the essential coordination? Who should take the initiative in effecting coordination?

Should a District Use Stock Plans?

Many school district superintendents and school boards with the necessity to build school facilities are faced with pressures from individuals in the community who push for a stock plan.

Persons advocating a stock plan, a plan that has already been used by the district or another district, claim that the use of these plans would save the district funds and speed up the construction of schools.

In an analysis of the stock-plan issue, one needs to look at the basic question—can districts benefit by the stock-plan approach? The superintendent faced with this issue in his community should be prepared to analyze the pros and cons. Architects claim that no two school buildings can be built with identical plans and specifications. The typical school has many details that are similar to other schools. At the same time the chance for the exact duplication of a school site is very small. Different sites require different grading orientation of the school on the site, plus a myriad of other changes including service roads, play areas, and utility and service connections.

In looking at the question of re-using plans or using plans from other districts, the superintendent and board should study practices in their own and other states. A number of states including Georgia, Missouri, and Wisconsin have tried and rejected or discouraged the stock-plan approach.

In answering the basic questions regarding the benefit to the district, thought needs to be given to the long-range effects of not involving the local staff and community in planning a school. Should the staff and community members accept the planning decisions that have been made by other individuals not at all familiar with the particular needs of the children and staff in the local district?

Any examination of this issue is going to require a study of the impact of court decisions regarding "equalizing" expenditures for pupils. Will this increased move toward more state control of funds effect planning for schools? Will states be forced into pushing for standardization of school plants as a parallel to equality in funding for educational programs?

Should Schools Be Renewed?

Increased costs of construction and voter rejection of school bond issues have sharpened the issues regarding modernizing existing facilities.

The firm of Mcleod, Ferrara, and Ensign, AIA, architect/planners, Washington, D.C., prepared a detailed report on school renewal for the West Hartford, Connecticut, Board of Education under the sponsorship of Educational Facilities Laboratories. A summary statement in their report covers the issue in an effective manner.

> Present schoolhouses constitute a tremendous investment, and realistically they cannot be soon abandoned and replaced. Nor should they be. Age itself need not be the sole indicator of obsolescence, and our national conscience now recognizes this fact. Over ¼ million of our classrooms and over one-third of our schools in large urban areas have been in use for over half a century. In their present state, most are incapable of meeting today's demands, and the challenge is to recognize the potential of these venerable buildings and renew them to serve useful contemporary functions. Added to the problem of the aged schools is the unpleasant fact that many of the facilities completed in the last few years have rigid plans and structures that seriously hinder the processes of learning used today. These too need a new lease on life.
>
> Renovations and additions have always been an important part of annual school outlays, constituting in the past few years almost one-third of the total educational construction dollar volume. The emphasis, however, has been on replacement and repair of equipment and materials and on updating to meet safety codes; meeting *building* standards, in other words. But it is predictable that within a few years the share of the dollar spent for modernization will pass the 50 percent mark, and much greater emphasis will be spent on making our outmoded buildings serve new *educational* standards.
>
> The possibilities of using existing buildings for effective educational programs extends beyond updating traditional schoolhouses. In our society,

populations shift rapidly. Facilities and services essential at one time become available for other needs. In the past we have not been alert to such opportunities, but more and more, noneducational buildings are being converted to school purposes.

Modernization in itself is not the panacea for the school system's economic ills but it is an important option available to the prudent administrator.[23]

Can educationally desirable learning space be achieved at defensible costs through renewal?

What Shall Be the Role of State Departments of Education in the Field of Schoolhousing?

State departments of education have in some instances had a rather different relationship to schoolhousing than they have had in regard to other aspects of education. Schoolhousing has continued to be regarded almost exclusively as a local matter in some states. In other states an increasing amount of state control, even of details, is apparent. These developments have been related to the programs of state financing of capital outlay that have developed. Without going into the financing question, which is treated elsewhere in this book, it is extremely important to look at the problem of the role of the state department of education and the matter of state controls. It would appear that the state department of education should discharge the following responsibilities:

1. The state department of education should be the administrative agency with which or through which the local school districts and their agents make all school plant arrangements. If it does not provide all the needed state services, it can coordinate the services of all state agencies involved.
2. It should be responsible for seeing that minimum standards of safety and health are established and observed in all school plants.
3. It should exercise a general supervision over school plant provisions to ensure minimum desirable space for learning.
4. The state department of education should be responsible for the planning, coordination, and implementation of research in the schoolhousing field. Quite possibly, much of the research should be done in local systems and in organized programs in the university. Through the development of adequate research programs, the state department should encourage that expansion of knowledge which may improve programs of schoolhousing. The operations of the School Development Group in the Ministry of Education in England is a challenging illustration of a desirable research operation.
5. It should accept as its role the stimulation and guidance of local systems as they develop schoolhousing programs. Emphasis upon this aspect of responsibility may eventually result in the virtual elimination of concern regarding the minimum school plant provisions referred to before.

[23] *School Renewal* (New York: Educational Facilities Laboratories, 1972), p. 3.

In carrying out these responsibilities the state department of education, as well as the legislature, needs to avoid exercising detailed controls that stifle local initiative. A state department of education that loses its way in legalisms and minute detail denies itself the chance to provide leadership. Not only must it avoid resisting new ideas—but it must avoid even the development of the suspicion that it does so. Unless it is acutely aware of this trap, it can easily be caught, and architects and educators may prepare plans that will be readily approved, rather than plans designed to facilitate the best situations. The recent and necessary growth of state financing of capital outlay needs to be carefully watched, or inadvertently the control of details may follow. It need not, but it may, if local districts, the overall plan, and the prevailing philosophy of administration are inadequate. State control of detail has occurred to too great an extent in some states, although "no one" involved in the service consciously sought this end.

How can state departments of education exercise leadership in an effective manner?

SELECTED REFERENCES

BAAS, ALAN M., *Building Renovation and Modernization.* Eugene, Oregon: Education Facilities Review Series, Eric Clearing House on Educational Management, 1972.

CASTALDI, BASIL, *Creative Planning of Educational Facilities.* Chicago, Illinois: Rand McNally & Co., 1969.

Educational Change and Architectural Consequences. New York: Educational Facilities Laboratories, 1960.

ENGELHART, NICKOLAYS L., *Complete Guide for Planning New Schools.* West Nyack, New York: Parka Publishing Co., 1970.

Guide for Planning Educational Facilities. Columbus, Ohio: Council of Educational Facilities Planners, 1969.

Guide for Planning School Plants. East Lansing, Michigan: National Council on Schoolhouse Construction, 1964.

LEU, DONALD J., *Planning Educational Facilities.* New York: Center for Applied Research in Education Inc., 1965.

Open Place Schools. Washington, D.C.: American Association of School Administrators, 1971.

PIELE, PHILIP K., *Educational Specifications.* Eugene, Oregon: Educational Facilities Review Series, Eric Clearing House on Educational Management, 1971.

17

Business Administration Operations and Services

The primary purpose of business administration is to help assure that maximum educational returns will be received per dollar invested in education. The purpose definitely is not to hold educational expenditures to a minimum, though too often that concept has prevailed. Economical efficient administration does not mean parsimonious administration. Business administration should be the servant of the educational program, not the master. Leaders of business and industry have long known that the investment of additional funds in an enterprise will frequently return more profits per dollar invested than could be obtained from a smaller investment. There is much evidence available showing that this same principle applies to the educational enterprise. On the other hand, the wasteful or unnecessary expenditure of funds does not bring the desired returns in either business or education.

MAJOR CONCEPTS AND PROCEDURES

Many concepts of sound business management are equally applicable to education. However, the purpose of a business enterprise is to earn profits and the purpose of an educational enterprise is to produce desired educational outputs. Profits in business are returned to the investor annually, monthly, weekly—even daily. Educational benefits may not be returned to the investor until years after the original investment. Business can, therefore, evaluate its policies much more quickly than can education. Some of the major operations of school business management are presented below. It will be noted that business management operations and educational objectives are closely interrelated.

Management of Resources

The Association of School Business Officials, after extensive study, developed a useful conceptualization of resource management called ERMS or Educational Resources Management System.[1] The Association conceptualized business administration services as a component of the total educational system provided for the purpose of facilitating the attainment of educational objectives. ERMS was explained as follows:

> An ERM System should be viewed as a basic conceptualization of a planning, programming, budgeting, evaluating system (PPBES) application. The system is designed for the management of educational resources in local school districts.[2]

The ERMS conceptualization had its origin in the planning, programming, and budgeting systems (PPBS) used in industry and the federal government. The Association adapted PPBS to education, renamed it PPBES, and described it as an educational resources management system. Following are the basic assumptions upon which ERMS is based:

1. The resources available to a school district are less than equal to the demands of that district.
2. The school district exists to produce a set of outcomes—to achieve certain objectives expressed as specific changes in characteristics of the learners.

[1] William H. Curtis, *Educational Resources Management System* (Chicago, Ill.: Research Corporation of the School Business Officials, 1971).
[2] *Ibid.*, p. 37.

3. Objectives of a school district can be achieved theoretically in a multitude of ways (program plans), some of which are more effective than others.
4. Productivity of a school district can be increased by the organization of learning activities and supporting services into programs specifically directed toward achieving previously defined goals and objectives.
5. Better decisions regarding the selection of program plans and greater benefits from their operation result when the costs thereof are considered on a long-term (multi-year) basis.
6. Better decisions regarding the selection of program plans and greater benefits from their application result when outcomes are related methodically to objectives.[3]

The processes of the ERM System were considered by the Association to be planning, programming, budgeting, and evaluating. Those processes were defined as follows:

1. Planning is the process of guiding internal change so that the school adapts effectively to the dynamic society of which it is a part.
2. Programming is the process of developing program plans.
3. Budgeting is the process which includes in addition to final reconciliation of programs and available resources according to established priorities, the preparation of the budget documents, the approval by a board of education, and the execution of the budgetary plans.
4. Evaluting is the process of assessing the attainment of objectives and the worth of programs.[4]

It is interesting to note that the Association of School Business Officials is using the systems approach in its recommendations for the establishment of a management system. Business management, per se, is seen not as an end in itself, but as a means to attain educational objectives. The processes of systematic strategic and management planning are discussed in detail in Chapter 6. Programming and budgeting policies and procedures are discussed in this chapter, and evaluation and accountability in Chapter 19.

Management Information Systems

Educational administrators are being urged by the business community and many legislators to install mangement information systems. There

[3] *Ibid.*, pp. 37–39.
[4] *Ibid.*, pp. 45–51.

is no doubt that educational administrators and boards of education need relevant information when they are making management decisions. This has always been true. However, some of the enthusiasts for management information systems assume that such as system, when installed in a school system, can be programmed in a computer so as to give optimum answers to all educational problems without the necessity of thinking and evaluating on the part of educational administrators, teachers, and boards of education. As will be pointed out in this chapter and also in Chapter 19, this is an erroneous assumption.

The implementation of PPBES involves research. Planning involves the determination of purposes and goals and the projection of the possible consequences of the acceptance of alternate purposes and goals. The intelligent selection of purposes and goals cannot be done without the availability of needed information. Programming cannot be accomplished without considering alternate programs. This requires cost effectiveness and cost benefit analyses. These analyses cannot be made without relevant information. Adequate budgeting requires information concerning programs, object, function, locus, revenues, and so forth. Evaluation requires the measurement of actual output as compared with expected output. This requires appropriate information. A management information system is designed to obtain the information necessary for planning, programming, budgeting, and evaluating. It is pointed directly to the implementation of these processes. Electronic data processing (EDP) is not an information management system (MIS) although it is essential to that system. EDP is simply the processing of information while MIS is "a planned arrangement for assuring that appropriate data are communicated in the proper form to the correct decision points at the appropriate time so that it facilitates organizational and managerial planning and operational decision making."[5]

Granger has pointed out that fully mechanized systems are myths which will never attain full possibility or reality. He made the following insightful evaluation of MIS:

> As a result of an accumulation of experiences in MIS, EDP, and other system procedures, administrators have become aware of the need for considering administrative philosophies and theories as well as techniques in the planning of organizational operations and related information networks. At one time bureaucratic theories led to the planning of information networks which centralized all important decisions in accordance with the "one big brain" concept of organizational leadership and decision-making. It was

[5]Robert L. Granger, *Educational Leadership* (Scranton, Pa.: Intext Educational Publishers, 1971), pp. 177–178.

predicted that middle managers, including school building principals, would soon be unnecessary and obsolete components of organizations. Experience has proved these oversimplified bureaucratic theory applications to be wrong.

Modern interdisciplinary organizational theorists believe that organizational optimization is best approached by designing MIS systems which encourage decision-making to be decentralized to the lowest point in an organization where the necessary skills and competence and sufficient legitimate authority intersect to permit the most useful application of new information in the making of a meaningful decision.[6]

Operations Research

As pointed out above, operations research is essential to efficient management. Johns and Morphet have suggested the following relationships of the operation of the educational enterprise to financial inputs:

1. If additional financial inputs will increase the individual and social benefits of the educational system more than the amount of the investment, the financial input should be increased.
2. If the same individual and social benefits of the educational system can be produced on a smaller financial input, then the financial input should be reduced accordingly.
3. If the school administrative unit itself or the individual schools within that unit are too small to achieve the economies of scale necessary to maximize the educational benefits per dollar of input, the school system or schools should be reorganized appropriately.
4. If the organizational structure does not function efficiently and effectively to maximize the educational benefits per dollar or input, it should be modified.
5. If any educational policy or program or operation is dysfunctional, ineffective, or inefficient, it should be changed.[7]

Both cost benefit and cost effectiveness studies would need to be made in order to apply these guides. Cost benefit studies as applied in industry commonly express benefits in terms of relative dollars of profit for different alternatives. It is difficult to express relative benefits in education in terms of dollars. This is especially true of the social benefits of education. However, individual benefits in education can be expressed in dollars and both social and individual inputs can be expressed in dollars.

[6]*Ibid.*, p. 179.
[7]Roe L. Johns and Edgar L. Morphet, *The Economics and Financing of Education* (Englewood Cliffs, N.J.: Prentice-Hall, Inc., 1969), p. 478.

Cost effectiveness studies are particularly useful in evaluating educational alternatives. For example, the relative costs of alternative educational delivery systems to attain a given educational objective, such as a given reading level, can be computed. An example would be comparing the cost and effectiveness of performance contracting with the cost of attaining the same objective as effectively in a public school.

Management Techniques

It is beyond the scope of this book to describe various techniques of management. Operations research has been producing some new and promising management techniques. An example of this is PERT (Program Evaluation and Review Technique).

PERT was developed by the Navy's Project Office in order to program the development of the *Polaris* missile. Its use was credited with reducing the anticipated time of the production of this missile by almost three years. The technique has been most useful in programming non-repetitive operations, such as the production of a missile, the construction of a school plant, or the programming of any major innovation. It is now being adopted by many business, industrial, and educational organizations. PERT is essentially a planning technique which was originally developed to control time in production, but it is also now being used to control costs. PERT time is described very briefly below.

The method of PERT is quite simple. In fact, the elements of this technique have been used by successful administrators for many years. The steps are as follows:

> First, every significant event that must occur to realize the end objective is selected and defined. . . .
> Second, the sequence and interdependency between events is established. This is done graphically by means of a flow chart, which in PERT jargon is called a network. . . .
> Third step in the process is to put a time value upon each activity. PERT requires three such time estimates: (1) optimistic, (2) most likely, and (3) pessimistic. . . .
> Fourth in the series of PERT steps, the three estimates are computed to find "expected" time for completing the activity. . . .
> Fifth, the computer then totals "expected" times along every possible path of the network to determine the "critical path"—the longest distance in time between beginning and end. . . .

In the sixth and final step, what derives from this series of computations is a report card in the form of standard printouts that "focus management attention on those areas where corrective action is most needed and can do the most good."[8]

Any shortening of the time for the completion of a project can be accomplished only by shortening the time required for the "critical path." This might be accomplished by such methods as overtime or shifting of materials and manpower from a path with "slack time" to the critical path.[9]

Although PERT was designed to control complex operations by means of digital computers, it can readily be used for less complex operations that do not require the use of computers. For example, it is now being used by many researchers to schedule and control research projects.

SCHOOL BUDGETING

A school budget is an aggregate of educational plans with an estimate of the receipts and expenditures necessary to finanace the services and facilities required to provide the desired educational programs. School budgets are usually made for a period of one fiscal year, although budgetary needs are sometimes projected for some years into the future. The school fiscal year should include a complete scholastic year in order to simplify the estimating of expenditures. Furthermore, the school fiscal year should coincide with the tax levying and collecting year, in order that the flow of revenue may coincide with the flow of expenditures during the school year. The most commonly used fiscal year, and perhaps the best for boards of education, is the year beginning July 1 and ending June 30. A fiscal year beginning on January 1 is particularly unsuited to school operations, because fractions of two different operating years must be budgeted within one fiscal year.

Almost all school systems in the United States now operate on some type of budget. These budgets may vary all the way from simple lump sum estimates of receipts and expenditures listed on a few sheets of paper to

[8]Howard Simons, "PERT: How to Meet a Deadline," *THINK*, May 1962, pp. 13–17. (Reprinted by permission from THINK Magazine, published by IBM, Copyright 1962 by International Business Machines Corporation.)
[9]See PERT Orientation and Training Center, PERT *Fundamentals*, Vol. I, *Networking* 0–712–769 and Vol. II, *Scheduling and Planning* 0–712–770 (Washington, D.C., U.S. Government Printing Office).

comprehensive documents of a hundred pages or more setting forth detailed programs and estimates of receipts and expenditures with accompanying material fully interpreting the budget. The budgetary process may be nothing more than ascertaining the revenue that will be available and allocating it in such a manner as to minimize complaints. On the other hand, the budgetary process may involve carefully studying educational needs, estimating the revenue necessary to meet educational needs, and planning the procurement of the necessary revenue to implement the educational program agreed upon. The latter type of budgetary process has been found to be most effective in promoting the development of adequate educational programs.

The school budget is the instrument through which the people can determine both their educational and their financial policy. Therefore, effective school budgeting must include:

1. The preparation of the budget in such a manner as to provide an educational program that gives effect to educational policies previously determined;
2. The budget document, which may be defined as a systematic plan and statement that forecasts the expenditures and revenues of a school system during a stated period of time;
3. The presentation, consideration, and adoption of the budget;
4. The administration of the budget;
5. The appraisal of the budget.

Some of the procedures necessary for modern school budgeting are presented in the following paragraphs.

Educational Planning

As has been pointed out in Chapter 1, the purposes of education must be defined and agreed upon before meaningful educational plans can be developed, as explained in Chapter 6. Definite plans for implementing the philosophy and purposes of the school system must be developed before action can be taken. Educational plans must present the quantity and quality of educational services being proposed. The statement of the proposed educational plans will include both short-range plans for the scholastic year and long-range plans reaching some years into the future. They will include information on such questions as the following:

1. Who should be educated? That is, will educational opportunities be limited to grades 1 to 12, or will the program include kindergartens, a junior college, and adult education opportunities?
2. What will be the probable enrollment in each age group or school program during the next five to ten years?
3. What additional sites, buildings, equipment, and personnel will be needed during the next five to ten years?
4. For how many days during the year will the school be kept open?
5. Should sufficient staff be employed to operate the schools during the summer months for enrichment and recreational purpose?
6. Should the school plants be planned to serve community purposes as well as the regularly organized school program?
7. What should be the pupil load per teacher?
8. What level of qualifications should be possessed by teachers?
9. What provisions should be made for exceptional children?
10. What provisions should be made for clinical and guidance services?
11. What provisions should be made for pupil transportation?
12. Should senior high schools be comprehensive high schools, or should vocational schools be provided?
13. Should special teachers of art, music, and physical education be provided for elementary schools, or should elementary rooms be self-contained?
14. What variety of educational programs should be provided in junior and senior high schools?
15. Should a school lunch program be provided, and what should be its characteristics?
16. What health services should be provided by the school system?
17. What special provisions should be made for the culturally different?

This is an incomplete list, but decisions must be made on matters of this kind before a budget incorporating educational plans can be constructed. Taxpayers are much more reluctant to support a lump sum increase in the budget than an increase they understand. Increases should be analyzed in terms of the educational program. For example, the public can evaluate a $200,000 increase for initiating kindergartens but it has no basis for evaluating an unexplained $200,000 increase in the budget.

Preparing the Budget

Once the educational program is agreed upon, estimates can be prepared indicating the probable costs. The word "costs" is used deliberately, because there are different costs for different levels of quality in many components of the educational program. Therefore, several alternative budgets and subbudgets should be prepared before the final budget is adopted. These alternative budgets will show the additional costs necessary to provide additional services or a higher quality of service. Whenever possible data on cost benefit or cost effectiveness for alternatives should be provided for those participating in making the budget. Representative citizen committees, classroom teachers, principals, supervisors, and other interested parties should be given adequate opportunity to share with the board and the superintendent the responsibility of developing the educational plan. Representative advisory groups should be given broad opportunities to study alternative educational plans and to present their recommendations to the board. This process results in communitywide participation in the educational planning and budget making. Only through the process of participation in the planning can there be genuine understanding of the budget.

Unfortunately, in the typical school system the superintendent and his staff, with perhaps a committee of the board, prepare the budget document. A notice that the board will have a public hearing on the budget on a certain date is published in the newspaper. Usually, no one attends the hearing with the exception of a few people interested in keeping the tax rate down and perhaps a few newspaper reporters hoping to get a story from attacks being made on the budget. The people who are genuinely interested in the school budget do not usually attend the public hearing, because it is a "cut-and-dried affair" and there is no genuine opportunity to participate. This common but primitive method of budget preparation is partly responsible for lack of adequate financial support of the schools in many districts.

As previously mentioned, the formal budget should incorporate a definite statement of the educational program in the form of a programmed budget as well as a statement of receipts and expenditures in terms of required function and object accounts. Other interpretive material might include various types of unit cost analyses, data for comparable school systems, trends in receipts and expenditures adjusted for variations in the purchasing power of the dollar, and any other information that will help the board and the public to make intelligent decisions concerning the budget.

Presentation and Adoption of the Budget

The budget should be formally presented to the board several weeks before it is adopted, and it should be approved prior to the beginning of the fiscal year for which the budget is made. It should not be inferred that the budget is "news" to the board when it is first presented. Board members should have been appropriately participating in the preparation of the budget throughout the year. For instance, the board should have been making decisions throughout the year on educational programs and policies that must be reflected in the budget. Therefore, the budget when it is presented should actually present largely a summary of decisions that have already been made by the board after careful studies involving many people. Wide publicity should be given to the budget during its preparation, and opportunity should be given for public hearings. But public hearings without a planned process for broad participation are almost worthless. Although mass means of communication should be used in publicizing the budget, little is accomplished by publishing only a formal statement of receipts and expenditures. Most of the publicity should center around the educational services and facilities being considered.

Administration of the Budget

There should be a centralized administration of the budget. No budget can be kept in balance if numerous persons make expenditures without preauthorization. The superintendent or his representative must have the responsibility for administering the budget.

If the budget is to have any meaning, it must be put in operation. A budget is not an effective instrument for implementing the educational program if it is filed away and referred to only at long intervals. Programs must be organized; persons must be employed; supplies must be purchased; buildings must be constructed, equipped, maintained, and operated; and many types of services must be provided. These and many other things all cost money, and unless the budget serves as a real guide there will be no money left for others. The choice then is to fail to finance certain items in the budget or to incur a deficit. Either alternative prevents the full achievement of educational goals. Therefore, the budget is the instrument used to keep all expenditures in balance, in order that the total educational plan is made a reality.

The detailed amounts budgeted for receipts and expenditures should be entered into the account books or machine records for receipts and expenditures. Most standard forms provide space for listing the budget amount for each budget appropriation. However, it should not be assumed that real budget controls are being exercised unless accounting is on an accrual basis. It should be obvious that cash accounting alone is insufficient to provide the information necessary for budget control. If one adds the expenditures to date for a particular expenditure account and subtracts the sum from the amount budgeted for that account, the difference does not represent the real balance available in that account, because it does not take into consideration the obligations against that account that have not yet been paid. Under accrual accounting (1) estimated revenues are counted as available when earned, even though the cash has not been received, but the estimates are adjusted periodically for gains or losses; (2) as soon as contracts or purchase orders are signed, the obligations so incurred are charged immediately to the amount affected as encumbrances, and when the corresponding bill is paid, the procedure is to credit the account with the original encumbrance and charge the final payment to it. Under accrual accounting, therefore, the unencumbered balance in an account is the difference between the amount budgeted and the sum of cash expenditures plus the encumbrances that have not been credited. In other words, the real balance in an expenditure account is the difference between the amount budgeted and the sum of cash expenditures plus obligations made against that account that have not yet been paid.

FINANCIAL ACCOUNTING AND ADMINISTRATION

School financial accounting systems should furnish: "(1) an historical record of receipts and expenditures; (2) a basis for evaluating the faithfulness of stewardship, and; (3) a partial basis for both fiscal and educational management with respect to budget preparation, control, cost analysis and reporting."[10] Therefore, accounting is far more than bookkeeping. Very few school administrators are trained accountants. Even if an adequate financial accounting system could be described here, state laws or regulations would prevent the use of exactly the same system of accounting in all states. School systems vary greatly in size, and accounting needs differ. Furthermore, much published information is already available setting forth the details of school accounting. The U.S. Office of Education has published a number of handbooks on school accounting.[11] The most recently revised handbook of the U.S. Office of Education on school accounting gives major emphasis to program accounting and cost accounting in order to implement PPBES (Program, Planning, Budgeting, Evaluating System). This revised handbook on school accounting contains the following statement concerning accounts:

[10]John Guy Fowlkes and Abner L. Hansen, "Business Management-Accounting, Auditing and Reporting," in *Problems and Issues in Public School Finance,* ed., R. L. Johns and E. L. Morphet (New York: Bureau of Publications, Teachers College, Columbia University, 1952), Chap. 14.
[11]The most recent handbook is Charles D. Roberts and Allan R. Lichtenberger, *Financial Accounting Classifications and Standard Terminology for Local and State School Systems.* U.S. Department of Health, Education and Welfare, Office of Education. (Washington, D.C.: U.S. Government Printing Office, 1973).

The chart of accounts in this manual has been structured to enable planners to budget, program, and evaluate the resources, processes and effectiveness of the various objectives of a school system.[12]

This handbook also states:

The purpose of classifying expenditures is to provide a basis for grouping expenditures for meaningful analysis. Expenditures are classified by function (why purchased), object (what purchased), organization unit and activity (for whom), and fiscal year (when).[13]

The primary purpose of this section is to describe what should be accomplished by an adequate accounting system.

Objectives of School Accounting

Budgeting, accounting, and reporting are physically separate operations, but from the standpoint of business management they must be so integrated as to result in a total structure that is internally consistent. For this reason the objectives of school accounting cannot be described in isolation from other operations. Following are some of the business management operations in which the accounting system plays a vital part.

1. A method must be provided for authorizing expenditures. The approved budget itself is a general authorization for spending money. But budget controls are necessary and preaudits of expenditures must be provided for. But preaudits of expenditures cannot be made unless cash and accrual accounting records are available.
2. In order for schools to operate, purchases must be made and contracts must be let. Pruchases include a wide variety of supplies, equipment, services, materials, real estate, and other items. Contracts are made for personnel services, building construction and repairs, insurance, leans, and other transactions. Authorized procedures must be followed and forms developed for recording these transactions.
3. The board must pay for the obligations it has incurred. Therefore, the board must develop procedures by which it can ascertain what it owes. Invoices must be checked to see that the board has received the goods it purchased and that it is paying the price agreed upon. The length of time worked by employees must be verified and the amount owed employees under contract determined. Buildings under construction must be inspected and the proportionate part of the contract due at a particular time determined.

[12] *Ibid.*, p. 4.
[13] *Ibid.*, p. 38.

4. The payments made by the board must be recorded systematically, and the records must show at least to whom or to what agency or organization payment was made and for what purpose.
5. The board must have revenue if it is to pay its obligations, so revenue must be procured by local taxation, state and federal appropriations, or other sources. These receipts must be systematically recorded by source and by the fund or purpose for which they can be used. Special fund accounts must also be kept in order to meet the requirements of law and to discharge trust obligations. Receipts may be for current purposes, for debt service, for capital outlay, or for trust and agency purposes.
6. The board must make reports of its financial operations to the public. Therefore, account classifications of the budget, the accounting system, and the financial reports should be consistent.
7. Reports are made to the state and the U.S. Office of Education. Therefore, the accounting system must meet state requirements, and the information provided should be comparable with that provided by other school systems.
8. Alternative programs and policies need to be evaluated, and budgets must be prepared for succeeding years. Therefore, the accounting system must provide the information necessary for appropriate research. Cost analyses are of particular importance in evaluating certain policies. For that reason, the accounting system should lend itself to making the needed cost analyses.

This is not a complete list of what should be accomplished by the accounting system, but it can be used as a rough check on whether a board has a reasonably adequate system of financial accounting.

Financial Reports

Financial reports should be made to the board monthly and to the general public at least annually. The monthly financial report should be reconciled with the budget. The primary purpose of the monthly financial report is to provide the board with necessary evidence to evaluate whether proper budget controls are being implemented. Regular financial reports also serve as a stimulus to keep records up to date and to locate promptly any accounting errors. Boards of education commonly publish technical annual financial reports. Although this is usually necessary to meet the requirements of law, such reports are unintelligible to most laymen. The most valuable financial reports for laymen are reports that relate financing to the educational programs and services provided. Progressive school systems periodically publish reports of this type.

Purchasing and Payment Procedures

Central purchasing should be provided for the total school system except for necessary petty cash accounts. Competitive bids should be obtained on sizable purchases. These bids should be based on appropriate specifications, locally prepared or obtained from some reputable source. Teachers, principals, custodians, and others who use supplies and equipment should participate in preparing the specifications for the items in which they are respectively interested. Competitive bids usually save the board money and also improve public relations. The policy of quantity purchasing should be followed when possible, because better prices are obtained. Quantity purchasing requires advance planning and storage facilities, but both usually promote economy and efficiency.

The importance of the participation of teachers, principals, and supervisors in the preparation of specifications for instructional materials and equipment cannot be overemphasized. This is essential in order to provide assurance of the educational value of the items purchased. But performance tests should also be made of items purchased. Many items of equal educational value may vary greatly in durability and safety. Large school systems may find it desirable to establish their own performance-testing laboratories. Other school systems should avail themselves of the services of state, regional, or national testing bureaus or laboratories.

Auditing

As mentioned previously, the business staff should continuously preaudit all financial transactions. But the board should have an independent external audit annually. It is essential that the audit be made by a competent person or persons not under the control of the board. Some states provide state auditors. In other states, the school system employs certified public accountants. State audits can be very valuable or of limited value, depending upon the training of the auditors and the policies of the auditing department. Audits made by certified public accountants who are familiar with school accounting are quite valuable; others are limited in value.

The objectives of the audit program as stated in the proceedings of the Association of School Business Officials are as follows:

1. To safeguard money, property, and employees.
2. To determine the adequacy of the methods of internal check.
3. To maintain adherence to the established standards, policies, and procedures—financial, accounting, and operating.
4. To check condition and use of property and equipment, particularly from the standpoint of adequate return.

5. To maintain and coordinate internal auditing procedures with those of the public accountant.
6. To present accurate, complete, and unbiased statistics with respect to the operation of the educational system.[14]

Therefore, auditors should limit their activities to these objectives and avoid making recommendations in the area of educational policy.

BUSINESS ADMINISTRATION SERVICES

The business administration services discussed in the following paragraphs are not always organized as a part of business administration. But these services are all closely related to business management. The efficiency of business administration is promoted if the business and financial operations described in this chapter are coordinated by one person. In medium- and large-sized school systems this person usually bears the title of "assistant superintendent for business affiars." In fact, communications and services are usually improved if the central administrative office and the facilities described next are all located either on the same site or in close proximity to each other. A number of school systems have recently constructed all their central facilities on one large site centrally located in the district. It is usually very unsatisfactory to house the central office of the school system in the city hall or the county courthouse. This practice usually results in inadequate facilities and unnecessary involvement in partisan politics.

Supply Management and Storage Facilities

When a board of education purchases supplies, equipment, and materials, it has simply converted money into physical things that are needed by the school system. Therefore, its responsibility for accounting does not cease. The goods purchased must be received, stored, delivered, and a control record system must be established. These are the functions of supply management. The ultimate objective of supply management is to get supplies and equipment to the point of need at the time needed and in the required quantity without loss or damage. Quality service must also be rendered at a minimum cost of time and money. This requires skillful

---

[14]Thor W. Bruce, "The Why and Where of Auditing," *Proceedings, Association of School Business Officials* (Kalamazoo, Mich.: Association of School Business Officials of U.S. and Canada, 1950), p. 236.

management indeed. Therefore, the person in charge of supply management, especially in medium- and large-sized school systems, has a very important responsibility. He can either be of great assistance in implementing the educational program or he can be a hindrance. He can either save the board money or he can waste money.

When something is ordered by the board, it must be received by some responsible person. That person must check the goods received against the bill of lading and the purchase order, and either attest to the accuracy of the shipment or give written notification to the business office of discrepancies in quantity, condition, or quality. Items purchased may be delivered by vendors to a warehouse, a school, a shop, or the central office. A copy of the purchase order should be sent to the point of delivery when purchases are made. When the deliveries have been checked, the purchase order with appropriate notations thereon, along with the invoice or other paper accompanying the shipment, should be sent to the business office. These papers constitute some of the vital original documents upon which financial accounting is based.

Central purchasing is essential to good business administration, because money is saved by quantity purchasing. Decentralized spot purchasing is wasteful in time and money. Quantity purchasing creates the need for storage space. When things are stored, the problem of getting them out of storage is immediately created. But the final objective is to get the supplies to the point needed, when needed, in the quantity needed, without loss or damage. Each school system planning its system of supply management must keep all these problems in mind. The size of the system will affect the magnitude of each problem, but not its nature.

School Plant Operation

School plant operation is concerned with the cleaning, heating, lighting, and other activities necessary to keep the plant open and in condition for daily use. School plant maintenance consists of the repair of buildings and the repair and replacement of equipment. They are separate but closely related operations. In school systems large enough to provide central services, school plant operation and maintenance are usually placed under the same person, bearing some such title as superintendent or supervisor of buildings and grounds.

Efficient operation is essential to the health, safety, and comfort of pupils and teachers. Furthermore, plant operations can either hinder or help the program of educational activities. School custodians have close relationships with pupils, and they can either be an asset or a liability. Modern school plants are expensive and contain complicated mechanical and electrical equipment. The operation of this equipment can either save money or waste money.

Obviously, it is poor educational and financial policy to turn the job of operating the physical facilities of the school over to an ignorant, untrained custodian of questionable character. Not so many years ago, it was the custom of some district boards to put the job of school custodian up for bids. The job went to the lowest bidder, and the custodian was frequently one of the least respected individuals in the community. This practice was never justified, and it is unthinkable today.

It is not the purpose of this section to describe detailed procedures for proper school plant operation but to present guides for administrative policies aimed at assuring adequate custodial services. Following are some guides for school custodial policies that should be considered by the administrator.

1. School custodians should be carefully selected. Consideration should be given to health, character, education, experience, and willingness to learn. The principal should recommend the custodian or custodians to the superintendent after consulting with the superintendent of buildings and grounds, if one is available.
2. A salary schedule should be provided for custodians giving due recognition to experience and quality of service. This schedule should be high enough to attract responsible and competent employees.
3. An in-service training program should be provided for school custodians. Only rarely are boards of education able to employ custodians who are already trained for the job. If a superintendent of buildings and grounds is available, he should direct this training program. If not, outside consulting help should be employed. Principals who are uninformed about school plant operation should participate in this or some other type of training program until they are able to give proper supervision to the custodians at their respective schools.
4. The job of school custodian should be defined and a work schedule developed. The superintendent of buildings and grounds should provide principals with consulting help for this task. Custodians should be trained to make simple repairs and adjustments in equipment but should not attempt complicated tasks. This will save time and money. Close coordination with the school plant maintenance department is essential, because the borderline between operation and maintenance is not always clear.
5. The custodian should be under the direct administration and supervision of the principal. If there are several custodians at a school, one should be appointed as head custodian. Direct orders to custodians should come through appropriate channels. Nothing is more frustrating to the custodian trying to complete his schedule of work than to be interrupted by a classroom teacher who suddenly orders the custodian to do something. Exceptions should be made in emergencies, of course, but the administrative principle that no employee should be required to take direct order from more than one person also applies to custodians.
6. Custodians should be employed for twelve months if possible. Many school systems put some custodians under the administration of the plant maintenance department during the summer months. This practice has much to commend it, because the maintenance staff usually needs to be expanded during the summer months and custodians need work.

7. A sufficient number of custodians should be employed to do a satisfactory job. It has been suggested that one custodian should be employed for every ten teachers, or one custodian for every 16,000 square feet of floor area to be cleaned. These are very rough ratios and cannot be equitably applied to individual school buildings. The labor required to clean and operate buildings varies with the condition and type of floor, the type of heating system used, the amount of ground maintenance required, the availability of labor-saving equipment, and other factors. Custodians can accomplish more work if given the proper equipment in any type of building, but some buildings are more adapted to labor-saving machinery than others.
8. When a local school faculty is considering policies affecting plant operation, custodians should participate in the faculty meeting. Custodians tend to have more interest in implementing policies that they help develop. Custodians should participate in such meetings as peers with the faculty. This is a rare practice, unfortunately.
9. Custodians should have the benefits of retirement, group insurance, sick leave, vacation leave, social security, and workmen's compensation.

These policies are based on the assumptions that the proper operation of the school plant is essential to a functioning educational program and that custodians are valued members of the school organization.

School Plant Maintenance

It has been estimated that an average of 1.5 to 2 percent of the replacement cost of a building must be spent annually for maintenance in order to keep it in good condition. School buildings have an average life of approximately fifty years. If 2 percent of the cost of a building is spent on it annually for fifty years for maintenance and repairs, the cost of repairing and maintaining the building over its life is as great as its original cost, assuming no change in the purchasing power of the dollar. If a building can be so constructed as to reduce maintenance cost to 1 percent annually, half the original cost of the building can be saved during its term of use. Therefore, the maintenance program starts with the construction and equipment of buildings. There is no economy in cheap, shoddy construction or flimsy equipment. Such construction requires a much higher percent expenditure for maintenance and repairs than the figures just cited, the plant will not have as long a life, and it is never as useful a tool as a properly constructed and equipped building. Industry and business have long recognized this as a sound principle, but some taxpayers seem to believe that somehow school plants are exempt from it.

Some large school systems have a school plant planning division as well as a school plant maintenance section. Other systems, usually not the largest, combine school plant planning with school plant maintenance. Whether these services are combined or separated in the organization, provisions should be made for close coordination of the two services.

The board of education must develop some type of plan for maintaining and repairing school plants. The alternatives are as follows: (1) outside contracting, (2) school employees, or (3) a combination of the two. Some of the most valid arguments for the board employing its own maintenance workers are as follows:

1. If the maintenance workers are school employees, the board can require a higher quality of service than it can obtain from many contractors.
2. Maintenance costs less because no profit is involved.
3. The time, cost, and trouble of advertising for bids and awarding contracts can be avoided.
4. School plant maintenance can be planned and scheduled more efficiently than by job contracting.

Some of the most valid arguments for outside contracting are as follows:

1. Some types of maintenance and repair require heavy, expensive equipment that the board would use so infrequently as to make it uneconomical.
2. Some types of jobs call for specialized mechanics that the board cannot afford to employ full-time.
3. The peak load for school maintenance and repair is during the summer months, and the board cannot do the necessary work in the time allocated.

The evidence seems to indicate that the best policy is a combination of school maintenance employees and outside contracting. Very small systems have no alternative to outside contracting. Small systems frequently find it desirable to employ one or two handy repairmen. When school districts are of efficient size, a school plant maintenance department should be established. This department should be headed by a man who is administratively responsible to the assistant superintendent for business affairs.

School Transportation

School transportation continues to grow in importance. In 1941, 18 percent of the pupils enrolled in the public schools were transported to school, and in 1971, approximately 42 percent. In 1971, more than 19 million pupils were transported to school at a cost of one billion dollars. It might have been assumed that the decline in farm population would have resulted in a reduction in the need for transportation. However, the increase in the suburban and rural nonfarm population has caused a much greater increase in the need for pupil transportation than the reduction caused by the decline in the farm population. The increased use of school transportation to achieve racial balance in the schools of a district is also contributing to increasing the number of pupils transported. It is anticipated that the increase in the need for pupil transportation will continue.

PURPOSES AND OBJECTIVES The development of pupil transportation was necessary for the attainment of the American ideal that every child, regardless of where he lives or his physical handicaps, has the right to an adequate educational opportunity. Modern school systems now provide transportation for normal pupils who live beyond a reasonable walking distance from school, for physically handicapped pupils who live any distance from school within its attendance area, for pupils who live on dangerous walking routes even if the walking distance is reasonable, and for educational trips for school classes. Therefore, school transportation should not be looked upon as a luxury any more than the school plant. It is an essential part of the total school program.

The use of school buses for educational trips is rapidly increasing. The school bus is thus becoming an extension of the classroom. This is sound educational policy. Technically, the school bus is a part of the school plant. It is just as logical to use the school bus to facilitate the learning experiences of pupils as to use a library or a laboratory.

SCHOOL BOARD POLICIES The operation of the school transportation program involves numerous policy and executive decisions. There is no area of school administration that requires a more definite and detailed statement of the board's policies than school transportation. If policies are not available to serve as a guide to executive decision making, too much of the school administrator's time will be spent on transportation problems, the program is likely to be wasteful, the service may not be adequate, and public relations may be damaged. The basic objectives of the board's transportation policies should be to provide safe, economical, and adequate transportation service to the pupils who need this service. Many factors contribute to such service. Some of these factors are discussed in the following paragraphs.

THE ROUTING AND SCHEDULING OF BUSES Basic to the organization of the transportation program is the determination of who should be furnished transportation services. This must be determined by board policy, subject to the limitations of state law. The board must determine (1) how far children must live from the school they attend in order to be entitled to transportation, (2) how far children must walk to the bus line before being entitled to special service on a spur route, and (3) what physically handicapped children are entitled to transportation. The definition of a reasonable walking distance to school varies among the states and the districts of a state. Some boards have defined reasonable walking distance as one mile and other boards two miles. The average practice seems to be approximately one and one-half miles. Some boards set different distances for different age groups.

When the board has determined its policies with respect to what pupils are entitled to transportation, a spot map should be made of those pupils. The next step is to plan the transportation routes necessary to serve the pupils. Following are some factors to keep in mind when planning bus routes.

1. It is more economical to operate one large bus than two small buses over the same route.
2. Pupils should not be required to spend an excessive amount of time on the bus.
3. The cost of operating the bus and the time for the route are unnecessarily increased if more stops are made than are required to give reasonable service.

After a map of transportation routes is made, it is then possible to determine accurately the number and size of bus units needed. The transportation map should be made annually because of rapid shifts in pupil population to be transported.

PUBLIC OWNERSHIP VERSUS CONTRACT TRANSPORTATION   One of the most important policy decisions for the board to make is whether it should own and operate its own buses or contract for transportation services. Numerous studies have been made of this matter in a number of states. The advantages usually found for public ownership are as follows:

1. It is more economical because fleet operation is more efficient than individual operation, and profits are eliminated.
2. Better service is provided, because school employees are more responsive to supervision than private contractors.
3. Better equipment is provided, because private contractors frequently cannot finance proper equipment.
4. Better drivers can be selected, because the board is not restricted to the man who can buy a bus.
5. Routing and scheduling are more efficient, because the board owns the equipment and can control it.
6. The educational program can be carried out more effectively, because the board can use its own equipment for educational trips more readily than it can use contracted equipment.

About the only advantages of contracting are as follows:

1. The board knows at the beginning of the year exactly what its transportation costs are.
2. The administration has less managerial responsibilities.
3. In some cities, the public transportation system can be used effectively for transporting some children.

The advantages of public ownership in most situations so overweigh its disadvantages that boards of education are rapidly changing to public ownership. At this writing, approximately 70 percent of the school buses of the nation are publicly owned.

THE SCHOOL-BUS MAINTENANCE PROGRAM If the board owns its own buses, a program for bus maintenance must be established. Attention has already been directed to the administrator's responsibility for routing and scheduling school buses and determining the services needed. The administrative and supervisory responsibilities for school transportation are so great that the superintendent needs a supervisor of school transportation if the board owns and operates twenty or more buses. In a small system the supervisor may work part-time as a mechanic. But with large fleets, he should spend his entire time in supervisory and administrative duties. These duties should include routing and scheduling of buses, supervision and in-service training of drivers and mechanics, dealing with the public on matters of transportation services, and many other transportation problems. If the school system is large enough to have an assistant superintendent for business affairs, the supervisor of school transportation should be directly responsible to him; if it does not have one, he should be directly responsible to the superintendent.

The supervisor needs a staff of mechanics and a school-bus garage in which they can work. The number of mechanics needed varies with the condition of the buses, the length of the routes, and the condition of the roads. One mechanic for every fifteen to eighteen buses is usually required for good service.

The soundest maintenance program is one that emphasizes preventive maintenance. Otherwise, all the district has is a repair program. The preventive maintenance program is based on regular, thorough, and systematic inspection to anticipate trouble and prevent it from occurring. Such a program minimizes road failures, promotes economy and safety, and provides better service. It is the job of the supervisor or his representative to make these inspections and to see that the necessary action is taken to correct deficiencies in equipment. It is also good business to employ good mechanics. Properly maintained school-bus bodies and chassis normally have a useful life of approximately ten years.

The School Food Service Program

The school food service program is now a major division of school operations. The National School Lunch Program alone cost more than $2,100,000,000 in cash and commodities in 1968–1969. Approximately 39 percent of the total enrollment in public and private schools were served food under the National School Lunch Program in 1968–1969.[15]

Basic economic and social changes have created the need for the school lunch program. The most important of these changes are as follows:

1. The consolidation of schools and the transportation of children have increased the length of time that children are away from home, and also have prevented children from going home for lunch.
2. Millions of mothers are now working, and they are not at home to prepare food for their children during the noon period.
3. There is an increased public awareness of the importance of good health and the contribution that proper nutrition makes to health.
4. There has been a change in the social thinking of the people. Formerly, it was generally assumed that each parent was responsible for providing the noon lunch for his own children and that school authorities had no responsibility. Compulsory attendance laws require parents to send their children to school. But schools are now organized and administered so that parents cannot discharge their normal responsibility for providing their children with a nutritious noon lunch. Therefore, the public now demands that school authorities assume at least a part of the responsibility for the food service program.

The school lunch operation is irrevocably an integral part of the public school program. It is operated for pupils in a publicly owned building by school employees under the supervision of school administrators and supervisors subject to the control of the board of education. Furthermore, teachers commonly use school lunch experiences for valuable learning activities. The school principal has the important responsiblity of organizing, supervising, and financing the school lunch program. He must operate it as a solvent enterprise without making a profit or incurring a loss. Many pupils, especially in communities with a low socioeconomic status, cannot pay for their lunches. He must somehow arrange for them to be fed. The school principal operating a lunch program in a poverty-stricken community is unfairly loaded with school-lunch financial burdens. Also, the labor cost is generally proprotionately greater for lunches served in a small school than in a large school.

The teachers inevitably become involved in these problems. In elementary schools particularly, teachers frequently collect the money from

---

[15] U.S. Department of Agriculture, Economic Research Service, *Food Service in the Nations Schools: A Preliminary Report* (Washington, D.C.: U.S. Government Printing Office, 1969).

pupils for their lunches. In high schools, pupils normally pay for their lunches at the principal's office or at the serving counter. In most states, the purchasing and accounting are done by individual schools. Consulting help may or may not be available from the central office. In many schools, therefore, too much of the principal's and even the teacher's time is spent in collecting and accounting for funds to operate an enterprise on a decentralized basis that is inherently inefficient and incapable of rendering the quantity and quality of service needed. Furthermore, the total cost per lunch served would be reduced by centralized financing, purchasing, and supervision, and by an increased volume of lunches served.

Following are some of the school lunch operating policies for public schools that are generally recommended by authorities in this field:

1. The board of education, the superintendent, and school principals accept responsibility for the school lunch program as an important part of the total program.
2. The financing of the school lunch program is centralized. All receipts of school lunchrooms are sent to the central office and pooled with state and federal funds available for the lunch program. This pooling of resources prevents the penalization of small schools and schools compelled to carry a heavy free lunch load because of the socioeconomic level of the population. In practice, federal funds and surplus commodities are largely used to remove inequalities.
3. All purchasing except for some authorized perishables is done on a wholesale basis by the central office. All payments are made and all financial accounts are kept by the central office. Budgets are made for each lunchroom, and cost accounts are kept for each lunchroom, but all lunchrooms are financed as one program.
4. In systems of efficient size, a trained school food-service supervisor is employed. The supervisor works closely with the principal and school lunchroom managers. He plans menus in cooperation with lunchroom managers; carries on an in-service training program for lunchroom workers; works closely with the business office in purchasing, storing, and distributing food, equipment, and lunchroom supplies; keeps the lunchroom accounts; and, in general, coordinates all phases of the lunch program. He is a part of the business management office.
5. Lunchroom managers and their assistants are appointed by the superintendent upon the recommendation of the principal. They are administratively responsible to the principal.
6. Lunchroom facilities are functionally planned for food service operations. Those operations include receiving, storing, preparing, and serving food; cleaning utensils; disposing of garbage; and keeping control records. The capacity of storage facilities provided for lunchrooms is coordinated with the capacity of central storage facilities.

SAFEGUARDING SCHOOL FUNDS, PROPERTY, AND PERSONS

The administrator has the responsibility of developing a program for safeguarding school funds, property, and persons. A comprehensive program of this type has many facets. It includes (1) insurance and bonding, (2) elimination of fire hazards from school buildings, (3) elimination from school plants of hazards to life and limb, (4) protection of pupils from traffic hazards, (5) removal of temptations to steal by protection of cash for which school employees are responsible and by adequate accounting and stock control records, and (6) protection of the health of pupils and school employees. Other measures could be added to this list; however this section is concerned only with safeguarding funds, property, and persons by insuring and bonding procedures.

Safeguarding School Funds

School funds are kept on either time or demand deposit in a bank or banks selected by the board of education as its depository. In some states, the depository must be approved by a state agency. If the balance in a school fund will not be needed for six months or more, it should be placed on time deposit or invested in high-rated government securities, because demand deposits usually draw no interest. These securities are normally short-term securities, because the maturity date of the securities purchased should correspond closely with the time the board will need its money. If balances are invested in long-term securities, the board must market its securities before maturity. An unfavorable change in the bond market would cause the board to lose a part of the principal of the investment. Security of principal is much more important to the board than rate of interest when it invests public finds. Time deposits have greater flexibility than bonds. This is an advantage to the board, especially for small balances or balances for which it is difficult to predict accurately the time of need.

When school funds are on either time or demand deposit, those funds should be fully protected at all times from loss due to bank failure. The Federal Deposit Insurance Corporation protects deposits up to $20,000. However, this protection is of little value to boards of education for large school systems that require operating balances of several hundred thousand dollars or even of a million or more dollars. Small school systems can secure adequate protection from the F.D.I.C. by depositing funds in several banks and securing $20,000 of insurance for each deposit. This procedure is not practicable for a medium- or large-sized school system because the protection would be far from sufficient. The standard procedure is to require the depository bank to place in escrow in another bank approved by the board collateral equal to the amount of funds on deposit. If the depository bank fails, as much of the collateral as is necessary to return the board's funds is sold. The board of education should approve as collateral only high-rating government securities.

Property Insurance

Boards of education have invested large sums of money in school buildings and equipment. This property is subject to heavy damage from fire and in some areas from storms and earthquakes. Heavy property losses result in serious budget difficulties and even financial disaster, especially for small school systems. Therefore, good management requires that a board of education protect itself against such contingencies. The purpose of insurance is to protect a board from a risk that it cannot afford to bear. Most boards of education carry fire insurance on buildings and equipment, and many others carry windstorm and other types of protection in addition.

The insurance needs of a board of education vary widely. A small school system of limited resources with only one or a few buildings proportionately carries a much greater risk than a large school system with several hundred buildings located on widely separated sites. The loss of one building not protected by insurance in a small school system will cause a financial crisis, but the loss of a single building in a large system may have but a limited effect on financial operations.

Fire insurance is expensive. A number of large city school systems with widely scattered risks have solved the problem of the high cost of fire insurance by becoming self-insurers. This is usually done by the board establishing an insurance reserve from funds that would have been paid to private companies for insurance. A few states, particularly Alabama and South Carolina, have established state insurance plans for insuring school buildings. Experience with well-managed self-insurance plans protected by adequate legislation has shown that from 40 to 50 percent can be saved in insurance costs. State insurance of school buildings or self-insurance by large school systems is practicable and it would save large sums of money, but this policy is bitterly fought by private insurance companies.

Following are some recommended procedures for obtaining maximum returns for the insurance dollar:

1. Procedures for accurately appraising the value of school buildings and contents should be developed in order to determine insurable value. This is necessary to determine the amount of insurance to carry and to appraise losses.
2. Coinsurance is the most economical plan of insurance. Except for large, low-risk fire-resistive buildings, 80 percent or more coinsurance should be carried. If a blanket district policy is used, there is some advantage in 90 to 100 percent coinsurance.
3. The most complete fire insurance coverage is obtained under the recently developed insurance form known as the Public and Institutional Property Plan. It is available only for public buildings such as schools. Under this plan, school buildings and contents can be insured for the replacement cost rather than depreciated value. Under this type of policy, buildings and contents are insured

for an agreed-upon amount in lieu of coinsurance, but this amount cannot be less than 90 percent of value which must be sworn to annually by the insured. At this writing this type of insurance is not popular with insurance companies and boards of education are finding it difficult to obtain an insurer.
4. A blanket type of insurance policy is easier to administer than specific insurance on each building.
5. A five-year term policy saves money, and it can be so scheduled that one fifth of the premiums due for the five-year term may be paid each year. This simplifies budgeting.
6. Construct buildings that have a low fire risk and consequently carry low rates of insurance.
7. Inspect buildings regularly for fire hazards and eliminate, as far as practicable, any factors endangering pupils and employees or causing higher rates. After factors causing higher rates are eliminated, take the necessary steps to secure rate reductions.
8. Boiler insurance should be included in the insurance program. One of the major benefits of this type of insurance is the inspection service provided. This service is designed to prevent boiler explosions, thereby safeguarding both persons and property.

Liability Insurance

The school board is not liable for the acts of its agents in the large majority of states. The courts generally hold that boards of education are not liable for negligence, unless the statutes of the state specifically make them liable. The immunity of governments has had a long history, but the trend of legislation and court decisions is to increase the liability of boards of education and other agencies of state and local governments.

Regardless of legal liability, every board has the moral responsibility of protecting the public, pupils, and even its own employees from the negligence of its agents. It is particularly important that persons be protected from personal injury and property damage caused by motor vehicles operated by the board.

The question of nonliability of boards of education has sometimes been raised by insurance companies when settling claims under a liability policy. This can be prevented by requiring the insurance company to include in the contract a waiver of the claim of nonliability of the board.

Boards of education should carry liability insurance of appropriate types to protect persons against bodily injuries and property damage caused by the negligence of agents of the board. If this is not done, the board of education has no legal authority in most states to reimburse persons who have suffered such injuries or damages.

Workmen's Compensation Insurance

Most states require that the employees of boards of education be given the protection of workmen's compensation insurance. It is not equitable to deny that protection to the employees of a board of education when it is given to the employees of business and industry. This protection should become universal. Some districts even provide workmen's compensation for students. Medium- and large-sized school systems can wisely be self-insurers for workmen's compensation. In small districts, insurance should be carried.

Surety Bonds

Boards of education are concerned primarily with three types of bonds as follows: (1) fidelity bonds to insure against dishonesty of employees, (2) public official bonds to insure against nonperformance or malperformance of duties by officials, (3) contract bonds to insure against nonperformance of contracts.

Fidelity bonds should be required of all employees who handle money. Such bonds not only protect the board against loss of funds but also stimulate the person bonded to keep proper records and to follow authorized procedures. Blanket bonds to cover all employees are now coming into common use.

Public official bonds cover much more than fidelity bonds. Under such bonds, the surety company is required to make good any misuse or misappropriation of funds as well as any funds lost by the dishonesty of the official. Such bonds are required of superintendents, board members, treasurers, tax collectors, and similar officials.

Contract bonds include bid bonds, labor and material bonds, and faithful performance bonds. It is particularly important that bonds of this type be required of building contractors. All bonds should be obtained from reputable surety companies. Personal bonds should never be accepted. Ordinarily, the board of education pays the costs of the bonds it requires.

Retirement and Survivors' Benefits

Retirement systems are in effect a type of insurance. It is in this type of insurance that the benefits of governmental operation have been fully demonstrated. The evolution of the federal Social Security System and the growth of state and local retirement systems of all types have made it imperative that boards of education obtain retirement benefits for all full-time employees. If this policy is not adopted, the board of education cannot bid successfully in the competitive manpower market. A complete retirement plan contains adequate provision for each of the following: (1) pension upon retirement, (2) a disability allowance, (3) survivors' benefits when an employee dies prior to being eligible for retirement.

Retirement systems were started by local school systems long before the states entered into this field. But experience has shown that state retirement systems are generally financially stronger than local retirement systems. Therefore, practically all states have retirement systems for teachers. Not all states, however, have retirement plans available for other full-time employees. Adequate retirement benefits should be provided for all school employees. There is no justification for providing no retirement or less adequate retirement benefits for different classes of school employees.

SOME IMPORTANT PROBLEMS AND ISSUES

The control of the school budget is a very live issue in a number of school districts. Who should be the immediate beneficiaries of school board spending is also an issue in some school districts. These two issues are presented in the following paragraphs.

Should the Local School Budget Be Approved by Some Agency Other than the School Board?

A board of education is fiscally independent when it is directly responsible to the people for its financial program and its educational policies. A board of education is fiscally dependent when its budget is subject to review, revisions, or approval by any noneducational agency or commission.

The principal arguments that have been advanced for fiscal independence of school boards are as follows:

1. Schools should be kept free of partisan policies.
2. Education is a state function. An intermediary authority standing between the state and the local school board makes it impossible for the board to be in fact responsible to the state and the people.
3. Fiscal control of school boards by noneducational governmental agencies leads to de facto control of educational policies.
4. Control of school affairs by municipal or other noneducational local governmental agencies often leads to coercion in professional and technical matters and in the management of expenditures.
5. Fiscal independence leads to greater stability and continuity in educational planning.
6. Fiscal dependence leads to competition for the local tax dollar, thereby intensifying controversies between local governmental agencies and school authorities.
7. Fiscal dependence complicates school administration.

8. Fiscal independence is the only sure way to protect school funds from diversion to nonschool purposes.
9. There is no evidence that fiscal dependence results in greater economy and efficiency.
10. The people should be able to express themselves on the important problem of education without having issues confused by a mixture with other governmental problems.
11. Separation of fiscal control from responsibility for educational results violates the basic administrative principle that authority and responsibility should go together.
12. It is desirable to keep educational control close to the people to preserve the elements of democratic government and to provide for the freedom essential for adaptability, adjustment, and invention.

The principal arguments that have been advanced for fiscal dependence of school boards are as follows:

1. There is a place for a unified and coordinated local financial structure. Intergovernmental relations are more complex and there is much duplication of effort and overlapping of functions when schools are independent of local government.
2. Determination of expenditures for all purposes should permit the weighing of the relative merits of each service. This recommends a single legislative authority.
3. Coordination of services in which the schools and local government are mutually interested is facilitated.
4. School services when delegated to local control and responsibility are in reality legitimate aspects of local government, the same way as police protection, public health, and similar services of general social significance.

The research on fiscal independence versus dependence affords little objective evidence to support either set of arguments. It is doubtful if this issue can ever be resolved by objective evidence, because it involves the determination of the relative importance of different social values. The determination of relative social values is a philosophical problem, and philosophical propositions do not readily lend themselves to statistical evaluation.

If one believes that centralization of the fiscal planning of all governmental services has greater social value than more direct determination of educational policy by the people, he will support fiscal dependence of boards of education. If one believes that the decentralized determination of educational policy is of greater social value than centralized fiscal management, he will support the fiscal independence of school districts.

Generally speaking, the states have imposed more rigorous statutory and constitutional tax limitations on boards of education than on city and county governments. What is the relationship between tax limitations on boards of education and fiscal independence?

Should Boards of Education Give Local Vendors Preferential Treatment?

Many boards of education are under considerable pressure to buy everything possible from local vendors, even at higher prices than would be paid to outside bidders. Some local contractors also bring pressure upon boards of education to award building contracts to local contractors, even though better bids can be secured from outside bidders. Local vendors and contractors advocating this policy argue that since they are local taxpayers they have a right to the board's business. This argument ignores the fact that schools are agencies of the state, and in most states, boards of education receive a large portion of their revenue from the state. To pay higher prices than are necessary in order to do business with local vendors and contractors is an unfair burden on the taxpayers of the community and the state and becomes something like a subsidy to local business interests.

Boards of education following sound business practices follow the policy of securing competivive bids on all items of any consequence purchased by the board. Bidding should be on the basis of specifications prepared by the professional staff of the board of education. The laws of most states require that building contracts be awarded to the lowest responsible bidder. However, sound practices with respect to many other types of important purchases are far from universal.

A few states have laws designed to give preference to local vendors. Under what circumstances, if any, should preference be given to local vendors?

SELECTED REFERENCES

ALLEN, CLIFFORD H., *School Insurance Administration.* New York: The Macmillan Company, 1965.

Association of School Business Officials of the United States and Canada, *Annual Volumes of Proceedings.* Evanston, Ill.: The Association, 1957 to date.

BANGHART, FRANK W., *Educational Systems Analysis.* Toronto, Ontario: The Macmillan Company, 1969.

CASEY, LEO M., *School Business Administration.* New York: Center for Applied Research in Education, Inc., 1964.

CURTIS, WILLIAM H., *Educational Resources Management System.* Chicago, Ill.: Association of School Business Officials, 1971.

FEATHERSTON, E. GLENN, and D. P. CULP, *Pupil Transportation: State and Local Programs.* New York: Harper & Row, Publishers, 1965.

FINCHUM, R. N., *Fire Insurance Economies Through Plant Management.* U.S. Department of Health, Education and Welfare, Office of Education. Washington, D.C.: U.S. Government Printing Office, 1965.

GARVUE, ROBERT, THELMA G. FLANAGAN, and WILLIAM H. CASTINE, Chap. 8 in *Planning to Finance Education,* Roe L. Johns, Kern Alexander and K. Forbis Jordan, eds. Gainesville, Fla.: National Educational Finance Project, 1971.

GRANGER, ROBERT L., *Educational Leadership.* Scranton, Pa.: Intext Educational Publishers, 1971.

JOHNS, ROE L., and EDGAR L. MORPHET, *The Economics and Financing of Education.* Englewood Cliffs, N.J.: Prentice-Hall, Inc., 1969, Chap. 14–18.

JOHNS, ROE L., IRVING J. GOFFMAN, KERN ALEXANDER, and DEWEY STOLLAR, eds., *Economic Factors Affecting the Financing of Education.* Gainesville, Fla.: National Educational Finance Project, Vol. 2, 1970, Chap. 11.

JORDAN, K. FORBIS, *School Business Administration.* New York: The Ronald Press Company, 1969.

KNEZEVICH, STEPHEN J., and JOHN GUY FOWLKES, *Business Management of Local School Systems.* New York: Harper & Row, Publishers, 1960.

ROBERTS, CHARLES D. and ALLAN R. LICHTENBERGER, *Financial Accounting Classification and Standard Terminology for Local and State School Systems.* U.S. Department of Health, Education and Welfare, Office of Education. Washington, D.C.: U.S. Government Printing Office, 1973.

STOLLAR, DEWEY H., Chap. 9 in *Planning to Finance Education.* Roe L. Johns, Kern Alexander and K. Forbis Jordan, eds. Gainesville, Fla.: National Educational Finance Project, 1971.

THOMAS, J. ALAN, *The Productive School.* New York: John Wiley & Sons, Inc. 1971.

WHITLOCK, JAMES W., *Automatic Data Processing in Education.* New York: The Macmillan Company, 1964.

18

Provisions for Financing Education

The development of provisions for financing the public schools is a fascinating story. An extensive treatise on the political, social, and economic development of the United States could be centered around the history of the development and financing of education.[1] Although they were not specifically addressing themselves to the history of financing the public schools, the following historians revealed their sensitivity to the effect of social, economic, political, and religious factors on school financing: Ellwood P. Cubberley in *Public Education in the United States;* Charles A. and Mary R. Beard in *The Rise of American Civilization;* Newton Edwards and Herman G. Richey in *The School in the American Social Order* and Merle Curti in *The Social Ideas of American Educators.* The names of many other historians cognizant of these issues could, of course, be added to this list.

---

[1] See Roe L. Johns, *Full State Funding of Education* (Pittsburgh, Pa.: University of Pittsburgh Press, Horace Mann Lecture for 1972).

Therefore, the study of the financing of education should not be considered an exercise in statistical analysis or a problem of data storage. *The school financing policies of a nation are a reflection of the value choices of the people, the order of priorities they establish in the allocation of their resources, and their political philosophy.*[2]

Only a limited treatment of school finance can be presented in one chapter. The following major topics are discussed briefly: (1) the early history of school financing in the United States; (2) the present status of school financing; (3) criteria for the evaluation of taxes; (4) the evolution of school finance theories; (5) the evaluation of state provisions for financing the public schools; and (6) alternative state school finance models.

EARLY HISTORY OF SCHOOL FINANCING

The financing of the public schools from public funds began in New England in colonial days. However, schools in the New England colonies were only partly financed from public funds. Before 1800, in all other states education was considered a family or church responsibility except for paupers. The sixteenth section of each township in the Northwest Territory was set aside for the support of education by the Ordinances of 1785 and 1787 but very little school revenue was derived from these lands prior to 1800. Therefore, prior to the beginning of the nineteenth century, the schools in all states, except the New England states, were financed primarily from philanthropy, fees, and rate bills.

Tax-supported public schools were not generally available in the United States during the first quarter of the nineteenth century. However, during the period 1830 to 1860 constitutional and statutory authority for tax-supported public schools was generally established in the Middle Atlantic and Midwestern states. Legal authorization for tax-supported public schools was not generally provided in the Southern and some of the Western states until the last quarter of the nineteenth century.

Despite the fact that legal authorization for tax-supported public schools had been provided in most states except the Southern states by the middle of the nineteenth century, the actual provisions for public education were very meager. According to the seventh census of the United States in 1850, only about half the children of New England were provided free education, one-sixth in the West, and one-seventh in the Middle States.[3] Therefore, constitutional and statutory authorization for tax-

---

[2] *Ibid.*, p. 3.
[3] Newton Edwards and Herman G. Richey, *The School in the American Social Order* (Boston: Houghton Mifflin Company, 1963), p. 292.

supported public schools did not result in substantial tax revenues for the public schools in most states for many years. In the South, with few exceptions, free education was provided only for paupers. Even in the New England, Middle Atlantic, and Western states, public education was confined largely to the elementary grades and tax funds were usually supplemented by fees and rate bills. It has been a long and arduous struggle to provide free public elementary and secondary education in the United States. Actually, free, tax-supported public schools did not become generally available in the United States until well into the first quarter of the twentieth century. In fact, secondary education, especially in rural areas, did not become generally available until after World War I.[4]

World War I had a significant impact on the financing of education. That war ended a long period of international isolation. We were rapidly becoming the greatest industrial nation in the world and a major migration from the farms to the cities began following that war. It became generally apparent to the people that a type of education that would suffice for an agrarian society was quite inadequate for a technological, industrialized society. This became even more apparent following World War II. The provisions for public education, including financing, have been extended steadily since the period following World War I. The data presented in Table 18-1 show this trend clearly. Average daily attendance increased 99 percent between 1930 and 1970. Expenditures per pupil in average daily attendance increased from $233 to $936 in terms of the purchasing power of 1969 dollars. This was a real increase of 302 percent. Education is given a much higher priority in the allocation of our resources today than it was given 40 years ago. In 1930 only 2.2 percent of the gross national product was allocated to the support of the public schools but in 1970 we allocated 4.2 percent of our gross national product for that purpose.

It should not be assumed from this optimistic picture that the problems of school financing have been solved. From the discussions that follow it will become apparent that many problems of school financing are still unresolved.

PRESENT STATUS OF SCHOOL FINANCING

In 1971–72, the revenue receipts for public schools totaled almost $47,000,000,000. Approximately 7 percent of these receipts was provided from federal sources, 41 percent from state sources, and 52 percent from local sources. Revenue receipts increased an average of $3,600,000,-000 annually during the four year period between 1967–68 and 1971–72.

[4] *Ibid.*, Chap. 9.

TABLE 18-1. Trends in Total Expenditures for the Public Schools 1930-1970 (Includes all Items for Current Expense, Capital Outlay and Interest on School Indebtedness)

Year	Expenditures in Current Dollars (Millions)	Consumer Price Index (1957-59 Prices = 100)	Expenditures in Terms of 1969 Dollars (Millions)	Average Daily Attendance (Thousands)	Expenditures Per Pupil in ADA in 1969 Dollars	Percentage of the Gross National Product Expended for the Public Schools
1929-30	$ 2,307	59.7	$ 4,935	21,165	$ 233	2.2
1939-40	2,331	48.4	6,149	22,042	279	2.6
1949-50	5,768	83.0	8,877	22,284	398	2.2
1959-60	15,613	101.5	19,641	32,477	605	3.2
1969-70	39,489	127.7	39,489	42,168	936	4.2
Percent Increase 1929-30 to 1969-70	1,612	114	700	99	302	91

Source: Data on expenditures and average daily attendance from the U.S. Office of Education except for the year 1969-70 which was estimated by the National Education Association. The price index is for the calendar year in which the school year began. Also, the gross national product for the calendar year in which the school year began is used in computing the percentage of the gross national product. Data for the price index were obtained from the Survey of Current Business.

The average annual increase during the ten year period 1961–62 to 1971–72 was approximately $3,000,000,000. These increases were due principally to the following factors: (1) annual decreases in the purchasing power of the dollar; (2) increases in attendance; (3) the public demand for an improved quality of education; and (4) the extension of school programs to meet the needs of children, youth, and adults who had previously not been served by the public schools. All these factors causing increases in school costs will continue to be with us in the decade of the 1970s with the exception of increases in the enrollment in grades 1–12. However, expected increases in kindergarten and prekindergarten will offset much of an expected decrease in grades 1–12. Therefore, we can look forward in the foreseeable future to continue increases in school costs. Furthermore, as will be pointed out in the following discussions, our present provisions for school financing are far from satisfactory.

Equalization of Educational Opportunity

Equalization of educational opportunity among the states and within the states is discussed under the headings that follow.

EQUALIZATION OF EDUCATIONAL OPPORTUNITY AMONG THE STATES.
The financial resources available for the support of education vary widely both among the states and within the states. There is considerable evidence that different levels of expenditure per unit of educational need affect educational output.[5] Therefore, it is rational to assume that wide differences in expenditures per pupil are usually accompanied by wide differences in the quality of education.

Differences in expenditures per pupil among the states are largely due to differences in wealth among the states. Table 18-2 gives the personal income per pupil and the school revenue available per pupil in eleven states ranging from the most wealthy to the least wealthy, selected by stratified sampling for comparison. It is noted that New York had approximately 2.4 as much personal income per pupil as Mississippi in 1970 and provided 2.2 times as much revenue per pupil as Mississippi in 1971–72. It is evident that Mississippi made a greater tax effort in proportion to its ability to support schools than New York in 1971–72 but it had less than half the amount of revenue available per pupil to support schools.

Table 18-2 shows that the amount of revenue available per pupil is fairly closely related to personal income per pupil for all these eleven states

[5] See Henry M. Levin, "The Effect of Different Levels of Expenditure on Educational Output," Chap. 6 in *Economic Factors Affecting the Financing of Education,* Roe L. Johns, et al., eds. (Gainesville, Fla.: The National Educational Finance Project, Vol. 2, 1970).

TABLE 18-2. *Personal Income Per Pupil and School Revenue Per Pupil in a Stratified Sampling of States Ranging from the Most Wealthy to the Least Wealthy*

State	Personal Income Per Pupil in Average Daily Attendance 1970 Amount	Rank Among the States	Revenue Receipts Per Pupil in Average Daily Attendance 1971-72 Amount	Rank Among the States
New York	$27,740	1	$1,639	2
Massachusetts	23,675	5	1,307	9
Maryland	20,292	10	1,400	5
Florida	18,702	15	962	29
Michigan	18,071	20	1,192	14
Virginia	16,723	25	1,033	22
Arizona	15,840	30	1,000	25
North Carolina	14,821	35	811	41
West Virginia	14,246	40	804	42
Alabama	13,040	45	637	50
Mississippi	11,461	50	750	45

Source: Research Division, National Education Association.

with the exception of Florida, which made a very low effort to support education during that year in comparison with its ability. Numerous studies[6] have shown that the states of least wealth on the average make as great or greater effort to support schools as the states of greater wealth. Therefore, the differences among the states in expenditures per pupil are largely due to differences in wealth. Up to the present time, sufficient federal funds have not been provided for the public schools to have a substantial equalizing effect.[7] All the federal funds are provided in the form of categorical grants and generally they are not apportioned for the purpose of equalizing the financial resources of the states.

EQUALIZATION OF EDUCATIONAL OPPORTUNITY WITHIN STATES. All the states, with the exception of Hawaii, finance schools in part from local taxes, levied and collected within the district. The percent of revenue

[6]See Roe L. Johns and Kern Alexander, eds., *Alternative Programs for Financing Education* (Gainesville, Fla.: The National Educational Finance Project, 1972), Chap. 10.
[7]See Edgar H. Bedenbaugh and Kern Alexander, "Financial Equalization Among the States from Federal Aid Programs," Chap. 8 in *Status and Impact of Educational Finance Programs,* Roe L. Johns, Kern Alexander, and Dewey Stollar, eds. (Gainesville, Fla.: National Educational Finance Project, 1971).

receipts derived from local taxes in 1971–72 ranged from none in Hawaii to approximately 90 percent in New Hampshire.[8] Approximately 98 percent of local tax revenue is derived from property taxes. Since 52 percent of school revenue at this writing is still derived from local sources, the value per pupil of taxable property in the school district is of great significance.

In 1971–72, there were approximately 17,000 operating school districts in the nation. The number of school districts in a state ranged from one (the state) in Hawaii to 1,335 in Nebraska. Eleven states had over 500 districts each and thirteen states had fewer than 100 districts each. In states with a small number of relatively large districts, the most wealthy districts usually have 5 to 10 times the wealth per pupil of the least wealthy district. In states with a large number of relatively small districts, the most wealthy district may have as much as 80 times the wealth per pupil of the least wealthy district.[9]

Most of the states have attempted to compensate to some extent for these inequalities in district wealth per pupil. The National Educational Finance Project made an extensive study including all 50 states in 1968–69 to determine the extent of inequalities among the districts of each state in school support. Only districts with 1,500 pupils or more and districts that operated both elementary and high schools were included in the study. It was found in many states that the most wealthy district per pupil had two to three times as much revenue available per pupil from state, federal, and local sources. In a few states, the difference was more than four to one. These ranges in revenue per pupil would undoubtedly have been greater if the smallest districts in each state had been included in the study.

This study also showed that the differences among the districts in revenue per pupil were largely due to differences in valuation of property per pupil.[10] In all states except Hawaii, the quality of a child's education depends, in part, on the per pupil wealth of the district in which he lives. The state and federal funds available are not sufficient nor are they allocated in such a manner as to fully equalize educational opportunity in forty-nine states.

RECENT COURT DECISIONS. The provisions for school financing have recently been challenged in the courts in a number of states. It is

---

[8]Research Division, National Education Association, *Estimates of School Statistics 1971–72* (Washington, D.C.: The Association, 1972), p. 35. These estimates include interest on deposits, fees, tuition, gifts, etc. in local school revenue. If those sources of revenue were deducted from total revenue receipts and tax revenues only included in revenue from state, federal, and local sources, the percent of tax revenue from local sources would range from zero to about 90 percent.

[9]Roe L. Johns and Kern Alexander, eds., *Status and Impact of Educational Finance Programs* (Gainesville, Fla.: National Educational Finance Project, Vol. 2, 1971), Chap. 3.

[10]A small part of the differences was due to variations in local tax effort in proportion to ability.

alleged in these cases that a school finance plan which makes the quality of a child's education a function of the wealth of the district in which he lives is a denial of equal protection under the law and therefore is a violation of the Fourteenth Amendment to the Constitution of the United States. The most famous of these cases is *Serrano v. Priest* in California.[11] In 1971 the Supreme Court of California ruled that education was a "fundamental interest" and that equal protection was denied when the state school financing "system conditions the full entitlement of such interest on wealth, classifies its recipients on the basis of their collective affluence and makes the quality of a child's education depend on the resources of his school district and ultimately upon the pocketbook of his parents." The court then ruled that the provisions for school financing in California violated both the state and the federal Constitutions.

Shortly thereafter, a three-judge Federal Court in Texas, in *Rodriguez v. San Antonio Independent School District*,[12] held that the Texas plan of school financing violated both the state and federal Constitutions. The reasoning in the *Rodriguez* decision followed the *Serrano* decision very closely. In 1973, the United States Supreme Court held that the Texas finance law did not violate the United States Constitution. The Court, however, did not endorse the Texas plan of financing, but suggested that it was the responsibility of the states to remedy the inequities in their school finance plans.

By the end of 1972, courts in a number of other states, including Michigan, Minnesota, New Jersey, Kansas, and Arizona, had held that the plans of school financing in these states violated either the state or federal Constitution or both.

These court decisions are destined to have a major impact on school financing. The ruling of the United States Supreme Court that the Texas finance plan did not violate the United States Constitution will not prevent state courts from ruling that their plans for school financing violate their state constitutions. These decisions have greatly stimulated the study of school financing in the United States and have highlighted dramatically the inequalities of educational opportunity in the nation.

CRITERIA FOR EVALUATION OF TAXES

Due[13] has recommended four major critiria by which a tax structure could be evaluated. Those major criteria are economic distortion, equity, compliance and administration, and revenue elasticity.

[11]*Serrano v. Priest*, 5 Cal. 3d 584, 487 P.2D 1241 (1971).
[12]*Rodriguez v. San Antonio Independent School District*, F. Supp. (W.D. Texas, 1971).
[13]John F. Due, "Alternative Tax Sources for Education," Chap. 10 in *Economic Factors Affecting the Financing of Education*, Roe L. Johns, et al., eds. (Gainesville, Fla.: National Educational Finance Project, 1970).

Summary of Due's Criteria

Following is a brief summary of Due's criteria:

ECONOMIC DISTORTION. The tax structure should be so organized that it will not cause people to behave economically in a way contrary to the objectives of society. Any tax that causes persons to change behavior to escape it will produce less revenue than could be obtained from the given tax rates if behavior were not altered. Five examples of distortions are (1) taxes may reduce output of some commodities relative to others or cause a loss in satisfaction on the part of those persons with high preferences for goods whose relative output is reduced; (2) taxes may interfere with efficiency in the conduct of production and physical distribution of goods by altering decisions about the selection of methods of organization and operation utilized; (3) tax differentials among areas may cause firms to select locations other than those that are optimal from the standpoint of efficiency; (4) taxes may cause some persons to drop out of the labor market or seek to work fewer hours; and (5) taxes may reduce the rate of economic growth.

EQUITY. Most people accept the principle that a tax should be equitable. A tax is usually considered equitable if it meets the following criteria: (1) equals are treated as equals (that is, persons in the same relevant circumstances should be taxed the same amount); (2) the distribution of the overall tax burden should be based on ability to pay as measured by income, wealth, and consumption; (3) persons in the lowest income groups should be excluded from tax on the grounds that they have no taxpaying capacity; and (4) the overall distribution of the tax structure should be progressive or at least proportional to income.

COMPLIANCE AND ADMINISTRATION. Taxes should be collectable to a high degree of effectiveness with minimal real costs to the taxpayers and reasonable costs to the government for collection.

REVENUE ELASTICITY. Tax revenue should keep pace at given rates to governmental expenditures which tend to rise at least in proportion to national income.

Major Types of Taxes

Personal income taxes, corporate income taxes, sales and gross receipts taxes, and property taxes produce 94 percent of all the tax revenue of the federal, state, and local governments.[14] It is beyond the scope of

[14]Roe L. Johns and Edgar L. Morphet, *The Economics and Financing of Education* (Englewood Cliffs, N.J.: Prentice Hall, Inc., 1969), p. 131.

this chapter to apply Due's criteria to these major types of taxes. Each type of tax ranks high on one or more of these criteria and each fails to rank high on one or more of these criteria. If equity alone is considered and ability to pay is the principle characteristic considered, the most equitable taxes in order are personal income taxes, corporate income taxes, sales and gross receipts taxes, and property taxes.

As previously noted, more than half of total school revenue in 1972 came from local sources and 98 percent of local school tax revenue was derived from property taxes. Therein lies much of the difficulty in school financing. The principal tax used to support the public schools is the property tax. The public generally regards the property tax as the most inequitable tax levied. Therefore, in recent years the people more frequently than ever before have failed to pass property tax levies for school operations and have also failed to pass bond issues serviced by property taxes. Heavy reliance on local property taxes for school financing not only creates inequalities in educational opportunity but also is inequitable for the taxpayer. These factors and others are causing a rising public demand for improvements in the tax base for the support of the public schools.

EVOLUTION OF SCHOOL FINANCE THEORIES

The deficiencies in the provisions for public school finance have long been noted by school finance theorists and researchers. Following is a brief summary of the contributions of some of these theorists.

Ellwood P. Cubberley

The development of theories of school support began with Cubberley who published his famous monograph *School Funds and Their Apportionment* in 1905. He and George D. Strayer, Sr., both received doctor's degrees from Teachers College, Columbia University, in 1905. These two men were among the first university professors of educational administration and they were largely responsible not only for the early literature on school finance but also for the entire area of educational administration.

Cubberley stated his basic theory of school financing as follows:

> Theoretically all the children of the state are equally important and are entitled to have the same advantages; practically this can never be quite true. The duty of the state is to secure for all as high a minimum of good instruction as is possible, but not to reduce all to this minimum; to equalize the advantages to all as nearly as can be done with the resources at hand; to place a premium on those local efforts which will enable communities to rise above

the legal minimum as far as possible; and to encourage communities to extend their educational energies to new and desirable undertakings.[15]

It is noted that Cubberley not only recommended that the state equalize educational opportunity but also recommended that the state provide a financial reward for local tax effort.

Harlan Updegraff[16]

Updegraff is not as well known as some of the other theorists in school finance but he developed an important concept. He proposed that state funds be allocated to local school districts in inverse relationship to the valuation of property per unit of educational need but in direct relationship to the local tax effort made by a district in proportion to its taxpaying ability. In other words, he proposed that districts of less wealth be apportioned more state funds per unit of need than districts of greater wealth but that any district could receive more state funds by increasing its local tax effort. Under Updegraff's formula, a poor district could have as much total revenue available from state and local sources as a wealthy district provided it made the same effort. Therefore, Updegraff proposed that the quality of a child's education should not depend upon the wealth per unit of need of the district but upon the local tax effort made by a district in proportion to its wealth. This concept of state support apparently was rediscovered 50 years later by John E. Coons, a Professor of Law at the University of California at Berkeley, who renamed it the "Power Equalizing Plan."[17]

George D. Strayer, Sr.

Strayer and Haig participated in a national study of school finance conducted by the National Educational Finance Inquiry Commission shortly after World War I. Strayer and Haig were responsible for Volume 1 of this study entitled *The Financing of Education in the State of New York*. They proposed the following theory of school financing in that volume:

[15]Ellwood P. Cubberley, *School Funds and Their Apportionment* (New York: Teachers College, Columbia University, 1905), p. 17.
[16]This section was adapted from Roe L. Johns, *Full State Funding of Education* (Pittsburg, Pa.: University of Pittsburg Press, Horace Mann Lecture for 1972).
[17]See John E. Coons, William H. Clune III, and Stephan D. Sugarman, *Private Wealth and Public Education* (Cambridge, Mass.: The Belknap Press of Harvard University, 1970), Chap. 6.

... The state should insure equal educational facilities to every child within its borders at a uniform effort through the state in terms of the burden of taxation; the tax burden of education should throughout the state be uniform in relation to taxpaying ability, and the provision for schools should be uniform in relation to the educable population desiring education. Most of the supporters of this proposition, however, would not preclude any particular community from offering at its own expense a particularly rich and costly educational program. They would insist that there be an adequate minimum offered everywhere, the expense of which should be considered a prior claim on the state's economic resources.[18]

These theorists recommended that the state equalize the financial support of a guaranteed minimum educational program throughout the state and that local districts be permitted to make local tax effort in addition to the minimum required, but they recommended against the state providing a financial reward for this additional effort because reward for effort was inconsistent with the equalization principle.

Paul R. Mort

Mort was one of Strayer's students and he developed the technology for implementing the theories of Strayer and Haig. He developed standard measures of "need" based on the "weighted pupil" concept which provides for necessary variations in per pupil costs for different educational programs and target populations. Mort theorized that in order to equalize educational opportunity it was necessary to take into consideration necessary variations in per pupil costs of the educational programs and services needed by pupils as well as variations in the per pupil wealth of local school districts. He also proposed that the following elements be included in the minimum program equalized:

1. An educational activity found in most or all communities throughout the state is acceptable as an element of an equalization program.
2. Unusual expenditures for meeting the general requirements due to causes over which a local community has little or no control may be recognized as required by the equalization program. If they arise from

[18]George D. Strayer and Robert Murray Haig, *The Financing of Education in the State of New York*. Report of the Educational Finance Commission, Vol. 1 (New York: MacMillan Co., 1923), p. 173.

causes reasonably within the control of the community they cannot be considered as demanded by the equalization program.
3. Some communities offer more years of schooling or a more costly type of education than is common. If it can be established that unusual conditions require any such additional offerings, they may be recognized as a part of the equalization program.[19]

Henry C. Morrison

Morrison is noted for being the first school finance theorist to advocate full state funding of the public schools. He noted the great inequalities of wealth among school districts that caused great inequalities in educational opportunity. He observed that constitutionally education was a state function and that local school districts had failed to provide that function efficiently or equitably. He asserted that attempts to provide equal educational opportunities by enlarging school districts, by offering state equalization funds—such as those advocated by Mort—or by offering state subsidies for special purposes had failed. He theorized that those measures would continue to fail to meet educational needs and, at the same time, to provide an equitable system of taxation to support schools. Therefore, Morrison proposed a model of state support whereby all local school districts are abolished and the state itself becomes both the unit for taxation for schools and for administration of public schools. He suggested that the most equitable form of tax for the state to use for the support of schools was the income tax.[20]

The defects that Morrison saw in local school financing are as evident today as in his time. Furthermore, educational opportunities are far from being equalized among school districts within most states, and there is more complaint about the inequities of local property taxes for schools than ever before. It is interesting to note that in recent years Hawaii has established a state system of education that is similar to the model advocated by Morrison. Morrison's model for state school financing is not as far outside the mainstream of American thought today as it was in 1930. However, as we move toward full state and federal fundings, most states will likely retain local school districts with boards of education. Hawaii is a very small state, both in population and in territory. The complete Morrison model is more applicable to a very small state than to a large state.

[19]Paul R. Mort, *The Measurement of Educational Need* (New York: Teachers College, Columbia University, 1924), pp. 6–7.
[20]See Roe L. Johns, "State Financing of Elementary and Secondary Education," Chap. 4 in *Education in the States: Nationwide Developments Since 1900,* Edgar Fuller and Jim B. Pearson, eds. (Washington, D.C.: National Education Association, 1969), p. 192.

EVALUATION OF STATE PROVISIONS FOR FINANCING PUBLIC SCHOOLS

The evaluation of plans for school financing in any nation must, of necessity, be based on the basic values, beliefs, and goals of the people of the nation. The National Educational Finance Project attempted to state the basic values and beliefs of the people of the United States relevant to school financing and then developed criteria for the evaluation of state finance plans based on those values and beliefs. These statements are discussed under the heading below.

Basic Values and Beliefs

Following is a brief summary of the National Educational Finance Project statement of what seems to be the basic values and beliefs of a majority of "We the people of the United States" that are relevant to school financing.

1. *Equalization of Educational Opportunity.* We believe that the opportunity to obtain a public education appropriate to the individual needs of children and youth should be substantially equal. We believe that the educational opportunity of every individual should be a function of the total taxable wealth of the state and not limited primarily to the taxing ability in the local school district.

2. *Social Mobility.* We believe that public education should tend to remove barriers between caste and class and promote social mobility. That is the essence of the American dream. Every child regardless of his race, national origin, religion or the economic condition of his parents should be given an equal chance in the public schools to develop his talents to the fullest in order that he may have equal access to the benefits of the American social, political and economic system.

3. *The Economy and Education.* We believe that an adequate investment in public education is essential to economic growth. Expenditures for education are an investment in people as well as a consumption expenditure. Education in this technological age has become essential to the growth of the economy and the survival of the individual.

4. *Equity of Tax Structure.* We believe that the public schools should be supported by an equitable tax structure.

5. *Accountability.* We believe that the educational output should be maximized per dollar of financial input.

6. *Control.* We believe that decisions concerning education should be made by the lowest level of government that can efficiently make that decision. By that, we mean that a decision should not be made by the

federal government if it can efficiently be made by the states and a decision should not be made by the state if it can efficiently be made by local school districts. Each higher level of government should impose its power on the lower one only to establish general policies for the common good, but not to destroy that diversity which enriches without harming others.

7. *District Organization.* We believe that school district lines should not be gerrymandered so as to segregate pupils by wealth, race, social or economic class. We believe that school districts should be organized in a manner that will achieve the greatest possible efficiency in the expenditure of school funds.

8. *Federalism.* We believe in the concept of federalism as applied to education. We believe that the federal government, the state governments and local school districts all have appropriate roles to play in providing for public education.

9. *Democracy and Education.* We have faith in American democracy and believe that a broadly based and adequately supported system of public education is essential to the preservation of "a government of the people, by the people, and for the people."[21]

Criteria for Evaluating a State's Finance Plan

A comprehensive state school finance plan must deal with at least three major kinds of public policy issues:

1. The scope, content, and quality of the public school program;
2. The organizational arrangements for providing public schooling; and
3. The level and method of financing public schools.

An adaptation of the criteria proposed by the National Educational Finance Project for the evaluation of a state's provisions for school financing is presented below.

CRITERIA RELATING TO PROGRAMS. The state school finance plan should:

1. Provide an educational program that meets the needs of all the educable children and youth of the state.
2. Include provisions for innovation and improvement in instructional programs.

[21] Adapted from Roe L. Johns and Kern Alexander, eds., *Alternative Programs for Financing of Education* (Gainesville, Fla.: National Educational Finance Project, Vol. 5, 1972), Chap. 1.

3. Include provisions for the identification and evaluation of alternative methods of accomplishing educational objectives.
4. Provide a system for local districts to develop program and financial data which permit accountability to the public.
5. Give children access to needed educational programs throughout the state.

CRITERIA RELATING TO ORGANIZATION. The state school finance plan should financially penalize or at least not financially reward:

1. The establishment or continuation of small inefficient school districts.
2. The establishment or continuation of small inefficient enrollment centers, except in cases resulting from geographical isolation.
3. The continuation or establishment of school districts which segregate pockets of wealth or leave pockets of poverty in the state or result in the segregation of pupils by race or socioeconomic class.
4. The continuation or establishment of school enrollment centers which result in the segregation of pupils by race or socioeconomic class.

CRITERIA RELATING TO FINANCE. The state school finance plan should:

1. Provide for equalization of educational opportunity by equalizing the financial resources of school districts in accordance with educational needs. The quality of a child's education should not be made dependent on the wealth of the district in which he lives nor should it depend substantially on the aspiration level of the people of that district.
2. Include all current expenditures and capital outlay and debt service in order to facilitate equitable budgetary planning for all phases of each district's educational program.
3. Recognize variations in per pupil program costs for local school districts associated with specialized educational activities needed by some but not all students, such as vocational education, education of exceptional or handicapped pupils, and compensatory education.
4. Recognize differences in per pupil local district costs associated with factors such as sparsity and density of population, e.g., pupil transportation, extra costs of isolated schools, and other necessary variations in the cost of delivering educational services and facilities of equivalent quality throughout the states.
5. Be funded through an integrated package which facilitates equitable budgetary planning by local school districts.
6. Utilize objective measures in allocating state school funds to local school districts.
7. Be based on a productive, diversified, and equitable tax system.
8. Integrate federal funds with state funds and allocate them to local districts in conformance with the proposed criteria to the extent permitted by federal laws and regulations.[22]

[22] *Ibid.*, Chap. 9.

ALTERNATIVE STATE SCHOOL FINANCE MODELS

No two of the fifty states have exactly the same state school finance plan; however, state plans can be classified according to two dimensions: the allocation dimension: and the revenue dimension.[23]

The Allocation Dimension

Following are the principal types of state school finance models classified according to the *allocation dimension:*

1. *Flat Grant Models.* Under this type of model, state grants are allocated to local school districts without taking into consideration variations among the districts in local taxpaying ability. There are two major variations of this model as follows:
    a. A uniform amount per pupil, per teacher, or some other unit of need is allotted without taking into consideration necessary variations in unit costs of different educational programs and services.
    b. Variable amounts per unit of need are allocated to local school districts which reflect necessary variations in unit costs.
2. *Equalization Models.* Under this type of model state funds are allocated to local school districts in inverse proportion to local taxpaying ability. In other words, more state funds per pupil, per teacher, or other unit of need are allocated to the districts of less wealth than to those of greater wealth. As in the flat grant models, there are two main variations in the equalization models as follows:
    a. In computing the cost of the foundation program equalized, a uniform amount is allowed per pupil, per teacher, or other unit of need without giving consideration to necessary variations in unit costs of different educational programs and services.
    b. Variable amounts per unit of need which take into consideration necessary variations in unit costs are used in computing the cost of the foundation programs.

The Revenue Dimension

Ignoring federal funds, following are the principal types of state school finance models classified according to the *revenue dimension:*

1. Complete state support model;
2. Joint state-local support model; and
3. Complete local support model.

If federal revenue is included the following additional revenue models can be added:

[23]*Ibid.,* p. 268.

1. Federal-state support model;
2. Federal-state-local-model;
3. Federal-local model; and
4. Complete federal support model.[24]

MEASURING THE COST OF THE PROGRAM

The development of a sound plan of state support must start with planning the educational program. Major policy decisions must be made with respect to the following:

1. Who should be educated? That is, what target populations should be served? (For example, pre-kindergarten, kindergarten, grades 1–12, and special categories such as exceptional or handicapped, those with vocational needs, culturally disadvantaged, and adult.)
2. What educational goals and objectives should be established for each of these target populations?
3. What kinds of educational programs are needed for these different target populations?

The services and facilities needed to provide the desired educational programs must be encompassed in the state school finance plan if the educational goals are to be attained. There is a demand on the part of some state legislators for a "simple" school finance plan. The simplest finance plan would be to allocate state funds on the basis of a uniform amount per pupil without taking into consideration variations among the districts in wealth per pupil or necessary variations in the per pupil costs of educational programs and services. Equalization of educational opportunity could not be attained under even a full state funding plan if necessary variations in unit costs are not taken into consideration. Variations in the per pupil costs of different educational programs are largely due to necessary variations in pupil-teacher ratios and costs of instructional equipment and supplies. Two methods, the weighted pupil method and the adjusted instruction unit method, have been developed for incorporating cost differentials in the program of state support.

The Weighted Pupil Method

This procedure is based on the assumption that pupil-teacher ratios are lower and operating and capital outlay costs are greater for some types of educational programs. The least expensive program per pupil is gener-

[24] *Ibid.*, pp. 268–269.

ally assumed to be the cost per elementary school pupil (excluding exceptional pupils) in a relatively large elementary school (300 pupils or more). The nonexceptional elementary pupil is then given a weight of 1 and the costs of all other programs are weighted in relation to the cost per pupil as compared with the nonexceptional elementary pupil. Following are some examples of weights that have been assigned to different target groups: equivalent full time kindergarten pupils, a weight of 1.2; grades 1–6 nonexceptional pupils, a weight of 1.0; grades 7–12, nonexceptional, nonvocational pupils, a weight of 1.2; special education, weights ranging from 1.5 to 3.0 depending upon the type of program; and vocational education weights ranging from 1.2 to 3.0 depending upon the type of vocational program.

It should not be assumed that these weights are recommended. However, they are typical of present practice. States using the weighted pupil or the adjusted instruction unit method of computing cost differentials should examine from time to time the validity of the weights being used.

Many states make an additional adjustment in weights assigned pupils enrolled in small schools which are necessarily isolated due to sparsity of population. Theoretically, adjustments should be made in weights due to variations among the districts in cost of living insofar as it affects the cost of delivering equivalent educational services. Adjustments could also be justified for hardship conditions such as teaching in ghettos or isolated rural areas. However, valid objective techniques for making these adjustments have not yet been developed.

The Adjusted Instruction Unit Method

The instruction unit method is based on the weighted pupil. Actually the adjusted instruction unit is simply a grouping of weighted pupils. If we assume that one instructor, supplemented by the necessary supporting staff and services, is required for 25 nonexceptional pupils in elementary schools of efficient size, then these 25 pupils become an "instruction unit." It is equivalent to a weight of 1. The weighted pupils represented in the previous paragraph can be converted into "instruction units" simply by dividing 25 by the appropriate weight. Thus, for example, 1 instruction unit would be allotted for 20.8 kindergarten pupils; 1 unit for 25 nonexceptional pupils in grades 1–6; 1 unit for 20.8 nonexceptional, nonvocational pupils in grades 7–12; 1 unit for 16.7 to 8.3 pupils in exceptional education depending upon the type of program offered; and 1 unit for 20.8 to 8.3 vocational pupils depending upon the type of program offered.

The costs of the state supported program can be calculated in terms of either weighted pupils or adjusted classroom units and the results would be the same. The adjusted classroom unit has the advantage of facilitating program budgeting and it is more readily understood by the lay public than the weighted pupil method.

Either the weighted pupil or the adjusted classroom unit method can be used to compute the cost of instruction and current expenses other than the cost of such items as transportation, school food service, and perhaps textbooks. For example, a weighted pupil could be assigned a value of $800. A comparable value per adjusted instruction unit would be 25 times $800 or $20,000.

Transportation

The need for transportation is determined by the number of pupils transported beyond the distances specified by state law or state policy. States commonly specify transportation beyond a distance of 1 to 1.5 miles for pupils in grades K–6, and 1.5 to 2.0 miles for pupils in grades 7 and above. Most states provide for transportation of physically handicapped pupils living any distance from school.

The per pupil costs of transportation vary greatly among the districts due principally to variations in the density of transported pupils. It is beyond the scope of this chapter to describe alternative formulas for allocating state funds for pupil transportation. These formulas generally provide higher amounts per transported pupil in districts with a low density of transported pupils than in districts with a high density.

School Food Service

State support for school food services has developed in only a few states and methods of calculating need for state assistance for school food service are in a primitive stage of development. At the present time state allocations are based on such factors as numbers served, number of free and reduced price lunches served, salaries of lunch managers, and other labor costs.

Capital Outlay and Debt Service

The costs of capital outlay and debt service can be calculated fairly equitably in terms of weighted pupils or adjusted instruction units. However, the capital outlay needs of school districts vary greatly largely due to adequacy of present school facilities and rate of growth in pupil population. All districts, even those with no growth in pupil enrollment, have annual depreciation of school facilities which will eventually require their replacement. Districts with a growing pupil enrollment not only have depreciation costs but also must construct additional facilities. Therefore, formulas for computing need for capital outlay and debt service should include provision for growth as well as provision for depreciation.

Financing the Total Program

The total state supported program should be financed in one package and not by a series of unintegrated categorical state grants. This facilitates the provision of a balanced, complete educational program and it reduces red tape in administration of school funds.

As pointed out above, the state has the alternatives of fully funding the educational program with no local support permitted, funding the program with a combination of state and local funds with state funds allocated on a flat grant basis, and funding the program with a combination of state and local funds with state funds allocated on an equalization basis. The allocation of state funds on an equalization basis requires the use of a measure of local taxpaying ability which is discussed below.

THE MEASUREMENT OF LOCAL TAXPAYING ABILITY

As previously pointed out, 98 percent of local taxes for schools is derived from the property tax. Therefore, the taxpaying ability of a school district is determined by the *true value* of property subject to taxation in that district. Actually what is being measured is the access to taxes open to local boards of education to support schools. If a board has access to local nonproperty taxes for schools, then the availability of such taxes should be included in the measure of local ability. However, it is not good public policy for the legislature to authorize the levy of local nonproperty taxes for schools. Studies made by the National Educational Finance Project show that the levy of local nonproperty taxes for schools unequalizes educational opportunity even more than the levy of local property taxes.[25]

The determination of the true value of property in a school district is a difficult matter in most states due to poor assessment practices. The ratio of assessed value to true value varies widely among the districts in most states. Local tax assessors are elected by popular vote in many states. Therefore, local tax assessors are usually not trained appraisers of property and they are more concerned in holding office than in assessing property equitably. Property assessments would be greatly improved if local asses-

---

[25]See Roe L. Johns, Kern Alexander, and Dewey Stollar, eds., *The Status and Impact of Educational Finance Programs* (Gainesville, Fla.: The National Educational Finance Project, Vol. 4, 1971), Chap. 6.

sors were appointed on the basis of suitable qualifications and if adequate state supervision of property assessments were provided.

In 1972, forty-two states apportioned one or more state funds on the equalization basis. These states need an equitable measure of local taxpaying ability because, under this plan, the computed local share is subtracted from the cost of the program in order to determine the state's share. Obviously, assessed valuation is not an equitable measure. Some states have established state agencies with the authority to compute the true value of property in each school district by the use of sales ratio and sampling appraisal techniques. The true value of property is then used as the measure of local taxpaying ability instead of assessed value.

In a few other states, an index of taxpaying ability based on economic factors is used to estimate the relative true value of property in each district. This method is better than using assessed valuation but it is not as equitable as appraisal by a competently staffed state agency.

Local assessors exercise a powerful fiscal control over school finances in states that have statutory or constitutional limits on tax rates for schools or the amount of school bonds that may be issued if these limits are set on the assessed valuation of property. The assessor can either decrease or increase local school revenues or the amount of bonds that can be issued simply by increasing or decreasing the percent of true value at which property is assessed. The arbitrary exercise of this power by assessors frequently creates artificial inequalities in local ability to support schools. Let us assume that the tax limit for school operations is $1.20 per $100 assessed valuation. If the assessor for District A assesses property at 100 percent of true value and the assessor for District B assesses property at 50 percent of true value, then the effective tax limit in District B is only $0.60. Tax limits and bond limits should be based on true value or a value equalized at a uniform percent of true value throughout the state and not on assessed value.

EVALUATION OF ALTERNATIVE STATE SCHOOL FINANCE MODELS

The National Educational Finance Project evaluated the characteristics of alternative school finance models on data from a prototype state. The prototype state was made up of actual school districts enrolling more than 1,500 pupils in more than one state in order to make it representative.[26]

[26] Roe L. Johns and Kern Alexander, eds., *Alternative Programs for Financing Education* (Gainesville, Fla.: The National Educational Finance Project, 1972), Chap. 10.

Following are some conclusions reached from testing a number of alternative models of state school finance plans.

1. State funds distributed by any model tested provide for some financial equalization but some finance models provide more equalization than others. Even the flat grant model provides for some equalization despite the fact that under this model each district, regardless of wealth or necessary variations in unit costs, receives the same amount of state money per pupil or other unit. This is due to the fact that the less wealthy districts receive more state aid per pupil than the revenue per pupil they contribute to the state treasury.
2. The flat grant model by which state funds are apportioned on the basis of a flat amount per pupil unit or other unit which does not take into consideration necessary variations in unit costs or variations in wealth per unit of need of local districts provides the least financial equalization for a given amount of state aid of any of the state-local support models tested.
3. The flat grant model under which necessary cost variations per unit of need are provided for but variations in the per pupil wealth of local districts are ignored provides for more equalization than the flat grant model described in 2 above. But it does not equalize financial resources as well as the equalization models providing for cost differentials and variations in wealth.
4. Equalization models under which necessary unit cost differentials are provided for in computing the cost of the educational program equalized and which take into consideration differences in the wealth of local school districts in computing state funds needed by a district are the most efficient models examined for equalizing financial resources in states which use a state-local revenue model for financing schools.
5. In equalization models the greater the local effort required in proportion to the legal limit of local taxes for schools, the greater the equalization.
6. In equalization models the greater the local tax leeway above the required local tax effort required for the support of the foundation program, the less the equalization.
7. Complete equalization is attained only under full state funding or under an equalization model which requires school districts to contribute the full legal limit of local taxes to the cost of the foundation program.
8. The higher the percent of school revenues provided by the state, the greater the equalization of financial resources under both flat grant and equalization models but there is always more equalization under an equalization model than a flat grant model for any given amount of state funds apportioned.
9. As full state funding is approached (100 percent of school revenue provided by the state) the difference between the equalization potential of flat grant models and equalization models begins to disappear, assuming that cost differentials are provided for under each model. For example, with 90 percent or more state funding of schools, the differences between flat grant models and equalization models in equalizing financial resources would not be significant but the equalization models would always be slightly superior until full state funding is reached.
10. As the percent of local revenue is increased, the possibility of equalizing financial resources decreases.
11. A complete local support model provides for no equalization whatsoever. In the prototype state under this model, the least wealthy district would have only 1/6 of the resources per pupil available in the most wealthy district.
12. The higher the percent of state funds provided, in relation to local revenue, the greater the progressivity of the tax structure for school support.

13. The higher the percent of federal funds provided in relation to state and local revenues the greater the progressivity of the tax structure for school support. This is due to the fact that federal taxes are on the average more progressive than state taxes and state taxes more progressive than local taxes.
14. Many states can increase the progressivity of state taxes by increasing the proportion of state revenue obtained from relatively progressive taxes.[27]

SOME IMPORTANT PROBLEMS AND ISSUES

There are a number of controversial issues in the field of school finance. A few of them are discussed in the following pages.

What is the Best Plan for Providing Federal Support?

As has been pointed out, the federal government provided only about 7 percent of public school revenues in 1971–72. If the federal government equalizes educational opportunity among the states and provides a more equitable system of school financing for all states, it would be necessary for the federal government to provide 30 percent or more of school revenues.[28]

Unfortunately, all federal aid to education is provided in the form of categorical grants. In a publication entitled *Guide to OE Administered Programs, Fiscal Year 1970,* the United States Office of Education listed 132 programs. Federal aid provided through narrowly restricted categorical grants results in undesirable federal controls and high administrative costs. It would be desirable if all or practically all categorical grants for the public schools were consolidated into a general aid or at least into a few block grants.

There is much controversy over the determination of the best plan for general federal aid. Following are four plans which have been proposed:

Plan I. A national foundation program for a minimum level of education for all states financed by a combination of federal, state, and local funds. Under this plan, the federal government would provide the differences between the cost of a national uniform foundation program of education in a state and the amount of funds that a state could raise in state and local school revenue from a nationally uniform tax effort in proportion to the ability of that state.

Plan II. Equal grants per student with no requirement of state or local effort to support education.

[27] *Ibid.,* pp. 246–248.
[28] *Ibid.,* p. 229.

Plan III. Equal grants per student for equal required state and local effort in proportion to ability. This is the same plan as Plan II except that each state, in order to receive its full entitlement of federal funds, would be required to make a nationally required minimum tax effort for schools in proportion to its ability.

Plan IV. A combination of Plans I and II. Each of the approaches emphasizes a different federal purpose. The purposes would be to:

1. Equalize educational opportunity among the states.
2. Transfer the administration and control of federal aid from Washington to the states.
3. Relieve the state and local tax burdens of all states.
4. Stimulate or at least preserve state and local tax efforts to finance education.
5. Develop a plan which would be politically acceptable to all or most of the states.[29]

To what extent do each of these plans satisfy these purposes? What other criteria could be used to evaluate these plans? What other plans for apportioning federal aid should be considered by Congress?

Is It Good Public Policy to Provide State Financial Incentives for Increased Local Tax Effort?

As has previously been noted in this chapter, Updegraff and Coons and others have recommended that the quality of a child's education should *not* be made dependent on the per pupil wealth of the district in which he lives but *should* depend on the local tax effort made by the district in proportion to its ability. For example, under such a plan, the state might guarantee all districts that levy 1 mill of taxes, $100 per pupil from a combination of state and local funds, 2 mills, $200; 3 mills, $300; 4 mills, $400; 5 mills, $500; 6 mills, $600; 7 mills, $700; 8 mills, $800; 9 mills, $900; 10 mills, $1,000; and so on. Theoretically such a plan would be open ended at both the top and the bottom. Practically, however, a state would probably set a minimum rate which all districts must at least levy and a maximum rate which the state would reward.

In a few states, the requirement is made that all districts make at least the minimum local tax effort required for the state guaranteed foundation program, and the state then matches with state funds on a percentage-

---

[29]National Educational Finance Project, *Future Directions for School Financing* Gainesville, Fla.: The Project, 1972), pp. 36–37.

equalizing or state-aid ratio basis the local funds raised in addition to the amount of local tax effort required for the foundation program.[30]

Both these plans are *"financially neutral"* in that the quality of a child's education does not depend on the per pupil wealth of the district in which he lives. However, under both these plans, the quality of a child's education is made to some extent dependent on the *aspiration level* of the people of the district in which he lives. Therefore, state financial reward for local financial tax effort disequalizes educational opportunity. Is this good public policy? Is it equitable for pupils? In some districts a high percent or even a majority of pupils attend private schools. In such districts are the voters likely to authorize high local taxes in order to improve the quality of the public schools?

It has already been pointed out in this chapter that property taxes are probably the most inequitable of the four major types of taxes. Is it good public policy to develop a state school finance plan which places a premium on increasing local property taxes? Are there better methods by which the state can provide incentives to local school districts for improving the quality of education?

Should Funds from Public Tax Sources Be Used to Support Programs and Services for Pupils Attending Nonpublic Schools?

The constitutions of most states provide that neither tax funds nor the income from the permanent school fund may be used for the support of sectarian or denominational schools. Such provisions seem to be in accord with the intent of the First Amendment to the federal Constitution providing for separation of church and state. They have been upheld by supreme court decisions in many states and have never been directly challenged in the U.S. Supreme Court. However, U.S. Supreme Court decisions have held that under certain conditions where state constitutions and statutes permit, funds may be used under the "child-benefit" theory for certain services to children. For example, in the case of *Cochran v. Louisiana State Board of Education,* the Supreme Court sustained a Louisiana statute authorizing that textbooks purchased from public funds be made available to children in nonpublic schools.[31] In the case of *Everson v. Board of Education,* the Supreme Court, in a sharply divided opinion, sustained

[30]See Roe L. Johns and Kern Alexander, eds., *Alternative Programs for Financing Education* (Gainesville, Fla.: National Educational Finance Project, 1972), pp. 337–342 for an analysis of this plan.
[31]281 U.S. 370, 50 Sup. Ct. 335.

the right of local school authorities under a New Jersey statute to provide transportation for children attending parochial schools.[32]

It has been argued by some parochial school leaders that it is constitutional to appropriate public funds to parochial schools provided the funds are spent for secular purposes. The Pennsylvania Legislature in 1968 appropriated funds for "purchasing" certain secular services from the parochial schools. In 1971 the Supreme Court of the United States ruled that act unconstitutional in *Lemon v. Kurtzman*[33] because it involved excessive government entanglement with religion. The Supreme Court summarized three tests for determining the constitutionality of a state statute. Those tests were (1) the statute must have a secular purpose; (2) its principal or primary effort must be one that neither advances nor inhibits religion; and (3) it must not foster excessive government entanglement with religion.[34] This ruling may place some limitations on the child benefit theory.

Some of the recent acts of Congress, such as the Elementary and Secondary Education Act of 1965, under which some of the funds provided for designated purposes are to be used for certain classes in public schools and services for children attending parochial schools, have resulted in considerable concern on the part of many people. Do any of these funds aid the nonpublic schools or do they merely assure better education for the pupils? If the "pupil-benefit" theory is carried to its logical conclusion, would parochial schools be aided as much as public schools, and if so, what would be the implications under the First Amendment? Should certain programs or services be recognized as more entitled to aid than others? If so, which ones, and why?

SELECTED REFERENCES

BENSON, CHARLES S., *Perspectives on the Economics of Education*. Boston: Houghton-Mifflin Company, 1963.

BURKHEAD, JESSE, *Public School Finance*. Syracuse, N.Y.: Syracuse University Press, 1964.

FULLER, EDGAR and JIM B. PEARSON, eds., *Education in the States-Nationwide Development Since 1900*. Washington, D.C.: National Education Association, 1969, Chap. 4.

---

[32] 330 U.S. 1, 67 Sup. Ct. 504.
[33] *Lemon v. Kurtzman*, 403, U.S. 602, 91 S. Ct. 2105.
[34] See Kern Alexander, Ray Corns, and Walter McCann, *1973 Supplement to Public School Law—Cases and Materials* (St. Paul, Minn.: West Publishing Co., 1973), pp. 14–24.

GARVUE, ROBERT J., *Modern Public School Finance.* Toronto: Ontario. The MacMillan Company, 1969.

JOHNS, ROE L. and KERN ALEXANDER, eds., *Alternative Programs for Financing Education.* Gainesville, Fla.: National Educational Finance Project, 1971.

JOHNS, ROE L., KERN ALEXANDER, and FORBIS JORDAN, eds., *Financing Education, Fiscal and Legal Alternatives.* Columbus, Ohio: Charles E. Merrill Publishing Co., 1972.

JOHNS, ROE L., IRVING GOFFMAN, KERN ALEXANDER, and DEWEY H. STOLLAR, *Economic Factors Affecting the Financing of Education.* Gainesville, Fla.: National Educational Finance Project, 1970.

JOHNS, ROE L. and EDGAR L. MORPHET, *The Economics and Financing of Education.* Englewood Cliffs, N.J.: Prentice Hall, Inc., 1969.

JOHNS, ROE L. and EDGAR L. MORPHET, *Planning School Finance Programs.* Gainesville, Fla.: National Educational Finance Project, 1972.

MORPHET, EDGAR L. and DAVID L. JESSER, eds., *Emerging Designs for Education.* Denver, Col.: Designing Education for the Future, 1968. (Republished by Citation Press, Scholastic Magazines, Inc., New York, N.Y.).

National Educational Finance Project, *Future Directions for School Financing.* Gainesville, Fla.: The Project, 1972.

President's Commission on School Finance, *Schools, People and Money.* Washington, D.C.: The Commission, 1972.

WISE, ARTHUR E., *Rich Schools, Poor Schools.* Chicago, Ill.: University of Chicago Press, 1968.

19

Evaluation and Accountability*

As explained in Chapter 3, any state or local system of education should be viewed as a social system that has certain stated or implied purposes and goals, is related in various ways not only to its many subsystems but also to other systems of education, and has an environment consisting of many other kinds of social systems each of which has certain purposes and goals that may or may not be consistent with those accepted by an educational system. A major purpose of all schools and other educational institutions should be *to contribute to the development of a dynamic, self-renewing society by assuming a major role in preparing the citizens, and especially the children and youth, to participate in and contribute effectively and constructively to the orderly development of that society.* The basic purpose

*Prepared with the collaboration of DAVID L. JESSER, Associate Director, Improving State Leadership in Education, and RUSSELL B. VLAANDEREN, Director, Research and Information Services, Education Commission of the States, Denver, Colorado.

should not be, as some have implied, either to develop a new social order or to perpetuate existing traditions, policies, or practices.

Every continuing social system finds it necessary to seek and attempt to achieve some kind of equilibrium. A *closed* system (one that tends to resist change) seeks what has been called *stationary* equilibrium. An *open* system (one that attempts to modify its goals and procedures to meet the needs of a changing society) seeks *dynamic* equilibrium—that is, equilibrium in the process of effecting needed changes.[1] In a rapidly changing society every system of education should be expected to be an open system that seeks equilibrium through the processes of planning and effecting needed changes, but many apparently have either resisted major changes or have accepted some changes on a fortuitous basis.

Because schools and educational systems have been so important in the development of this nation they have always been of special interest and concern to the citizens. The public schools and educational systems especially have been informally appraised and evaluated—commended and criticized—from the beginning. Every social system needs the insights that can be derived from periodic or continuing evaluation if it is to thrive and continue to contribute to the improvement of society. But such evaluations should be carefully planned and conducted—not based on unstated beliefs and assumptions which may result in conclusions that cannot be supported by valid evidence.

Appraisal, assessment, evaluation, and accountability are interrelated in many ways. *Appraisal* is usually concerned with estimating the value, nature, or quality of something and may be helpful as an initial step toward the *assessment* (determining the current status) or the evaluation of some educational processes, outcomes, or products. *Evaluation* requires the development and use of systematic and defensible procedures to determine the value and appropriateness of goals, policies, functions, procedures, and relationships of a social system, its subsystems, or the components. In education, as in other social systems, systematic evaluation (which should be concerned with emerging as well as with existing goals, problems, and needs) is essential to provide a sound basis for accountability which has only recently begun to receive appropriate attention. *Accountability* is concerned primarily with determining, on the basis of valid evidence, the validity and appropriateness of goals, the progress made toward achieving goals and objectives, the factors and conditions that have facilitated or retarded progress, and ways of effecting improvements. It should not—as

---

[1]For a more detailed discussion of this concept, see Robert Chin, "The Utility of System Models and Developmental Models for Practitioners," in *The Planning of Change*, Warren G. Bennis, Kenneth D. Benne, and Robert Chin, eds. (New York: Holt, Rinehart and Winston, Inc., 1969).

some people have assumed—be concerned merely or even primarily with stabilizing or reducing expenditures for education.

During the past few years there seems to have been an increasing "crisis in confidence"[2] in traditional provisions for and procedures in education and a continuing demand for changes. As one result, some major changes have been made in a number of "pioneering" school systems. Some of these apparently have been carefully planned but others have obviously been adopted or adapted without adequate study or consideration. Relatively few of these changes have been carefully analyzed and evaluated in terms of the implications for and effects on student attitudes and progress, teacher growth and competencies, long-range cost-benefits, or other similar matters.

Fortunately these and other developments have helped to direct attention to the need for systematic study and planning, for adequate research and development, for carefully monitored experimentation, for collecting and analyzing data and information pertaining to all developments, and for utilizing not only the talents and contributions of a wide range of competent personnel including teachers but also the appropriate technologies. In other words, these and related developments—including the quest for excellence in education and the concern of legislators and other lay citizens about the increasing costs and some of the problems and inadequacies in education under modern conditions—have served to emphasize the need for continuous evaluation of the processes and products of education and for attempting to develop valid criteria and establish appropriate procedures designed to ensure accountability in and for education. These demands and expectations present complex and difficult problems that are not likely to be resolved quickly or easily.

APPRAISAL AND ASSESSMENT

The terms "appraisal" and "assessment" are frequently used almost interchangeably. In education, however, the term assessment has gradually assumed a more scientific mantle. While appraisal usually is concerned with estimating the value, nature, or quality of some process or program and may be based on quite valid empirical evidence, it does not assume the precision inherent in assessment. Although lacking the criteria with which results of some measurement processes may be judged, assessment can utilize precise, scientifically developed, and sophisticated measurement tools to provide censuslike data about the status of processes, needs, or products. Assessment results may be arrayed in such a manner that careful

[2]James Allen, "Crisis in Confidence; The Public and Its Schools," *P T A Magazine,* October 1971, pp. 18–20.

study will yield insights into the subject of investigation, but only when these results are compared with present performance criteria—a process that yields publicly verifiable, objective judgments about the worth of the subject under investigation. Thus appraisal, assessment, and evaluation may be arranged hierarchically in order of precision, use of scientific methods, depth of understanding, and utilization of results.

In the early 1960s, as sharp criticisms were being made about education (usually challenged by a vigorous defense), a few people were beginning to realize that relatively little information was available upon which to base either criticism or defense. To be sure, the U.S. Office of Education, the National Education Association, and accreditation agencies collected and published substantial amounts of educational data concerned almost solely with items of *input* (although dropout statistics may be considered a rather gross measure of educational output). State departments of education were also collecting increasing amounts of information, most of which was related to regulatory functions or constituted an effort to establish an objective basis for the distribution of state monies in local school districts. Although Regents' Examinations in New York State provided some indications of output, they were administered for an entirely different reason and consequently were ill-suited to the type of evaluation under discussion here. Very few educational outcomes actually were being measured as a result of this increased flow of information. Moreover, none of this information was of the kind that could be used as a sound basis for criticism or defense of, or for proposing changes in, education. Measurement of educational *output* was urgently needed.

Financed by the Carnegie Corporation and the Fund for the Advancement of Education, the national assessment movement began with the appointment of a committee under the chairmanship of Ralph A. Tyler, who earlier directed the well-known Eight-Year Study and had developed a model of evaluation that placed priority on student behaviors and the definition of objectives in behavioral terms. This committee, called the Exploratory Committee on Assessing the Progress of Education (ECAPE) was charged with the responsibility for exploring ways in which educational progress might be measured, for developing procedures designed to measure progress (or lack of it) on a periodic basis, and for reporting the results to the nation. The Committee recognized that the development and administration of another series of standardized tests would not provide a solution to the problem, and concluded that, if a valid and defensible method of assessing educational progress were to be devised, new tools that would *measure outcomes in reference to goals and objectives* rather than norms would have to be developed and utilized.

One of the most ambitious, well-conceived, and far-reaching projects for the purpose of assessing educational *output* is known as "National

Assessment of Educational Progress," the design for which has been carefully and systematically developed.[3] New methods of sampling and statistical manipulation were invented to solve problems posed by the constraints imposed on the project, both by lack of full financing and by concern and suspicion on the part of many people involved in education. Test exercises were developed that were radically different from the usual test items on a standardized achievement test. New competencies had to be developed to prepare these exercises. It is anticipated that many side benefits will accrue from this project (now being directed through the Education Commission of the States), not the least of which will be the development of a prototype evaluation model that is based solely on output. In any event, as a result of this project, more information will be available about what children and young adults know than at any time in the history of formal education.

EVALUATION

As indicated earlier, there have been increasing concerns about the public schools, institutions of higher learning, and even about the entire system of education in this country. People from all walks of life have been questioning and criticizing virtually every facet of the educational system and are demanding both answers and some kind of action. In some instances, criticisms have been voiced with complete disregard for the data and information that are available. But regardless of the validity of the criticisms directed at education, the fact that they have been made, and will no doubt continue, clearly indicates the need for educational and other leaders to develop and be able to provide sound and defensible answers for difficult and complex questions. Information of this nature can only be gained from bona fide assessment and evaluative endeavors. Destructive, demoralizing, and unjust criticisms can often be countered or even converted into constructive channels when adequate information and data are available and utilized. Unfortunately, in many instances the needed data are either not available or are not utilized effectively. As one result, the general public has often been exposed primarily to the *opinions* of the critics or of school administrators, board members, or others. These opinions do not provide a satisfactory or defensible basis for making decisions about educational processes and programs.

The lack of adequate information may be explained in a variety of ways. It is, for example, often difficult to obtain valid information that can

---

[3]See Frank B. Womer, *What Is National Assessment?* (Denver, Colorado: Education Commission of the States, National Assessment of Educational Progress, 1970).

be utilized effectively. Partly because the roles and functions of evaluation in education have not been made clear, many involved in education—teachers, students, administrators, and board members—have been reluctant to participate in anything other than limited or superficial evaluative efforts. The lack of understanding about the roles and functions of evaluation has also caused many school systems to assign—at least by implication—a low priority to evaluative efforts. This perhaps can be best illustrated by the fact that during the past decade educational research (which is essential for evaluation) received less than one half of 1 percent of the amount spent on education in the United States.[4] The process of gathering and analyzing information about education requires that resources—both human and material—be allocated for that purpose. Educators and lay citizens need to identify ways of impressing upon legislators and governing boards the importance and significance of bona fide evaluation, and to assist them in re-ordering or establishing priorities.[5] If this is done, the resources needed for evaluation can be allocated and valid information can be made available and utilized to improve educational structures, programs, and procedures.

Purposes of Evaluation

Among educators and lay citizens alike there is often a tendency to perceive evaluation only or primarily as an effort to provide answers to questions such as "Did it work?", or "Did it accomplish what it purported to do?" When evaluation is treated in this context, only shallow or superficial determinations are feasible and these obviously should not provide a basis for important decisions. Educators certainly need to know what did or did not work, and sound research programs will be required to make this possible. But more important in any effort that has as its goal the improvement of some aspect of education is a determination of the *worth* or *value* of the effort. This, then, should be the primary focus of any evaluative endeavor. In order to determine the value, however, educational leaders should seek to develop and utilize evaluation procedures that go far beyond a determination of whether or not something worked. Teachers, supervisors, administrators, and citizen groups need reliable information relating to (1) what did or did not work or work well; (2) why it worked or did not work satisfactorily; and (3) modifications that may be needed.

[4]Edward Wynne, "Educational Research: A Profession in Search of a Constituency," *Phi Delta Kappan,* December 1970, p. 245.
[5]For a comprehensive discussion of priorities in education see Robert B. Howsam, "Problems, Procedures and Priorities in Designing Education for the Future," in *Cooperative Planning for Education in 1980,* Edgar L. Morphet and David L. Jesser, eds. (New York: Citation Press, 1969).

Information of this nature, when properly analyzed and made available to educators and concerned lay citizens, will make it possible for them to *make rational and defensible decisions about educational policies and procedures*—which is a major function of evaluation. More specific purposes are discussed in the paragraphs that follow.

Evaluation should provide a sound basis for making judgments and developing conclusions. Until recently, this has probably been the most commonly recognized purpose of evaluation. At the end of the year, for example, the local school board should want to know how well things have gone and what has been achieved. The emphasis on evaluation at the conclusion of a period of time is both useful and necessary for some types of decisions to be made about the instructional program. There is a distinct danger, however, that when evaluations are related primarily to student achievement, they may become the basis for judgments and decisions about other aspects of education. For example, some have proposed that student achievement be the criterion used for teacher employment and retention; others that teachers be paid on the basis of student achievement. Despite the emphasis in recent years upon the desirability of evaluating all aspects of the educational program, much testing during the last month of school still occurs, and it is likely that test-based evaluation of achievement will continue for some time to occupy a major role in the educational system.

Evaluation should ensure continually improving processes and programs of education. All educational institutions and agencies should accept this concept as a major purpose of evaluation and should devote considerable effort toward its attainment. New methods and procedures are constantly being developed, and it is imperative that these be considered and tested where applicable. Schools and school systems tend to change to some extent as society changes, yet all too often schools continue to operate as though they and society had never changed. Carefully planned evaluation programs, continuous in nature, are necessary if the schools and school systems are to eliminate wasteful procedures and to plan and effect needed changes.

Evaluation should enable schools and school systems to diagnose difficulties and to avoid destructive upheavals. Wherever evaluation takes place—in the classroom, at a board meeting, or in the total system—diagnosis should be considered an important purpose. Serious and bona fide evaluation of problem areas will usually provide the data that are necessary for defensible judgments and for developing appropriate policies. When suitable corrective steps are taken, it may be possible to avoid the potentially destructive developments that have been experienced in some school systems.

Evaluation should improve the ability of the staff and lay citizens to plan and effect improvements in the educational system. Although this may not be generally perceived as a purpose of evaluation, it should be considered one of the most significant. Meaningful improvements in education are not likely to be effected unless there is a demand on the part of the professional staff and lay citizens that such improvements be made. When those concerned are actively and constructively involved in evaluation of procedures and practices, they are likely to be supportive of the needed changes that become evident as a result of the evaluation.

Evaluation should enable school systems to test new approaches to the solution of problems. As school systems become larger and their operations more complex, there may be a tendency for them to be hesitant either to clearly identify problems or to search for effective ways of solving them. In some instances the problems seem to have assumed proportions of such magnitude that educators and lay citizens see little if any hope for solutions. Moreover, potent forces that seek conformity rather than experimentation will undoubtedly continue to exist. Schools and school systems should take the lead in developing and implementing action research programs that can be used as a basis for planning and effecting major changes in their provisions for education. Such programs should always incorporate sound provisions for evaluative procedures.

Types of Evaluation

Evaluation, as has been noted, is but one aspect of what should be perceived as the process of accountability. It is, therefore, closely identified with the other components of the accountability process. Moreover, evaluative efforts are sometimes difficult to categorize or classify because they may, in effect, be combinations of several kinds of efforts. It should be helpful to note some of the types of evaluation discussed briefly below in order to develop some understanding of the potential range and scope of evaluations.

GEOGRAPHIC AREA OR GOVERNMENTAL UNIT. Educational studies or evaluative efforts may be concerned with a program or an activity, a school, a school system, an area service agency, a state, or federal agencies or activities. Evaluation for accreditation purposes, for example, is usually concerned with only a single school,[6] while evaluation for systemwide improvement is, obviously, concerned with the total school system.[7] An emerging trend in evaluative efforts at the state level may be seen in the fact that nearly one-fourth of the states have, in recent years, enacted legislation relating to state testing, assessment, and evaluation.[8]

LIMITED OR COMPREHENSIVE. Educational evaluations may be quite comprehensive in nature, that is, be concerned with most or all aspects of

[6] See *Evaluative Criteria,* 4th ed. (Arlington, Virginia: National Study of Secondary Schools, 1969).
[7] See *Profiles of Excellence: Recommended Criteria for Evaluating the Quality of a Local School System* (Washington, D.C.: National Education Association, 1966).
[8] *Characteristics and Models for State Accountability Legislation* (Denver, Colorado: Cooperative Accountability Project, 1973).

education provided in a state or local school system. Evaluations of this comprehensive type are usually associated with state, regional, or local accreditation efforts, but may also be associated with other studies or self-improvement efforts. Evaluations of a more limited nature, in which attention is focused primarily upon a single area of educational service, are sometimes conducted by either a state or a local school system in an effort to improve a particular aspect of the curriculum, administration, or similar areas.

CONTINUOUS, PERIODIC, OR IRREGULAR. Some schools and school systems provide for a planned, continuous program of evaluation in which all aspects of education may be evaluated in a systematic manner during a specified period of time. When such provisions are made, some phase of the program or system is under study at all times. In some instances, evaluative procedures are established on a cyclical basis, with provision for recurring study of a specific aspect every five or six years. In other instances, school systems may stipulate that comprehensive evaluation be conducted periodically—perhaps every five years—and at the same time provide for more limited evaluations as the need may become evident. Either type of evaluation can be helpful to educational leaders and the lay public. The important concern is that evaluations be carefully planned and conducted in some continuing manner. All too often evaluations are conducted on an irregular, almost hit-or-miss basis. When evaluations are irregular and ill-defined, there is likely to be confusion as to purpose, too little involvement, and considerable difficulty in ensuring utilization of the evidence and conclusions.

OUTSIDE, INTERNAL, OR COOPERATIVE. In this context reference is made to those who assume the major responsibility for evaluative efforts. Is the evaluation to be conducted primarily by "outside" consultants, by members of the local school system, or does it involve some type of cooperative arrangement? Until recently, few local school systems had the kind of expertise on their staffs needed to conduct bona fide evaluations. As a result, many have sought the assistance of outside consultants for evaluative endeavors. Frequently, however, the outside consultants did not have adequate knowledge or insights concerning the local situation, and their reports were sometimes rejected, or at least not utilized for the purposes originally intended. An internal study or evaluation may also have disadvantages. For example, the local staff may not have the expertise needed, or may be too parochial or limited in outlook to make objective evaluations or comparisons. This situation, when added to a possible tendency to attempt to justify existing practices, may make the concept of internal evaluation untenable in many instances.

Because of the difficulties noted, many school systems and state education agencies have encouraged cooperative endeavors in which competent local resource personnel (educators as well as lay citizens) are utilized in cooperation with the talents of outside consultants. A team of this kind should have most of the advantages of both external and internal evaluations and be able to avoid most of the disadvantages of each. If the cooperative approach is to be effective, considerable effort must be devoted not only to development of appropriate plans and procedures, but also to the development and perhaps modification of attitudes and understandings held by those who participate in the effort.

Guidelines for Evaluative Efforts

Any defensible evaluation should be based on defensible criteria, many of which are commonly recognized. Generally, however, when reference in education is made to evaluation, the instructional program receives primary emphasis. Obviously, this is an integral and vital aspect of the educational system. However, many components of the educational system affect instructional and learning procedures and should be continually evaluated. The guidelines that follow, therefore, are directed toward the entire system of education.

- *Evaluation should be based on clearly stated educational goals and objectives.* The desirability, worth, or value of a given educational practice or product (such as a classroom, an administrative procedure, a teaching method, or a student's performance) can only be determined in relation to its contributions to the achievement of goals and objectives of the educational enterprise. When evaluations do not relate closely to stated goals and objectives, the results will likely be meaningless in terms of the purposes of evaluation.
- *When evaluations are contemplated or planned, the intent or purposes should be effectively communicated to all concerned.* In some school systems, as well as in other educational institutions and agencies, evaluations have been viewed as a kind of modern-day witch hunt. As a consequence, many educators have tended to resist evaluative efforts. Unfortunately, some of the fears and suspicions of educators have been well grounded. In many instances evaluations—of personnel especially—have been misused, or used for purposes other than those originally stated. For example, if the purpose of an evaluation is to determine the value or appropriateness of an educational program, it should be made clear that the program—not the teachers—is being evaluated. On the other hand, if the purpose is to evaluate the effectiveness of the instructors or facilitators of learning this should be made clear. In any evaluation, those concerned should be made aware of all aspects, including purposes, procedures, and how the results are intended to be utilized.
- *Bases or standards for evaluating should be established prior to any evaluation.* To conduct an evaluation without having identified the standards or criteria that are to be utilized for guidance or comparisons would be similar to not knowing where one is going—and consequently never knowing whether he

has arrived. For most types of evaluation, standards have been established. Some emanate from state education agencies, others from accrediting agencies, and still others from locally developed statements of philosophy or purpose. Whatever the source, however, effective evaluation requires the utilization of appropriate standards and criteria.

Recent Developments in Evaluation Methodology

Guba and Stufflebeam, among others, have regarded evaluation as a tool that should be used by educational managers in making decisions about educational programs and processes. They have defined evaluation as the *process of obtaining and providing useful information for making educational decisions.*[9] Evaluation thus becomes, under this concept, a tool to be used by management in the operation of the schools and is *decision oriented* rather than conclusion oriented. Although there can be no doubt that more valid empirical data should be available to educational decision makers than is presently the case, there is no guarantee that those charged with making decisions will have developed the level of competency necessary to utilize properly all empirical data in the decision-making process. Put quite simply, if empirical data differ from intuitive feelings, attempts may be made to find fault with the data and thus disrupt the rational decision-making processes that are essential for any defensible evaluation. Evaluation, however, should not only be decision oriented as indicated in the model briefly discussed in this paragraph, but it should also be *goal oriented* —should be concerned with goals and precise goal statements. Scriven has defined evaluation from a goal-oriented point of view in the following manner:

> Evaluation is itself a methodological activity which is essentially similar whether we are trying to evaluate coffee machines or teaching machines, plans for a house or plans for curriculum. The activity consists simply in the gathering and combining of performance data with a weighted set of goal scales to yield either comparative or numerical ratings, and in the justification of (a) the data gathering instruments, (b) the weightings, and (c) the selection of goals.[10]

One of the values of this concept of evaluation is the emphasis on goals and goal justification. Unfortunately many of the techniques needed to implement this model are not yet in existence but it offers some poten-

---

[9]Egon G. Guba and Donald O. Stufflebeam, "Evaluation: The Process of Stimulating, Aiding and Abetting Insightful Action," (An address to the Second National Symposium for Professors of Educational Research, Boulder, Colorado, Nov. 21, 1968), p. 24.

[10]Michael Scriven, *The Methodology of Evaluation,* AERA Monograph Series on Evaluation, No. 1, Robert E. Stake, ed. (Chicago: Rand McNally, 1967), p. 40.

tial benefits not inherent in other models. The efforts of state and local education agencies might well be directed to the development of greater sophistication in the area of goal-oriented evaluation. Such efforts would contribute significantly to the utilization of evaluation as an effective management tool.

The use of the computer is becoming more commonplace in evaluation efforts. Far greater amounts of data may be obtained and far more sophisticated analyses can now be made and implemented than was previously the case. However, sophisticated and complicated manipulation and analysis of crude data can lead only to crude results. Moreover, our confidence in sophisticated data massage tends to result in misplaced confidence in these crude results, and dangerous or misleading conclusions are apt to be forthcoming. Perhaps Christopher Jencks best summed up the state of the art when he said, "If I were to say what was the single major limitation of current research, I would say our capacity to measure the things we care about is still rather moderate."[11]

ACCOUNTABILITY

The concept of accountability, the parameters of which have not yet been fully defined, is one that is virtually certain to affect education and educators rather significantly in the years ahead. Unfortunately, this concept has not yet received adequate attention from scholars in the field and, as a theoretical construct, accountability is in its infancy. However, because of dramatically increased interest on the part of decision makers, particularly those in the political arena, more researchers are turning their attention to investigations of accountability and there is a small but growing body of literature dealing with the subject. Many legislators as well as state and federal government officials have emphasized the importance of accountability. For example, James E. Allen, Jr., former United States Commissioner of Education, said in his testimony to the Senate, "The strengthening of the concept of accountability in our educational system is imperative."[12]

Perhaps the most dramatic, although not the first, crude effort to impose accountability in or for education was the incident in which the citizens of Athens forced Socrates to swallow hemlock because they thought his influence on the youth was not in harmony with the values and perceived needs of their parents. The history of education is replete with examples of efforts to ensure accountability and, although it is not the purpose of this section to present a history of accountability in Ameri-

[11]Donald W. Robinson, "An Interview with Christopher Jencks," *Phi Delta Kappan,* December 1972.
[12]James E. Allen, Jr. (Testimony before the Senate Subcommittee on Education, Tuesday, Apr. 21, 1970).

can education, a few illustrations are in order. In 1642 the Massachusetts General Court passed its famous act requiring parents and masters to see to the education of the children under their control and levying fines on all adults who failed to do so. The town selectmen were charged with enforcing the law and authorized to hail negligent parties into court for punishment by fine. In 1647 the same General Court passed another far-reaching law requiring towns to establish schools and providing for penalties and fines for towns neglecting to do so. These acts provide the first examples in American education of colonial (state) efforts to require some measure of accountability on the part of local governments. Although the initiative remained in the hands of local school districts in the early part of the history of the United States, efforts in the early 1800s on the part of Mann and others resulted in a gradual shifting of initiative and responsibility to the state level. The federal Constitution, state constitutions, and especially recent court decisions relating to state school finance systems, have established the fact that the state is the political division primarily responsible for the education of its citizens.

A system of accountability and cost-benefit payments was proposed in England as early as 1862. According to Pfeiffer,[13] it was introduced by Robert Lowe, Vice President to Britain's Committee of the Privy Council for Education, as a "payment by results" plan. The plan provided that allocation of funds to schools would be based on the grades of pupils in the three Rs. The proposal and the ensuing emotional reaction resulted in Lowe's resignation two years later.

Legislation intended to accomplish accountability is becoming more common as legislators attempt to determine the results which are being achieved in relationship to moneys appropriated for education. One bill recently introduced in the Illinois Legislature would direct the Superintendent of Public Instruction to take over the operation of any school district in which test results showed that the students were below national norms.

Social Elements Leading to Accountability

Changes in the conceptual design discussed in Chapter 2 have set the stage for demands for accountability. Social unrest and dissatisfaction with social institutions—of which the educational system is only one—have led to the politics of confrontation by which results, rather than promises, are demanded. Parents are no longer content to leave the education of their children primarily in the hands of professional educators without some

[13]John Pfeiffer, *A New Look at Education* (New York: The Odyssey Press, 1968), p. 80.

accounting procedures being established. No longer are many of them willing to increase local mill levies for school purposes without having some evidence that the schools are achieving their goals and that additional moneys will result in increased achievement. Rapid changes in society, in value systems, and in technology—especially in communications technology—have resulted in a strong conviction on the part of the lay public that the schools, left to themselves, will not achieve for their children the long cherished American ideal of equal educational opportunity.

Identifiable Elements of an Emerging Concept

The dictionary is of little use in defining accountability. It gives as a synonym, "responsibility." While this is a beginning, the definition needs expansion if precision in meaning is to be achieved. Two people talking about accountability are likely to be talking about two different things. A legislator may believe that educators and the schools are accountable to the legislature because it appropriates money for school operations. Congressmen may believe that educators should be accountable for the manner in which federal moneys are expended for improving school programs. Some federal legislation currently in effect, and much proposed federal legislation, includes a requirement for evaluation of programs and projects that are supported by federal funds. On the other hand, educators are likely to believe that legislators should be held accountable for the kinds of laws adopted and for the manner in which they provide (or do not provide) financial support for the schools. Many may insist that, since education is a responsibility of the state and legislators set policies through legislation, these legislators should be held accountable to the public and the educational community. Thus, accountability has a number of facets and dimensions that have to be considered.

Who should be accountable to whom and for what? Most lay citizens, when confronted with this question, find it rather easy to "answer." They are likely to say schools ought to be accountable, and that they should be accountable to the taxpayers. This "answer" is illustrative of the present level of thought about the concept. Somehow, whenever accountability is mentioned, it seems to be in connection with money. While there is nothing wrong with a taxpayer's wish to get full value for the money provided, accountability goes beyond this level. Most people would agree that schools should be held accountable. But, to whom and for what should they be held accountable?

Obviously, the increasing demands for educational accountability call for a better understanding of the problems and procedures on the part of professional educators as well as the general public. Accountability, if it is to be an effective instrument for helping to bring about needed improvements in education, must be viewed by all concerned as a constructive tool, and not simply as a device for punishment or for busywork. It must be utilized to help educators, legislators, and lay citizens to determine what areas of education are developing or progressing according to plans, and which areas or aspects are failing to do so. To make some reasonable determination concerning successes or failures requires that, as indicated in Chapter 6, adequate planning be accomplished including:

- The development and refinement of meaningful goals, objectives, and priorities;
- The translation of goals and objectives into measurable terms;
- The development of criteria that are needed to determine the amount of progress made toward achievement of goals;
- The development of methods for effectively utilizing the criteria that are developed;
- The interpretation and analysis of the results of measurements;
- The formulation of recommendations pertaining to needed changes or modifications;
- The determination of strategies designed to bring about the changes that are needed; and
- The development and implementation of procedures appropriate for evaluation and for reporting on the progress that is or is not made.

When the necessary steps have been accomplished, educational leaders and others should be in a better position to answer questions about the *who* and *what* of accountability. In terms of the "who," several possibilities can quickly be identified. These would include taxpayers, boards of education, parents, legislators, governors, Congress, and state education agencies. Various beliefs that are expressed indicate that the schools should be held accountable to taxpayers because of the financial support they provide; school boards because they set policy and represent the community in its educational enterprise; parents because of their interest in and concern about the education their children receive; legislators because they set educational policy for the state and presumably provide financial support to implement those policies; governors because they are the chief executive officers of political entities (the states) which have the prime responsibility for education within their state boundaries; and state education agencies because of their leadership and regulatory functions.

The Importance of Goal Setting in Accountability

The importance of goal setting in education has previously been emphasized. In a very simple sense, schools are held accountable for helping students and personnel to reach pertinent goals. The *first* necessary condition of accountability is: *Lay citizens and educators must reach agreement on the goals they expect to be achieved primarily through the schools.* One can hardly expect school personnel to be held accountable for achieving a goal about which they know nothing, in the same sense that the captain of a ship cannot be held accountable for reaching a certain harbor if he is not told the name of the harbor. Recent manifestations of dissatisfaction with public education may not be so much the result of poor educational processes as of confusion over the goals of education.

Educational goals are frequently stated in such general terms that it is difficult to define them completely and precisely. One of the many goals that is proclaimed for education throughout the nation and included in practically all state and local statements of goals is "to educate pupils for good citizenship." A worthwhile goal indeed! Stated in this manner, however, it is not attainable in the sense that schools will know whether or when it has been attained. It must be analyzed and divided into its elements.

What is good citizenship? Is it keeping within legal boundaries set by society? Or paying one's income taxes? Or voting in an informed manner? Or participating in civic affairs? All these are elements of "good" citizenship in a democratic society (an added condition). How should success in achieving this goal be measured? Must schools wait to see whether their graduates vote in elections after having become informed on the issues? Certainly actual performance could be called a valid criterion. Unfortunately in some situations the method is cumbersome, costly, and its measurement too long delayed to be of any assistance in making educational decisions. To be sure, we can, in the aggregate, determine the percentage of eligible voters who actually vote in any election. We cannot tell, however, whether they voted on the basis of interest and information, strong biases, or because the precinct captain furnished their transportation. It is known that those who understand how elections are conducted and how to cast a ballot are more likely to vote than those who are ignorant about these matters. Such knowledge can be provided by schools. How much of this knowledge the student has mastered can be measured. Therefore a measurable objective can be established that, when reached, will contribute to the achievement of one of the elements of the general goal of good citizenship. Thus, a second necessary condition in accountability may be stated: *Goals and objectives must be stated in measurable terms.* This is the "what" of accountability.

The Accountability Partnership

Thus, accountability must include mutually agreed upon goals, and progress toward attaining these goals or their elements must be measurable. However, the definition is not yet complete. An additional element of accountability involves another aspect of mutually agreed upon goals. It relates to the question: Agreed upon by whom? Obviously, *goals should be agreed upon by (1) the person or organization empowered to hold another person or organization accountable, and (2) the person or organization to be held accountable.*

The conclusion stated above brings up some interesting questions. What agreements have been reached between whom in the field of education? The writers of the constitutions of the several states were aware of the value of education and provided for a system of free public education. In turn, the constitutions usually assigned to state legislatures the responsibility for providing for this system.

Provisions in most state constitutions require that legislatures provide for the establishment of local school districts. Thus the basic responsibility for providing education in these states has been assigned to the local school district level. If we assume for the purpose of simplification that the two parties primarily involved are the legislature (representing the state government) and the local school districts, it follows that the goals must be agreed upon between these two levels of government. There are numerous other pairings in the accountability partnership where goals must be mutually agreed upon—for example, student and teacher, teacher and supervisor, the board and administrator, and the state and local school systems. The state education agencies clearly have a major role in assisting all parties concerned to resolve the issue of goals and, in the process, to bring about some clarity in the interpretation of the responsibility for accountability in a state.

The Assignment of Responsibility

In an effort to arrive at other necessary conditions for the establishment of accountability, let us assume that the state holds local school systems responsible for preparing graduates who will make "worthy use of leisure time." Worthy is hardly a measurable term, but an agreement could be reached that one of the elements of worthy use of leisure time is interest and proficiency in one or more follow-up recreational activities —that is, an activity that a student is likely to continue after graduation, such as golf, tennis, swimming, hiking, camping, and the like. Inventories exist that can be used to measure interest, and proficiency can be measured against performance criteria. Assume further, however, that a recreation district is coterminous with a school district. Recreation districts typically offer diverse opportunities and attempt to foster interest in their activities and create proficiency in them. If interest and proficiency have been measured and both are found to be high, to which organization can the success be ascribed? Or, if both are weak, to which organization may the failure be ascribed? We could, of course, examine the number of lessons given, the number of students taught, the number of sessions held, then ascribe some value to these quantities and perhaps arrive at some tentative conclusions. These are measures of input, but input measures (of dollars, for example) have not always been demonstrated to have a high degree of correlation with goal achievement.

A *third* necessary condition of accountability that must be considered is: *The responsibility for goal achievement must, as nearly as possible, be assignable and be definitely assigned.* It is difficult to assign certain responsibilities uniquely to the schools since there is always the possibility, even probability, that much of what students learn is derived from their environment including parents, siblings, peers, television, and so on—their total gamut of experiences.

Conditions and Constraints

Thus far, accountability has been discussed as a responsibility that is clearly identified, measurable, and assignable. There is yet another element to be considered. In the real world in which the public schools are operating there are conditions and contraints over which the schools have little or no control. For example, expectations may be set at a higher level than available resources can support. Parents may be expecting certain results from the schools and at the same time may oppose an increase in the tax levy. By doing so they impose a condition or constraint within which the school district must operate. Unfortunately, expectations are seldom, if ever, reduced when constraints are imposed. Constraints are quite diverse and are not limited to the financial support provided for the schools.

The conditions that qualify goals and objectives must also be specified. If one of the objectives of a school is to teach young students to read at a certain level of proficiency, one of the conditions should be that it be accomplished within a specific period of time. It might also be specified that no more than a certain amount of money be spent in accomplishing the objective. These are the stipulations under which the goals must be achieved. A *fourth* necessary condition for accountability is: *The constraints and conditions must be specified.*

The increasing emphasis upon the state as the political subdivision primarily responsible for education (as exemplified by the report of the President's Commission on School Finance and some recent court opinions holding some state school finance systems unconstitutional) would seem to indicate that the state will become a focal point of any system of accountability. Adding to the weight of evidence is the shift in the conceptual design in an apparent return to a concept of creative federalism which places greater responsibility on the state rather than on the central government in Washington, D.C. Such a shift presages greater responsibility for state boards of education and state education agencies. The education policies adopted by the executive and legislative branches of state government will be increasingly of vital importance. Twenty-three states have adopted legislation of varying degrees of sophistication aimed at implementing a system of accountability. The number will undoubtedly grow rather than diminish. School administrators would do well to become acquainted with the many facets and problems of accountability and, indeed, seek to influence legislation relating to accountability.

Accountability Legislation

Analysis of the legislation existing in twenty-three states, and proposed thus far in an additional nine states, reveals rather sharply defined inadequacies in the understanding of the concept of accountability.[14] Most accountability measures passed by state legislators focus on some sort of state testing program utilizing norm-referenced or standardized tests of basic skills, the results of which are generally expressed in grade-level achievement. While there can be no disagreement that student output measures should be the focal point for a system of accountability, the reliance on norm-referenced tests in such an endeavor is an example of the misuse of test and test results. First, norm-referenced tests are of value in counseling each student relative to his weaknesses and strengths in relation to the group on which the test was standardized or in relation to his relative standing with other members of the school, but not with regard to his achievement or nonachievement of specified goals. Second, these standarized tests are composed of items which may have little or no curricular validity for the district in which they are to be used. Third, the tests were constructed, and norms calculated in such a manner that 50 percent of the population would fall above the mean and 50 percent below. Consequently, one of two situations arises: either the average becomes the goal (that is, what presently exists is the goal), or the goals are set by the test constructors. From our previous discussion of the importance of goal setting it should be obvious that goals should be mutually agreed upon before criteria for measuring their achievement are established. Manifestly, the use of standardized tests is not compatible with this concept.

[14] *Characteristics and Models for State Accountability Legislation.*

Other characteristics of legislation in the thirteen states which have passed accountability legislation with the main emphasis on testing programs are (1) administration and implementation of the program are assigned to the state board or department of education in all thirteen states; (2) options are available in seven states as to what segments of the school population are to be tested; and (3) results are to be reported to the legislature in nine states, to local school districts, boards and teachers in eight states, and to the citizens in six states. Multiple audiences are reflected in seven states.

The statutes in eleven states prescribe improved educational management methods either through Program-Planning-Budgeting Systems, Management Information Systems, or uniform accounting systems. The main characteristics of this type of legislation are (1) PPBS is emphasized in seven states and a uniform accounting system in the other four; (2) administrative control for the legislation is centered in the state board or department of education in ten states; (3) primary features of the requirements in seven states are a cost performance analysis, a program analysis for performance objectives, and a standard budget format; (4) programs are mandated for local school districts in seven states, for the state agency in three, and on a voluntary basis in one state; and (5) results have to be reported to the state legislature in seven states in conjunction with the state board or department of education and/or the citizens in four states.

Of interest to educators is the increased emphasis upon performance-based evaluation and certification of educational personnel. Legislation relating to this concept has been enacted in eight states. An examination of these enactments reveals these features: (1) the development of an evaluation system is the responsibility of the local school district in five states; (2) certified teachers are the subject of evaluation in six states and in conjunction with administrators and supervisors in four states; (3) procedures and techniques for assessing teacher performance must be developed and are required in six states; and (4) written evaluations must be discussed with educational personnel in four states, with the employee having the right to appeal in two states.

The Methodology of Accountability

As discussed earlier in this section, accountability can be accomplished only when two or more parties agree as to (1) the goals to be achieved, (2) the resources to be allocated for their achievement, (3) the evaluative criteria to be used to assess the degree of achievement, and (4) the conditions and constraints under which goals are to be achieved.

Perhaps one of the leading proponents of accountability in recent years has been Leon Lessinger who, in his publication *Every Kid a Winner: Accountability in Education,* examines several sound principles of accountability. His emphasis on the use of management support groups and performance contracting with private enterprise—with its implicit assumption that private industry has more expertise in education than publicly employed educators—may, however, lead some students of accountability to examine his other pronouncements with more skepticism than is warranted. His concept of the independent educational accomplishment audit deserves some scrutiny in that it seems to be an essential element of the methodology of accountability and is related to the previous discussion on evaluation. Drawing an analogy between fiscal and educational audits, Lessinger stated:

> If the same expense and effort now devoted to fiscal control were put into auditing our educational practices, we could swiftly weed out faulty procedures and programs that now persist thanks to dubious, unchecked claims of success and, more important, we could spot the workable programs and nourish them accordingly.[15]

Most experts agree that evaluations that are conducted by the same persons responsible for operating a program are liable to bias, or at least may be suspect because of the human tendency to emphasize successful aspects of one's own ventures and to deemphasize, if not actually ignore, the more unsuccessful ones. Consequently, the results of an independent evaluation may generally be regarded with more confidence than those obtained by an interested party. Whether the process chosen is an independent educational accomplishment audit or an evaluation by either internal or external personnel, in general, six phases occur in the process:

THE GOAL-SETTING PHASE. In this first phase, it is essential that the evaluator and program personnel (optimally including community representatives) agree on the *specific* objectives of the program or projects and the activities proposed to achieve these objectives. This stage partially achieves the first, second, and fourth of the necessary conditions listed previously.

THE DATA-IDENTIFICATION PHASE. The second phase consists of reaching agreement on the types of data necessary to indicate whether or not objectives have been met and on the procedures to be used in gathering these data. It is in this stage that the evaluative criteria are determined, thus

---

[15]Leon Lessinger, *Every Kid a Winner: Accountability in Education* (New York: Simon & Schuster, 1970).

fulfilling the second condition. Generally, where student achievement is to be measured, it is here that goals are translated into measurable objectives.

THE INSTRUMENTATION PHASE. During this phase existing data collection instruments are examined for appropriateness and the need for new instruments to be devised if existing ones are found to be inappropriate. In either event, the evaluator and program personnel agree on the instruments to be used in gathering the data agreed upon in the second phase.

THE PROCEDURAL PHASE. Evaluator and program personnel agree, in this phase, on what is frequently referred to as a *review calendar*. This is a written document which may assume a variety of formats from a simple narrative to a highly complicated PERT chart. Regardless of the degree of sophistication, it essentially represents an agreement on the part of all interested parties as to the specific instruments to be used, the places and times of the administration of the instruments, and the methods to be used in the analysis of the data thus gathered. Such an agreement assists in assuring the public that all aspects of the program will be examined and that failures as well as successes will be reported on an impartial, scientific basis.

THE IMPLEMENTATION PHASE. This is the action phase in which the procedures agreed to in the review calendar are implemented by the evaluator. He collects the data, utilizing the instruments and procedures agreed upon. Any deviations from the agreement should be the subject of negotiations between the agreeing parties as soon as the possibility of such a deviation is foreseen, and new agreements should be reached. (For example, any deviation which is beyond the ability of the evaluator to control or forecast, such as some event which causes excess absenteeism or closing of school completely on the scheduled day of the administration of an instrument).

THE REPORTING PHASE. The final step is the presentation of a *public report* in which the results of the evaluation are presented in an impartial manner that depicts fairly the degree to which the objectives have been reached. Some authorities recommend that the report should also include proposals for improvements in the program. However, it should be pointed out that such a procedure would result in the evaluator's possibly being in the position of evaluating his own recommendations during the next year of the program, or might result in the necessity for changing evaluators in order to maintain impartiality. The report should also account for deviations from the review calendar if any exist.

If these stages of evaluation are adhered to by competent persons, a system of accountability can be established which will be impartial and also will allow educators and the concerned lay people collectively to make decisions about goals and programs in a professional, orderly manner rather than in an emotional outburst of energy during a time of crisis when charges and countercharges, based on nonscientific information, are used by both sides of a dispute.

SOME IMPORTANT PROBLEMS AND ISSUES

A few of the many problems and issues relating to evaluation and accountability are discussed briefly in this section. What others are also important and how should they be resolved?

How and by Whom Should Appraisals, Assessments, and Evaluations of Developments in or Relating to Education Be Made?

As noted or implied in most chapters in this volume and in many other recent publications, those involved or interested in education must be concerned with the future as well as with past and current developments. Why is this orientation essential, yet so often given inadequate attention? Is it, as Alvin Toffler has indicated in his *Future Shock,* because most people tend to ignore many of the facts and their implications when dramatic changes are occurring, or are there other important reasons?

Perceptive appraisals of policies, practices, and trends in education and society should be helpful in providing a basis for planning and effecting improvements, but many informal appraisals by individuals and groups during recent years seem to have been primarily negative or critical. Until substantial agreement is reached on appropriate goals and policies for the future, the situation will probably continue to be chaotic and confusing for many, and progress, at least in some important areas, is likely to be limited. Which of the procedures or combinations of procedures suggested below would be most helpful? What others should be considered? What would be the advantages and disadvantages of each?

- The school board and the staff make a careful appraisal of present programs and of their own functions and procedures, and the board then informs the public concerning changes to be made.
- The legislature, after reviewing criticisms of the schools and proposals for changes in education, approves a proposal requiring that certain changes be made in all school systems.
- As a first step toward planning and proposing changes that may be needed in educational goals, policies, and procedures, the governor, a committee designated by the legislature, and the state board of education cooperate in selecting a commission or committee composed of competent lay citizens and educators that, with the assistance of qualified consultants, will be responsible

for (1) attempting to identify, appraise the significance of, and determine the most important implications for education of prospective major changes in society; (2) making an appraisal and assessment to determine (a) the extent to which present (stated or implied) goals of education are being achieved in various kinds of schools and school systems in the state, and (b) the respects in which these goals are and are not consistent with the needs of present-day society; (3) proposing new or revised goals designed to meet emerging needs; and (4) disseminating and encouraging study and discussion throughout the state of the findings, conclusions and proposals.

What Kinds of Appraisals and Evaluations Should Be Made in Local School Systems?

In a dynamic society all local school systems as well as other educational agencies and institutions must constantly seek to become self-actualizing and self-renewing organizations. This is a difficult goal to achieve because there is always a tendency for people to assume that what seems to be working reasonably well should suffice to meet future conditions and needs. How can this tendency be avoided or minimized by local school board members, administrators, teachers, and other staff members, and by other citizens in the community?

One essential seems to be continuous study of the problems and needs of the schools and school system with the cooperation of everyone involved in or concerned about education. Satisfactory answers to questions such as the following should be sought: Are the school board members among the most competent, knowledgeable, and perceptive citizens in the community who are interested in improving education? Is the board making a serious and sustained effort to involve the citizens, the staff, and the students in identifying, agreeing on, and helping to achieve appropriate goals? Are the administrators, members of the supporting staff, and teachers seriously involved in this process and in developing suitable procedures for appraising developments, assessing and reporting on problems and progress, and in devising appropriate strategies to facilitate the quest for excellence in education for every student in accordance with his needs?

Continuing self-appraisal or evaluation of perceptions and attitudes relating to education by board members, staff, and students, and even by parents and other citizens seems to be another essential. Constructive self-appraisals to which others contribute under favorable conditions should result in increasing the understanding of problems and needs in education and in more effective contributions to their solution.

Many of the larger local school systems currently seem to be so involved in attempting to deal with crisis situations that they apparently have inadequate time, energy, or resources to devote to systematic appraisals or assessments of existing policies and procedures. Moreover, many of the smaller systems may not have any staff members who have the competencies or time needed to make or direct valid appraisals or assessments. Under these conditions, assistance may be sought from a regional service agency, the state education agency, an institution of higher learning, or perhaps even from a commercial group organized to make such studies for a substantial fee. However, *unless such studies help to develop the competencies of the staff to conduct appropriate studies,* little progress may have been made from a long-range point of view. In such situations, perhaps a better plan would be to obtain and utilize the services of consultants who, in the process of helping to plan and conduct needed studies, can assist the administration and staff to develop the perceptions and competencies needed to direct and conduct such studies in the future.

What hazards and handicaps do school districts face in attempting to make their own appraisals and evaluations? Under what conditions is an assessment or evaluation likely to be most beneficial? How can the value of studies made by an outside group or those made with the assistance of a consultant best be determined? How can such groups or consultants best help the staff to develop appropriate insights and competencies?

What Are the Advantages and Disadvantages of Statewide or Other Testing Programs?

One of the developments resulting at least in part from the increasing concern about improving the quality of education for all students in every school has been the demand for and increasing use of external tests and uniform state testing programs. There should be no doubt about the need for more and better information about students and their needs, and about problems and progress in and through schools. Such information is essential not only for effective counseling and guidance, the planning of remedial programs, the evaluation of experimental programs, and similar purposes, but also for helping to determine why some students fail repeatedly, why others graduate from high school without having learned to read at a functional level, and so on.

There, however, seem to be valid reasons for concern about the heavy reliance on and current use in some states and local school systems of standardized achievement tests, most of which are norm-referenced. For example, the evidence indicates that, at least in one state, some children from homes in which the parents do not speak English have been improperly assigned to classes for the mentally retarded. Other factors resulting in concern include the number of tests sponsored in secondary schools which overlap and may be extremely time consuming; the tendency for that which is tested to be regarded as synonymous or of equal importance;

the improper or limited use of results; the extreme belief by some in their validity, objectivity, and scientific quality; their impact on the study habits of students; and the control which they exercise on the curriculum and instructional procedures.

Provision should be made for incorporating external tests as a part of the program of evaluation only to the extent to which the results justify this action. Even statewide programs—if properly planned and administered, with adequate flexibility and safeguards provided, and if local school systems are encouraged to develop programs designed to meet their own needs—may be defensible. However, the experiences of other societies which have seen their schools reduced to the pursuit of rigid, conforming, test-ridden programs of study should not be ignored. Rather, as a result of their experiences and with a knowledge of the limitations of current programs of testing and evaluation and of the hidden threats of some programs, it should be possible to develop programs of evaluation that will ensure far more adequate knowledge regarding students and more competence in utilizing the results.

Is there any evidence indicating that some tests tend to be culturally oriented? If so, what are the implications? Under what conditions are "criterion-referenced" tests more appropriate than "norm-referenced" tests? Why? What guidelines and cautions should be utilized for developing and using the results of statewide testing programs? For using test results in making an evaluation of a school or school system?

How Do Accreditation Procedures Relate to Evaluations?

If there are to be national, regional, or state accreditation agencies for any aspects of education, the procedures must be based at least in part on some presumably valid and rather comprehensive information that can be analyzed to provide a reasonably sound basis for an appraisal or evaluation. The rather comprehensive type of accreditation study that has become common in recent years is a great advance over the kind of inspection by an individual that formerly provided the basis for being accredited. The *Evaluative Criteria* developed by the Cooperative Study of Secondary Standards in 1940 (and revised every 10 years since then) have served as guides to evaluation that are much superior to former aids of this type, partly because attention is directed to the many aspects of the life of the school and the need for considering the philosophy of the institution under study is recognized. Concise statements of what is judged to be good practice are provided as a basis for the evaluation.

As one result of these developments, attempts at accreditation have increased. Forms have been developed for the evaluation of elementary schools, with the implication, in some instances at least, that they may also be rated. Somewhat similar instruments have been developed for other levels and special programs. However, many question the manner in which these aids are used and the long-range influence they may have. A most worthwhile or desirable use of such appraisal guides is for purposes of self-evaluation. A staff, with the cooperation of citizens and students, can well afford to engage periodically in a careful evaluation of the type made possible by the use of one or more of these guides. Such an evaluation will bring together many kinds of data and point out many problems that may otherwise be overlooked. It is a good procedure for a staff to utilize in order to develop competence in recognizing and providing for the problems of the school. Moreover, extensive self-evaluation can be carried out as a part of the appraisal for accreditation purposes.

Even if the immediate effect of accreditation evaluations may be good because they bring shortcomings to attention and therefore stimulate action, their long-range effect may be unfortunate because the mere use of certain forms may tend to narrow the range of approaches to the solution of problems. The use of these forms may help poor schools to approach those that are better. But does it really challenge the better schools to push ahead into new territory? *Isomorphism*[16] —the tendency of institutions to grow more alike and narrower in range—is especially dangerous in a society in which conformity is highly valued. It would appear necessary for our society to seek variety of practice rather than conformity in education. These questions and comments probably relate also to the unfortunate use of standard tests in some schools and to the much too common tendency to accept norms as standards.

Is it possible to develop the needed provisions for education in a climate of conformity—a climate that may result in more uniformity of practice and less vigorous exercise of initiative than would necessarily result from the operation of a highly centralized government? Why or why not? How can appraisals and evaluations be planned and conducted so they will release initiative and encourage the acceptance of responsibility for narrowing the gap between the ideals and commitments of society and its practices? How can appraisals avoid the norm and facilitate the attainment of equality rather than identity of opportunity?

What Kinds of Aids Are Needed for Appraisal or Evaluation?

Unless an appraisal or evaluation of any aspect of education is systematically planned and conducted it may have little or no value. An

---

[16]See discussion of this problem in David Riesman, *Constraint and Variety in American Education* (Lincoln: University of Nebraska Press, 1956).

adequate plan should include (1) a clear statement of the purpose, scope, and procedures; (2) a description (supplemented by pertinent factual information) of the current situation including present goals and objectives; (3) if appropriate, a statement giving some current assumptions about the future, which, everyone should understand, are to be reexamined as the study proceeds; and (4) a statement concerning the expected time of completion and the resources, including staff and special services (such as consultants) that will be available. If a district has developed an adequate Educational Resources Management System or a Management Information System and has access to computers, the necessary studies can more readily be made than would otherwise be possible.

Although many helpful criteria, guidelines, checklists, scorecards, tests, and other instruments and devices have been developed for almost every aspect of education ranging from student achievement through buildings and finance, these materials will need to be examined carefully to determine which, if any, are appropriate. In many cases, adaptations will need to be made or new instruments and procedures devised. Some important cautions should always be kept in mind; for example, (1) certain approaches may result in a picture that represents only one point of view or one aspect of an operation; and (2) in most complex situations, the use of an instrument without careful study could easily result in unfair and indefensible conclusions. In the process of making the necessary studies and developing conclusions, every implied or stated assumption or apparent bias should be clearly identified and continuously examined. Any such recognized or unrecognized bias or assumption can easily lead to indefensible conclusions or proposals.

What are some of the limitations in using instruments developed by other school systems or organizations? How should an evaluation of a state or local school system be related to its purposes and goals?

What Policies and Procedures Are Needed to Facilitate Accountability?

The terms "responsibility" and "accountability" are closely related. There is, however, a potentially significant difference in that the latter more clearly conveys the concept of being able to provide valid and presumably objective evidence of progress or accomplishment than the former.

In this country, the people (that is, the citizens of a community) have always been responsible for providing schools at least for some of the children, and for selecting a committee or board to be responsible to them for appointing teachers and for the operation of the school or schools. In turn, the teachers were responsible to the board for the operation of the school and for the conduct and progress of the students. As the nation developed, however, the concept of responsibility became more complicated and sometimes confusing as policies and sometimes detailed requirements were established by the legislature; regulations were adopted by the state board; superintendents, principals, facilitating personnel, and teachers were appointed by local boards; and the concept of education was expanded to include not only all children and many adults but also many kinds of educational programs and activities in addition to the original "three Rs."

During recent years many people have begun to recognize some of the weaknesses in the rather common, but indefensible, interpretation of the term "responsibility" that permitted heavy reliance on subjective judgments with little or no attempt to obtain or seriously consider all pertinent information as a basis for reaching conclusions. Over the years many teachers and other employees have been unfairly dismissed, numerous students failed, and many schools criticized or handicapped primarily on the basis of subjective, and often biased, judgments. Most people now understand the necessity for, and importance of, valid information that can be utilized not only for eliminating such practices but also for more constructive purposes. They want both bona fide responsibility and accountability in and for education.

A troublesome question relating to education is: Who should be responsible or held accountable for what? The voters who elect poorly informed members to the legislature, legislators who vote for statutes that handicap the schools, or those who neglect to provide them with adequate information? The parents who show little interest in the education of their children, the people or the members of the board who are satisfied with mediocre schools, the colleges at which inept teachers have been "prepared," the teachers, or the students who may not be interested in school? Many similar questions will need to be raised and carefully considered in the process of planning defensible policies and procedures relating to accountability. Other troublesome questions relate directly to the kinds of information needed, how it can best be obtained and analyzed, and how it should be utilized. Fortunately some states and local school systems have already made significant progress in developing and establishing plans and provisions for accountability and much can be learned from their experiences.

What policies and procedures should be utilized in planning for and implementing accountability in a school system? What should be the role of the state education agency, institutions of higher learning, and of local boards of education? What are some of the important cautions and potential hazards or pitfalls that should be kept in mind? Some people believe one of the best ways to facilitate accountability in public agencies is to help students, teachers, administrators, and even parents to develop better self-evaluation and self-accountability. Is that feasible or desirable? If so, how can it best be done?

In one state, in which there is a strong demand for accountability, the following bills are being considered by the legislature:

- Providing that the state education agency, with the assistance of a competent committee and necessary consultants, make the necessary studies and develop a report including a proposed plan for establishing accountability in and for education in the state, which is to be submitted to the legislature for consideration at its next session. Funds have been appropriated to meet the estimated cost of the study.
- Requiring all districts to give standardized tests (to be designated by the state board of education) each year to all students and to publish the results and send a copy to the state board. The bill also provides that, after the first year, the amount of funds apportioned to a district in which the average test score any year is more than 10 percent below the average for state, would be reduced by 10 percent.
- Requiring the state education agency to evaluate once every five years all school systems in the state having more than 2,000 students (except city systems) and report the findings and recommendations to the legislature.
- Requiring all districts to develop and establish within two years an accountability system that will include procedures for evaluating teachers and replacing those whose work is found to be unsatisfactory.

What are the strengths and weaknesses of each of these bills? Which seems most defensible? Least defensible? Why? If none seems to be satisfactory, what should be included in a bill relating to accountability?

SELECTED REFERENCES

BLOOM, BENJAMIN S., J. THOMAS HASTINGS, and GEORGE F. MADAUS, *Handbook on Formative and Summative Evaluation of Student Learning.* New York: McGraw-Hill Book Company, 1971.

BRICKELL, HENRY M., *Organizing New York State for Educational Change.* Albany: University of the State of New York, State Education Department, 1961.

DAVIS, JOSEPH L., ed., *Educational Evaluation: Official Proceedings of a Conference.* Columbus, Ohio: Ohio Department of Education, 1969.

Evaluative Criteria, 4th ed., Arlington, Virginia: National Study of Secondary School Evaluation, 1969.

HAWTHORNE, PHYLLIS, *Legislation by the States—Accountability and Assessment in Education.* Denver, Colorado: Cooperative Accountability Project, 1972.

KNEZEVICH, STEPHEN J., and GLEN G. EYE, eds., *Instructional Technology and the School Administrator.* Washington, D.C.: American Association of School Administrators, 1970.

LESSINGER, LEON, *Every Kid A Winner: Accountability in Education.* New York: Simon and Schuster, 1970.

MORPHET, EDGAR L., and DAVID L. JESSER, eds., *Emerging State Responsibilities for Education.* Denver, Colorado: Improving State Leadership in Education, 1970. (See especially Chap. 8.)

MORPHET, EDGAR L., and DAVID L. JESSER, eds., *Planning for Effective Utilization of Technology in Educaton.* New York: Citation Press, 1969.

National Society for the Study of Education, *Educational Evaluation: New Roles, New Means.* Chicago: National Society for the Study of Education. 1969.

PAYNE, DAVID A., *The Specification and Measurement of Learning Outcomes.* Waltham, Massachusetts: Blaisdell Publishing Company, 1968.

Phi Delta Kappan, December 1970, and October 1972. (Issues devoted primarily to accountability.)

Profiles of Excellence: Recommended Criteria for Evaluating the Quality of A Local School System. Washington, D.C.: National Education Association, 1966.

Testing, Testing, Testing. Washington, D.C.: American Association of School Administrators, Council of Chief State School Officers, National Association of Secondary School Principals, 1962.

WILHELMS, FRED T., ed., *Evaluation as Feedback and Guide.* Washington, D.C.: Association for Supervision and Curriculum Development, 1967.

Index

Abbott, Max G. and John T. Lovell, 104
Accountability:
 conditions and constraints, 547
 goal setting in, 544
 legislation, 548
 methodology of, 549
 partnership, 545
 policies and procedures for, 557
 responsibility for, 546
 social elements leading to, 542
 state education agency, 278
Accreditation and evaluation, 555
Adams, Brooks, 22
Administrative behavior, 117–18
 model for study of, 143–45
Administrative process, 145
Adult and continuing education, 411
Alexander, Kern, Ray Corns, and Walter McCann, 528
Allee, W. C., 90, 154
Allen, James E., Jr., 532, 541
Alternatives in education, identification and analysis of, 398
Alves, Henry F. and Edgar L. Morphet, 300
American Association of School Administrators, 203, 282, 406
Appraisal:
 accreditation, 555
 assessment of education, 532

Appraisal: (cont.)
 in local systems, 553
 responsibility for, 552
 staff, 428
 testing programs, 554
Argyris, Chris, 109, 110, 111, 186
Arthur D. Little, Inc., 317

Bailey, Stephen K., Richard T. Frost, Robert C. Wood, and Paul E. Marsh, 77, 272
Barnard, Chester I., 68, 69
Bartholomew, Paul C., 47
Beach, Fred F., 265, 267
Beach, Fred F. and Andrew H. Gibbs, 265
Beach, Fred F. and Robert F. Will, 261, 263
Bedenbaugh, Edgar H. and Kern Alexander, 507
Behavioral Science, 60
Bennis, Warren G., 102, 316, 318
Bennis, Warren G., Kenneth D. Benne, and Robert Chin, 160
Benson, Charles S., 78
Berelson, Bernard and Gary A. Steiner, 96, 121, 129, 139, 141, 142, 156
Better Teaching in School Administration, 113
Blau, Peter M. and W. Richard Scott, 86, 88, 89, 123
Bloom, Benjamin, 407
Bloom, Benjamin, Allison Davis, Robert D. Hess, 409

561

Board of education:
  and the administrator, 323
  appraisal of educational services, 322
  duties, 311
  ensure competency of, 319
  fiscal independence, 498-99
  organization and functioning, 312
  selection of members, 310
  standing committees, 321
Bogue, E. G., 318
Bollens, John C. and Henry J. Schmandt, 198, 336, 337, 338
Bowles, Frank, 170
Brown v. Board of Education of Topeka, 34, 49, 231
Bruce, Thor W., 484
Budget:
  administration of, 479
  approval, 498
  fiscal independence of school boards, 498
  preparation of, 477
Budget of the U.S. Government, 1973, 247, 248, 249
Burkhead, Jesse, 307
Business administration:
  budget, 475
  financial accounting, 480
  food service, 492
  liability insurance, 496
  management of resources, 470
  property insurance, 495
  safeguarding school funds, 493
  school plant maintenance, 487
  school plant operation, 485
  supply management, 484
  transportation, 488
  Workmen's Compensation insurance, 496
Butts, R. Freeman and Lawrence A. Cremin, 16

California Attorney General Opinion, 42
California State Department of Education, 407, 452, 455
Callahan, Raymond E., 150, 151, 326
Campbell, Roald F., Luvern L. Cunningham, and Roderick F. McPhee, 19
Campbell, Roald F. and Russell T. Gregg, 127, 143, 145, 146
Carlson, Richard O., 12, 73, 74, 75
Cartwright, Derwin and Alvin Zander, 121, 128
Castetter, William B., 416
Catholic Canon Law, 27
Centralization, 24
Chambers, Ernest W., 295
Change:
  cooperation, kinds of, 183, 185
  effecting, 180-83, 186
  in facilities, 443-47
  implications for education, 9
  implications for organization and administration, 11-12
  interrelations with planning, 180
  mandated, 185
  significance of, 8
Charters, W. W., Jr., 22
Chin, Robert, 61, 62, 531
Cillie, F. S., 346
Clinchy, Evans, 460
Coffey, Hubert S. and William P. Golden, Jr., 145, 399
Coladarci, Arthur P. and Jacob W. Getzels, 58, 59, 359
Coleman, James S., 191
Collective negotiations:
  and the principal, 375

Collective negotiations: (cont.)
  process, 437
  strikes—arbitration, 441
Committee for Economic Development, 198, 200, 337, 340
Committee on Education and Labor, 227
Community education, 402-3
Community education center:
  attendance area, 379
  and decentralization, 376
  decision making in, 359-61
  organization of staff, 366
  organization of students, 379
  the principal, 361-64
  staff patterns, 378
Community, state and national development, 23-24
Community power structure, 76-77
Community study:
  action based on, 213-14
  implications of, 212
  procedures, 211
Compartmentalization, avoiding, 414
Compliance relationship, 70-71
Conant, James Bryant, 34
Conflict, 157-58, 196
Confrontation, 197
Constitutional provisions:
  federal, 36-37
  state, 38
Cook, Katherine M., 300
Coombs, Philip H. and Jacques Hallak, 350
Coons, John E., William H. Clune III, and Stephan D. Sugarman, 512
Cooper, Shirley and Charles O. Fitzwater, 294
Cooperative Accountability Project, 537, 548
Counts, George S., 16
Court decisions:
  role of courts, 46-48
  state supreme court, 51-52
  United States Supreme Court, 49-51
Cubberley, Ellwood P., 256, 512
Culbertson, Jack A., 169, 314
Curriculum development programs, 201, 403
Curtis, William H., 470, 471

Davie, Ronald, Neville Butler and Harvey Goldstein, 193
Dean, Howard, 266
Decentralization:
  of budgeting, 377
  in city school systems, 347
  and community school center, 376
  of large districts, 298
  in metropolitan area, 345
  and roles of professionals, 354
Dennis et al. v. United States, 341 U.S. 494, 233
Department of Elementary School Principals, 365
Designing Education for the Future, 273
Dewey, John, 393
Dubin, Robert, 146
Due, John F., 509
Durkheim, Emile, 16
D'Urso, S., 282

Eaton, Wallazz B., 109
Economic Opportunity Act, 202
Educational administration and the behavioral sciences, 13-15
Educational Facilities Laboratory, 445, 446, 454, 459, 460, 462, 467
Educational organization and administration:
  issues relating to, 6-7

Educational organization and administration: (cont.)
  provisions for, 20–22
  purposes and goals, 5–6, 26
  what kind, 27
Educational organizations, 204
Educational planning, 476–77 (see also Planning)
Educational Policies Commission, 16, 19
Educational Resources Management System, 470
Educational services coordinated with related services, 331–33
Education in the United States:
  centralization, 24–25
  conceptual design, 31–33
  control of, 25–26
  purposes, policies and values, 18–19, 26
  purposes and social policy, 19–20
  structural pattern, 35–36
  unique features of, 15–17
Education programs and procedures:
  avoiding mediocrity in, 413
  changing concepts, 390–92
  characteristics of effective, 400
  determination of needs, 398
  implementing plans for improving, 399
  purposes, goals, objectives, 395–97
  role of leadership, 401
Edwards, Newton, 44, 228, 229, 233, 281
Edwards, Newton and Herman G. Richey, 503, 504
18 Washington, (2d)37, 286
Equality of educational opportunity, 194
Equalization of educational opportunity, 506
Etzioni, Amitai, 70
Evaluation of education:
  accountability, 541
  guidelines, 539
  innovative developments, 412
  purposes of, 535
  recent developments in, 540
  types of, 537
Evans, Richard I., 182
Executive behavior, 149

Fabricant, Solomon, 77
Facilities for education (see School housing):
  changes within the school, 444
  changes in the system, 446
  in an era of change, 443
  technological change, 445
Farrar, Carroll D., 118
Fayol, Henri, 93
Federal and state activities, impact of, 206
Federal constitutional authority:
  equal protection, 231
  general welfare clause, 229
  limitations on the states, 230
Federal education agency:
  National Institute of Education, 251
  United States Office of Education, 250–51, 252–53
Federal government:
  activities prior to 1958, 239
  activities since 1958, 243
  how much federal control desirable, 253
  land grant colleges, 235
  land grants for public schools, 234
  and metropolitan areas, 344–45
  Ordinance of 1787, 234
  relief measures, 237
  Smith-Hughes Act, 237
  Smith-Lever Act, 236
Fesler, James W., 329, 339

Financial accounting:
  auditing, 483
  financial reports, 482
Fisher, John H., 462
Fosmire, Fred and Richard A. Littman, 15
Foundations, 203
Fowlkes, John Guy and Abner L. Hansen, 480

Galbraith, J. K., 266
Garber, Lee O., 37, 52
Gardner, John W., 9, 10
Gault, 87 S. Ct. 1428, 50
Getzels, Jacob W., 69, 70
Gibson, John S., 396
Gittell, Marilyn, 354
Goldhammer, Keith, 359, 363, 365, 374
Goodlad, John I. and M. Frances Klein, 367
Gores, Harold, 460
Gouldner, Alvin W., 72, 124
Granger, Robert L., 64, 472, 473
Griffiths, Daniel E., 23, 61, 75, 78, 81, 82, 86, 91, 92, 120, 146, 147, 148, 363
Griffiths, Daniel E., David L. Clark, D. Richard Winn, and Laurence Innaccone, 22
Gross, Bertram M., 14, 150
Gross, Neal and Robert E. Herriott, 369
Guba, Egon G. and Donald O. Stufflebeam, 540
Gulick, Luther, 93

Hack, Walter A., 194
Hall, Donald Ellis, 43
Halpin, Andrew W., 143, 144
Halpin, Andrew W. and Don B. Croft, 115
Hamilton, Robert A. and Paul R. Mort, 31, 35, 47, 54
Hans, Nicholas A., 6
Hanson, Nels W., 289
Harman, Willis W., 19, 169
Haskew, Lawrence D., 296
Hearn, Gordon, 60, 61
Helvering v. *Davis,* 46, 230
Hemphill, John K., 134, 144
Henderson, Lee G., 372
Hofstadter, Richard, 152, 153
Homans, George C., 90, 135, 136, 137, 142
Hooker, Clifford P. and Van D. Mueller, 295, 296, 297
Hooper, Robert L. and Robert E. Bills, 132
Howsam, Robert B., 173, 182, 535
Hudgins, H. C., Jr., 49
Huefner, Robert P., 173
Hunter, Floyd, 76, 146, 208

Illich, Ivan, 445
Immegart, G. L., 63
Improving education, alternatives for, 187
Innovation and change, 118
Institute of Administrative Research, 290
Instituto de Estudos Rurais, Fundacao Escola de Sociologia e Politica de Sao Paulo (Brazil), 24
Intermediate units:
  emerging concepts and policies, 296
  organization and role, 295
International concerns, 3

Jackson, Penrose B. and Delores A. Steinhilber, 246
Jacob, Philip E. and Henry Teune, 207
Jencks, Christopher, 191
Jesser, David L., 163, 530
Johns, Roe L., 502, 503, 512, 514

564 INDEX

Johns, Roe L. and Kern Alexander, 507, 508, 516, 517, 518, 519, 523, 525, 527
Johns, Roe L., Kern Alexander, and Dewey Stollar, 522
Johns, Roe L. and Edgar L. Morphet, 78, 473, 510
Johnson, Donald W. and Donald R. Miller, 176, 180
Johnstone, W. C. and Raymon J. Rivera, 411

Kandel, I. L., 7, 26, 346
Katzenbach, Edward L., 405
Keesecker, Ward W., 257
Kerr, Clark, 327
Kimbrough, Ralph B., 77, 271
Kimbrough, Ralph B. and R. L. Johns, 76
Kropotkin, Peter, 153
Kurth, Edwin L., 243

La Barre, Weston, 154
Lazarsfeld, Paul F., 14
Leadership:
  concepts of, 126–30
  environment for, 388
  external and internal environment, 388–89
  generalizations on, 139–42
  group, 135–39
  Homans' Exchange Theory, 142
  informal group characteristics, 134
  interaction or group approval, 133–34
  planning improvements in, 393
  resources for, 404
  studies of traits, 130–133
Leavitt, Harold K., 102
Leeman v. *Sloan,* 231
Legal provisions:
  bases for, 31
  board policies, standards, regulations, 44–45
  laws relating to education, 39–44
  sources of law, 33
  Warren Court decisions, 34
Lemon v. *Kurtzman,* 231, 528
Lessinger, Leon, 550
Leu, Donald and I. Carl Condoli, 446, 449, 450, 462
Levin, Henry M., 506
Lipham, James M., 127, 129
Local education agency, significance of, 305–8
Local responsibility for education, 292
Local school districts:
  characteristics of effective districts and schools, 286
  development of, 280–83
  factors affecting organization, 283
  fostering initiative within, 330
  kinds, 285
  reorganization of, 288–93
  significant trends, 284
Lonsdale, Richard C., 22, 62, 168

McGregor, Douglas, 119, 149
Mackenzie, Gordon N. and Stephen M. Corey, 402
MacLean, Malcolm and Edwin H. Lee, 20
McLure, William P., 294, 302
Management information systems, 471
Mann, Horace, 33
March, James C. and Herbert A. Simon, 78, 88, 99
Marsh, William Robert, 76
Masters, Nicholas A., Robert A. Salisbury, and Thomas H. Eliot, 273

Matlin, John P., 356
Metcalf, Henry C. and L. Urwick, 157
Metropolitan area:
  achieving reorganization, 351
  city vs. surrounding area, 339
  decentralization in, 345
  definition of, 336
  district structure in, 340
  encouraging developments, 343
  governmental structure for education, 353
  inner city, 336–37
  large resources and larger needs, 198–99
  local governments in, 199-201
  "mosaic of social worlds," 337
  planning and development in, 348
  reorganization for education, 350
  reorganization of districts, 342
  from rural to, 197–98
  and state and federal governments, 344
Miles, Matthew B., 13, 361
Miller, James G., 61, 62, 65, 66, 75, 78, 93, 94, 97, 99, 129, 130
Miller, Van, 394
Milstein, Mike, 268
Minzey, Jack, 373
Montagu, Ashley, 154
Morphet, Edgar L., 167, 184, 258, 259, 288
Morphet, Edgar L. and David L. Jesser, 165, 176, 177
Morphet, Edgar L., David L. Jesser, and Arthur P. Ludka, 172, 183, 278, 390, 397, 404
Morphet, Edgar L. and John G. Ross, 289
Morphet, Edgar L. and Charles O. Ryan, 176
Mort, Paul R., 514
Myers, Robert M., 131, 132, 140

National Citizens Commission, 167
National Council of Chief State School Officers, 166, 267
National Council on School House Construction, 455
National Education Association, 43, 357, 358, 368, 375, 380, 508, 537
National Educational Finance Project, 526
National Society for the Study of Education, 160, 167
National Study of Secondary Schools, 537
NEA Committee on Tax Education and School Finance, 269
Nix, Charles, 175
Nolte, M. Chester, 30
Nonpublic education (*see also* Parochial schools), 27, 527
Nyquist, Ewald B., 183

Odiorne, George G., 426
163 U.S. 537, 231
Operations research, 473
Organization, typology of, 73–75
Organizational changes:
  among schools, 382
  classroom, 380
  within the school, 381
Organizational democracy, 438
Organizational development and personnel administration, 441
Organization and administration:
  bureaucratic concept, assumptions underlying, 105–8
  communication, 116
  emerging pluralistic, collegial concepts, 109

Organization and administration: (cont.)
  monocratic, bureaucratic and pluralistic, collegial concepts, 114–18
  pluralistic, collegial concepts, assumptions underlying, 111–14
  provisions for, 20–23
  structural, 115
  traditional monocratic, bureaucratic concepts, 102
Organization and the individual, 68–69
Organizations:
  attainment of goals, 95
  characteristics of, 87
  classification of, 88
  decision making, 91
  determination of roles, 94
  informal and formal, 89–90
  need for, 90
  selecting a leader, 93–94
  two-tier district structure, 350
  types of, 88
  typology of, 73–75

Parker, J. Cecil, T. Bentley Edwards, and William H. Stegeman, 395, 401
Parochial schools, 17, 204
Parsons, Talcott, 64
Parsons, Talcott and Edward S. Shils, 67
Participation, limits of, 222–23
Pennsylvania School Boards Association, 440
People v. Draper, 39
Perkins, Lawrence B., 461
Personnel and counseling services, facilitating, 405
Personnel function:
  planning of, 420–22
  structuring of, 418–20
Personnel performance (*see also* Staffing):
  academic freedom, 435
  appraisal, 428
  compensation, 431
  development, 430
  improving, 427
  maintaining and improving, 433
  participation, 437
  protection against arbitrary treatment, 436
  retirement, 436
  security, 434
  strikes—arbitration, 441
  tenure, 435
  tenure laws, 440
PERT, 474
PERT Orientation and Training Center, 475
Pfeiffer, John, 542
Phi Delta Kappan, 194, 403
Pierce, Douglas Richard, 70
Planning:
  concepts and guidelines, 166
  Council of Chief State School Officers, 166
  and heterogeneous community, 461
  initiation of, 171
  kinds of, 169
  in metropolitan areas, 348
  nature and processes of, 173
  organizational structure, 172
  politics and economics of, 170
  preparation for, 168
  priorities, 179
  processes of, 177–80
  rationale, 165–66
  schoolhousing, 463
  system approach, 176
  technologies of, 174–76
  time frames, 175
Pluralism, 195

Policy and procedure guide, 318–19
Polley, John W., 353
Power:
  and authority, 146
  community structure, 76–77
  in local district area, 205
  organizations, 208
  professional, 195
  P.T.A. and other groups, 221–22
  structures, 206
PPBS, 470
President's Commission on National Goals, 395
Presthus, Robert, 72
Principal:
  and the central staff, 364–66
  and collective negotiations, 375
  of community education center, 361–64
  competencies, 363
  defining the role of, 353, 374
  as instructional leader, 369
  working with staff, 368
  working with students, 370
  working with the community, 371
Principles of administration, 85–87
Principles of organization:
  division of labor, 99
  evaluation, 101
  flexibility, 100
  security, 101
  single executive, 97
  span of control, 100
  stability, 100
  standardization, 99
  unity of command, 98
  unity of purpose, 97
Proposals for legislation, evaluation of, 53
Public opinion and educational practice, 217–18
Public relations and educational purposes, 219–20
Purposes and goals, 5

Quattlebaum, Charles A., 228, 234, 240, 250

Ramseyer, John A., 148, 149
Regional service agencies, 294
Reller, Theodore L., 297, 331, 349
Reller, Theodore L. and Edgar L. Morphet, 4, 28
Reorganization of school districts, 288–92, 301–4
Report to the President, 7
Riesman, David, 556
Rights of individuals, 54–55
Roberts, Charles D. and Allan R. Lichtenberger, 480, 481
Robinson, Donald W., 541
Rodriguez v. San Antonio Independent School District, 509
Ronken, Harriet O. and Paul R. Lawrence, 326
Ross, D. H., 10
Ryan, Mary Perkins, 27

Salinger, Herbert E., 443
School-community action, 214–16
School community integration, 207
School District of Abington Township v. Schempp, 231
School finance:
  alternative state models, 518
  early history, 503
  equalization models, 518
  equalization of educational opportunity, 506

INDEX

School finance: (cont.)
  evaluation of alternative state models, 523
  evaluation of state provisions, 515–17
  evolution of theories, 511
  flat grant models, 518
  measuring cost of program, 519–21
  measuring local taxpaying ability, 522
  present status, 504
School housing (see Facilities for education):
  adequate educational planning, 463
  administrative time for, 449
  determining needs and ability, 450
  educational specifications, 455
  estimating student population, 450
  evaluating existing plants, 452
  and instruction, 447
  needs, 448
  planning and heterogeneous community, 461
  quality of space, 460
  renewal of schools, 466
  role of state departments of education, 467
  school plant planning and city coordination, 464
  selecting and employing an architect, 453
  selecting sites, 454
  sketches and plans, 456
  space for learning, 459
  stock plans, 465
  supervising construction, 457
School system and individual schools, 328
Schools:
  ambiguity of goals, 194
  and education, 191
  efficacy of, 190
  an isolated social agency, 192
  and other educational centers, 293–94
Schultz, Theodore W., 77
Scientific management theory, 150–51
Scriven, Michael, 540
Secord, Paul F. and Carl W. Backman, 128
Serrano v. *Priest*, 48, 509
Shedd, Mark R., 345
Silberman, Charles E., 359, 389
Simon, Herbert A., 23, 78, 85, 91, 146
Simons, Howard, 475
Smith, Louis M. and Pat M. Keith, 361
Southern States Cooperative Project in Educational Administration, 87
Southern States Work Conference, 167
Special provisions and programs, 406
  adult and continuing education, 411
  early childhood, 407
  for the gifted or talented, 409
  for the handicapped, 408–9
  for vocational-technical and career education, 410
Spurlock, Clark, 49, 51
Staff:
  organizational patterns, 378
  organization of, 316
  organizing, 366–368
Staffing the system:
  induction process, 426
  manpower planning, 422
  recruitment, 423
  selection, 425
State education agency:
  accountability, 278
  and metropolitan area, 344
  relations with other agencies, 267
  responsibilities for research, 276
  role in schoolhousing, 467–68
  staff organization and functions, 275
State ex rel. Anderson v. *Brand*, 232
State leadership and coordination, 269

State-local partnership, 308–9
State policies and standards, 269
State provision for education:
  state board of education, 260–63, 274
  state constitution, 258
  state department of education, 264–65
  state education agency, 259
  state legislation, 258
  state school officer, 263–64, 274
State responsibilities for education, 265–67
State systems of education, 256–57
Stogdill, Ralph M., 131, 132
Strayer, George D. and Robert Murray Haig, 513
Structural pattern of education, 35–36
Superintendent of schools:
  defensible position, 325
  expectancies, 325
  responsibilities of, 315
  security, 327
  selection of, 314
Swift, Fletcher Harper, 234
Systems:
  characteristics of social systems, 61–63
  entropy, 63
  equifinality, 64
  and research, 65–66
  the school as, 64–65

Taxes, evaluation of, 509
Taylor, Frederick, 87, 150
Texas Education Agency, 455
Theory:
  of action, 67–68
  general systems, 59–61
  innovation and change, 72–76
  mathematical models, 78
  mutual-aid, 153
  role in research, 81–82
  scientific management, 150
  "survival of fittest," 151–52
  X and Y, 119
Thompson, Victor A., 73, 105, 107, 108, 109, 110, 155
330 U.S. 1, 231, 528
333 U.S. 203, 231
347 U.S. 483, 233
Thurston, Lee M. and William H. Roe, 256
Tinker v. *Des Moines School Board*, 50, 54
Tumin, Melvin M., 391
Turner, John M., 63
208 U.S. 412, 233
281 U.S. 370, 527

U.S. Department of Agriculture, 492
United States v. *Butler*, 230

Vlaanderen, Russell V., 530
von Bertalanffy, Ludwig, 60

Walsh, Annamarie Hauck, 348
Walton, John, 371
Weber, Evelyn, 388
Weber, Max, 103, 104, 105
Wiles, Kimball, 147
Womer, Frank B., 534
Woodard, Prince B., 362
Wynne, Edward, 535

Yntema, Theodore O., 401